Description et mesure du bilinguisme

Description and Measurement of Bilingualism

Description et mesure du bilinguisme:

un colloque international

Université de Moncton

6-14 juin 1967

rédacteur: **L. G. KELLY**

Publié en collaboration par
la Commission canadienne pour l'Unesco
et University of Toronto Press

Description
and Measurement
of Bilingualism:
an international seminar
University of Moncton
June 6-14,1967

L.G. KELLY, editor

**Published in association with
Canadian National Commission for Unesco
by University of Toronto Press**

Copyright, Canada, 1969, by

University of Toronto Press

Printed in Canada

Reprinted, 1971

ISBN 0-8020-1666-9

LC 75-449041

PREFACE

"En raison du caractère à la fois multidisciplinaire et international de l'étude du bilinguisme et du multilinguisme, il serait hautement souhaitable que tous les experts fournissent le maximum d'efforts pour être compris par les spécialistes d'autres disciplines, d'autres cultures et d'autres langues."

Voeu exprimé par deux congressistes

Why should the Canadian National Commission for Unesco organize a major international seminar on bilingualism? The answers to this question - which has been asked many times over the past two years - reflect both our international responsibilities and our domestic interests.

Internationally, bilingualism is the essential element in communication between different language groups and the cultural traditions they represent. All exchange between cultures requires a bilingual person somewhere in the chain; either one is bilingual or else one reads a translation or listens to an interpretation. Meaningful exchange also requires a whole range of bilingual institutions and situations through which ideas and arts expressed in language can reach wider audiences. As our world shrinks into a network of neighbourhoods, the importance of communication between linguistic communities spreads beyond frontier areas to involve everyone.

In Canada, Centennial Year has marked new levels of research and reflection about the significance of bilingualism in our national life. Preoccupied with their own concerns, Canadians have not always been conscious that the very great opportunities - and the attendant difficulties - implied by two languages are not unique to our country. Indeed, most of the nations of the world are bilingual or multilingual, although we in Canada may be especially fortunate that both our major languages are important world languages as well. The seminar was not concerned except incidentally with bilingualism in Canada, but we hope to contribute in a small way towards bringing international insights to bear on our domestic situation, and towards making available some of our current thinking to specialists in other parts of the world.

Despite the widespread appearance of the phenomenon, we do not yet have a satisfactory general theory of bilingualism. Indeed, it was not until this century that attempts were made to analyze the phenomenon scientifically, and to assess its effects on human behaviour and its influence on social structures. From what evidence we have of earlier periods, bilingualism appears as a rare and unusual quality, suspect except in those societies which valued another language as a key to culture. Indeed, in former times the word had overtones of deceitfulness, and a little of this aura still hangs about it.

Educators were probably the first to undertake scientific inquiry into the phenomenon. Studies of bilingual children are found as early as the Renaissance and works on foreign-language teaching appear with the first textbooks. In the early part of this century, psychologists began to link bilingualism with human behaviour, although some of them were convinced that facility in a second language had an adverse effect on the development of intelligence. In certain countries demographers concerned themselves with the incidence of bilingualism, if only to show the need for a firm educational policy directed towards stamping it out. Still more recently, sociologists and linguists have started to examine the phenomenon for its own sake.

Each discipline has its own methodology, and interdisciplinary exchanges have been limited by imperfect understanding of the first principles, concepts and vocabulary taken for granted in other lines of research. The same kind of problem has existed between scholars of different languages and intellectual traditions who have not always been in close touch with the major current work of their more distant colleagues. Difficulties are increased by the sheer volume of current publication. The Moncton seminar thus succeeded to the extent that it identified significant questions, and contributed to improved communication between specialists from different traditions, languages and disciplines.

In organizing the seminar, participants were invited from as many relevant disciplines and traditions as possible, although we could not accommodate all who would have liked to come and whom we would have liked to receive. We sought to confront linguists, psychologists and sociologists, representing a wide range of scientific and intellectual insights, so that the discussions and this report would represent an authoritative and useful statement of current knowledge. In addition to about 30 invited specialists, about 100 observers added a still wider range of experience to the discussions. All the participants took part in a personal capacity.

Bilingualism was not only the subject of the seminar but a fact of the meetings themselves. The official languages were English and French, the working languages of Unesco and the two main languages of Canada. Simultaneous translation was provided for all sessions. Many other languages were, of course, used in informal conversations. The setting of the seminar in a bilingual community offered continuing evidence of the practical relevance of the discussions.

In this report, the theme papers and invited commentaries are printed in the language in which they were presented. The reports of the discussions and the resolutions are recorded in both official languages since individual contributions have not normally been identified. In the bibliographies, the entries appear only in the language of the work cited.

In the organization of the report, each session of the seminar is recorded as a separate chapter. The chapter is introduced by the paper commissioned on the topic, followed by formal invited commentaries and a summary of the conference discussion. In some chapters the session Chairman has added his own "last word". Each chapter concludes with a selected bibliography suggested by the author of the principal paper and the commentators, with a few other titles cited in the discussion. In recording the commissioned papers, the authors' spelling and usage has been retained and, accordingly, this will vary from place to place within the report. A "finder's list", cross-referencing all bibliographical entries, is provided at the end of the report.

The Editor was asked to condense and summarize the discussion reports to keep them to manageable length, eliminate repetition and present coherent lines of argument. He has transposed some material, even from session to session, so that each section of the report will focus on the prime subject of discussion. We are grateful to a number of members of the Organizing Committee and others for reading sections of the report and offering most helpful comments; the final decisions were necessarily made by the Editor, and responsibility for errors and omissions accordingly rests solely with the National Commission.

May I pay particular tribute to the hospitality and warm generosity of the Université de Moncton. Our thanks go to our host, the Reverend Clément Cormier, then Rector of the University, and to the Reverend Brother Léopold Taillon, Director of the Department of Linguistics, whose original suggestion gave rise to the seminar and whose thoughtfulness during the meeting was appreciated by everyone. Mr. Rhéal Bérubé provided for our needs - both official and personal - with great good humour and impressive effect. The clerical staff of the University willingly accepted the extra load of work we imposed, as did the catering and maintenance staff. To the people of Moncton, whose hospitality we had no way to repay, we offer our sincere thanks.

Travel expenses of overseas delegates were largely covered by a generous grant from Unesco headquarters in Paris and we record our appreciation to the Director-General, Mr. René Maheu, and to his associates on the secretariat, not only for their financial assistance but for their sustained interest.

For the National Commission the primary responsibility for organizing the seminar was carried by Miss Shirley Cull, now Mrs. Dale Thomson. Mrs. Thomson was assisted by Miss Micheline Paré, who managed the papers and the participants with great efficiency and charm. The Commission made a happy choice in retaining Dr. Louis Kelly, now Acting Chairman of the Department of Linguistics at the University of Ottawa, as Technical Secretary for the meeting and Editor of this report.

We particularly appreciate the assistance of Dr. V. Vildomec and Mr. Tremblay and their colleagues of the International Centre for Research on

Bilingualism at Laval University for the co-ordination and verification of the bibliographies. Our thanks go to Mrs. Suzanne Lalonde for her work in preparing the masters from which this report was printed, and to Mr. Roger Brûlé for his inspired redrawing of the contributers' diagrams.

We are especially grateful to Mrs. Beatrice Weinreich for granting us permission to reproduce a diagram (p.193) from her late husband's doctoral thesis.

For a meeting characterized by bilingualism in fact as well as in substance, the task of interpreters and translators is clearly of critical importance. We are accordingly indebted to our team of simultaneous interpreters who handled obscure and difficult vocabularies skilfully and who, in less formal discussions, contributed important insights from their own professional experience. Translation of documents was directed with his habitual competence by Mr. Mario Lavoie of the Canada Council's secretariat in Ottawa.

When the National Commission accepted Brother Taillon's original suggestion that we sponsor the seminar, it was clear that the logistics could be arranged but that the intellectual substance and scientific content would be quite beyond us. Thanks of a different order must therefore go to the Organizing Committee, and particularly to its Chairman, Dr. William F. Mackey, Director of the International Centre for Research in Bilingualism at Laval University. The report which follows is the best evidence of the scholarship and support of Dr. Mackey and his colleagues, and of the other distinguished specialists from many parts of the world who took part in the seminar.

D. W. Bartlett

December 31, 1968   Canadian National Commission for Unesco

PREFACE

"En raison du caractère à la fois multidisciplinaire et international de l'étude du bilinguisme et du multilinguisme, il serait hautement souhaitable que tous les experts fournissent le maximum d'efforts pour être compris par les spécialistes d'autres disciplines, d'autres cultures et d'autres langues."

Voeu exprimé par deux congressistes

Pourquoi ce grand colloque international sur le bilinguisme, qu'a organisé la Commission canadienne pour l'Unesco? Maintes et maintes fois, depuis deux ans, cette question a été posée. La réponse se trouve du côté de nos responsabilités internationales comme dans les caractéristiques propres de notre pays.

Sur le plan international, le bilinguisme est indispensable à toute communication entre les collectivités linguistiques et entre les mondes culturels qu'elles représentent. Tout échange entre deux cultures passe obligatoirement par quelqu'un de bilingue, qu'il s'agisse des auteurs de l'échange eux-mêmes, ou d'un traducteur. Pour les échanges suivis, il faut un ensemble complexe d'institutions bilingues et de situations de bilinguisme, afin que les idées et les oeuvres nées dans l'une des langues puissent atteindre les publics de l'autre. Les distances, sur notre globe, disparaissent rapidement; aussi devient-il nécessaire à chacun, et non plus seulement aux populations frontalières, de pouvoir communiquer avec les autres collectivités linguistiques.

Au Canada, le Centenaire a fourni l'occasion de recherches et de réflexions approfondies sur l'importance du bilinguisme dans la vie du pays. Tout à ses préoccupations, le Canadien n'a pas toujours vu que les grandes possibilités, et aussi les grandes difficultés, découlant de la présence de deux langues ne sont pas particulières à son pays. En fait, la plupart des pays sont bilingues, quand ils ne sont pas multilingues. Mais tous n'ont pas l'avantage d'avoir comme nous, pour idiomes nationaux, deux des principales langues du monde moderne. Le colloque n'a pas porté directement sur le bilinguisme canadien, mais nous espérons éclairer, ne serait-ce que dans une modeste mesure, notre situation nationale par des comparaisons plus larges, et d'autre part faire bénéficier de nos réflexions les spécialistes des autres pays.

Si répandu soit-il, le phénomène du bilinguisme n'a pas fait l'objet encore d'une théorie générale satisfaisante. On n'avait jamais essayé avant notre siècle de l'analyser scientifiquement, ni de mesurer ses effets sur le comportement des gens, son influence sur les structures sociales. D'après ce que nous savons des époques révolues, le bilinguisme a souvent été jugé comme exceptionnel, un peu étrange, et plutôt suspect, sauf là où la connaissance d'une autre langue était enviée du point de vue intellectuel. On peut dire que le bilingue, avant notre époque, était un peu redouté, comme un rusé compère; cette crainte n'a pas disparu entièrement.

Les premiers qui aient examiné scientifiquement le phénomène ont été sans doute les éducateurs. On relève des études sur des enfants bilingues dès l'époque de la Renaissance, et les premiers manuels scolaires furent accompagnés d'ouvrages sur l'enseignement des langues. Au début de notre siècle, des psychologues ont établi un lien entre le bilinguisme et le comportement de l'homme, certains estimant toutefois que la facilité dans l'utilisation d'une seconde langue nuisait au développement de l'intelligence. Dans certains pays, les démographes se préoccupaient de l'incidence du bilinguisme, mais bien souvent à seule fin de réclamer une politique d'éducation propre à faire disparaître le phénomène. Enfin, plus récemment, sociologues et linguistes ont commencé à examiner celui-ci en tant que tel.

Comme toute discipline a sa méthodologie propre, les échanges interdisciplinaires ont été limités de part et d'autre par la connaissance imparfaite que l'on avait des principes premiers, des concepts et du vocabulaire de l'interlocuteur. Des problèmes analogues se sont posés entre chercheurs se servant de langues différentes et obéissant à des traditions intellectuelles différentes, parce qu'ils ne suivaient pas toujours de près les travaux de leurs confrères lointains. L'abondance même des publications ajoute un obstacle. Le colloque de Moncton aura donc eu du succès dans la mesure où il aura permis de poser nettement des questions valables, et fait communiquer davantage et mieux, entre eux des spécialistes représentant différentes traditions, différentes langues et différentes disciplines.

Les organisateurs du colloque y ont invité des représentants d'un aussi grand nombre que possible de disciplines et de traditions concernées, même s'ils n'ont pu répondre au voeu de tous ceux qui auraient voulu venir, de tous ceux qu'ils auraient voulu voir venir. Ils se sont efforcés de mettre en présence linguistes, psychologues et sociologues, c'est-à-dire une large gamme de disciplines scientifiques, de façon que les discussions et le présent compte rendu fassent le point, avec autorité, de l'état actuel des connaissances. A côté d'une trentaine de spécialistes, une centaine d'observateurs apportaient les ressources de l'expérience particulière à chacun. Les participants avaient tous été invités au colloque à titre personnel.

Le bilinguisme n'a pas été seulement l'objet même du colloque; il en a été une caractéristique. L'anglais et le français, langues de travail de l'Unesco et langues principales du Canada, y étaient les deux langues

officielles. Il y avait interprétation simultanée à toutes les séances. Inutile
de dire qu'entre eux les participants se servaient d'une foule d'autres langues. Le caractère bilingue de l'endroit où se déroulait le colloque ajoutait
encore au caractère d'actualité de celui-ci.

Dans le présent compte rendu, les communications et les commentaires
officiels paraissent dans la langue de l'original. Le compte rendu des discussions de même que les résolutions sont publiés dans les deux langues officielles, ce qui était d'autant plus nécessaire qu'en général les interventions
individuelles sont consignées sans les noms de ceux qui les ont faites. Dans
les lites d'ouvrages, la langue employée est celle de l'ouvrage même.

Le compte rendu consacre un chapitre distinct à chaque séance. On reproduit d'abord la communication du début de la séance, puis un compte
rendu des commentaires qui étaient officiellement au programme, et enfin un
résumé de la discussion générale. Dans certains chapitres, le président de la
séance a ajouté des observations en postface. Chacun des chapitres se termine
par une liste d'ouvrages indiqués par l'auteur de la communication et par les
commentateurs, augmentée parfois de quelques titres cités dans la discussion.
Les textes des communications conservent l'orthographe et le mode de présentation que leur ont donnés les auteurs; il n'y a donc pas toujours uniformité
dans l'ensemble du compte rendu. Celui-ci se termine par un index des
ouvrages cités.

On s'est efforcé de condenser et de résumer le compte rendu des discussions, d'en éliminer les redites et de présenter de façon cohérente la suite
des arguments. Certains éléments ont été transposés, parfois d'une séance à
l'autre, de façon que chaque partie de l'ensemble porte sur un thème unique.
Plusieurs membres du comité d'organisation, et d'autres personnes aussi, ont
bien voulu relire des parties du compte rendu et faire des observations qui se
sont révélées précieuses. Les décisions définitives ont été prises, naturellement, par celui que la Commission canadienne pour l'Unesco avait chargé du
travail de mise au point; aussi la Commission assume-t-elle la responsabilité
de toute erreur ou omission que l'on décèlerait.

L'Université de Moncton mérite un hommage particulier pour sa bonne
hospitalité et sa générosité constante. Il convient de remercier particulièrement le R.P. Clément Cormier, alors recteur de l'Université, et le R.F. Léopold Taillon, directeur du Département de linguistique, lequel a eu le premier l'idée du colloque et n'a cessé de se dévouer à sa réalisation. M. Rhéal
Bérubé a répondu aux besoins de chacun, sur le plan officiel et sur le plan
personnel, avec bonne humeur et efficacité. Le personnel de secrétariat de
l'Université, de même que les responsables de l'alimentation et de l'entretien des locaux, ont accepté de gaieté de coeur le surcroît de travail que
notre présence leur a imposé. Toute la population de Moncton, enfin, mérite
des remerciements pour sa bonne hospitalité.

Une généreuse subvention du Siège de l'Unesco, de Paris, a couvert les
frais de déplacement des participants venus de l'étranger. Il y a lieu de

remercier ici le directeur général de l'Unesco, M. René Maheu, et ses collaborateurs du Secrétariat, non seulement pour le secours financier qu'ils ont accordé au Colloque, mais tout autant pour l'intérêt qu'ils n'ont cessé de lui porter.

A la Commission canadienne pour l'Unesco, les tâches d'organisation ont été confiées à Mlle Shirley Cull, devenue depuis Mme Dale Thomson. Mlle Micheline Paré a été chargée de tout ce qui regardait les textes et les participants, et s'en est acquittée avec charme et efficacité. La Commission a retenu les services de M. Louis Kelly, devenu depuis lors directeur intérimaire du Département de linguistique de l'Université d'Ottawa, comme secrétaire technique du colloque, chargé de la mise au point du présent compte rendu.

M. V. Vildomec, M. Tremblay et leurs collègues du Centre international de recherches sur le bilinguisme de l'université Laval ont bien voulu coordonner et vérifier les listes d'ouvrages et les indications complémentaires. Nous tenons aussi à remercier Mme Suzanne Lalonde qui a dactylographié la copie à reproduire, et M. Roger Brûlé qui a refait avec tellement d'éclat les dessins des participants.

Nous sommes très reconnaissants à Mme Béatrice Weinreich de sa permission de reproduire un diagramme tiré de la thèse de son mari.

A ce colloque bilingue sur le bilinguisme, le rôle des interprètes et des traducteurs n'était pas d'une mince importance. Le vocabulaire difficile et souvent obscur des spécialistes n'a pas désemparé les interprètes, et dans des discussions hors cadre ils ont plusieurs fois apporté le poids et les richesses de leur expérience professionnelle. M. Mario Lavoie, du secrétariat du Conseil des Arts du Canada, avec sa compétence habituelle a traduit ou fait traduire la documentation pertinente.

La Commission canadienne pour l'Unesco, lorsqu'elle a approuvé l'idée de colloque proposée par le R. F. Taillon, s'est bien rendu compte qu'elle pouvait faire en sorte que cette manifestation ait lieu, mais non pas en assurer la qualité intellectuelle et scientifique. C'est donc à un titre tout à fait particulier qu'il convient de remercier, pour finir, le comité d'organisation du colloque, présidé par M. William F. Mackey, directeur du Centre international de recherches sur le bilinguisme de l'université Laval. Le rapport qui suit constitue une preuve éloquente de la haute compétence de M. Mackey et de ses collègues, comme des autres spécialistes distingués venus de l'extérieur prendre part au colloque.

D. W. Bartlett
de la Commission canadienne pour l'Unesco

le 31 décembre 1968

Contents/Table des matières

Address of Welcome/Accueil aux congressistes

Rev. Clément Cormier, c.s.c.

Monsieur le Président, Mesdames et Messieurs,

J'ai plusieurs raisons particulières de me réjouir de votre présence ici et de vous accueillir chaleureusement. D'abord à titre de Recteur de l'Université, je prends plaisir à souligner l'honneur que vous nous faites en tenant votre colloque chez nous. Notre institution est encore toute jeune. Comme vous pouvez le voir, les chantiers de construction ne manquent pas; et autour des édifices encore tout neufs, (c'est peut-être plus visible aujourd'hui qu'en temps ordinaire) nous n'avons pas encore eu le temps de parachever le gazonnement.

Vous pouvez vous demander comment il se fait que cette réunion de savants ait lieu à Moncton. La réponse, bien, c'est une délicieuse petite histoire: A l'occasion d'une promenade sous le ciel d'Italie, deux rêveurs canadiens eurent une idée impossible. C'était après le colloque qui avait eu lieu au pays de Galles. Ils ambitionnèrent d'inviter les linguistes au Canada, à l'occasion de l'année du Centenaire dans le but d'approfondir le problème fondamental de la nation canadienne. Le premier de ces deux rêveurs était le regretté Félix Walter qui s'occupait des problèmes de l'enseignement de langues de l'Unesco, et à qui a succédé monsieur Albert Legrand qui est ici aujourd'hui. Le second était mon collègue, le frère Léopold Taillon, qui n'a jamais de sa vie abandonné une idée à mi-chemin, surtout lorsqu'il s'agit d'un projet comme celui-ci, ne fusse que pour rendre hommage à la mémoire de son ami, M. Walter. Je ne connais pas le détail des plans d'attaque de ces deux stratèges. Je fus probablement l'une des premières victimes à me laisser ensorceler pour endosser un projet utopique qui, j'en étais convaincu, n'avait aucune chance de réussite. Mais la réaction de la chaîne fit son chemin et un à un les attaqués tombaient dans le panneau: le Premier ministre de la province du Nouveau-Brunswick, le Secrétaire d'Etat du gouvernement central, le Secrétariat de la Commission canadienne de l'Unesco, les linguistes canadiens et enfin, vous tous Mesdames et Messieurs. Qu'un organisme international de l'importance de l'Unesco ait accepté notre invitation de réunir sous notre jeune toit autant de sommités de réputation internationale, nous en sommes touchés et nous remercions la Commission canadienne de l'Unesco de sa bienveillance. On est porté à se demander comment se fait-il que l'Unesco ait assumé la responsabilité d'un colloque

sur le bilinguisme. Je vous livre mon interprétation. L'Unesco est un organisme d'envergure international qui, d'après l'article premier de l'Acte
constitutif est voué à "contribuer au maintien de la paix et de la sécurité en
reserrant par l'éducation, la science et la culture, la collaboration entre les
nations". Cette collaboration est à base de communication et étant donné au
départ la multiplicité des langues, les communications sont impossibles, sans
le bilinguisme. Si nous étions tous des unilingues, parlant chacun uniquement
notre langue maternelle, nous ne pourrions guère nous comprendre. Plus nous
arriverons à maîtriser la technique du bilinguisme, plus nous serons en mesure
de mieux promouvoir la fraternité entre les peuples, et il me semble qu'il
entre tout à fait dans l'esprit et le champ d'action de l'Unesco de promouvoir
une étude scientifique poussée sur le bilinguisme par les experts du monde
entier. Nous sommes honorés de la présence d'un représentant de l'Unesco
international, monsieur Albert Legrand, dont j'ai souligné la présence tout à
l'heure. La Commission canadienne de l'Unesco était idéalement placée pour
rendre ce colloque possible et en faire un succès. Elle est unie d'une filiale
de la grande organisation internationale, un corps non-gouvernemental, abrité
par le Conseil des Arts du Canada. Elle est pourvue de fonds dont elle peut
disposer pour des fins dignes de mérite. Mais surtout elle dispose de ressources
humaines capables de mener à bon port un projet comme ce colloque. Nous
sommes tous redevables au Président de la Commission canadienne, monsieur
Napoléon LeBlanc, et à son Conseil et tout particulièrement au Secrétaire et
à son adjointe, le Secrétaire, monsieur David Bartlett, et Mlle Shirley Cull,
son adjointe, qui ont été les maîtres-organisateurs de cette rencontre. La
Commission canadienne a contribué l'aide financière et l'organisation. Nous,
à l'Université nous nous efforcerons modestement à pourvoir aux besoins maté-
riels mais l'âme du congrès, c'est l'effort de penser autour d'un thème. Et
au nom de tous les participants, je me permets de rendre hommage à monsieur
William Mackey, et aux membres de son comité d'organisation qui ont préparé le programme et garanti la participation des experts.

I think I should give a sample of bilingualism by summing up what I just
said. I witnessed the birth of the idea of this seminar being held in Moncton
and its incredible growth toward maturity. It was cultivated with great care,
and it has been exposed at just the right time under the right climate to the
right influences, born under Italy's radiant sky, it received an early ray of
sunshine from the Government of New Brunswick, then the Government of
Canada. It was nurtured by the Canadian National Commission for Unesco
and then it was submitted to the extra care of our own Canadian specialists
before entering its final stage. And here we are gathered in Moncton to take
a deep insight into the theme of international scope that is bilingualism. Why
should Moncton have any special appeal? It is a modest city of between
60,000 and 70,000 inhabitants and I am sure you will find it welcoming. You
will come to like it as you discover its charm and its special tourist attractions.
If there is one particular feature that will be of special interest to you, because

it will be a living illustration on the theme of your seminar, I refer to the typically bilingual character of our city. Canada is a federation of 10 provinces, one of these provinces is 90% French speaking, that is Quebec. Eight others are predominantly English speaking, only in New Brunswick is there such a balanced ratio of 60%/40% and the city of Moncton retains that same proportion. It will be a pleasure for us Monctonians to be your hosts and at the same time to serve as a model of bilingualism. Perhaps you are aware that at this time in Canada, we have a particular problem arising from the very fact that we are a predominantly bilingual country. The problem was such that in 1963 the federal Government set up a Royal Commission to enquire into the whole question of bilingualism and to make recommendations.

La Commission royale sur le bilinguisme et le biculturalisme m'a chargé de vous présenter des hommages et vous souhaiter le plein succès dans vos délibérations. Un de mes collègues à la Commission, un distingué linguiste, que plusieurs d'entre vous connaissent, M. Rudnyckyj est présent avec nous aujourd'hui et il est possible que d'autres membres de la Commission nous rendent visite au cours de la semaine. Depuis bientôt quatre années, notre Commission travaille assidûment à analyser le phénomène du bilinguisme au Canada. Nous avons visité le pays d'un océan à l'autre, nous avons reçu au-delà de 400 mémoires et nous avons poursuivi des recherches approfondies sur une quantité d'aspects de la question. Sans doute le point de vue qui nous intéresse n'est pas précisément le même que le vôtre. Mais nous nous rendons bien compte que c'est sur des hommes de vos spécialités qu'il nous faut compter pour jeter les bases des structures qui répondent aux besoins sociologiques d'un pays bilingue. C'est ainsi que la Commission a eu souvent recours aux lumières du Président de votre comité d'organisation, M. Mackey, qui nous a apporté une très précieuse collaboration. J'ai étudié les titres des travaux qui vous sont présentés au cours du colloque, et ils sont tous du plus grand intérêt pour notre Commission royale.

Mesdames, Messieurs, c'est un grand honneur que vous nous faites en séjournant parmi nous et, en vous souhaitant la plus cordiale des bienvenues, je voudrais vous assurer que nous nous efforcerons de rendre votre séjour agréable et de faire tout en notre pouvoir pour que le séjour soit confortable.

INTRODUCTION

HOW CAN BILINGUALISM BE DESCRIBED AND MEASURED?

COMMENT DEFINIR ET MESURER LE BILINGUISME?

Outline of the Problems/Esquisse des problèmes

W.F. Mackey

Puisqu'il m'incombe de fournir, pour ce colloque, une introduction, je me propose de commencer en le plaçant dans son contexte national et international. D'abord, on peut se demander pourquoi un colloque international sur le bilinguisme devrait se tenir au Canada en 1967. On pourrait dire que c'est pour fêter le centenaire d'un pays bilingue. C'est que le Canada passe à travers une crise du bilinguisme dont la première phase est à la veille de se terminer. A la suite de nombreuses manifestations — voire, d'explosions — le grand public est devenu conscient du problème, et son gouvernement a engendré la cueillette d'une masse considérable de faits et de rapports. Il est maintenant temps de réfléchir, de voir le problème en toute objectivité, de considérer le bilinguisme en tant que phénomène qui ne se limite pas au Canada, mais qui se trouve un peu partout dans le monde sous des aspects multiples. C'est pourquoi il a fallu une rencontre internationale pour étudier ce qui est le plus objectif dans l'étude du bilinguisme.

Si c'était nécessaire de tenir un tel colloque au Canada, c'est tout à fait naturel que l'endroit désigné soit la province la plus bilingue du pays et, en particulier, la région la plus bilingue de cette province, au sein de son institution de haut savoir qui est l'Université de Moncton.

Puisque le colloque est bilingue, je vous prie de me permettre de continuer mes propos dans l'autre langue, non seulement pour respecter le principe du bilinguisme national, mais également pour souligner le fait que les deux langues de travail de ce colloque sont celles de l'Unesco, sans l'appui de laquelle ce colloque n'aurait jamais eu lieu.

Ladies and gentlemen, if at this point, it is appropriate for me to switch over to English, it is neither to exemplify switching mechanisms nor to illustrate the fact that this Seminar is about bilingualism, but simply because English and French happen to be the international working languages of our Unesco sponsors and co-incidentally, also the official languages of the country in which this Seminar is being held.

All of us are in some way concerned with bilingualism, in one or more of its multiple manifestations. In fact, it is a great source of gratification that we have been able to gather here for a few days so many of the leading specialists for whom the scientific study of bilingualism is, or has been, the chief concern.

The fact that we have dared today to bring people together from all over the world for a seminar on the measurement of bilingualism is itself a measure of the progress which has been made in this field over the past few decades. Twenty years ago, we were still groping for a working definition of bilingualism. People wishing to undertake research in this field were uncertain what to consider as bilingualism. There were almost as many definitions as there were reports, and articles. The literature on bilingualism emanating from such fields as education, psychology, and linguistics did not seem to referring to the same thing. Much of the reasoning was circuitous and many experimental results contradictory.

Thanks to the pioneering work of a number of eminent specialists, some of whom we have the honor to have with us today, it has been possible to undertake systematic research in the field.

One of the most outstanding contributions to the unification of the field was the basic theoretical work of Uriel Weinreich whose recent and premature passing we all regret. And I think it only fitting that I should pause here to pay tribute to him. It was not without reason that his basic work was quoted again and again by most subsequent writers in the field. But it is those of us who knew him and admired his sense of intellectual responsibility, his devotion to scholarship, his modesty and sense of humour, who most regret that he is not among us today. For, if it is possible for us at this time to dare to establish measures of bilingualism, to talk objectively about languages in contact, it is partly as a result of the theoretical framework which he gave us only fifteen years ago. If this seminar were to be dedicated to anything, it would be most appropriately dedicated to his memory.

The fact that today we can talk about the measurement of bilingualism is also a tribute to the scholars who have attempted to define the phenomenon. But since all of these did not agree in detail, it is important that we, in this seminar, come to some understanding. For it would be futile to devote time to measuring something before making sure that we know exactly what we are measuring.

When the members of the international planning committee, who kindly consented to give their time to the organizing of this seminar, held their first meeting to select a theme, the sole criterion used was the permanent contribution which it might make to the scientific study of bilingualism. It was unanimously agreed that the most important and immediate problem was that of measurement. For, as Lord Kelvin, once remarked, "When you can measure what you are speaking about and express it in numbers, you know something about it". It was thought that if ways could be found to arrive at standard measures of the various dimensions of bilingualism, it would be possible to compare results of experiments and analysis in various parts of the world.

We soon realized that, at the present state of our knowledge, it was impossible to isolate the measurement of bilingualism from its description. It is therefore to the description and measurement of bilingualism that this seminar is devoted. This involves identifying the variables, isolating and validating their indices and establishing valid measures for them.

Such an ambitious undertaking, however, is beyond the scope of any single science. For language permeates all human activity. It is so much part and parcel of human life that it is normally taken for granted. It is when the problem of choice of language presents itself that the extent of human dependence upon it becomes obvious. We then become conscious of language as language, of its forms and references, its role in thinking and communication, its social and political functions. When bilingualism enters into the activities of man, the problems are not only linguistic, or social, or psychological; they may interest any of the several disciplines dealing with human activity—any and all of the human sciences. It was therefore necessary that a seminar dealing with the description and measurement of bilingualism be multi-disciplinary, in the hope that its results might become inter-disciplinary.

Thus it is that we have here today representatives of a number of human sciences—not however of all the sciences that can be interested in bilingualism. It was necessary to limit the number of dimensions that could be studied with profit, in a seminar such as this, to those most likely to yield some results. It was decided to limit the study to six main aspects of bilingualism—developmental, psycholinguistic, linguistic, socio-cultural, socio-linguistic, and demographic.

In order to promote inter-disciplinary discussion, it was decided to elimi-nate the oral reading of papers. Free time was allocated in the programme to permit participants to read and annotate the relevant preliminary documents before these come up for discussion. These documents form the basis for the final report of the proceedings of the seminar. All participants will be given an opportunity to modify their statements before they appear in print. But since most participants will probably have more leisure to do this here than when they return to their numerous commitments, it would be wise to do as much editing as possible before the end of the seminar.

This is another reason why so much free time has been allocated. It is also because the main purpose of the seminar is to arrive, through controlled discussion and systematic criticism, at some measure of understanding and agree-ment on the establishment of suitable measures of bilingualism. To this end, at the beginning of each session, the author of the preliminary document is given an opportunity to sum up his findings and to reply to the written com-ments distributed beforehand; the chairman then recognizes the official com-mentators before opening the discussion to the floor.

It is hoped that enough free time has been included to permit small groups of three or four persons to hammer out their differences and to come up with concrete proposals which may be submitted for inclusion in the final report. A secretariat is placed at the disposal of any such groups studying the measure-ment of bilingualism. It is hoped that some groups may re-think the basic hy-potheses and implicit assumptions upon which currently used measures are based.

It is expected that people holding different theories in their respective discipline may wish to defend them.

It is possible that one theory may be better than another in providing models for the description and measurement of bilingualism. This we can dis-cuss. Arguments on general theories pertinent only to a particular discipline, however, are beyond the scope of this seminar. For we must avoid making our seminar a battle-ground for conflicting theories in psychology, sociology, or linguistics. Let it be sufficient, for the moment, to state these differences; not to settle them.

Given the broad definition which has evolved over the past two decades, it would be fruitless to quibble about what bilingualism really means, or to try to find out at what point a person becomes bilingual. Let us rather limit our discussion to methods of description and measurement. If we have made any progress in the analysis of bilingualism over the past twenty years, it has been

in the recognition of bilingualism as a relative, complex, and multidimen-
sional phenomenon, best described through quantitative methods.   The basic
assumption of the seminar is that bilingualism, being a variable phenomenon,
can be measured.
       To begin with the concept of bilingualism poses basic problems of identi-
fication and delimitation, such as those between language and dialect, between
dialect and idiolect, between idiolect and discourse, between code and message—problems made more complex by the bilingual situations in which each
language functions.

I. The Description of Bilingualism

       How can we therefore describe bilingualism? Let us rather ask how bi-
lingualism has been described.   It has been described by category, dichotomy,
and scale.

I.I Categories

       By category, it has been described, according to proficiency, and ac-
cording to function. From the point of view of proficiency, such categories
as "complete bilingual", "perfect bilingual", "partial bilingual", "incipient
bilingualism", and "passive bilingualism" have become current.   From the
point of view of function, we have heard of "home bilingualism", "school
bilingualism", "street bilingualism", and similar terms, denoting the use to
which bilingualism is put.
       The disadvantage of categories in the description of bilingualism is that
either they are impossible to delimit (When does a person become a perfect
bilingual?), or that they overlap (Bilingualism of the street can also penetrate
the home).

I.2 Dichotomies

       Secondly, bilingualism has been described by the use of dichotomies.
For example, there are co-ordinated versus compound bilinguals, individual
versus national bilingualism, stable versus unstable bilingualism, balanced
versus unbalanced bilingualism, pure versus mixed bilingualism, simultaneous
versus sequential bilingualism, comprehensive versus limited bilingualism,
organized versus incidental bilingualism, general versus specific bilingualism,
regressive versus progressive bilingualism, and so forth.
       The difficulty in describing bilingualism through dichotomies has been
that they are rarely mutually exclusive and that individual cases are rarely an
either/or proposition.   If they are made up of variables, we shall have to ask
ourselves whether some of these could not be converted into scales and whether
a number of such scales could not interlock to provide profiles.

1.3 Scales   *with a typology which is appropriate to the study*

This leads us to the third type, that of the scale. Bilingualism has sometimes
been described in scales. For example, there is the dominance configuration,
profiles of bilingual background, and bilingual semantic differentials. The
difficulty here is that many such scales presuppose standard units of measure,
which do not exist, and valid procedures for their delimitation. And such
units presuppose an understanding of the nature of what is measured. For
example, before time could be measured, there had to be a concept of time;
before energy could be gauged, there had to be an idea of what heat was.
These concepts of time and energy, led to the creation of units—hours, minutes,
seconds,—watts, volts, and horsepower.

Although the creation and standardization of units create a practical difficulty, the basic research required constitutes a theoretical advantage, since
it forces us to establish valid measures for each of the many dimensions of bilingualism. It is also this type of description which is pre-requisite and most
conducive to the establishment of measures.

2.   The Measurement of Bilingualism

Our second question is: How can bilingualism be measured? Bilingualism
has been measured according to the function, stability, and distribution of the
languages involved, in relation to their location, origin, and dominance.
These dimensions can apply both to the individual and the group.

Most measures presuppose the creation of units. In the measurement of
bilingualism, this is rendered difficult by the fact that these units are not self-
evident. They are, therefore, often simply measures of indices which are assumed to reflect certain variables of bilingualism—dominance, skill, regression,
etc. Are these true indication of such variables? What does the presence of
a certain feature really indicate?

Before being used as basis for units of measurement, such indices require
validation. The problem has been three-fold. First, there is the validation of
suitable indices. To what extent, for example, is word-association skill an
index of individual language dominance? What sort of data can be used as
indices for the proportion of bilinguals of a certain degree in a given area?

Secondly, the obtaining of valid samples has often been difficult. For
example, questionnaires have been used to measure language proficiency.
Recorded samples have been obtained for the measurement of language function.

Thirdly, the elaboration of units of measurement poses a number of problems. Type-token ratios have been used as measures of interference. Percentage of loan-words have been used as measures of language dominance.
Some measures have been based on various branches of statistics and information
theory.

3. Fields of Enquiry

The business of this seminar is to examine systematically all these indices, sampling techniques, and units of measure, to see the extent to which they are valid, to discard or modify some, and to propose others. The identification and delimitation of variables, the validation of appropriate indices, the choice of effective and acceptable units, and the elaboration of measurement techniques are the steps which we will have to take to achieve the aims of this seminar. We shall limit our enquiry to six aspects of the study of bilingualism: developmental, psycholinguistic, linguistic, sociolinguistic, socio-cultural and demographic.

3.1 Developmental Aspects

We shall first discuss the indices, sampling and measures used in case studies. In this field of enquiring, researchers have used written questionnaires, oral recording, and descriptive introspection. Most studies, however, have taken into account only the bilingual's out-put.

Few of them, if any, have also recorded in-put, that is, what the developing bilingual hears and reads.

3.2 Psycholinguistic Aspects

Secondly, we shall study the indices, sampling and measures of bilingual proficiency, capacity, and performance.

Most measures of this dimension of bilingualism have been based on tests, ranging from the conventional and modern-type, skill-based language tests, through time-reaction tests on rapid word-translation, oral reading of homographs, and mixed word lists, word detection and word completion tests, reading of color names written in colors other than the name indicates, and a number of local tests invented for specific experiments.

What needs to be discussed here is the extent to which such tests are indices of bilingual proficiency or capacity.

Does a standard word-translation test, for example, measure only language proficiency, only translation skill, switching facility, or all three skills—and to what extent?

3.3 Linguistic Aspects

We then turn our attention to the measurement of interference and language distance. One of the main problems here is that of distinguishing between code and message, that of identifying each item in the bilingual's chain of speech and allocating it to one language or the other in the idiolect of the individual. The fact that the bilingual uses an item from the other language is not necessarily an indication of interference if this item has already become part of that individual's language norm. Among measures used, there have been word-counts and type-token ratios in running texts.

3.4 Sociolinguistic Aspects

After studying the measurement of how well the bilingual knows his languages, we study what he does with them. This fourth dimension of our study has to do with language function. Various models and configurations of dominance, bilingual background profiles, and other measures have been used, most of the data coming from questionnaires.

One of the main problems here is to make sure that the measures give an accurate picture of the distribution of both languages throughout the entire behavior of the individual.

3.5 Socio-cultural Aspects

From the individual, we pass to the bilingual group as a group. How can we describe and measure the behavior of bilingual groups? The first problem here is the isolation of behavioural features of the bilingual group which are distinct from those of each unilingual group with which there is contact. This behavior may be both linguistic and non-linguistic. It may reflect group attitudes and prejudices, group values and customs. The description of these may range from the anecdotal to the statistical. Measurements have included such direct tests of group attitudes and indirect tests based on questionnaires and pre-recorded voice guises.

3.6 Demographic Aspects

Finally, we turn to the measurement of bilingual populations.

In many countries, this is a practical problem of great importance.

Several countries keep language statistics, but these either say very little or are largely meaningless. The problem is first that of collecting large meaningless. The problem is first that of collecting large masses of data with simple questionnaires, and second, that of finding out how to classify people as bilinguals from the evidence of their answers to a question which, for practical reasons, has to be simple. What sort of question should this be? This will depend of course on the arbitrary significance which we can give to the word bilingual. And here, we come full circle and are again faced with the problem of definition. This seminar could look into the possibility of devising a series of questions which would design a profile of language contact, thus obviating the problem of definition and that of deciding on a dividing line.

In the study of these six dimensions of bilingualism, we will find that we are faced with different types of data normally dealt with by such diverse disciplines as psychology, linguistics, sociology, anthropology, and perhaps politics, law, and government.

Each discipline has been in the habit of categorizing and representing these data according to its own conventions and dealing with the results in its own way to arrive at its own theory of bilingualism.

If we are to succeed in our object, we must attempt to elaborate common categories and common or related types of representation of the same phenomena to describe such inherent differences as may exist between the bilingual and the unilingual, the differences among bilinguals themselves, the inter-personal and inter-group relation among and between bilinguals and unilinguals. A great help here would be a general and unified theory of bilingualism.

In our search for measures, however, it might be salutary to remember that, in the final analysis, all measures are arbitrary. Even the hours and minutes which are so much part of our daily lives are simply arbitrary measures of time. The important thing is that they have been so efficient for the sort of time measures which we required.

We can hardly expect measures of bilingualism to be less arbitrary.

But we can insist that they effectively measure what we shall agree to call the constituent elements of any given dimension of bilingualism.

Nor can we reasonably expect immediate and unanimous adoption of our proposals, when we consider that little over two centuries ago, some twenty competing thermometer scales were still in use, and England, after a hundred and seventy years of hesitation, had finally got around to adopting the Gregorian calendar. So there is still hope for the decimal monetary unit, the centigrade thermometer and the metric system. And also, we hope, for universal measures of bilingualism.

1

HOW AND WHEN DO PERSONS BECOME BILINGUAL?

COMMENT ET QUAND DEVIENT-ON BILINGUE?

THEME

R. M. Jones

The question of time When does a child become bilingual? is certainly no easier to answer than the other time question When does a child become monolingual?

As the infant moves over the border-line between non-language and language, we are forced to a certain precision in definition. When exactly does the infant enter language? The further question When has the child completed his language learning? (in the sense of completing his vocabulary and mastery in manipulating optional syntactic structures) would seem to be easier to answer with an emphatic never; but an adaptation of this latter question may be the point that is really required, as the phonology and the basic grammatical apparatus are completely acquired at a comparatively early age.

The child inevitably enters language with an act of recognition(1) (or decoding), which contains the whole primary organisation of any linguistic act, apart from the mechanism of utterance. He may be bilingual in this sense before the end of his first year, as was Leopold's child: a preferable way of describing it would be, however, to say he entered each of his languages at such and such an age, and from then on he possessed such and such a degree of bilingual attainment, reaching one key point of development when the whole of his phonology(2) was in place and another when he had acquired all his basic grammatical(3) machinery.

The second question of manner How does a child become bilingual? depends on whether he has acquired both his languages at home in the usual, comparatively undeliberate fashion, or whether his second language was

---

(1) Ronjat 1913 p.3; Lewis 1936 pp.105-106; McCarthy 1946 pp.497-500; Leopold 1949 III:162-167; Carroll 1961 337-338

(2) Voegelin & Adams 1934; Grégoire 1937/1947; Velten 1943; Irwin & Chen 1946; Leopold 1947 II; Cohen 1952; Leopold 1953; Jakobson & Halle 1956 pp.37-54; Leopold 1956; Albright 1956; Burling 1959

(3) Sechehaye 1926; Leopold 1949 II; Berko 1958; Braine 1963; Miller & Ervin 1964; Brown & Fraser 1964; Jenkins & Palermo 1964; Menyuk 1964; Brown & Bellugi 1964; Lenneberg 1964

taught subsequently and planned. If we require information about the first process, then a fair amount of evidence is already available. And indeed, it is not impossible that detailed knowledge of this first process may assist us in improving the effectiveness of the second.

The concensus of informed opinion has swung around during recent years from favouring the postponement of the introduction of a second language (until the child is comparatively stable and mature in his first language) to favouring an early introduction to the learning of a new language. The reasons for this change are fourfold:-

Psychological:(4) By commencing second language learning early, a process of unconscious habit formation can be followed, similar to the natural way a first language is acquired. The child's world is less complicated at this level; and the inhibitions of puberty with its consolidation of personality, its moods and perplexities, do not yet provide a stumbling-block to the spontaneity so valuable in language learning. The young child is able to make his behavioural adjustment more easily because his imitative impulse, his preparedness to identify himself with others, his carefreeness in committal of ridiculous oral errors, all coincide to determine this as the optimum period of learning.

Neurological and Physiological(5): Despite a certain amount of opposition, the mass of expert opinion favours the view of Penfield and Glees in seeing a connection between the growth of brain mechanisms and the development of verbal behaviour: at an early age the brain seems to possess a greater plasticity and specialised capacity for acquiring speech.

Experience of Teachers(6): Teachers and linguists in various parts of the world have commented on the success of infants in learning a second language, compared with the laborious efforts of adolescents.

Political and Social: The desirability of learning a language early so that it can be used throughout a person's educational development has become increasingly imperative for a variety of social reasons in a world that has increasingly become nationally and internationally conscious. And sociologically, the child will accept his school's linguistic environment without questionning at this age: the presence of the language is sufficient motivation, whereas later other motivations have to be ensured.

The opposition that formerly came, though inconsistently, from early research on the effects of bilingualism tended to break down when it was shown that the case remained unproven when major didactic factors such as the comparative quality of text-books or teaching materials in different linguistic situations, the attitudes of teachers and children, the appropriateness of the age

---

(4) Tomb 1925; Huse 1945 p.6; Haugen 1956 p.73; Langer 1958 pp.109-110; Perren 1958; Lee 1960; Larew 1961
(5) Penfield 1953; MLA 1953; Penfield & Roberts 1959; Milner 1960; Glees 1961
(6) Andersson 1953; Gurrey 1959 p.170; Parker 1961 p.17; Breunig 1961

for commencing formal teaching, as much as socio-economic differences, were ignored and might entirely account for the disadvantages so often wildly attributed to the fact of bilinguality. And so, the climate became favourable for the report on Foreign Languages in Primary Education, published by the UNESCO Institute for Education, Hamburg in 1963.

Early second language teaching has to militate against an established tradition of late second language teaching. As a result, some infant courses (Ollman 1962) tend to be over-ambitious in vocabulary and grammar, and outrun the children in concept formation. Methods tend to be too self-conscious and condescending, for the simple reason that we do not yet know how relaxed we may be in our 'language bath', how much so-called 'passive knowledge' can be built up before expecting language production, how best to utilise gesture, intonation, song and rote imitation. The teachers, like the children, are still in their infancy. It is regrettable that so much work in bilingualism has been done on measuring the possible effects of bad early teaching before any scientific efforts have been made to improve that teaching.

No satisfactory conclusions can be made from measurements of bilingualism until the significance of the didactic factors is calculated, until the various aspects of importance in language acquisition are distinguished. If scientific progress is to be made in the relationship between didactics and bilingualism, the whole process of language learning and teaching has to be broken down— language analysis, method analysis and teaching analysis. At present, for example, there is no agreed principle for outlining a typology of exercises in language didactics. W. F. Mackey's outline (Mackey 1965) is the most thorough, and it is on his insights that agreement will be built in the future. The only widely accepted division of exercises at the moment is according to the four skills, listening, speaking, reading and writing; and as oral work is exclusively obligatory for infant learning, only the first two of these are necessary in our present teaching analysis.

At present, "convenience" (at the particular age involved) alone dictates general principles of analysis of infant exercises: we do not yet know what procedures make significant divisions. Comparative measurement of effectiveness of courses is in dire need of basic principles of description. Reviewing the three second language infant courses published in Wales (Rosser 1964; 1965; 1965a) since the Hamburg report, we may suggest Singing as a rough division, because at this age singing is a very common and useful activity in teaching. Movement represents another category that has major importance at this age.

	Saying (talk or story)	Singing
I Movement (the central form for teaching infants)	1. Action for imitation (drama – at the most complex)	2. Dance (ballet) and Action–songs
	3. Action for resolution (i.e. games)	4. Musical games
II Still (the rest form for teaching infants)	5. Ostensive (limited to objects isolated or in situation)	6. Ostensive
	7. Pictorial: (i) Still picture (Cards, wall-pictures, flannelgraph) (ii) Motion-film	8. Pictorial

But is this an adequate means of analysis? Across this broad division of eight types of exercises we have the aforementioned split between receptive and productive (or decoding and encoding): for example, type one would be divided into miming (receptive) or play-acting (productive). A further division would be between the two types of repetition suitable at this age, namely rote and operational. Thus the grand total would be brought to 32 types of exercises (and these are limited by the assumption that there would be no phonemic exercises in isolation: i.e. without meaning).

Within each of these types, further kinds of exercises of various forms may be devised, of course; and these will vary at the different grades in the work. For instance, types five and six will involve Naming Exercises, particularly at the beginning of the learning process. Plain naming is an essential infant activity.(7) William Stern, the great pioneer in Child Language of the first half of this century, said: 'The demand that some name must belong to every object whatever its nature, we may consider as a real—perhaps the child's first—general thought.' (Stern 1924 p.163) All evidence points towards the fact that naming is deeply rooted in the early development of the child. Says A. H. Arlitt: 'In the so-called "Naming stage," children appear to be fascinated by the mere pointing at objects with some form of demand that the name of the objects be told.' (Arlitt 1946 p.376)

---

(7) Sully 1896 p.161; Trettien 1904 p.140; Bühler 1930 p.148; Cassirer 1944 p.132; Luria 1961 pp.3-4; Warfel 1962 pp.46-47

These are three types of Naming exercises for young children, according to the means for conveying meaning. They are (apart from their inter-combination):-

(i) Naming and pointing (at an object);
(ii) Naming and onomatopoeia;
(iii) Naming and movement-imitation.

Onomatopoeia(8) looms disproportionately large in the early stages, and the interest shown in it should be taken advantage of. In the analysis of the vocabulary of my own daughter at three years of age, of her 1690 words 58 were noted as Onomatopoeia and Interjection. The onomatopoeic style of speech must seem close to natural expression to the child and easy to adopt, as if 'the idea and the word appear almost simultaneously' (Preyer 1898 p.90). It cannot be denied that onomatopoeia is inevitably conventionalised; but the infants' tendency to duplicate sounds as well as the attempt in the patterns themselves to 'represent the sounds of the situations in which they are spoken' (Lewis 1936 p.118) is a definite help to the infant's memory.

The plan of an exercise at the infant stage has to be extremely simple, and plain naming needs very little disguise to make it into a palatable exercise. One elementary example of what we have been talking about would be a repetitive chant ending in onomatopoeia: e.g. Here's a donkey, here's a donkey, here's a donkey, hee-haw, hee-haw, hee-haw (and so on with pig, dog, bird, etc.)

In a typical course (Rosser 1964) for teaching a second language to infants, the naming of still objects in the room, of animals and of clothes, is followed by the naming of movements. What was once still, now begins to move. The animals, for instance, now begin to perform their own particular actions—the birds to fly, the fish to swim, the frogs to jump and so on. And the children themselves begin to move freely about the room in imitation. Movement introduces them to the names of crafts and modes of employment—the policeman, postman, soldier, doctor, and so on. And from there, we lead on to simple games such as "The Cat and the Mouse."

One archetypal pattern in children's play seems to appear consistently in courses of this type, and that is the imitation hunting game. Particularly between three and four years of age, this sort of activity makes an immense appeal to the child and can be adapted to his language teaching needs. Combined with imitation of a variety of human and animal characters, vocabulary can be extended and simple sentence patterns drilled repeatedly. The cat and mice opposition can be replaced by owl and mice, crow and little birds, wind and leaves, duck and frogs, dog and cats, policeman and bad men, dog and balls, man and rabbits, fisherman and fish, sun and snowflakes. With each variation in the game, a different brief dialogue can be taught and repeated between the opposing factions.

_____

(8) Sully 1896 p.143; Preyer 1898 pp.90-91; Jesperson 1922 pp.150-151; Lewis 1936 pp.115,118,135,141; McCarthy 1946 p.503; Leopold 1949 III; Lewis 1957

Good infants teachers know how important it is to appeal to the senses in such games as these. If the children are to be snowflakes, they don't undertake the task anyhow. They are told to feel like snowflakes, cold and crisp and light, easily blown about, rising and falling, running forward and backward, and all the time shivering. Imitation is done thoroughly at this age, with a strong appeal to the imagination; and so the language link is forged in an active imaginative experience.

In the development from naming stationary beings to naming their movements, we have the possibility of a parallel between presentation itself and the development in content, from the one-element sentence to the two-element sentence: from the naming of the thing to the naming of the thing plus its action or its quality. The linguistic development is reflected in the development of exercises.

Let us trace briefly some of the child's linguistic development. The first stage is a fairly extended one of recognition (or decoding) without expression. Recognition always precedes use, and under normal conditions the compass of recognition continues to be broader than use. Here, for example, is a table of my own daughter's progress to the end of her first year, in understanding individual 'words' as contrasted with her ability to utter 'words': (Jones 1966a p. 54)

Words understood	Words said
14	0
26	1
26	2
52	3
53	4
55	5
62	6

During the period of plain recognition, the rudiments of independent expression or recall are forming; and this process continues thereafter into the later period of expression itself. Look-and-listen exercises (and perhaps occasional drills of phonetic identification) are the first group that have to be devised for this primary period in language development.

The next stage is what we may term the period of one-element sentence expression.(9) The nature of this particular element itself is as important as the fact that the child starts with a single element. The element cannot be the definite article nor the copula, however much word frequency should dictate their advantages: nor can it be a preposition, a pronoun, or a conjunction, for it has to support itself from its own internal necessity. Nor is it a verb

---

(9)   Bateman 1917; Sechehaye 1926 pp. 17, 44–46; McCarthy 1946 pp. 500–504; Leopold 1949 III p. 2.n.4 (a brief bibliography on the 'one-word' stage); Leopold 1953 p. 10; Slama-Cazacu 1961 p. 203

incorporating person or number, as that by its very nature demands a broadening of oneness beyond the primary scope. The significant adopted—if it is not an interjection—possesses what Guillaume would term <u>internal incidence</u>: i.e. it signifies 'in such a way that the semantic meaning and the support of the meaning coincide in the same word.' (Gallup 1962 p.31; Guillaume 1964 p.37) It will eventually support an adjective or personal verb (i.e. an element of external incidence.) The explanation of naming by a total reliance on the notion of reference has been refuted by Chomsky. It remains to be seen whether the notion of incidence is in any way superior. For the child it has to be equal to a substantive: though it may turn out to be an adjective or an adverb later on, it stands alone now, naming a notion, self-sufficient and autonomous vis-à-vis the situation. <u>This stage is the one that demands Naming exercises of varying types.</u>

<u>From here we lead on to exercises of combination, and the multi-element sentence.</u>(10) When the child has mastered the one-element conception, i.e. combined the relationships necessary in his own mind for the expression of single 'words', he now faces (in Indo-European languages) the conception of further combining these accomplished simple elements to form more complex thoughts. He combines his first wholes into new wholes.

We are concerned primarily not with transforming kernel sentences, but with constructing the kernel sentences themselves. There are two major syntactical steps: firstly, building the superior permanent positions that structure sentences (which are more than an indiscriminate sequence and include a series of cast-iron relationships); and secondly, developing the transformation machinery that operates within these basic channels.

Any element that is now added to the primary prop of the one-element sentence possesses what Guillaume terms <u>external incidence</u>: i.e. it leans for support on the first and is subordinated to it. It also has the quality of a predicative part of speech (Moignet 1961 pp.17-18), that is to say it is a noun, a verb, an adjective, or an adverb; and the child's early sentences are usually bereft of any linking devices.

If we can imagine an infants teacher with her second language group, we would see her first of all establishing the pivotal notion of KING (i.e. the word <u>king</u> would be the emphasised element in her sentence). She would, by appealing to their senses, convey to them the feeling of being a KING: she would puff with importance, feel the weight of the crown on her head, smoothe the velvet in her royal cloak, look around proudly at her court, and acknowledge the homage of the crowds. Having ascertained that every child has become a KING, then she would begin walking: THE KING'S WALKING. THE KING'S WALKING. The person (or thing) is combined with an action. And

---

(10)   Leopold 1949 III pp.20,28-41; Leopold 1953; Wittwer 1959 p.29; Berko & Brown 1960 pp.517-557; Brown & Fraser 1962; Braine 1963 pp.1-18; Descoeudres 1946

then, that same action is brought into juxtaposition with other persons, animals or things that the children are acquainted with, each according to his
own character. And so the substantive one-element sentence would adopt a
subordinate additional element.

Before suggesting some possibility of clear co-operation between development in presentation, grammar and vocabulary, something should be said of
the classification of vocabulary itself. This could be carried out situationally
following the basic contrastive divisions already made between stable and
moving (Jones 1966b p.169):

SITUATION

THING	ACTION
A. The House: family, children; and personal- parts of body	A. Playing, cleaning, washing, ironing, sleeping—indoor activities.
B. Outside: (1) Wild (a) trees, flowers, animals, birds. (b) weather—wind, rain, sun. (c) places— sea and countryside.	B. (1) Wild (a) growing, climbing, jumping, crawling. (b) blowing.
(2) Civilised (a) places—town, shops, circus, fair. (b) jobs— policeman. (c) vehicles—cars, boats, aircraft. (d) food. (e) various.	(2) Civilised— (a) shopping, buying, selling. (b) working (c) driving, sailing, flying.

Just as listening precedes saying, so the thing mentally precedes its
action, and naming precedes asking. Thus, we could have a roughly parallel
development between grammar, presentation and vocabulary that may be outlined in this way:

	GRAMMAR	VOCABULARY	PRESENTATION
STEP I	One-element sentence (Internal Incidence)	Names of (a) things actions	Saying or singing:- (a) (i) pointing (ii) onomatopeia (b) imitating movement
STEP II	Multi-element sentence (External Incidence	Combining things and action, e.g. brushing hair, bird flying	Thematic combination - story, drama (puppets, costumes, masks, films), games (doll's houses, shops, telephones)

In the field of language didactics, if we look around for scientific research that may assist us in the preparation of materials such as these and in determining means of presenting a second language at the infant level, the only works available are case-studies of young children acquiring language. At present, such case-studies of the acquisition of two languages can be counted on the fingers of one hand, namely Ronjat 1913, Pavlovitch 1920, Leopold 1939-50, Burling 1959, Jones 1966;(II) and although amongst these we can boast that one—namely Leopold's—is also the major study in infant language in general, the lack of variety in languages and in circumstances greatly inhibits any significant conclusions as regards infant bilingualism.

———

(II) (i) Ronjat 1913: When contrasted with Leopold's substantial work, to which this brief study of 150 pages is in no way comparable, Roniat is seen to lean more towards bilingualism than to language growth. The book has been written by a linguist, and the parallel phonetic development of the two languages is traced together with a discussion of special problems such as assimilation and dissimilation. The author concludes that bilingualism in no wise retards the acquisition of a correct pronunciation. He deals with borrowings from one language into the other and the growing consciousness of bilinguality. And he compares his results with the conclusions made in other less rigorous observations of bilingual children. The work concludes with an appendix dealing with general intellectual development, including such matters as curiosity, memory, colours, number, aesthetic sense, reading and writing.

However, as there does not seem to be any notable difference in the manner of acquiring either of the two languages, nor between the acquiring of one and acquiring two (apart from a problem of interference), the whole study of the

------

(II) cont'd.

(ii) Pavlovitch 1920: In this study bilingualism plays a subordinate role; but linguistically, it goes into more detail than Ronjat. After a historical and methodological introduction, the book is divided into three parts. The first surveys the general development of the child's language to two years of age, dealing with babbling and then with basic problems such as memory and imitation. The second part is exclusively concerned with phonemics—vowels, consonants, and 'the structure of the verbal image'. The third part treats the development of vocabulary, morphology, and syntax. The child's bilingualism is discussed in a conclusion, side by side with an attempt to discover the general principles of development in child-language. One question that seems to loom large behind this study is—What role does child language play, and what is the significance of changes made by children from the adult norm, in the historical evolution of a language?

(iii) Leopold: This is the standard linguistic case-study not only of the first two years of a bilingual child but of any child. The first volume deals with Vocabulary Growth. A detailed account for the first two years of the phonetic, grammatic and semantic development of every English, German and Non-standard word is given, followed by a word-count and analysis of the mortality in certain words with a discussion of the reasons why words become obsolete, and an analysis of the ratio between the three linguistic components (German, German-English, and English) and of the rate of progress, together with a classification in semantic groups which is of great interest in the situational development of the child and her linguistic development.

The second volume is entirely devoted to studying sound learning. Every vowel, diphthong and consonant is examined in detail, and relationships traced between the sounds of the standard languages and the sounds of the child. Particular problems are analysed, such as assimilation, dissimilation, metathesis, metanalysis, onomatopoeia and accent; and the various theories that attempt to explain systematically these sound developments are discussed.

The third volume deals with syntax and morphology. Simple, compound and complex sentences are analysed for length and structure. The growth of inflections is traced in nouns, adjectives, adverbs, pronouns, numerals and verbs. The verb in particular is discussed in detail in its various forms— infinite, imperative, present indicative, progressive, auxiliaries, modals, past participle, past, future, passive and subjunctive. A special section is given to studying the growth of certain concepts—such as colour and number, abstracts in general, original word-formation and creation, the

early acquisition of a single language as well as bilingual acquisition, is of interest to those who are involved in teaching a second language to infants. And in this latter field, as the various surveys or summaries of research(12) show, and as we see by the standard bibliographies, there is an enormous amount of information of varying degrees of value. (Leopold 1952; 1959; Nostrand et al. 1965)

Of what practical use are the various studies of child language to the educationist who wishes to prepare an early second language course? He can

---

(11) cont'd.

use of paraphrases to explain a meaning, child etymology, semantic changes through extension and restriction. Aspects of the learning process are dealt with, such as imitation, motivation, gesture, echolalia, memory, and stages in language learning. This is followed by a discussion of the interplay of two languages in the learning of the child, the struggle of bi-lingual synonyms and of shifts in vocabulary from one language to the other, and the influence of bilingualism on words and sounds, on forms and on syntax.

Volume four contains the diary entries for Leopold's two daughters, Hildegard from the age of two to fifteen years seven months, and Karla from the age of two to eight. Each volume concludes with critical refer-ences to an essential bibliography.

(iv) Burling 1959: This record begins by describing the initial construction of a single phonemic system for both Garo and English, the writer finding it largely possible to ignore the existence of the two languages. The vowel and consonant systems of the two are progressively differentiated, but the author finds a minimal amount of interference. The development is traced too in morphology, syntax and semantics; and in bilingualism a conscious-ness of translation appeared early. A brief comparison is made with the results found by Leopold and Velten.

(v) Jones 1966: Bilingualism is mentioned only incidentally in this thesis, as the child was still almost monoglot Welsh at the age of three (in the English-Welsh word proportion of 95:1595). Part I deals with the relevance of case-studies for the early teaching of a second language. Part II out-lines the language acquisition of a child in a Welsh home, but within a bilingual community. Part III attempts to extend Jakobson's theory of contrast in child phonology to other aspects of language, by applying the psycho-mechanical techniques of analysis associated with the name of Gustave Guillaume.

(12) McCarthy 1954 pp.492-630; Kainz 1960 pp.1-161; El'Konin 1960 pp.249-61; Carroll 1960 pp.744-52; Brown and Berko 1960 pp.515-57; El'Konin, D. B. 1960; Kainz 1960 II pp.1-161; Ervin & Miller 1963 pp.108-143; Diebold 1965 pp.242-251

be told exactly what phonemes mature late, what vocabulary to expect, and this vocabulary may be analysed situationally for teaching. He will know too what concepts—such as colour and number—to avoid for a while. He will know in what order the grammar of the first language was learnt (although this may not necessarily be of use to him in the second language). In the field of interference he can be told what forms will give particular difficulty. And even in the field of presentation he may glean some interesting pieces of information. All this may not amount to much; but it is a start in the right direction.

Naming, for instance, is a complex process that depends on the parallel but not simultaneous sensory and perceptual development of concepts in a variety of fields. (Lenneberg 1957; 1964) The development of colour, number and time concepts is a function of age and the educational development of the child. In other words, naming is not a simple phenomenon uniformly available to the young child in all basic conceptual fields.

For the task of presentation, some suggestions that are forthcoming may seem contradictory. For instance, Ruth Weir in her study of soliloquies carried on by a child in bed before sleeping, noticed that the child seemed to practise patterns or sentence series in a manner similar to the modern technique of oral drills (Weir 1962). She was preceded in this discovery by Vinogradov 1930 and Chukovsky 1956, but hers is the best treatment of this phenomenon in English. She concludes: 'the pleasure of play is structured so that it serves as a linguistic exercise' ... 'The child finds great joy in practising his discovery that linguistic units can be combined freely up to a point, but subject to rules which he is exploring.' However, lest in our zeal we should be tempted to introduce full-blown pattern practice to infants, we are reminded by Goldstein 1948 that sound combinations made involuntarily by young children may be quite impossible on demand or by voluntary repetition. Unconscious imitation is one thing: conscious imitation is quite another. And Weksel 1965 warns us that a great deal of experimental research on the imitative process in language acquisition is challenged by the possibility that there may be developmental factors which inhibit the child's ability to repeat utterances on demand.

From the point of view of linguistic analysis, one of the major steps forward in the study of child language was made when Roman Jakobson(13) saw a path through the seemingly anarchic jungle of child phonology. Instead of trying to discover a sequence of sounds in the usual way, he directed his attention to the sequence of acquiring sound categories, the contrastive mechanics of utterance, such as dental versus labial, oral versus nasal, and so on. The child distinguishes at first only the coarser contrasts, leaving the finer, more subtle contrasts until later. Since this important discovery, others—

---

(13) Jakobson 1941; Jakobson 1949 pp.367-379; Jakobson & Halle 1956;
      Leopold, W. F. 1953 pp.1-14; Leopold 1956 pp.265-8

like Berko and Braine (Berko 1958; Berko & Brown 1960; Braine 1963)—have been trying to seek a similar contrastive development in the field of morphology.

The emphasis of recent linguistics is on the fact that grammar is not made of more or less autonomous parts, but is a related system, a complex set; and this, it is claimed—by Moore 1964 and Weksel 1965—highlights the inadequacy of learning theories in psychology. The question, how does the brain operate in learning such structures, still remains unanswered. Language learning does not follow the traditional pattern of individual adjustment to a stimulus on the part of the organism just like any other behaviour, for language itself is a structured analysis of the universe, and not a list of responses. The child in learning a language is constructing a unified edifice, and not collecting an indiscriminate or infinite number of words.

One theory recently revived by Brown and Fraser 1964, that 'child speech is a systematic reduction of adult speech,' seems to imply that the child is concerned not only with what he uses but also with what he does not use. Such a hypothesis may have resulted from viewing the child's relationship to adult language as transformational. As a result, the linguist may become concerned immediately with discovering why and how the child omits particular par parts: he may concentrate on the child's motives for calculated elimination and the methods whereby he transforms a larger piece ot material into a smaller smaller piece by means of "some simple mental switch that activates the baby grammar." Brown and Fraser assume that children 'make a communication analysis of adult speech.'

What seems striking to the observer, as the child constructs his own system face-to-face with a mature adult system, is the way he chooses always those materials that are within his grasp, ignoring the rest indiscriminately. That is to say, his system can best be followed not from what he omits but from what he includes, from construction rather than reduction: we examine the language from within his own values and not from without.

The child starts linguistically from nil and ends up with the whole system of the particular language being learnt. If eventually he will use transformational techniques, turning certain results into other results, his primary task is not transformation, but building the major parts of the sentence, establishing basic constructions. Very perversely, he begins with those sentences that seem to be the bugbear of linguists and that have been brushed off with a variety of descriptions—'subjectless', 'elementless' categories, containing 'elliptical' or 'zero' elements, 'inert constructions which hardly enter into transformations,'—'abbreviations' with 'suppression of elements.' In other words, he starts from the centre of the language with those elements that will eventually support the whole of the sentence structure: he names concepts.

We are in need, at the moment, of a great deal of structural analysis of child grammar, closely linked to case-studies of the acquisition of language. We will hardly see many, if any, more attempts on a scale similar to Leopold's, that take in the whole gambit of this process. In the future, we must expect

emphasis or specialisation on certain aspects. One of the sub-products derived from Leopold's great study is the realisation of our need for detailed
individual records of each sector and problem.

In the field of early second language teaching, comparative experiments
are wanted on the various materials and ways of presenting these materials.
Inadequate descriptions of the spoken language and lack of any contrastive
analysis with the first language have been in the past a stumbling block not
only in teaching minority languages such as Irish and Welsh, but also those
languages possessing a wider and more lucrative market. Although we have
a certain amount of selection of vocabulary and grammatical forms for older
learners, little exists for the infant; and no reliable experimentation has been
carried out in the gradation of what is taught. We know very little of the
structure of attitudes, and to what extent the various teaching equipment and
techniques contribute to their formation.

In the evaluation of language teaching methods, the identification of
variables and definition of the problem carried out by Mackey 1965a have
opened up a new opportunity for standardising tests and verifying experiments
in a field where research has hitherto proved of little significance. What has
been said of early language teaching is equally true of latter introduction, or
even of the education of children who begin their education bilingual. So
often in the past irresponsible assertions have been made about the advantages
or disadvantages of bilingualism that may very well be due merely to adequacy or inadequacy in the teaching itself. It is time for bilingual research
to take account of the factors involved in learning and teaching. So often
in countries where bilingualism still remains a matter of controversy, research
workers with a veneer of statistics precipitating claims to its advantages or
disadvantages, have ignored, even deliberately refrained from examining experimentally the cruciality of such basic questions as—What is the best age
for introducing the second language? What is the best method of presentation?
How best can materials be arranged? How much time should be devoted in a
school to each of the two languages? After presenting a second language,
what is the best way of organising a subsequent bilingual education?

COMMENTARIES/COMMENTAIRES

Susan M. Ervin-Tripp

The topic assigned to Professor Jones is a complex one. It concerns, as the
other sessions do not, the analysis of the process of becoming bilingual. The
bilingual-in-process might be a child growing up in a bilingual adult milieu,
or an adult who has moved to a different linguistic milieu; the learning process
might be casual or systematic pedagogy. Since Dr. Jones has elaborated the
possibilities of child second-language teaching extensively, I shall touch this
aspect briefly and bring some other points before the seminar.

Pedagogy and Age

    <u>Phonology</u>. There is strong evidence that for children under eleven lan-
guage is sound, for adults, sense. Children generalize more between words
alike in sound, give more clang associations, confuse the meanings of similar-
sounding words. (Ervin-Tripp 1967b pp. 62-63) In adults, similar behavior appears in feeblemindedness and under drugs. One might say that for adults language is transparent, since adults rapidly penetrate the surface of an utterance
to its meanings, to a network of connected thoughts. (Strunk Sachs 1965)
Children attend more to the surface, just as they also connect speech more to
the immediate situation in which it occurs.
    The basis for this difference between children and adults is unknown. If
this difference is neurological, (Lenneberg 1967) or if it lies in the loss of an
ability (like the traditional notion of eidetic imagery) then there is a clear pedagogical implication: children must be exposed to different teaching methods
than adults, since their abilities differ. If the difference in behavior is a consequence of shift of set or attention (like the shift from color-sorting of blocks
to form-sorting), or if the difference is a result of the adults' greater richness
and skill in semantic association, then the implications are quite different.
First, one would have to find out what the age curve is, for specific items, to
see if an age difference in learning rate affects new sounds where there is no
negative transfer, (1) and if the curve matches the generalization curve

---

(1) In second language learning, either positive or negative transfer may occur,
or prior training may be simply irrelevant. Unfortunately, most emphasis
has been placed on negative transfer. For sophisticated application of these
psychological concepts to second language learning, see Brière 1966

mentioned above. If so, then one might seek to simulate in adults the conditions of attention to sounds and play with sounds that are common in child use
of language. In one experiment, attention to sound was increased by simply
delaying semantic information (glosses) for a few days. Phonological skill in
this group was no better than in a control group with no delay.(2)

Lexicon. Children's lexicon is composed almost entirely, in Osgood's
terms, of signs rather than assigns. (Osgood, Suci & Tannchbaum 1957 p. 8)
New words are normally learned in the context of visual-motor activity, whereas much of the adult's vocabulary is learned in a purely verbal context so that
its meanings are verbal. Asher has claimed dramatic increases in learning rate
and retention when adults were treated like children with respect to learning
context, i.e. when they were taught to recognize words referring to actions
they performed and objects they handled. (Asher 1965)

Grammar. Differences between adults and children in grammatical capacity may arise from limitations in memory and "programming capacity" rather
than limitations in the character of the grammatical rules they can process.
That is, the differences may be more quantitative than qualitative. At six,
there do appear to be some limits in the grammatical rules used by English-
speaking children. There are some specific details of the English system to be
worked out, such as nominalizations of verbs, pronominalizations, participial
verb complements, and semantically complex structures like "if" and "so"
clauses, and perfect aspect.(3) Children do not know the rules involving rare
structures, or those used in various styles. But it is impressive to see in a variety of studies in different languages how early most grammatical patterns and
sociolinguistic variations are acquires.(4)

In order to know whether control of a grammatical pattern in one language
will facilitate learning an analogous pattern in another language, one needs an
underlying theory of the logical structure of grammatical rules. The results
from studies of grammatical development have so far not been stated in a sufficiently abstract form, transcending the specific structures of each langue, and
even of langage. The emphasis of general cognitive research on children has
been on development before two and after five, so we know little about the
cognitive operations children develop during this age period, which is most
critical for language. But judging from the child language diaries it appears

---

(2) Japanese was taught in taped lessons to American students with structure
     drills based on a contrastive analysis. For a third of the sessions no gloss
     was given. There was no difference in pronunciation between the students
     who first learned the Japanese sequences without gloss, and those who
     learned meanings along with the sequences. See Sawyer et al. 1963
(3) Menyuk 1963a. In addition sentence imbedding increases with age, sug-
     gesting that children's "programming capacity" increases quantitatively.
     See, for example, the increasing use of clauses reported by Templin 1957
(4) Ervin-Tripp 1967b; Lenneberg 1967; Slobin 1966

that there must be, by school age, an extraordinary capacity for grammatical learning. There is no evidence of basic intellectual barriers to learning new language structures quite early, provided (a) the semantic distinctions are not difficult ones, such as the conditional, and (b) the training input is not too complex quantitatively, in terms of the amount of imbedding, or the co-occurrence of new meanings with new grammatical structures. It may be that even these limitations are sufficiently inconvenient so that from the standpoint of learning grammatical patterns, unlike the learning of sounds, early teaching is no distinct advantage.

Imitation. Studies of input-output relationships in imitations appear to be a fruitful way to characterize the linguistic system as it changes. Here I shall draw on some pioneering work of Charles Welsh, who has been developing a process model of utterance imitation for a two-year-old child. This model can predict the output for any input. While processing models have been offered before,(5) the convenience of imitation is that both input and output are fully specifiable.

The Welsh model(6) contains first a phonological analyzer. Both segments and phonotactic patterns are analyzed according to the child's rules. For example, the child may consistently convert "banana" to ['mana] , and "gramma" to ['ŋama] and "gun" to [ŋət], through a general analyzer which perceives all nasals as in initial position but preserves other features of the initial consonant.(7)

The second component in the model is a dictionary with category markers, which assimilates what is heard to familiar words, within certain limits. Thus "Chomsky and Veritas are crying" became "Cynthia and Tasha cry" but "cui bono is the quarter" became "cui bona a quarter." If the sentence is less than five words long, a new item could enter the child's dictionary, receiving the category marker inferred from its position.

The third component is an auditory storage device for holding material while further analysis occurs. In one model(8) this analysis consists of predic-

---

(5) Presidential address of Charles Osgood before the American Psychological Association, (Osgood 1963) This is a general model which does not yield as specific predictions as an input-output model.

(6) Charles Welsh is a graduate student in psychology at the University of California, Berkeley, and has presented an outline of his model informally at the Institute for Human Learning. His dissertation will contain a more fully-developed version.

(7) A nasal anticipation rule is probably common in child language in the second year. For another example of such a rule see Ervin & Miller 1963

(8) Thorne et al. n.d. In this computer program, English sentences were given rapid syntactic interpretations, using only a dictionary of functions and syntactic category sequence predictions. This might be a hypothetical processing model for actual perception of sentences, as the title implies.

tions, rather like a Markov chain. In Welsh's current thinking, there is a set of pre-analyzed templates in the form of category sequences. The surface structure of the sentence, in terms of category markers, is scanned and the appropriate template is selected, which includes "encounter-operate rules" for what to do when standard order (e.g. English S-V-O) is violated. It is these templates which result in the return of "The boy the chair hit was dirty" as "Boy hit the chair was dirty," and "The man who I saw yesterday runs fast" as "I saw the man and he run fast," and "The pencil and some paper are here" as "Some pencil here and some paper here."

An analysis of such rules at various stages of second language learning would prove highly enlightening.(9) One can expect that there might be sharp changes in comprehension and imitation as new templates or new encounter-operate rules are acquired.(10) It is important to note that these models are not logical models of the rules of a language, such as those of a linguist, but an attempt to characterize the processing algorithms of real speakers. They will therefore contain quite different components and types of rules.

Imitation is often used as a pedagogical device, and it is frequently considered both a necessary and sufficient account of language learning. Recent evidence suggests that it is neither, at least in terms of structural learning. (Ervin 1964 pp.163-190) Spontaneous imitations of two-year-olds, whose linguistic systems are undergoing rapid change, are as simple as or simpler syntactically than their free speech. Many adults and some children learn languages without any overt imitation, as well as without correction, to a degree beyond that required for intelligibility. Thus we do not in fact know how to account for the fact that the linguistic system changes very rapidly, except to refer to changes in the system of comprehension. For example, children may say "otherbody" before they say "somebody," "tomorning" before they say "tonight," and "do-ed" before any regular past tense. This evidence suggests that children's structural analysis of what they hear, rather than any rote imitation, is the key to systematic change.(11)

---

(9) For example, the dictionary might be changed first, by the addition of diamorphs employing similar category-markers in the translation "equivalents."

(10) The template change conveniently accounts for the rapid learning of certain high-frequency phrase structure rules, mentioned below, such as S-V-O order in English. In a phenomenological analysis of learning to comprehend Hebrew during a year in Israel, Robert Epstein, in a term paper, reports bursts and plateaus in comprehension though vocabulary increased at a more constant rate. Epstein suggests these bursts involve shifts in "listening technique," at first involving selective attention (e.g. attention to first and last words) and later "methods of ordering the syntax of sequences." If such sudden shifts can be objectively confirmed, they may correspond empirically to the development of templates or encounter-operate rules.

(11) Ervin-Tripp 1967b. On the learning of semantic shifts, see Earle 1967

Elicited imitation in the classroom probably has two values: motor drill and the manipulation of attention. The first, of course, refers to a peripheral skill in articulating sequences. The second is more interesting. It may be that elicited imitation is like disconfirmation in logical or cognitive development. Disconfirmation can draw attention to features hitherto ignored as noisy or irrelevant. Short simple sequences might be repeated to a point which violates former processing rules, thus forcing the rule system to change. The imitation of verses, songs, and dialogues, advocated by Jones, thus has value only if there is evidence that the learner comprehends the components and produces imitations that are phonologically or grammatically superior to free speech. Even this kind of practice may not succeed in altering the structures for sentence production, of course. If the imitations used in the classroom are consistently filtered through the existing processing device of the pupil without any effect on that device, then they are not pedagogically useful for learning the linguistic system, though they may have other uses.

Social Milieu of Learning

The above discussion pertains to school teaching of a second language or of the mother tongue. In almost all respects other circumstances of bilingual acquisition are dissimilar: in social support of the two languages, values, norms of correct usage, and sociolinguistic rules for speech. I shall touch on each of these points briefly.

By social support of bilingualism, I mean that the learner hears speech in several languages outside the classroom, either because he moves between two monolingual communities or because there are consistent rules governing alterations in a bilingual community.

Social support appears to be of greater importance to children than to adults. It is a common complaint of sojourners abroad that their children both learn and forget languages too readily, whenever the linguistic milieu is changed. It could be that when the milieu is reinstated there would be marked savings on re-learning, so that there is not so much "forgetting" as lowered availability. On this point we sorely need systematic research. Perhaps children's selection of linguistic variety is more dependent on the social milieu and less dependent on private motives than the adult's. Adults can sometimes alter the language used to a given interlocutor at will. In addition, their rich inner speech and their access to reading may provide a form of support, FLES programs may have serious problems in the event that there is continuous exposure to a language neither in the school nor outside.

Values play an important role in determining whether a given condition of social support will produce or sustain learning. At a gross level, beliefs about the ease or appropriateness of becoming bilingual may affect the probability of child or adult learning. In India it is assumed that children will readily become multilingual; in the United States bilingualism is taken as a matter of course only where the second language is English. Speech markers of social identity carry a strong value which may promote or retard learning. Labov, for example, has noted that the speech features of the women teachers in New York may not be learned readily by working class boys, who fear a threat to their "machismo." (Labov 1965b)

In addition to altering the effects of a fixed social milieu, the learner's values may lead him to increase or decrease exposure to the second language. Thus Japanese women married to Americans learned fluency as a simple function of years in the United States, but beyond the needs of rudimentary communication there were vast differences in the degree of learning of phonology and grammar and even of American ideas, related largely to their values and education. (Ervin-Tripp 1967a)

Values should enter prediction at two points. If circumstances do not guarantee exposure, values may lead to seeking out conditions for listening and inner speech. If the social milieu provides support, then the social meaning of linguistic markers will determine how far second language learning progresses beyond lexical alternations and the basic syntax necessary for intelligibility.

Primary Language Data

Any full analysis of the process of learning must contain realistic specific action of the actual input system, or in this case the "primary language date," including the stable and variable features, the social meaning of each variable, and the co-occurrence rules. While other papers in this seminar have dealt more fully with the specification of norms, I wish to emphasize that it is the norms of the face-to-face community which influence bilingual speech. (Blom & Gumperz 1966; Gumperz 1964)

In school learning, for example, the pupil may never use L_2 in a monolingual setting, nor learn the sociolinguistic rules of that setting. Even in social milieux where two monolingual communities are nearby, there usually is at least a bilingual belt between, and only interpreters and travelers would have occasion to frequent both communities, with resultant constraints on their linguistic behavior.

Probably most bilinguals live among others like themselves; they may have contact with only one or with no monolingual community. The bilingual is likely to be exposed to a single set of semantic and phonetic ranges for many linguistic categories. An American Indian child in the Southwestern United States hears about him a form of English with inter-vocalic glottal stops and simplified final consonant clusters. The Canadian francophone hears considerable common lexicon in both speech varieties, so that "sink", "hotel", and "table" are shared, but "homme" and "man" are not. One is likely to find maximal separation of varieties and maximal co-occurrence restrictions only in the highly self-conscious, carefully monitored formal and written registers. (Gumperz 1967)

Even in bilingual communities maintaining considerable linguistic separation, there may be sociolinguistic convergence. American Nisei have not learned Japanese speech etiquette, and appear rude in Japan; American Lebanese may lack classical Arabic allusions appropriate to formal situations; the familiarity and status distinctions carried by the second person pronoun or inflection of the verb in many languages may be lost by American bilinguals so that the speaker sounds presumptuous. Thus even if the classical "true bilingual" existed, he might be a social boor.

Interference

In all studies of language learning, there must be some way to characterize the linguistic system of the learner. Traditionally, this analysis has consisted of noting from tapes or writing the deviations of the learner's output from some ideal norm. When these deviations can be attributed to structures in another language, they are called interference.

There are at least three general classes of phenomena which have been included in this term. These are features in the systematic norms of the bilingual community, or its language and sociolinguistic rules; systematic features of the learner's language at a particular point in time; and performance errors.

Community norms. In the language of a bilingual community there may be fixed or compound features shared by both linguistic varieties. This is especially likely to be the case with semantic and phonetic features. In the example given above, sink is a lexical item common to both the French and English linguistic milieux for representing the same semantic category.

Second, there may be systematic alternations between the two varieties, which are part of the sociolinguistic norms of the community and carry social meaning which the members can identify. Blom and Gumperz have found that even when speakers can recognize the social meaning of switching, they may not be able to control switching consciously when they talk among themselves. (Blom & Gumperz 1966) They refer to situational switching for the case when the variety is predictable from the interlocutors, setting, or topic. Metaphorical switching occurs within a given situation for connotative purposes.

Learner's idiolect. A newcommer, whether child or adult, to a new linguistic milieu must master a new system. If the milieu is bilingual, he must master as well the rules for alternation between the two varieties. These rules can be characterized by either a linguistic model or a performance model. He must learn general grammatical categories, rules of arrangement of those categories, phonetic and semantic distinctions, and particular morphemes which represent semantic and grammatical categories. It frequently is the case that in lieu of learning all of the new features, he continues to employ the same distinctions, the same grammatical categories, the same rules of arrangement, and even may import morphemes into the new variety. In the process of learning he may over-generalize newly learned features and alter the initial system accordingly. For example, a Frenchman speaking English may regularly use

"who" as the subject of relative clauses, as in "That's the book who is on the
table." He has a common syntactic rule in both varieties and merely alternates "qui" and "who" as diamorphs.(12) In such cases, whether it be L_1 or
L_2 which is affected, we speak of interference because features are used in
common in both languages which are not shared in the speech community from
which the norms derive.

However, it also happens that learners employ patterns common to neither
language. When this happens, we may find something analogous to the interesting idiolectal rules in child language development. A frequent occurrence
is the omission or overgeneralization of morphemes in the new variety, even
where the appropriate semantic or syntactic category exists in the primary language. We might call such instances simplification. By using a reduced set
of distinctions, by omitting inflectional morphemes, the learner cuts down the
task in sentence production. Possibly the morphological and syntactic simplifications of second-language learners correspond to some simplifications common among children learning the same language. (13)

Performance errors. While the speaker may control and recognize a norm
for speech, he does not always realize in his output the rules which he knows.
This is true of practiced speakers as well as learners, of bilinguals as well as
monolinguals. Performance errors are inconsistent, and tend to occur in fatigue or under stress, or when sentences are long, grammatically complex, or
contain novel lexicon. They arise from overtaxing the "programming capacity" of the speaker. The bilingual's speech system contains more complex rules,
both linguistic and sociolinguistic, than the monolingual's, and therefore his
performance errors may violate co-occurrence restrictions socially or linguistically, producing interference.

It would be of great interest to psycholinguists to know whether there is a
non-random distribution of performance errors. For example, it appears in
English texts of Frenchmen that loanshifts are frequent following cognates.
In a system undergoing constant change, there may be oscillation between
rules from two adjacent stages of development in the learner's dialect. It
might be a characteristic feature of performance errors that they include forms
of interference or simplification typical of an earlier stage of learning. For
this reason, it is of value to supplement textual data with tests in the form of
comprehension or imitation measures which provide richer criteria of those

---

(12) "If two morphemes have phonemic shape or semantic function in common,
they will often be identified by bilingual speakers....Such semantic and
morphological overlapping has been described as producing a 'compound
sign'; in pursuance of my suggestion for the phonemic identification, I
shall refer to this as a diamorph." (Haugen 1955)

(13) For some examples in an inflectional language, see Slobin 1966

regularities which occur under all conditions of performance.(14)

If the distinctions between different types of interference are correct, then the second kind of analysis, the analysis of the learner's system, is central to an understanding of the process of bilingual learning.

A series of studies in which the social conditions of learning and the primary language data are specified should predict outcomes in terms of the learner's idiolect, or the language of a group of learners. For example, a child of an isolated Italian immigrant couple hears English and Italian morphemes both realized with many Italian phonological features. He is likely, like his parents, to use a common phonological system with lexical alternation. But he may adopt the English phonological system of his peers, interpreting his parents' phonology as idiosyncratic, since it is not uniquely joined to Italian lexicon by co-occurrence restrictions.

The rate of acquisition of different features under specified learning conditions would be of great interest. In my data, semantic compounding is very common, affecting both L_1 and L_2. But among native speakers of French in the United States, the lexicon seems to be the conscious marker of the language being spoken, so little morpheme borrowing occurs when language is controlled by instructions. The rate at which new syntactic rules are acquired varies considerably. Sequences which affect the "basic grammatical relations":(15) modifier-head, subject-predicate, verb-object, are learned very fast and learners rapidly acquire coordinate rules for representing these relations. Thus French bilinguals almost always maintained a difference in noun-adjective sequence for English and French, and Japanese newcomers to English and S-O-V in Japanese. On the other hand, they have great difficulty in maintaining separate rules for adverb placement, and in learning the sub-categorization of English verbs according to objects and complements, so that they say "he put", but never "he them put." Transformations reflecting basic grammatical relations may be learned faster and be more resistant to change than those reflecting secondary relations or subcategorizations.

---

(14) Examples of such tests can be found in Slobin 1967. This is a draft manual to coordinate studies of first-language acquisition and language socialization in various societies.

(15) It has been argued that these relations apply to the deep structure of sentences, and are universal constraints on grammars. "They supposedly describe an aspect of children's capacity for language....Evidence exists that the basic grammatical relations are honored in children's earliest patterned speech, if not before." This evidence is presented by David McNeill in "The capacity for grammatical development in children," in D. I. Slobin (Ed.) The ontogenesis of grammar: facts and theories, (forthcoming). From a paper presented at a symposium of the Am. Ass. Advancement of Science, Dec., 1965

Differences in the rate of acquisition of new rules, and the permeability of old rules to convergence with the new, cannot be predicted entirely on the basis of contrastive analysis. The facility with which the order rules for the basic grammatical relations are learned arises either from their fundamental importance for intelligibility, or from their role in strategies for listening to the speech of others. In this respect, as in many others, the problems in the analysis of the process of becoming bilingual are very similar to those in the study of monolingual child language acquisition.

Wilga M. Rivers

My particular emphasis in this commentary will be on the pedagogical implications of Dr. Jones's paper, as this is the area in which I am most competent.

In examining the two questions which were presented to him, Dr. Jones has considered it most useful to concentrate on the first: How do persons become bilingual? I agree with his contention that the second question: When do persons become bilingual? is difficult to answer without further precision, which may well be supplied in the discussion of the next question before the seminar: How can one measure the extent of a person's bilingual proficiency? In order to make my discussion of the points in Dr. Jones's paper coherent, it seems essential to set down first what I myself understand by the term "bilingual". I doubt whether it is helpful to talk of an "entrance into" a language when we are probably witnessing what is more akin to a "dawn": a gradual process of increasing recognition; we may observe that the child does in fact recognize or comprehend on a particular occasion although we may not be able to pinpoint an actual moment when he reached this stage. I would hesitate to term the child "bilingual" at this point. The moment when the process of second-language acquisition can be observed to have begun cannot usefully be regarded also as a moment of completion of acquisition, even to a relative extent.

For purposes of discussion, an arbitrary decision must be taken as to the stage of the process at which we will consider the child to be bilingual. I prefer to use the word "stage" because, with a gradual process, we will not be able to say "at this moment the child is bilingual; a moment ago he was not". Since growing competence in the second language is reflected in both recognition and production, discussion of the moment of occurrence of an act of recognition is irrelevant and misleading. I would choose, therefore, for my part of the discussion, to consider the child bilingual as soon as he is able to understand and make himself understood within his limited linguistic and social environment (that is, as is consistent with his age and the situation in in which he is expressing himself). I would not, then, state without qualification that he possessed "such and such a degree of bilingual attainment", but rather that in the communication of his own message in the world of his particular age-group he demonstrated such and such a degree of control of the phonological, syntactical and lexical systems of performance. With the second language, as with the first, maturational factors will determine the degree of control the young child attains in certain of these areas.

In considering the question "How does a person become bilingual?" we also need to delimit precisely our field of discussion. Dr. Jones has taken up the question from the point of view of the child learning a second language which is not spoken in his home: a language taught to him "subsequently and planned". Here we need to distinguish between two situations: the language the child is being taught as a second language may be in common use in the community in which he is living, either as a prestige or as a non-prestige language(l), or it may be a language the child will not hear frequently outside the teaching situation. It seems from my reading of his paper that Dr. Jones has been considering the second situation rather than the first, and I shall limit my comments on his paper in accordance with this assumption. Where the child comes in frequent contact with the second language outside the classroom, what he learns in school will be a small part of his total language acquisition and the process and progress of its acquisition will be more difficult to describe or predict.

A final precision which needs to be made before discussion is possible on common ground is a statement of the age at which the language is being learned in the situation being described. For effective language teaching it is essential to adapt procedures and contrived learning situations to the stage of maturation and of conceptual development of the children involved. After discussion of the desirability of beginning the teaching of the second language at an early age, Dr. Jones has limited his considerations to the teaching of three- and four-year olds: that is, to the stage of the preschool or "infant courses". This is, then, all we can discuss at this point.

Dr. Jones asserts that "by commencing second language learning early, a process of unconscious habit formation can be followed, similar to the natural way a first language is acquired". He then proceeds to describe various imitative activities which may be introduced in order to develop these language habits. In the statement quoted, Dr. Jones has made two assumptions which are highly controversial and which recent research has tended to make less and less tenable: first, that the learning of a first language is a process of unconscious habit formation resulting from imitation of utterances and, secondly, that procedures for the teaching of a second language to three- and four-year-olds may legitimately be based on what is known about the process of acquisition of the first language.

(l) H. H. Stern (1963 pp.25-26) draws attention to the social and emotional factors involved in the learning of prestige and non-prestige languages as second languages.

Recent studies of the way in which a child acquires his first language have
cast very serious doubts on the validity of an "unconscious habit formation" view of
the process. On the contrary it would seem that there is an active inductive
process involved; this is evidenced by the fact that the child casts aside certain
well-practised habits of speech at various stages as he attains further concepts
of the syntactic structure and morphological features of the language system.
This subject has been developed at length by Susan Ervin (1964), D. McNeil
(1966), D. I. Slobin (1966), and R. Brown & C. Fraser (1964) Slobin quotes
El'konin, one of the Soviet Union's leading developmental psychologists as
saying: "It is perfectly clear that (language acquisition) is not a mechanical
process in which the child acquires each separate linguistic form by means of
simple repetition." (2) The elaboration of this aspect of the subject I shall leave
to Susan Ervin-Tripp.

 The assumption that three- and four-year-olds in an artificial learning situation will acquire a second language in exactly the same order of development
as they learned their first language is difficult to maintain when the position is
examined more closely. The three- or four-year-old already possesses a well-
developed language system, approximately to that of his community, and this
system he is using constantly to express his interests, emotions and needs. Experience in preschool situations where attempts are being made to teach a language other than the mother tongue of the majority of the students has shown
that even at this age children show evidence of native-language interference. (3)
They try at first to adapt the new language items to the syntactic system which
is basic to their acts of communication in their native language. This individual syntax may not be as yet the full system of their language, but they are
already functioning at a stage of development beyond the one- and two-element
sentences of early infant speech. Pedagogical procedures will need to take
these factors into account.

 For the reasons outlined, I would not agree that "in the field of language
didactics, if we look around for scientific research that may assist us in the
preparation of materials ... and in determining means of presenting a second
language at the infant level, the only works available are case-studies of young
children acquiring language". In view of the lack of evidence that the two
situations are basically similar, guidelines for a language teaching program
for three- and four-year-olds should be sought rather in pedagogical principles. These should be formulated with due attention to what is known of the
nature of language and of the communication process, of the developmental

------

(2) Slobin (1966 p.132) quoting D. B. El'Konin, "The Development of Speech
     in Preschool Age" (Moscow: Akad. Pedag. Nauk RSFSR, 1958)
(3) L. B. Rivers, formerly Headmistress of Neena School, Hyderabad, A. P.,
     India, in which children of Urdu and Telugu speaking backgrounds were
     being taught English (personal communication).

characteristics of children of this age, and of the type of learning situation which is most appropriate for them. It is consistent with studies of child development to state, as Dr. Jones has done, that children of this age learn a second language more readily and with fewer inhibitions than older children, and that neurological studies would indicate that at this stage of physical development they learn it with more facility. They will learn it more rapidly and effectively, however, if exercises are designed with due consideration for such factors as their interests, their attention and memory span, and their mobility in comparison with older children. Despite the statement quoted at the beginning of this paragraph, Dr. Jones has taken many of the observed characteristics of preschool children into account in the exercises he has suggested: the child's love of imitation and mimicry, his spontaneity and pleasure in acting out roles, his unquestioning acceptance of the learning situation in which he is placed, his love of movement and verbal play (onomatopoeia, reduplication of syllables, rhyme, alliteration, and repetitive singing).

Dr. Jones's analysis has, however, taken little account of the nature of the speech and comprehension abilities he is endeavouring to develop. Language is hierarchical in operation. The intention to be expressed demands a certain overall construction or sentence type, and certain combinations of segments within this general construction. These combinations for the most part belong to closed systems with rigidly determined interactions (morphological and lexical). Teaching based on a theory of habit formation endeavours to ensure that the learner of a second language can automatically produce the acceptable inter-relationships at this lower level and can articulate them in an appropriate fashion to convey the full import of the message. Facility of operation at this lower level requires much practice, both in reception and production. It is, however, one small part of the production of a spontaneous utterance. The language learner also requires much practice in making the selections at a higher level which determine which of these lower-level inter-relationships are appropriate for conveying of the intended message. Practice at one level without practice at the other level will lead either to selection with inaccurate production, or inability to do more than make acceptable relational adjustments while being unable to express one's personal meaning. What is required, then, at any age of second-language learning is a continual interplay of manipulative and creative activities designed in accordance with the stage of cognitive development and with the interests and preferred activities of the age-group to which the students belong.

With these facts in mind, let us examine the learning activities proposed by Dr. Jones. On page 15, he suggests a fundamental "split between receptive and productive (or decoding and encoding)" exercises, this division corresponding to the necessity for training in listening and speaking. At this point, I would suggest a three-way division of exercises into receptive, imitative and productive. In reception, the child is increasing his competence through familiarity with the language system, as he listens to stories, verse and songs. He is able to comprehend much more than he can produce. In imitative exercises he is playing with language combinations, learning to manipulate them in ways which are consistent with the inter-relationships within closed systems. Here we provide for the young child's love of language, his pleasure in rhyme, rhythms, sonority and repetition, and his urge to express himself vocally. He will be able to imitate more than he can comprehend(4), but by repeating words and phrases himself he will gradually come to understand more and more of what he hears. In production he is learning to select in order to express his own personal meaning within the limits of his developing skill.

I have already stated my inability to accept the premise on which Dr. Jones has based his development of language activities (pages 18-9), that is, that it should follow the order of first language learning. I cannot, therefore, see the necessity for returning the child to the stage of one-element and two-element sentences, when, through the learning of phrases memorized as vocabulary items in dialogues, rhymes, exercises and games, he can expand the basic structure of his small utterances so that they are similar in length and form to those he is currently using in his first language. The naming exercises Dr. Jones describes, followed by simple games and exchange of dialogue, are appropriate early activities, as are the various activities listed on page 15 I would question the necessity to limit the choice of types of exercises to two of those suggested by Mackey: rote and operational. (Mackey 1965a pp.258-259) The incremental type seems particularly appropriate at this level, where such rhymes as "The House that Jack Built" are listened to and repeated with delight. By imitating such expansions, children learn some of the combinatorial possibilities of the second language. Variational exercises are also useful, as long as the variations do not require complicated transformational changes; they are particularly appropriate for conversion into language games with much repetition.

While realizing that Dr. Jones was setting himself a task of analysis which necessitated the listing of fundamental elements of language exercises, I feel that the recommendations which result from this analysis are too atomized to be appropriate at preschool level. At this age children are unable to concentrate their attention on any one type of activity for very long. They must express the thoughts which come into their minds immediately and overtly in speech or action. They interrupt spontaneously and interpolate. There must, therefore, be a constant interplay of activities, of restful exercises and movement, of reception, imitation and production, with the form of the exercise following the changing interests and attention of the group. For these reasons, language exercises must be more situationally based, with active involvement of the children, than appears in Dr. Jones's exposition.

Instead of look-and-listen exercises there should, from the beginning, be listen-do-repeat exercises where actions illustrate the meaning. Children

_____

(4) For a discussion of Fraser, Bellugi & Brown 1963, see McNeill 1966

of three and four love to imitate sound and action. The children should be encouraged to repeat everything from the beginning, even when they do not comprehend fully. In this way they are learning the phonology in close association with the surface features of the system. In look-and-listen exercises even the young child with an already established first language is likely to resort to quick mental translation. In listen-do-repeat exercises he becomes absorbed in the game and concentrates on the meaning expressed through his actions as he repeats. In all such actions, the phrases he is hearing and repeating must refer to visible objects and functional activities of his small world. As a result he will be able to identify himself with what he is saying and repeat it later in his autonomous activities where its relevance is apparent to him because of the similarity of the situation and of his own actions. Instead of "the King is walking," phrases such as "Mummy's making the bed," "Dolly's sleeping" will transfer easily to the child's own play activities where he may reinforce his own learning by repeating the phrases in what is for him a very real situation. In such exercises the patterns and lexical content will be chosen because of their appropriateness to the child's activities, not because of any arbitrary decision about the order of presentation of structural features. At this age language will grow out of the situation and the environment in compatibility with the child's level of expression rather than being artificially imposed according to some adult criterion. Language activities will not be limited to statements, but children will learn to obey orders and prohibitions, repeating them after the teacher. In this way, they will be learning language in an immediately useful form, enabling them to tell others what to do, to tell their dolls and toys what to do and to give themselves instructions, as little children frequently do, as they follow through a series of inter-related actions.

Many children's rhymes and songs are ideal for role-identification. Stories with much repetition, listened to often, with the children contributing as they remember what was said and done, can be followed by play drills where the children, identifying themselves with a character from the story, make simple substitutions and expansions. Repetitive rhymes, songs and stories of this type may be recorded on tape and allowed to play softly for children who want to come close and listen and imitate and involve themselves whenever they feel so inclined. Before long, the children will wish to use the phrases they have heard again and again in their make-believe activities, with the child talking to himself about what he is doing or being.

It may seem over-optimistic to suggest that in a preschool where all his activities are in the first language which is the language of his teacher and of his companions, the child will wish to use the second language spontaneously. He will be aided in this stage of development if the second-language activities are associate consistently with a certain area of the room and with certain dolls and toys. Such a corner will provide a second-language focus which encourages the child to wander over and play at roles and activities in an atmosphere where the teacher too addresses him only in the second language. Time spent in the second-language corner then becomes a regular feature of his play routine which he accepts as part of the preschool reality.

In a preschool where the second language is actively taught, there must of necessity be one person who is fluent in the second language. A further, and even more effective, language-focus will be provided if that teacher or helper speaks to the children only in the second language in all situations. If this person is indispensable for other activities which must be conducted in the first language, then the schedule of activities should be so arranged that he may use each of the languages exclusively on alternative days or at least for half-day periods. In a country where there is an urgent need for developing bilingualism in two sections of the population, each speaking one of the languages, an exchange system should be established so that native speakers of the two languages work side by side, each speaking only his first language in his relations with the children. In this way a second-language environment will be created in which, with the types of activities outlined, the child will develop in the creative use of the language within the limits of his knowledge and experience.

One last question remains which cannot go unconsidered. Enlightened efforts at teaching a second language in preschool may lead to the attainment of a satisfactory degree of bilingualism on the part of the children. This in itself will mean nothing for the future if a similarly enlightened program is not available as they enter the primary grades, and further appropriate instruction provided as they proceed up the school. It is a matter of common observation that young children forget a second language very rapidly when they no longer have the opportunity to use it. How does the child become bilingual? is one thing. How does the child remain bilingual? is another. I raise this question only; to discuss it would require another session and another paper.

E. G. Malherbe

Introductory remarks

I have been asked particularly to comment on Dr. R. M. Jones' paper "How and when do persons become bilingual", as a preliminary contribution to this Seminar.

My comments will be confined mainly to two questions:

1. how bilingualism is acquired, and
2. the stages of bilingualism in terms of practical use or function.

To define bilingualism so as to cover all its possible connotations will be too complicated a task to be attempted in the allotted space and will therefore not be embarked upon here.

For the present purpose I would simply describe bilingualism as the co-existence in the same individual or community of two distinct sets of linguistic symbols of communication (i.e. two languages).

The degrees of effectiveness with which these languages function respectively as a means of communication will be described when I come to deal with the stages of bilingualism. I shall not attempt to discuss the mutual influence of a purely linguistic nature which two co-existing languages exert on each other in regard to grammatical structure, vocabulary, accent, etc. This is one of the important consequences of bilingualism and one which merits special treatment.

How does a child become bilingual?

Here I want to associate myself fully with Dr. Jones in his criticisms of "the established tradition of late second language teaching". The weight of evidence in South African experience seems to be in favour of exposing the child already from infancy to both languages, provided that this process is confined only to the hearing and speaking of the two languages during the child's early years. Reading, for obvious reasons, should come later, and writing still later. Where the two languages differ widely in their phonic symbols, as Afrikaans and English do, it has been found that the child is confused and retarded in his reading and spelling if these didactic exercises in the second language are introduced before the child's reading and spelling habits are more or less firmly established in the first language (i.e. the mother tongue). Afrikaans spelling is almost consistently phonetic, whereas the spelling of English is notoriously unphonetic. On the whole (and subject to the above provisos) there are, as Dr. Jones shows, distinct advantages in learning two languages concurrently rather than consecutively.

Natural and artificial bilingualism

It is useful to distinguish between natural bilingualism acquired in a spontaneous and unplanned fashion and artificial bilingualism which is the result of deliberate and systematic teaching. These two processes are, however, not mutually exclusive: they can mutually reinforce each other. Dr. Jones shows very clearly how the didactic situation becomes effective in proportion as it simulates the natural situation, particularly during the early years.

In this connection I would like to refer also to the advantages of the direct method of learning a language, (i.e. when words are associated directly with environmental events), over the indirect method, i.e. when words in the other language are used as stimuli. The available evidence shows that the direct method results in both faster learning and better retention.

Natural bilingualism is developed where the surrounding social needs and pressures which cause the child to acquire a second language are strong and pervasive. This process is more or less natural when a child grows up in a bi-lingual home, neighbourhood or community.

Becoming bilingual under such circumstances is quite different from simply "learning a foreign language". For example, the environmental pressure to learn English, on a Welsh child in Wales, or on an Italian immigrant in New York, or on an Afrikaans child in South Africa, is more immediate and urgent than when English is merely studied at school as it is done in many European countries like France, Germany, Holland, etc.

In the former cases a command of English is not a personal attribute simply, it is a function of a person's communal awareness. This is not to deny that problems of bilingualism in bilingual communities and problems of learning foreign languages do not overlap.

Communal pressures

I am inclined to agree with E. Glyn Lewis where he writes
"If the study of bilingualism is to lead to a more thoughtful appraisal of the administrative and educational attitudes which should be adopted, the distinction between the two should be recognised. This distinction is based upon a consideration of the context in which the child is learn-ing the languages and the existence of social conditions and communal pressures which conduce to the learning of more than one language, no matter how disinclined or how devoid of native wit and aptitude for learn-ing the child may be." (Bilingualism 1965 p.110)

How these pressures apply also in adult learning is illustrated by the re-markable facility with which the Bantu in South Africa acquire one or both of the country's official languages—English and Afrikaans—in addition to their own vernaculars—Zulu, Zosa, Tswana, etc., when they live in association with White people. The prestige of a language is a powerful motivating force. The extent to which the White man's language has prestige over the Bantu verna-cular is illustrated by what a prominent chief in the Transkei told me when he encountered the plea for mother tongue instruction. He said: "Yes, it is good to learn one's mother tongue. If I know that, I am like a chicken pecking in-side a hen-coop. But when I know the White man's language (English), I can soar like an eagle'."

(Incidentally it may be mentioned that out of about 11, 000, 000 Bantu, over $1\frac{1}{2}$ million speak English; 2 1/4 million speak Afrikaans. Of these about one million can speak both English and Afrikaans. These Bantu are therefore trilingual for practical purposes).

If one takes all the non-Whites in South Africa (i.e. Bantu, Coloured and Asiatic), about 12% are bilingual in the sense of being able to speak both the official languages English and Afrikaans. The percentage for the Whites only is 66% and for the total population (White and non-White) 22%. The latest available figure for bilinguals speaking both French and English in Canada is 12%).

Many Bantu also come from outside the borders of the Republic to work on contract in the mines. In order to enable all these various Bantu vernacular groups to communicate with one another and also to instruct them in connection with their work, there has been developed on the mines a lingua franca called Fanagalo. It consists of a mixture of common words taken from various Bantu vernaculars in order to serve as a basic vocabulary suited to the practical needs of the work on the mines. Thus it happens that many Bantu Africans become in fact quadrilingual for practical purposes. These "practical purposes" operate generally at the oral level, and reading, if any, is limited to "look and say" of notices giving directions and warnings against danger. Written words are thus recognised merely by their shape as pictorial symbols.

Bilingualism is functional

Bilingualism in a bilingual country is largely functional. It develops in proportion as it functions in a certain social context. This context of pressures and attitudes can be viewed in the form of a series of concentric and ever-widening circles. For the young child the innermost circle is the intimacy of the home. Gradually it widens to include his playmates from the neighbourhood; then come the school, the local community, and later, in adulthood, the ever-widening circles according to social and occupational needs.

I find this functional approach useful in discussion the two questions as to (a) how bilingualism is acquired, and (b) how it can be graded or measured. In each case one must consider the purpose (implicit or explicit) or practical use. "Bilingual for what" is to be the criterion.

How bilingualism is acquired

Let us take the case of the infant growing up in a bilingual community. It is doubtful whether such a child initially recognises that there are amongst the many sound symbols it hears two distinct structured sets of symbols, in other words, that two languages exist in his infant invironment. It is only later when the child finds out that certain oral symbols are associated with certain persons under certain circumstances that it begins to differentiate. This differentiate. This differentiation or realisation that these symbols constitute different languages is facilitated when these are consistently associated with different persons or sets of persons, for example, where the father consistently speaks one language and the mother another, or where the infant hears different members of the family or friends consistently speak different languages. I find that in a bilingual country like South Africa a child has no difficulty in operating linguistically in different universes of discourse. It becomes naturally bilingual because it finds out very soon that certain persons are "persons-to-whom-English-is-spoken", that other persons are "persons-to-whom-Afrikaans-is-spoken", and that, say, the Zulu domestic servants are "persons-to-whom-Zulu-is-spoken". It is very rarely that a child who grows up in such a linguistic context mixes these languages when communicating severally with any of these persons or groups of persons.

It is quite a common occurrence to find that White infants who grow up in Natal and have Zulu nannies, can speak Zulu before they can speak either English or Afrikaans. Zulu is in such cases their "first language", chronologically at least, if not their "mother tongue".

Obviously, this is a transient condition which does not last long and the child very soon picks up English or Afrikaans or both, depending on the language or languages of the home.

Bilingual homes

In a survey I conducted of the home language background of 18,000 White South African pupils in Stds. IV to X inclusive in over 200 representative schools, I found that in 25% of the homes only Afrikaans was spoken; in 32% only English, and in 43% both English and Afrikaans in varying degrees. In these bilingual homes Afrikaans was preponderant in 12% and English in 8%, thus leaving a central group of 23% of homes where English and Afrikaans were used more or less equally. In such homes, therefore, it is quite common that children, as they grow older and have learnt both languages at school, will speak English in certain circumstances, e.g. when a unilingual English-speaking person is present. This is generally done as a matter of courtesy, irrespective of what the usual home language may be. In these cases bilingualism is functional and operated colloquially as a result of indigenous social sanctions impinging on the home and in the intimate neighbourhood.

Bilingualism in the school

To continue with the South African situation: at school the position is more artificially regulated. Here children are segregated according to their home language (or mother tongue) into separate-medium schools or parallel-medium classes. In a relatively few schools to-day the Afrikaans and English-medium children are not thus segregated but receive their instruction through dual medium, i.e. using the two languages alternately as media, or using Afrikaans as a medium in certain subjects and English in other subjects.

Except in these last-mentioned schools, the use of the second language is confined to the language lesson of one class period a day and is not used functionally as a medium of communication in the way it is used outside the school in the South African context where the two cultural groups are widely interspersed and where, as has been pointed out, 66% of the White persons of 7 years and older speak both English and Afrikaans.

This hard and fast segregation by Government regulation of children into separate-medium schools is of relatively recent origin, i.e. it has been progressively enforced during the last quarter of a century. This administrative measure has deprived children of normal and free association and of the hearing

of the other language on the school playground. In this way natural and valuable adjuvants to language learning have become lost, particularly in the
oral use of language as a second language.

Before this "mother-tongue medium" principle was so rigorously enforced
by the Government, a large proportion of South Africa's White children received their instruction through the medium of the other language, usually
English, according to the parents' choice. In other words, the second language was used functionally at school and not merely confined to a language
lesson; which is often the dullest kind of lesson. The result of this functional
use was a significant increase in the percentage of people who became bilingual. Thus it increased steadily from 43% in 1918 to 73% in 1951, according
to the census figures.

Since, however, the Nationalist regime came into power in 1948, the
artificial hard and fast segregation of children into two distinct linguistic
groups, ignoring the very considerable central group where both languages are
used at home, bilingualism in South Africa has deteriorated in recent years.
Between the two censuses of 1951 and 1960 the percentage of Whites able to
speak both English and Afrikaans dropped from 73% to 66%. Amongst the Coloured population the drop was from 46% to 37% during the same period and for
the same reasons.

On analysing the statistics this drop was found to be due to the fact that
the Afrikaans-speaking section of the population (which had always been more
bilingual than the English-speaking section) showed an increase of from 11% to
18% of persons who could not speak English, whereas the English-speaking
section who could not speak Afrikaans remained constant at 15% between the
two censuses of 1951 and 1960.

These facts seem to support my main contention that a language is not
learned in a vacuum. It is essentially a tool. It develops in proportion as it
is used in connection with something that matters. Subjects in a school curric-
ulum are things that matter in school as well as after the pupil leaves school.
The use of both languages must therefore, be functional in school as well as in
the life of the individual outside the school in a bilingual country.

The use of two languages as school media

To what extent bilingualism can be fostered by using both languages as
media of instruction has been demonstrated by the results of the above-
mentioned survey which I conducted in 1938. The results were published in
The Bilingual School and can be summarised as follows. This survey involved
the testing of the scholastic and linguistic achievements of over 18,000 pupils
with a view to comparing the effects of having them in unilingual and bilingual
medium schools respectively. In 1938 bilingual schools were still common and
Afrikaans and English-speaking children very frequently had the opportunity of
associating with one another and hearing the two languages spoken on the playground. In these bilingual schools a child would generally receive his primary

level instruction through the mother tongue or his first language. Beyond the primary stage his instruction would be through both media, at least partially if not completely, except of course in the language lessons. In the unilingual-medium school which is attended by children from one home language group only, one medium is used throughout, except, of course, when teaching the second language.

In comparing the scholastic and linguistic achievement in these two types of school, the children's intelligence and home language were kept constant. As regards attainment in the second language on the part of both English and Afrikaans-speaking pupils, we found a considerable superiority amongst those pupils who attended the bilingual school. The English-speaking pupils, being the less bilingual to start with, gained more in Afrikaans than the Afrikaans-speaking pupils gained in English; in fact, the gain was more than four times as big. As regards the first language or mother tongue, whether English or Afrikaans, there was no loss whatsoever on the part of those pupils attending the bilingual school. The highest degree of bilingualism, i.e. that obtained by adding the Afrikaans and English scores together, was obtained by bilingual children attending bilingual schools. Next came the bilinguals and Afrikaans home-language children attending English-medium schools, next bilinguals in Afrikaans-medium schools. The lowest on the list were the unilingual home language pupils attending unilingual-medium schools where the medium was the same as the home language, English and Afrikaans single-medium schools being about equally poor.

Our results showed also that Afrikaans children in unilingual-medium Afrikaans schools were about two and a half years behind in English compared standard for standard with English children in English medium schools. Similarly English children in English-medium schools were about three years behind in Afrikaans when compared standard for standard with Afrikaans-medium schools. This disparity was found to be considerably lessened when children from unilingual homes attended bilingual medium schools.

While it can be expected that the partial or exclusive use of the second language as a medium of instruction does improve the pupil's proficiency in that language, the question arises: Is this linguistic gain not accompanied by a loss in the pupil's attainments in the content subjects which are taught through the medium of the second language?

One of the purposes of the survey was to find an answer to this question. In doing so intelligence and home language background had to be kept constant. This was statistically possible because of the large number of pupils tested (18,773).

The results showed that where the second language was totally unknown to the child as a result of his unilingual home environment, there was a definite handicap in the lower standards. This handicap tapered off as the child went on in the school. In subjects like arithmetic where language does not play such a big role, the initial handicap was smaller than in subjects like geography and history where language plays a greater role both in communication to and expression by the pupil. The results showed further that, whatever initial handicap there was as a result of the partial or exclusive use of the second language as a medium, this handicap proved to be almost precisely in proportion to the relative strangeness of the language used as a medium, and practically disappeared when the child's knowledge of the second language approximated that of his first language. By the time pupils in the bilingual medium school reached Std. VI, i.e. the end of the primary school, they were in no way behind in their content subjects as a result of their second language being used as a medium of instruction.

At the high school level the use of the English medium showed considerable advantages in content subjects which required wide reading, because there is a wider selection of reference material in libraries available in the English language than in Afrikaans. Children who have had English medium instruction read such books with greater facility than those who studied English merely as a school subject.

There is a theory that while the clever child may survive the use of the second language as a medium, the duller child suffers badly. We therefore made the comparison at different intelligence levels and found that not only the bright children but also the children with below normal intelligence do better school work all round in the bilingual school than in the unilingual school. What is most significant is that the greatest gain for the bilingual school was registered in the second language by the lower intelligence groups. Not only do they more than hold their own in the first language, but in their second language their gain was nearly twice as big as that registered by the higher intelligence groups. It would seem that the linguistic experience gained by contact with the second language in the playground and in other concrete ways in the bilingual school is vital in the case of the dull child and should be capitalised as a means of learning the second language. It appears that when the school uses both channels available in the South African situation for communicating knowledge, it gives not only intelligent children but also less intelligent children a greater advantage over those who use only one channel of linguistic experience in communicating school subjects. This is quite apart from making children more bilingual.

Attitudes

In dealing with the whole question of bilingualism, there is one aspect which seems to be of crucial importance (at least in the South African situation), and that is the emotional aspect—the attitudes which children, parents and teachers have towards the other tongue and towards the persons whose mother tongue it happens to be. It depends on whether it is regarded as a means of opening up new cultural vistas and contact or as the language of a people feared, hated or despised. This is where history as well as geography plays a role.

The child's whole learning process is affected by attitudes. It is influ-

enced not only by his home environment but also by the type of school organisation in which the child finds himself, i.e. whether the children living in
the same community are artificially segregated on linguistic lines into separate
schools or go to the same school. The effects which this factor has on children's feelings of social distance to the other language group have been demonstrated and measured in the above-mentioned survey. (Malherbe 1946)

The extent to which teachers' attitudes affect even research and experimental work in this field is shown in the "Experiment Involving the Use of the
Second Official Language as a Medium of Instruction" which was conducted
by the Department of Public Education of the Cape Province during the period
1944 to 1951. Those teachers who wanted to make a success of the experiment
reported positive results; those who were apathetic or antagonistic found all
sorts of difficulties in the way.

The measurement of bilingualism

The term "measurement" implies the use of units of a quantitative nature
which have objectivity irrespective of the measurer. In "measuring" language
one is, however, confronted with a very complex situation which does not
easily lend itself to mathematical treatment. It is true that there are quantitative aspects of language such as range of vocabulary, speed of reading and
comprehension, which can be fairly objectively assessed. But then even in
vocabulary a distinction must be made between the range of words understood
and the range of words used. One finds a considerable difference here in the
case of both children and adults learning a language.

But there are also qualitative aspects such as elegance of expression which
are not so readily amenable to objective measurement. Furthermore, there
are differences according as one deals with the written or the oral aspects of
language respectively. In the latter case accent and enunciation are also
involved. These aspects do not easily lend themselves to quantitative measurement.

Though separate tests and scales have been devised and even standardised to measure vocabulary range, reading ability, spelling and composition,
I am not aware of the existence of a general language test which has been
standardised similar to the widely used tests of general intelligence for individuals and groups. Here is a challenging field for research. It will,
however, require language experts who are also well versed in the statistical
techniques necessary for constructing tests which will have validity as well as
reliability.

Assuming that this can be done in the case of each of several languages
by themselves, one is faced with a further problem when dealing with the coexistence of two languages at different stages of development within the same
individual. Bilingualism does not necessarily connote equilingualism. In bilingualism one has to do with two variables, each one of which may differ in
range from almost zero to 100% in an infinite variety of combinations which

may be found in individuals who are all called bilingual. Then, too, age is a factor and must be taken into account as in the case of measuring a child's intelligence quotient (I.Q.) with a view to arriving at his bilingualism quotient (B.Q.). The problem of measurement in this field is therefore exceedingly complicated.

Functional Bilingualism

It is doubtful whether bilingualism per se can be measured apart from the situation in which it is to function in the social context in which a particular individual operates linguistically. The only practical line of approach to this complicated problem which I can suggest is to assess bilingualism in terms of certain social and occupational demands of a practical nature in a particular society. Here again the criterion is to be "bilingualism for what." Purpose and function are the main determinants. It should be possible to work out graded steps or stages of bilingual proficiency in particular situations or occupations. In certain occupations, for example, all that may be required may be an ability to follow an ordinary conversation in the second language without being able to speak or write that language. This may be regarded as the lowest step of binguality, but at the same time it may prove perfectly adequate in the case of a farm labourer or a miner operating in a bilingual country like South Africa. At the top end of the scale one would have the stage of bilingualism which is reached by only a few persons, probably language scholars, who command a greater facility and power in the use of both languages than, say, 90% of the people who use either of the two languages as their first language. In between these two extreme points there will be stages of proficiency in the two languages such as will be required, for example, from shop assistants, bus conductors, waiters, civil servants, teachers, etc. respectively. In South Africa, for example, tests for bilingualism are applied in the case of civil servants and of teachers. Here oral as well as written proficiency in the two languages is required. These tests, however, have never been properly standardised, i.e. as regards validity and reliability and the results vary very frequently according to the subjective judgment of the examiner.

The problems connected with the various degrees of bilingualism have been more fully discussed in my book The Bilingual School and also in the inaugural address which I delivered on the occasion of the International Seminar on Bilingualism in Education which was held at Aberystwyth, Wales, in 1960, under the auspices of the United Kingdom National Commission for Unesco, published by H. M. Stationery Office in 1965. In my book The Bilingual School I described the use and the results of standardised tests in assessing the growth of bilingualism in school children under various situations in a bilingual country like South Africa. These tests had a high validity in determining the degree of bilingualism reached by groups of children.

There is still great scope for research in the field of standardised tests which can be used in determining bilingualism not only in the written form but also in the oral form. I refer to the technique used by Professor Ben Taute in his scales for the Determination of the Ability of School Pupils to Speak the Second Language and of the Intercorrelations Between this Ability and Certain Other Abilities and Factors. (Taute 1948)

DISCUSSION

English Version

Dr. Jones told the meeting that his paper on how and when people became bilingual was entirely concerned with the description rather than the measurement part of the terms of reference. Originally it had been suggested that he should concentrate on case studies and child bilingualism.

He postulated that consideration of bilingualism from the point of view of acquisition of language led us to one other typology to add to the already interminable typologies of bilinguals:

a) Those with whom the manner of learning—whether it be in the family or in the community at large—is unorganised didactically, although the learners themselves follow a distinct order in their learning, which does not differ greatly from that of the first language.

b) Those who acquire the second language more deliberately, and whose learning is organised and "artificial". This was amplified by a comment from a commentator that in determining the question of whether bilinguals possessed two codes or not, one must know what the input is from the environment. Where both languages are spoken in the subjects' environment, it would be difficult to separate one from the other to establish what a bilingual's "languages" are. It was pointed out that human beings tend to take the way of least resistance and that Dr. Gumperz's work showed that language systems tend to coalesce. The question of whether bilingualism was harmful in itself was briefly debated, Dr. Jones defending his point of view by showing that the evidence failed to distinguish between bilingualism itself and the educational and social factors which surround it.

Dr. Jones made the point that, as no reliable experimental research exists for determining the value of various language exercises or deliberate courses for infants, the main question raised and to a great extent, left unanswered, in his paper was: of what practical importance are descriptions of "natural" acquisition (Bilingualism type 1) for the field of didactics (Bilingualism type 2) Despite incompatibilities between these two types it may be possible now to review their more positive relationship.

There are essential differences between first and second language acquisition. The fact of interference between what already exists and what is being learnt is the obvious factor, but there are important motivational and psychological differences as well. The basic structures of one's first language are learnt before the age of 4 years, and this produces a psychological set which makes it difficult to conform entirely to the norms of the second language. In spite of those considerations, though experts do their best to avoid it, it is tempting to borrow concepts from the field of first-language learning as these do cast some useful light on second-language learning. The field of second-language learning is one in which considerable basic research is still needed before we have a clear idea of the processes involved.

According to one participant, part of the problem lies in the different degrees of sophistication of adult and child speech behaviour. Children pay more attention to sound than do adults who tend to go through sound to the meaning of the sentence. Because of this love of sound, children tend to use more demonstrative sentences, to use language as a plaything, and their information-giving is not so well organised. The child tends to learn his lexicon through visual motor activity, while the adult is more verbally oriented, though visual motor activity can play a part in his learning. The child becomes very deeply involved in the situation in which he finds himself through his reliance on activity. In a bilingual situation this involvement in the situation can cause confusions between the signifier and the signified. The meeting was told that in Alsace where children are taught the concrete vocabulary of French by means of plastic models, they tend to reserve the French word for the model and the native Germanic word for the real thing. This confusion does not disappear until relatively late in the child's career at kindergarten.

Psychological factors held a large place in the discussion. In support of an early start, it was pointed out that a child enjoys playing with strange sounds, a characteristic which favours an early start. Adolescents are very often embarassed by the strange phonemes of another language and the contortions necessary to produce them. Against this point of view several speakers pointed to the importance of social considerations in language learning. If a language has social value to a child and his peers, this could accelerate learning. It was agreed that differences in social situations will entail differences in approach. In bilingual countries, due to social needs, an early start would seem to be necessary. In other countries, because the second language is taught more for cultural reasons, a latter start would be reasonable. In bilingual communities, one delegate remarked, language serves as one method of identifying parts of the environment. For instance, children often class people according to the language in which they are to be addressed: thus one person is one to whom English is spoken, another is one to whom French is to be spoken. Even animals tend to be identified according to the language of their owner.

The decision on methodology to be used is one each community is to make on its own, judging by its own linguistic situation. Apart from social factors, methodology should suit the ages and capabilities of the pupils, a principle that is often ignored. Thus methodology designed for children should make more use of their liking for activity, and adult methodology should be based on the adult's preference for verbal types of learning.

Emotional factors play a large part in the efficiency of learning. It was pointed out that a child wants to use the second language in the sort of situation in which he uses his first language. If he is made to feel that it is not possible, the whole thing takes on an air of unreality and motivation suffers. The prestige of the language and attitudes of both peers and superiors is of capital importance.   One delegate told of an inspection he made of English teaching in a small South African school.   The performance of the pupils was considerably inferior to that of the classes of roughly the same ability in a school about five miles away.   When the teacher was asked to give a demonstration lesson he sighed and said: "Come children, let us wrestle with the enemy's language." The inspector drew the obvious conclusion. An observer suggested that research he had carried out in one of the Ontario school systems showed that poor performance in first language lessons adversely affected interest in a second language. The reasoning seemed to be that as the first language is so difficult, a second will be impossible.

There was some comment on Dr. Jones' discussion of the importance of habit formation in language learning. Though commentators agreed that there was a place for "unconscious habit formation" and, indeed that it was present in all language learning situations, the fact that a child follows a definite sequence in language learning shows that there are many other elements besides habit formation. Dr. Jones felt he had been misinterpreted on this point and hoped that his brief Guillaumean interpretation of the growth of child language would have suggested how opposed his own approach would be to any limited ideas of habit formation. The very fact that the child follows his own definite order in acquisition, whatever habits an adult would wish to inculcate, gives the lie to mere habit formation. The fact that there is an almost obligatory order in the acquisition of parts of speech, in the persons of the pronoun, in the tenses of the verb, in number with nouns, and in the comparison of adjectives, and so on, such facts direct our attention to the type of process under way, which is far removed from mere habit formation. Nevertheless, while agreeing on that, and while taking up a totally different position, Dr. Jones would be loth to state categorically that habit formation is absent at this stage, nor would he deny that it is a considerable aid. He remarked that when we start, quite rightly, weeding out matters such as "habit" in our description of infant language, we must be careful not to throw out the baby with the bathwater.

He was supported by other speakers who said that a child learns to interpret language before learning how to use it. Habit formation is valuable provided that a child is encouraged to move beyond habits by integrating his new language into his ordinary activities. Dr. Jones thought that Dr. Rivers' three-way analysis of exercises (receptive, imitative, and productive) would lead to confusion. There is on one hand, a differential reception of phonemes, that is to say, the child nearns to distinguish the hearing of sounds. There is also the production of phonemes. Imitation is not an additional process to either of these: it is no half-way house. If a child is imitating vocally, he is producing. Expressive vocal imitation is merely one type of reproduction. This was accepted by Dr. Rivers, but she wanted to see it laid out as such. Imitation was important in fixing sound elements and kinesthetic images, and this type of exercis e should be resorted to very often. Activities should be integrated into listen-do-repeat exercises for efficacy in learning; but such exercises should always be followed by application in real situations. The early stages of language learning are a very good point at which to introduce natural situations, formulas of courtesy, etc., in play form. But any such procedures must be based on solid research.

Some comments were made on the needs linguistic analysis could fill. One delegate agreed with Dr. Jones' uneasiness over transformational approaches to bilingualism. Emphasis on generation from kernel sentences lead to quite unnatural assumptions when dealing with bilingualism. Mention was made of the forthcoming articles by Michael Halliday on Transitivity and Theme in English in the Journal of Linguistics. In these articles emphasis is on the psychology rather than on the logic of grammar which is the concern of the transformationalists. This could be an important contribution to the study of bilingualism. There is also need to distinguish the grammar of monologue from that of dialogue. It is quite possible that in children dialogue is developed first.

The question of one-element sentences was briefly debated. Dr. Jones remarked that the need for identification of environment is peculiar to one's first language. But grammatically and syntactically this type of construction is basic even in adult language. This sentence form is so often mistreated by some linguists who attempt to approach it from other types of sentences. Hill, who finds great difficulty in situating this type of utterance, designates it as an " Elementless" sentence, and explains the term by saying; "In all but a few single-construction sentences, it is impossible to identify the content of the sentence with any of the sentence elements such as subject, predicator, complement or adjunct." Likewise transformationalists find the form resistant to their approach. Harris, in dealing with such sentences as "yes", finds them "inert construction which hardly enter into transformations." Certain presuppositions are here being made about language that do not work with one of its major forms. Sleator has criticized justly this ad hoc treatment meted out to items which don't fit into the a priori constructional frame: "The treatment may consist of setting up a special class of items on the basis of their not having features required by the general rule, or of setting up "elliptical" or "zero" elements or classes like "subjectless" and "elementless" to account for the "absence" of some regularly required element."

Some linguists, in ignoring this sentence-type, begin with particular results of their choice and turn them into other results. Their technique presupposes certain kernel sentences (without explaining how these came about in their particular form), and shows how to analyses them or how it is possible to derive other sentences from them. The child, on the other hand, starts linguistically from nil, and ends up with the whole system of the particular language being learnt.

If the sentence structure is to develop, he must begin it with a central support, as it were a "thing" or a thing equivalent (i.e. a noun-equivalent). This is true of the one-element sentence, even when the sign adopted turns out in the maturer language system to be a verbal form, an adjective or adverb: it begins as if it were a thing. Subsequently, in Indo-European languages, a verb or an adjective equivalent may be said about this. But the starting-point or central prop of the sentence is the thing that is identified. And this particular grammatical achievement remains with him on into adult sentences. Another speaker confirmed that one-element sentences were not restricted to things: actions can also form the subject of such sentences, as they are one means of identifying the environment. The question of basing exercises and games on contrastive analysis was raised. This principle was accepted as important but the question arose of contrast with what. Analyses of child language are quite sparse. In comparing the child's language with that of the adult we tend to contrast spoken with written. We need analyses of the spoken language to make valid contrasts. A delegate spoke of the work of Remacle who is analysing his children's language from a structural point of view as well as a phonetic, and drew the attention of the delegates to the work of Mme Ruke-Dravina on bilingual children. Both scholars show that analogy is a very important factor in the development of child language.

The question of bilingual schooling took up much of the discussion. In bilingual countries the assumption is that the attainment of bilingualism is a desirable thing from the point of view of the individual and the society. The most important question is: How can it be acquired with the least ill effect? South Africa was used as an illustration of what could be done. There, over 70% of the white population speaks both English and Afrikaans. Children are widely exposed to both and to Bantu languages as well. In 1938 an analysis of home language showed that in 43% of the homes in South Africa both languages were spoken, in 32% only English and in 25% Afrikaans. Every child is taught both languages at school. This is done in two ways: through language lessons, and by using the second language as a medium of instruction. If a child has to live in a bilingual society he has to interpret life in bilingual terms. As school subjects are just crystallisations of life experience to be interpreted to school children, using both languages as media of instruction duplicates the bilingual environment outside the school.

In South Africa there are unilingual medium schools and bilingual medium schools. The second type sometimes teaches certain subjects through the other medium, sometimes uses different languages on alternate days. There are also some schools in which part of the lesson is given in one language and part in the other. Handicaps are possible if the child's home environment is linguistically so poor that he has trouble following the lessons. But the general experience indicates that pupils gain immeasurably from the experience and that there is no lasting handicap in their knowledge of the subject. The handicap actually decreases as one moves up the school.

Some of these conclusions have been submitted to experiment. A psychologist at the University of Capetown selected 60 boys from an Afrikaans-medium school, the same number from English-medium and bilingual schools. IQ and other factors were controlled. The 180 children were observed over a period of years and those from bilingual schools did best. The psychologist ventured

the explanation that children tend to ignore the recapitulation cycle of a lesson when it is given in the same language as the exposition, but that if it is in
another language, there are always additional nuances which enrich the learning process.

The experience from other countries contradicted much of this evidence.
In countries like Australia and Holland, as the second language was not spoken
outside the classroom, as far as the children were concerned, bilingual schools
would be unreal. In Belgium, similar experiments to the South African one
gave notably different results, so that bilingual teaching was not feasible there.

One delegate suggested that one should always assess an educational process against the background of the system. There are five types of system possible:

	Medium	Branch	Auxiliary Language
a	L1	L2	--
b	L1&2	L1&2	--
c	L2	L1	--
d	L2	--	L1
e	L2	--	--

The first pattern is the unilingual school; the third a common minority pattern.

There was common agreement that teacher training was a key question.
The question of imitating the NDEA institutes of USA was mentioned. The
question of training parents was mentioned in connection with certain adult
education programmes in Wales. These have as their main aim not the creation
of bilinguals, but implanting certain favourable attitudes towards Welsh so
that the children will not be discouraged from studying the language or using
it. Parental collaboration was essential if the school was to do its job.

DISCUSSION

Version française

M. Jones déclare que sa communication relative à la manière dont on devient bilingue et aux circonstances dans lesquelles on le devient porte uniquement sur la partie description, plutôt que sur la partie mesure, du sujet proposé au colloque. On l'avait invité au début à traiter surtout des études de cas individuels et du bilinguisme chez l'enfant.

Il postule d'abord que l'examen du bilinguisme du point de vue de l'acquisition d'une langue fait apparaître une typologie de plus, qui s'ajoute à la liste déjà interminable des typologies de bilingues:

a) Ceux dont la manière d'apprendre (que ce soit dans le milieu familial ou dans l'ensemble de la collectivité) n'est pas tributaire d'une méthode d'enseignement, même s'ils apprennent dans un ordre nettement perceptible et qui diffère peu de celui dans lequel ils ont appris leur première langue.

b) Ceux qui acquièrent plus délibérément leur seconde langue, d'une manière organisée et "artificielle". Un commentateur appuie sur cette distinction en notant que, pour savoir si un bilingue se sert de deux codes, on doit connaître l'importance de ce qu'il reçoit du milieu même. Si les deux langues se parlent autour de lui, on pourra difficilement des séparer l'une de l'autre pour déterminer quelles sont "ses langues". Quelqu'un fait observer que les gens ont tendance à emprunter la voie de moindre résistance et que les systèmes linguistiques, d'après les travaux de M. Gumperz, ont tendance à se fondre ensemble. On discute brièvement des inconvénients propres du bilinguisme. M. Jones maintient son point de vue, faisant observer que les arguments apportés ne distinguent pas suffisamment entre le bilinguisme en tant que tel et les facteurs sociaux qui l'entourent.

Comme il ne s'est pas encore fait, dit-il, de recherches expérimentales permettant d'établir avec certitude la valeur de divers exercices de langue ou cours d'études destinés aux enfants en bas âge, la grande question qui ressort de sa communication, et à laquelle, dans une grande mesure, il n'a pas été apporté de réponse, est la suivante: Quelle est l'importance pratique des descriptions de l'acquisition "naturelle" (bilinguisme de type 1) pour le domaine de la didactique (bilinguisme de type 2)? En dépit de certaines incompatibilités entre ces deux types de bilinguisme, peut-être est-il possible aujourd'hui d'examiner ce qu'il peut y avoir de positif dans leurs rapports mutuels.

Il existe des différences fondamentales entre l'acquisition de la première langue et celle de la seconde. L'interférence entre ce que l'on possède déjà et ce que l'on apprend entre nécessairement en ligne de compte, mais il y a

en outre des considérations de motivation et de psychologie à ne pas négliger.
On apprend les structures fondamentales de la langue première avant l'âge de
quatre ans, ce qui met en place un système psychologique rendant difficile
l'obéissance totale, par la suite, aux normes d'une seconde langue.   Cependant, et bien que les spécialistes s'efforcent de ne pas le faire, on est tenté
d'emprunter des concepts au domaine de l'apprentissage de la langue première,
car ils éclairent de façon utile la manière dont s'apprend la langue seconde.
Il reste pourtant bien des recherches fondamentales à faire avant que l'on per-
çoive clairement les mécanismes d'apprentissage de la langue seconde.

D'après l'un des participants, le problème tient jusqu'à un certain point
à l'inégal développement du langage chez l'adulte et chez l'enfant.   Ce dernier s'arrête davantage aux sons que ne le fait l'adulte, lequel cherche toujours à travers les sons la signification de la phrase.   L'enfant, parce qu'il
aime les sons, a recours à des phrases plus démonstratives; pour lui, parler est
un jeu, et la valeur d'information de ce qu'il dit est moins sûre que chez l'a-
dulte.   Il apprend son lexique par une activité motrice surtout visuelle, tandis
que l'adulte, même s'il apprend lui aussi visuellement, le fait surtout verba-
lement.   L'enfant, parce qu'il est actif avant tout, s'engage très profondément dans toute situation où il se trouve.   Dans une situation de bilinguisme,
son engagement profond donne lieu parfois à une certaine confusion entre signifiant et signifié.   En Alsace, où l'on enseigne aux enfants le vocabulaire
français des objets concrets au moyen de modèles en matière plastique, il arrive
que les écoliers réservent le nom français au modèle et continuent de donner à
l'objet réel son nom allemand.   La confusion ne se dissipe que bien des mois
après l'entrée à la maternelle.

La discussion fait une place importante aux facteurs psychologiques.   On
fait observer, en faveur de l'apprentissage de la langue seconde dès l'âge ten-
dre, que l'enfant aime jouer avec les sons étrangers, ce qui facilite son bilinguisme.   L'adolescent, lui, est souvent retenu par sa timidité devant la mimi-
que nouvelle que lui imposeraient les phonèmes de l'autre langue.   Contre ce
point de vue, plusieurs participants mettent l'accent sur les considérations
d'ordre social qui entrent en jeu.   Une langue s'apprend parfois plus rapidement lorsqu'elle présente une utilité sociale pour l'enfant et pour ses camara-
des.   On reconnaît que toute différence entre les situations sociales peut en-
traîner des différences d'attitude.   Dans les pays bilingues, il semble que l'apprentissage de la langue seconde devrait commencer plus tôt, en raison de son
utilité sociale.   Il en sera autrement là où l'utilité de la langue seconde se
manifeste surtout sur le plan de la culture.   Dans les collectivités bilingues,
note un participant, la langue constitue l'un des éléments d'identification du
milieu où l'on vit.   Les enfants, par exemple, étiquettent les personnes suivant
la langue dans laquelle ils doivent leur parler: à celle-ci on parle en anglais,
à celle-là en français.   Même les animaux, parfois, sont anglais ou français
suivant la langue de leur maître.

Le choix de la méthodologie à adopter appartient à chacune des collectivités, qui tiendra compte de sa situation linguistique particulière.   La métho-

dologie doit répondre, non seulement aux conditions sociologiques, mais à l'âge et aux aptitudes des élèves, ce qu'on oublie souvent. Les enfants, par exemple, ont besoin d'une méthodologie fondée sur l'activité; les adultes, de méthodes surtout verbales.

Le rôle de l'affectivité est important. L'enfant désire parler sa langue seconde dans le même genre de situations que sa langue première. S'il en vient à sentir que ce n'est pas possible, tout son effort s'enveloppe d'irréalité, ce qui diminue sa motivation. Autres éléments d'importance capitale, le prestige de la langue dont il s'agit et l'attitude des égaux et des supérieurs. L'un des participants se rappelle une visite d'inspection qu'il fit à une petite école d'Afrique du Sud. Les élèves y étaient beaucoup moins forts en anglais, classe pour classe, que ceux d'une école semblable située à cinq milles de là. L'instituteur, prié de donner une leçon de démonstration, dit aux enfants avec un soupir: "Allons-y, les enfants, essayons de venir à bout de la langue de l'ennemi!" La conclusion était facile à tirer. Un observateur assure que, d'après des recherches qu'il a faites dans l'un des systèmes scolaires de l'Ontario, de mauvais résultats dans l'étude de la langue première retentissent sur l'intérêt que l'élève peut porter à la langue seconde. Sans doute se dit-il que, s'il est si difficile d'apprendre une langue, il est impossible d'en apprendre une seconde.

Les observations de M. Jones sur l'importance de l'acquisition d'habitudes, dans l'apprentissage d'une langue, alimentent divers commentaires. On est d'accord pour admettre la réalité de l'acquisition inconsciente de certaines habitudes, et même pour y voir un phénimène constant dans toute étude de langue. Toutefois, le fait que l'enfant qui apprend une langue observe une succession nettement définie révèle l'intervention de nombreux autres éléments que l'acquisition d'habituees. M. Jones estime qu'on l'a mal compris à ce sujet; il aurait cru que sa brève interprétation à la Guillaume, en ce qui concerne le développement du langage de l'enfant, aurait montré à quel point sa manière de voir est étrangère à tout exclusivisme en faveur de l'acquisition d'habitudes. Le fait même que l'enfant acquiert des habitudes dans l'ordre qui lui convient personnellement, quelles que soient les habitudes que les grandes personnes s'efforcent de lui inculquer, est révélateur à cet égard. Il existe par ailleurs un ordre quasi obligatoire pour l'apprentissage des parties du discours, de la déclinaison de certains pronoms, de la conjugaison des verbes, du nombre des substantifs, des degrés de comparaison des adjectifs, et ainsi de suite; cela suffit à nous renseigner sur la nature des processus qui interviennent, fort différents de la simple acquisition d'habitudes. M. Jones, pourtant, tout en étant d'accord là-dessus, mais à partir d'une position entièrement différente, n'irait pas jusqu'à soutenir catégoriquement que toute acquisition d'habitudes est absente à ce stade, non plus qu'à en nier la grande utilité. Lorsque l'on écarte, d'ailleurs à juste titre, les habitudes et autres éléments en parlant du langage de l'enfant en bas âge, il ne faut pas, dit M. Jones, jeter le bébé avec l'eau sale du bassin...

D'autres participants soutiennent le même point de vue: l'enfant apprend à interpréter la parole avant d'apprendre à s'en servir lui-même. L'acquisition d'habitudes a son utilité, mais à condition que l'on encourage l'enfant à faire davantage et à donner à sa langue nouvelle un rôle dans son activité ordinaire. D'après M. Jones, l'analyse que fait Mme Rivers des exercices, et son tryptique réception-imitation-production, risquent d'engendrer une certaine confusion. D'une part, les phonèmes ne sont pas perçus de la même façon par chaque enfant qui les entend et qui apprend à les distinguer. Il y a aussi la production des phonèmes. Quant à l'imitation, elle ne constitue pas une opération distincte, un stade intermédiaire. L'enfant qui imite un phonème produit un phonème, tout simplement. Ce n'est là qu'un des modes possibles de production. Mme Rivers admet cela, mais elle voulait que ce soit dit nettement. L'imitation joue un rôle important dans la fixation des éléments des sons et dans celle des images kinesthésiques, et l'on doit donner très souvent des exercices du genre écouter-faire-répéter comportent la participation active de l'enfant, et soient toujours suivis d'une application à des situations réelles. Les premiers stades de l'étude d'une langue conviennent très bien à la familiarisation avec des situations naturelles, avec les formules de courtoisie, etc., tout cela par manière de jeu. Il faut toutefois, que les méthodes employées se fondent sur des recherches sérieuses.

Certains participants signalent des besoins auxquels l'analyse linguistique pourrait répondre. L'un des délégués éprouve comme M. Jones une certaine inquétude devant les attitudes "transformationnistes" face au bilinguisme. En insistant trop sur la transformation à partir de "phrases-noyaux", on en arrive à formuler, au sujet du bilinguisme, des hypothèses fort discutables. Il est question, au cours de la discussion, des articles de Michael Halliday qui paraîtront sous peu dans le Journal of Linguistics sous le titre: Transitivity and Theme in English. Ces articles mettent l'accent sur la psychologie de la grammaire plutôt que sur sa logique, à la différence de ce que font les transformationnistes. Ils exerceront peut-être une importante influence sur l'étude du bilinguisme. La grammaire du monologue, d'autre part, doit être distinguée de celle du dialogue. Chez les enfants, il n'est pas impossible que le dialogue précède le monologue.

On discute brièvement la question des phrases à élément unique. M. Jones note que le besoin d'identifier l'environnement n'est satisfait que par la langue première. Cependant, du point de vue grammatical comme du point de vue syntaxique, les phrases à élément unique constituent la base du langage, même chez les adultes. Cette construction de phrase est souvent maltraitée par des linguistes qui l'abordent à partir d'autres genres de phrases. Hill, qui éprouve de grandes difficultés à la situer, l'appelle phrase "dépourvue d'éléments", ce qu'il explique ainsi: "Dans toutes ou presque toutes les phrases de construction aussi simple, il est impossible d'identifier le contenu de l'énoncé à l'aide de l'un ou l'autre des éléments de phrase que sont le sujet, l'attribut ou le complément". Les transformationnistes, eux aussi, trouvent ce genre de phrase réfractaire à leur mode d'examen. Harris voit dans les phrases comme "oui" des "constructions inertes qui ne participent à peu près jamais à des transformations".

De tels propos s'appuient sur des postulats qui ne cadrent pas avec l'une des formes principales du langage. Sleator a critiqué à juste titre ce traitement spécial réservé aux faits de langage qui n'entrent pas dans un cadre préétabli: "Ce traitement consiste par exemple à établir une classe spéciale pour les faits de langage qui n'ont pas les caractéristiques prévues par la règle générale, ou à créer des éléments "elliptiques", ou "zéro" ou des catégories de phrases dites "sans sujet", ou "dépourvues d'éléments", afin d'expliquer l'"absence" de tel ou tel élément habituellement présent".

Certains linguistes, qui ignorent aussi cette forme de phrase, partent de résultats choisis par eux et les transforment en d'autres résultats. Leur technique présuppose certaines "phrases-noyaux" (sans expliquer de quelle façon elles se sont présentées sous une telle forme), et indique la façon de les analyser ou d'en faire dériver d'autres phrases. L'enfant, lui, part linguistiquement de zéro et aboutit à une connaissance globale de la langue qu'il apprend.

Pour que la structure de la phrase puisse se développer, l'enfant doit lui donner au départ un point de support central, comme un objet ou l'équivalent d'un objet (par exemple un nom de chose). Il en est ainsi dans le cas de la phrase à élément unique, même si le signe utilisé correspond, dans le système de langage d'une personne plus développée, à un verbe, un adjectif ou un adverbe: celui-ci est d'abord utilisé comme une chose. Ultérieurement, dans les langues indo-européennes, l'équivalent dont l'enfant se servira sera peut-être un verbe ou un adjectif. Mais le point de départ ou le support central de la phrase, c'est la chose identifiée. Et cette opération grammaticale sert encore à l'enfant lorsqu'il en arrive à construire des phrases d'adulte.

Un autre participant confirme le fait que les phrases à élément unique ne reposent pas seulement sur des objets: elles peuvent reposer aussi sur des actes, car les actes constituent un moyen d'identifier l'environnement. Quelqu'un pose la question des exercices et des jeux fondés sur une analyse de contrastes. L'importance de ce principe est admise, mais il reste à préciser entre quels termes il y a contraste. Les analyses du langage enfantin sont assez rares. Lorsque l'on compare le langage de l'enfant et celui de l'adulte, on a tendance à établir un contraste entre langage parlé et langage écrit. Pour établir des contrastes valables, c'est d'analyses du langage parlé que l'on a besoin. Un délégué cite les travaux de Remacle, qui analyse le langage de ses enfants du point de vue structurel aussi bien que phonétique, et il signale aux participants les travaux de Mme Ruke-Dravina sur les enfants bilingues. Tous deux montrent l'importance de l'analogie dans le développement du langage enfantin.

La question du bilinguisme à l'école retient longuement l'attention des délégués. Dans les pays bilingues, on pose au départ que le bilinguisme est souhaitable, tant pour l'individu que pour la société. La principale question qui se pose est donc de savoir comment arriver au bilinguisme en réduisant au minimum les inconvénients de l'opération. L'Afrique du Sud offre un exemple de ce qu'il y a moyen de faire. Plus de 70 pour cent des blancs y parlent et l'anglais et l'afrikaans. Les enfants entendent tous les jours parler ces deux langues, de même que les langues bantoues. En 1938, une analyse des langues parlées dans les foyers a révélé que dans 43 pour cent de ceux-ci on parlait les deux langues, dans 32 pour cent l'anglais seulement et dans 25 pour cent l'afrikaans seulement. Tous les enfants apprennent les deux langues à l'école. On les leur enseigne de deux manières: par l'étude même de chaque langue et en utilisant la langue seconde comme langue d'enseignement. L'enfant qui est appelé à vivre dans une société bilingue doit pouvoir interpréter la vie dans les deux langues. Comme les matières scolaires ne sont que des cristallisations de la vie réelle, à interpréter aux écoliers, le recours aux deux langues pour l'enseignement ne fait que reproduire la situation de bilinguisme qui règne à l'extérieur de l'école.

Il existe en Afrique du Sud des écoles moyennes unilingues et des écoles moyennes bilingues. Dans ces dernières, l'enseignement de certaines matières se fait parfois dans l'autre langue, parfois alternativement dans l'une et l'autre langues, selon le jour. Certaines écoles donnent une partie de la leçon dans une langue, et le reste dans l'autre. L'enfant dont le milieu familial est pauvre en ressources linguistiques peut avoir du mal à suivre et en subir un certain désavantage, mais en général, on constate que les élèves tirent un immense profit de ce bilinguisme de l'enseignement, et n'en subissent pas d'inconvénients durables quant à la connaissance de la matière. Ces inconvénients diminuent même à mesure que l'élève atteint les classes supérieures.

Certaines de ces conclusions ont fait l'objet d'une expérimentation. Un psychologue de l'Université du Cap a choisi 60 garçons dans une école moyenne afrikaans, un nombre égal dans une école moyenne anglaise, et autant dans une école bilingue. Il y a eu contrôle des quotients intellectuels et des autres éléments pertinents. L'observation des 180 garçons s'est poursuivie sur plusieurs années. Or ce sont les élèves des écoles bilingues qui ont réussi le mieux. Le psychologue a formulé l'hypothèse que les élèves ne prêtent qu'une attention distraite au cycle récapitulatif des leçons lorsqu'il se fait dans la même langue que l'exposition première; lorsqu'il se fait dans l'autre langue, de nouvelles nuances apparaissent, et l'enfant comprend d'une manière plus complète ce qui lui a été enseigné.

Les résultats obtenus dans d'autres pays contredisent pour une bonne part ces constatations. En Australie et aux Pays-Bas, par exemple, où les enfants ne parlent plus la langue seconde une fois sortis de la classe, l'institution d'écoles bilingues ne collerait pas à la réalité. En Belgique, des expériences analogues à celles d'Afrique du Sud ont donné des résultats notablement différents, en sorte que l'enseignement bilingue ne paraît pas possible dans ce pays.

D'après l'un des participants, il faut toujours évaluer un procédé d'enseignement en tenant compte de la situation d'ensemble du système. Cinq genres de systèmes sont possibles:

	Langue	Matière	Langue auxiliaire
a	L1	L2	--
b	L1 et L2	L1 et L2	--
c	L2	L1	--
d	L2	--	L1
e	L2	--	--

Premier genre: l'école unilingue; troisième, le cas d'une minorité ordinaire.

On s'accorde à reconnaître l'importance primordiale de la formation des maîtres. Un participant cite l'exemple des instituts de la NDEA des Etats-Unis. La question de la formation des parents est évoquée à propos de certains programmes d'éducation des adultes mis en oeuvre au pays de Galles. L'objet principal n'en est pas de rendre les parents bilingues, mais d'implanter chez eux des attitudes favorables à la langue galloise, afin que leurs enfants ne se sentent pas découragés à l'idée d'apprendre cette langue ou de s'en servir. La collaboration des parents est indispensable au succès de l'école.

CHAIRMAN'S SUMMARY/BILAN DE LA SEANCE

W. F. Leopold

It is not easy to state in which respects the session brought progress in bilingualism research. Each paper reported about matters with which the author is familiar, without a unified approach. But that was probably the chief benefit of the session, apart from personal contacts: every participant became conscious of the wide variety of geographic and sociological situations in which bilingualism manifests itself, of the difference of interests and methods which linguists, psychologists, educators, and sociologists contribute to the study of bilingualism. In the past there has been some inbreeding in the exploration of the field, representatives of one discipline paying scant attention to the work done in neighboring fields. The interdisciplinary as well as international basis of the seminar contributed to the widening of horizons.

Personally I should have liked to see more emphasis on the genesis of individual bilingualism for which the topic of the session seemed to call. But perhaps this must still be left to demonstration by case studies with their recording of countless details which are not easily summarized. The growth of "natural" bilingualism was mentioned, but the emphasis of the papers and of the discussion was on induced bilingualism, on the teaching of infants and primary school pupils. This approach reflects the interests of the participating scholars and the needs of their countries.

It can safely be assumed that no participant felt disappointed in the session. We all benefited from the meeting of so many minds from so many parts of the world and different disciplines.

BIBLIOGRAPHY/BIBLIOGRAPHIE

Albright, R. W. & J. B.
1956   "The Phonology of a Two-Year-Old Child," Word 12, 382-390

Anderson, Theodore
1953   The Teaching of Foreign Languages in the Elementary School,
        Boston, D. C. Heath

Arlitt, Ada Hart
1946   Psychology of Infancy and Early Childhood, 3 ed., New York &
        London, McGraw-Hill

Arsenian, Seth
1937   Bilingualism and Mental Development: a Study of the Intelligence
        and the Social Background of Bilingual Children in New York
        City, New York, Teachers College, Columbia University (Con-
        tributions to Education 712)

Asher, James J.
1965   "The Strategy of Total Physical Response; an Application to Learn-
        ing Russian," International Review of Applied Linguistics in Lan-
        guage Teaching 3, 291-300

Bateman, W. G.
1917   "Papers on Language Development," Pedagogical Seminary 24,
        391-398

Bellugi, U. & Brown, R. (eds.)
1964   The Acquisition of Language; Report of the Fourth International
        Conference Sponsored by the Committee for Research in Child
        Development, Lafayette, Indiana, Monograph of the Society for
        Research in Child Development, 29:1 no. 92

Berko, Jean
1958   "The Child's Learning of English Morphology," Word 14, 150-177

-----& Brown, R.
        "Psycholinguistic Research Methods," in Handbook of Research
        Methods in Child Development, Mussen, P. H. (ed.) New York
        & London, John Wiley & Sons, 517-557

Bilingualism and Education, Report on an International Seminar. Aberystwyth,
        Wales, 1960, Organised by U. K. National Commission for UNESCO,
        E. Glyn Lewis (ed.)
1965   London, H. M. Stationery Office

Blom, Jan-Petter & Gumperz, J.
1966   "Some Social Determinants of Verbal Behavior," Unpublished Paper
        presented at the American Sociological Association

Braine, M. D. S.
1967   "The Acquisition of Language in Infant and Child," in The Learning
        of Language, Carroll Reed, (ed.) in press

1963   "The Ontogeny of English Phrase Structure; the First Phase,"
        Language 39, 1-13

Breunig, Marjorie
   1961   Foreign Languages in the Elementary Schools of the United States,
              1959-1960, New York, MLA
Brière, E.
   1966   "An Experimentally Defined Hierarchy of Difficulties of Learning
              Phonological Categories," Language 42, 768-796
Brown, Roger & Bellugi, Ursula
   1964   "Three Processes in the Child's Acquisition of Syntax," Harvard
              Educational Review 34, 133-151
-----& Berko, Jean
   1960   "Psycholinguistic Research Methods," (In) Handbook of Research
              Methods in Child Development, P. H. Mussen (ed.), New York,
              London, John Wiley and Sons, Co., 517-557
-----& Fraser, Colin
   1963   "The Acquisition of Syntax," (In) Verbal Learning and Verbal Be-
              havior; problems and processes, C. N. Cofer and B. S. Musgrave
              (eds.), New York, McGraw-Hill, 158-209
-----& Fraser, Colin
   1964   "The Acquisition of Syntax," (In) Bellugi & Brown 1964
Buhler, Karl
   1930   The Mental Development of the Child; a summary of modern psy-
              chological theory, London, K. Paul, Trench, Trubner and Co.
              Ltd., New York, Harcourt, Brace and Co.
Burling, Robbins
   1959   "Language Development of a Garo and English Speaking Child,"
              Word 15, 45-68
Buxbaum, Edith
   1949   "The Rôle of a Second language in the formation of Ego and
              Sperego," Psychoanalytic Quarterly 18, 279-289
Cape Provincial Department of Public Education, Report on the Experiment
              Involving the Use of the Second Language as a Medium of Instruc-
              tion, Cape Town, 1951
Carroll, John B.
   1960   "Language Development," (In) Encyclopedia of Educational
              Research, C. W. Harris (ed.), New York, The Macmillan Co.,
              744-752

   1961   "Language Acquisition, Bilingualism and Language Change," (In)
              Psycholinguistics; a book of readings, S. Saporta (ed.), New
              York, Holt, Rinehart and Winston, 331-345
Cassirer, Ernst
   1944   An Essay on Man; an introduction to a philosophy of human culture,
              New Haven; Yale University Press, London, H. Milford, Oxford
              University Press

Cazden, Courtney
  1965   Environmental Assistance to the Child's Acquisition of Grammar,
          Ed. D. Dissertation, Harvard
Chukovskii, Kornei Svanivich
  1956   Ot Dvukh Do Piati, Moscow
Clarke, Fred
  1934   Quebec and South Africa; a study in cultural adjustment, London,
          Pub. for the Institute of Education by Oxford University Press,
          H. Milford
Cohen, Marcel
  1952   "Sur l'étude du langage enfantin", Enfance, 181-249
Dawes, Thomas Richard
  1902   Bilingual Teaching in Belgian Schools; being the report on a visit
          to Belgian Schools as Gilchrist Travelling Student, Cambridge
          University Press
Descoeudres, Alice
  1946   Le développement de l'enfant de deux à sept ans; recherches de
          psychologie expérimentale, 3ᵉ éd., Neuchâtel-Paris, Delachaux
          et Niestlé
Diebold, A. R.
  1965   "A Survey of Psycholinguistic Research 1954-64," (In) Psycholin-
          guistics; a survey of theory and research problems, C. E. Osgood
          & T. Sebeok (eds.) Bloomington, Indiana University Press
Dimitrijevic, N. R.
  1965   "A Bilingual Child," English Language Teaching 20, 23-28
Earle, M. J.
  1967   "Bilingual Semantic Merging and an Aspect of Acculturation,"
          Journal of Personality and Social Psychology 6, 304-312
El'konin, D. B.
  1960a   Detskaia Psikhologiia, Moscow

  1960b   "Nekotorye itogi izuchenii psikhicheskoyo razvitiia detei doshkol
          nogo vozrasta," Psykhologicheskaia nauka 11, 228-285
Ervin, S. M.
  1961   The Verbal Behavior of Bilinguals. The Effect of Language of Report
          on the Thematic Apperception Test Content of Adult French Bi-
          linguals, Microfilm AC-1, No. 12,571, Michigan University
          Library

  1964a   "Imitation and Structural Change in Children's Language," in
          Lenneberg, 1964, 163-189
-----& Miller, W. R.
  1963   "Language Development," (In) Child Psychology, H. W. Stevenson
          (ed.), Chicago, Chicago University Press, 108-143 (62nd Year-
          book of the National Society for the Study of Education)

Ervin-Tripp, S. M.
  1967a   "An Issei Learns English," Journal of Social Issues 23, 78-90

  1967b   "Language Development," (In) Review of Child Development
            Research, Lois & Martin Hoffman (eds.), Vol. 2 Russel Sage
            Foundation
Fodor, J. A.
  1966   "How to Learn to Talk: some Simple Ways," (In) Smith & Miller
            1966
Fraser, C., Bellugi, U., Brown, R.
  1963   "The Control of Grammar in Imitation, Comprehension and Pro-
            duction," Journal of Verbal Learning and Verbal Behavior 2,
            121-;35
Gallup, John R.
  1962   "An Approach to the Theory of Declension," The Canadian Journal
            of Linguistics 8, 26-32
Glees, Paul
  1961   Experimental Neurology, Oxford, Clarendon Press
Goldstein, Kurt
  1948   Language and Language Disturbances; aphasic symptom complexes
            and their significance for medicine and theory of language,
            New York, Grune and Stratton
Grégoire, Antoine
1937-47   L'apprentissage du langage, Liège, Faculté de philosophie et
            lettres, Paris, E. Droz
Guillaume, Gustave
  1964   Langage et science du langage, Paris, A. G. Nizet
Gumperz, J.
  1964   "Linguistic and social interaction in two communities," (In)
            J. J. Gumperz and Dell Hymes (eds.), The ethnography of
            communication. Amer. Anthropol. 66, No. 6, Part 2,
            137-153

  1967   "On the linguistic markers of bilingual communication,"
            J. Soc. Issues 23, No. 2, 48-57
Gurrey, P.
  1959   Letter to English Language Teaching 13, 170
Haarhoff, T. J.
  1938   The Stranger at the Gate; aspects of exclusiveness and cooperation
            in ancient Greece and Rome, with some reference to modern
            times, London, New York, Longmans, Green and Co.

          "Bilingualism" (article in the Oxford Classical Dictionary)
Hartshorne, K. B.
  1967   The Teaching of English as a Second Language in South Africa,
            The English Academy of South Africa, Johannesburg

Haugen, Einar
  1955   "Problems of bilingual description," General Linguistics, 1, 1-9

  1956   Bilingualism in the Americas; a bibliography and research guide,
          American Dialect Society, University of Alabama
Hoffman, M. N. H.
  1934   The Measurement of Bilingual Background, New York City,
          Teachers College, Columbia University, Contributions to
          Education No. 623
Hughes, John
  1937   "The Social Psychology of Bilingualism," (In) Educational Adapta-
          tion in a Changing Society, E. G. Malherbe (ed.), Cape Town,
          Juta and Co., 73-81
Huse, Howard R.
  1945   Reading and Speaking Foreign Languages, Chapel Hill, The Uni-
          versity of North Carolina Press
Irwin, O. C. & Chen, H. P.
  1946   "Development of Speech during Infancy; survey of phoneme types",
          Journal of Experimental Psychology 36, 431-436
Jakobson, R.
  1941   Kindersprache; aphasie und allgemeine lautgesetze, Uppsala,
          Almgvist and Wiksells boktryckeri a.-b.

  1949   "Les lois phonétiques du langage enfantin et leur place dans la
          phonologie générale," (In) Troubetzkoy, N. S., Principes de
          phonologie, tr. Cantineau, J., Paris, Klincksieck
  -----& Halle, M.
  1956   "Phonemic Patterning," (In) Jakobson, R. & Halle, M. (eds.),
          Fundamentals of Language, Gravenhage, Mouton, 37-51
Jenkins, J. V. & Palermo, D. S.
          "Mediation Processes and the Acquisition of Linguistic Structure,"
          (In) Bellugi & Brown 1964
Jespersen, Otto
  1922   Language; its nature development and origin, London, G. Allen
          and Unwin Ltd.
Jones, R. M.
  1966a Astudiaeth o ddatblyiad icithyddol plentyn hyd at dair blwydd oed
          mewn cartref cymraeg, Ph. D. Thesis, University of Wales
  ----
  1966b "Situational Vocabulary," International Review of Applied Lin-
          guistics 4, 165-173
Kainz, F.
  1943   Psychologie der Sprache, Vol. 2, Stuttgart, Ferdinand Enke
Kotze, W. J.
  1964   "Bantu Languages in Education," Bantu Education Journal 10,
          434-436

Labov, W.
1965a   Progress Report for Office of Education

1965b   Stages in the Acquisition of Standard English in Social Dialects
         and Language Learning, Proceedings of the Bloomington,
         Indiana, Conference 1964, Roger W. Shuy, Ednor; Alva L.
         Davis, Director; Robert F. Hogan, Assistant Director; Champ-
         lain, Ill., National Council of the Teachers of English

Lambert, W. E.
1963   (compte rendu par) "Psychological Approaches to the Study of
         Language, Part II, on Second Language Learning and Bi-
         lingualism,"Modern Language Journal 47, 114-121

-----& Gardner, R. C., Barik, H. C.
1963   "Attitudinal and Cognitive Aspects of Intensive Study of a Second
         Language," Journal of Abnormal and Social Psychology 66,
         358-368

Landreth, C.
1966   The Psychology of Early Childhood, New York, Alfred A. Knoff

Langer, S. K.
1958   Philosophy in a New Key; a study in the symbolism of reason,
         rite and art, 9th printing, New York, New American Library

Lanham, L. W.
1965   "Teaching English to Africans," Optima 15, 197-204

Larew, L. A.
1961   "The Optimum Age for Beginning a Foreign Language," Modern
         Language Journal 45, 203-206

Lee, W. R.
1960   Letter to English Language Teaching 14, 75-76

Lenneberg, E. H.
1957   "A Probabilistic Approach to Language Learning," Behavioral
         Science 2, 1-12

----- (ed.)
1964   New Directions in the Study of Language, Cambridge, M. I. T.
         Press

1964   "The Capacity for Language Acquisition," (In) The Structure of
         Language, J. Fodor and J. Katz (eds.), Englewood Cliffs,
         N. J., Prentice-Hall, 579-603

1967   Biological Foundations of Language, with appendices by Noam
         Chomsky and Otto Marx, New York, Wiley

Leopold, W. F.
1939-49 Speech Development of a Bilingual Child; a linguist's record,
         Evanston, Illinois, Northwestern University Press, (North-
         western University Studies, Humanities Series 6, 11, 18, 19

———————

1952   Bibliography of Child Language, Evanston, Illinois, Northwestern
          University Press, (Northwestern University Studies, Humanities
          Series 28)

———————

1953-54   "Patterning in Children's Language Learning," Language Learning 5,
          1-14

———————

1956   "Roman Jakobson and the Study of Child Language," (In) For Roman
          Jakobson, The Hague, Mouton, 285-288

———————

1959   "Kindersprach," Phonetica 4, 191-214
Lewis, M. M.
1936   Infant Speech; a study of the beginnings of language, London,
          K. Paul, Trench, Trubner and Co., Ltd.

———————

1957   How Children Learn to Speak, London, Harrap
Lisker, L. & Cooper, F. S., Liberman, A. M.
1962   "The Uses of Experiment in Language Description," Word 18, 82-106
Lowie, R.
1945   "A Case of Bilingualism," Word 1, 249-259
Luriia, A. R.
1961   The Role of Speech in the Regulation of Normal and Abnormal Be-
          haviour, New York, Pergamon Press
MLA
1953   "When should Second Language Learning Begin?" FL Bulletin 1
Mackey, W. F.
1965a   Language Teaching Analysis, London, Longmans
McCarthey, D. A.
1954   "Language Development in Children," (In) Manual of Child
          Psychology, Leonard Carmichael (ed.), New York, John Wiley
          and Sons, 492-630
McConkey, W. G.
1951   "An Experiment in Bilingual Education," Journal for Social Research
McNeil, D.
1966   "Developmental Psycholinguistics," (In) Smith and Miller 1966
          76-82
McRae, K. D.
1964   Switzerland; example of cultural coexistence, Toronto, Canadian
          Institute of International Affairs, (Contemporary Affairs 33)
Malherbe, E. G.
1946   The Bilingual School; a study of bilingualism in South Africa,
          London & New York, Longmans Green

1967   Demographic and Socio-Political Forces Determining the Position
        of English in South Africa, Johannesburg, English Academy of
        South Africa

Marshall, M. V., Phillips, R. H.
1942   "Effect of Bilingualism on College Grades," Journal of Educational
        Research 36, 131-132

Menyuk, P.
1963a   "Syntactic Structures in the Language of Children," Child Develop-
        ment 34, 407-22

1963b   "A Preliminary Evaluation of Grammatical Capacity in Children,"
        Journal of Verbal Learning and Verbal Behavior 2, 429-439

1964   "Comparison of Grammar of Children with Functionally Deviant
        and Normal Speech," Journal of Speech and Hearing Research 17,
        109-121

Miller, W., & Ervin, S.
1964   "The Development of Grammar in Child Language," (In) Bellugi
        & Brown 1964

Milner, P. M.
1960

        "Book Review of Penfield and Roberts," Canadian Journal of
        Psychology 14 , 140-143

Moignet, G.
1961

        L'adverbe dans la location verbale; étude de psycho-systématique
        française, Québec, Presses de l'Université Laval, (séries:
        Cahiers de psychomécanique du langage 5)

Moore, O. K.
1964   "Comments and Conclusions," (In) Bellugi & Brown 1964

Nostrand, H. L., Foster, D. W., Christensen, C. B.
1965   Research in Language Teaching; an Annotated International Bibli-
        ography, 1954-64, 2 ed., Seatle University of Washington Press

Ollman, J. J. (ed.)
1962   MLA Selective List of Materials for Use by Teachers of Modern
        Foreign Languages in Elementary and Secondary Schools, New
        York, MLA

Osgood, C. E.
1963   "On Understanding and Creating Sentences," American Psychologist
        18, 735-751

-----, Suci, G. & Tannenbaum, H.
1957   The Measurement of Meaning, Urbana, University of Illinois Press

Parker, W. R.
   1961   The National Interest and Foreign Languages; a discussion guide,
           3 ed., Washington, U. S. Government, Printing Office
Paton, A.
   1942   "New Schools for South Africans," Mentor 24
Pavlovitch, M.
   1920   Le langage enfantin, acquisition du serbe et du français, par un
           enfant serbe, Paris, E. Champion
Penfield, W.
   1952-53 "A Consideration of Neurophysiological Mechanisms of Speech and
           Some Educational Consequences," Proceedings of American Aca-
           demy of Arts and Sciences 2, 199-214
-----& Roberts, L.
   1959   Speech and Brain Mechanisms, Princeton, N. J., Princeton
           University Press
Perren, G. E.
   1958   "Bilingualism or Replacement? English in East Africa," English
           Language Teaching 13, 18-22
Pintner, R. A. S.
   1937   "The Relation of Bilingualism to Verbal Intelligence and School
           Adjustment," Journal of Educational Research 31, 255-263
Preyer, W.
   1888-89 The Mind of the Child; observations concerning the mental devel-
           opment of the human being in the first years of life, New York,
           D. Appleton and Co. (International Education Series 7, 9)
Public Service Commission Report 1950, Union of South Africa, Pretoria,
           Government Printer (1951)
Reyburn, H. A.
   1943   "Bilingual School; a criticism refuted," Trek 8
Roberts, M.
   1945   "The Crises in Finnish Bilingualism," Standpunte (July Issue)
Ronjat, J.
   1913   Le développement du langage observé chez un enfant bilingue ,
           Paris, H. Champion
Rosser, M.
   1964   Cymraeg i Blant Bach, Cardiff Priory Press Ltd.

   1965a   Cymraeg fel Ail Daith (Babanod), Sir Gaernarjon, Pwyllgor Addysg
----
   1965b   Cynllum Cymraeg i Ysgolian Babanod, Pwyllgorr Addysg Morgannwg
Rousseau, H. J.
   1967   Die Invloed van Engels of Afrikans, Kaapstad, M. Miller, Reperk
Salisbury, R. F.
   1962   "Notes on Bilingualism and Linguistic Change in New Guinea,"
           Anthropological Linguistics 4:7, 1-13

Sawyer, J., Silver, S., Ervin, S. M., D'Andrea, J. & Aoki, H.
1963   "The Utility of Translation and Written Symbols during the First
        thirty Hours of Language Study," International Review of Applied
        Linguistics in Language Teaching I, 157-192

Schmidt, C. H.
1926   The Language Medium Question; the relation between language
        and thought, Pretoria, J. L. Van Schaik

Sechehaye, C. A.
1926   Essai sur la structure logique de la phrase, Paris, E. Champion

Slama-Cazacu, T.
1961   Langage et contexte; le problème du langage dans la conception
        de l'expression et de l'interprétation par des organisations con-
        textuelles, Gravenhague, Mouton (Janua linguarum, Series
        major 6)

Slobin, D. I.
1966   "The Acquisition of Russian as a Native Language," (In) Smith &
        Miller 1966
------- (ed.)
1967   Field Manual for the Cross-Cultural Study of the Acquisition of
        Communicative Competence, Berkeley

Smith, F. L., Miller, G. A., (eds.)
1966   The Genesis of Language; a psycholinguistic approach, Cambridge,
        M. I. T. Press

Spoerl, D. T.
1943   "Bilinguality and Emotional Adjustment," Journal of Abnormal
        and Social Psychology, 38, 37-57

Stern, W.
1934   Psychology of Early Childhood up to the Sixth Year of Age,
        Translated from the 3d ed., New York, H. Holt and Co.

Stern, H. H. (ed.)
1963   Foreign Languages in Primary Education; the teaching of foreign
        or second languages to younger children, Hamburg, Unesco
        Institute for Education

Stone, L. J., Church, J.
1957   Childhood and Adolescence; a psychology of the growing person,
        New York, Random House

Strunk Sachs, J.
1965   Recognition Memory for Syntactic and Semantic Aspects of Con-
        nected Discourse, Ph. D. Dissertation, University of California

Sully, J.
1896   Studies of Childhood, New York, D. Appleton and Co.

Swanepoel, J. F.
1926   The Teaching of the Second Language in the Primary School, Paarl

Taute, B.
   1948   "Die befaling van die mondelinge beheer van skoolkinders oor die
            tweede taal," Annale van die Universiteit van Stellenbosch,
            24B, 1
Templin, M.
   1957   Language Skills in Children, University of Minnesota Institute of
            Child Welfare Monograph 26, 94
Thorne, J. P., Dewar, H. M., Whitfield, H., Bratley, P.
            "A Model for the Perception of Syntactic Structure," Eng. Lang.
            Res. Inst., Edinburgh U. P., n. d.
Tireman, L. S.
   1944   "Bilingual Children," Review of Educational Research 14, 273-278

   1951   Teaching Spanish-Speaking Children, Albuquerque, University of
            New Mexico Press
Tomb, J. W.
   1925   "On the Intuitive Capacity of Children to Understand Spoken
            Language," British Journal of Psychology 16, 53-55
Trettien, A. W.
   1904   "Psychology of the Language Interest of Children," Pedagogical
            Seminar 11, 113-177
Turner, J. D.
   1967   Language Laboratories and the Teaching of English in South Africa,
            Johannesburg, the English Academy of South Africa
Van Zyl, H. J.
   1965   "Interesting Experiment by Unesco on Mother Tongue Instruction,"
            Bantu Education Journal 11, 7-10
Velten, H. V.
   1943   "The Growth of Phonemic and Lexical Patterns in Infant Language,"
            Language 19, 281-292
Vinoyradov, G.
   1930   Russkij detskij folklor, Irkutsk
Voegelin, C. F., Adams, S.
   1934   "A Phonetic Study of Young Children's Speech," The Journal of
            Experimental Education 3, 107-116
Von Raffler Engel, W.
   1965   "Del bilinguismo infantile," Archivio Glottologico Italiano 50,
            175-180
Warfel, H. R.
   1962   Language, a Science of Human Behavior, Cleveland, H. Allen
Weir, G. M.
   1934   The Separate School Question in Canada, Toronto, The Ryerson
            Press
Weir, R. H.
   1962   Language in the Crib, The Hague, Mouton

Weksel, W.
   1965   "The Acquisition of Language," by V. Bellugi and R. Brown,
           Reviewed by W. Weksel, Language 41, 692-709
West, M. P.
   1926   Bilingualism; with special reference to Bengal, Calcutta Govern-
           ment of India, Central Publication Branch (India, Bureau of
           Education, Occasional reports, 13)
Wittwer, J.
   1959   Les fonctions grammaticales chez l'enfant; sujet, objet, attribut,
           Neuchâtel, Delachaux and Niestlé
Yoshioka, J. G.
   1929   "A Study of Bilingualism," Journal of Genetic Psychology 36,
           473-479

2

HOW CAN ONE MEASURE THE EXTENT OF
A PERSON'S BILINGUAL PROFICIENCY?

COMMENT MESURER LE BILINGUISME D'UNE PERSONNNE?

THEME

John Macnamara

Before setting out to obtain measures of bilingual proficiency, it is essential to determine quite precisely the purpose for which such measures are required. The reason is that proficiency in a language, and a fortiori in two languages, is not a single skill but rather a combination of numerous skills, so it is necessary to bear clearly in mind which skills one wishes to evaluate.

One of the major effects of recent developments in linguistics and sociolinguistics is an increased awareness of the complexity of language skills. Sociolinguistics has been much concerned with the varieties of language usage which were formerly treated as "free variation"; uninteresting and largely irrelevant variation in phonology, syntax and vocabulary. Such variation is now known to be closely related to such variables as social class, social situation, topic, etc. (see Ferguson and Gumperz 1960; Fishman 1967; Hymes 1967; Labov 1966). Furthermore, it is now clear that some bilinguals do not model their speech on any variety used by unilingual speakers of their languages, but rather on local bilingual usage which shows considerable linguistic fusion (see Gumperz 1967). It is therefore a question of some importance, and one which cannot readily be dismissed, which variety of each of the languages to the same extent over the whole range of social settings, topics, etc. In other words, most bilingual situations are to some extent diglossic, i.e., the functions of communication are not matched for the two languages (see Ferguson 1959; Gumperz 1964; Fishman 1967); and so in at least some bilingual settings there is an a priori assumption that bilingual proficiency will show quite marked variation with topic, situation, etc. This does not make the measurement of bilingual proficiency impossible or useless, but it does affect expectations as to the outcome of such measures, and it also indicates possible pitfalls in attempts to obtain global, undifferentiated measures of bilingual proficiency.

Alongside the linguistic variations which have been the object of sociolinguistic study must be considered the division of skills which have long been traditional in linguistics. Two of these, listening and reading, are decoding skills and two, speaking and writing, are encoding skills. In each of these, four aspects can be distinguished. Thus, for example, in speaking, there are the semantic, the lexical, the syntactic and the phonological aspects. The complete matrix of four aspects in each of the four skills is set out in Figure 1. Bilingualism, of course, involves two such matrices or, because not all bilinguals possess all four skills, at least sections from two such matrices. Preschool bilingual children, for example, generally cannot read or write either of their languages, while persons who have been educated in only one of their languages may be quite unable to read and write the other, especially if the two orthographies differ greatly. Furthermore, there are examples of bilinguals who can understand but cannot speak one of their languages. This is sometimes called receptive bilingualism and it typically occurs in homes where parents are immigrants to a country which differs in language from their country of origin.

Figure 1. Matrix of four aspects of each of the four language skills

Encoding		Decoding	
Speaking	Writing	Listening	Reading
Semantics	Semantics	Semantics	Semantics
Syntax	Syntax	Syntax	Syntax
Lexicon	Lexicon	Lexicon	Lexicon
Phonemes	Graphemes	Phonemes	Graphemes

If now we allow the double four-by-four matrix to covary with the language varieties which sociolinguistics have studied we get a good impression of the complexity of the bilingual skills which we are attempting to measure. Obviously the complexity is such that it would take a team of psycholinguistics and sociolinguistics several years to study even a limited number of bilinguals, and so far as I know such a task has been undertaken only by Dr. Joshua Fishman and his collaborators who are studying Spanish-English bilingualism among the Puerto Ricans of New York. Fortunately we will be hearing about this very important investigation from Drs. Cooper and Gumperz. However, it is quite clear that the psychologist and the educational psychologist will rarely be able to undertake anything so elaborate. Thus it is essential for such investigators to find a simple and direct path through the intricate maze of bilingual skills. Usually it is possible to do so if the investigator bears clearly in mind the purpose for which he requires measures of bilingual proficiency. He need only measure those skills and those aspects of skills with which he is directly concerned.

As examples of bilingual studies which employed the above solution may be cited two studies of bilingual performance with the Stroop test, Preston 1965 and Lambert 1967. The test consists of a series of names of colours printed in various colours, e.g. the word blue printed in green, the word red printed in blue. Subjects are required to disregard the printed word and name the colour of the ink. In both the studies mentioned, a bilingual (English and French) version of the Stroop test was employed, and subjects were needed who, for the purposes of the test, were equally proficient in English and French.

In both studies the bilinguals named colours equally rapidly in the two languages. However, the main interest was in the interference effect of the printed
word when the language of that word and the language of response differed.
This interference was measured by comparison with performance in a condition
in which the response and printed word were in the same language. Once again
performance in this unilingual condition was equal across languages. Thus a
completely satisfactory test of relevant bilingual proficiency was built into the
design; other preliminary data, such as responses to a language background
questionnaire, served only as a rough screening device. For similar designs
see Macnamara and Kellaghan 1967 and Macnamara 1967.

    The point just made is of such importance that it needs to be underlined.
Where possible it is best to measure bilingual proficiency in precisely those
skills which the psychologist wishes to study. However, there are numerous
studies in which so simple a solution to the problem of bilingual proficiency is
not available. For example, many educational psychologists have attempted
to determine the relationship between bilingualism on the one hand and intellectual development (Darcy 1953; 1961), language learning (Macnamara 1966),
or attainment in such subjects as mathematics, geography, etc. (Macnamara
1967) on the other hand. Since bilingual proficiency varies, it is essential to
such studies to have some measure of it which can be employed in estimating
the effects of bilingualism. The rest of this paper is devoted to the discussion
of such measures. The paper does not, however, deal directly with procedures
for the employment of bilingual persons. Such procedures demand an altogether
different treatment, since they focus on a person's capacity in each of his languages rather than on the status of his two languages relative to one another.

Degree of Bilingualism

    The term bilingual is used here to connote persons who possess at least one
of the langage skills listed in Figure 1 even to a minimal degree in their second
language. That is, I shall consider as bilingual a person who, for example, is
an educated native speaker of English and who can also read a little French.
This means that bilingualism is being treated as a continuum, or rather a series
of continua, which vary among individuals along a variety of dimentions. That
there can be variations in an individual's degree of bilingualism from speaking
to listening, and from reading to writing, is well kn own (Weinreich 1953).
That there can be variation in any or all these skills from, say, formal to informal style, is becoming widely recognized (Ferguson and Gumperz 1960;
Hymes 1967). But it has scarcely been noticed that there may also be variations within a single modality, such as listening, from one aspect (Figure 1)
of linguistic performance to another. For example, it is quite possible for a
person to be almost equally skilled in the syntactic analysis of French and
English, but not in the ability to perceive spoken French and English. The
possibility is not so far-fetched as one might suppose, since an individual
might have considerable practice at reading a language such as French without

having had much opportunity to hear it spoken, with the result that he might
be able to analyse the syntax of spoken French quite well if only he could make
out the words which were being used. Nor is the point merely a matter of hypothesis, since some progress has been made in examining bilingual proficiency
in its various linguistic aspects (see Macnamara 1967). All this is not to claim
that the sixteen cells of Figure 1 represent skills which are independent of one
another. However, the figure does set out the minimum level of complexity
to be dealt with, since the cells are at once logically and empirically distin-
guishable.

The term "balanced" is commonly used to describe persons who are "equally skilled in two languages in all aspects and all styles of the language skills
he possesses. Thus if he is an educated person, it is implied that he is balanced
in all sixteen cells of Figure 1 in each of the several styles he can employ.
Clearly, however, the term is generally intended, implicitly if not explicitly,
in a more limited sense: the claim is that a person is balanced in understanding or in speaking two languages, or at least in some particular facet of linguistic competence.

How are we to measure degree of bilingualism and categorize bilingual
performance along the relevant continua? Lado 1961 shows the complexities
involved in composing appropriate tests of skills in a single language; the complexities involved in establishing comparable measures in two languages are,
if I may be permitted to quantify, far more than double. To illustrate the
point, the measurement of listening comprehension will suffice.

To begin with, even if standardized tests of listening comprehension are
available in two languages, they may not be appropriate for the population one
wishes to test. Thus an English test standardized in the United States or in
Britain and a French test standardized in France may not, because of regional
variations, be suitable for use with French-English bilinguals in Quebec. Additionally the sorts of content which may be appropriate for use with persons
in Britain or France may not be appropriate for use with bilinguals in Quebec.
Furthermore, many tests of listening comprehension are designed to test the
proficiency of students taking the language as a second language and so such
tests are unsuited for use with native-speakers or persons with near native command of the language. Still further, such tests are almost invariably in the
formal, standard style of a language and do not test a person's capacity to understand informal, intimate conversation.

Difficulties such as these must be considered when testing any bilingual
skill, but there is no reason to suppose that they are insurmountable, especially if one bears in mind the purpose for which measures of bilingualism are required. Thus, for example, if the purpose is to measure capacity to communicate in a classroom setting where a formal style of language is used, the last
point made above ceases to be a difficulty.

Indirect Measures of Degree of Bilingualism

In order to get around the difficulties involved in "directly" measuring degree of bilingualism by means of tests of reading, writing, speaking and listening, a number of "indirect" measures have been devised. By indirect measures I mean brief, economic measures which have been used to assess undifferentiated degree of bilingualism. Some of these tests obviously measure some aspect of linguistic skill directly, yet in the sense that this aspect is thought to indicate overall proficiency in two languages, the tests may be termed indirect measures of overall proficiency. Indirect measures may be loosely classified under four heads: rating scales, tests of verbal fluency, flexibility, and dominance. Although there is an abundance of such tests, it is fair to say that investigations of their validity have been inadequate. In particular, their users have paid little attention to the facet or facets of linguistic competence which each measures, or to the comparative strength of the different indirect measures, or to the comparative strength of the different indirect measures as indicators of bilingual proficiency. As a first step towards remedying this inadequacy, I conducted over the past several months an investigation among sixth grade pupils (N=158) in four Montreal schools under the direction of the Montreal Catholic School Commission.(1) The schools were selected by the Commission as being most likely to contain large numbers of bilinguals. There were three French schools in predominantly English-speaking districts, while one was an English school in a predominantly French-speaking district. Because of limitations in time and resources no attempt was made to cover all the skills enumerated in Figure 1. However, four sets of tests which sample these skills widely were administered to each S in each of his languages: tests of reading, writing, comprehension of spoken French and English, and ability to speak French and English. In all, fifteen measures of competence in each language were obtained. In each case a S's 'French' score was subtracted from his 'English' score to yield a difference score. The fifteen sets of difference

(1) This study was financed by a generous grant from the French-Canada Studies Programme, McGill University. I also wish to acknowledge my debt to Professor William Mackey of Laval University and Professor Wallace Lambert of McGill University in planning the study; to the Montreal Catholic School Commission for permission to carry it out and for help in selecting the schools; to the staff and students of the four schools in which the study was done: Ecole St-Antonin, 5010, ave. Coolbrooke; All Saints School (Annex), 4975 Amos St.; Ecole Ste-Catherine-de-Sienne, 7065, ave. Somerled; Ecole St-Richard, 7450, Côte St-Luc; to my assistants who did the bulk of the testing, Miss Marie Fletin, M. Louis Laurencelle and M. Pierre Blanchette; and finally to Dr. George Madaus, New England Catholic Education Center, Boston College, who saw the data through the computer for me.

scores were employed as criterion measures against which fourteen indirect measures were assessed. These indirect measures, which are described in greater detail below, were: word completion, word detection, reading speed, word meaning, semantic richness, language background questionnaire (sections on self, father, mother, siblings, environment of home), self-ratings (speaking, listening, writing, reading). Fifteen regression analyses were then run in each of which the multiple regression of one of the criterion measures on the indirect measures was calculated. The regressions were run "step-wise" so that we know the efficiency with which different sets of indirect measures predict a particular criterion (Experiment A).

In using the Montreal study it must be borne in mind that the findings apply only to sixth grade French-English bilinguals in Montreal. The results might well have been different if the study had been made with a different age-group or in a different bilingual setting. The choice of indirect measures was arbitrary; different results might be expected if the choice of measures had been different. However, on the assumption that the direct measures which were used are reasonably valid measures of what their names imply the study does have general interest in showing us what sorts of results to expect when indirect measures are employed to determine degree of bilingualism. In general, the control of criterion variance was quite satisfactory.

Rating Scales

The technique most frequently employed in the past to determine degree of bilingualism is the language background questionnaire (LBQ). Most questionnaires of this type derive from the work of Hoffman 1934 and require the subject to estimate the extent to which each of his languages is used in his home and in the home environment. The questions can generally be classified under five headings: Those which deal with the subject's own language usage, those which deal with that of his father, his mother, his siblings, and usage in the environment of the home (church, T.V., Radio, etc.). Hitherto answers to all questions have been combined to yield a single rating for a subject. Arsenian 1937 reports estimates of the reliability of such ratings which are of the order of $r = .8$ or better. Arsenian also cites validity estimates of about $r = .8$ obtained by correlating LBQ ratings and ratings of linguistic proficiency made by interviewers.

In the Montreal study LBQ contributed significantly to the prediction of only 10 of the 15 criterion scores. In each case except one the contribution was made by only one of the five sections of the LBQ; there was little consistency as to the particular section. In the one case where two sections contributed to the regression, one beta was positive and one negative. In no case was LBQ the best predictor. In general, too, it would appear that little is lost by combining the five sections to form a single rating. However, the value of LBQ information will almost certainly be found to vary from country to country, owing to varying social pressures to exaggerate or understate the use of a particular language. For example, the Irish government makes a grant of £10 per annum per child to parents who make Irish the home language. It is not difficult to imagine the effect of these grants on the validity of LBQ responses.

A second form of rating scale used to measure bilingualism is self-rating for language skills. Typically the subject is required to rate himself in the four skills; speaking, listening, writing, and reading in each of the two languages, and typically all the ratings are combined to form a single over-all rating.

In the Montreal study the four ratings were kept distinct, and found to be powerful predictors of the criterion measures. In fact, they were considerably more powerful than LBQ. They made a significant contribution to twelve of the fifteen regressions, while two in combination made significant contributions to four of the regressions. In eight of the regressions a self-rating was the best predictor, though curiously self-rating on ability to read the two languages turned out to be the most powerful of the four self-ratings right across the range of direct measures—reading, writing, speaking and listening. These are interesting findings since in bilingual studies LBQs have generally been taken as the best measure of bilingual proficiency. The results also show that little accuracy is lost by combining all four self-ratings to form a single one.

While the new findings are encouraging it is necessary to bear in mind that social pressures which may distort LBQs may also distort self-ratings. Additionally, I found self-ratings less powerful than a "richness of vocabulary" test (to be described below) in distinguishing between groups clearly differing in experience in two languages. In that study it seemed that self-ratings were contaminated by the influence of examination marks. Many subjects (college students) rated their skills in their second language above those in the first language if their marks in the second language were higher than those in the first, although the marks were patently non-comparable.

Fluency Tests

There are a number of economic and ingenious tests of speed of responding to verbal stimuli or speed of verbal production in two languages. One such is Ervin's picture naming test which yields times for naming pictures of certain objects. (Ervin 1961) Times thus obtained correlated highly with assessments of language background. A second test is described by Rao 1964 which measures the speed with which bilinguals follow simple instructions given in their two languages. Several other tests of fluency are due to Lambert and his associates. (Lambert et al. 1955; 1959; 1967) In one test they measured response times to instructions to press keys; in another, they counted the number of French and English words beginning with a pair of letters which bilinguals were able to write in a given time; in a third, they timed the reading of passages in two languages. In each case, resulting difference scores were found to be related to language background. Johnson 1953 and Macnamara (in press) had similar findings with a "word-naming" task in which subjects were required to say as many different words as they could in one language, and later in the other, within a limited period. On the other hand, several studies (Lambert, Havelka and Gardener 1959; Treisman 1965; Macnamara, Krauthammer & Bolgar 1967; Macnamara, in press) found that neither speed of translation nor speed of switching languages (without translating) is related to degree of bilingualism.

In my recent study, I included three fluency tests: word-completion, speed of reading, and word-naming. Word-completion contribution signifi- cantly to the prediction of certain measures of bilingual proficiency in speaking and writing. In no regression was it the best predictor, and in general it is not a powerful measure. Speed of reading in contrast is a very powerful predictor of all four major linguistic skills. It contributed significantly to eleven of the fifteen regressions and in six of them was the principal contributor. In fact, of all the indirect measures it proved to be the most valuable not only in the size of its contribution to regression but also in the number of regressions to which it contributed. Word-naming, on the other hand, is a weak predictor of bilingual proficiency. It contributed significantly, never as principal con- tributor, to reading comprehension and to certain aspects of speech.

Flexibility Tests

By flexibility tests I mean tests which require a subject to change linguis- tic set rapidly within a confined framework. One such test I call a richness of vocabulary test. (2) It consists of a series of phrases of the type, "He is drunk" (later the same item occurs in translation), and subjects are asked to write as many words or expressions as they can which are synonymous or nearly synonymous with the word underlined in the phrase. The idea behind this is that bilinguals seem to have far more ways—some formal, some informal, some humourous—to express a concept in their strong than in their weak language. A possible objection to this is the fact that languages vary in the number of ways in which a particular concept can be expressed. However, this is not important as long as there are a number of ways in each language; this allows of variation across a range of bilinguals and one can determine the extremes independently by administering the test to monolinguals.

In my study of this I had three clearly distinguished groups of Irish-English bilingual college students in Dublin (N=117): native Irish-speakers who had learned English at school and in the English-speaking environment of Ireland; native English-speakers who had had their secondary schooling in preparatory colleges where half the students were native Irish-speakers and all the work of the college was conducted in Irish; native English-speakers who had been edu- cated throughout in the medium of English, but had learned Irish in school for not less than twelve years. The numbers 1, 2, 3 were assigned to the three

----

(2) The idea of such a test was suggested by my brother-in-law, Oisin O'Siochru.

groups respectively and regression analysis was used to determine how well subjects could be classified by their performance on the richness of vocabulary test.   There were eleven pairs of phrases in the test, each yielding a differ- ence score which was used as an independent variate in the regression analysis (see Experiment B).   It was found that by selecting the five independent varia- bles which were significant at the 5% level, 79% of the variance in the cri- terion variable could be controlled.   This is extremely encouraging, but further study is needed to determine how well richness of vocabulary predicts various aspects of bilingual competence.

The richness of vocabulary test was not included in my recent study; pre- liminary try-outs indicated that it was too difficult for children.   However, a complementary test, a "semantic richness" test was included.   Ideally this would consist of a number of words, and subjects would be required to give as many meanings as possible for each.   For use with children (at Dr. Mackey's suggestion) a modified form was prepared which consisted of a series of sen- tences each with a blank which was to be filled by a multiple choice tech- nique.   The correct answer was always a common word used in one of its sec- ondary senses.   For example:

Après les longs voyages pendant l'hiver il se......... à la fatigue.

      (a) triste
      (b) grondait
      (c) sortait
      (d) faisait

The correct response is faisait in which the verb faire is not used in its pri- mary sense, to make, but in the sense, to become accustomed to.

This test proved to be a moderately powerful predictor of the criterion scores, turning up significant in six of the fifteen regressions, once as best predictor (criterion = reading vocabulary), and contributing to the prediction of all four major linguistic skills.

Lambert's word detection test may also be classified as a flexibility test. It requires subjects to identify as many words (from two languages) as they can in a long nonsense word, for instance, the French and English words in the string DANSONODENT.   Lambert found that data obtained with this test correlated highly with LBQ ratings.   In the recent study it contributed signi- ficantly to only four of the fifteen regressions (never as principal contributor). As might have been expected it contributed significantly to the prediction of vocabulary scores, but strangely it also contributed significantly to the pre- diction of grammar scores, both in speech and in writing.

Dominance Tests

A dominance test is one in which a bilingual is confronted with an ambig- uous stimulus (which could belong to either language) and asked to pronounce or interpret it.   The language most frequently used is the dominant one.   One example of such a test is that devised by Lambert et al. 1959 who presented bilinguals with a list of words to be read aloud of which some items were ambiguous, e.g. pipe which is both English and French, but pronounced differently in the two languages. Measures obtained with the test correlated with measures of degree of bilingualism based on linguistic background. However, it was not included in the Montreal study and so it remains to be seen how well it predicts scores in the various aspects of the major bilingual skills.

Discussion

Lambert, Havelka and Gardner 1959 have gone further than most students in this field and have administered to a group of bilinguals a battery of tests in which all four types of indirect measures were represented: rating scales, fluency, Flexibility, and dominance tests. They found that all such measures are intercorrelated and could be interpreted as measuring a single factor. This is encouraging as the various tests appear at first sight to measure quite distinct skills. It is also strange, since results of factorial studies of the linguistic performance of monolinguals (Thurstone and Thurstone 1941; Carroll 1941; Guilford et al. 1956; Vernon 1961) show that verbal functioning can be interpreted as comprising many factors, and that some of these factors, for example, verbal fluency, can be subdivided into several factors. At their face value the indirect measures used by Lambert et al. appear to measure different factors. However, the findings of monolingual studies do not apply directly to work with bilingual measures of the type described. Typically, indirect measures of bilingualism have been used to derive difference scores by subtracting scores for performance in one language from those for performance in the other. Thus, from the resulting difference scores has been removed the influence of all factors which contribute equally to performance in the two languages. So it is hardly surprising that the factor structure of difference measures should differ from that of the original measures.

My own study supports Lambert et al. in that it too found the indirect measures to be intercorrelated. This, however, does not mean that all indirect tests are equally good measures of bilingual proficiency, or of its various divisions, as the new regression study clearly reveals.

One finding of the regression analysis deserves underlining, the relatively poor predictive power of the LBQ data. In the past what work has been done on the validity of indirect measures has consisted in relating the latter to LBQ ratings. It is now apparent that LBQ ratings are weak criteria, and that they seem in fact to be weaker than some of the measures which they have been used to validate.

How well can degree of bilingualism be determined by means of the indirect measures alone? The answer is to be found in the multiple Rs (Experiment A). The amount of error (suspected, but unmeasured) in the criterion variables suggests an upper limit somewhere in the region of .85 for R; so it seems likely that the indirect measures are as effective in determining degree of bilingualism over a wide range of linguistic skills as the direct measures. Indeed, except for skill in writing, the indirect measures fare surprisingly well. These remarks, however, apply only to a formal style in both languages.

To sum up, the psychologist who wishes to obtain subjects of a certain degree of bilingualism in order to study some aspect of bilingual behaviour is best advised to measure degree of bilingualism with those very skills which he wishes to manipulate in the course of his investigation. As a rough screening device he will probably find self-ratings and speed of reading aloud, rather than an LBQ, the most satisfactory indirect measures. If his subjects are unable to read, however, he may still be able to employ an orally administered form of the self-rating. But further research is necessary to determine the validity of oral forms of such measures. Where it is impossible to determine degree of bilingualism by measuring those skills which the psychologist wishes to manipulate for experimental purposes, reasonably good results may be obtained by selecting (from Experiment A) the appropriate combination of indirect measures and the appropriate weightings. In a wide sward of studies, however, where the investigator is interested in the effect of bilingualism on intellectual development or on language learning, that is if the investigator needs to know his subjects' proficiency at some point in time prior to the beginning of the investigation—for example, the time when his subjects started school—the best measure available to him is the LBQ. If, on the other hand, such studies are to be conducted on a long term developmental basis, then bilingual proficiency can be measured directly (where possible) or indirectly (when direct measures are either unavailable or inappropriate) without undue reliance on the LBQ. Finally, in investigation of bilinguals' relative capacity to learn through the medium of their two languages it will often be possible to determine degree of bilingualism by means of those linguistic skills which they will use in the learning tasks (Macnamara 1967; Macnamara and Kellaghan 1967) or to use an appropriate combination of indirect measures. However, the limitations of the study upon which these conclusions are based should not be forgotten.

EXPERIMENT A

Results of Montreal Study of the validity of indirect measures of degree of
bilingualism

Criterion Variables: English

1. Reading comprehension: Gates Reading Survey, Form 1
2. Reading vocabulary: Gates Reading Survey, Form 1
3. Spelling mistakes
4. Grammar mistakes   Written essay: mistakes and
5. Syntactic interferences from French   interferences expressed as a
6. Lexical interferences from French   proportion of the total number
7. (only intelligible as difference score)   of words in an essay. Count
8. Number of words   was made of "different" mis-
                                                takes and interferences.
9. Listening comprehension: Specially constructed test con-
                                                sisting of short stories followed
                                                by questions: numbers (e.g. 3,
                                                10, 121, 1971); snatches of radio
                                                messages followed by questions
                                                (suggested by Prof. W. Mackey).

10. Grammar mistakes
11. Phonetic mistakes   Speech: retelling a story.
12. Rating for rhythm   Count was made of "different"
13. Rating for intonation   mistakes, which were then
14. (intelligible only as difference score)   expressed as a proportion of
15. Number of words   the total number of words.

Criterion Variables: French

1. Reading comprehension: Test de lecture silencieuse, Joly
2. Reading vocabulary   Test de vocabulaire, Binois &
                                                Pichot: plus special supplement
                                                of 10 common words (specially
                                                constructed).

3. Spelling mistakes   Written essay: count was made
4. Grammar mistakes   of "different" mistakes and inter-
5. Syntactic interferences from English   ferences, which were then expres-
6. Lexical interferences from English   sed as a proportion of the total
7. (intelligible only as difference score)   number of words.
8. Number of words

9.   Listening comprehension: Constructed on lines similar to
                                    the corresponding English test.

10. Grammar mistakes
11. Phonetic mistakes   Speech: retelling a story
12. Rating for rhythm   Count was made of "different"
13. Rating for intonation   mistakes, which were then ex-
14. (intelligible only as difference score)   pressed as a proportion of the
15. Number of words   total number of words.

Where tests differed across languages in the total number of questions, raw
scores obtained on the longer test were divided by a constant in order that the
"expected" raw scores for balanced bilinguals should be roughly equal. All
"French" scores and ratings were subtracted from the corresponding "English"
scores to obtain a set of 15 difference scores for each subject.

Two essay themes were used. Each was one of La Fontaine's fables which
was first told to a class with the aid of a filmstrip. The story was told in simple
prose in the appropriate language. Variable 7 was calculated as follows. Each
subject's scores on variables 3 to 6 in each language were added. His "French"
total was then subtracted from his "English" one, to obtain an index of the
overall relative standing of his two essays. Subjects were then ranked (across
all subjects) on this index, and their ranks were entered as Variable 7.

Two of La Fontaine's fables were also used to obtain samples of subjects'
speech. These were told in the appropriate language with the aid of filmstrips
to small groups of children before they tape recorded their retelling of the
stories. The children's version were then typed. Using both tapes and typed
pages Mme Yolande Séguin, a French-Canadian teacher with training in linguistics, counted the number of grammar and phonetic mistakes made by each
subject, and rated him on a five point scale for rhythm and intonation. In e-
valuating phonology she only took account of errors which showed a subject to
be a non-native French speaker. In other words, no account was taken of the
deviations of Joual from educated French-Canadian or Parisian French. The
corresponding work on the English tapes was done by Miss July Adams, an
English-Canadian teacher with training in linguistics. Variable 14 is based on
variables 10 to 13 in the same way as Variable 7 is based on variables 3 to 6.

It should be noted that the expected regression of the criterion variables
on the predictor variables is not constant in sign. The expected regressions of
variables 1, 2, 8, 9, 12, 13, 14 and 15 are positive, the remainder negative.
The reason is that in the remainder what has been calculated is an index of errors: naturally, the more errors the poorer the knowledge of the language. In
order to avoid confusion, however, I have expressed the results below as though
the expected regression in all cases (except the regression on variable 19—see
below) was positive. This does not alter the statistical significance of the values in any way.

Predictor variables

As these have been described in the text they will only be listed here:

17. Word completion
18. Word detection
19. Reading speed (prose passages of equal number of words in the two languages)
20. Word naming
21. Semantic richness
22. Self ⎤
23. Father ⎟
24. Mother ⎟ Language Background Questionnaire
25. Siblings ⎟
26. Environment of home ⎦
27. Speaking ⎤
28. Listening comprehension ⎟ Self-ratings
29. Writing ⎟
30. Reading ⎦

Scores or ratings on variables 17 to 30 were obtained for each of the two languages. In each case the "French" score or rating was subtracted from the corresponding English one; the difference score or difference rating was used in regression analysis. In general it can be said that the faster one reads aloud in a language the better one's knowledge of that language. So scores on variable 19 19 are in the opposite "direction" from those obtained on the other predictor variables. That is, the regression of criterion variables on variable 19 is expected to lie in the opposite direction from those of the criterion on the other predictors. This difference in expected sign has been preserved in the tables below.

In giving the results I shall mention the criterion variable and list beneath it only those variables which contribute significantly to regression at the 5% level. The regression was calculated step-wise. What is given below is the regression at the point at which the inclusion of additional variables ceased to contribute significantly to the control of criterion variance. Since the distribution of all scores was normalized before being analysed, the regression coefficients are directly comparable.

RESULTS

1. Reading comprehension   R = .8312

Predictors   Beta

19. Reading speed   -.20

21. Word naming	.15
22. LBQ: self	.33
25. LBQ: siblings	−.13
30. Self-rating: reading	.37

2. Reading vocabulary   R = .8231

Predictors	Beta
18. Word detection	.25
19. Reading speed	−.17
21. Semantic richness	.26
26. LBQ: home environment	.21
27. Self-rating: speaking	.14

3. Spelling (essay)   R = .5557

Predictors	Beta
18. Word detection	.24
19. Reading speed	−.39

4. Grammar mistakes (essay)   R = .5453

Predictors	Beta
18. Word detection	.20
19. Reading speed	−.24
22. LBQ: self	.23

5. Syntactic interferences (essay)   R = .5134

Predictors	Beta
19. Reading speed	−.26
30. Self-rating: reading	.30

6. Lexical interferences (essay)   R = .4643

Predictors	Beta
19. Reading speed	−.34
26. LBQ: home environment	.20
28. Self-rating: listening	.30
29. Self-rating: writing	−.38

7. Rank on variables 3 to 6   R = .7405

Predictors	Beta
17. Word completion	.23
19. Reading speed	-.17
21. Semantic richness	.21
29. Self-rating: writing	.26

8. Number of words (essay)   R = .7357

Predictors	Beta
17. Word completion	.17
19. Reading speed	-.18
21. Semantic richness	.18
30. Self-rating: reading	.33

9. Listening comprehension   R = .8355

Predictors	Beta
21. Semantic richness	.23
22. LBQ: self	.20
27. Self-rating: speaking	.35
30. Self-rating: reading	.25

10. Grammar mistakes (speech)   R = .6246

Predictors	Beta
18. Word detection	.19
19. Reading speed	-.25
21. Semantic richness	.29
23. LBQ: father	.22
28. Self-rating: listening	-.23

11. Phonetic errors (speech)   R = .5348

Predictors	Beta
19. Reading speed	-.27
23. LBQ: father	.15
27. Self-rating: speaking	.25

12.   Rhythm (speech)   R = .7185

Predictors   Beta

17. Word completion   .24
20. Word naming   .20
27. Self-rating: speaking   .18
30. Self-rating: reading   .26

13.   Intonation (speech)   R = .7440

Predictors   Beta

17. Word completion   .16
20. Word naming   .16
24. LBQ: mother   .22
27. Self-rating: speaking   .18
30.   Self-rating: reading   .23

14.   Rank on variables 10 to 13 (speech)   R = .7426

Predictors   Beta

17. Word completion   .25
19. Reading speed   -.32
20. Word naming   .17
23. LBQ: father   .19

15.   Number of words (speech)   R = .6743

Predictors   Beta

21. Semantic richness   .31
22. LBQ: self   .22
30. Self-rating: reading   .25

EXPERIMENT B

Results of the Dublin study of richness of vocabulary

The criterion variable, described in the text, was a ranking of three groups of Irish-English bilingual adults. The predictor variables were the number of synonyms or near synonyms written by subjects for the underlined words in the following phrases:

1. The reason I did it
2. He is angry
3. He is drunk
4. He is a proud man
5. I am tired
6. I think
7. A is like B
8. I agree with you
9. The mountain is big
10. He can run quickly
11. He is a clever boy

Richness of Vocabulary   R = .8895

Predictors	Beta
1. Reason	.12
2. Angry	.08
4. Proud	.07
9. Big	.19
11. Clever	.12

COMMENTARIES/COMMENTAIRES

Leon A. Jacobovits

I greatly enjoyed reading Dr. Macnamara's paper, and I am glad to have this opportunity to make a few general comments on it. I would like to begin with his proposal that the investigator interested in measures of bilingual proficiency "need only measure those skills and those aspects of skills with which he is directly concerned" (p. 81) Dr. Macnamara proposes in his figure 1 (p.81) 16 cells in each language representing the various skills which are potentially involved in language proficiency. A relevant question that ought to be raised in this connection is whether it is possible, in practice, to measure the various skills tabulated in this scheme independently. That is, assuming for example, that one were interested in measuring a person's skill in understanding the syntax of oral speech—which is one of the 16 cells in the figure—can one use a test which would measure this skill independently of skills represented in adjacent cells, such as semantic and phonemic decoding? Even a superficial analysis of this problem suggests that such cannot be the case. Phonemic decoding is essential in the meaningful perception of an utterance and semantic disambiguation must precede or accompany syntactic analysis. Examination of the "direct" measures used by Dr. Macnamara and presented in the appendix leads to the same conclusion. Thus, criterion variable, 9, which is a listening comprehension skill, logically involves all four of the cells under the "decoding - reading." Other criterion variables such as reading vocabulary, syntactic variable 1, which is reading comprehension, involves all four cells under the heading "decoding - reading." Other criterion variables such as reading vocabulary, syntactic interferences, number of words, and so on, also involve two or more cells in the schematic figure. Given this situation, one must interpret Dr. Macnamara's admonition that we must limit ourselves to those measures with which we are directly concerned in terms of the traditional four-way classification of listening, reading, speaking, and writing. However, we must consider the fact that even these more global skills are not independent of each other. One can hardly imagine (except in abnormal situations involving various forms of aphasic dysfunctioning) someone proceeding in writing skills without a prior or parallel achievement in reading skills, nor is it likely that one could develop speaking skills without any kind of listening skills. In view of these interdependencies, it would appear that some global measure of language proficiency is necessary and that it is difficult to imagine that an investigator could limit himself to the measurement of sub-skills that in fact do not develop or exist independently.

My second point, relates to the distinction made by Dr. Macnamara between "direct" and "indirect" measures of language proficiency. In principle, such a distinction would seem to be potentially useful if by "indirect" measures one would mean to refer to tests that are assumed to be mediated by language competence but that, on the surface, involve some apparently unrelated skill such response latency in motor behavior, which in fact is involved in Lambert's automaticity measure of bilingual dominance. Similarly, a language background questionnaire and self-evaluation ratings of bilingual proficiency can be conceived of as indirect indices. But in what way can one say that fluency tests, word completion tests, semantic richness tests, and tests of reading speed are "indirect" measures of language proficiency? Surely all of these measure skills directly involved in the four basic aspects of language use and it is a matter of complete arbitrariness to call them "indirect" as opposed to "direct." This issue is not purely one of terminology since in Dr. Macnamara's analysis one is treated as criterion for validation while the other is treated as tests to be validated. Hence the important issue of validation is completely vitiated by this arbitrariness. The most that could be done in this case, given the absence of a global validating measure of language proficiency, is to present a table of intercorrelations of the 29 measures and the problem of their validation remains unsolved.

I come now to Dr. Macnamara's method of indexing bilingual proficiency. Since this estimate is based on a difference score between the various language proficiency tests referred to above, all the difficulties just mentioned will also apply to the measure of bilingual proficiency. But there is an added difficulty here which ought now to be taken up. The rationale for using the difference score is that the investigator wishes to eliminate and control out that part of the variance which is attributable to monolingual skills. For example, if we wish to estimate the bilingual's relative ease in reading speed in his two languages, we are told to subtract his reading speed in the second language from his reading speed in his first language and, in some cases, the difference score must be divided by the reading speed in the first language to obtain a percentage difference of imbalance. The assumption underlying this procedure is that the two measures are mediated by a common type of competence and that the same factors influencing one measure will also influence the other measure in a similar manner. How valid is such an assumption?

Let us take the case of bilingual proficiency in fluency as measured by the ratio—difference score of ratings of word frequency. In this test, as it is described in the paper by Dr. Cooper (p.198), the subject rates the frequency of words chosen from particular domains in his two languages. The ratio—difference score, when computed, allows him to make such statements as "the respondent's English dominance over Spanish for words in the home domain is 10% while her English dominance for words in the school domain is 29%," and so on. The assumption implicit in this conclusion is that the aptitude underlying the two indices, namely verbal fluency, is the same in the two languages since the respondent acts as her own control. My point is that this assumption is not necessarily true and that despite the fact that the aptitude involved in verbal fluency is constant, the actual performance of fluency—factors which are not necessarily comparable in the two languages. The evidence which I can suggest for this assertion is only informal but nevertheless compelling. It relates to a psychological aspect of bilingualism which, to my knowledge, has not been extensively investigated although it has often been described subjectively in what I might call "folk bilingualism" following Hoeningswald's proposal for a "folk linguistics." The phenomenon manifests itself as a décalage between the psychological states involved in bilinguals using their two languages. In extreme instances, such as might be the case with co-ordinate bi-cultural bilinguals, one might even speak of a schizophrenic type de-duplication of the bilingual's personality, such that when he speaks language one he is not the same person as when he speaks language two. This difference in personality may exhibit itself in different ways of perceiving the environment, different interpersonal perceptions and behaviors, different role expectations and role manifestations, tations, all of which, by the way, are objectively measurable. I believe that these manifestations are present to a greater or lesser extent in all bilinguals. The consequences of this kind of a psychological décalage on linguistic performance are potentially very great. The difference score involved in the measurement of bilingual proficiency is completely confounded by these effects and to my mind invalidates its use. This problem involved in the measurement of bilingual proficiency is connected with the failure on the part of Dr. Macnamara and others in this field, to heed Chomsky's warning that performance measures in general and in principle are inadequate estimates of competence. In the present instance, the performance measures involved in the measurement of bilingual proficiency are potentially affected by non-linguistic extraneous factors that vary differentially in the two languages and that were not taken into account.

The solution to these problems is not an easy matter, but it seems to me that it does not lie in direct comparison of measures in the form of simple difference scores. There is a difficult dilemma here. On the one hand, I am suggesting the use of a global monolingual measure to be standardized in relation to the performance of monolinguals and with due attention to the difficulties of estimating competence from performance. On the other hand, I would not want to have neglected the purely bilingual nature of knowing two languages, which comes about by the unique fact of a co-location of two different linguistic and cultural systems in the brain of a single individual, the investigation of which is pursued in studies on interferences and on translation. It may be that these two aspects, that is, monolingual competence in each of two languages and bilingual interferences, may have to be studied separately.

Before I attempt to summarize my remarks I would like to make note of the absence among the various measures proposed and used by Dr. Macnamara of tests that are relevant to the individual's bilinguality per se. I don't know if this is the best way to refer to this type of a test, but what I have in mind includes the potential linguistic and psycholinguistic advantages of being bilingual. I am intentionally putting it in terms of the positively evaluative term of "advantages" to counteract the implied negative evaluation in the universally used term of "interferences." It may help to remind ourselves that the notion of "linguistic interference" in the speech of bilinguals stems from the psychological concept of transfer and despite the fact that it is well known that transfer effects may be either negative or positive, its negative aspects in linguistic interferences have been generally emphasized in experimental reports to the exclusion of an interest in any positive effects. An examination of the literature on the problem of the effects of bilingualism on education and intellectual development, such as the excellent review in Dr. Macnamara's book, reveals an exclusive interest on the part of researchers in this area in the negative effects of bilingualism. The supporters of bilingualism are apparently quite happy in demonstrating that there is no evidence for negative effects of bilingualism. The Peal and Lambert study which has demonstrated the superiority of a bilingual group of children in the Montreal setting is a notable exception to this trend, and these authors have permitted themselves to at least examine the possibility that early bilinguality may contribute to greater cognitive flexibility in the child. Lado, in his book on language testing, devotes one or two paragraphs to the problem of measuring linguistic and psycholinguistic skills that are facilitated by the learning of a second language. Among these he mentions an increased awareness of the arbitrariness of the sound-meaning relation, an increased flexibility in the manipulation of alternative ways of expressing analogous ideas and a keener realization of the polysymous and homophonous nature of words. To these we may add the proposal of a weakening of linguistic chauvinism and a broadening of linguistic intuitions relating to language particulars and language universals. I have no specific proposals for procedures to measure any of these skills, but a recognition of their existence and importance would undoubtedly lead other to implement the development of such measures.

And now, I would like to briefly summarize my remarks. My first point was that the subdivision of language skills beyond the four basic ones of listening, reading, speaking and writing, while theoretically possible, cannot in fact be achieved by tests, and therefore the suggestion that the investigator limit himself to those aspects that he is interested in, as opposed to paying attention to more global skills, is to my mind a weak proposal. My second point was that the distinction between "direct" and "indirect" measures, unless it is based on a clear theoretical criterion, is in fact arbitrary, and this arbitrariness vitiates the attempt to validate some measures by means of others. Thirdly, I argued that the difference score as proposed for a measure of bilingual proficiency is inadequate in principle due to the fact that correlated non-linguistic factors may differentially affect scores on proficiency tests in the two languages, hence rendering their direct comparison questionable. These considerations follow from the principle that performance measures cannot be taken as simple and direct indices of competence. Finally, I pointed out the apparent exclusive interest shown in bilingual interference on the negative transfer side to the detriment of measures dealing with the potentially positive linguistic effects of bilingualism.

I would not want to end my comments with an enumeration of my criticisms of Dr. Macnamara's paper. It is a strange fact that a commentary, more often than not, turns out to be a negative piece of work. In this instance, my commentary thus far, fails to reflect the great interest with which I have read and reread Dr. Macnamara's contribution and the personally useful function which it fulfills as a summary of the measures that investigators have used in this area. At several places in his paper, Dr. Macnamara furthermore shows the same perspicacity and lucid evaluation of certain central issues in bilingualism that he has previously demonstrated in his excellent book on bilingualism and education, as well as in his editorship of the recent issue of the Journal of Social Issues dealing with bilingualism and to which he has contributed several articles. We surely owe him an expression of gratitude for taking upon himself this useful task.

Andrée Tabouret-Keller

Le titre de la conférence de ce matin "Comment mesurer le bilinguisme d'une personne" se réfère à deux concepts: le concept de mesure et le concept de bilinguisme qualifiant une personne, concepts à propos desquels je souhaite faire quelques remarques.

Voici d'abord les commentaires se rapportant au concept de mesure: l'idée de mesurer le bilinguisme ou de mesurer l'efficience bilingue d'une personne est étroitement liée au contexte socio-économique de notre type de société. Nous souhaitons mesurer le bilinguisme pour contrôler les résultats de notre enseignement d'une part et d'autre part pour sélectionner la personne bilingue qui convient le mieux à telle ou telle occupation dans un secteur professionnel défini. C'est parce que les mesures sont ainsi liées à une double idée d'efficacité que la tendance est répandue d'attribuer une note au bilinguisme, une bonne note ou une mauvaise note. Dans le premier cas (contrôle des résultats de l'enseignement scolaire ou de l'enseignement des adultes), en mesurant le bilinguisme, ce sont en fait les résultats de l'application d'une méthode pédagogique que l'on mesure et à laquelle on attribue une bonne ou une mauvaise note. Cette note traduit également les conditions matérielles de l'enseignement: par exemple, l'enseignement d'une seconde langue donnera des résultats différents dans une classe de vingt élèves et dans une classe de quarante élèves.

Dans le deuxième cas, - la sélection d'une personne pour un emploi, - mesurer l'efficience bilingue revient à estimer les connaissances que la personne examinée a dans les deux ou les trois langues dont elle aura besoin dans la profession en question. Celà revient également à avoir un aperçu de son degré de motivation pour cet emploi: plus elle est motivée mieux elle se sera préparée à cette épreuve de bilinguisme et de plurilinguisme. En fin de compte les notes attribuées aux résultats des tests reflètent, dans notre type de société, la valorisation des emplois allant, par exemple, du responsable d'un service commercial d'une grande firme qui sera payé beaucoup et pour lequel l'efficience bilingue exigée sera très élevée, à l'employé des tramways dont l'emploi est beaucoup moins bien rémunéré et pour lequel les exigences d'efficience bilingue sont également nettement moins élevées. Cette réflexion me conduit directement à une question qui n'a pas encore été posée explicitement ici. Pour quelle raison, tel ou tel gouvernement ou tel ou tel groupe de personnes milite-t-il en faveur du bilinguisme ou, au contraire, en défaveur du bilinguisme? Pour quelle raison telle personne particulière souhaite-t-elle améliorer son bilinguisme ou au contraire est-elle tout à fait indifférente à la manière dont elle parle les deux langues? Etre bilingue, d'accord, mais pour quoi faire?

Un certain nombre de faits sur lesquels se base l'exposé de Monsieur Macnamara et sur lesquels se basent également les travaux de l'Ecole de Lambert dont cet exposé s'inspire, font appel à des indices très fins de l'efficience bilingue, à la vitesse de réaction et aux modalités de la perception visuelle dans des épreuves qui mettent en jeu la lecture silencieuse, par exemple. Est-ce que cette catégorie de mesure ne concerne pas autant, sinon plus, l'individu particulier en question que son bilinguisme? Il est problématique de prétendre que c'est le bilinguisme qui a été estimé: en réalité les indications obtenues portent sur l'état de fonctionnement et l'état d'entraînement d'un certain nombre de fonctions psycho-physiologiques fondamentales de l'individu, qu'il soit bilingue ou qu'il soit unilingue.

Dans la plupart des travaux un aspect de la personne bilingue qui nous concerne au plus haut point et qui est proprement psychologique a été laissé de côté: quelle est l'image que la personne se fait de son propre bilinguisme et quel est le système de valeurs sociales et même de valeurs morales dans lequel elle inscrit ses propres aspirations au bilinguisme ou bien son rejet du bilinguisme? Est-ce que mesurer le bilinguisme n'est pas aussi d'une certaine manière intervenir dans l'histoire individuelle d'une personne? Le test aussi objectif soit-il, constitue une intervention dans une histoire personnelle, elle-même généralement liée au passé d'un groupe de population et aux rapports de ce groupe avec une histoire linguistique. Le test est objectivement le même pour tous les candidats mais chacun d'eux l'appréhende subjectivement d'une manière différente, au décours même de son histoire particulière, ce qui ne saurait manquer d'influer sur les performances.

Toutes les mesures ont à la fois l'avantage et l'inconvénient d'être des estimations strictement synchroniques. A un moment donné nous prenons une mesure rigoureusement circonscrite à une activité très particulière. Il semblerait pourtant plus important d'avoir un aperçu sur les potentialités d'une personne: que peut-elle devenir, comment peut-elle évoluer si elle est mise dans d'autres conditions? Or, ce que nous mesurons généralement ce sont les ré-

sultats d'un mode de vie préalable, d'un mode préalable d'usages linguistiques, ceci au moment même où les conditions de ces usages doivent changer,
par exemple, au moment où la personne cherche à s'engager dans un autre
métier, au moment où elle doit passer un examen de fin d'études ou d'entrée
dans une activité professionnelle. Ce mode d'intervention synchronique que
constituent les tests nous empêche de prévoir, et même de nous demander comment la personne va réagir et comment elle va évoluer si elle est mise dans des
conditions différentes: problèmes que nous avons ignorés jusqu'ici.

Enfin j'aborderai rapidement les problèmes de la fidélité et de la prédic-
tivité des tests. D'une manière tout à fait générale, l'on sait très bien que
c'est seulement pour des déciles tout à fait supérieurs et tout à fait inférieurs
d'une distribution gaussienne que les tests ont une valeur prédictive. Pour la
grande masse des résultats moyens, les tests ont une valeur prédictive strictement relative: savoir à un moment donné que les résultats d'une personne donnée correspondent à la zône moyenne de la distribution des résultats d'une population de référence. On admet que le test possède un certain degré de fidélité indépendant des individus auxquels il s'applique (1); on admet également qu'un sujet possède de façon stable un certain degré d'aptitude (2) qu'il
soit ou non soumis à un test. En fait le degré d'aptitude ne peut être défini
de façon précise que par la description d'une opération expérimentale donné
(ici le test); on ne peut pas attribuer à l'aptitude une "mesure" absolue indé-
pendante de cette opération, ni d'ailleurs au procédé de mesure une vertu in-
dépendante des matériaux mêmes à partir desquels il fut élaboré et auxquels sa
pertinence se limite. La mesure et son objet sont complémentaires; dans le cas
du bilinguisme, cette relation et la nature linguistique du test (3) et de ce
qu'il estime mériteraient une rigueur méthodologique particulière. La question de savoir ce que l'on mesure avec un test est dépourvue de sens si elle
implique l'existence de réalités autonomes antérieures à leur mesure et indé-
pendantes d'elle et qui pourraient être connues sans que la mesure soit utilisée.
Dans ces conditions il paraît pour le moins hasardeux de se limiter à la question ici posée "comment mesurer le bilinguisme d'une personne": d'un simple
point de vue méthodologique on ne peut simplement pas le mesurer. La même
remarque est valable pour la question portant sur la mesure des comportements
des groupes humains bilingues.

La deuxième remarque que m'a suggérée la lecture du texte de Monsieur
Macnamara concerne le concept de "bilinguisme d'une personne" et le problème plus général d'une typologie des bilinguismes. Il me semble que si l'on
se mêle de mesurer le bilinguisme ou l'efficience des bilingues, c'est que

----

(1) A condition d'opérer dans des populations où la dispersion réelle reste la
     même.
(2) Dans le cas du bilinguisme, certains parleraient plutôt d'inaptitudes!
(3) Le fait que le test ne soit pas verbal n'y change rien.

l'on a déjà admis l'idée d'une classification. Il y a une question que nous pourrons difficilement éviter ici et qui est de savoir ce que cela présuppose et ce que cela entraîne de qualifier les bilingues ou les bilinguismes et de faire des typologies. Nous nous sommes, dans ce colloque, lancés tête baissée dans la bataille sans nous mettre d'accord sur un minimum de définitions nécessaires. Or les typologies des bilinguismes sont nombreuses, presque chaque auteur a la sienne et chaque fois qu'on arrive dans une contrée bilingue les gens vous disent: "Ah, mais vous savez, chez nous c'est tout à fait particulier, nous avons ici une typologie spéciale, nous avons des bilingues comme ceci et des bilingues comme cela". C'est pour cette raison que je me permets de terminer mon commentaire par une remarque plus générale concernant la définition des bilinguismes. Les nombreuses typologies qui ont été proposées jusqu'à présent, ici ou dans différents textes, sont toutes entachées de la même faiblesse méthodologique qui consiste à qualifier le bilinguisme d'une épithète qui renvoie en réalité au point de vue adopté pour mener l'analyse du phénomène bilingue en question. Il est question de bilinguisme individuel, de bilinguisme social, régional, culturel, horizontal, vertical, symétrique, pré-scolaire, etc.... or, toutes les terminologies se réfèrent aux méthodes d'analyse et au concept de trois disciplines seulement: la psychologie, la sociologie et la linguistique. J'écarte la psycho-linguistique parce qu'elle n'a pas de système conceptuel propre et se réfère pour chaque théorie qu'elle prétend vérifier aux concepts propres à cette théorie. Dire par exemple qu'un bilinguisme est pré-scolaire c'est privilégier une optique génétique qui se rattache à la psychologie, voire à la psycho-pédagogie. Dire d'un bilinguisme qu'il est social ou individuel ou dominant, c'est privilégier une optique sociologique qui se rattache au système conceptuel d'une discipline donnée: la sociologie.

En réalité quelle que soit la situation et l'individu ou le groupe considérés, il convient de préciser le point de vue selon lequel l'analyse a été menée, parce que c'est ce point de vue qui détermine à la fois le type de réduction et le mode d'intelligibilité que des cadres conceptuels particuliers ont imposés à l'analyse. Nous travaillons toujours dans le cadre d'un système conceptuel et il ne faut surtout pas, — je pense que cela nous arrive souvent dans ce colloque —, confondre ce que nous apporte ce cadre conceptuel avec des propriétés qui appartiendraient en propre au bilinguisme. En fait, le bilinguisme est toujours un phénomène complexe qui relève d'une analyse multi-disciplinaire. Il est parfaitement justifié de ne l'analyser que d'un seul point de vue mais il ne faut pas oublier que c'est toujours une réduction que nous opérons au sein d'une réalité beaucoup plus complexe. Par leur généralité les notions de bilinguisme (ou de plurilinguisme) englobent toutes les situations qui entraînent la nécessité de l'usage parlée et dans certains cas écrit de deux ou plusieurs langues par un même individu ou par un groupe. Une telle définition implique que pour la compréhension de l'ensemble du phénomène de bilinguisme, il soit fait appel non seulement à la description des faits proprement linguistiques, ce qui entraîne l'étude structurale du processus de contact et de ses conséquences, mais également aux faits sociologiques qui définissent la situation de contact et sa transformation ainsi qu'aux faits psychologiques qui touchent au locuteur ou au groupe de locuteurs et aux rapports originaux qu'il entretient avec ses différents langages.

Emile Th. G. Nuytens

Any psychological approach to the problem of bilingualism needs a firm theoretical basis to be laid in collaboration by linguists and psychologists. It seems to me that attempts at measuring bilingual proficiency will remain amateurish as long as we do not know the linguistic and psychological factors well enough. As an advisor in a project of research into the knowledge of the mother tongue in secondary schools in Holland (carried out by the Nijmegen laboratory of Psychology), I have found that practically all the psychological tests for various forms of language are very defective. More than ever before, has it become clear to me that there is still a great deal of research to be done before we can approach such a complicated phenomenon as bilingualism by tests and similar means.

In reading Macnamara's paper it surprised me somewhat to see that he did not mention Osgood's work. It seems to me that in measuring bilingualism we should be aware of the possibilities of his semantic differential method (cf. Measurement of meaning and his publications on bilingualism). The more so, as with this method, unexpected results have been obtained also in the field of bilingualism. Macnamara's research does not make it clear how the data obtained has been processed. Has a calculation been made of the correlation between the data of the various tests? Has a factor-analysis been applied? Is it not desirable to establish in addition to the rate of delivery the length of pauses and their nature and frequency? It must further be possible to estimate the progress of a learner of a second language on the basis of a quantitative analysis of style, i.e. by establishing word frequencies.

Confusion data also seems to me to offer unexpected and fascinating information. This approach can be of the greatest importance to the "pure" linguist as well, because it may offer him insights into the structure of language which could hardly be obtained in any other way. Mathematical psychology has succeeded in designing a satisfactory processing technique for this kind of data. In the phonological field, this method has already yielded good results. But it is my experience that the psychological tests in existence can hardly be a basis for linguistic research. Measuring is desirable and necessary, but one should have some idea of what one is measuring. The interesting but endless discussion of the way in which words are recognized in tachistoscopic presentation cannot but lead one to the conclusion that "they" don't know, and will undermine any confidence in the use of the Stroop test for linguistic purposes, although it may be useful for the selection of airplane pilots. This does not mean that a tachistoscope may not be valuable aid to the linguist also for measuring bilingual proficiency.

In conclusion I would like to state that I do not think we have got to the measuring stage yet, but that much preliminary research is still required on the basis of a close co-operation between linguists and psychologists.

DISCUSSION

English Version

Dr. Macnamara began the discussion by remarking how complicated the field of bilingualism had become. What had once been a fairly simple job of psychological measurement, was now extremely complex because of the increasing emphasis by linguists and socio-linguists on factors like social context, interlocutor and topic. In duscussion his own techniques he stated that the figures given in the appendix to his paper were valid for 12-year-olds from a couple of schools in Montreal. The most reliable were probably the self-ratings, as at that age there are probably no pressures to hide language loyalties.

In measuring bilingualism most people try a short inexpensive test to cover all variables. The usual measure of bilingualism is the difference score obtained by subtracting the score for performance in one language from that of another. This allows us to place people on a continuum of language skills ranging from unilingualism in one language to unilingualism in the other. Variables in a difference score react according to the following diagram:

French proficiency = French + confidence + intelligence + memory + ...
English proficiency = English+ confidence + intelligence + memory + ...

One can cancel out the variables which are the same in both equations and we are left with the languages themselves. When we measure reaction time by difference tests we measure the sum of the following variables:

Knowledge of (English + Error + Reaction Speed
              (French

The difference we arrive at is a measure of the different knowledge of two languages. Under the conditions imposed by time and place the reaction speed and error are the same unless the subject feels that a certain rhythm belongs to one of the languages. This point needs proof. The concept of bilingual balance is closely linked to difference scores: it is important to see what happens as difference is being dwindled to balance.

Two questions were raised by other participants: What device would Dr. Macnamara suggest to ensure that texts in two different languages were of equal difficulty? How is the difference in achievement on two language tests a measure of bilingualism? It was assumed that the continuum of ability went from 1 to 100. If a person has 60 in French and 40 in English, is this a measure of difference in ability? In answer to the first question Dr. Macnamara suggested a cross-over technique. A group of bilinguals of known and equal ability in both languages was to be divided randomly in two. One age group was given form A in one language and form B in the other. A few days later

108

the groups were to be switched over. If there was any difference this would show discrepancies in the test. In answer to the second question the speaker said that if the measures had been properly standardised, they would indicate the position of the bilingual in relation to the whole population that speaks the language, assuming that the distribution was normal in both languages.

Another important point was that tests measure specific aspects of bilingual skills: learning of various types, naming skills, speed of reaction etc. Many of these measures have been treated by Lambert and his team at McGill. In answer to the criticism in Dr. Jacobovits' first paragraph, Dr. Macnamara commented that we have to realise that we are dealing with a matrix made up of the four language skills. Though he himself did not break each skill down into its component parts he would not deny that it could not be broken down. Most aspects of language performance are covered somewhere in the matrix. Some variables can be used as predictors for others, but the question is, how well do they do it?

The tests used came under attack from several quarters. One participant repeated Dr. Jacobovits' question: Was there any proof for the assumption that the basic reaction speed was the same no matter what the language? Is knowledge of the language in question the only factor which causes variation? The questioner thought not, putting forward the idea that, under test conditions, a difference in reaction time could be due to some imponderable in the situation. He claimed that in assuming that differences were necessarily due to differing commands of both languages, Dr. Macnamara was confusing his working hypothesis with reality.

In the difference equation as Dr. Macnamara had it, according to another speaker, certain interaction factors were disregarded. Reactions within each equation can be different, and no amount of cancelling out will remove them. As yet, we do not know how to remove them, but we must recognise their existence.

The meeting's attention was called to the distinction between the use and study of language. Language is a tool like a hammer. It is there for us to use, not to discuss its uses. It seemed that several of the tests mentioned did not test what you do with language, but make you enumerate what you could do with it. The flexibility test, in requiring the subject to enumerate certain of its uses, does not test the automatic skills of language, but book-learning. A subject may be able to use many different synonyms in different situations, but not be able to think of them when he is asked. In any case, the better a person knows a language the better he knows the finer distinctions between words, and the less he is able to feel that words like surprise, astonishment and bewilderment are synonyms. So it could be argued that the more synonyms a subject produces, the less sensitivity he has to the language he is operating in. Even if this opinion is a little strong, the critic submitted that this test hardly gave a good impression of language competence.

There was much comment on the value of difference scores in measuring bilingualism. One delegate marked the absence of tests for the intelligibility of bilinguals' speech to monolinguals of either group. Though difference scores tell us about dominance and balance, what information do they give about success in communication? In his eyes, the meeting had forgotten the problem aspect of bilingualism. He went on that bilingualism is a form of behaviour imposed by a dominant group on a dominated one. For the dominant group, it is a transient stage in the assimilation of the dominated, while the dominated see bilingualism as a threat to their very existence as a group. So if we are to measure bilingualism, we must balance handicap against opportunity and measure the size of handicap. So far this had not been done. The Chairman reminded the meeting that these areas, though important, were not part of Dr. Macnamara's mandate for his paper. In any case, as yet prestige and intelligibility do not count as <u>measures</u>.

One important question raised was whether we were yet at the testing stage as regards bilingualism. This speaker claimed that the psychological and linguistic bases were, as yet, far from sound. We can not say anything about bilingualism until we know the grammar of spoken language and about related questions like kinesics. To save themselves from lamentable mistakes, psychologists should read modern linguistic theory, as expounded by Chomsky, Pike, Uhlenbeck and Malmberg. In their turn, linguistics can not avoid reading psychologists like Miller, Osgood, Brown, Suci and Lenneberg. Both psychologists and linguists should be familiar with the mathematical theories of Coombs. It is only by interdisciplinary cooperation that we will get results. Another speaker differed from this view, remarking that to measure something it was not really necessary to know what it was. He cited intelligence, which can be measured even if we do not really know its nature.

The meeting was told of the difficulties one participant had in relating the deviations of bilingual standards to unilingual norms. He found that unilingual reference point was useful only in classroom situations. But this is not really what scholars in the field are doing. As an illustration the speaker described his difficulties in finding norm groups for assessing the linguistic proficiency of Japanese immigrants to the United States. There is really no native norm group, as, owing to social conditions, these immigrants have evolved differently from their peers who stayed home. This could be what has been going on in French Canada. In these cases, the appropriate norm groups could be bilinguals of the group, and not monolinguals. An observer noted that the above remarks could apply to civil servants in Ottawa who having been taught the metropolitan norm find it is not entirely suitable for work conditions as the linguistic norms of the two places are different.

The points raised by the commentators were answered as follows. Dr. Macnamara considered Dr. Tabouret-Keller's points about improving bilingual skills and testing men for their suitability for employment as quite important, but added that the consideration of these points did not come into the ambit of his paper. He and Dr. Lambert both doubted whether a subject could influence the validity of difference scores by deliberate cheating on the test. The assumption was that <u>under the conditions of the test</u> a subject's basic reaction time was

the same. Dr. Jacobovits defended the utility of testing but was convinced
that unless the results in some way recognise the goals of linguists and other
people interested in language, nobody but psychologists would take any notice
of them.

Dr. Macnamara added that the tests under discussion were predictor tests.
A person faced with such a test would do certain things which would allow the
tester to draw certain conclusions. The criticisms voiced could be made about
criterion tests, but here they do not apply. He further emphasized that terms a
are comparable across equations—it is the same intelligence and the same memory
reacting with English and French. To substantiate the point that they are different one would have to assume that a person changed personality in changing
language—a doubtful hypothesis. Though it is the same intelligence that is being used in the second language, it is not being used as efficiently. People who
understood problems in their second language did not solve them as well. He
suggested as an explanation that while one is digesting the latter part of the
problem, one forgets the first parts.

There was even a suggestion that unless people could not produce better
tests that those criticised they should not comment on them. This was met by
the idea that, even if one is not a psychologist, one can detect faults in the
results of the tests and ask the psycgologists to take into account neglected factors in elaborating further tests.

The sociologists present were far from satisfied about the validity of difference tests. One of them claimed that the flexibility test would not give the
same sort of result with upper-class and lower-class speakers. But it was suggested that one could compare restricted-code speakers with elaborate-code
speakers by this means. As the second group perform better in context-free situations, they (i.e. middle-class speakers) should perform better under laboratory conditions. This application of flexibility tests should work as well in monolingual as in bilingual situations.

One participant called for a clearer taxonomy of bilingualism. If bilingualism is treated mainly as a scale, it would be impossible to avoid the question of social aspects of acquisition. The internalisation of social structures
takes place largely through language acquisition. This concept could be studied
by taking up the ideas of repertoire and variety as developed by Dr. Gumperz
and others. Language acquisition in a classroom is an affair totally different
from normal language acquisition. Jacobovits's social décalage may refer more
to this case than to the other. In a native bilingual there is not the schizophrenic split one finds in the others. The bilingual community is a type of complex society with linguistic complexities of a special order. The bilingual's
two languages allow him to comprehend social diversity, and do not form two
competing systems. The proficiency of the artificial bilingual should be treated
as a separate problem. Except in the hands of teachers and testers who try to
treat the languages as separate and discrete units on the model of the standard
languages spoken in unilingual areas, bilingualism is not a problem. For the
natural bilingual both of his languages are his mother tongue, and tests based
on the interference theorem are not applicable to him.

DISCUSSION

Version française

M. Macnamara ouvre la discussion en faisant remarquer que le domaine du bilinguisme est devenu très complexe. On se contentait naguère de mensurations psychologiques assez simples, mais aujourd'hui, linguistes et sociolinguistiques tiennent compte de plus en plus du contexte social, de l'interlocuteur, du sujet traité et d'autres facteurs semblables. A propos de ses propres techniques, M. Macnamara déclare que les chiffres donnés dans l'appendice de sa communication s'appliquent à des enfants de 12 ans, élèves de deux écoles de Montréal. Les résultats les plus sûrs sont probablement ceux des auto-évaluations, car à cet âge, rien ne pousse vraisemblablement les jeunes à masquer leurs allégeances linguistiques.

Pour mesurer le bilinguisme, on a le plus souvent recours à un test court et peu coûteux qui tient compte de toutes les variables. La mesure habituelle du bilinguisme est la note différentielle, qu'on obtient en soustrayant la note attribuée pour la compétence dans une langue de la note attribuée dans une autre langue. Cette méthode permet de classer les sujets selon une échelle continue allant de l'unilinguisme dans une langue à l'unilinguisme dans l'autre. Les variables exprimées par une note différentielle suivent le schéma suivant:

compétence en français= français + assurance + intelligence + mémoire + ...
compétence en anglais = anglais + assurance + intelligence + mémoire + ...

Si l'on élimine les variables qui sont les mêmes dans les deux équations, il ne reste plus que les langues elles-mêmes. Si l'on mesure le temps de réaction au moyen de tests différentiels, on mesure la somme des variables suivantes:

Connaissance de (anglais + erreur + temps de réaction)
(français + erreur + temps de réaction)

La différence qu'on obtient est une mesure de la différence de connaissance des deux langues. Dans les conditions imposées par le temps et par le lieu, le temps de réaction et l'erreur sont les mêmes, à moins que le sujet ne trouve qu'une des langues exige un rythme particulier, ce qui reste à prouver. L'idée d'équilibre entre les langues est étroitement liée aux notes différentielles: il importe donc de voir ce qui se produit à mesure que les différences s'amenuisent et qu'on se rapproche de l'équilibre.

D'autres participants soulèvent deux questions: quelle méthode M. Macnamara préconiserait-il pour s'assurer de l'égale difficulté des tests employés dans deux langues différentes? Comment la différence des résultats obtenus dans deux tests de compétence linguistique peut-elle constituer une mesure du bilinguisme? A supposer que la compétence s'échelonne de 1 à 100, et qu'un sujet obtienne 60 en français et 40 en anglais, est-ce là une mesure de l'écart de compétence? En réponse à la première question, M. Macnamara propose une méthode de croisement. On prend, par exemple, un groupe de bilingues connus comme également compétents dans les deux langues, et l'on divise ce groupe en deux, au hasard. Pour l'un des groupes, on utilise la formule A dans une langue et la formule B dans l'autre, et quelques jours plus tard, on intervertit les formules. Si l'on obtient des résultats différents, c'est que le test est défectueux. En réponse à la seconde question, le conférencier déclare que si les tests ont été bien normalisés, ils exprimeront la position du bilingue par rapport à l'ensemble de la population que parle la langue en question, à supposer que la distribution soit normale dans les deux langues.

Une autre considération importante, c'est que les tests mesurent des aspects particuliers du bilinguisme: diverses formes d'apprentissage, aptitude à nommer les choses, temps de réaction, etc. Un grand nombre de ces mesures ont été étudiées par M. Lambert et son équipe à McGill. Relevant la critique formulée par M. Jacobovits, dans son premier paragraphe, M. Macnamara rappelle qu'il s'agit ici d'une matrice comprenant les quatre éléments de la compétence linguistique. Sans donner lui-même les composantes de chacun des éléments, il ne nie pas la possibilité d'identifier ces composantes. La plupart des aspects de la compétence linguistique sont englobés dans cette matrice. Certaines variables peuvent servir à prédire les autres, mais il reste à savoir avec quelle exactitude.

Plusieurs participants critiquent les tests employés. L'un d'eux répète la question de M. Jacobovits, a-t-on des raisons de supposer que le temps de réaction est fondamentalement le même, quelle que soit la langue? La connaissance de la langue en question est-elle le seul facteur de variation? L'interrogateur pense bien que non, car selon lui, à l'occasion d'un test, une différence dans le temps de réaction pourrait être due à un élément impondérable de la situation. A son avis, M. Macnamara, en supposant que les différences sont nécessairement attribuables à une inégale maîtrise des deux langues, confond son hypothèse de travail avec la réalité.

Selon un autre participant, M. Macnamara ne tient pas compte, dans son équation, de certaines influences réciproques. Les réactions, dans les deux équations, peuvent être différentes, et l'on aura beau éliminer des chiffres, les différences n'en subsisteront pas moins. A l'heure actuelle, nous ne savons pas comment les faire disparaître, mais nous devons reconnaître leur existence.

On rappelle la distinction qui existe entre l'utilisation et l'étude des langues. La langue est un outil, à la manière d'un marteau. Elle est là pour qu'on s'en serve, non pour qu'on en discute les emplois. Il semblerait que plusieurs des tests mentionnés, au lieu d'étudier l'utilisation de la langue, ne font qu'amener le sujet à énumérer ce qu'on pourrait en faire. Le test de souplesse, en demandant au sujet d'énumérer certains emplois de la langue, ne détermine pas les automatismes linguistiques, mais les connaissances livresques. Un sujet peut être capable d'utiliser de nombreux synonymes dans des situations différentes, mais être incapable de se rappeler ces synonymes sur demande. De toute façon, plus une personne connaît une langue, mieux elle connaît les nuances entre les mots, et moins elle est portée à voir des synonymes dans des mots comme surprise, étonnement et ahurissement. On pourrait donc affirmer que plus un sujet produit de synonymes, moins il est sensible à la langue dans laquelle il s'exprime. Tout en admettant que cette opinion est peut-être un peu forcée, le critique n'en affirme pas moins que ce test ne donne guère une bonne appréciation de la compétence linguistique.

On a beaucoup discuté la valeur des notes différentielles pour mesurer le bilinguisme. Un délégué a signalé l'absence de tests permettant de mesurer l'intelligibilité de l'expression orale des bilingues pour les monolingues des deux groupes. Les scores différentiels nous renseignent sur la langue dominante et sur l'équilibre des langues, mais que nous disent-ils du succès dans la communication? A ses yeux, on a oublié ce qui fait bilinguisme un problème. Selon lui, le bilinguisme est une forme de comportement imposé par un groupe dominant sur un groupe dominé. Pour le groupe dominant, c'est une étape dans la voie de l'assimilation du dominé, tandis que les dominés voient dans le bilinguisme une menace à leur existence collective. Si l'on veut mesurer le bilinguisme, il faut donc peser les avantages et les inconvénients, et déterminer l'importance relative des inconvénients, ce qu'on n'a pas fait jusqu'ici. Le président rappelle que ces questions, quoique importantes, n'entraient pas dans le sujet proposé à M. Macnamara. De toute façon, les questions de prestige et d'intelligibilité ne comptent pas encore comme mesures.

Un participant soulève l'importante question de savoir s'il n'est pas encore trop tôt pour vouloir établir des tests de bilinguisme. Selon lui, les fondements psychologiques et linguistiques de ces tests sont encore loin d'être solides. On ne pourra rien affirmer au sujet du bilinguisme tant qu'on ne connaîtra pas la grammaire de la langue parlée et qu'on ignorera d'autres questions comme la cinesthésie. Pour éviter de tomber dans des erreurs lamentables, les psychologues devraient lire des ouvrages de théorie linguistique moderne, comme ceux de Chomsky, Pike, Uhlenbeck et Malmberg. Les linguistes, pour leur part, se doivent de lire des psychologues comme Miller, Osgood, Brown, Suci et Lenneberg. Psychologues et linguistes devraient se familiariser avec les théories mathématiques de Coombs. Ce n'est que par une collaboration entre les diverses disciplines qu'on obtiendra des résultats. Un autre participant s'oppose à ce point de vue, faisant remarquer que pour mesurer une chose, il n'est pas indispensable de savoir ce qu'elle est. Il cite l'intelligence, qu'on peut mesurer, mais dont on ne connaît pas vraiment la nature.

Un participant fait part des difficultés qu'il a eues à rattacher à des normes unilingues les déviations des normes de bilinguisme. Il a constaté qu'un point de référence unilingue ne peut être utile dans une salle de classe. Mais ce n'est pas là ce que font les chercheurs qui travaillent sur le terrain. A titre d'exemple, il cite la difficulté qu'il a eue à trouver des groupes témoins pour mesurer la compétence linguistique des immigrants japonais aux Etats-Unis. Il n'existe vraiment pas de groupes indigènes pouvant servir de norme, car selon

les conditions sociales, les immigrants ont connu une évolution différente de
celle de leurs congénères qui sont restés chez eux. C'est peut-être ce qui s'est
produit au Canada français. Dans ces cas, il y aurait peut-être lieu de considérer comme groupe normal les bilingues, plutôt que les monolingues. Un observateur a fait remarquer que ces propos pourraient s'appliquer aux fonctionnaires de l'état à Ottawa qui, ayant appris à utiliser la norme métropolitaine,
constatent qu'elle n'est pas applicable telle quelle dans des conditions de travail, étant donné que les normes linguistiques des deux endroits sont différentes.

Voici les réponses données aux questions soulevées par les commentateurs.
M. Macnamara reconnaît l'importance des arguments invoqués par Mme Tabouret-
Keller au sujet de l'amélioration du bilinguisme chez les personnes et de la nécessité de mesurer l'aptitude à remplir un emploi, mais il ajoute que ces questions n'entraient pas dans le cadre de son étude. Lui-même et M. Lambert
doutent qu'un sujet puisse altérer la validité des notes différentielles en trichant
délibérément dans le test. On prend comme postulat que dans les conditions du
test, le temps de réaction fondamental d'un sujet est le même. M. Jacobovits
affirme l'utilité des tests, mais se dit convaincu que si leurs résultats ne tiennent pas compte de quelque façon des objectifs des linguistes et des autres personnes qui s'intéressent à la langue, tout le monde s'en désintéressera sauf les
psychologues.

M. Macnamara ajoute que les tests dont il est question sont des tests de
prédiction. En présence d'un tel test, le sujet fera certaines choses qui permettront à l'administrateur du test d'en tirer certaines conclusions. Les critiques qu'on a formulées seraient valables pour des tests normatifs, mais ne s'appliquent pas ici. Il rappelle en outre que les deux termes de l'équation sont
comparables: c'est la même intelligence et la même mémoire qui interviennent
en anglais et en français. Pour prouver qu'il y a différence, il faudrait postuler qu'une personne change de personnalité lorsqu'elle change de langue, ce
qui est douteux. Même si c'est la même intelligence qui intervient dans la
langue seconde, elle n'est pas utilisée avec la même efficacité. Les personnes
qui comprennent des problèmes dans leur langue seconde ne réussissent pas aussi
bien à les résoudre, peut-être parce qu'en digérant les derniers éléments du
problème, elles oublient les premiers éléments.

Un participant va jusqu'à dire que les personnes incapables de produire de
meilleurs tests que ceux qu'elles critiquent devraient s'abstenir de les critiquer.
A cela il est répondu que, même si l'on n'est pas psychologue, on peut déceler
les lacunes dans les résultats des tests et demander aux psychologues de tenir
compte des facteurs négligés dans la mise au point de nouveaux tests.

Les sociologues présents sont loin de se montrer satisfaits de la validité des
tests différentiels. L'un d'eux prétend que le test de souplesse ne donnerait
pas les mêmes résultats avec des sujets de classes sociales différentes. Mais ce
moyen permettrait de comparer les locuteurs disposant d'un code restreint aux
locuteurs disposant d'un code complexe. Comme le second groupe obtient de
meilleurs résultats dans les situations hors-contexte, ce groupe (c'est-à-dire
les locuteurs de classe moyenne) devrait obtenir de meilleurs résultats dans des

conditions de laboratoire. Cette application des tests de souplesse devrait valoir aussi bien dans les situations de monolinguisme que dans les situations de bilinguisme.

Un participant réclame une taxonomie plus claire du bilinguisme. Si l'on considère le bilinguisme surtout comme une question de degré, il est impossible d'éviter la question des aspects sociaux de l'acquisition. L'intériorisation des structures sociales se fait, dans une large mesure, par l'acquisition de la langue. On pourrait étudier cette conception en s'inspirant des idées de répertoire et de variété mises de l'avant par M. Gumperz et par d'autres. L'acquisition d'une langue à l'école est une chose tout à fait différente de son acquisition dans des conditions normales. L'idée de décalage social de Jacobovits se rattache peut-être plus à ce cas qu'à l'autre. Chez un bilingue de naissance, on ne trouve pas la même rupture schizophrénique que chez les autres. La collectivité bilingue est un type de société complexe ayant des complexités linguistiques d'un ordre particulier. Les deux langues d'un bilingue lui permettent de comprendre la diversité sociale, et ne forment pas deux systèmes rivaux. La compétence du bilingue artificiel doit être considérée comme une question à part. Sauf pour les éducateurs et les administrateurs de tests qui s'efforcent de considérer les deux langues comme les unités séparées et discrètes selon le modèle des langues ordinaires parlées dans les régions unilingues, le bilinguisme n'est pas un problème. Pour le bilingue naturel, les deux langues sont des langues maternelles, et les tests fondés sur la théorie de l'interférence ne s'appliquent pas à son cas.

BIBLIOGRAPHY/BIBLIOGRAPHIE

Arsenian, Seth
   1937   Bilingualism and Mental Development; a study of the intelligence
              and the social background of bilingual children in New York
              City, Teachers College, Columbia University

Carroll, J. B.
   1941   "A Factor Analysis of Verbal Abilities," Psychometrika 6, 279-307

Coombs, C.
   1964   The Theory of Data, New York, Wiley

Darcy, N. T.
   1953   "A Review of the Literature on the Effects of Bilingualism upon
              the Measurement of Intelligence," Journal of Genetic Psy-
              chology 82, 21-57

Ervin, S. M.
   1961   "Semantic Shift in Bilingualism," American Journal of Psychology
              74, 233-241

Ferguson, Charles A.
   1959   "Diglossia," Word 15, 325-340

------- & Gumperz, John
   1960   "Introduction," International Journal of American Linguistics 26,
              3, 2-18

Fishman, Joshua A.
   1967   "Bilingualism With and Without Diglossia; Diglossia With and
              Without Bilingualism," The Journal of Social Issues 23, 2,
              29-38

Guildford, J. P., Kettner, N. W., & Christensen, P. R.
   1956   "The Nature of the General Reasoning Factor," Psychological
              Review 63, 169-172

Gumperz, John J.
   1964   "Linguistic and Social Interaction in Two Communities," American
              Anthropologist 66, 6, Part 2, 137-153

   1967   "On the Linguistic Markers of Bilingual Communications," The
              Journal of Social Issues 23, 2, 48-57

Hoffman, M. N. H.
   1934   The Measurement of Bilingual Background, New York City,
              Teachers College, Columbia University

Hymes, Dell
   1967   "Models of the Interaction of Language and Social Setting,"
              The Journal of Social Issues 23, 2, 8-28

Johnson, G. B.
   1953   "Bilingualism as Measured by a Reaction Time Technique and the
              Relationship Between a Language and a Non-Language Intel-
              ligence Quotient, Journal of Genetic Psychology 82, 3-9

Krauthammer, Marcel

A Comparison of Performance on Linguistic and Non-Linguistic Tasks in English-French Bilinguals, Unpublished thesis, McGill University

Labov, William

1966   The Social Stratification of English in New York City, Washington, Center for Applied Linguistics

Lado, Robert

1961   Language Testing: the Construction and Use of Foreign Language Tests; a teacher's book, London, Longmans

Lambert, W. E.

1955   "Measurement of the Linguistic Dominance of Bilinguals," The Journal of Abnormal and Social Psychology 50, 197-200

1966-67   Psychological Studies of the Interdependencies of the Bilingual's Two Languages, Paper presented at the meetings of the Linguistic Society of America, Los Angeles; in press as an article in a series with University of California Press

-----, Havelka, J., & Gardner, R. C.

1959   "Linguistic Manifestations of Bilingualism," American Journal of Psychology 72, 77-82

Macnamara, J. T.

1966   Bilingualism and Primary Education; a study of Irish experience, Edinburgh, Edinburgh University Press

----

1967a   "The Linguistic Independence of Bilinguals," Journal of Verbal Learning and Verbal Behaviour, to appear in Oct.

1967b   "The Effects of Instruction in a Weaker Language," The Journal of Social Issues 23, 2, 121-135

-------& Kellaghan, Thomas

1967   "Reading in a Second Language," (In) Reading Instruction; an international forum, D. Jenkinson (ed.), Newark, Delaware, International Reading Association, 231-240

Mol, H.

1963   Fundamentals of Phonetics, 1; the Organ of Hearing, Mouton, The Hague

Osgood, C. E. et al.

1957   The Measurement of Meaning, Urbana, Illinois University Press

Preston, M. S.

1965   Inter-Lingual Interference in a Bilingual Version of the Stroop Color-Word Test, Unpublished Ph.D. thesis, McGill University

Rao, T. S.

1964   "Development and Use of the Directions Test for Measuring Degree of Bilingualism," Journal of Psychological Researches 8, 114-119

Thurstone, L. L., & Thurstone, T. G.
   1941   "Studies of Intelligence," Psychometric Monographs 2
Treisman, Anne M.
   1963   "The Effects of Redundancy and Familiarity on Translating and
             Repeating Back a Foreign and a Native Language," British
             Journal of Psychology 56, 369-379
Vernon, P. E.
   1961   The Structure of Human Abilities, 2nd ed., London, Methuen
Weinreich, Uriel
   1953   Languages in Contact; findings and problems, New York, Lin-
             guistic Circle of New York, (Series: Linguistic Circle of New
             York, Publications, No. 2)

3

HOW CAN WE MEASURE THE EFFECTS WHICH ONE LANGUAGE MAY
HAVE ON THE OTHER IN THE SPEECH OF BILINGUALS?

COMMENT MESURER LES EFFETS EXERCES PAR UNE LANGUE SUR
UNE AUTRE DANS LE LANGUAGE DES BILINGUES?

THEME

Nils Hasselmo

1. The problem

The problem which I have been asked to discuss has been described in the recent literature on bilingualism as follows: Speech is produced in accordance with certain norms. A bilingual differs from a monolingual in one fundamental respect. Instead of being in possession of one set of norms, he is in possession of at least two sets (Haugen 1956 p.8), referred to below as L1 and L2. The presence of more than one set of norms in one and the same speaker may lead to linguistic interference, defined in an often quoted passage as 'those instances of deviation from the norms of either language which occur in the speech of bilinguals as a result of their familiarity with more than one language, i.e. as a result of language contact....' (Weinreich 1953 p.1) The question of how to measure interference has accordingly been viewed as consisting of the three partial questions of how to identify interference, how to describe interference, and how to quantify and tabulate interference.

2. Attempted solutions

2.1 The identification of interference

The identification of interference requires norm specification and contrastive analysis.

(1) Norm specification. Norm specification entails a detailed description of the phonology, grammar, and lexicon of the languages available to the speaker, including those features, originally characteristic only of one language, that can be regarded as integrated with another. The problems involved are extremely complex, especially those arising in connection with the specification of the lexicon of a language. Variations that are an aspect of a certain code must be distinguished from those that are due to the presence of another code; interference in speech must be distinguished from interference in language.

The distinction between interference in speech and in language was first introduced by Uriel Weinreich, with reference to de Saussure's concepts of parole and langue. The former is characteristic of a certain discourse, it is momentary, and it is due to the speaker's first-hand knowledge of another language; the latter is part of the norm, it is a feature of another code that has become habitualized, and it is learned by monolingual speakers in the same

way as originally native features of the norm. (Weinreich 1953 p.11) William
Mackey reserves the term interference strictly for what Weinreich calls interference in speech, the first step of his analysis consisting of a rigorous determination of the local code on the basis of 'availability tests'. These tests,
one of the most notable efforts to establish a procedure for norm specification,
focus entirely on the social dimension of interference phenomena, establishing
'the extent and uniformity of the local standard' by investigating the 'way(s)
of expressing something' used by monolinguals. If a word or phrase represents
the only way of expressing something, it is regarded as part of the local language regardless of whether it belongs to one language or the other historically
or in other communities. 'Once the local code is established, any divergence
from it in the samples of speech of a bilingual as a result of the other language
may be analyzed as a case of bilingual interference.' (Mackey 1956 p.241)

Einar Haugen restates the question of whether a given instance of interference is interference in speech or in language. After having pointed out
that 'any item that occurs in speech must be a part of some language if it is to
convey any meaning to the hearer', he continues: 'The real question is whether a given stretch of speech is to be assigned to one language or the other.'(1)
In his opinion, Weinreich's terminology does not furnish any criterion for making this decision. Haugen regards the linguistic criteria of phonology and
morphology as basic and expresses strong misgivings concerning the social criterion of appeal to one or more speakers. He accepts as a consequence of the
application of his criteria the fact that some items may have to be assigned to
two languages simultaneously. The result of Haugen's discussion is a three-
fold classification of phenomena. Code-switching refers to the use of successive stretches of two languages, i.e., to the extreme of complete lack of adaptation of items from one language to the phonology and morphology of the other
language; interference (in the strict sense) refers to the overlapping of two languages, i.e., to the simultaneous application of the patterns of two languages
to the same item; integration refers to the extreme of complete adaptation of
items from one language to the phonology and morphology of the other language. (Haugen 1956 p.40)

(2) Contrastive analysis. Contrastive analyses specify the similarities and
differences between languages by comparing equivalent subsystems. Instances
of partial similarity are of special interest from the point of view of interference
since they may lead to false interlingual identifications. A considerable number of such analyses have appeared in recent years, mostly for the purpose of
foreign language teaching. So far attention has been limited almost entirely
to phonology and grammar. (2)

---

(1) Haugen 1956 p.39   Italics in the original.
(2) A comprehensive bibliography of contrastive analyses in Hammer & Rice
    1965   Of special importance is the Series of contrastive studies published
    by the Center for Applied Linguistics, Washington, D. C.

2.2 The description of interference

The following criteria have been employed in the description of interference.

(1) Levels of analysis. The discussion of levels of analysis is relevant to the present survey only insofar as it relates the levels to mechanisms of interference. The minimum number of levels distinguished in any analysis of interference is two, the phonemic and the morphemic level. Haugen has argued that this twofold distinction is not only sufficient but that it also best reflects the mechanism of interference. He maintains that the threefold distinction used by Weinreich and others, which involves the separation of the grammatical and the lexical level at the outset of the analysis, leads to redundancy and actually obscures the fundamental similarity between interference involving grammatical and lexical morphemes. (3) Weinreich's argument for a separation of the grammatical and the lexical level is that 'many morphemes do have a designative function distinct from their purely grammatical function.' (Weinreich 1953 p.47 fn.1) Mackey makes a distinction between 'referential' and 'structural' (or 'sequential') modification that reflects the separation of levels preferred by Weinreich. (Mackey 1965b p.244; 1966 p.87)

Available descriptions of interference also recognize such other linguistic levels and domains as the phonemic versus the allophonic level, the morphemic versus the allomorphic level, grammatical morphemes versus grammatical relations versus obligatory categories, and different form classes.

The most extensive investigations of phonemic versus allophonic interference are those of Weinreich. He distinguishes between interference that involves phonemic under- or over-differentiation or phonemic reinterpretation and interference that involves phone substitution. (Weinreich 1953 pp.18ff; 1957 pp.5ff)

Little attention has so far been devoted to the parallel distinction between morphemic and allomorphic interference. An analysis of this type forms the basis for a statement such as the following: 'When English -s is introduced into the Welsh plural system, it is hardly more than a new allomorph of the pre-existent plural morpheme.' (Haugen 1954 p.386) It is possible that Weinreich's distinction between different types of lexical integration of morphemes could be interpreted as a distinction of the same type. The introduction of items with 'entirely new content' or with a new grammatical function and the specialization of content or function between native and foreign items would then represent morphemic interference, 'confusion in usage' of native and foreign items allomorphic interference. (Weinreich 1953 pp.54ff)

A full-fledged application of immediate constituent analysis is found in Mackey's work. His scheme, which is designed specifically for the analysis

---

(3) Haugen 1954 p.386 Cf. also Haugen 1956 p.50

of texts, recognizes all the levels in the hierarchical structure of sentences, from the sentence itself over clauses, phrases, words, morphemes, and phonemes down to the distinctive features. (Mackey 1965b p.243)

(2) Mode of interference. For the present purposes it is convenient to conceive of a language as made up of inventories of units which have identity and distribution. One of the most common criteria used in the description of interference can then be summarized as follows: interference can take the form of the introduction into L1 discourse of L2 identities or L2 distributions. The identities are the phones and the morphs, the distributions the permissible sequences of phonemes and the patterns of arrangement and the grammatical or designative functions of morphemes.

This distinction between the introduction of identities and of distributions has been applied most consistently by Haugen, who considers it relevant on the phonemic as well as the morphemic level. He uses the terms importation for the introduction of identities, substitution (redistribution) for the introduction of distributions, viewing the two modes of interference as an aspect of integration, i.e., of the relationship between an L2 model and an L1 replica of this model. (Haugen 1953 pp.388, 402; 1954 p.386) Weinreich, following the practice of previous studies, has applied the distinction only on the morphemic level(s). He thus separates the transfer of morphemes from the reproduction of morphemes. (Weinreich 1953 p.47)

The distinction between the two modes of interference also figures to some extent in Mackey's analysis, viz., in the form of constituents that are bilingual by the combination of identities from two languages versus those that are bilingual by modification, i.e., by the occurence of an L2 distribution with L1 identities. (4)

Various classifications of loanwords embody the distinction between the introduction of identities and of distributions. Thus loanword and pure loanword refer to borrowed identities, loan translation and loanshift to borrowed distributions, and hybrid loan and loanblend to items that represent both modes and interference. (Haugen 1950; 1953 pp.402ff; Weinreich 1953 pp.407ff)

(3) Degree of linguistic integration. Linguistic integration is a matter of the adaptation of imported items to the phonology and grammar of the recipient language. In the form of considerations of sound substitution and of the adaptation of loanwords to the native grammatical system it has long standing in the literature. (5) The degree of phonological integration forms the basis for the distinction between loanwords (Lehnwörter) and foreign words

---

(4) Mackey 1965b p.243ff; 1966 p.87 'Bilingual by combination' in Mackey's terminology includes not only combinations of L1 and L2 constituents but also combinations of an L1 constituent with a constituent that is itself bilingual (supposedly by combination or by modification).
(5) See, e.g., Paul 1920 p.394ff; Bloomfield 1933 p.445ff.

(Fremdwörter) that is sometimes made. (6) Haugen's threefold division into integration, interference, and code-switching is the most explicit statement of degrees of integration. This scheme is based primarily on 'linguistic integration' (adaptation) but does to some extent reflect 'social integration' (adoption) as well, viz., insofar as integration is represented by 'established loans'.

The point has been made by Weinreich that a speaker's intention is a matter of a binary choice, i.e., that at the moment of first use, he chooses either to render a foreign item in its original form or to adapt it (completely) to the language spoken. (7) The fact that items often show a form that can be said to reflect two different systems is thus interpreted as a matter of speech production, not of choice of mechanism.

(4) Degree of social integration. The question of the degree of 'social integration' of instances of interference has so far received relatively little attention. (8) Mackey's 'availability tests' suggest one possible approach. Of considerable interest is also the work of Dell Hymes, John Gumperz, Trevor Hill, William Labov, and others which focuses on the often subtle alternation between 'different languages' in what Hymes has called the 'speech economy' of a community. (9)

It has been suggested that degree of 'social integration' may at times be signalled by phrases such as 'as we say in English' or by vocal quotation marks such as stress, pitch, changes of tempo etc. (Weinreich 1953 p. 73; Haugen 1965 p. 75)

(5) Literal versus approximate renditions of models. This distinction has been applied in the description of lexical loans that represent reproduction of compounds and phrases. (10)

(6) Conditioning of interference. On the phonemic level, Weinreich has distinguished between syntagmatic and paradigmatic factors, the former involving the segmentation of sound sequences and permissible sequences, the latter phonemic contrasts and the distinctive feature analysis of phonemes. (Weinreich 1957 pp. 2ff)

On the morphemic level, Haugen has distinguished between homophonous, synonymous, and homologous extention on the basis of whether the model and the replica show phonetic or semantic similarity or both. (Haugen 1953 p. 402)

The variety of extra-linguistic factors that have also been discussed in the literature under such headings as prestige, need, and oversight cannot be

---

(6)   See, e.g., Schuchardt 1928 p. 178; Jesperson 1922 p. 208

(7)   Weinreich 1953 p. 26, footnote 30   Cf. Pap 1949 pp. 101-2

(8)   However, both Paul and Bloomfield recognize that the adoption of a foreign item is distinct from its adaptation. Paul thus speaks of making an item usuell (Paul 1920, 393) and Bloomfield of how an item 'embarks upon a career of fluctuation in frequency' (Bloomfield 1933 p. 445)

(9)   Hymes 1962; 1964; Gumperz 1964; Hill 1958; Labov 1966

(10) Betz 1939 pp. 33-5; 1949

surveyed in the present report. (11)

(7) Configurations and conditioning of code-switching. A few attempts
have been made to describe code-switching in terms of the configurations of
two languages that occur in texts or in terms of conditioning. Haugen has
pointed to the lexeme as the minimal unit introduced in this manner and to the
fact that switching rarely takes place within one and the same breath group.
He has also pointed to the fact that the change of language can be more or
less 'clean', i.e., involve different degrees of overlapping. (12) The role
of vocal quotation marks has been mentioned by Haugen and Wienreich.
(Haugen 1953 pp.65; Weinreich 1953 p.73) In a study of Swedish-English
code-switching, I have attempted to describe the configurations of code-
switching in terms of limited and unlimited switching, viz., the introduction
of complete immediate constituents of sentences or complete discourse segments
versus the introduction of stretches which are not describable in terms of such
units; in terms of clean and ragged switching, viz., the absence or presence
of phonic and/or morphic overlapping; in terms of marked and unmarked switching, viz., the presence or absence of signals of a change of language; and in
terms of triggered and triggering stretches of speech. (13) In Indian communities where code-switching has been part of social interaction for centuries,
Gumperz has established the existence of what he terms 'code-switching varieties' of the languages involved. These varieties are characterized by minimal language distance; in extreme cases only a handful of markers remain
to distinguish the two codes from each other. (Gumperz 1964) Quotations have
been pointed to by Haugen as a factor conditioning code-switching. (Haugen
1953 p.65) Michael Clyne has distinguished between consequential and anti-
cipational triggering, viz., changes of language due to a preceding and a following ambiguous item respectively, and contextual triggering, viz., changes
due to the fact that the speaker is talking about a situation linked with the
other language. (14) I have attempted a distinction between different types
of primary conditioning, viz., conditioning by receiver, setting, channel,
topic, functions of speech, linguistic structure, and/or discourse structure,
and secondary conditioning, viz., conditioning by what occurs in the stream
of speech. (Hasselmo MS) Gumperz has made a distinction between transactional and personal switching, based on whether the speaker switches because
of a particular social role relationship or for purposes that might be termed

---

(11) See, e.g., Weinreich 1953 p.56ff Cf. also (7), below.
(12) Haugen 1956 p.50 Cf. also Diebold 1963
(13) Hasselmo, Ms. Cf. section 5 Proposal 2
(14) M. Clyne, Monash University, Victoria, Australia, in correspondence.
      Clyne has also introduced the term 'multiple transference' for code-
      switching to conform with a terminology based on the concept of 'trans-
      ference'. A book by Clyne is forthcoming, entitled Transference and
      Triggering.

stylistic. Joshua Fishman has explored patterns of language choice in terms of 'who speaks what language to whom and when'. (Fishman 1965)

(8) Direction of interference. Distinctions have been made between a speaker's primary language, the one with which he is most familiar, and his secondary language, his 'other' language. The classical and somewhat doubtful statement is the so-called 'Windisch's Law': It is not the language learned that is most subject to interference but the learner's original language. (Windisch 1897) This question has been discussed extensively by Andreas von Weiss. (15) Work by psychologists and sociologists on language dominance is relevant to this aspect of interference. (16)

(9) Production versus perception. Weinreich has introduced a distinction between interference in the production of speech as opposed to interference in the perception of speech. (17)

(10) Effect on communication. The effects of interference have been found to vary from a complete breakdown of communication to subtle misunderstandings, from complete blocking of speech production to a slight speech retardation. (18)

(11) Other criteria. Other criteria that have been used are desirability, need, and the speakers and their attitudes. (Haugen 1956 pp. 59-60)

2.3 The quantification and tabulation of interference

One of the objectives of the kind of classification described in the previous section has been the identification of what might be referred to as 'units of interference'. Broadly interpreted, the units consist of identities ranging from single L2 phones to sequences of sentences introduced through code-switching and of distributions ranging from a feature of L2 phonotactics to complex word order patterns or the designative functions of sentences or even longer stretches of speech. (19) This type of quantification of interference is less complex than that which attempts to relate a unit of interference to the total number of units of potential interference. Some efforts of the latter type will be discussed in the survey of measurements, below.

Three types of measurements will be considered: measurements of interference on specific levels and in specific domains, comparisons between

---

(15) v. Weiss 1959 passim. Concerning Mackey's distinction between 'main language' and 'secondary language', see below.

(16) See, e.g., Lambert 1955; Fishman 1964

(17) Weinreich 1957 pp.1-2. He uses the terms 'rendition' and 'analysis'. See further under 2.3 (3), below.

(18) See further under 2.3 (3) and (7), below.

(19) Descriptions of interference in terms of successful and unsuccessful communication can perhaps be said to deal with units of interference equalling communication events. Cf. (3), below.

domains, and measurements of total interference.

(1) Measurements of lexical interference. The most common type of measurement of interference is the loanword count, i.e., a measurement of interference in language. Lexical interference has been studied in relation to the
total lexicon of the recipient language. One actual count performed on the
vocabulary of one single informant is reported by Haugen. (Haugen 1953 p.94)
More common are statements to the effect that a certain language has a lexicon
consisting almost entirely of loans. (Meillet 1921 p.83; Bloomfield 1933 p.467;
Haugen 1956 p.67) An approach that occupies a position between measurements in terms of a total lexicon and measurements in terms of lexical subsystems has been used by A. Richard Diebold. For Huave he established the number of imported lexical items that were part of the current version of the 100-
word lexicostatistics list. (Diebold 1961 p.107) Studies of lexical subsystems
have focussed on semantic fields and on form classes. One study of the former
type included 'spheres of activity' ranging from 'autos and bicycles' and
'city life' to 'church' and 'parts of the body'. (Haugen 1953 p.94) The need
for a careful selection of fields has been emphasized by Weinreich. (Weinreich
1954 p.168) Haugen has supplemented a count of loans by form class by a comparison with the share of the total lexicon that represents each form class of a
variety of the language found in a non-contact situation. (Haugen 1953 pp.
406-7)

Investigations of texts normally deal with the number of loanword tokens
in relation to the total number of word tokens in the texts. Such studies have
been undertaken by, e.g., Haugen for American-Norwegian and by Learned
and Springer for Pennsylvania-German. (20) More recently Veroboj Vildomec
has published detailed analyses of written multilingual texts, including some
information on lexical interference in terms of types and tokens. (Vildomec
1963 pp.123ff) In a discussion of what is variously called the 'transferability'
and the 'adoptability' of morphemes, Weinreich has pointed out the need for
measurements of the text frequencies of loans representing different form classes, especially in terms of tokens. He has also stressed the need for comparing these frequencies with those of the corresponding classes in the source
language and the recipient language. (Weinreich 1953 p.36)

(2) Measurements of grammatical interference. No methods designed
specifically for the measurement of grammatical interference are known to me.
Such function words as prepositions and confunctions are often included in
measurements of lexical interference.

The rather extensive literature on foreign language testing is mentioned
in this report only in passing. Some of the procedures, including check lists
and scales of 'seriousness' of errors, can be regarded as methods for measuring
grammatical interference. (21)

---

(20) See, e.g., Learned 1889 p.288; Springer 1943; Haugen 1953 p.95
(21) Cf. 2.3 (3) and (6), below.

(3) Measurements of phonological interference. Statements about the addition or loss of phonemes and about the addition or loss of positions in the distribution of phonemes are the only available measurements of phonological interference in relation to phonological systems. (22)

A method for measuring phonological interference in terms of successful and unsuccessful communication has been developed by S. Saporta, R. Brown, and W. D. Wolfe. (Saporta, Brown & Wolfe, 1959) It is based on four types of communication events.

Communication event	Source	Receiver	Description of event
1	A ⟶ A A ⟵ A		Correct confirmation
2	A ⟶ B B ⟵ B		Correct rejection
3	A ⟶ A B ⟵ A		Incorrect rejection
4	A ⟶ B A ⟵ B		Incorrect confirmation

A message is sent from a source to a receiver and returned for confirmation or rejection as 'correct' or 'incorrect'. A   A stands for correct, A   B for incorrect reception. When the message is returned to the source, it will be confirmed or rejected. Confirmation: A   A or A   B; rejection: B   A or B   B. In the experiment either the source or the receiver is a bilingual while the other is a monolingual. On the basis of the assumption that 'interference is measured by the proportion of communication events which are not correct confirmations', the authors proceeded to test the amount of interference caused by phonemic under-differentiation, phone substitution, and distributional differences. The procedure allows for separate measurements of interference in perception and production.

Tests of interference in perception have been used in experimentation for language teaching purposes. In one such test a group of Japanese students of English were twice (before and after a period of learning) presented with twenty-five problems involving distinctions between vowels, between consonants, and between sequences, occurring in identical environments. The purpose was to determine the amount of phonic interference before and after training and to rank English phonological features according to degree of

---

(22) See, e.g., Bloomfield 1933 pp.445ff.; Diebold 1961 pp.106-7

difficulty for speakers of Japanese. (Strain 1963) A ranking of interlingual phonic relationships on a scale of difficulty was also the purpose of an investigation of the order in which a German learning English mastered various type of syntagmatically and paradigmatically conditioned difficulties. (Green 1963)

(4) Measurements of code-switching. Apart from statements concerning the number of changes of language that take place in a given text, no effort has been made to measure code-switching. (Haugen 1953 p.65; Mackey 1965b; 1966)

(5) Comparisons of interference in different domains. Weinreich has drawn attention to the fact that comparisons of the amounts of interference found in different domains require a type of quantification which has not yet been accomplished: 'Indeed, it seems necessary first to devise ways of formulating the degree of integratedness of a system, and to measure the affected proportion of the domain, before meaningful comparisons can be made'. (23) The same problem has confronted v. Weiss in his efforts to compare different types of 'errors' made by German-Estonian bilinguals. He comments briefly on the need to relate the number of errors in a certain domain to the total number of possibilities for error (Fehlermöglichkeiten) if a statement concerning the absolute frequency of a certain error is to be made. (Weiss 1959 p.109) His only attempt to perform such a measurement consists of relating 513 'word usage errors' to the estimated total of 200,000 word tokens in his samples. (Weiss 1959 p.114) Instead he concentrates on relative frequencies, relating the number of errors of a certain type, or in a certain domain, to the total number of errors occurring in texts in a certain language and to the number of errors of an equivalent type, or in an equivalent domain in texts in the other language. His analysis includes statements concerning relative amounts of interference for three types of bilinguals. Mackey's approach makes possible a comparison between the amount of interference on different levels of the immediate constituent structure of sentences, both in terms of the proportion of interference and in terms of the rate of alternation between languages. (24)

Statements concerning the direction of interference of the following type can be regarded as elementary comparative measurements which do not require quantification: 'A has exerted no influence on B phonemics but has influenced the B lexicon while B has influenced A phonemics and A grammar as well as the A lexicon'. (Weinreich 1953 p.67; Vildomec p963 pp.137ff)

(6) Measurements of total interference. There seems to be general agreement that there is no way of measuring total interference short of a specification of the amounts of different types of interference. Weinreich states it this way: 'No easy way of measuring or characterizing the total impact of one language on another in the speech of bilinguals has been, or probably can be,

---

(23) Weinreich 1953 p.67 Cf., e.g., Whitney 1881; Dauzat 1927 pp.49-55; Pritzwald 1938

(24) See further under (6), below.

devised. The only possible procedure is to describe the various forms of interference and to tabulate their frequency'. (Weinreich 1953 p. 64) Weinreich
refers to the efforts of, e.g., M. E. Smith to compute the frequency of specific types of interference in the English of Hawaiian children with different
mother-tongues. (Weinreich 1953 p.63; Smith 1939) Various types of 'error
counts' for pedagogical purposes also fit into this category, e.g., a 'German
error count' which provides a very detailed check list of errors and a number
of tables summarizing the amounts of interference of different types. (Hathaway
1929) The report includes an estimate of the total number of word tokens in the
samples but no specification of the possibilities for errors of each types.

The common type of language proficiency tests has been suggested as a tool
for measuring total interference. (25) However, their obvious deficiencies have
also been noted: the oftentimes inadequate classification of 'errors', the arti-
ficiality of the testing situation, etc. Weinreich has also pointed to the absence of a measure of 'poverty of expression' in most of these tests, although
this phenomenon may be due to interference. (Weinreich 1953 p.63) Such a
measure is part of v. Weiss' scheme. Under his category of 'idiomatic norm
errors', which he admits may be due to interference between different varieties of the same language but keeps distinct from 'mixing errors' (due to interference between Estonian and German), he includes 'lack of words' (Wortnot)
and 'empty words' (leere Worte) and computes the frequencies of these errors.
(Weiss 1959 pp.66ff) The purpose of v. Weiss' total measures is to show the
difference between a person's primary and secondary language and between
different types of bilinguals. His total measures of interference in speech
(spontane Sprachmischung) include four partial measures, those of 'word usage',
'morphology', 'syntax', and 'word order'. (Weiss 1959 pp.86–88)

Specimen Measurement of Interference (after Mackey 1965 p.247)

Specimen: (Reference to specific text in corpus)

Main language: French	ML – Main language
Secondary language: English	SL – Secondary language
Place: Home	B – Bilingual unit
Style: Recounting	To – Tokens
Context: Work	Ty – Types
	∿ – Alternation

Levels	Combination					Modification				∿
	ML		SL		B	REF		STR		
	To	Ty	To	Ty		To	Ty	To	Ty	%
Sentences	312	309	197	194	82	3	3	2	1	6
Clauses	155	152	88	87	61	5	4	5	3	8
Phrases	102	96	44	38	59	8	6	7	6	9
Words	98	69	53	47	58	11	8	12	10	7
Morphemes	61	46	30	23	41	6	6	6	7	6.5
Phonemes	164	36	73	17	11	3	2	8	6	7.5

(25) For information concerning testing procedures, see Yamagiwa 1956–57;
    Lado 1961

Mackey's focus is one specific text, produced in a specific place, style, and context. (Mackey 1965b p.243ff; 1966 pp.87ff) After an immediate cons- tituent analysis of the text, he distinguishes between units representing the main language (ML) and the secondary language (SL) and units that are bilin- gual (B) by combination or modification. The measurement of the proportion of interference tabulates for each level the number of units that represent ML and SL or that are bilingual, distinguishing between ML and SL tokens and types. The units that represent only ML or SL respectively are thus gradually separated from the bilingual units, i.e., the units that show interference within their boundaries. Thus B units are in turn subjected to further analysis on the next lower level. The measurement of the rate of interference tabulates the number of times the speaker changes languages between complete ML and SL units on a given level, expressed in terms of the number of changes per 100 oc- curences of units on that level.

(7) Psychological measurements of interference. An ordinary foreign lan- guage test that involves a time factor can be regarded as the simplest form of psychological measurement of interference. (26) Response times have also been studied through oral tests for the purpose of measuring interference. (Gali 1928; Saer 1931; Weinreich 1953 p.63; Lambert 1955; 1963 p.118) General speech hesitancy has been interpreted as an effect of interference and used as an index of deficiencies in a language. (Taute 1948) However, on the whole psychol- ogists have in recent years been 'less interested in the linguistic quantification of interlingual interference than in dominance, associative interferences, re- call, and biculturalism'. (Diebold 1965 p.253)

3.   Critique of attempts to date

3.1 The identification of interference.

The work in contrastive analysis has so far been focussed almost entirely on the phonological and grammatical systems of paired languages, an emphasis with which one can hardly quarrel. Nevertheless, the neglect of lexicon and 'discourse structure', in its broadest implications, is a serious deficiency.

Another deficiency is the absence of investigations of the nature and role of variation, of 'alternation between equivalents', in the behavior of mono- linguals and bilinguals alike. If the distinction between interference in speech and in language is to be truly meaningful, these phenomena must be clarified. The recent interest in grammaticality and in speech economies may lead to clarification. (27) The discussion of grammaticality is concerned with ranges

---

(26) Gali 1938; Sear 1931; Weinreich 1953 p.63; Lambert 1955; 1963 p.118
(27) Concerning grammaticality, see Chomsky 1957; 1961; 1964; Maclay and Sleator 1960; Hill 1961; Coleman 1965. Concerning speech economies, cf. footnote 9 above.

of variation within a given norm, that of speech economies with the function
of variation in communication. Both impinge on the problems of norm specification. The various tests of grammaticality that have been suggested and applied may be useful in the pursuit of norms. The concept of the speech economy, of the total patterning in the use ot the means of communication, should
alert us to the fact that each of a bilingual's languages may consist of several
different registers and that the 'social integration' of foreign material may be
limited to a specific register. The norm in one situation is not necessarily the
norm in another; and the specialization of functions for native and foreign
lexemes is not only a matter of referential meaning but also a matter of situational appropriateness. What has sometimes been regarded as 'confusion in
usage' between a native and a foreign item may turn out to be specialization
of functions describable in terms of different registers.

3.2 The description of interference

The need for including new levels of analysis in contrastive descriptions
and in descriptions of interference was mentioned above. It remains to be seen
whether analysis in terms of a transformational approach can throw new light
on the mechanisms involved. (28) Regardless of the exigencies of the debate
of linguistic theory, it is likely that the distinction that has here been expressed in terms of the introduction of identities and distributions will remain via-
ble, in one form or another. With reference to Mackey's analysis, one might
raise a question concerning the best definition of 'bilingual by combination'.
Assuming that a unit A has two constituents, the following three possibilities
are of interest:

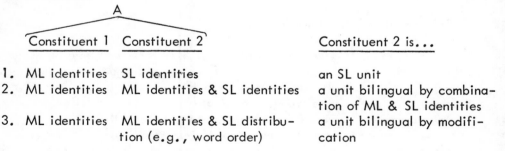

	Constituent 1	Constituent 2	Constituent 2 is...
1.	ML identities	SL identities	an SL unit
2.	ML identities	ML identities & SL identities	a unit bilingual by combina-tion of ML & SL identities
3.	ML identities	ML identities & SL distribu-tion (e.g., word order)	a unit bilingual by modifi-cation

Does the interpretation of all three versions as 'units A bilingual by combination', an interpretation which tends to obscure the distinction between the
introduction of identities and of distributions, best represent the nature of interference or would it be better to set up special categories for versions 2 and
3? (29)

---

(28) Concerning the use of a transformational approach to contrastive analysis,
      see Dingwall 1964 and Wyatt 1966
(29) See further the discussion of Mackey's scheme under 3.3, below.

One critical comment that seems to be applicable to most analyses of interference in language is that the impact on the receiving language of the introduction of a foreign element is not satisfactorily described. Weinreich's treatment of lexical integration is an important advance in this area as is his emphasis on the 'rearrangement of patterns' that follows the introduction of a foreign element. (30) However, the full impact of these concepts has not been established by analysis of subsystems that have adopted foreign elements. In this context the question of morphemic versus allomorphic interference also needs further study. Meaningful quantification of interference in language can hardly be achieved without considerations of 'impact'.

It is important to emphasize the distinctness of the 'linguistic' and 'social dimensions' of integration, i.e., the dimensions of adaptation and adoption, in spite of the difficulties encountered in the study of the latter. There is undoubtedly a rather high degree of correlation between the two but they are not completely parallel. Complete linguistic adaptation is possible in the case of foreign identities that show a low degree of regularity of occurence in the context of speech representing L1 and, conversely, items that show a high degree of regularity of occurence in such a context may show a low degree, or even complete lack, of adaptation to L1. The higher the level of analysis, the more important this distinction becomes. Identities larger than words are often not subject to phonological and/or grammatical integration but it is not uncommon that they exhibit a degree of regularity of occurence in the context of speech representing L1 that makes it necessary to speak of them as in some sense 'socially integrated'. We thus have to consider two spectra of degrees of integration:

| Complete linguistic integration | ———— | Partial linguistic integration | ———→ | Complete lack of linguistic integration |
| Complete social integration | ←———— | Partial social integration | ———→ | Complete lack of social integration |

The concept of social integration needs further clarification. (31)

The question of the extent to which a speaker makes a binary choice between the mechanisms of integration (momentary adaptation) and code-switching (lack of adaptation) also needs further clarification.

_____

(30) Weinreich 1953 p.54   Cf. Vogt 1949 p.35, and for a comment on
     Weinreich's approach, Vogt 1954 p.369
(31) What from a synchronic point of view is described as the frequency and
     spread of a certain item in a speech community is, of course, from a
     diachronic point of view a stage in linguistic change.

Choice of the mechanism   Choice of the mechanism
of integration   ◄─────────────►   of code-switching

As has been pointed out, the realization of an item can be ambiguous, supposedly a matter of imperfect integration or imperfect code-switching. The
question then arises: How is one to decide which mechanism is involved?
The answer is obviously that one cannot, except perhaps if additional criteria
are considered. I will limit myself to posing these questions: To what extent
can markers of switching serve as an additional criterion? To what extent
should social integration be considered? Are integration and code-switching
really two distinct modes of behavior even from the point of view of the speaker's 'intention'? Another question also belongs in this context. If it turns
out to be necessary, on the basis of a high degree of regularity of occurence
in the context of speech representing L1, to include certain 'discourse units'
that represent L2 phonology and/or morphology as part of the norms of such
speech activity, with what are these discourse units integrated? With a code
that includes the 'discourse level' as well as phonology, grammar, and lexicon
or with something that might be called a 'mode of speaking'?

Efforts have been made to limit the term 'interference' to include only
the overlapping of two languages. It can be argued that unless one insists on
a strict definition of overlapping in terms of simultaneity, the determination
of whether there is overlapping or not is a matter of the 'frame' used. If,
e.g., an L2 word is introduced into L1 discourse without phonic or morphic
substitution, there is no overlapping on the word level but there is in a sense
overlapping on the level. (Cf. Haugen 1956 pp.39ff)

With regard to code-switching there are two supplementary approaches,
that of starting with the broad patterning of use of two languages in a community and working down toward a finer and finer analysis of code-switching in
a given discourse and that of starting with a minute analysis of a set of recorded discourses and working up toward the broader patterning in the community
as a whole. While both approaches have been explored, no theory linking the
two has yet emerged. Such a theory is obviously an important desideratum.

3.3 The quantification and tabulation of interference

Some of the gaps in the measurements of lexical interference are the lack
of studies of the relative frequency of importation and substitution, if items
showing different degrees of integration, and of morphemic and allomorphic
interference. (32)

The most serious shortcoming of the available loanword counts is the general lack of information concerning the degree of 'social integration' of the

─────────

(32) See the check list in Proposal 3, below.

'loanwords' included in the counts. Have the 'loanwords' been adopted by
an entire speech community or are they used only by certain groups or individuals? Are the 'loanwords' used as the sole expression for given contents or
grammatical functions? Do they combine freely with 'inherited' items in the
language or are they restricted to combinations with other 'loanwords'? Are
the 'loanwords' characteristic only of some varieties of a language or of all?
These are some of the very basic questions which have not been answered in
most of the available loanword counts.

The measurements based on successful versus unsuccessful communication
are of considerable interest and the possibility of extending this type of measurement to levels other than the phonemic should be investigated. (One draw-
back is the fact that the communication events may have to be of such an elementary type that little is learned about the role of interference in everyday
events). One possible effect of interference on communication is a change in
predictability. It is well known that successful communication to some extent
depends on the receiver's ability to predict what the sender is going to say
after he has uttered some part of a sentence, or possibly even of some larger
unit. The question of the effect of code-switching, or of any form of alternation between two norms, on a receiver's ability to make such predictions has
not been pursued. (33)

Mackey's method of measuring interference in texts represents a new de-
parture which appears to hold considerable promise. The table in which he
summarizes the 'proportion of interference' and the 'rate of interference'
gives the kind of condensed characterisation of a text that is necessary for the
patterning of bilingual communities in terms of types of speakers and types of
situations. He has offered some suggestions for the refinement of his method
as described above. One possibility is the extension of the analysis to the
level of distinctive features, which would require the use of instrumental techniques, another the inclusion of distinctions between different types of structural modification. Other possibilities also suggest themselves. There are,
e.g., ways of including further subclassification under modification: a distinction paralleling that between 'extension' and 'creation' in Haugen's terminology, i.e., between new uses of existing patterns and new patterns; and
a distinction between modifications based on 'homonymy', 'synonymy', and
'homology' respectively. Naturally, the amount of subclassification included
must be adjusted to the purpose of the measurement. Mackey has also experimented with different measurements of alternation. What he calls the '-B
method' includes only alternation between complete ML and SL units on a given
level while the '+B method' includes alternation between ML and SL units as
well as between these and B units. More attention could be given to different
types of alternation, e.g., in the form of an investigation of the types of units
introduced through code-switching that would go beyond a statement of whether

---

(33) See Proposal 6, below.

the change of language involves sentences, clauses, phrases etc. This would mean focussing attention on the total stretches in the 'other language' that are introduced in each case and on the possible functional relationship of these stretches to the contexts in which they occur. This has implications for the quantification of interference since units of interference that are not immediate constituents on any level will be considered and also units larger than sentences.

The B units in Mackey's analysis can be regarded as units of interference in a sense other than that mentioned earlier. A sentence may thus be classified as bilingual because it contains one single phone from the 'other language' The table does show, although only indirectly, the proportion of sentences etc. that are bilingual because of the occurrence of foreign units on different levels, viz., through the gradual analysis of the B units and through the statement of the rate of alternation. It may nevertheless be worth considering the possibility of stating more directly the number of units that are bilingual on each level because of the occurrence of foreign identities or distributions that actually function on that level.

A question that may have a bearing on the separation of the phonemic and the morphemic levels can also be raised with regard to Mackey's method. The progressive measurement of proportions of ML, SL, and B units would end on the morpheme level for a sentence that consisted of ML units except for one SL morpheme represented completely by SL phonemes. The analysis would include also the phoneme level if the SL morpheme were represented by a combination of ML and SL phonemes. How would one handle a unit classified as a SL morpheme which showed complete phone substitution? It would not be bilingual by combination of ML and SL phonemes, yet its phonemic status should be noted in a measurement of proportion.

4. What remains to be done

(1) Further development of techniques of contrastive analysis; inclusion of lexicon and 'discourse structure' in such analyses in addition to phonology and grammar.

(2) Clarification of the concept of 'social integration'.

(3) Investigation of the relationship between 'linguistic' and 'social integration'.

(4) Investigation of the mechanisms of integration (momentary adaptation) and code switching (lack of adaptation) in order to clarify their relationship to each other, especially testing of the hypothesis that they are distinct modes of behavior as far as the speaker's 'intention' is concerned.

(5) Investigation of code-switching in terms of configurations.

(6) Quantification of interference, presumably so that it will be possible to speak of 'one unit of interference' as related to the 'total number of units of potential interference' both in a given subsystem or domain of a language and in a given text.

(7)   Clarification of the concept of 'impact on a system'.

(8)   Investigation of amounts of morphemic interference including all the types of measurements suggested in the check list in Proposal 3, below.

(9)   Investigation of amounts of phonemic interference including all the types of measurements suggested in the check list in Proposal 4, below.

(10)   Investigation of the concept of 'grammaticality' ('acceptability') with reference to bilingual communities.

(11)   Investigation of successful and unsuccessful communication involving messages of varying complexity and different types of interference.

(12)   Testing of different versions of the type of measurement proposed by Mackey.

5. Research proposals

Proposal 1: Investigation of degrees of 'social integration'. (a) Establishing patterns of alternation between L1 and L2 'equivalents'. Informants should be presented with a list of 'equivalents' that have been found in use in the community (possibly in identical linguistic environments) and asked to indicate how or when one item or the other would be used. The test could also include the task of choosing the appropriate expression for situations typical of the community. Since direct questioning of this type mostly yields only limited results, even if the situations chosen represent extremes on the formality scale, it must be supplemented by investigations of alternation in recorded texts. For very frequent items, e.g., conjunctions, it is possible to construct diagrams which show the clustering of the respective members of the pairs of equivalents in texts. (b) Establishing patterns of combinability. L2 items that have occurred in L1 discourse should be tested with regard to their potential for appearing in construction with L1 items, e.g., L2 adjectives with L1 adjectival inflection and with L1 nouns or L2 adverbs with L1 word order. Concerning testing procedures, see Proposal 5, below. Again, extensive recorded texts are essential. (c) Establishing patterns of use of markers of degree of integration. The use of pause, inflections of the voice etc. and of phrases such as 'as we say in English' should be studied with the help of recorded texts. (34)

Proposal 2: Investigation of configurations of code-switching. On the basis of extensive recorded texts, a study should be made of the configurations of L1 and L2 stretches of speech. If a change of language takes place between sentences, is the unit that is introduced simply one sentence or is it a sequence of sentences or is it one complete sentence plus the first clause, phrase, word etc. of the following sentence? Furthermore, a study should be made of whether the stretch introduced has a functional relationship to the environment in which it occurs or not. Is an immediate constituent of a sentence, clause etc.

---

(34) The examples mentioned in Proposal 1 have proved to be of interest in a study of American-Swedish discourses.

involved, and only it (limited switching), or is the stretch such that it is not in its entirety describable in terms of one unit on any level (unlimited switching)? This distinction could be applied on the discourse level as well as on the sentence level. Is a stretch consisting of one complete sentence or of a sequence of sentences one unit of discourse in some sense or is it not describable in such terms? The 'discourse units' that may figure in code-switching include stretches that can be described as 'content units', e.g., 'quotations', 'translations', 'stories', 'expressive routines', or 'preformulated arguments', or as 'discourse markers', e.g., 'channel establishing, reinforcing, or closing signals'. Finally, a study should be made of whether it is possible to establish a preference for introducing stretches in the 'other language' in certain positions. Would it be possible to measure preferences with regard to the introduction of phrases and words in sentences as, e.g., subjects, objects, adverbials, or subjective complements or with regard to introduction 'early' or 'late' in sentences? These questions can also be phrased in terms of 'weak points' in the structure of sentences. (35) Do bilinguals tend to switch at certain types of boundaries? Do they possibly differ with regard to their sensitivity to boundaries? Are some bilinguals 'unit switchers', others 'spill-over switchers'? Are some 'sentence switchers', others 'word switchers'? This also has a bearing on the conditioning of switching. The suggested measurement of 'unit' versus 'spill-over switching' may reflect differential sensitivity to conditioning factors or differences with regard to what Weinreich has called 'switching facility'.

Proposal 3: Investigation of interference on the morphemic level. This proposal consists simply of a check list of measurements: (1) The proportion of items representing interference of the total inventory of items (including a distinction between types and tokens for investigations of interference in speech); (2) the proportion of items representing interference in relation to different form classes and semantic fields; (3) the proportion of the total inventory of foreign items representing each form class, compared with the distribution of native items among the form classes in a variety of the language found in a non-contact situation; (4) the proportion of items representing 'importation' and 'substitution'; (5) the proportion of items representing morphemic and allomorphic interference; (6) the proportion of items representing different degrees of 'linguistic' and 'social integration'; (7) the proportion of items representing interference due to 'homophony', 'synonymy', and 'homology'.

Proposal 4: Investigation of interference on the phonemic level. This proposal also consists simply of a check list: (1) The proportion of items representing interference of the total inventory of items (again including a

---

(35)   Could this type of study of 'weak points' supplement the 'click experiments' undertaken in order to study the psychological reality of phrase structure?

distinction between types and tokens for investigations of interference in speech); (2) the proportion of items representing interference in relation to different subsystems; (3) the proportion of items representing phonemic and allophonic interference; (4) the proportion of items representing syntagmatic and paradigmatic interference.

Proposal 5: Measurement of degrees of grammaticality (acceptability). Tests should be constructed including sentences representing as many types and degrees of interference as possible, from completely 'native' sentences to sentences representing extremes of code-switching (perhaps including sentences that represent neither L1 nor L2 but some other 'grammar'). The tests should be administered to different groups of bilinguals as well as to monolinguals. One purpose of the testing would be to find out whether it is feasible to try to measure interference in terms of degree of grammaticality as viewed by members of a speech community; another purpose would be to find out the possible differences between the responses elicited from different groups of bilinguals and from bilinguals as compared with monolinguals.

Proposal 6: Measurement of success of communication. Elementary communication events have been used in testing phonic interference. Elementary events, consisting of one-sentence messages that are sent and returned for confirmation or rejection, could also be constructed for testing interference on the grammatical and lexical levels. Specifically, the possibility of testing the effect of the use of less than fully integrated lexical items, including outright code-switching, should be investigated. The test could consist of pairs of sentences that differed only in one respect, administered in random order so that the paired items could not be regarded as translations of each other. Various forms of 'noise' (other than that caused by the interference) could be used if necessary to distinguish responses.

Proposal 7: Testing of different versions of the type of measurement suggested by Mackey. (a) Testing of versions that include as many as possible of the distinctions between types of interference suggested above. (b) Testing of versions that include different combinations of distinctions. The purpose of the testing would be to find out what versions are best suited for general typologies of bilingualism, for typologies of speakers, for typologies of situations, and for the measurement of ranges of variation.

COMMENTARIES/COMMENTAIRES

R. B. LePage

1.   In preparing this discussion paper I have—as I imagine most other people have—been bedevilled by the fact that the kind of answers we ought to give to the question asked by Professor Hasselmo depends to such a large extent to the kind of approach taken in the other papers being given at the Conference. Professor Hasselmo's own paper has suffered from this same consideration. He has summarised admirably a great many approaches to the problem, but each of these approaches has its own framework of reference and the net effect of summarising them all together has been that the distinctions between these frameworks of reference has on the whole been lost sight of—although made explicit at the beginning of his paper. My own framework of reference does not coincide wholly with any of those to which he refers although it has I think most in common with that of Professor Mackey.

2.   I need really go no further than the title of the paper in order to discover that my own approach differs from those to be discussed: if I were to use my own terminology with exactness and consistency I would never say that one language had an effect on another language. I am unlikely to use my own terminology in this way and I shall from time to time use the word language in a colloquial way but I must outline my own approach to such problems in order to put you on your guard against drawing conclusions from colloquial statements which I might make which I would not draw myself.

3.   One further point of general difficulty about Professor Hasselmo's paper and about what I know at the time of writing of other papers for the seminar is that nowhere are we told why we want to describe and measure bilingualism. Upon the answer to this question why will depend to a certain extent the validity of any particular approach to the practical problem. I have myself one very good reason for wishing to measure what is commonly referred to as interference—I would dearly like in my work to find some means of using the extent of interference as a measure of the direction and degree of acculturation of individuals living in multilingual communities. The reason for this is that I feel very strongly that educational programmes in those multilingual communities with which I am particularly concerned—the newly independent countries of the Commonwealth such as East Africa—must be feasible in terms of the resources available and the wishes and inclinations of the local population. Very often we find that educational policies such as a decision to teach in language x up to a certain age and then switch to language y, or to use language x in certain areas and language y in other areas—may produce short-term results

at a superficial level but run counter to deeper and longer lasting changes in the linguistic habits of the population and are therefore doomed as realistic long term programmes. Further, such decisions often tend to make the educational process more artificial and more remote from the people at large than it need be. We wish to give realistic advice about feasible educational programmes in the developing countries and to ensure that financial aid is not squandered on bolstering non-feasible programmes—if we can use verbal behaviour as a barometer of the economic, social, political and cultural pressures operating at the deeper level then we shall be making a major contribution to the social sciences concerned with these countries. I recognise that my objective may be quite different from that of those who are concerned with a relatively simple bilingual situation in, for example, Canada or in Wales—not that the emotional attachments are any simpler to resolve, nor the political decision simpler to put into effect, but the situation frequently must be simpler to describe in these countries.

4.   Each of us is conditioned, in our approach to bilingualism and interference, by our own experience. My experience has been of multilingualism on the one hand and of Creole and contact language situations on the other. The framework of reference which I would prefer to adopt is one which increasingly has been forced upon me by my efforts to describe Creole languages and contact varieties of English; it is one which has also been adopted by my colleagues at York to a large extent, notably Dr. M. W. S. De Silva and Dr. Rebecca Posner. Dr. De Silva has worked on Creolization and contact situations within India, Ceylon and the Maldive Islands; Mrs. Posner has been concerned with historical Romance linguistics and with West African language situations. I do not wish to imply their necessary endorsement of what I am going to say, but simply to acknowledge the help which they have given me in my discussion of the problem with them.

5.   A language is an abstraction from the area of overlap between the verbal habits of two or more people. It has no existence independent of those who speak it. Interference can only be observed at the level of the verbal habits of the individual, although the results of interference can be observed in the descriptions of the area of overlap referred to (i.e. langue), since these descriptions will change according to the historical period, the size of the community, its geographical location and so forth.

6.   If an individual is truly bilingual, having two sets of norms one of which is used consistently in one context and the other in another context, there is by definition no interference although there may be code-switching. As the environment changes, so the switch is made. This means that the Sikh shopkeeper in Kuala Lumpur who habitually even when speaking Punjabi quotes prices in English, is not code-switching, because the environment has not changed, but he is using a language common among the Sikh community in Kuala Lumpur in which prices are quoted in English. We can call this language Kuala Lumpur Punjabi, and describe its norms in the way Professor Mackey suggests. This language is not subject to interference, but is the product of linguistic

change. It can of course be compared with other varieties of Punjabi and the nature and extent of the differences stated in terms on the one hand of sets of contrastive features, and on the other of the functional load carried by each set.

The Sikh shopkeeper speaks English to me, a variety of English in which, for example, some allophones are unknown in my English (retroflex /d/ for example) but well-known in Punjabi, and in which he introduces a number of grammatical constructions and words common in Malayan English but unfamiliar outside Malaya; these are generally borrowed from Chinese or Malay, in some cases from Portuguese. He is therefore bilingual in Kuala Lumpur Punjabi and Malayan English (as a matter of fact he also speaks Bazaar Malay). He speaks English to me, Punjabi to other Sikhs, Malay to the Malays and Chinese. But code-switching is an established and frequent practice among all races in Kuala Lumpur, and so it might be said that there is a mode of behaviour common to a greater or less extent to all members of the community, with large areas of behaviour restricted in each case to the Sikhs, the Malays, the English, the Tamils, the Cantonese and so on and so on. How under these circumstances can we specify a norm at all? or interference between norms?

7. What I am leading up to is that the very idea of a norm derives from an examination of the verbal behaviour of a number of people. There is no such thing as a language except in so far as the verbal habits of two or more people overlap. It may therefore be misleading from the outset to speak of interference in the case of bilinguals possessing two sets of norms; interference occurs precisely because and to the extent that people are not bilingual and do not possess two sets of norms. The best one can say is, in a clear cut case:
Group A exhibits usage a consistently
Group B exhibits usage b consistently
Mr. X behaves on some occasions, and/or in some respects, like Group A, and on other occasions and/or in other respects like Group B. If there are other people whose usage overlaps with that of Mr. X, there is a language x.
a can be described only by observing the usage of many members of A, and stating those features common to all, in terms of structure and functional load.
b likewise.
Mr. X's usage can be described first in terms of its own structure and functional load, and these can then be accounted for historically in terms of interference between a and b in the production of x.

8. We can however distinguish between the man whose English, say, is always affected by his native language, and the man whose English is only spasmodically affected. Phonological features tend to be constant, lexicon highly spasmodic, grammar more constant than spasmodic. But if interference is constant, it ceased to be interference because it has become the norm. This implies a new way of defining the norm—it is what the individual most usually says, rather than what most individuals say. The only alternative, I feel, is to accept Einar Haugen's concept of true interference, which Professor Hasselmo refers to on page 123.

interference (in the strict sense) refers to the overlapping of two languages, i.e., to the simultaneous application of the patterns of two languages to the same item.

It seems therefore that we should distinguish between linguistic usage which is the product of consistent interference, and which if common to a group of speakers in the same situation represents linguistic change; and linguistic usage in an individual which is the product of sporadic interference between two cod codes which normally he keeps separate. These codes must be defined and des- cribed in terms of the individual's consistency of behaviour, not primarily by reference to other people's behaviour. That comes later.

9.   Perhaps I may now play you an example of what I mean. (1) This little girl lives in British Honduras, near the borders of Guatemala. Her mother is Mexican, her father was Creole. The lingua franca of her village is Creole, in a version which has itself been influenced by Spanish, but her Creole is more noticeably influenced by Spanish in its phonology than that of other children. Nevertheless, this is her Creole; it is her first language; normally she speaks it consistently, and does so when she gets into the body of her story. But at school she is taught in English by English nuns for examinations set and marked in England; she is aware that im leave is not acceptable in school for the past tense, and towards the beginning of her story she uses this, the usual Creole form, first, and then corrects herself to im lef. Here her speech shows inter- ference in her Creole from British English, of which she has limited knowledge. Later she re-tells the story in Spanish—her mother's language. She is not quite so fluent in this as in Creole, and her story is an Anansi story which she her- self has always heard told in Creole; and so from time to time she forgets to say hermano Hicatee and says Bra Hicatee. Her Spanish is interfered with by her Creole. Creole English itself is of course the product of interference in their English by the West African verbal habits of the 17th century and 18th century slaves.

10. I am aware that I am throwing at least part of Saussure's concept of langue out of the window. It is only useful as a means of referring to abstractions from the area of overlap between the verbal habits of two or more speakers. Beyond that point it becomes a myth, but a very powerful myth which has bedevilled linguistics for far too long, which lies behind the worst excesses of the gener- ative grammarians just as much as it lies behind ideas of linguistic purity. It is easy to see how strong are the forces which support the idea of a code ex- ternal to and more permanent than the users of the code; the idea that books, dictionaries and grammars are the repositories of the code rather than simply— as I see them—conditioning instruments. But one must resist this myth. It is basically false, and very misleading. The idea that there is a language to which we gain access is false, except in so far as we are progressively condi- tioned by other people and by books etc.

---

(1) A short tape was played at this point.

11. I must apologise for dwelling on this point of view, but it colours very much my reaction to some of Professor Hasselmo's own statements as well as those he cites from other people. I cannot accept what seems to me the confusion between interference and linguistic change which runs through this paper—and which I must confess derives to a certain extent from Professor Hasselmo's attempt to summarise rather diverse approaches. If Mr. X uses words he has acquired from French but pronounces them in an English way and uses them with an English functional load, and if his family all do the same, then their language can be said to contain Anglicised (or if you like X-icised) French loanwords, but these are not examples of interference in Mr. X's speech. The classification of loan-words on p.125 does not therefore seem relevant to interference, nor does it seem to me right to speak (p. 125 (3)) of imported morphemes—each of us creates our own stock of morphemes. Weinreich is quoted to the effect that the speaker may choose 'either to render a certain item in its original form or to adapt it (completely) to the recipient language'—once again, an independent identity of languages and of linguistic units seems to be assumed. What is 'the original form'? How can we speak of a 'binery choice' in such a connection? The citation on p.128 referred to as 'Windisch's Law' seems to me far more unacceptable than even Professor Hasselmo implies ('somewhat doubtful'): "It is not the language learned that is most subject to interference, but the learner's original language". Neither language is subject to interference. (And in any case, even if one accepts a colloquial use of language here, I should have thought the truth was usually very much the reverse: West African slaves did not modify their Twi when learning English, but reproduced a form of English modified by the structural features of Twi. So also Gallic Latinists, Congolese Gallicists, Chinese Anglicists, etc. etc.)

12. In practical terms my argument means that many of the methods of classification and measurement suggested are appropriate only to the language of the community, whilst others are appropriate to the idiolect of the individual; that the first type of statement will be essentially a diachronic statement, the second a synchronic statement. The first type will be made in terms of linguistic structures, at the level of abstraction of phoneme, morpheme, syntagmeme, lexeme; the second in terms of phones, morphs etc.—it is to the confusion between these two types, I think, that we owe para. (2) on page 129. A description of the Sikh shopkeeper's Kuala Lumpur Punjabi will include the statement that certain features of this language derive from English; a description of his behaviour when using Malayan English may include the fact that under conditions of stress or when he is at a loss for words he will slip into Punjabi. The first kind of behaviour is by definition highly predictable, the second only very roughly so, and dependent on psychological and environmental factors. Predictability, or internal self-consistency, suggests itself at the most coherent way of describing the degree of interference in any particular individual. I find myself here fairly closely in agreement with some aspects of Professor Mackey's approach. Professor Hasselmo mentions psychological measurements of interference on p. 133, but only to report that in recent years the psychologists appear to have lost interest in problems of quantification.

13. What remains to be done:

13.1 A consistently behavioural approach to linguistics—on the lines of Pike's Language in relation to a Unified Theory of the Structure of Human Behaviour— is the only approach which seems to me satisfactory in handling problems of multilingualism. Within this framework the distinction between contrastive analysis at the language level and descriptions of interference at the idiolectal level must be clearly maintained. It must be realised that linguistic systems are much more complex than is normally stateable, and that even in a fairly simple monolingual situation people shift frequently between different registers of their idiolect depending on the context. Contrastive analysis must necessarily be based on rather simple abstractions, descriptions of langue. Interference statements can make use of these descriptions as a matter of reference but hardly as a means of quantification. Interference is frequently so complex that I must confess that in spite of my great wish for Professor Hasselmo's programme to be fulfilled, I fear that items 6, 8 and 9 of para. 4 at least are impossible.

13.2 It is significant that Professor Hasselmo, in his research proposals, starts with what is in fact a piece of sociolinguistic research. In linguistic terms it is simply not possible to assign 'items' to 'languages'—how, for example, can we say that phonemic contrast between [i] and [ɪ] belongs to English rather than Twi?—and any system of measurement based on such an attempt is, I feel, fallacious. In short, I feel that the best hope for the future is to describe the 'normal ' registers of an individual, and then to describe the nature and context of departures from these normal registers without attempting quantification in linguistic terms—simply in sociological terms. For this reason I myself get people to tell stories in their usual home language, and then get them to tell me again in any other languages they speak. In the first case, they become more and more relaxed as they get into the body of their story; in the second and third and sometimes fourth 'languages' they reveal progressive degrees of interference—but without knowing the relationship of the story-matter or the circumstances under which they learned it to the everyday circumstances of their lives, I feel that attempts at exact quantification are likely to mislead more than they help. I hope soon to have a joint research team (consisting of a linguist, a social anthropoligist and a social psychologist) working, first in East Africa, and then in Mauritius to see what correlations are possible between changes in verbal behaviour and changes in the context or environment.

Els Oksaar

In order to answer this question the main problems, as seen by Mr. Hasselmo, are how to identify, describe and to quantify and tabulate interference. My

commentary will first discuss some general questions associated with his paper
and then give some further research and bibliographical information.

1.1 Generally we distinguish between speech and language and due to this we
claim that interference in speech must be distinguished from interference in
language. In this complex problem I want to call attention to a methodical
point. In the case of spoken language we must always take into account the
factor of performance. When we observe that a bilingual speaker deviates from
the norms of the language he is using, we must be careful not to interpret this
as an interference. It can depend on extra-lingual factors that can influence
performance: a person may be tired, in a hurry, etc. Performance problems
of bilinguals must be compared with those of monolinguals.

1.2 If we want to identify interference, we must in each case know which language is being used. If we take the statement of Haugen: "any item that occurs in speech must be part of some language if it is to convey any meaning to
the hearer" (Haugen 1956 p.39) (compare Wienreich: "every speech event belongs to a definite language" cit. Lotz,) (Weinreich 1953 p.7) and the definition of interference given by him: "a linguistic overlap, when two systems are
simultaneously applied to a linguistic item" (Haugen 1956 p.40) we have a
situation where a person uses simultaneously elements from two languages but
speaks only one. Which one? The following analysis helps to clarify this in-
consistency. When somebody uses elements from language A when speaking
language B this can only happen, if we have a state where this element from
A has a "quasi-existence" in language B. At its first appearance in speech a
new item cannot belong to the system of language, otherwise it would not be
new. It will be used as if it belongs to it, that is, in the context of that language. This is the point also when we have items from another language.
Because of the fact that interference in speech is a process, we cannot explain
it from the purely static point of view. How can we, then, distinguish between
code-switching and interference? We have to consider that in cases where
there are many interferences, where the sentences are short or the languages
in contact are similar, it will be difficult to decide to which language the
speech belongs and hence the difference between interference and code-
switching are not so distinctive.

1.3 Haugen has stated: "a complete language switch is possible at any lexeme
boundary and may embrace only one lexeme". (Haugen 1956 p.68) Why is it
not possible in the case of the morphemes of the lexeme? What criteria play a
role here? Lexeme, too, are not entirely independent, they are parts of structures as, for example, sentences, syntagmas, etc., they serve in a simulteneous
syntactic process. Hence, depending on the type of syntactic relations, what
we may look at as code-switching can from another point of view be an overlapping. The question is also: in what kind of distribution in language B are
the relations so close that an element of language A will not be looked upon as
an independent A-element, but as belonging to B-speech. We have to work
out dominance relations between linguistic elements on the syntactic level.(1)

(1) See the method of Saumjan, explained by Luelsdorff 1966

1.4 As to the levels of analysis the investigations carried out by Weinreich on the phonemic level are the most extensive. His fourfold distinction, phonemic under- and overdifferentiation, phonemic reinterpretation and phone substitution (Weinreich 1953 pp.18ff), is a mechanism that can be reduced to a two-fold category, because his reinterpretation of distinctions actually combines the under- and overdifferentiation. (Haugen 1954 p.384) Furthermore, the types 2 and 3 are established on criteria that do not necessarily belong to interference. A classification founded on interference seems to be more convenient. It would be useful to distinguish between: 1) interference that cover the distinctive features of the secondary system, 2) those where only irrelevant features are embraced.

1.5 As to configurations and conditioning of code-switching it seems to me that Gumperz's distinction between transactional and personal switching, based on the social role of the individual and stylistic devices, cannot always be kept apart. Many people use different styles of their language in monolingual situations according to their social roles and the same can occur when they use two languages. What Clyne classifies as contextual triggering I have in a study of Estonian-Swedish bilingualism distinguished as situational switching, whereas contextual switching is a purely linguistic matter. (Oksaar MS.) My observations with a three year old bilingual child (Estonian-Swedish) show that the switch over in conversation with others does not take place so frequently when the surroundings remain the same. It happens when he is alone, speaking to himself, when playing and before falling asleep: when he comes to think about events that happened in situations where the second language was used. --- Interesting cases are pointed out by Elwert.

1.6 An important point is norm specification. I think we must face the problem by trying to analyze the functions of interference and pay more attention to the situation and the correlations between the linguistic and social dimensions of interference. My observations prove that there is a great deal of correlation between certain kinds of interference phenomena and the social factors of discourse. Estonian bilinguals in Sweden who know each other well, do not use loan translations or loan shifts very often, but use instead of that borrowed identities. They interfere with Swedish words, often combined with Estonian morphemes. This tendency decreases in relation to the decreasing degree of acquaintance. One reason fo this many of them have given is, that they do not wish to be locked upon as affected, which would be the case when they build Estonian loan translations. Integration and code-switching can really be two distinct modes of behavior even from the point of view of the speaker's intention. We have, therefore, also to ask about the motives and take into considerations such factors as prestige, need and other social indicators as well as emotive devices.

1.7 As to the question whether a transformational approach can throw new light on the mechanisms involved in interference, we must reply in the affirmative. Transformations can reveal the differences among related structures. The constituent-structure already shows the points where even monolinguals

usually make the most mistakes. Johnson's interesting hypotheses in this area
can be tested on bilinguals too. (2) The hierarchical model shows us more of
the process. A new approach is developed by Bolinger; his concept of trans-
formulations can be useful in contrastive structure studies.

1.8 Mr. Hasselmo raises the question whether we should include version three
in his scheme when we want to define "bilingual by combination". I think we
should include it, because the SL distribution often plays an important role.

2.1 The need for further contrastive analysis and for further refining of its
technique must be stressed. It is, therefore, important to investigate the studies on levels other than phonology and grammar. Numerous attempts have been
made to identify and to describe "the various lexical structures into which our
words are organized". (Ullmann 1964 p.10) For contrastive analyses the concept of lexical fields has been fruitful. As early as 1941 Reuning has compared Joy and Freude. A solid structural basis for semantic contrastive analyses
is given by Leisi. For semantical techniques Weinreich 1966 is valuable as
well as Bendix. An attempt to measure lexical interference is made by Herdan.
Among his results the following is of interest: "Anteil der Fremdsprache im
Gesamtvokabular ist proportional dem Logarithmus der Textlänge". (Herdan
1965 p.99; cf 1966)

     The contrastive analysis of semantical items on the connotational level can
be successfully carried out by the Osgood semantic differential method. This
method makes it possible to test certain grammatical aspects too, such as gen-
der, in its relation to the semantical structure. Hofstätter has investigated
the words for sun and moon in German, French and Italian in this respect. I
have measured connotative variations of occupational terms in Swedish and
German. (3)

2.2 Ervin and Osgood differentiate between compound and coordinated bilingualism. The equivalent words house – Haus will give various results on the
semantic differential in these two categories. Lambert, Havelka and Crosby
have empirically confirmed this hypothesis. Among other attempts to find me
methods for measuring semantic structure are those of Jakobovits and Lambert,
and Fischer.

2.3 Among the means for quantifying the probability of occurrence, we ought
to make use of the concepts of "entropy" and "bit" where possible. (4)

2.4 It is necessary to analyse the determinants of language choice. Herman
has discussed the problem why a bilingual speaker chooses one language rather

---

(2) The rank order of the constituents correlates with that of the frequency of
     mistakes.
(3) "Semantisch-soziologische Code-Veränderungen", in press.
(4) See the works described by Plath (1961), 30ff. and Akhmanova a.a.
     (1963)

than the other in situations where either language could serve as a medium of conversation.

2.5 Mr. Hasselmo points out that it is necessary "to describe the impact on the receiving language of the introduction of a foreign element". With regard to these and other questions that arise when we wish to quantify interference, the question must be investigated whether Vogt's statement holds: "One might think that linguistic interference affects the system only in so far as the foreign elements correspond to some of these innovation possibilities offered by the receiving system". (Vogt 1954 pp.366ff) A way to approach this area would be to investigate why a certain kind of interference is impossible: a loan translation in the case of teenager in German (German has now der Teenager), whilst that is possible in Swedish: tonaring, Finnish: teiniikäinen. (Oksaar 1961 pp.388ff)

2.6 A very important question is that of social integration and its relation to the linguistic one. There are several investigations that can be mentioned. Labov uses five main phonological indices. Their realization in the speech of the members of various social classes (that are identified by objective socio-economic indices from 0 to 9) is "plotted against a scale of speech styles" (from "casual speech to reading style"). The author tries to establish an "objective distribution of linguistic features and delineating class norms".

Sommerfelt calls attention to the fact that "a certain correlation seems to exist between the presence or the absence of certain types of phonemes and the more or less archaic character of societies".

Stewart presents a typology of sociolinguistic language types and functions. Types: standard, classical, vernacular, creole, pidgin, artificial and marginal. They are differentiated by means of history, standardization, vitality, homogeneity. The functions of language are: official, group, wider communication, education, literary, religious, technical. -- Currie proposes research into the social significance of language in all respects. (It is to be noted that these works give a basis to the necessary analysis in one language.) -- We have further to distinguish social dialects along the factors of sex, rank, occupation and profession. The best survey of these problems today is given by Hertzler.

2.7 Lewis tries to classify the varieties of bilingual situations. Bilingualism as a social institution should be separated from bilingualism in the life of the individual, in order to get a right basis for the investigations.

Mackey points out that structural-linguistic borrowing is determined by social and linguistic factors. The former includes type, degree and duration of bilingual contact. The linguistic factors are, among other things, compatibility, structural function, class-size and frequency.

2.8 In connection with the hypothesis that integration and code-switching are distinct moods of behavior not only the study of Estonian-Swedish bilinguals mentioned above (1.6) (5) could give some evidence and show the complexity

(5) To be published in a forthcoming work "Erscheinungsformen sprachlicher Kontakte".

of the problem. In another connection (Oksaar 1965 p.6ff) there could be
stated that negative feelings favoured code-switching: many Estonians swear
in Swedish, but would not switch over by declarations of love! The same happens with bilingual Laps: they switch over to Finnish when quarreling. (6)
Psycholinguistic problems must be taken into account, the emotive devices
constitute only a part of them.

      The question whether bilinguals tend to switch at certain types of bounda-
ries can best be answered by tests of the kind described by Johnson.
2.9 As an example of impact on the first language one may mention the case
(to which Haas calls attention) of avoiding in the first language words that
sound like the taboo words in the second.
2.10 Approaches like that of Winthrop will provide methods to study the effect
of communication. He tests various kinds of message distortion in translation.
A method for comparing efficiency has been discussed among others by Ray,
who distinguishes between text frequency and list frequency. The former compares two lexical forms in their repetitions with a body of discourse. The latter
compares two lexical forms in their repetitions of pairing with other lexical
forms.

Berthe Siertsema

Professor Hasselmo's paper represents a comprehensive and instructive assembly
of the state of knowledge with respect to the measuring on language interference in the speech of bilinguals. Above all it shows three things very clearly:
1) how much work has already been done in this field; 2) how little we know
about the field in spite of this amount of work; 3) how much there remains to
be done.
1.   As regards the first point: the amount of work already done with respect
to the measuring of language interference; this is dealt with in the first half
of the paper. The survey given there is, as was said, comprehensive, and in
view of its comprehensiveness it has had to be made concise. Almost too concise for readers who, like the present writer, do not know all the literature
discussed. Such readers would no doubt have liked more illustrative examples
from actual language to clarify statements such as: "In a study of Swedish-
English code-switching, I have attempted to describe the configurations of
code-switching in terms of limited and unlimited switching, viz., the introduction of complete immediate constituents of sentences or complete discourse

----

(6) Information from Nils Hansegard.

segments versus 'spill-over'; ... and in terms of triggered and triggering stretches of speech"; or "Under his category of 'idiomatic norm errors', which he admits may be due to interference between different varieties of the same language but keeps distinct from the 'mixing errors', he includes 'lack of words' (Wortnot) and 'empty words' (leere Wörte) and computes the frequencies of these errors".

However, the lack of explanatory remarks and examples in the survey does have the effect of an instigation to read the works themselves—as far as they are available (Professor Hasselmo's paper referred to above has not yet been published).

2.   Already in reading the first half of the paper, showing the great amount of study given to the problem so far, does one realize what was put as the second point of this commentary: how little we know as yet about the problem of interference.

In the second half of the paper Professor Hasselmo rightly points out many shortcomings of the research carried out up to now and many problems that need investigation, but it seems to me there is even more to be cleared up than he mentions before we can hope to obtain anything like a reliable method of measuring linguistic interference. For one thing, in his fourth chapter: "What remains to be done" Prof. Hasselmo mentions three concepts that need clarification, viz. 'social integration' (pt. 2), 'impact on a system' (pt. 7), and "'grammaticality' ('acceptability')" (pt. 10) pp.138-41. But when the present writer was reading through the survey of existing literature, she came across several other concepts that to her mind were equally in need of clarification. For instance (p. 125):

a) when do we speak of two codes? As far as my own experience of interference goes (Frisians speaking Dutch and Africans speaking English), bilinguals often seem to be in the possession of at least three codes. Many Frisians speak their own local dialect when at home, "town-Frisian" when in Leeuwarden, and Dutch outside their own province. African students, who in college speak "received English" to their teachers but "African English" to their friends, use two very different codes of "English" according to social circumstances—apart from which they each possess the code of their own various mother-tongues. These cases are different from the one mentioned by Epstein of a native Yiddish speaker who had "two accents for Russian". Epstein 1915 p.82, quoted by Weinreich (in Saporta and Bastian, "Psycholinguistics, a Book of Readings", 1961 p.390). Epstein's case was one of different degrees of interference of two codes, whereas in the Frisian and African instances mentioned above there would seem to be three codes.

b) Can we ever obtain a rigorous determination of (a) code at all? Does not every code contain elements which are on their way out (e.g. archaic or old-fashioned idioms of pronunciations) and elements which are "on their way in"—wherever they may have come from? The "ways of expressing something used by monolinguals" will always differ slightly from one individual to the next, especially as regards the amount and use of "foreign" words. Is not there something to be said for Hjelmslev's distinction of 'schema', 'norm' and 'usage' instead of the one rigorous 'code'? Professor Hasselmo rightly stresses the need for clarification on this point, too, when he mentions the phenomenon of "alternation between equivalents" in the behavior of monolinguals and bilinguals alike and the function of such variation in communication (p. 133. It is true that a study of various degrees of grammaticality may bring some some light here as he says, but the phenomenon is not one of grammar only, as he realizes (p. 134)

c) In this connection a third question arises: when can a loan be said to have reached integration? How is it that so often, as Haugen observes, "the criteria which satisfy the linguist that a borrowed word has been integrated will not disguise it to the consciousness of bilingual speakers, who will continue to call an English loanword English in spite of its adapted shape". (Haugen 1954 p. 387)

It is because there may be other, more hidden criteria which so easily escape the linguist. In Yoruba (Nigeria, W. Africa) for instance, an initial vowel indicates that the word is a non-verb: true Yoruba nouns begin with a vowel.

But owing to large scale borrowing from English for over a century, Yoruba has by now a great number of nouns which sound perfectly Yoruba but which begin with a consonant: Lọyà, 'lawyer'; télọ̀, 'tailor'; burẹ́dî, 'bread', etc. Moreover, a word like télọ̀ deviates from true Yoruba in its combination of vowels: true Yoruba words have partial vowel harmony and present either e C o ... or ẹ C ọ, not e C ọ (o = [ɔ];   e = [ɛ]; Siertsema 1959 pp. 386-387) Now what is the status of this word télọ̀ in Yoruba: is it "integrated"? Or is it still a case of "interference"? These concepts, too need further determination. And as we are paying attention to the matter of terminology, it might be mentioned in passing that Professor Hasselmo's terms "L 1" and "L 2", for the two codes a bilingual has at his disposal, should not be confused with Weinreich's "P" (primary language) and "S" (secondary language) respectively, for they indicate just the opposite. Hasselmo's "L 1" is the language which suffers interference (he speaks of "the introduction into L 1 discourse of L2 identities or L 2 distributions". This is Weinreich's "S", whereas Hasselmo's "L 2" is Weinreich's "P" ("the language which causes the interference"). (cf Weinreich 1957 p. 1)

3. In observing this need of clarifying concepts and terms, we have reached the third point to be made in this commentary: how much there remains to be done.

Professor Hasselmo rightly emphasizes the distinction between the interference which concerns "identities" and that which concerns "distributions" (p. 129): a simple but extremely valuable characterization of the essential criteria for the description of interference, criteria to be applied on all levels, it should be said, not only on that of phonemes or of morphemes. Here a word might be put in a defence of the distinction between the level of the distributions of morphemes into words and the higher levels usually called "syntax"—

which distinction Prof. Hasselmo too seems to make when he advocates "inclusion of lexicon and discourse structure in (contrastive) analyses in addition to
phonology and grammar" (p.138) On the level of syntax, indeed, we find a
feature which is sadly missing in most of the literature on linguistic interference
and which nevertheless is of first importance: the feature of intonation.

Professor Hasselmo gives a long list of desirata "to be done" with which
one cannot but agree whole-heartedly. But if he wants "discourse structure"
to be included in contrastive analysis (p.138), and if he wants an "investigation of successful and unsuccessful communication involving messages of varying complexity and different types of interference" (p.139), there will be no
escape from the task of tackling intonation phenomena and investigating the
extremely complex and bewildering functions of intonational contours on these
levels. If there is one thing that makes "African English" difficult to understand for an Englishman newly arrived in Africa, it is its intonation which shows
many characteristics of the speakers' mother tongues. Thus a Yoruba will pronounce every English relative pronoun or adverb on a high tone, as he does in
his mother tongue—which high tone the Englishman, however, perceives as a
stress: "the book which I bought". (Siertsema 1959 p.9) But nearer home, too,
for instance when Dutchmen speak English or French, communication may be
hampered by a wrong intonation (cf. Siertsema 1962 p.394)

Intonation contours indeed present another vast field of research hardly
looked at so far from the point of view of language interference. Their investigation should be urged with a double purpose, for little is known of this aspect in any language, and it may well be that the "contrastive analysis" advocated by Professor Hasselmo, if applied to intonation, will not only shed
more light on interference phenomena but will turn out to be the means "par
excellence" to discover some more about intonation itself and its function in
general.

How such a contrastive analysis is to be carried out, however, is still an
open question. As long as opinions are still as divided as they are regarding
the number of intonation contours and their semantic functions in any one language, any attempt at contrastive analysis comparing two or more languages on
this point would be senseless.

The implication of the fact are more far-reaching for the problems posed
at this conference than the present writer had thought at first sight—that is why
she adds this paragraph to her commentary.

For in spite of the above-mentioned lack of agreement on intonational
details, linguists are at one in recognizing the fundamental importance of
intonation in the functioning of language. As long as different intonational
features can alter the entire meaning of one and the same "phatic" utterance, can even change it into its opposite as in irony or sarcasm, what sense
is there in measuring phatic material only (supposing all the time that this
would indeed be possible)? Had not we better drop the whole idea of
"measuring" in the study of bilingualism?

Armand Boileau

1. Considérations préliminaires

1.1 L'exposé qui suit se limite volontairement aux aspects spécifiquement belges du bilinguisme, dans la mesure où ceux-ci sont susceptibles d'éclairer les
différents problèmes abordés par M. Hasselmo dans son rapport: identification,
description, évaluation et classification des interférences. Cette limitation se
justifie par le fait que le bilinguisme belge est un phénomène séculaire et essentiellement stable, et que les méthodes utilisées pour étudier le bilinguisme
tel qu'il apparaît dans les pays neufs, où il est dû principalement à l'immigration des groupes relativement restreints d'éléments alloglottes, ne lui sont pas
toujours applicables.

1.2 Plusieurs savants belges qui se sont penchés sur les problèmes des interférences linguistiques (Van Loey, Grootaers) estiment qu'il est indispensable de
faire une distinction fondamentale entre "bilinguisme" et "diglossie". Le diglotte connaît (parfois très bien) deux langues: sa langue maternelle et une
langue étrangère acquise par une étude raisonnée; le bilingue sent et pense
(mais parle parfois très mal) en deux langues. (Van Loey 1951 p.24) Un Flamand qui use du français quand le besoin s'en fait sentir est très souvent un
bilingue (au sens restreint), tandis qu'un Wallon qui est capable de se servir
du néerlandais est presque toujours un "diglotte"; un Bruxellois qui se sert in-
différemment de l'une ou de l'autre langue nationale est aussi un bilingue,
mais il lui arrive de n'être pas capable de dire laquelle des deux langues est
sa langue première et il les parle l'une et l'autre avec une égale imperfection.
La distinction qui est ainsi faite entre "bilinguisme" et "diglossie" peut paraître subtile, mais elle répond à une réalité psychologique que nous pouvons
schématiser de la façon suivante: (Boileau 1946 chll)

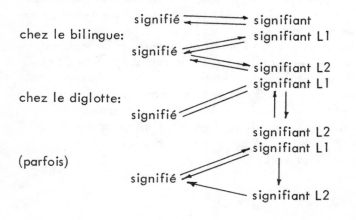

chez le bilingue:

chez le diglotte:

(parfois)

Cela signifie que, dans le cas du diglotte, il y a entre le signifiant L2 et le signifié un intermédiaire (le signifiant L1 correspondant) et que les interférences affecteront davantage la langue seconde. Dans le cas du bilingue proprement dit, les associations entre le signifié et les signifiants se produisent sans intermédiaire, ce qui ne veut pas dire qu'il n'y a ni perturbation ni interférences; au contraire, celles-ci risquent d'être plus profondes et plus durables et, chose plus grave, d'affecter davantage la langue première, parce que les deux images acoustiques peuvent apparaître simultanément et se confondre dans le même concept. Cependant, la perturbation est souvent atténuée par le fait que le signifié ne renferme pas que le concept seul mais qu'il englobe les circonstances qui l'environnent. Par exemple, chez un enfant en bas âge parlant français avec son père et flamand avec sa mère, il y a un lien entre le concept qu'il veut exprimer et la personne à laquelle il va s'adresser. Ce lien apparaît au moment même de l'élaboration du concept, de sorte que le signifié présente en réalité un aspect double. Chacun de ces aspects (que nous pouvons symboliser respectivement par x et x') forme avec le signifiant correspondant un signe linguistique distinct:

$$\text{signifié} \left\langle \begin{array}{l} x \longleftarrow\!\!=\!\!=\!\!=\!\!\longrightarrow \text{signifiant L1} \\ x' \longleftarrow\!\!=\!\!=\!\!=\!\!\longrightarrow \text{signifiant L2} \end{array}\right.$$

De toute façon, comme le faisait observer Michel, "le vocabulaire des bilingues est toujours unilingue dans certains éléments" (Michel 1939 pp. 32-33), ceux-ci devant être précisés selon des critères psychologiques et sociaux.
1.3 Il apparaît nécessaire de préciser les buts des recherches que nous poursuivons sur le bilinguisme. L'évaluation quantitative des interférences ne peut constituer un but en soi, mais un moyen permettant d'atteindre ces buts.

La finalité des études sur le bilinguisme correspondant aux préoccupations spécifiquement belges est double:

a. sur le plan de la psycho-pédagogie linguistique: (a) essayer de savoir si le bilinguisme scolaire est nocif ou s'il l'est moins qu'on le croit (problème d'actualité à Bruxelles); (b) rechercher une réponse à la question de savoir à quel moment il convient de commencer l'étude de la seconde langue dans les régions unilingues. Ces préoccupations ne nous intéressent pas directement ici mais méritent d'être mentionnées.

b. sur le plan de la linguistique diachronique: l'observation des faits actuels de bilinguisme dans les régions linguistiquement hétérogènes et dans les régions où règne un bilinguisme (voire un trilinguisme) généralisé de la population autochtone (comme c'est le cas, p. ex. au Grand-Duché de Luxembourg et, en Belgique, en certains endroits bien déterminés) peut permettre de résoudre des problèmes concernant le passé linguistique de notre pays. A cet égard, une évaluation quantitative des effets du bilinguisme sur la "langue" régionale (le mot "langue" étant employé ici par opposition à "parole") peut s'avérer très utile. Cependant, il apparaît plus urgent de procéder au préalable à une évaluation qualitative de ces effets. C'est sur cet aspect du problème que je m'arrêterai plus longuement. Mais au préalable, il est nécessaire d'esquisser brièvement la "carte" du bilinguisme en Belgique.

2. Aspects géographiques du bilinguisme en Belgique

2.1 Entre les parlers romans (wallons, picards, lorrains) d'une part, qui sont en usage dans la partie méridionale de la Belgique, et les divers parlers germaniques (flamands, brabançons, limbourgeois, rhénans, luxembourgeois) d'autre part, qui sont en usage au nord et à l'est, il existe une ligne de démarcation séculaire bien nette: la "frontière linguistique". Décrire la configuration de cette ligne qui sépare les parlers populaires (dialectes) romans et germaniques est une tâche relativement aisée pour le dialectologue impartial, pour autant que le critère choisi soit celui de l'homogénéité des parlers locaux, comme l'a fait Legros dans un mémoire publié par la Commission royale de Toponymie et de Dialectologie. (Legros 1948 pp.48sv) Cette tâche devient pourtant délicate à partir du moment où l'on veut et où il faut tenir compte à la fois des parlers populaires, qui partout sont restés très vivaces, et des langues de culture, qui sont, au nord, le néerlandais, au sud, le français, et à l'est l'allemand. Le manque de concordance existant çà et là entre la F.L. réelle et la limite des langues telle qu'elle est définie par la loi a prêté et continue à prêter à contestation, voire à des affrontements sur le plan politique. Les régions "contestées" sont, en fait, des régions où il y a (ou bien: où il y a eu dans le passé) "divorce" entre le parler populaire et la langue littéraire du même groupe. (1)

2.2 Les régions contestées ne sont pas nombreuses; elles sont en général peu peuplées, à l'exception toutefois de la capitale, Bruxelles, et de l'agglomération bruxelloise, qui dialectalement reste flamande, mais qui, par suite de vastes mouvements démographiques notamment, est très fortement francisée et où la langue littéraire du même groupe, le néerlandais, n'occupe plus, en fait, qu'une place secondaire. Chacune de ces régions "contestées" a ses caractéristiques. Elles sont les seules à connaître un régime administratif bilingue: à Bruxelles, les deux langues sont placées sur pied d'égalité; ailleurs on a instauré un régime dit de "facilités". Dans quelques cas cependant, la langue officielle unique (le français) est différente du dialecte local, mais il existe chez les habitants de ces régions un bilinguisme de fait, assez généralisé. Par contre, la région allemande est officiellement bilingue (allemand avec "facilités" pour le français), alors que la population autochtone est incontestablement unilingue.

2.3 Il résulte de ce qui précède que l'étude du bilinguisme en Belgique

---

(1) Sur le "bilinguisme combiné" dans certaines localités mixtes (connaissance des 2 patois + une ou les deux langues communes correspondantes), cfr Boileau 1954 p.10)

nécessite que soit pris en considération le bilinguisme du type "patois + langue commune", non seulement dans les zones linguistiquement hétérogènes (p. ex.: dialecte flamand + langue française, ou - comme c'était le cas à Malmedy, d dans l'est du pays, avant 1920: dialecte wallon + langue allemande), mais aussi en région homogène (dialecte wallon + langue française, dialecte flamand + langue néerlandaise).

3.   Influences réciproques des parlers en présence

3.1 La description et la mesure du bilinguisme des patoisants en région homogène intéresse à la fois les praticiens de l'enseignement de la langue cultivée et les dialectologues: (a) Dans quelle mesure le dialecte local influence-t-il la langue commune? (b) Dans quelle mesure l'implantation de la langue commune appauvrit-elle les dialectes locaux?

Dans son traité de prononciation néerlandaise, Blancquaert, auteur des atlas régionaux des dialectes flamands, s'est principalement attaché à utiliser toutes les ressources offertes par la connaissance approfondie qu'il avait des patois locaux pour inculquer aux Flamands une prononciation correcte du néerlandais. Poursuivant un but essentiellement didactique, son livre ne nous fournit toutefois pas des données permettant de caractériser le néerlandais cultivé tel qu'il est parlé en Belgique, ni de faire la distinction entre ce qui est dû à l'emploi (encore très généralisé) du dialecte et ce qui est dû à d'autres causes.

L'article de Remacle (auteur du tome I de l'Atlas linguistique de la Wallonie) sur le sujet "Bilinguisme et Orthophonie", malgré sa brièveté, est plus instructif à cet égard. Il a relevé 28 traits du français régional "issus directement des habitudes articulatoires propres au patois ou aux patoisants" plus une demi-douzaine d'autres "dont les rapports avec le patois sont moins clairs, obscurs ou inexistants". (Remacle 1943 pp.125-128-131-132) Parmi les conclusions générales auxquelles il aboutit, nous retiendrons: (a) "Fixées autrefois dans une population dont la plupart des membres employaient les deux langues, les habitudes de prononciation se perpétuent aujourd'hui traditionnellement; sans doute subsisteraient-elles, même si personne ne parlait plus le patois, comme un témoignage ultime, résistant et peut-être actif encore, du substrat définitivement enfoui". (Remacle 1943 p.120) (b) "L'action de l'enseignement (de la prononciation française) n'est pas vaine, puisqu'elle paraît même atteindre, par contre-coup, la phonologie patoise. On ne peut douter qu'à l'avenir, aidés comme ils le seront par tous les facteurs modernes de nivellement (...), les maîtres de français n'arrivent encore à d'autres résultats". (Remacle 1943 p.134) Comme on le voit, les deux questions posées ci-dessus n'ont jusqu'à présent donné lieu à des réponses que dans le domaine de la phonétique. Signalons en passant que Warnant, auteur d'un excellent "Dictionnaire de la prononciation française", met actuellement sur pied à l'Université de Liège une enquête en vue de l'élaboration d'un "Atlas phonétique du français en Belgique", englobant, je crois, non seulement le français parlé en Wallonie, mais aussi le français parlé par les Flamands, Bruxellois et Germanophones bilingues. Cette enquête se fait sur la base d'un questionnaire de 600 phrases comportant chacune un trait phonétique typique, complété par l'enregistrement d'un texte libre. Ce nouvel "Atlas" (prévu pour dans 5 ou 6 ans) permettra des recherches menées dans le sens indiqué par la Proposition no 4 de M. Hasselmo.

En ce qui concerne le lexique, il n'existe guère que des recueils non exhaustifs du type "Ne dites pas... mais dites..." poursuivant des buts strictement didactiques: tout reste donc à faire dans ce domaine. En ce qui concerne le passage d'une langue à l'autre (code-switching) dans le langage des bilingues patoisants, on trouve quelques observations précieuses dans le tome III de la "Syntaxe du parler wallon de La Gleize" de Remacle. (Remacle 1960 pp. 286-288) En ce qui concerne le néerlandais en Belgique, il serait intéressant d'étudier la langue d'écrivains tels que Cyriel Buysse, Félix Timmermans, Ernest Claes, etc., qui était fortement teintée de dialecte et fourmillait de traits étrangers au néerlandais cultivé tel qu'on l'enseigne actuellement en Belgique comme aux Pays-Bas.

3.2 Le bilinguisme des régions non homogènes (patois + langue commune de type différent) a donné lieu à des recherches plus poussées, notamment par Bertrang (Arlon), Warland (Malmedy), Boileau (n.-e. de la province de Liège); les résultats obtenus, sans être exhaustifs, permettent, si on le souhaite, de procéder à une évaluation quantitative de l'influence de la langue commune (L2) sur le dialecte local (L1) en ce qui concerne le lexique. (Bertrang 1921 pp.259sv; Warland 1940 pp.48sv) et le nivellement toponymique. (Boileau 1954) Il a été constaté en général que l'influence de L2 sur L1 se situe en effet presque exclusivement sur le plan lexical; la structure interne de L1 (morphologie et syntaxe) reste plus robuste; la phonologie de L1 semble ne pas s'appauvrir, mais plutôt s'enrichir d'éléments empruntés à L2. D'autres études concernant la Flandre française (Pée) et certaines considérations d'ordre général sur la situation linguistique dans le Grand-Duché de Luxembourg (Bruch) tendent cependant à infirmer ce qui précède ou tout au moins à montrer qu'il ne s'agit pas là d'une règle sans exception: "Sous la surface de son bilinguisme officiel, le Luxembourg garde jusque dans la structure intime de son patois germanique l'empreinte profonde de l'empire occidental de Charlemagne".(2)

Seules quelques études sur le bilinguisme bruxellois (Wind, Van Loey) font état de l'influence du patois (L1) sur le français (L2), les premières en ce qui concerne le lexique, les secondes en ce qui concerne en outre la syntaxe et la morphologie. (Wind 1937; Van Loey 1951)

En dépit du caractère fragmentaire de la documentation dont nous disposons, nous pouvons dire que dans les zones bilingues non homogènes de la frontière linguistique, il existe une dualité de mode d'expression mais une unité de base d'articulation. Cette base d'articulation régionale commune s'observe surtout chez les autochtones bilingues, mais elle atteint également, par une

---

(2) Bruch 1954 p.87 L'argumentation employée n'est pas convaincante.

sorte de "mimétisme linguistique", les immigrés venant de l'autre région linguistique, même s'ils restent unilingues. Ce phénomène ne se produit toutefois qu'à partir de la seconde génération; la base d'articulation commune évolue elle-même imperceptiblement mais indépendamment de L1 et de L2.
3.3 La frontière linguistique constitue une barrière entre les communautés
qu'elle sépare, mais dans un pays comme la Belgique, moins que partout ailleurs, une telle barrière n'est nullement infranchissable. Des échanges, principalement lexicaux, se sont effectués dans le passé et continuent à s'effectuer entre parlers germaniques et romans. Nous pouvons observer le présent,
mais nous souhaitons en outre essayer de reconstituer le passé. Dans cette perspective, de nombreuses études ont été consacrées aux emprunts germaniques
en wallon et aux emprunts romans dans les patois flamands et allemands voisins.
Deux d'entre elle au moins font autorité en la matière: celle de Warland sur
les emprunts germaniques (surtout allemands) en wallon malmédien et celle de
Geschiere sur les emprunts néerlandais en wallon liégeois. Je m'en voudrais
de ne pas mentionner à côté d'elles celle de Van Doorne, qui leur est anté-
rieure, sur les mots français dans le dialecte west-flamand de Wingene. (Van
Doorne 1939; Warland 1940; Geschrere 1950) Le classement des termes d'emprunt qui caractérise ces ouvrages est surtout intéressant en ce sens qu'il mon-
tre sous quel angle et dans quels domaines de la vie publique, sociale et pri-
vée l'influence de l'autre langue s'est fait sentir. C'est surtout la comparaison entre le contingent des différentes catégories et sous-catégories qui est
instructive. Un tel classement nous fournit en outre des indications concernant
les causes de l'emprunt. Mais ce qui nous intéresse avant tout, c'est de pouvoir mesurer la profondeur des contacts qui ont présidé aux échanges lexicaux
dans le passé (évaluation qualitative). Le classement par catégories idéelles
n'est pas, à cet égard, pleinement efficace et il est souhaitable qu'on lui en
superpose un autre par catégories grammaticales, tenant compte en outre du
phénomène psychique de l'intellection, c.-à-d. de l'effort qu'à nécessité
chez l'emprunteur la compréhension des vocables étrangers. Ceci afin de
"peser" l'emprunt de façon répondant mieux à la réalité des faits.

   La question se pose, en effet, de savoir si certaines régions aujourd'hui
unilingues n'ont pas été bilingues dans le passé. On s'est demandé, p.ex.,
si la Wallonie (et avec elle tout le nord de la Gaule romane) n'aurait pas été
bilingue à l'époque franque (Petri). Warland, qui ne s'est pas borné au dé-
nombrement et au classement des mots d'emprunt qu'il a étudiés, a analysé
plus de 600 substantifs d'origine germanique en usage à Malmedy et empruntés
aux différentes époques, depuis la période franque jusqu'à celle allant de
1876 à 1920, durant laquelle a régné à Malmedy un bilinguisme de fait "wallon + allemand". Il a constaté que tous les substantifs, à l'exception de ceux
qui appartiennent à cette dernière couche, adoptent lors de leur passage en
wallon un genre grammatical qui est "déterminé en ordre principal par une
coïncidence de caractéristiques formelles. (...) Il n'y a dérogation au principe de l'assimilation analogique que dans un seul cas: quand les deux langues en présence sont connues, et qu'il se produit comme une fusion de deux

complexes d'instincts grammaticaux, laquelle a pour effet une conservation
plus fidèle du substantif et de son genre grammatical." (3)

J'ai pour ma part essayé d'étudier le même problème sous l'angle de la
sématique en analysant les phénomènes psychologiques accompagnant l'emprunt
des verbes germaniques par le wallon liégeois. J'en suis arrivé à la conclusion
que "des verbes qui nous apparaissent aujourd'hui comme abstraits (ce qui pourrait nous inciter à postuler à la base de l'emprunt un certain bilinguisme de la
part de l'emprunteur) décrivent avant tout des attitudes (...) Même si leur
étymon a eu un sens abstrait, l'emprunt le leur a d'abord enlevé." (Boileau
1960 p.99)

Dans quelle mesure les emprunts impliquent-ils un bilinguisme des intermédiaires? L'importation opérée par un bilingue isolé "ne s'impose qu'avec
peine et (...) elle reste souvent superficielle et réduite en comparaison de ce
que produit le bilinguisme dura le de certains groupes ethniques importants
(...)" (Deroy 1956 p.211) Telle est la portée générale de la question évoquée
dans cette partie de mon exposé. Deroy y répond de la manière suivante: "Si
le bilinguisme n'est pas nécessaire pour justifier l'emprunt de la plupart des é-
léments lexicaux, c.-à-d. des noms à valeur concrète, des adverbes, des inter-
jections, des préfixes et des suffices (ces derniers étant sentis comme des membres de composés), il paraît, en revanche, que seuls les bilingues peuvent re-
prendre à l'étranger des noms abstraits, des éléments flexionnels, des syntagmes
et des sens. Le calque implique aussi le bilinguisme, tandis que j'hésite à appeler de ce nom le minimum de connaissance linguistique que supposent certains
emprunts d'adjectifs et de verbes." (Deroy 1956 p.213) Il y a dans la réalité
tant de cas méritant chacun un examen particulier du point de vue étymologique comme du point de vue sémantique, que l'évaluation qualitative des interférences se produisant par-dessus les frontières linguistiques reste avant tout une
oeuvre de patience exigeant beaucoup de temps et de minutie. Cette tâche
est cependant inséparable de nos recherches sur le bilinguisme actuel, dont M.
Hasselmo nous a montré la complexité. En effet, si le présent doit nous aider
à entrevoir le passé, la réciproque est également vraie: c'est en connaissant
le passé que nous pourrons comprendre le présent.

4. Conclusions

J'ai expliqué en commençant les raisons pour lesquelles je désirais limiter
mon "commentaire" aux aspects spécifiquement belges du problème traité ici.
Le moment est maintenant venu de conclure et de résumer où je voulais en
venir.

Je souhaiterais que deux propositions soient ajoutées à celles de M. Hasselmo (auxquelles je me rallie sans réserves).

---

(3) Warland 1935 p.74; cf aussi Warland 1940 pp.260-273

La première de ces propositions complémentaires insisterait sur la nécessité qu'il y a de procéder à une évaluation qualitative des interférences tenant compte des procès psychologiques particuliers que ces interférences impliquent, ceci dans le but de permettre aux historiens de la langue de comprendre, en se basant sur nos recherches, le "pourquoi" et le "comment" de l'importation de termes étrangers dans une langue donnée.

Ma seconde proposition complémentaire a une portée plus générale et est d'ordre essentiellement pratique. Elle vise tout simplement à donner un nom à l'objet de nos recherches sur le bilinguisme et à délimiter leur portée, compte tenu qu'elles intéressent à la fois la linguistique, l'histoire, la sociologie, la psychologie et la pédagogie. Je proposerais d'adopter le terme "interlinguistique" et de le définir comme suit: l'interlinguistique a pour but d'étudier et d'analyser les actions réciproques que deux (ou plusieurs) idiomes (langues, dialectes, patois) exercent dans un territoire donné où ils sont en contact permanent, 1. en comparant les structures des parlers en présence (analyse linguistique différentielle (Mackey 1965a pp.80-97); 2. en observant la nature et le degré des contacts existant entre les différentes communautés linguistiques (sociologie linguistique); 3. en décrivant le mécanisme de la pensée et de la parole chez les bilingues (psychologie linguistique: analyse de cas individuels (4), ainsi que la base d'articulation propre aux individus bilingues et la norme constatée dans la communauté bilingue dont ils font partie (phonétique); 4. en procédant à des recherches approfondies concernant (a) les échanges d'un idiome à l'autre (emprunts lexicaux et autres, calques, etc.), (b) la toponymie ancienne et moderne, dans laquelle se reflètent indirectement mais fidèlement la situation linguistique dans les zones de contact et les interférences que celle-ci implique (5), (c) les problèmes posés par l'existence de "frontières linguistiques", notamment celui de leur origine et celui de leur configuration ancienne et actuelle et, éventuellement, des fluctuations qu'elles ont subies (6); 5. en évaluant (quantitativement et qualitativement les interférences

---

(4) Cf notamment les ouvrages de Ronjat 1913, Elwert 1959, Ruke-Dravina 1967 Le dernier ouvrage cité, qui vient de sortir de presse et qui intéresse autant la psychologie et la sociologie du langage que la linguistique, contient une très riche bibliographie "interlinguistique" et peut servir de modèle à nos recherches.

(5) Sur les "aspects du bilinguisme toponymique" en Belgique (Aspekten van de tweetalige toponymie) et l'intérêt que présente ce type de recherches, voir Bulletin de la Commission royale de Toponymie et de Dialectologie, XXXVIII, 1964, pp.3-5 et 13-15 (résumé d'une communication).

(6) Il peut arriver qu'une frontière linguistique recule ou avance parce qu'une population autochtone s'est laissé assimiler par des immigrants alloglottes. Cette assimilation présuppose une période plus ou moins longue de

(suite de la note à la page suivante)

résultant des contacts observés; 6. l'interlinguistique appliquée s'étendrait à tous les problèmes d'ordre psycho-pédagogique que posent, d'une part, la nocivité (réelle ou supposée) du bilinguisme précoce et, d'autre part, la nécessité unanimement reconnue d'apprendre et d'enseigner une ou plusieurs langues étrangères (7), ce qui implique tout naturellement l'analyse scientifique des diverses méthodes d'enseignement des langues (8).

---

(6)   (suite de la note de la page précédente)
bilinguisme, qui laisse des traces plus ou moins profondes (substrats et superstrats). Les divers facteurs indispensables pour rendre possible cette assimilation doivent être conjugués. Comme ce n'est que très rarement le cas, il s'ensuit que le phénomène est exceptionnel. De fait, en Belgique, à l'époque historique, on n'a constaté de variations de la ligne que très sporadiquement (cf Boileau 1946 chp. IV; Legros 1948 pp. 5-29). Il n'en est pas de même dans le nord-ouest et le nord-est de la France (cf Pée 1957; Toussaint 1955). Sur les origines de la frontière linguistique en Belgique, voir notamment Kurth 1896-98; Des Marez 1926; Petri 1937; Legros 1942; Draye 1943 (3è partie); Warland 1943; Verlinden 1955; Stengers 1959.

(7)   Le problème du bilinguisme a été envisagé sous cet angle notamment par Verheyen 1928; Braunshausen (1932?); Malherbe 1946; Weijnen 1949; Taillon 1959; Closset 1963 et bien d'autres.

(8)   C'est ce qui a été tenté par Mackey dans son remarquable ouvrage Language Teaching Analysis (1965)
L'oeuvre qui fait autorité en Belgique en matière d'enseignement linguistique est la Didactique des langues vivantes de F. Closset, qui préconise une méthode active éclectique, donnant la primauté à l'acquisition d'automatismes tant sur le plan de l'intellection que sur celui de l'expression orale et écrite, mais visant avant tout à respecter la personnalité de l'élève. Le Professeur Closset (décédé en décembre 1964) insistait sur la nécessité de donner "un enseignement concret qui fasse appel aux sens des élèves en même temps qu'à leur intelligence" (p. 187); il a, le premier en Belgique, recommandé le recours aux techniques audio-visuelles, en insistant toutefois sur leur caractère de simple auxiliaire du maître et de l'étudiant: "Systématiquement imposé, il (=l'entraînement mécanique facile et utilitaire") est sans aucun doute contraire à l'esprit même des Humanités et de la formation à laquelle on vise, en général, au niveau de l'enseignement secondaire" (Closset 1963 p. 74). Dès 1963, cependant, la méthode "structuro-globale" de l'Ecole dite de Saint-Cloud - Zagreb a été expérimentée, puis, après le décès du Professeur Closset, avec les encouragements des autorités pédagogiques, introduite dans de nombreuses classes d'enseignement secondaire. Les principes de cette méthode ont été excellement exposés et défendus par R. Renard (cf Bibliogr.)

Elisaveta Referovskaya

En conformité avec l'opinion émise dans l'exposé du professeur Nils Hasselmo, je crois qu'une langue se trouvant en contact perpétuel avec un milieu linguistique étranger, ne peut pas rester isolée de l'interférence plus ou moins considérable avec ce milieu.

1) Les niveaux d'une langue les moins résistants à l'influence hétérogène sont la prononciation et l'intonation.   Le dessin mélodique est essentiel pour la caractéristique d'une langue parlée et c'est justement ce domaine qui souffre en premier lieu du contact avec une autre langue parlée.

2) La couche d'une langue qui est aussi susceptible à l'influence étrangère est évidemment le lexique.   Les emprunts lexicaux se divisent en plusieurs groupes:

a)   Les emprunts des mots peuvent accompagner ceux des notions et des objets.   Ces emprunts enrichissent la langue aussi bien que les idées et les objets nouveaux enrichissent le monde matériel et intellectuel des emprunteurs, y comblent des lacunes éventuelles.

b)   Mais il arrive souvent que les mots étrangers évincent les mots de valeur lexicale correspondante de la langue maternelle.

Ce phénomène moins logique que le premier s'explique par l'habitude de se trouver constamment dans l'ambiance des mots appartenant à la langue des interlocuteurs, par le désir d'être mieux compris par ceux-là au cas où on leur parle en sa propre langue.

c)   S'il s'agit du contact de deux langues apparentées ou ayant un fonds lexical commun, on peut signaler une influence qui fait changer les acceptions des mots de la langue maternelle en les modelant à la façon des mots correspondants de la langue voisine.

C'est le plus dangereux aspect de l'influence d'une langue sur une autre langue sur une autre puisqu'il est complètement inconscient et passe inaperçu. D'ailleurs, il n'est possible qu'entre deux langues ayant un fonds lexical commun.

3) La structure grammaticale est incontestablement le domaine le moins sujet aux troubles provoqués par un contact immédiat avec une langue étrangère. Néanmoins, même cette partie de la langue peut être atteinte d'une contagion linguistique.   Ainsi naissent les constructions syntaxiques inusitées, l'emploi inexact des prépositions, etc.

D'ailleurs les emprunts grammaticaux ne sont jamais nombreux, surtout en comparaison avec ceux du vocabulaire.

4) Le bilinguisme qui est essentiel pour la communication des groupes de population de différentes expressions linguistiques crée des conditions favorables

à l'épanouissement de l'emprunt dans tous les domaines de la langue. Le contact des porteurs de deux ou de plusieurs langues différentes s'accomplit surtout dans les villes qui attirent de tous les côtés des nouveaux venus au préjudice de la campagne.

Au point de vue social et culturel, le rôle du bilinguisme est immense.

Au point de vue linguistique, il possède deux traits caractéristiques:

1) Un trait positif - servant de moyen d'enrichissement de la langue emprunteur.

2) L'autre négatif - contribuant aux modifications souvent inutiles de cette langue.

L'Union soviétique peut servir d'exemple d'un pays où le bilinguisme est largement répandu.

La population du pays consiste en 233 millions d'habitants. L'Etat de l'URSS comporte 53 subdivisions nationales. Les habitants de l'URSS parlent en tout plus de 100 langues. Il y a des républiques et des régions dont la population est formée de groupes apparentés entre eux, mais dont les parlers sont différents.

La langue russe est la langue maternelle de la majorité de la population (120 millions, ce qui fait plus de 50%).

Le russe occupe le centre européen du pays et la plus grande partie de la Sibérie, en Asie.

La langue russe relie les nombreuses nations à l'intérieur du pays. C'est la langue administrative du gouvernement central. Mais dans les établissements administratifs et dans la vie officielle des républiques et des régions nationales on emploie les langues locales.

En Union soviétique il y a encore deux langues slaves: l'ukrainien parlé par 46 millions et le biélorusse - langue maternelle de 9 millions d'habitants.

Les langues slaves prédominent dans le pays. Ce sont des langues qui ont une longue histoire, qui traduisent une grande culture, qui contribuent au développement de la littérature, de la science et du théâtre soviétiques.

Des nations moins nombreuses vivent dans les régions marginales. Les parlers turcs y occupent la place la plus importante. Ce sont les langues des Ouzbeks, Kazakhs, Tatares, Tchouvaches, Kirghiz, Bachkirs, Azerbaidjanais, Turkmènes, Yakoutes, des peuples d'Altai, de Tuva etc. Ce qui fait un total d'environ 30 millions d'habitants.

Le groupe finno-hongrois est représenté par les Estoniens, Caréliens, Komi, Oudmourtes, Mordvines, Mansis etc., en tout près de 4 millions.

Les langues baltiques sont parlées par les Lithuaniens et les Lettons - 5 millions environ. Le groupe des parlers arméniens compte plus de 2 millions. Une langue romane, parlée en Moldavie, 3 millions environ. Les parlers iraniens (les langues des Tadjiks, Kourdes, Ossètes) - près de 3 millions. Les nombreuses langues du Caucase (le géorgien, avarien, lesghien etc.) - plus de 4 millions.

Les habitants des régions nord ne sont pas très nombreux - en tout près de 150 mille, - mais chaque groupe national y parle aussi sa propre langue. Il y

en a plusieurs: les Evènes, Evenques, Nénéens, Tchouktchis, Koriaks, Es-
quimos, Nanaïens etc.

Avant la Révolution de 1917, la situation culturelle et politique des nations de la vieille Russie était différente. Il y avait des peuples de grande et
ancienne culture, tels que les Lithuaniens, les Arméniens, les Géorgiens et
beaucoup d'autres.

En même temps, le niveau culturel de la plus grande partie des petits peuples habitant le Nord et les régions asiatiques du pays était très bas: ils n'a-
vaient même pas de langues écrites.

Maintenant, non seulement ils possèdent des langues écrites (dans la plupart des cas sur la base de l'alphabet russe), mais ils ont développé leurs lit-
tératures nationales, leurs arts nationaux, ils participent à la vie intellectuelle, scientifique et politique de tout le pays.

Dans les républiques et les régions nationales, l'enseignement obligatoire
de huit années est donné en langues locales.

Chacun peut employer sa langue maternelle dans tous les domaines de son
activité. Mais pour être compris dans tout le pays il faut avoir recours à la
langue russe qui sert d'intermédiaire entre les nombreux groupes nationaux du
pays et qu'on enseigne dans toutes les écoles.

De cette façon, les porteurs des langues nationales, ayant reçu l'instruction obligatoire, deviennent bilingues. C'est un bilinguisme conscient, ou
plutôt c'est déjà une diglossie, dont la langue maternelle n'a pas à souffrir.

De cette façon, le russe peut servir de source d'enrichissement pour les
jeunes langues littéraires qui adaptent, en se développant, des éléments de la
langue russe, puisent dans le trésor du vocabulaire immense des langues slaves.

Par exemple, les langues des Turkmènes, Kazakhs, Ouzbeks, Kirghiz,
Oudmourtes, Mansis, Nénéiens. Evènes ont adapté les mots russes завод,
usine, самолет, avion.

Oudmourtes et Tchouvaches emploient les mots russes больница, hô-
pital; врач, médecin;   кресло, fauteuil.

Le mot russe живописъ, peinture entré dans les langues des Tchouvaches,
Kazakhs et Kirghiz.

Le mot шлюз, écluse est maintenant employé par les Ouzbekhs, Turkmènes, Tchouvaches, Kazakhs.

Les Evenques ont pris dans le russe марка, timbre;   сталь, acier, et
beaucoup d'autres mots.

Les Tadjikhs ont adopté железобетон, béton armé;   водопровод,
conduite d'eau;   верфъ, chantier naval, etc.

Les mots empruntés du russe peuvent être compter par centaines. Ils sont
devenus indispensables pour désigner les notions et les objets nouvellement
connus.

La langue russe joue aussi le rôle d'intermédiaire entre les langues des
pays occidentaux et les langues des nations de l'Union soviétique, en trans-
mettant dans ces langues plusieurs mots internationaux, tels que téléphone,
télégraphe, radio, téléviseur, énergie atomique, président, académie, bi-
bliothèque, etc.

L'introduction des éléments de la langue russe dans les parlers des nombreux groupes nationaux, contribue à la formation d'une nouvelle et commune culture et des langues littéraires propres au niveau des exigences de l'époque. Les traits essentiels des parlers nationaux n'en souffrent point. Leur structure reste intacte.

Le bilinguisme - source de danger pour les langues-emprunteurs - porte en soi-même un contrepoison. Mieux on connaît une langue étrangère, moins est nuisible son influence. Il faut savoir profiter cu contact, surtout si la langue en question est à même de contribuer au développement de la langue-emprunteur. D'autre part, mieux on connaît sa propre langue, moins on est tenté d'y introduire des éléments hétérogènes inutiles.

Dans ces conditions, tout emprunt paraît motivé et raisonnable.

Seulement les emprunts inconscients et immotivés peuvent être jugés superflus et indésirables.

Le bilinguisme contribue généralement à l'interaction des deux langues, mais il existe une différence essentielle entre le bilinguisme des groupes d'immigrants qui se trouvent dans un milieu étranger privilégié, puisque la population originaire du pays parle la langue de ce pays, et le bilinguisme d'une population dont tous les groupes d'expression linguistique différente appartiennent par leur origine au même pays.

Dans le premier cas, la langue de la minorité peut se trouver sur la voie d'assimilation, en particulier, si on ne fait pas d'efforts conscients pour la maintenir. Dans une telle situation, le bilinguisme serait, pour ainsi dire, unilatéral. La minorité serait bilingue, non pas la majorité.

Dans le second cas, il n'y a pas de question d'assimilation linguistique, chaque groupe parlant, écrivant et développant sa propre langue, qui, au point de vue social, est égale à toutes les autres langues parlées dans le pays.

Il ne reste qu'à choisir une langue qui puisse servir d'intermédiaire entre les groupes de la population d'expression linguistique différente. Et, si c'est une langue apprise, et bien apprise, il n'y aura pas d'interférence nuisible entre elle et les langues maternelles de différents groupes de la population. Ce qui est caractéristique pour les nombreuses langues de l'Union soviétique.

Ainsi, il me semble que le bilinguisme, ayant un côté linguistique très intéressant et très important, relève plutôt des conditions sociales.

DISCUSSION

English Version

The discussion revolved around the questions of norm specification and identification of code. Dr. Hasselmo pointed out that the measurement of interference demands description and quantification. In their turn, these operations
require identification of interference, which finally requires norm specification.

The key concept in norm specification is consistent co-occurrence in a
given frame. The frame can be any speech event, even a sentence or a word.
A norm may be defined as internal consistency in a speaker's usage. In all
speech there is a neat hierarchy of levels. Norms defined on certain levels
may include alternation between lower levels. If speakers show features of one
norm co-existing within the frame of another, then interference has taken place.
Interference can only be observed in the speech of individuals as deviation from
a given norm. Dr. Lepage's discussion would seem to suggest that we should
reject the notion that one language influences another. Dr. Hasselmo would
agree with this point of view in that it implies that individuals are not expected to adhere consistently to one set of norms in a given stretch of discourse.
Most discussions tend to obliterate the distinction between interference in
speech and interference in language. If it would clarify matters we could call
the first interference, and the second linguistic change.

To this linguistic notion of norm, a sociologist present added another dimension. Two meanings of norm are generally found: the first is what people
normally do; the second is what they expect. The danger with the second sense
is that we tend to substitute linguists' expectations for those of speakers. The
concept of norm is vital for the sociology of language. There is no way of
measuring role and status apart from language. We must at least start with some
idea of norm, otherwise we are not necessarily measuring behaviour. But the
concept of a particular norm is far from fixed; it is merely a working hypothesis.

An objection was raised that sociologists have begun with a definition of
role and status based on income and residence and other non-linguistic factors,
and then related this to linguistic data defined according to the various norms
of American English. In reply, it was pointed out that Dr. Labov had not been
satisfied with this technique and had gone into the problem of eliciting roles
and certain styles of speech from his subjects. His results were due to his techniques, rather than to correlations between role and status.

A norm definitely has a social dimension. What the individual usually says
leads to some conception of what people usually say. People are constantly
conditioned by the desire to behave like other people. We must define norms

in terms of internal consistency.

The question of defining norms for a bilingual community had already been partially discussed during the second session. It was proposed that one should take as a norm the speech habits of those on the fringe of bilingual communities, at least where these communities were the result of migration. This, according to the proposer, would be more accurate, assuming proper matching for sociological factors, than a norm based on monolingual usage in the parent communities or the usage of bilinguals who had already been settled for some time.

The idea that as analysis becomes finer one discovers more norms caused some problems. Could this statement be squared with the possibility of a rigorous definition of a code? From a social point of view words like the Yoruba télò were integrated, but was this true from a linguistic angle? The fact that we may have to speak about norms on different levels without any one-to-one matching on the lower levels makes it doubtful whether we can speak in any general sense about code. The whole speech economy was the code. There would probably always be areas that would lie beyond rigorous determination, probably because they were not rigorously determined as far as the speakers were concerned. At the moment there seemed to be no satisfactory answer to the question posed in Dr. Siertsema's paper.

Some attempt was made to separate the concepts of interference and code-switching. Interference is the application of two or more norms to the same item. In discussing the whole question of interference a participant cited a number of different situations:

1. The situation in which two languages with clearly defined literate norms are in contact. (e.g. French and German). A speaker deliberately keeps the two norms separate according to the immediate situation but, from time to time, will lapse into the preferred language.

2. At the other end of the scale there is the situation in which neither language in contact has prescribed literate norms. In such situations the degree of interference will often depend on differences between structures. If they are very different, it will probably be easier to keep them apart.

3. Between these extremes there is the situation in which literate codes are in contact with non-literate. There is a continuum including all possible situations between the extremes.

We will have to recognise a large spectrum of situations among those we are dealing with. This delegate suggested designing a "quantum linguistics" to deal with states of transition and with systems in motion rather than the static descriptive models we have available at present. He noted that cooperation between psychologists and linguists was necessary for this end.

Some agreement seemed to be reached that interference is what a person says once or twice with a low degree of consistency if the item is borrowed from another norm, phonological, grammatical or lexical. This would distinguish it from code-switching which implies some sort of consistency. There was a suggestion that interference was an unconscious feature in speech. Reference was made to the Prague school, who used the term in this sense. But some delegates did not like the term as it carried a stigma. Where a new element filled a gap in the receiving language, it could not be regarded as interference; where it drove out a perfectly good native word, it could.

So far the assumption had been that spoken languages were the usual source of interference. But in the case of contact between regional patois and metropolitan languages, or between local and colonising languages, interference was affected through the written language. One speaker noted that when French replaced Latin as a written language in the territory in which it is now the metropolitan language, Alsatians and Occitans learnt it from written scripts, pronouncing it with their native phonemes. The same thing happened in French Oceania, for instance, where the language spoken by native-born teachers was French with a phonology affected by native speech habits, and in the East with English. There was agreement that one could speak of bilingualism where there was a classical language involved.

One commentator, who illustrated his paper with tapes of a girl from British Honduras telling the same story in Creole English and Spanish, felt that in dealing with such subjects we have to assume two phonemic systems, and that we must try to state conditions when they move from one to the other. No matter the code, there are all sorts of compensatory features. The subject under discussion carried into Spanish the intonation patterns of her Creole English and compensated for missing features with marginal features such as interaction of phonotactic groups.

While interference was not generally considered to be part of an existing norm, code-switching could. It can be part of a high-level norm and was defined as the use of successive stretches of two languages in speech. To a bilingual, his languages can be merely different registers in the same over-all pattern of speech behaviour. Even in unilingual situations, many people use different registers according to their social roles and role expectations. Often they will mix registers. The functional approach of the Prague school is an important starting point in the methodology of the question.

Certain combinations of phones with in a word constitute interference if not used consistently. Lexical items which incorporate phones and/or grammatical norms from a system other than the speaker's habitual system can be regarded as another lexical system. Since lexical items may possibly occur only once with certain phonological features, it is necessary to consider the social dimension on this level. Thus lexical items which occur consistently with phonological and grammatical features of one type constitute one norm; items occurring with others constitute another norm.

In discussing the problems of norm and interference, the question of integration is important. The dichotomy integrated/unintegrated is easy to state but impossible to impose in any strict sense. Dr. Hasselmo would judge that the Yoruba nouns, cited by Dr. Siertsema on the basis of social criteria, are integrated into the language. A study of link-words in American Swedish, and, och, men, but show a strange type of integration in the function of sequence signalling. And is used in about 25% of the occurrences and och 75%. This

brings up Dr. Oksaar's problem of the quasi-existence of items in speech.
Such items are not part of the norm in any given event, and are defined by the
norm of occurrence. Here the norm must be defined without any social correlate. The question was further complicated by the fact that integration and
code-switching can really be two distinct types of behaviour from the point of
view of the speaker. In this case linguistic and social norms must be viewed
together. Each case must be viewed on its peculiarities.

Dr. Lepage's idea that where a person X behaves on some occasions like
a member of Group A and on others like a member of group B, and this mingling
of behaviour is shared there is a language X is definitely a description of one
sort of norm that may or may not depend on integration or code-switching.
This statement lead to a discussion of the validity of Saussure's concept of language. Dr. Lepage's statement that langue was a harmful abstraction was modified by another speaker who pointed out that unless the idea was taken as a
working hypothesis, it seems to make a unit out of a complex of systems which
are loosely integrated and subject to change.

The question of how interference passes to switching or integration was
debated. The question had two dimensions, a social and a linguistic, and the
main problem was where to cut the continuum. Integration is used to charac-
terise the substitution of native features used in an item taken from another language, but is not integrated in a social sense until it is habitual. Where do
we cut the continuum? It was postulated that when items of interference become habitual, they are no longer interference but become part of the code.
This creates difficulties, but by using Dr. Lepage's approach, we can at least
begin to deal with the problem.

Dr. Haugen commented that his early works had been extensively used by
both speakers and commentators. As these had been written ten to fifteen
years ago they were now subject to revision. He wished to clarify his thinking
before the meeting. In his own thinking the concept of interference had been
absent until the appearance of Uriel Weinreich's Languages in Contact (1953).
In his Norwegian Language in America (1953) it did not appear, but in Bilingualism in the Americas (1956) it did. The term seemed to be a good substitute
for "borrowing", partly because "borrowing" implies reciprocity, and it also
implies a lack to be met. After using the term "interference", he became un-
easy as it could not apply to foreign items well established in the language.
Yet they came into the language by the deliberate choice of a speaker. At
that point they were examples of interference, which can be defined as the
simultaneous use of rules from two languages. The exact use of a phonemic
sequence will depend on the skill of the borrower. If he knows the original
language well, he will produce its phonemes fairly accurately; if not, he will
make them conform to his own language. If features of the foreign language
are consistently preserved as in the examples from Yoruba given by Dr. Siertsema, it means that the host system has changed. Such conflicts between linguistic and social acceptance are far from rare.

If we develop a new linguistics it may be that a new and integrated grammar will allow us to do a better job of stating the position of interference. Each item of interference and borrowing will have to be stated as a rule in the level of grammar in which it occurs. Grammar must have room for the description of alterations that are drawn from more than one style or register. The question of the number of norms we are to recognise is a problem.

As far as one delegate was concerned, the fore-going discussion had left undefined the difference between testing and measuring, and had indeed confused these two areas. Even in such an "objective" activity as measuring it is impossible to avoid subjectivity—results have to be interpreted. The meeting had also neglected to define a language. For him it still had to be proved that there was a difference between animal and human language.

DISCUSSION

Version française

La discussion tourne autour de la définition des normes et de l'identification des codes. M. Hasselmo signale que la mesure de l'interférence exige un travail de description et de quantification, opérations qui nécessitent elles-mêmes l'identification des phénomènes d'interférence, laquelle exige enfin une définition des normes.

L'idée centrale, dans la définition d'une norme, c'est la reproduction constante d'un même phénomène dans un cadre donné. Ce cadre peut être n'importe quel fait de langage, même une phrase ou un mot. Une norme peut se définir ainsi: la constance interne du mode d'expression d'un locuteur. Dans tout langage parlé, il existe une nette hiérarchie des niveaux. Les normes définies pour certains niveaux peuvent comprendre une alternance entre des niveaux inférieurs. Si l'on relève chez un locuteur des traits appartenant à une norme et coexistant dans le cadre d'une autre norme, c'est qu'il y a eu interférence. L'interférence dans le parler d'un individu ne peut être observée que comme une déviation à partir d'une norme donnée. Les propos de M. Lepage semblent indiquer qu'il faudrait rejeter l'idée qu'une langue influence une autre langue. M. Hasselmo partage ce point de vue en ce sens qu'il ne droit pas qu'on doive s'attendre à ce qu'un individu s'en tienne constamment à un ensemble de normes dans une tranche de discours donné. Dans la plupart des discussions, on a tendance à oublier la distinction entre l'interférence dans le parler et l'interférence dans la langue. Si cela peut aider à établir les distinctions qui s'imposent, on peut appeler la première interférence, et l'autre modification linguistique.

A cette notion linguistique de norme, un sociologue présent ajoute une autre dimension. Le mot norme s'emploie généralement dans deux sens: il désigne en premier lieu ce que les gens font ordinairement, et en second lieu ce qu'ils attendent des autres. Ce qui rend le second sens sujet à caution, c'est que nous avons tendance à substituer des prévisions de linguiste aux prévisions des locuteurs. L'idée de norme est fondamentale pour la sociologie de la langue. Il n'y a aucun moyen, si ce n'est pas le langage, de mesurer le rôle et le prestige des personnes. Il faut commencer par avoir au moins une idée de la norme, sans quoi nous ne mesurerons pas nécessairement le comportement. Mais l'idée d'une norme particulière est loin d'être fixe: ce n'est qu'une hypothèse de travail.

Un participant objecte que les sociologues ont commencé par définir le rôle et le prestige en fonction du revenu, de la résidence et d'autres facteurs non linguistiques, et qu'ils les ont ensuite rattachés à des données linguistiques établies en fonction des diverses normes de l'anglais américain. On lui répond que M. Labov ne s'est pas contenté de cette technique, et qu'il s'est attaqué au problème de tirer de ses sujets des rôles et certains styles de discours. Ses résultats sont attribuables à ses techniques plutôt qu'à des corrélations entre rôle et prestige.

Chose certaine, une norme comporte une dimension sociale. Ce qu'une personne dit permet habituellement de se faire une idée de ce que les gens disent habituellement. Les gens sont constamment conditionnés par le désir de se comporter comme les autres. Il faut définir les normes en fonction d'une constance interne. On a déjà étudié partiellement, au cours de la seconde séance, la question de la définition des normes pour une collectivité bilingue. On a proposé de prendre comme normes les habitudes de langage des personnes vivant à la frontière des collectivités bilingues, au moins lorsque ces collectivités sont le produit d'une migration.

D'après le participant qui a émis cette idée, ce serait là une méthode plus exacte, dès lors que l'on tiendrait compte des influences sociologiques, que de tracer la norme d'après l'usage unilingue des collectivités d'origine ou d'après l'usage des bilingues établis déjà depuis un certain temps.

La possibilité, toutefois, que plus l'analyse sera poussée, plus on découvrira de normes ne laisse pas de poser des problèmes. Peut-elle se concilier avec la possibilité de la définition rigoureuse d'un code? Des mots tels que télò, en yorouba, sont intégrés du point de vue social, mais le sont-ils du point de vue linguistique? Comme il faut peut-être dégager des normes à des niveaux différents, sans pouvoir établir de correspondances norme pour norme aux niveaux inférieurs, on peut douter qu'il soit possible de parler d'un code dans un sens le moindrement général. C'est l'ensemble de l'économie du langage qui constitue le code. Certaines zones échapperont sans doute toujours à une détermination rigoureuse, probablement parce qu'elles ne sont pas rigoureusement déterminées dans l'esprit des locuteurs. Aucune réponse satisfaisante ne paraît pouvoir être donnée pour le moment à la question que pose la communication de Mlle Siertsema.

Les participants s'efforcent jusqu'à un certain point de distinguer l'un de l'autre. L'interférence consiste en l'application de deux ou plusieurs normes à un même élément de langage. Au sujet de l'interférence en général, un participant indique plusieurs situations différentes:

1. Contact de deux langues possédant des normes étudiées et nettement définies (le français et l'allemand, par exemple). Le locuteur fait un effort conscient pour ne pas mêler les deux ensembles de normes, dans la situation immédiate où il se trouve, mais de temps à autre il revient malgré lui à celle des deux langues qu'il préfère.

2. A l'autre extrémité de l'échelle, contact de deux langues dont ni l'une ni l'autre ne possède de normes étudiées et prescrites. Dans les situations de ce genre, le degré d'interférence tient souvent aux différences qui existent entre les structures des deux langues. Lorsque les structures sont très

différentes, il est sans doute plus facile de ne pas confondre les normes.

3. Entre ces extrêmes, il y a le cas du contact entre une langue dont le code est pleinement évolué et une autre dont le code ne l'est pas. On trouve entre les deux extrêmes toute la diversité possible des situations.

Il faut reconnaître l'existence d'une très large gamme de situations parmi celles qu'examine le colloque. Le délégué voudrait que soit mise au point une "linguistique de quantums" pour le cas des états de transition et celui des systèmes en évolution, afin de remplacer les modèles descriptifs statiques dont on dispose à l'heure actuelle. Il note qu'une collaboration est nécessaire à cette fin entre psychologues et linguistes.

On est apparemment d'accord pour juger qu'il y a interférence lorsqu'une personne s'exprime d'une certaine manière une fois ou deux seulement, avec un assez faible degré de constance, en empruntant l'élément de langage dont il s'agit à une autre norme, soit phonologique, soit grammaticale, soit lexicale. L'interférence diffère du passage d'un code à un autre, celui-ci se produisant d'une manière plus constante. Quelqu'un demande si l'interférence ne serait pas un fait inconscient du langage. On cite l'école de Prague, qui attribue ce caractère à l'interférence. Certains délégués, toutefois, n'aiment pas ce terme, qui serait quelque peu péjoratif. Il n'y a pas interférence lorsque l'élément nouveau répond à un besoin de la langue d'accueil, mais lorsqu'il déplace un mot de la langue d'accueil qui répondait déjà à ce besoin.

On est toujours parti de l'idée que la source ordinaire d'interférence était une langue parlée. Pourtant, dans le cas du contact entre les parlers régionaux et les langues métropolitaines, comme entre les parlers locaux et les langues de colonisation, l'interférence a été le fait de la langue écrite. Un des participants rappelle ce qui s'est passé lorsque le français a remplacé le latin comme langue écrite sur le territoire où il est aujourd'hui la langue métropolitaine: les Alsaciens et les Occitans ont appris le français à partir de textes écrits et lui ont donné la prononciation de leurs phonèmes propres. Il est arrivé la même chose en Océanie française, par exemple, où les instituteurs indigènes parlaient français avec une phonologie reproduisant certaines habitudes de leurs parlers. La même chose s'est produite en Orient pour l'anglais. Les participants reconnaissent que l'on peut parler de bilinguisme même lorsque l'une des langues en cause est une langue classique.

Un commentateur, dont la communication comporte des enregistrements réalisés par une jeune fille du Honduras britannique qui reprend une même histoire en anglais créole et en espagnol, est d'avis qu'il faut tenir compte de deux systèmes phonémiques dans les cas de ce genre, et qu'il faudrait définir les conditions dans lesquelles le locuteur passe d'un système à l'autre. Quel que soit le code, on trouve de très nombreuses caractéristiques de compréhension. La jeune fille des enregistrements fait passer en espagnol les intonations de son anglais créole et supplée les caractéristiques manquantes par des caractéristiques marginales telles que l'interaction de groupes phonotactiques.

L'interférence n'est pas considérée d'ordinaire comme relevant d'une norme existante, mais le passage d'un code à un autre pourrait, par contre, relever d'une norme supérieure et se définir comme le recours à des fragments successifs de deux langues différentes lorsque l'on parle. Dans le cas d'un bilingue, ses deux langues peuvent ne constituer que des registres différents d'un même mode général d'expression par la parole. Même dans les situations d'unilinguisme, nombreuses sont les personnes qui ont recours à des registres différents suivant le rôle social qu'elles jouent et les exigences de ce rôle. Souvent elles confondent les registres. Le point de vue fonctionnel adopté par l'école de Prague fournit un important point de départ pour la méthodologie de cette question.

Certaines combinaisons de phonèmes à l'intérieur d'un mot constituent des cas d'interférence lorsqu'elles ne se reproduisent pas de façon constante. Les éléments lexicaux au sein desquels sont incorporés des phonèmes ou des normes grammaticales provenant d'un autre système que celui dont se sert habituellement le locuteur peuvent être considérés comme constituant un troisième système lexical. Comme il arrive que des éléments lexicaux ne se présentent qu'une fois avec certaines caractéristiques phonologiques, il y a lieu de tenir compte, à ce niveau, de la dimension sociale. Les éléments lexicaux qui se reproduisent constamment avec le même genre de caractéristiques phonologiques et grammaticales constituent une norme; ceux qui se présentent avec d'autres caractéristiques constituent une norme différente.

Dans l'examen des problèmes que posent les normes et l'interférence, la question d'intégration ne laisse pas d'être importante. La dichotomie intégré et non intégré est facile à énoncer, mais impossible à imposer effectivement. D'après M. Hasselmo, les substantifs yoroubas que cite Mlle Siertsema en se fondant sur des critères sociaux sont intégrés dans le langage. L'étude de certains mots-charnières du suédois américain (and, och, men, but) fait apparaître un mode étrange d'intégration par une fonction d'indication de séquence. And est employé dans 25% des cas environ, et och dans 75% des cas. Cela évoque le problème de Mme Oksaar, celui de la quasi-existence de certains éléments dans le langage. Les éléments de ce genre n'appartiennent à la norme d'aucune situation; ils se définissent par la norme au sein de laquelle ils apparaissent. Cette norme doit se définir sans corrélatif social. La question se complique du fait que l'intégration et le passage d'un code à un autre sont parfois, en réalité, deux modes distincts de comportement, du point de vue du locuteur. Dans ce cas, les normes linguistiques et sociales doivent être considérées ensemble. Il faut tenir compte des particularités de chaque cas.

L'idée de M. Lepage suivant laquelle, lorsqu'une personne X se comporte en certaines occasions comme faisant partie du groupe A et en d'autres occasions comme faisant partie du groupe B et que ce comportement mixte est aussi celui de son entourage, et que par conséquent il existe une langue X, cette idée indique nettement l'existence d'un genre de norme qui peut dépendre ou ne pas dépendre soit de l'intégration, soit du passage d'un code à un autre. A partir de là, la discussion s'engage au sujet du concept de langue de Saussure. Alors que M. Lepage voit le terme langue comme une abstraction nuisible, un autre participant fait observer que, si l'on ne se sert pas de cette idée comme d'une hypothèse de travail, le mot langue paraît réunir sous une même dénomination un ensemble complexe de systèmes peu intégrés et en constante modification.

On discute ensuite de la manière dont l'interférence devient soit passage d'un code à un autre, soit intégration. Cette question a une dimension sociale et une dimension linguistique, et il s'agit de savoir à quel point précis se divise le continu. L'intégration consiste dans la substitution de caractéristiques indigènes à certaines caractéristiques d'un élément de langage emprunté à une autre langue, lequel n'est intégré socialement qu'une fois devenu habituel dans la langue d'accueil. Où se divise le continu? On pose en postulat que les éléments d'interférence, lorsqu'ils sont devenus habituels, ne constituent plus une interférence mais font partie du code. Cela pose certaines difficultés, mais cette méthode de M. Lepage permet au moins d'aborder le problème.

M. Haugen fait observer que les auteurs de communications et les commentateurs ont eu recours abondamment à ses premiers ouvrages. Comme ceux-ci remontent à dix ou quinze ans, ils ont besoin d'une certaine révision. Il tient à préciser sa pensée. D'après lui, le concept d'interférence n'a fait son apparition que lors de la publication de Languages in Contact d'Uriel Weinreich, en 1953. Il n'en était pas question dans son Norwegian Language in America (1953), mais on le trouve dans Bilingualism in the Americas (1956). Ce terme lui paraît meilleur que le mot "emprunt", d'abord parce que tout emprunt suppose réciprocité et suppose aussi une lacune à combler. Après s'être servi du terme "interférence", il en a été inquiet, ce terme ne pouvant être appliqué aux éléments étrangers qui sont déjà installés dans la langue. Il reste pourtant que ces éléments sont entrés dans la langue par un choix de la part d'un locuteur. A ce moment-là, ils ont constitué des cas d'interférence, c'est-à-dire de recours aux règles de deux langues. La façon dont est utilisée une séquence phonémique dépend de la compétence de l'emprunteur. S'il connaît bien la langue d'origine, il en reproduit avec assez d'exactitude les phonèmes; s'il la connaît mal, il en assimile les phonèmes à ceux de sa propre langue. Lorsque les éléments de la langue étrangère sont uniformément conservés, comme dans les exemples de Mlle Siertsema, tirés du yorouba, c'est que le système de la langue d'accueil a été modifié. Les conflits de ce genre entre l'acceptation linguistique et l'acceptation sociale ne sont pas rares.

Si l'on met au point une linguistique nouvelle, peut-être une nouvelle grammaire intégrée permettra-t-elle de préciser la position qu'occupe l'interférence. Chacun des cas d'interférence et d'emprunt devra être présenté comme constituant une règle au niveau de grammaire auquel il appartient. La grammaire doit faire sa place à la description des modifications provenant de plus d'un style, de plus d'un registre. Il restera à voir combien de normes doivent être reconnues.

Un délégué fait observer que la discussion n'a pas abouti à une définition de la différence qui existe entre épreuve et mesure, et même qu'elle a mis plus de confusion encore entre les deux. Même dans une activité aussi "objective"

que le mesurage, il est impossible d'éviter toute subjectivité: on doit interpréter les mesures que l'on a trouvées. La discussion, d'autre part, a négligé
d'établir une définition du langage. A son avis, rien ne prouve encore qu'il
y ait une différence entre le langage de l'homme et ceux des animaux.

BIBLIOGRAPHY/BIBLIOGRAPHIE

Akhmanova, O. S., Mel'chuk, J. A., Frumkina, R. M., Paducheva, E. V.
   1963   Exact Methods in Linguistic Research, Berkeley, University of
           California Press

Bendix, E. H.
   1960   "Componential Analysis of General Vocabulary; the semantic of a
           set of verbs in English, Hindi and Japanese." International
           Journal of American Linguistics 32, 2, Part 2, 1-190

Bertrang, A.
   1921   Grammatik der Areler Mundart, Bruxelles, M. Lamertin

Betz, W.
   1939   "Zur Erfarschung des 'inneren Lehnguts'." (In) 5th International
           Congress of Linguists, Réponses au questionnaire, Brugge, 33-35

   1949   Deutsch und Lateinisch; die Lehnbildungen der althochdeutschen
           Benediktinerregel, Bonn, H. Bouvier

Blancquaert, E.
   1953   Practische Vitspraakleer van de Nederlands taal, Vierde uitgave,
           Antwerfen

Bloomfield, L.
   1933   Language, New York, H. Holt & Co.

Boileau, A.
   1946   "Le problème du bilinguisme et la théorie des substrats". Revue des
           langues vivantes 12, 113-125, 169-193, 213-214

   1949   "Het noordoosten van de provincie Luik, kriusfunt van drie kulturen,"
           (In) Handelingen van het 18de Vlaamse Filologencongres, Gent

----

   1954a   Notes sur les parlers du nord-est de la province de Liège, Liège

----

   1954b   Enquête dialectale sur la toponymie germanique du nord-est de la
           province de Liège, Liège, P. Gothier

   1960   "Les procès sémantiques de l'emprunt populaire observés à travers
           quelques verbes wallons d'origine germanique," Bulletin du dic-
           tionnaire wallon 20, 81-99

Bolinger, D.
   1966   "Transformulation; structural translation," Acta Linguistica
           Hafniensa 9, 130-144

Borsu, A.
   1923   La bonne forme; sens des mots, prononciation, orthographe, ex-
           pressions vicieuses, Bruxelles, Office de publicité

Bottequin, A.
   1937   Le français contemporain, incorrections, difficultés, illogismes,
             bizarreries, ou le bon usage du français d'aujourd'hui, Bruxelles,
             Office de publicité
Bruch, R.
   1954   "Aspects linguistiques du Luxembourg", Revue des langues vivantes
             20, 82-87
Braunshausen, N.
   1934   Le bilinguisme et les méthodes d'enseignement des langues étran-
             gères, Bruxelles (Cahiers de la Centrale du P. E. S. de Belgique
             no 7)
Chomsky, N.
   1957   Syntactic Structures, Gravenhague, Mouton

   1961   "Some Methodological Remarks on Generative Grammar," Word 17
             219-239

   1964   "Degrees of Grammaticalness," (In) The Structure of Language;
             reading in the philosophy of language, Jerry Fodor & Ferrold
             Katz (eds.), Englewood Cliffs, New Jersey
Closset, F.
   1956   Didactique des langues vivantes, 3 ed., Bruxelles, M. Didier
   ----
   1963   "Le problème du bilinguisme et l'enseignement des langues vivantes",
             Revue des langues vivantes 29, 70-75
Coleman, E. B.
   1965   "Responses to a Scale of Grammaticalness," Journal of Verbal
             Learning and Verbal Behavior 4, 521-527
Dauzat, A.
   1927   Les patois; évolution-classification-étude, Paris, Delagrave
Deharveng, S. V.
   1928   Corrigeons-nous; aide-mémoire et additions, Bruxelles, Dwitt
Deroy, L.
   1956   L'emprunt linguistique, Paris, Les Belles lettres
Des Marez, G.
   1926   Le problème de la colonisation franque et du régime agraire en
             Belgique, avec cartes, plans et figures, Bruxelles, M. Lamertin
D'Harve, G.
   1923   Parlons mieux! Nouvelles recherches et trouvailles lexicologiques,
             Bruxelles, Office de publicité
Diebold, A. R.
   1961   "Incipient Bilingualism," Language 37, 97-112

   1963   "Code-Switching in Greek-English Bilingual Speech," Georgetown
             University Monograph Series on Languages and Linguistics 15,
             53-59

1965   "A Survey of Psycholinguistic Research, 1954-64,"(In) Psycholin-
        guistics; a survey of theory and research problems, C. E. Osgood
        & T. A. Sebeok (eds.), Bloomington, Indiana

Dingwall, W. O.
1964   "Transformational Generative Grammar and Contrastive Analysis,"
        Language Learning 14, 147-160

Draye, H.
1941-2 "De studie van de Vlaamsch-Waalsche taalgrenslijn in België
        gedurende de hedendaagsche periode," Leuvensche Bijdragen.
        Tijdschrift voor Moderne Philologie 33, 61-112; 34, 1-37

1941-3 "De gelijkmaking in plaatsnamen," Handelingen van Koninklijke
        Commissie voor Toponymie ne dialectologie 15, 357-394; 16,
        43-63; 17, 305-390

Elwert, W. T.
1960   Das zweisprachige Individuum; ein Selbstzeugnis, Wiesbaden, In
        Kommission bei F. Steiner

Epstein, I.
1915   La pensée et la polyglossie; essai psychologique et didactique,
        Paris, Payot & Cie

Ervin, S. M. & Osgood, Ch. E.
1965   "Second Language Learning and Bilingualism," (In) Psycholinguis-
        tics; a survey of theory and research problems, C. E. Osgood &
        T. A. Sebeok (eds.), Bloomington, Indiana, 139-

Fisher, H.
1966   "A New Approach to the Measurement of Meaning," Linguistics
        22, 24-33

Fishman, J. A.
1964   "Language Maintenance and Language Shift as a Field of Inquiry;
        a definition of the field and suggestions for its further develop-
        ment," Linguistics 9, 32-70

Galand, V.
1891   Les 600 expressions vicieuses belges recueillies et corrigées, 2^e
        éd. Charleroi, Michel Hubert

Gali, A. M.
1928   "Comment mesurer l'influence du bilinguisme", (In) Le bilinguisme
        et l'éducation, travaux de la conférence internationale tenue à
        Luxembourg du 2 au 5 avril 1928, Genève, Bureau international
        d'éducation-Luxembourg, Maison du Livre, 123-136

Geschiere, L.
1950   Eléments néerlandais du wallon liégeois, Amsterdam, Noord-
        Hollandsche Vitg. Mij. (Series: Verhandeling der Koninklijke
        Nederlandsche Akademic van Wetenschaffen. Afd. Letterkunde.
        Nieuwe reeks, Jeel 53, No. 2)

Green, E.
  1963   "On Grading Phonic Interference," Language Learning 13, 85-96
Grootaers, L.
  1948   "Tweetaligheid," Album Prof. Dr. Frank Baur, Antwerpen, Brussel,
           Standaard-Boekhandel, vol. 1, 291-296
Gumperz, J. J.
  1964   "Linguistic and Social Interaction in Two Communities," American
           Anthropologist 66, 6, Part 2, 137-153
Haas, M. R.
  1951   "Interlingual Word Taboos," American Anthropologist 53, 338-344
Hammer, J. H. & Rice, F. A. (eds.)
  1965   A Bibliography of Contrastive Linguistics, Washington, Centre for
           Applied Linguistics
Hatheway, L. V.
1928-9   "A German Error Count; an experimental study," The Modern Lan-
           guage Journal 13, 512-533
Haugen, E. I.
  1950   "The Analysis of Linjuistic Borrowing," Language 26, 210-231

  1953   The Norwegian Language in America; a study in bilingual behavior,
           Philadelphia, University of Pennsylvania Press

  1954   "Languages in Contact; findings and problems," by Uriel Weinreich
           ..., reviewed by Einar Haugen, Language 30, 380-388

  1956   Bilingualism in the Americas; a bibliography and research guide,
           American Dialect Society, University of Alabama Press
Herdan, G.
  1965   "Eine Gesetzmässigkeit der Sprachenmischung," Mathematik und
           Dichtung, ed. Helmut Kreuzer, München, Nymphenburger Verlags
           handlung, 85-106

  1966   "How can Quantitative Methods Contribute to Our Understanding
           of Language Mixture and Language Borrowing?" (In) Statistique
           et Analyse linguistique, Paris, Presses universitaires de France,
           17-39
Herman, S. N.
  1961   "Explorations in the Social Psychology of Language Choice," Human
           Relations 14, 149-164
Hertzler, J. V.
  1965   A Sociology of Language, New York, Random House
Hill, A. A.
  1961   "Grammaticality," Word 17, 1-10
Hill, T.
  1958   "Institutional Linguistics," Orbis; bulletin international de documen-
           tation linguistique 7, 441-445

184 Bibliographie/Séance 3

Hofstätter, P. R.
  1963   "Uber sprachliche Bestimmungsleistungen: Das Problem des gramma-
          tikalischen Geschlechts von Sonne und Mond," Zeitschrift feier
          experimentelle und angewandte Psychologie 10, 91-108
Hymes, D.
  1962   "The Ethnography of Speaking," (In) Anthropology and Human Be-
          havior, T. Gladwin & W. C. Sturtevant (eds.), Eashington,
          D. C. 13-53

  1964   "Introduction: Toward Ethnographies of Communication," American
          Anthropologist 66, 6, Part 2, 1-34
Jakobovits, L. A. & Lambert, W. E.
  1961   "Semantic Satiation among Bilinguals," Journal of Experimental
          Psychology 62, 576-582
Jespersen, O.
  1934   Language; its nature, development and origin, London, G. Allen
          & Unwin, Ltd., New York, H. Hold & Co.
Johnson, N. F.
  1965   "Linguistic Models and Functional Units of Language Behavior,"
          (In) Directions in Psycholinguistics, Sheldon Rosenberg (ed.),
          New York, Macmillan, 29-40
Kurth, G.
1895-8   La frontière linguistique en Belgique et dans le nord de la France,
          Bruxelles, F. Hayez, imprimeur de l'Académie royale des scien-
          ces, des lettres et des beaux-arts de Belgique
Labov, W.
          Phonological Indices to Social Stratification, Paper presented to
          the 1963 Meeting of the American Anthropological Association,
          San Francisco
Lado, R.
  1961   Language Testing: The Construction and Use of Foreign Language
          Tests; a teacher's book, London, Longmans
Lambert, W. E.
  1955   "Measurement of the Linguistic Dominance of Bilinguals," The
          Journal of Abnormal and Social Psychology 50, 197-200
-----, Havelka, J. & Crosby, C.
  1958   "The Influence of Language-Acquisition Contexts on Bilingualism,"
          Journal of Abnormal and Social Psychology 56, 239-244

  1963   "Psychological Approaches in the Study of Language, Part II; on
          second language learning and bilingualism," The Modern Language
          Journal 47, 114-121
Learned, M. D.
  1889   The Pennsylvania German Dialect, Baltimore I. Friedenwald

Legros, E.
    1948   La frontière des dialectes romans en Belgique, Liège, Vaillant
            Carmanne, (Commission royale de toponymie et de dialectologie,
            section wallonne, Mémoires no 4)
Leisi, E.
    1961   Der Wortinhalt, seine Struktur im Deutschen und Englischen 2,
            erweiterte Hufl, Heidelberg, Quelle und Meyer
Lewis, E. G.
    1964   "Conditions Affecting the Reception of an Official (Second/Foreign)
            Language, in Symposium on Multilingualism; second meeting of
            the Inter-African Committee on Linguistics, London, Committee
            for Technical Cooperation in Africa, 83-102
Luelsdorff, P. A.
    1966   "Applicational Generative Grammar," Lingua 16, 225-237
Mackey, W. F.
    1953   "Bilingualism and Linguistic Structure," Culture 14, 143-149

    1965a   Language Teaching Analysis, London, Longmans

    1965b   "Bilingual Interference; its analysis and measurement," The Journal
            of Communication 15, 239-249

    1966   "The Measurement of Bilingual Behavior," Canadian Psychologist 7,
            75-92
Maclay, H. & Sleator, M. D.
    1960   "Responses to Language; Judgments of grammaticalness," Interna-
            tional Journal of American Linguistics 26, 4, 275-282
Malherbe, E. G.
    1946   The Bilingual School; a study of bilingualism in South Africa,
            London, New York, Longmans, Green
Meillet, A.
    1921   Linguistique historique et linguistique générale, Paris, E. Champion
Nichol, L.
    1939   "Réalités psycho-sociales et degrés du bilinguisme," (In) 5e Congrès
            des linguistes, réponses au questionnaire, Bruges, 32-33
Oksaar, E.
    1961   "Kaksikielisyyden ongelmaste," Virittäjä 65, 388-395

    1963   "Om tvasprakighetens Problematik," Spraklärarnas Medlemsblad
            19, Stockholm, 1-20
Pap, L.
    1949   Portuguese-American Speech; an outline of speech conditions among
            Portuguese immigrants in New England and elsewhere in the U-
            nited States, New York, King's Crown Press

Paul, H.
1920   Prinzipien der sprachgeschichte, Halle A. S., M. Niemeyer
Pée, W.
1957   Anderhalve eeuw taalgrensverschuiwing en taaltoestand in Frans-
        Vlaanderen; lezing, gehouden voor de Dialecten commissie der
        Koninkligke Nederlandse Akademie van Wetenschappen op 23
        Juni 1956, Amsterdam, Noord-Hollandsche Uity. Mij.
Petri, F.
1937   Germanisches volkserbe in Wallonien und Nordfrankreich, Bonn,
        Ludwig Röhrscheid verlag
Plath, W.
1938   "Mathematical Linguistics," (In) Trends in European and American
        Linguistics 1930-1960, Edited on the occasion of the ninth Inter-
        national Congress of Linguists, C. Mohrmann, A. Sommerfelt &
        Joshua Whatmough (eds.), Utrecht, Spectrum, 1963, 21-57
Pritzwald, K. S. von
1938   "Sprachwissenschaftliche Minderkeitenforschung; ein Arbeitsplan
        und eine Statistik," Woerter und Sachen 1, 52-72
Ray, P. S.
1962   "Language Standardization," (In) Study of the Role of Second Lan-
        guages in Asia, Africa, and Latin America, Frank A. Rice (ed.)
        Washington, Centre for Applied Linguistics of the Modern Lan-
        guage Association of America, 91-104
Remacle, L.
1943   "Bilinguisme et orthophonie," Bulletin de la Commission royale de
        toponymie et de dialectologie 17, 115-136

1948   "La structure interne du wallon et l'influence germanique," Bulle-
        tin de la Commission royale de toponymie et de dialectologie 22,
        353-397

1952   Syntaxe du parler wallon de la Gleize, 3 vols., Paris, Les Belles
        Lettres, 56-60
Renard, R.
1965   L'enseignement des langues vivantes par la méthode audio-visuelle
        et structuro-globale de Saint-Cloud-Zagreb, Bruxelles, Didier
Reuning, K.
1941   Joy and Freude; a comparative study of the linguistic field of pleas-
        urable emotions in English and German, Swarthmore, Pennsylvania,
        distributed by the Swarthmore College bookstore
Ronjat, J.
1913   Le développement du langage observé chez un enfant bilingue,
        Paris, H. Champion
Ruke-Drawina, F.
1967   Mehrsprachigkeit im Vorschulalter, Lund

Saer, H.
1931   "An Experimental Inquiry into the Education of Bilingual Peoples,"
         (In) Education in a Changing Commonwealth, Wyatt Rawson (ed.)
         London, the New Education Fellowship, 116-121
Saporta, S. & Bastian, J. R. (eds.)
1961   Psycholinguistics; A Book of Readings, New York, Holt Rinehart &
         Winston
-----, Brown, R. E. & Wolfe, D. W.
1959   "Toward the Quantification of Phonic Interference," Language and
         Speech 2, 205-210
Schuchardt, H. E. M.
1922   Hugo Schuchardt-brevier; ein vademekum der allgemeinen
         sprachwissenschaft, als festgabe zum 80. gebrtstag des meisters
         zusammengestellt und eingeleitet, von Leo Spitzer...Mit einem
         porträt Hugo Schuchardts... Halle (Salle), M. Niemeyer
Siertsema, B.
1959a   "Stress and Tone in Yoruba Word Composition," Lingua 8, 385-402

1959b   A Test in Phonetics; 500 questions and answers on English Pronoun-
         ciation and how to teach it in West Africa, The Hague, M. Nijhoff
         Nijhoff

1962   "Timbre, Pitch and Intonation," Lingua 11, 388-398
Smith, M. E.
1939   "Some Light on the Problem of Bilingualism as Found from a Study
         of the Progress in Mastery of English among Pre-School Children
         of Non-American Ancestry in Hawaii," Genetic Psychology Mo-
         nographs 21, 110-284
Sommerfelt, A.
1957   "Phonetics and Sociology," (In) Manual of Phonetics, E. Kaiser
         (ed.), Amsterdam, North-Holland Publishing Co., 364-371
Springer, O.
1943   "The study of the Pennsylvania German Dialect," Journal of Eng-
         lish and Germanic Philology 42, 1-39
Stengers, J.
1959   "La formation de la frontière linguistique en Belgique, ou de la lé-
         gitimité de l'hypothèse historique", Bruxelles - Berckem,
         Latomus Revue d'Etudes latines (Collection Latomus no 41)
Stewart, W. A.
1962   "An Outline of Linguistic Typology for Describing Multilingualism,"
         (In) Study of the Role of Second Languages in Asia, Africa, and
         Latin America, F. A. Rice (ed.), Washington, Centre for Applied
         Linguistics of the Modern Language Association of America, 15-25
Strain, J. E.
1963   "Difficulties in Measuring Pronunciation Improvement," Language
         Learning 13, 27-224

Taillon, L.
1959   Diversité des langues et bilinguisme, 2e éd. Montréal, les Editions de l'Atelier

Taute, B.
1948   Die belaping van die mondelinge beheer van sckoolkinders oor die korrelasies tussen hierdie bekeer en sekere bekwaamhede en faktore ('n voorlopige ondersoek), Kaapstad, Nasionale Pers, Beperk

Toussaint, M.
1955   La frontière linguistique en Lorraine; les fluctuations et la délimitation actuelle des langues française et germanique dans la Moselle, Paris, A. & J. Picard

Ullman, S.
1964   Language and Style; collected papers, New York, Barnes & Noble

Van Loey, A.
1951   "Tweetaligheid," (In) Handelingen van het 19de Vlaamse Filologengencongress, Brussel, 21-32

Van Doorne, A.
1939   "De Franse woorden in het dialect van Wingene," Handelingen van de Koninklijke Commissie voor Toponymie en Dialectologie 13, 297-360

Verheyen, J. E.
1928   "Le bilinguisme en Belgique," (In) Le bilinguisme et l'éducation, travaux de la Conférence internationale tenue à Luxembourg, Genève, Luxembourg, Maison du Livre, 137-145

Verlinden, C.
1955   Les origines de la frontière linguistique en Belgique et la colonisation franque, Bruxelles, Renaissance du Livre

Vildomec, V.
1963   Multilingualism Leyden, A. W. Sythoff

Vogt, H.
1949   "Dans quelles conditions et dans quelles limites peut s'exercer sur le système morphologique d'une langue l'action du système morphologique d'une autre langue? Et de quelles conséquences sont ces actions pour l'accession des langues moins évoluées au rôle de langues de culture? (In) Actes du sixième congrès international des linguistes, Paris, librairie C. Klincksieck, 31-40

1954   "Language Contacts," Word 10, 364-374

Warland, J.
1940   Glossar und grammatik der germanischen lehnwörter in der wallonischen mundart Malmedys, Liège, Faculté de philosophie et lettres

----
1935   "Le genre grammatical des substantifs wallons d'origine germanique", Bulletin du dictionnaire wallon 20, 53-86

1943   "Bild und Bildung der germanisch - romanischen Sprachgrenze in
          Belgien," (In) Album Verdeyen, Brussel - Manteau, & Den Haag,
          Nijhoff, 387-398

Weinreich, U.
1953   Languages in Contact; findings and problems, New York, Linguistic
          Circle of New York (Series: Linguistic Circle of New York,
          Publications, No. 1)

1955   "The Norwegian Language in America, a Study in Bilingual Be-
          havior," by Einar Haugen, Reviewed by Uriel Weinreich, Word
          11, 165-168

1957   "On the Description of Phonic Interference," Word 13, 1-11

1966   "Explorations in Semantic Theory," (In) Current Trends in Linguis-
          tics III; theoretical foundations, Thomas A. Sebeck (ed.), The
          Hague, Mouton, 395-477

Weijnen, A.
1949   Tweetaligheid, Tilburg
Weiss, A. von
1959   Hauptprobleme der Zweisprachigkeit; eine Untersuchung auf Grund
          deutsch/estnischen Materials, Heidelberg, C. Winter
Whitney, W. D.
1881   "On Mixture in Language," Transactions of the American Philolo-
          gical Association 12, 1-26

Wind, B.
1937   "Les contributions néerlandaises au vocabulaire du français belge",
          Neophilologus 23, 81-98, 161-167
Windisch, E.
1897   "Zur Theorie der Mischsprachen und Lehnworter," Verhandlungen
          der Sächsischen Gesellschaft der Wissenschaften 49, 101-126
Winthrop, H.
1966   "A Proposed Model and Procedure for Studying Message Distortion
          in Translation," Linguistics 22, 98-112
Wyatt, J. L.
1966   "Contrastive Analysis Via the Chomskyan Verb-Phrase Formula,"
          Language Learning 16, 41-48
Yamagiwa, J. K.
1956-7   "A Check-List of Tests for Various Types of Proficiency in a Foreign
          Language," Language Learning 7, 3-4, 99-124

4

HOW CAN WE MEASURE THE ROLES WHICH A BILINGUAL'S LANGUAGES
PLAY IN HIS EVERYDAY BEHAVIOUR?

COMMENT DEFINIR ET MESURER LE ROLE DES LANGUES D'UN BILINGUE
DANS SON COMPORTEMENT QUOTIDIEN?

THEME

Robert Cooper

When a group is in the process of culture contact, the functions formerly served by one language sometimes come to be divided between two or more (Barker 1947). Interest in the resulting functional specialization of languages or language varieties is a relatively recent phenomenon, although such differentiation is probably as old as multilingualism itself. Haugen (1966), for example, points out that in classical Greece the "dialects" referred to written varieties of Greek which were each associated with a specific literary use, e.g., Ionic for history and Attic for tragedy. The present paper reports some current attempts to devise techniques for the measurement and description of a bilingual's differential use of two languages, i.e., his language choice behavior within a bilingual speech community.

Functional Typologies

Among those who have discussed the intragroup functional specialization of language varieties are West (1926), Kloss (1929), Schmidt-Rohr (1933), Frey (1945), Barker (1947), Weinreich (1952, 1953), Haugen (1956), Ferguson (1959), Mackey (1962, 1966), Fishman (1964, 1965), and Reimen (1965). A number of classificatory schemes have been used to describe such specialization, and these differ both in the number and type of functions specified. Reimen, for example, employed 20 functional categories to describe the language choice behavior of bilinguals in Luxembourg, whereas Frey used only three to describe that of the Pennsylvania Dutch. Functions have been specified in terms of various dimensions, including those of institutional context, domain, or sphere of activity, e.g., family, church, school; medium of communication, e.g., the press, letters, sermons; mood or style, e.g., formal informal; topic, e.g., technical, nontechnical; and interpersonal distance, e.g., intimate, non-intimate.

One of the best known discussions of functional specialization is that of Ferguson, who described the division of labor performed by pairs of language varieties in four settings of stables, intragroup bilingualism. He noted that in each case one variety was associated with formality, ritual and literary tradition, whereas the other was associated with informality, intimacy, and ordinary, everyday affairs. Barker's description of the language usage of Mexican-Americans in Tuscon, Arizona employed a fourfold division of social functions: intimate or familial, informal, formal, and intergroup. Weinreich's classification (1952) used seven categories: literature, church, administration, school, public addresses, family, and everyday business. In the following diagram (figure 1) Weinreich represented the functional differentiation in Switzerland between Schwyzertutsch and Standard German. The functional categories were arranged along a continuum of conservatory usage, with literature the category use of Schwyzertutsch, the area with thin stripes denotes the proportion of use of the standard language, and the area of cross hatching represents the functional overlapping of the standard and the dialect.

Figure 1: Functional Division between Schwyzertutsch
             and Standard German (from Weinreich 1952
             p.449)

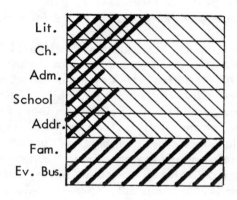

Most of the functional classifications which have been proposed were made to describe bilingual usage in specific speech communities. The differences which can be observed in the various classificatory schemes suggest what has been pointed out before, namely that there is probably no unvarying set of language functions found in all speech communities (Hymes 1962; Fishman 1964)

Previous Psychological Measures of Bilingual Behavior

Inasmuch as the techniques which the present paper describes are "psychological" in their methodological orientation and in their application to the measurement of individual differences, we shall attempt to relate them to previous psychological investigations of bilingual performance.(1)

Fishman (in press) has characterized most previous psychological measures of the verbal behavior of bilinguals as undifferentiated with respect to functional categories or to the situational contexts which serve as the settings for

(1) For a recent review of psychological measures of bilingual performance,
     see Macnamara (1967)

language use. There have been few attempts to relate the verbal traits which have been studied (such as degree of bilingualism, linguistic independence, and the coordinateness of semantic systems) to social correlates. Psychologists, in other words, have usually studied the verbal behavior of individual bilinguals as if the latter were self-contained units and not part of a social system with rules for appropriate language usage.

Although there have been few if any psychological measurements of bilingual performance which have been tied to an explicit sociolinguistic model, not all psychologists have been insensitive to the complexity of bilingual performance or to its relationship to social variables. Saer (1931), for example, selected the stimulus words for her bilingual word association experiment from categories which represented objects, persons, and situations which "should have entered significantly into the life of the child by the time he was three years of age."(2) The bilingual ratios derived from her data were not applied to the categories themselves, however, but to the individual items comprising each category.

The work of another early investigation, Hoffman (1934), appears to have been based on at least an implicit assumption that the use of two languages may involve functional differentiation. He devised a "bilingual background" questionnaire for New York City school children, which asked them to rate the degree with which languages other than English were used, for various purposes, by themselves and by certain relatives (for example, "Do the following read any newspaper in a language other than English? a) Father, b) Mother, c) You"). For each person and purpose specified, the respondent was asked to rate non-English usage on a five-point scale ("never, sometimes, often, mostly, always"). As Haugen (1956) points out, however, only a single global bilingual score was computed for an individual's ratings, although these responses covered many different activities which were to some extent incommensurable. No distinction was made between intergroup and intragroup bilingualism nor was a model of domain appropriate usage followed.

An explicit recognition of functional differentiation in the language usage of bilinguals has been demonstrated in the recent work of at least two psychologists, Herman (1961) and Ervin-Tripp (1964). Herman formulated several hypotheses to account for bilingual language choice behavior. He advanced these in terms of three variables: background situation, personal needs, and immediate situation. The speech behavior of immigrants in Israel was used to illustrate and test his views.

Ervin-Tripp reviewed some of the variables employed in sociolinguistic research, and she experimentally manipulated three of them—topic, listener, and code—in a study of the speech behavior of Japanese-American bilingual

---

(2)   The categories employed by Saer were as follows: members of the family, familiar animals, natural phenomena, activities, moral situations, the house, and eating and drinking.

women. She found that her subjects' speech was disrupted when they were asked to speak in English about Japanese topics to Japanese interlocutors. More hesitation pauses, deviant syntax, and borrowing of Japanese words were found when the social rule requiring the use of Japanese for this combination of topic and listener was artificially suspended.

Three Sociolinguistic Variables

If most psychological measurements of bilingual verbal behavior have not been related to socially relevant dimensions, at least part of this failure can be attributed to the lack of a generally accepted sociolinguistic theory which could serve as a framework for psychological investigation. The model which serves as the framework for the techniques reported in the present paper has been elaborated by Fishman (1964, 1965, in press) and draws upon several constructs, notably those of the dominance configuration and domains of language use, as suggested by Schmidt-Rohr (1933) and reintroduced by Weinreich (1953), and those of the social situation and interaction type as formulated by Gumperz (1964) and Blom and Gumperz (1966).

The techniques to be reported have been constructed within a framework formed by three of the variables in this model: domain, role-relationship, and interaction type. Each of these constructs will be briefly described in connection with the specific techniques related to it.

Some Psychological Measures of Language Choice Behavior

The techniques to be reported can be classified into two types: those that can be used to investigate the relationship between language choice behavior and a single variable of the sociolinguistic model and those that can be used to measure the relationship between performance and the combined effect of more than one of the variables. These classifications are referred to as "univariate" and "multivariate" techniques, respectively. The speech community upon which the development of these techniques has been focussed is that of the Puerto Rican community in greater New York. The preparation of the techniques has been part of a larger venture which is seeking to develop integrated measures of bilingual behavior by means of psychological, sociological, and linguistic methods.(3) Thus, the psychological techniques have been tried out with bilinguals for whom sociological and linguistic data pertaining to bilingualism have also been gathered, thereby affording an opportunity to relate psychological data to other relevant criteria.

---

(3) United States Department of Health, Education, and Welfare. Office of Education. Contract No. 6-2817. "The measurement and description of language dominance in bilinguals". Joshua A. Fishman, Yeshiva University, Project Director.

Univariate Techniques - Domain

The univariate techniques have been devised to assess the relationship between language choice behavior and the most abstract of the three variables, domain. By domain is meant an institutional context, sphere of activity, or set of interactions for which implicit rules of appropriate behavior exist. Examples of domains (which must be empirically determined for any speech community) might be home, neighborhood, church, school, and work sphere.

According to the model we are employing, the domains of language use represent an arena not only for speech but also for the enactment of community values. In terms of this model, language varieties are maintained within a community when each is associated with a complementary set of community values. For example, one set or "value cluster" might be described in terms of participation in high culture and aspiration toward social mobility. Another set might be described in terms of the maintenance of comradeship, intimacy, and solidarity. A bilingual's identification with each value cluster results in his use of the language variety associated with it. He typically acts out each set of values and employs each language within a corresponding set of domains. For example, the values of solidarity, along with the use of one language, might be enacted most frequently or typically in the domains of home and neighborhood, whereas the values of high culture and mobility, along with the use of the other language, might be enacted most characteristically in the domains of school, church, and work.

Five univariate techniques, devised to explore the relationship between language choice behavior and the domains of language use have been constructed and are in the process of being tried out. These are word naming, picture naming, word association, word recall, and word frequency rating. All but the last of these have been previously used or suggested for the measurement of degree of bilingualism. Inasmuch as the first four devices have been used only in connection with the measurement of a trait which has been viewed as global and undifferentiated, our work with them represents an attempt to contextualize them so that a bilingual's performance on these tests can reflect differences in his language use associated with different contexts or situational domains.

The techniques have been contextualized in terms of five domains: home, school, church, work sphere, and neighborhood. It should be emphasized that these represent hypotheses as to the actual situational domains of Puerto Rican life in New York City. These may later be added to, modified, collapsed, or omitted on the basis of ongoing ethnographic research.

Word Naming. In the word naming task, respondents were asked to name, in English and in Spanish, as many objects or concepts appropriate to a given situational domain as they could within a one-minute time limit, for example, items found in a kitchen or subjects which can be studied in school. The number of words produced in each language is compared by domain. The advantage of this technique over the other univariate devices to be described is that the respondent structures the domain himself. In the other univariate tasks, the investigator must provide items (pictures or discrete words) that "represent" each context.

Picture Naming. Macnamara (1967) found that a task which required bilingual respondents to supply in each language as many synonymous words or phrases as possible for certain stimulus words was an excellent predictor of degree of experience with each language when experience was globally defined. His task has been adapted via a picture naming technique. Five sets of pictures have been collected, each set consisting of illustrations of objects, activities, or personnel that appear to be appropriate to a given domain. Respondents were asked to give as many different ways as possible of naming or labelling each picture in both languages. The number of synonymous words or phrases is compared by language and domain.

Word Association. Five sets of fifteen words have been compiled in English and Spanish. Each set consists of names of objects, activities, or personnel that seem to be appropriate to a given domain, i.e., to have a higher frequency of use in that domain (or in talking about that domain) than in the others. An attempt was made to match the English and Spanish sets for average word frequency as tabulated by published word counts.(4) The words representing a domain in one language have from 9 to 12 translation equivalents in the other. The items have been checked with Puerto Rican informants to make sure the words are in active use in the Puerto Rican community in Greater New York. The word lists were used for both discrete and continuous word association tasks. In the former, the respondent was asked to give the first word that came to mind when he heard the stimulus word. His average speed of response by language and domain is computed. In the continuous word association task, he was asked to give as many words as came to mind when he heard the stimulus word. The total number of words produced by language and domain is counted. In both tasks, the words were presented aurally. In the continuous association task, however, only a few words from each list were used to present a domain in order to prevent too great an overlapping of responses.

Recall. The word lists employed in the discrete word association task were also used to assess the respondent's ability to recall words in each language. The items representing a given domain were read off by the interviewer and the respondent was asked to recall as many as he could. The number of words recalled is counted by domain and by language.

Word Frequency Rating. The word frequency rating task was suggested by the finding that English speaking monolinguals can rank the frequency of occurrence of English words with a relatively high degree of agreement with the

-----

(4) The attempt to match lists for word frequency may have been a somewhat futile enterprise inasmuch as the published frequencies may not have resembled the frequencies of oral usage in the Puerto Rican community of New York. The published counts employed were those by Thorndike and Lorge (1944) and Eaton (1961) for Spanish.

Thorndike-Lorge frequency counts (Howes 1954; Carroll 1966). The word lists which were employed in the association and recall tasks were also used for the frequency rating task. The frequency that was rated was not the word's occurrence in terms of some kind of community norm (5) but instead the degree to which the respondent himself heard or uttered the word. It is plausible that the relative frequency with which he encountered a domain appropriate set of words in two languages will provide an index of his relative use of each language in that domain. Unlike the other univariate tasks, which elicit responses that are assumed to reflect practice (i.e., greater use of one language in a given domain is assumed to result in more responses or faster responses to domain appropriate stimuli in that language), the word frequency task provides an estimate of practice by means of a self-report technique.

In the word frequency rating task, the items were presented either aurally or in paper and pencil form to the respondent, who rated the frequency with which he encountered them on an eight-point scale. The points on the rating scale are bunched at the higher frequencies and spread out at the lower frequencies in order to correspond somewhat to the skewed distributions that are typically observed in word frequency counts.

An Example.(6) The performance of a small group of respondents on the word frequency estimation task, during a preliminary tryout, can be described to provide an example of the type of data gathered by the univariate techniques. The respondents were adolescent boys attending a Catholic high school in New York City. They were members of that school's chapter of a city-wide organization of high school and college clubs which had been formed to encourage Puerto Rican youngsters to continue their education, promote pride in the Puerto Rican heritage, and develop leadership within the local Puerto Rican community. The respondents were presented with the word frequency estimation task in paper and pencil form. Half the group rated the Spanish list first and half rated the English list first. Their scores are summarized, by domain and by language, in table 1. For the English list, the domain with the highest average frequency rating was school, whereas for the Spanish list, the domain with the highest average rating was home. Such a result would not be unexpected. Note, however, that the difference between the average frequency ratings for the English and Spanish lists, where all items are combined, was slight.

----

(5)   However, if word frequency counts were available for English and Spanish oral usage in the New York City Puerto Rican community, the degree to which a respondent could predict these frequencies might indicate the degree of his participation in that community.

(6)   (Editor's note) In the original working paper prepared for the seminar, Dr. Cooper cited the example contained in the appendix on pp. 207-208. The Example in the final text (pp. 198-199) was presented orally.

Table 1: Summary Data, Word Frequency Rating Scores (N = 8)

Language	Item	Domain					
		Home	Neigh.	Church	Work	School	Total
Spanish	X	5.7	4.2	3.9	4.1	5.0	4.6
	SD	1.4	1.3	1.3	1.4	1.6	1.3
English	X	5.7	4.4	4.7	4.4	6.1	5.1
	SD	1.1	1.3	1.1	1.2	.8	1.1

Note: — Words were rated on the following scales: 7 = more than once a day,
6 = once a day, 5 = every other day, 4 = once a week, 3 = once a
week, 2 = once a month, 1 = less than once a month, 0 = never.

The difference between the average total English and Spanish ratings was
in fact not statistically significant. An analysis of variance of the scores, presented in table 2, indicates that there was no significant main effect for language. That is, variation in item ratings cannot be attributed to the effect of
the language of the item alone. However, a significant main effect was observed for domain, which is to say that variation in item ratings was due at
least in part to differences in the domains involved. We can thus reject the
hypothesis that the semantic items comprising the different domains were all
drawn from the same pool or field. More important, a significant interaction
between domain and language was observed. That is, deviations of individual
item ratings from the average of all ratings combined were due not to the effect
of domain acting alone but to the joint effect of domain and language acting
together. Stated in another way, the coincidence of language and domain produced systematic variation in the ratings. We can reject the hypothesis then,
that the between-language differences by domain were all equal. The extent
to which English and Spanish ratings differed depended on the domain from
which the items were drawn.

The average ratings by language, all items combined, may be compared
to the scores obtained from global, undifferentiated tests of bilingual performance. Note that in the present example no statistically significant difference
in the total language average ratings was observed. Such a finding would be
analogous to a "balanced" ratio obtained from a task on which the score in one
language equalled the score in the other. In the present example, however,
when the total "global" scores were broken down into componential subscores,
obtained in an attempt to contextualize global performance, between-language
differences emerged. Such a preliminary finding supports the observation that
bilingual tasks which elicit global, undifferentiated, uncontextualized

performance may be insufficiently revealing of bilingual functioning and may thus mask whatever differences exist (Fishman 1964; in press).

Table 2: Analysis of Variance of Word Frequency Rating Scores

Source of variation	d.f.	Sum of squares	Mean square	F	F .95
Subjects	7	23382	3340		
Language	1	1189	1189	3.03	5.59
L X S	7	2750	393		
Domain	4	7575	1894	34.44	2.71
D X S	28	1548	55		
L X D	4	535	134	3.44	2.71
L X D X S	28	1082	39		

Multivariate Techniques – Domain, Role Relationship, and Interaction Type

The multivariate techniques have been devised to tap the relationship between language choice behavior and the combined effect of more than one of the sociolinguistic constructs of our framework: domain, role relationship, and interaction type.

In terms of the model we are following, language usage and identification with community values are, typically, simultaneously realized in a corresponding set of domains. Each domain is comprised of a set of social situations, each of which is composed of combinations of specific times, settings, and role relationships.

A role relationship can be described in terms of the culturally defined set of mutual rights and obligations that constrains the interaction between two occupants of complementary statuses, as for example, between husband and wife, student and teacher, or father and son. Role relationship is one component of a social situation and is thus in some sense hierarchically related to the constructs of domain and value cluster, although the same role relationship can enter into more than one social situation and domain.

Bilingual role-relationships can be classified into two broad types of social network (Gumperz 1964). In "closed network" role relationships, behavior is constrained by a single, overriding set of norms which typically are realized in one language only. In "open network" role relationships, speakers are not so constrained. They can allude to alternative value systems, which can be realized in different languages.

Interaction type, a notion formulated by Gumperz (1964), refers to the saliency of status distinctions implied by the function of an interaction.

Gumperz distinguishes two types of interaction, "transactional" and "personal".
In transactional interactions, speakers enact a specific, socially defined task,
e.g., a job interview. In such encounters, the interlocutors "suspend their in-
dividuality" in order to act out the mutual obligations of their role relationship.
In personal interactions, on the other hand, speakers are free to express themselves as individuals rather than as participants in a socially defined task. The
relaxed conversation between two members of a peer group provides an example
of a personal interaction. With respect to each type of interaction, the choice
of language is easier to predict for transactional encounters, where the acting
out of the relevant statuses implies a given system of values. Language choice
becomes harder to predict for personal interactions—at least among members of
open networks, who can imply alternative views, interests, and values by
switching language.

The relationship among these constructs is diagrammed in figure 2. The
degree of abstractness of each construct is indicated by its vertical position,
with the most abstract at the top of the diagram and the least abstract at the
bottom. Each construct can be viewed as a potential source of variance accounting for language choice behavior.

As an example of these constructs, let us take a hypothetical conversation
between two New York City Puerto Rican high school students. They are talking in school, after class, and in English about a homework assignment. The
social situation in which they are participating can be described in terms of
the setting (classroom), time (school hours), and role relationship (fellow students). This social situation is one of a set of situations which are constrained
by a common set of behavioral norms and which comprise the domain of
"school", which in turn is one arena for the enactment of the value cluster
"high culture and social mobility". The students' role relationship is part of
an open network inasmuch as they also share another, complementary set of
values related to their participation in and identification with the Puerto Rican
community in New York. Should they switch from English to Spanish during
the present conversation, they could be alluding to that alternative set of community values and interactions. Their conversation about the homework constitutes a personal interaction inasmuch as they are speaking as individual in a
non status-stressing situation and not as participants in a socially defined task.
Again, it should be emphasized that the classifications employed to describe
the conversation in this example are hypothetical ones.

Two types of multivariate technique have been constructed, one a self-
report, the other a proficiency measure. The self-report technique was devised in an attempt to relate language choice behavior to two of the sociolinguistic constructs, domain and role relationship. The performance measure was
constructed to relate language choice to all three constructs.

Figure 2: Interaction constructs

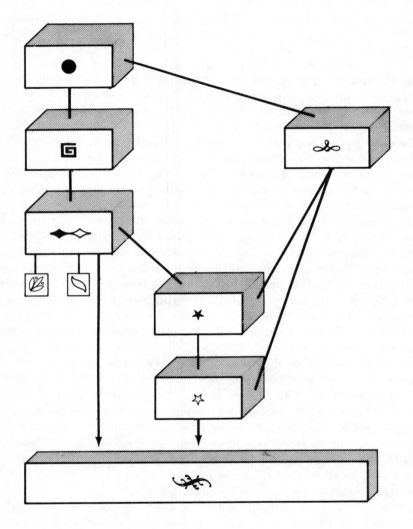

● Value Cluster - Set of community values characteristically enacted in a corresponding set of culturally defined, behavioral domains.

🄶 Domain - Cluster of social situations typically constrained by a common set of behavioral rules.

◆ Social Situation - Encounter defined by intersection of setting time, and role relationship.

✎ Network Type - (open and closed) Cluster of role relationships defined by extent to which they are governed by a single (or multiple) set of community values.

✶ Role Relationship - Set of culturally defined mutual rights and obligations.

✩ Interaction Type - (personal and transactional) Function of interaction defined by degree to which participants in social situation stress the mutual rights and obligations of their role relationship.

✎ TIME   ◗ SETTING   🦎 SPEECH

Spanish Usage Rating. In the Spanish usage rating procedure, the respondent was asked to rate the frequency with which he uses Spanish, with interlocutors who know both English and Spanish, in various domains. For example, he was asked to rate the frequency with he uses Spanish with fellow students at school, his brothers and sisters at home, and his friends in his neighborhood. We are interested here in the degree to which he uses Spanish not with all interlocutors but only with those who make it possible for language choice to exist, that is, where the constraints on language choice are not those of mutual intelligibility. For each domain, persons holding different role relationships with the respondent are specified in terms of sex and age. In this technique both domain and role relationship are specified in an attempt to account for the joint contribution of these constructs to language choice behavior.

Bilingual Conversation Technique. The multivariate proficiency tests employ as stimuli tape-recorded conversations representing a variety of social situations. The conversations were elicited from members of the Puerto Rican community of New York by means of role playing techniques. The elicitation procedure was typically as follows. A small group of friends, gathered in the home of one of the group, would be asked to agree upon a story-line for an encounter between bilingual Puerto Ricans in New York. The encounter had to represent a social situation commonly found in the New York Puerto Rican community and one which would require the use of both Spanish and English. After the "plot" had been determined, the substance of what was to be said (but rarely the exact words) was agreed upon. Next, the members of the group assigned the roles among themselves and acted out the story. The recorded conversation was then played back and if the group was not satisfied with the "naturalness" of the recording, the skit was redone. Thus, the group members acted as their own "writers" (although no scripts were used), directors, actors, and critics.

Respondents were asked to listen to a conversation and then to repeat as much as possible of what was said, using each language where it had been employed in the conversation. In addition, they were asked questions to determine their comprehension of both the surface (manifest) and latent (social) content of the conversation. Included were question concerning the appropriateness of the language choices made in each story. Respondents were also asked to repeat some of the routines which were used in the stories (such as greetings and invitations) and then to give equivalent routines in the other language. Thus, the bilingual conversation technique should permit analyses in terms of productivity, fluency, listening comprehension ability, and knowledge of stylistic (social) constraints upon the interpretation of conversations, and it should provide an opportunity for describing the covariation of these abilities, in both English and Spanish, with the three sociolinguistic constructs represented in the conversations.

Four Measurement Dimensions

The psychological measures described can be summarized in terms of four dimensions: the observer, the number of constructs specified or represented, the degree of "directness", and the trait measured. As for the first dimension, we can distinguish between retrospective observations made by the respondent about his own behavior and observations made by another about the respondent's ability to perform on a series of standardized tasks. Thus, we can dichotomize our techniques in terms of self-report (word frequency rating, Spanish usage rating) and test method. As for the second dimension, number of constructs specified, we have already characterized our techniques in terms of univariate and multivariate types. The third dimension, "directness", a quality noted by Macnamara (1967) in his discussion of tests of bilingual performance, refers to the degree to which the behavior elicited from the respondent (or the behavior on which the respondent is asked to report retrospectively) corresponds to the behavior in which we are ultimately interested. For example, the performance required by the multivariate bilingual conversation technique would, on its face, appear to bear a closer correspondence to the respondent's naturally occuring speech behavior .than would performance on the discrete word association task. Few if any respondents need to give speedy associations to discrete items of lexicon in their everyday behavior. All, however, must be able to interpret conversations heard in different social contexts. We can, therefore, characterize our measures as "direct" or "indirect" according to the extent to which the elicited behavior, or behavior reported on, resembles the criterion behavior. Finally, we can characterize our techniques according to whether the trait measured is one of proficiency or frequency of usage. The test methods employed provide measures of proficiency. The self-report methods provide measures of frequency of usage (although self-report techniques can be used to provide an estimate of proficiency as well). It is true that one might want to make inferences about frequency of usage from measures of proficiency, on the assumption that the greater the frequency of usage, the greater the "practice", and thus the greater the proficiency. Indeed, such an assumption provides the basis for our using proficiency measures to predict or estimate differential usage. However the two traits are theoretically distinct and probably are, at least in part, independent. The assignment of our techniques to each of the four dichotomized variables is presented in figure 3.

Summary

We have described some psychological techniques which have been constructed to investigate an individual's differential use of two languages or language varieties within a bilingual speech community. The techniques have been devised to reflect the influence of three sociolinguistic constructs: domain, role relationship, and interaction type. The measures have been tried out with members of the Puerto Rican speech community or Greater New York as part of a larger project which is collecting sociological and linguistic data from some of the same respondents, thereby providing an opportunity to compare and contrast the usefulness of the techniques which have been des-cribed.(7)

Figure 3: Classification of Reported Techniques in Terms of Four Dimensions

	Proficiency		Frequency of Usage	
	univariate	multivariate	univariate	multivariate
Self-Report				
direct				SUR
indirect			WFR	
Test Method				
direct		B. Conv.		
indirect	WN,WA,PN,R			

Note: — SUR = Spanish Usage Rating, WFR = Word Frequency Estimation
        Rating, B. Conv. = Bilingual Conversation, WN = Word Naming,
        WA = Word Association, PN = Picture Naming, R = Recall.

(7) The author gratefully acknowledges the helpful comments, on earlier drafts of this paper, of Joshua A. Fishman, John J. Gumperz, and John Macnamara.

Appendix

Table 1: Average Word Frequency Ratings, Respondent 14

Item	Domain				
	Home	School	Church	Work	Neighborhood
English	1.8	1.7	6.0	3.3	2.3
Spanish	2.0	2.4	6.9	3.8	3.2
Ratio (s-e) s	.10	.29	.13	.13	.19

Note: Rating of 1= "more than once a day". Rating of 7= "less than once a month".

Table 2: Correlations between Frequency Ratings of Translation Equivalents, Respondent 14

Item	Domain				
	Home	School	Church	Work	Neighborhood
r	.96	.10	-.02	.04	.7
number translation equivalents	12	10	11	11	12

The respondent is an eighteen-year-old college student, a native of New York City whose parents were born in Puerto Rico. She reported that she had learned both English and Spanish before she entered school. Spanish is restricted primarily to conversations with her parents, but she said that she also speaks in English to both parents.

In table 1 the highest rating ("more than once a day") is given the value of 1 and the lowest rating ("less than once a month"), the value of 7. For each domain her average English rating is subtracted from her average Spanish rating, and the difference is expressed as a ratio to the Spanish rating. Thus, positive ratios would be obtained if the respondent reported that English words were encountered more frequently than the Spanish words, and negative ratings would be obtained if the reverse were true. If no difference were reported a zero ratio would result.

Note that each domain received a higher rating in English than in Spanish. However, the resulting ratios are not constant. The smallest ratio was observed for "home" and the greatest for "school". These data suggest that she uses the least Spanish in school and the most Spanish at home, an influence which is consistent with her self-report.

When the ratings of translation equivalents were correlated for each domain list (table 2) substantially no relationship was found for the domains of school, church, or work sphere. For home and neighborhood however, the coefficients are statistically significant. That is, in these domains, translation equivalents tended to be ranked in the same order. Such coefficients may be useful in describing the relative compartmentalisation of English and Spanish in various situational domains. The significant coefficients observed in this example may suggest that the respondent engages in more bilingual switching in the domains of home and neighborhood than in the other situational domains. Again, this inference is not inconsistent with her self-report.

COMMENTARIES/COMMENTAIRES

Shirô Hattori

1. Until some hundred years ago Japan was a closed country and had no official intercourse or trade with Western countries: the shogunate government
of Tokugawa had been following an isolationist policy for more than two and a
half centuries. Since the Meiji Restoration our people have been doing their
utmost to catch up with the advanced occidental nations by endeavoring to absorb their culture including literature, the humanities, social and natural
sciences, medicine and all sorts of technology. However except for the fact
that a number of students went to Europe and America and a few Western teachers came or were invited to our country, this was done primarily through books.

We, Japanese, have a thousand-year-old tradition of learning foreign languages through books; and again, a firm tradition of learning English, French
and German as written languages has been established during the last hundred
years. Especially before the end of the World War II, the Japanese intelligent-
sia were able to read Western books, though most of them could not speak foreign languages. At the same time, owing to compulsory primary education,
which has been given in Japanese and has developed with an unparalleled ra-
pidity among our people, illiteracy has been almost exterminated. On the
other hand, the recent development of radio, talking movies and television has
greatly helped the diffusion of standard spoken Japanese all over Japan and now
it is possible to say that all persons in our country are able to communicate with
each other orally. In this sense, pre-war Japan was an exceptionally monolingual country, so I was unable to imagine such a serious problem of bilingualism as is found in Canada.

On the other hand, however, it could be said that we are endeavoring to
make bilingualism or multilingualism grow in our country. We are trying to
improve the methods of teaching foreign languages by adopting an oral approach, and are trying to develop it in order to teach students and others to
speak them. Therefore, we look forward with great interest to the publication
of the proceedings of this International Seminar.

However, if we could successfully foster bilingualism in Japan, this extremely difficult task would result in a bilingualism or multilingualism quite
different from that of present-day Canada, because every Japanese would have
full command of the national language, Japanese.

For this reason, to my regret I am unable to contribute to this Seminar by
presenting to you Japanese examples of bilingualism. However, I have some
experience of observing peculiar cases of bilingualism and will give some

comments on Doctor Cooper's paper in terms of these examples.

2. It seems to me very common for the language of a minority without prestige to be influenced by that of the more privileged majority, and to assimilate in the course of time more and more to the latter. It is a well-known fact
that the second generation of immigrants who make up the minority group
usually speak the language of their parents more or less imperfectly, especially
when they are educated in the schools of the majority group.

Thus I was able to observe the speech behavior of the Tatars when I stayed
in northern Manchuria for about two and half years from 1933 till 1936, studying the Altaic languages there. Besides the Mongol tribes and various small
Tungusic-speaking groups, there lived several hundred Tatars among the Russian immigrants, making their minority communities in Harbin, Hailar and other
cities. They were bilinguals although the older people spoke bad Russian.
They had their own primary schools at least in Harbin and Hailar, and children
were educated there in Tatar which is a language quite different from Russian,
and was written in Arabic script. They usually spoke Tatar at home, so that
all the children were able to speak it fluently. At the same time they learned
to speak Russian too, because they also played with Russian children. If they
wanted to receive higher education, they were obliged to enter Russian high-
schools and colleges. I met several young Tatars who had received high-school
or college education, and noticed the tendency that the younger they were, the
purer the accent of their Russian. Some of these young people spoke Tatar and
Russian which were mutually influenced to some extent not only in vocabulary
but also in phonology and grammar. For instance, Tatar and Russian rounded
mid-back vowels are fairly different from each other, the Tatar vowel being
half-closed, out-back and lax [e] in IPA, while the Russian one in a
stressed syllable is fairly open, fully back and rather tense [ɔ] . For instance,
[tette] "he took it", [terde] "he stood up" in Tatar, [ktɔ] "who", [doˈtgə]
"for a long while" in Russian. The aforementioned Tatar youth, however, pronounced instead a vowel which was something in between the two, i.e., [o̞]
both in Tatar and in Russian. They were unable to pronounce e.g. the Russian
word [ktɔ] but pronounced [kto̞] instead, and pronounced e.g. the Tatar
words [tette][terde] as [to̞tto̞][to̞rdo̞] , especially when asked to utter
them distinctly. Similarly, they had only one hushing sound which was something
in between the Tatar apico-alveolar [ʃ] and the Russian retroflex [ʂ].
The grammar of their Tatar was influenced by Russian especially in word order.
For example, they said [kiræk kitærgæ] "necessary to go" instead of the
genuine Tatar expression [kitærgæ kiræk] "to go, necessary", because
the usual Russian word order is nado pojitti "necessary to go". I will give you
another remarkable example. I found such an utterance:

[bar -də   yəz -mə   bøtøn ɟir-lər -egez-gæ
  go/(Past)/you/ (?)/ all/place/(pl)/ your / to/

qaja   tijeʃ   idegez   barəγa]
where/ obliged/ you were/ to go

"Did you go everywhere you were supposed to go?"

The genuine Tatar utterance would be something like:

[bar -acaq bøtøn   ɟir -lær   -egez -gæ
  go/should/   all/   place/(plural)/ your/   to/

  bar - də   -yez/   -mə]
  go/ (Past)/ you/   (?)

In this way it seemed that the morphology was in general untouched, and they usually did not decline the borrowed Russian adjectives. However, they freely borrowed such Russian emphatic particles as ze (Tatar [ʒe]) and to (Tatar [te] For instance, [minʒe baram] "I will go" (Russian javze pojdu), [minte belmim] "I don't know" (Russian ja-to ne znaju). They spoke Tatar fluently when they were engaged in daily conversation, but they had to switch it into Russian when the topic concerned higher culture, simply because their Tatar lexicon was very poor in this respect and did not have words enough to express such matters. This is why the Tatar youth, when they felt it necessary or desirable, spoke Russian to each other even at home.

I should like to ask Mr. Cooper and others to investigate whether one can detect or not such phenomena as this in the Spanish language of the younger generation of the Puerto Rican community in New York. It seems to me necessary at least to add the item topic to the right of Social situation in Figure 1 on page 202.

At the same time I have received the impression that Dr. Cooper assumes that the English and the Spanish of the younger Puerto Rican generation were independent languages, and the structures had no mutual influence.
3.   If the minority group of immigrants is not reinforced with new-comers from their home land, the third generation will speak their mother tongue imperfectly or even ungrammatically, and if the situation remains the same the final result will be complete assimilation to the majority language, that is, the extinction of this minority language. Similar process of extinction have apparently taken place in the case of Manchu and Ainu. Manchu, a Tungusic language in northeastern China is completely extinct and Ainu in northern Japan is on the point of extinction. In 1955 and 1956 we searched for good informants all over Hokkaido, the northern-most island of Japan, and found only a few good speakers of Ainu, all of them very old people.

Before a language dies out completely, however, it sometimes happens that the language survives for a while as a secret jargon. In this case it need not preserve its linguistic system as a whole. A secret jargon usually is a language with its own peculiar basic and special vocabulary, but its phonology and grammar (especially syntax) are the same as those of the ordinary language, so that the aforementioned secret language which is the continuation of the minority language can have the phonology and grammar of the majority language to which it has assimilated.

I think this is the case with Afghanistan. The Moghols are a people of the Mongol origin who are supposed to be descendants of the garrison of Gengis Khan. When I made an expedition to the district east to Herat in northwestern Afghanistan in 1961, I found them to be bilingual between Persian and Moghol. While their Persian was clearly a simple regional variety of Persian and did not exhibit Moghol influence, I noticed, however, that the phonology and syntax of their so-called Moghol language were the same as those of their Persian dialect, and that the only difference between them was the fact that their Moghol had preserved some morphological features and several hundred non-Persian i.e. Moghol words in its basic lexicon. It seemed to me very probable that the sociolinguistic function of Moghol was rather that of a secret jargon. Even the Ainu sometimes use several Ainu words in their own Japanese utterances in order to make them incomprehensible to the Japanese bystanders. The aforementioned Tatars often used Tatar for this purpose, too.

In order to describe correctly this kind of speech behavior, I think we have to add to Dr. Cooper's three sociolinguistic constructs, i.e. domain, role-relationship and interaction type, a fourth, i.e. the presence of third person(s).

The acts of speech are conducted by the addresser with the intention to communicate his message to the addressee. If someone nearby is able to hear his utterance, the addresser may or may not want him to understand it. In case the bystander does not understand the minority language, the addresser will utter his message in the majority language when he wants or permits the third person to understand it or when he does not want to be impolite, but he will utter it in the minority language when he does not want the bystander to understand it. In the latter case, the minority language functions as a secret jargon.

When only the addressee who understands both languages is present, the addresser can switch languages at will. In such a situation it is possible to imagine such an extreme case in which the addresser mixes up, in very relaxed chatter, the words of the two languages to a great extent, because he only intends to communicate with the addressee and need not care in any way about the "purity" of the medium of communication.

4. I would like to say a few words about the word-frequency rating technique used by the author. The respondent whose data is given in the appendix to the paper reported that her use of Spanish was restricted primarily to conversations with her parents. In commenting on Table 1 of the appendix the author states: "Note that each domain received a higher frequency rating in English than in Spanish. However, the resulting ratios are not constant. The smallest ratio was observed for 'home' and the greatest for 'school'. These data suggest that she uses the least Spanish in school and the most Spanish at home, an inference which is consistent with her self-report". I think, however, that in Table 1, the ratio of the domain of neighborhood .19 should be corrected to .28. If I am right, then does this datum mean that the respondent uses as little Spanish in the neighborhood as in school? And does this not contradict the author's inference that the respondent engages in more bilingual switching in the domains of home and neighborhood than in other situational domains?

Is it possible to infer from the data of Table 1, i.e. the relatively small numbers of Spanish, that Spanish is used not only at home but also in the domains of school, neighborhood and work to a considerable degree? In my opinion, however, these data may be indications that she learned the Spanish words of these domains from her parents and that she uses them not infrequently also in conversations with her parents at home.

A. Haudricourt

L'exposé de R. Cooper concerne un cas précis: bilinguisme d'un groupe d'immigrants, mais il existe bien d'autres situations:
1)   Différentes par la nature sociale des langues en contact:
      Langues de large communication
      Langues nationales
      Langue de nationalité
      Dialecte
      Patois local
2)   Différentes par les groupements sociaux en contact: importance numérique et situation économique sociale de ces groupes.
    Je ferai remarquer l'importance du cas-limite, instauration du bilinguisme sans contact réel: par exemple, dans une île polynésienne où un instituteur autochtone enseigne le français en l'absence de tout européen ou colon. A ce point de vue (commentaire sur l'exposé de N. Hasselmo) je dois signaler qu'en France la langue nationale s'est d'abord propagée comme langue écrite, et qu'on ne peut pas expliquer la prononciation du français d'Alsace, ou du français de Marseilles par l'influence de la phonologie du dialecte sur un français prononcé à la parisienne. (La confusion de [e] et [ɛ] dans le midi de la France, ne s'explique pas par la phonologie de l'Occitan, qui distingue <u>séz</u> (soi) et sèr (serpent).
    Le français est arrivé comme langue écrite, remplaçant le latin et les é è qui n'étaient pas distingués dans l'orthographe ne l'ont pas été dans la prononciation.
    Toute étude quantitative et qualitative du bilinguisme doit être précédée d'une étude sérieuse des états de langues qui sont réellement en contact.
    L'abandon d'un bilinguisme peut être catastrophique pour la langue survivante. Lorsqu'en France, dans une région fortement patoisante (dans un cialecte occitan ou franco-provençal), les paysans refusent de parler patois aux enfants et leurs parlent toujours "français" pour qu'ils ne soient pas retardés à l'école, c'est ce français à phonologie patoise, à vocabulaire pauvre que les enfants apprennent et non pas le français de l'instituteur. Tandis que si l'instituteur avait su le patois et avait enseigné comment passer d'une langue à l'autre, la richesse du vocabulaire et les facilités d'élocution seraient conservées. Un autre cas: au sud de la Nouvelle Calédonie, les petits enfants de 5 à 10 ans refusent de parler la langue mélanésienne de leurs parents (dont

c'est la langue normale), mais on entend des solécismes, "le chaise", "la fauteuil". Les régions mélanésiennes ont toujours été bilingues, mais il s'agissait d'un bilinguisme passif et égalitaire. Passif parce que l'on comprend la langue des voisins (il y a intermariage), mais on ne la parle pas: ce serait ridicule. Egalitaire parce que chacun est fier de sa langue maternelle et méprise un peu celle des voisins.

Les missionnaires ont changé cela; il y a maintenant les langues qui s'écrivent, dans lesquelles les évangiles ont été traduits, et que doivent apprendre les pasteurs. Sur la vingtaine de langues (Nouvelle Calédonie et Loyalty), quatre ou cinq ont été écrites et doivent être comprises des pasteurs indigènes qui font au temple une traduction publique du texte évangélique. Dans certaines réserves où il coexiste trois langues, le pasteur traduit dans une langue (sa langue maternelle) et deux diacres dans chacune des deux autres langues.

Je résumerai mon opinion en disant que le bilinguisme est essentiellement un fait sociologique qui a des conséquences psychologiques linguistiques. Les méthodes ou procédés de mesures que le linguiste ou le psychologue peut élaborer pour mesurer le bilinguisme n'ont de sens que si le problème sociologique est correctement posé.

Knut Pipping

In his paper, Dr. Cooper purports to devise techniques "for the measurement and description of a bilingual's differential use of two languages, i.e. his language choice behavior in a bilingual community". If I have understood him correctly, he deals exclusively with interaction between bilinguals who are quite fluent in both languages which, in my opinion, is to restrict the problem unduly; and in my comments I should like to concentrate on some other aspects of the problem.

Few bilinguals are equally proficient in both languages; most know one language better than the other, and most bilinguals, at least in Finland, identify themselves with one speech community and label themselves accordingly. Few, if any, bilinguals live in a completely bilingual society; all, or almost all, live simultaneously in two adjacent, or overlapping, monolingual speech communities. (This statement is a simplification: The bilingual Puerto Ricans in New York City live simultaneously in a bilingual and a (probably) monolingual Spanish speech community and a partly monolingual, partly multilingual English speech community). From this follows that only a part of a bilingual's interaction is with other bilinguals, and that most bilinguals are obliged to interact more or less frequently and regularly with monolingual—or virtually monolingual—members of each monolingual speech community. Since, moreover, an individual's proficiency in a given language sets limits for his interaction with

other speakers of the same language, we must treat proficiency as a basic independent variable.   Hency, if we want to study the roles which a bilinguals
languages play in his everyday behavior, we need, to begin with, three fundamental sets of data:

(1) A measure of the bilingual's proficiency or competence in each language.
Since this problem will be dealt with at another session of the symposium, I
shall deal with no technical details here.

(2) A measure of the "amount" and "content" of the bilingual's interaction
with other bilinguals and with monolinguals from each speech community.

(3) A measure of the proficiency or competence in each language of the bilingual's interaction partners.

I assume that the discussion concerning the measurement of a person's bilingual proficiency, will show that 'proficiency' is a rather complicated compound variable.   As Macnamara has pointed out in his paper, we must keep
apart four skills and four aspects of each skill when trying to measure proficiency.   To this variable are, however, several other variables causally linked
so that they, together with 'proficiency' form a still more complex "double
compound" variable which we, not quite unambiguously, might call 'competence', whose structure can be tentatively represented as follows:

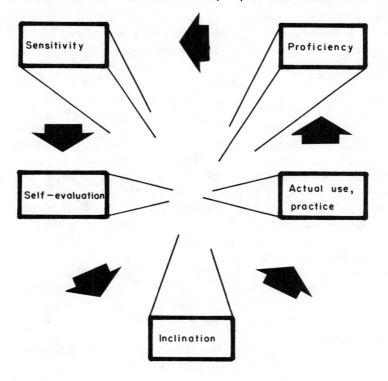

From other experimental work we know that self-evaluation and performance of a given task to correlate, but that this correlation seldom is perfect and that the relationship not necessarily is linear. Assuming further that a subject's evaluation of his own proficiency in, and his inclination to use a language also correlate positively; that a similar positive relationship exists between his inclination to use the language and his actual use of it; and between his actual use of it and his proficiency, we may establish the above model, where any of the four (five) variables can be treated as the independent variable.

None of the variables depends, of course, entirely on the other variables in the model. A subject's self-evaluation of his own proficiency depends, except on his personality, on the proficiency of his interaction partners; his inclination to speak depends on, among other things, his identification with the speech community and his ideological commitment; and his actual use depends on, e.g., the number of agreeable interaction partners within a given domain.

Since single individuals can show much variation not only between different skills, but also between the separate aspects of each skill, it is not quite clear whether it is appropriate to regard 'proficiency' as a single continuum; and since the same individuals certainly will differ considerably along each of the other variables in the model, it is far from certain that 'competence' can be treated as one continuum, however desirable it might be. The problem here, as when representing 'proficiency' as one continuum, will be to assign proper weights to the different components—self-evaluation, inclination, practice; the skills and the aspects—however we go about, the weights must always be arbitrary. As long as we keep this in mind it need not be an unsurmountable theoretical obstacle, but it will nevertheless cause many methodological difficulties.

From a technical point of view it would, indeed, be very agreeable if a subject's degree of bilingualism could be represented as his position in a orthogonal coordinate system with his competence in language A shown on the abscissa and his competence in language B on the ordinate. But since I fear that such a picture will be of questionable value, I would rather suggest a factorial model, in which a subject's competence in languages A and B—and why not, in C, D and E—can be expressed as his position in a factorial space.

As to the second set of basic data which we need, I fully agree with Dr. Cooper that it is very important to contextualize the bilingual's language use and to ascertain what other values are realized through action in different domains. But I should like to stress the necessity to take into account also: (1) how well the subject is, or has been able to enact these values; (2) to what extent he feels that a certain level of proficiency is a sine qua non for being able to enact these values; and (3) how important to him enactment of these values is in comparison with enactment of other values in his value-hierarchy. I think that the last point is particularly important as it may decisively affect the subject's motivation and his inclination to speak the language in question, and thus, as my model shows, his proficiency.

Data about bilinguals' interaction with other bilinguals and/or monolinguals can fairly easily be obtained through direct questioning. I have collected some (yet unpublished) data of this kind in my home town Abo (population
in 1965: 126 000 Finnish and 9 500 Swedish speaking inhabitants).   Similar
data can certainly be secured by the univariate techniques presented by Dr.
Cooper. At an earlier stage of my research in Abo I planned to use an association technique similar to Dr. Cooper's, but abandoned it as it seemed not
to separate well enough Swedes who were moderately, almost perfectly, and
perfectly proficient in Finnish, as most Swedes in Abo are.

It will, of course, be extremely laborious to test the proficiency of all—
or only the key—interaction partners of bilingual interviewees even in a sample
of moderate size. Therefore some labour and cost saving technique would be
welcome. Now, it can be argued that it is not the actual proficiency or competence of my interaction partners which matters, but my perception of his proficiency because peoples' ability to judge the quality of their interaction
partners' speech varies. A less discriminating person or somebody with little
schooling may accept as perfect a performance which a more discriminating individual classifies as inadequate. Therefore we need not necessarily measure
the quality of the interaction partners' speech; for our purposes it is enough to
know how the interviewees experience it. This could be done with a method
similar to Dr. Cooper's multivariate technique and Dr. Macnamara's listing
comprehension tests: in collaboration with linguists and phoneticians a series
of tape recordings are made, where the speaker(s) use different degrees of broken speech (with respect to pronounciation, grammar and vocabulary). These
recordings are then played back to the interviewees who are asked, after each
stimulus, to (1) name those of his regular interaction partners whose speech resembles the recorded talk, (2) compare his own speech with it, and (3) rank
the stimuli with respect to proficiency. Thus we can measure not only the subject's evaluation of his partners' speech, but also his self-evaluation and his
ability to discriminate, his sensitivity, which may be an important fifth variable in the competence model outlined above. (By 'sensitivity' I mean something more than the 'listing comprehension' measured and described by Macnamara; 'sensitivity' being affected not only by the other variables in my competence model, but also by the listener's expectations vis-à-vis, and his conception of, the role of the speaker. Many people in Finland are more sentitive
to the speech of e.g. a post-office clerk than that of an errand boy.)

When we measure a bilingual's proficiency and self-evaluation in this way,
these measures are against an objective standard, the tape recordings. But I
think that we also ought to measure what I should like to call—alluding to the
distinguished sociologist Charles H. Cooley—his 'looking-glass proficiency',
i.e. his perception of how he thinks or feels that his interaction partners experience and judge his own speech. I believe that most subjects, when judging
a partner's proficiency, make an estimate also of the partner's sensitivity,
which estimate, in turn, affects their self-evaluation.

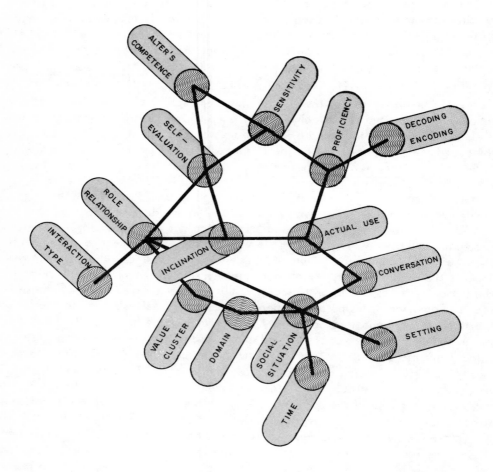

It might even be necessary to measure the subject's 'looking-glass competence', for when evaluating his partner's reaction upon himself, the bilingual probably forms an opinion of how his partner experiences and judges not only his proficiency, but also his sensitivity, self-evaluation, inclination and amount of practice. How this can best be done I do not know, but do not doubt that it is possible.

All the variables outlined above are probably difficult to operationalize and to isolate; and the relationships between them are hypothetical. But I think that model building of this kind, which pays due attention to the complicated and subtle feed-back mechanisms that always operate when bilinguals interact (cf Gumperz pp.384sqq.), will help us to construct fruitful experiments both in real-life situations and in the laboratory. Thus I think that Dr. Cooper's model is very helpful in this respect, as it focusses attention on the relationships between some important variables. I also think that, by combining it with my model above, some other important relationships will be emphasized (see facing page).

S. M. Katre

1-   The paper suggests a two-fold approach to measure the relative strength of the use of one or the other language of a bilingual in situations where both can be used or are found used. In one case the subject's ability to name objects in a given domain, to name pictures dealing with it, to recall items bearing on it, to associate words to given items, or to rate the frequencies of words, are utilised to know to what extent one language is more in use than the other in the domain chosen for the purpose. In the other approach situations of a more specific and concrete nature are presented to him to elicit from him his comments and his grasp of the theme to ascertain indirectly what he thinks of the use of one or other language in that situation. While the univariate approach is straight forward and the responses can be measured with some accuracy, this cannot be done in the case of the multivariate approach and hence its use is of no great value in measuring the intensity of use of one language as against the other. If we can simplify the situation and present the subject with a large number of well thought-out concrete cases and ask him to name which of the two languages will be used in them, it will be possible to ascertain in greater detail the functions of the two languages and in cases where both are thought possible, we can request him to rate them on the scale of greater probability or propriety. By using a larger number of subjects it is possible to calculate the results in more precise terms as in the case of the first approach.

2 – What is in need of greater clarification in this problem is to state the nature of abilities which are really measured in these experiments. There are three coordinates which are used as frame-work for these experiments, viz. domain, role-relationships and interaction types. Here the network used appears to be too gross and requires greater fineness. In fact by controlling the other features one can use the experiments to expand them to a wider extent. For instance, by fixing the relation between the interlocutors (say two friends) and the type of interaction (as purely personal) one may measure the vocabulary items in different domains and grade them according to the range of the vocabulary. The same can be done with the other variables.

3 – The ultimate purpose of these measurements is not clear. It is used to suggest the process by which one language is going to be replaced by the other, or is it meant to assess situations? Or is it intended to see how functional differences separate the use of the two languages against their concurrent use? Much depends upon the final aim.

4 – An experiment of a similar nature will be of capital importance in the Indian context at this juncture. One of the burning questions of education today is the so-called three-language formula, which is being discussed without any evidence of what the actual situation is at present. The regional language, the national language and a world language are meant to be taught to most students thus producing a kind of multilingualism and it is thought that the skill in these should suit the use to which they should be put. As a thorough mastery of all three is considered an undue burden on the memory and time of the students it is necessary to ascertain their precise uses to determine the scope of teaching them, on which again depend questions like the number of years for teaching, the stage at which they should be introduced and the choice of material and the proficiency to be attained.

5 – There are too many variables in this situation and hence some amount of simplification is necessary. Thus the relative use of Hindi and English in the Hindi speaking area will be simpler than where the regional language is some other Indian language. One may first ascertain the use of English and Hindi in the Hindi speaking area and between Hindi and the other Indian language in outside Hindi speaking area. By conflating the two one can prepare a spectrum of domain of the use of these three languages in actual use.

The use of Hindi and English in the Non-Hindi speaking areas will give us a situation of bilingualism very close to the one dealt with in this paper and the use of the different languages could be used to determine the strenght of the two languages in these areas. This will give us an idea of what the practice at present is in the use of these two languages and will help the policy maker to decide how to introduce them in the teaching programme.

6 – Similar experiments may help us decide which are the favoured role relationships for any two of the languages taken in pairs and an index of correlation can be worked out for all three. This may help us in the choice of the material to be used for teaching for different groups or classes. The relative strength

of the two languages in formal and informal situations may be of some use in this context, though a much more differentiated grid will have to be used in this dimension. Besides interviews and personal talks we will have to consider situations like writing out applications, formal talks, group discussions, sermons etc.

7 - What is being attempted in such an approach is to detail with a fair amount of exhaustiveness the use of one of the three languages in different situations to be classified into different domains with subdivisions, different role-relationships under each one of them and an indication of the amount of formality or lack of it and conventional predetermination involved in them. This is likely to make clear not only the exact amount of bilingualism in the given group but its more precise nature as well.

8 - While evaluating the results of such an investigation it is essential to realize that the three dimensions used in this type of work are not quite independent of each other and a kind of relationship among them is presupposed but will become clear from the results themselves. A personal conversation is likely to be more frequent in the domain of home and neighbourhood, while a transactional one is more appropriate in the domain of work. The relationships like those between the teacher and student and child and parents will also show a different distribution among different domains and so on. A highly complex network is expected as the result of interaction of all three and the role of each language has to be stated in relation to this complex.

DISCUSSION

English Version

Dr. Cooper began by pointing out that his problem was the measurement of the differential use of two or more languages in a speech community, for example, the Puerto-Rican speech community of New York. What are the considerations that will elicit Spanish and those that will elicit English, assuming both are intelligible? The terms used in the discussion were defined as follows: The "variates" refer to three hypothetical constructs taken from the work of Fishman and Gumperz: domain, role-relationship, interaction type. Of the three, domain is the most abstract, refering to the sphere of activity in which language takes place. It includes a set of social situations which have in common a set of expectations held in common by the speakers who participate. Role-relationship refers to a set of obligations of rights and duties obtaining between two people, e.g. father and son; parent and child. The interaction type is concerned with the purpose of the interaction and is often defined in terms of status considerations.

The five domains defined for the Puerto-Rican speech community (i.e. home, neighbourhood, church, work, school) were all defined in terms of regularities of expectations in situations. In the original experiment, reported in the appendix to the paper, Dr. Cooper gave results of analysis of a single individual. In the paper itself he has the results of a project involving eight children at a Roman Catholic high school in the Bronx. The respondents were asked to rate the frequency with which they uttered a set of English or Spanish words. For each language he gave a list of fifteen words per domain. Within each list they were randomly arranged except that every fifth word pertained to the same domain. Unlike the other test this was given in a written form. The rating scale varied from 7 for the most frequent to 0 for the least frequent. There was no difference for the home domain, and the difference was small for neighbourhood and work, and significant for church and school.

Dr. Cooper was questioned on his use of the concept domain. If one takes domain as a situation where a common set of norms of expectations apply, are these norms established? Domains in the sense of home or school could break down if common expectations exist in them. Do Dr. Cooper's results bear directly on the school as an institution or on role-relationships at school? The closest connection so far was with topic, and not with domain. Dr. Cooper replied that at the moment his notions of domain were largely hypothetical and that they could be modified or abandoned. What he expected to get from his data was consistencies explainable in terms of domains or role relationships that enter into them. Dr. Gumperz reminded the meeting that Dr. Cooper's paper was the result of a project jointly undertaken by Drs. Fishman, Cooper and himself. At the moment he did not see how domain related to what he himself was doing; all he was worried about was people interacting. He could see that there was some idea of norm as part of the cultural knowledge brought to the interaction, but he could not see how this related to domain. He postulated that we can only learn what domain is after we have finished our analysis. Another participant thought that for Dr. Cooper it was the semantic domain which was important while he himself saw a domain as linked to the real activity of the bilingual.

One commentator repeated his request that the concept, topic, should be added to the three variates under discussion. This was supported by another participant who illustrated the point by telling the story of a Basque priest who arrived in Paris to minister to his fellow-countrymen. One night as he was hearing confession, an old man began to reel off a long catalogue of sins and the priest asked him how long it was since his last confession. The penitent replied that it did not matter, for forty years he had been going to confession in French and at last he was going to make a valid confession in Basque. It was agreed that topic was important, but it probably operated in different ways in different linguistic communities. It could be important if it triggered that Dr. Gumperz called metaphorical switching, where a topic reminds people of certain special relationships they have to each other, e.g. two friends who are both residents of the same village as students of the same university will speak dialect, but on a topic related to university affairs will switch to the standant language. One's training in a subject will often trigger the use of the language one was trained in.

Dr. Cooper agreed with Dr. Hattori that third party or interlocutor was important as that was part of the social situation. So far he had been dealing only with situations in which all participants spoke both languages. Professor Hattori's comments opened up an interesting line of enquiry. On the possibility of the extinction of Spanish in New York, Dr. Cooper said that the question was far from clear. There was continual travelling back and forth and so the Puerto Rican community in New York have constant relationships which require the use of Spanish.

The question of language prestige and language survival in a bilingual situation was brought up. The meeting was reminded that bilinguals tend to unify their language systems. But if the first language, even of a minority group, has a certain prestige, there is much less danger of its disappearance. Thus Flemish speakers in Wallonia tend to assimilate in the third generation. But French-speaking Walloons keep their language even without recourse to the school. But the fact of assimilation in the two directions is illustrated by French-speakers and Flemish-speakers who have names from the other language. One difficulty in India was that of kinship terms which are peculiar to social groups. In Kannada (a Dravidian Language) and Marathi (an Indo-European language) to fall asleep is translated by to sleep-fall. One language is obviously the donor. So to predict what is likely to be used in a given situation, given certain sociological and psychological factors, and to show what roles languages play, we must take into account a translation-set.

There was some criticism that the question of quality of language use did not enter into the thinking of the main speaker. The question of quantity did not matter much, if quality did not come into the picture. One speaker commented that during a visit to the lobster factory at Shediac he had noticed that the signs were bilingual, but while the English was perfect the French was shot through with all sorts of elementary errors, like misent with the value of a past participle. For him the quality of the work language was important. This question was closely tied up with that of proficiency, treated by Dr. Pipping. Though the work of Dr. Macnamara, among others, made it difficult to treat it as a separate variable, it would be useful if we could develop a measure of technical proficiency which would enable us to rank a number of subjects along just one continuum.

In this way, using the model in Dr. Pipping's paper, proficiency could be described not merely by difference scores, but by position relative to the vertical and horizontal axes. In sociological work, it is desirable to treat proficiency as one variable. There are many things affecting proficiency. Proficiency is not only a matter of psychological constructs, but also of social norms. Self-evaluation is in part determined by sensitivity. In such an assessment, a speaker sees one of three linguistic relationships between himself and his interlocutor:

$$\text{He speaks} \left\langle \begin{array}{c} \text{better than} \\ \text{as well as} \\ \text{worse than} \end{array} \right\rangle \text{I do}$$

A feedback between inclination and role-relationship depends on the extent to which one can enact certain values when using language. Norms must enter into the model. In all bilingual situations some norms exist which determine where one should use language A and where one should use B. The connection with actual language use depends on domains. The variables can be manipulated. If some can be kept constant for different types of situation, we can then measure self-evaluation and language use and see how these variables vary according to the total situation. The ultimate validity of this model is doubtful, but it should help us to locate the important variables.

One participant commented that for self-evaluation and inclination, one should substitute self-report and attitude, as these were the current terms. This Pipping model should be placed over the Fishman one as it reflects different kinds of data that describe context and functions of bilingual behaviour. Dr. Cooper commented that the model was useful for two reasons: a. his own model was an over-simplification; b. if some of the variables, e.g. sensitivity and self-evaluation were operationalised and identified, they might help us account for better or more rapid learning of English in the New York Puerto-Rican Community.

For one commentator, the basic problem was coming to terms with the second language. While this is going on two things can happen:
a. One can make an unintentional mistake in identifying a morpheme. E.g.,
when a consignment of German goods arrived in India they were lettered:
DIE DEUTSCHEN WAREN FÜR INDIA
which was translated as "The Germans were for India".
(waren (goods) taken as part of the verb sein)
b. One might attempt a literal translation.
Tu as raison   you have right.
This could also happen on the phonological and structural levels, as Professor
Hattori had shown. This was probably why bilinguals tend to unify diverse systems to make behaviour in the second language much easier, but very often the
result falls outside both language systems.

There was much discussion on techniques arising out of these general principles. Dr. Nuytens repeated his criticisms of the measures used as weak. In
response to challenges he referred to what he had said in the second working
session and referred again to Coombs. Another participant remarked that the
notion of measure had its annoying side. Testing is not measuring as the tester
works from standard worked out according to a given population, will measuring
relates everything to absolutes. One reason for the lack of understanding between linguists and other scholars was the following: linguists usually work from
quantified data, while sociologists and psychologists work on distributional data.

On the plane of phonetics, one of the other commentators remarked that,
in his view, Dr. Hattori's representation of the production of Tatar /o̦/ was too
crude. For an assessment of vowel movements one must use a distinctive feature
analysis. For example, in Saramacca and Sranan, both languages spoken in
Surinam, the first retains the tonal features of West African, the second uses
a stress system akin to that of English. There is a complex movement between
tonal intonation to English stress.

A participant pointed out that the main problem of methodology is determining which of the socio-linguistic aspects can be studied by which means.
It is difficult to determine which components are amenable to self-report, as
not all of these components are part of social consciousness. Relationship between self-report and reality are notoriously unreliable, and, according to the
different degrees of sophistication of the speaker, relationships between self-
report and language behaviour take on a different meaning. Various ways of
getting round the difficulty were suggested. One was using Fries' technique
of analysing phone conversations. This would give us all the data we were asking for. Unfortunately it is not possible to check on the rigour of Fries' work
as Bell Telephone have never allowed Fries to release his raw material (i.e. recorded conversations) to the public. Another suggestion was based on an experiment in Malaya. 200 students had been asked to report on language behaviour
in their homes. Eventually all three generations were to report on each other
and the data was to be backed up with recorded samples of language behaviour.
Yet another suggestion rose out of the comments on quality of language used.

Tape recorders were to be put under factory benches without the workers' knowl- and turned on at random. From analysis of the conversations one would have a clear idea of both the quantity and quality of language used, and if necessary, take measures accordingly.

Dr. Cooper used yet another method. In analysis involving multivariate techniques he used as stimuli conversations involving role relationships. At first he tried to write them himself. Finally he recruited a group of four ado- lescents to whom he submitted situations and asked them to comment on their possibility and suggest how they would go. One such was that of a boy ringing up a friend's sister to invite her to the movies with him. If the girl's mother answers he is closely questioned and then the girl herself is sent to the phone. She does not immediately accept but offers to ring back after talking it over with Mother. The team proposed a dialogue and acted the situation out. These conversations were recorded and submitted to outsiders for comment. This tech- nique serves as a discovery technique. It can show what is meant by a switch from Spanish to English and back again.

While another participant wished to congratulate Dr. Cooper on his paper and welcomed approaches along these lines, the question of how research re- sults fit the original situation is primarily a statistical one, and until the three disciplines involved in testing and measuring bilingualism agree on the variables to be quantumised, so significant progress is possible. At present there is no such agreement and all sorts of different measures are being used. It is now ne- cessary to reduce all factors to something measureable by computer. With the solutions proposed at this meeting, we have made a promising beginning.

The meeting was agreed that a social typology of bilingual situations is desirable. There is a basic difference between the behaviour of natural bi- linguals who can be said to have two mother tongues and others who acquire their second languages by formal instruction. The criteria for judging rules are different in both cases: background study is necessary to establish the quantums to be measured which would indicate different language uses and different deg- rees of proficiency against which we can assess the case of the second group of bilinguals. With reference to this group a peculiar situation existed in India, especially before 1947. People educated in English had shown a peculiar tend- ency to code-switching in all situations. Such code-switching does not help us work out roles. It is partly this tendency which has caused Indian educators to recommend the state languages for education rather than the proposed official language.

One participant posited a difference between the bilingualism of immig- rant and native groups. In the first case the minority language could be assi- milated and the minority, not the majority would be bilingual. In the second case each linguistic group speaks his own language and they are all equal. The only thing left was to choose a language to act as communication between the groups. If this auxiliary language is well learnt, there will be not harmful interference between the two. This was the case in the Soviet Union. It was underlined by this participant, among others, that in spite of the linguistic importance of bilingualism, it takes its rise from social conditions.

An observer was at pains to underline the interdisciplinary interest of bilingualism and pointed out that from the point of view of the group it was often a necessary condition for survival. He suggested three contexts in which it should be studied:

1. Individual bilingualism for cultural ends;
2. Group bilingualism to enable two groups to occupy the same territory on an equal footing;
3. Group bilingualism in a minority situation to ensure national survival. The speaker suggested that it would give direction to future seminars to deal with questions in function of one of these three situations, preferably the third, as most bilingual groups found themselves in minority situations.

DISCUSSION

Version française

M. Cooper souligne d'abord le fait qu'il s'agit pour lui de mesurer l'inégalité d'utilisation de deux ou de plusieurs langues au sein d'une collectivité linguistique, par exemple au sein de la collectivité porto-ricaine de New York. Dans quelles circonstances parlera-t-on espagnol et dans quelles circonstances anglais, lorsque l'on comprend également les deux langues? D'abord établir la définition des termes employés au cours de la discussion: les "variées" sont trois catégories de circonstances hypothétiques empruntées aux travaux de Fishman et Gumperz: domaine, relation de rôle, genre d'influence réciproque. La plus abstraite des trois catégories est le domaine, c'est-à-dire la sphère d'activité dans laquelle se produit le fait de langue. Elle englobe un ensemble de situations sociales ayant en commun un ensemble d'attentes qui sont communes aux locuteurs prenant part au fait de langue. La relation de rôle est un ensemble d'obligations, de droits et de devoirs existant entre deux personnes, par exemple, entre père et fils, entre parent et enfant. Le genre d'influence réciproque qui s'exerce se situe sur le plan de l'objet visé et se définit souvent du point de vue de la situation personnelle.

Les cinq domaines qui ont été définis pour la collectivité linguistique porto-ricaine (c'est-à-dire le foyer, le voisinage, l'église, le travail, l'école) l'ont tous été du point de vue de la régularité des attentes dans des situations données. Dans l'étude originale, dont les résultats sont présentés en appendice, il s'agit d'un seul individu. Dans sa communication même, M. Cooper fournit les résultats d'une étude portant sur huit enfants d'une école secondaire catholique de Bronx. Ces enfants avaient été priés d'indiquer par une cote la fréquence de l'emploi dans leur parler d'un certain nombre de mots anglais et de mots espagnols. Il y avait pour chacune des deux langues une liste de quinze mots par domaine. Chaque liste était présentée dans un ordre établi au hasard, avec cette particularité qu'à tous les cinq mots elle revenait au même domaine. A la différence de l'autre test, celui-ci a été passé par écrit. Les cotes données par les enfants vont de 7 (emploi le plus fréquent) à 0 (emploi le moins fréquent). Dans le cas du domaine foyer, la différence est nulle; elle est faible dans le cas du voisinage et du travail, et marquée dans le cas de l'église et de l'école.

On pose diverses questions à M. Cooper sur le recours à l'idée de domaine. Si l'on considère le domaine comme une situation à laquelle s'applique un ensemble commun de normes d'attentes, les normes dont il s'agit ont-elles été précisées? Les domaines foyer et école pourraient bien n'en faire qu'un,

si dans l'un et l'autre les attentes sont les mêmes. Les résultats obtenus par
M. Cooper concernent-ils l'école en tant qu'institution ou bien les relations
de rôle à l'école? Le rapport le plus pertinent paraît exister, pour l'instant,
avec le thème bien plus qu'avec le domaine. M. Cooper répond que l'idée
qu'il se fait des domaines reste encore hypothétique dans une grande mesure et
qu'elle peut encore être soit modifiée, soit abandonnée. Il compte déceler à
partir des données obtenues des persistances s'expliquant par les domaines ou
par les relations de rôle. M. Gumperz rappelle que la communication de M.
Cooper est le fruit d'une étude entreprise par MM. Fishman, Cooper et lui.
Il ne voit pas encore de quelle façon l'idée de domaine peut avoir un rapport
avec ses travaux à lui; ce qui le préoccupe, c'est l'influence exercée réci-
proquement par les gens les uns les autres. Il perçoit jusqu'à un certain point
des normes dans les connaissances culturelles concurant à cette influence réciproque, mais il ne voit pas comment cela peut se rapporter aux domaines. Il
pose en postulat qu'on ne pourra se prononcer sur la nature du domaine qu'une
fois terminée l'analyse entreprise par la Conférence. D'après un autre participant, ce qui importe pour M. Cooper, c'est le domaine de la sémantique;
tout domaine devrait se rattacher, selon lui, à l'activité réelle du bilingue.

Un des commentateurs demande de nouveau que l'idée de thème soit ajou-
tée aux trois variées en question. Un autre participant, appuyant cette demande, raconte une anecdote. Un prêtre basque, arrivé à Paris pour faire du ministère auprès des gens originaires de son pays, entend un soir la confession
d'un vieillard qui lui défile une longue série de péchés. Le prêtre demande
depuis combien de temps il s'est confessé. Le pénitent répond que cela n'a
pas d'importance, que depuis quarante ans il se confesse en français et qu'il
peut enfin cette fois se confesser pour vrai, c'est-à-dire en basque. Tous sont
d'accord pour juger que le thème a son importance, mais que cette importance
n'est probablement pas la même d'une collectivité linguistique à une autre.
L'importance du thème, du sujet, peut grandir beaucoup lorsque celui-ci déclenche ce que M. Gumperz appelle un aiguillage métaphorique, c'est-à-dire
lorsque le sujet dont parlent les locuteurs leur rappelle certains liens spéciaux
qui existent entre eux; par exemple, deux amis du même village qui étudient
à la même université parlent entre eux en dialecte, mais dès qu'ils abordent
un sujet d'intérêt universitaire ils emploient la langue de l'établissement. La
formation reçue dans une discipline déclenche souvent le recours à la langue
dans laquelle cette discipline a été étudiée.

M. Cooper reconnaît avec M. Hattori que le tiers interlocuteur joie un
rôle important, car il fait partie de la situation sociale. Ses propos n'ont porté
encore que sur des situations dans lesquelles tous les participants peuvent parler
l'une et l'autre langues. Pour ce qui est de la possibilité de la disparition de
l'espagnol à New York, M. Cooper est d'avis que la question est loin d'être
tranchée. Les déplacements sont continuels entre Porto Rico et New York, et
ils entraînent des rapports personnels constants qui nécessitent l'emploi de
l'espagnol.

La question des langues bénéficiant d'un prestige et celle de la survivance d'une langue dans une situation bilingue viennent sur le tapis. On rappelle que les bilingues tendent à unifier leurs deux systèmes linguistiques. Cependant, lorsque la langue première, même si elle est la langue d'une collectivité minoritaire jouit d'un prestige marqué, elle est moins menacée de disparaître. C'est ainsi que les Flamingants de Wallonie s'assimilent en général dès la troisième génération, tandis que les Wallons francophones conservent leur langue, même sans l'aide de l'école. Le fait d'une assimilation jouant dans les deux sens n'en est pas moins démontré par les noms flamands de locuteurs français et français de locuteurs flamands. En Inde se pose la difficulté des termes apparentés qui appartiennent spécifiquement à certaines catégories sociales. En langue kannada (langue dravidienne) et en mahrate (langue indo-européenne), l'idée de s'endormir se rend par un mot composé groupant les deux idées dormir et tomber. Il est évident que l'une des deux langues a donné cette expression à l'autre. Donc, pour prédire la façon dont on s'exprimera dans une situation donnée, dans un ensemble précis de conditions sociologiques et psychologiques, et pour montrer le rôle que jouent les langues, il faut tenir compte du jeu de la traduction.

Certains participants reprochent à l'orateur principal d'avoir laissé de côté la question de la qualité de la langue employée. La question de la quantité n'aurait guère d'importance si l'on ne tenait aucun compte de la qualité. Un des participants note qu'à Shediac, où il a visité une usine de préparation du homard, les affiches et écriteaux sont bilingues, mais que les inscriptions anglaises sont correctes tandis que les inscriptions françaises sont parsemées de fautes grossières, telles que misent pour mises. La qualité de la langue de travail, d'après ce participant, est d'une grande importance. Cette question se rattache étroitement à celle de la connaissance approfondie de la langue, abordée par M. Pipping. Bien qu'il soit difficile, depuis les travaux de Mr. Macnamara et d'autres linguistes, de considérer cette question comme une variable distincte, il serait utile de pouvoir établir une mesure de la compétence technique qui permettrait d'aligner de façon continue un certain nombre de rubriques.

A partir du modèle élaboré par M. Pipping, on pourrait définir le degré de connaissance, non pas seulement d'après les points de divergences, mais d'après la position sur les axes verticaux et horizontaux. Du point de vue sociologique, il est souhaitable que le degré de connaissance soit considéré comme constituant une seule variable. De nombreux éléments interviennent dans la détermination du degré de connaissance. Dans son modèle, M. Pipping s'est efforcé de rattacher les travaux de Cooper et de Macnamara aux siens propres.

Le degré de connaissance n'est pas seulement affaire de catégories psychologiques, mais aussi de normes sociales. L'évaluation de soi-même par le locuteur est déterminée pour une part par sa sensibilité de perception. Le locuteur, en effet, a conscience de l'une des trois relations linguistiques suivantes entre lui et la personne qui lui parle:

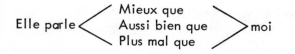

Elle parle ⟨ Mieux que / Aussi bien que / Plus mal que ⟩ moi

Entre inclination et relation de rôle, il n'y a d'influence que dans la mesure
où l'utilisation de la langue dont il s'agit vient à l'appui de certaines valeurs.
Il faut introduire des normes dans le modèle.   Dans toutes les situations de bilinguisme, il existe des normes qui permettent de décider du moment où l'on
doit se servir de la langue A et du moment qui convient pour la langue B.   Le
rapport avec l'utilisation effective de chaque langue dépend du domaine.   On
peut manier séparément les variables.   S'il est possible de faire en sorte que
certaines restent constantes dans divers genres de situations, il sera possible de
mesurer l'évaluation de soi-même et l'utilisation de la langue et d'en suivre
la variation dans l'évolution de l'ensemble de la situation.   On peut douter
que ce modèle soit retenu longtemps, mais sans doute aidera-t-il à découvrir
les variables les plus importantes.

L'un des participants souhaite que l'on substitue à l'évaluation de soi-
même et à l'inclination des termes "self-report" et aittitude, d'usage plus cou-
rant.   Le modèle Pipping devrait être superposé au modèle Fishman, car il
tient compte d'autres genres de données, relatives au contexte et aux fonctions
du comportement du bilingue.   M. Cooper exprime l'opinion que ce modèle
est utile pour deux raisons:
a.   son modèle à lui constitue une simplification exagérée;
b.   si l'on pouvait "opérationnaliser" et identifier certaines des variables, par
exemple la sensibilité de perception et l'évaluation de soi-même, ces variables aideraient peut-être à comprendre les cas d'apprentissage meilleur ou plus
rapide de l'anglais dans la collectivité porto-ricaine de New York.

Aux yeux de l'un des participants, le problème fondamental consiste à
maîtriser la langue seconde.   Pendant qu'on s'y efforce, il peut se produire
deux choses:
a.   On peut se méprendre sur le sens de tel morphème.   C'est ainsi qu'un ar-
rivage de marchandises allemandes en Inde portait l'inscription:
DEUTSCHEN WAREN FÜR INDIA, ce qui fut traduit par "Les Allemands étaient
pour l'Inde".   (Le mot waren, signifiant marchandises, avait été pris pour un
temps du verbe sein, être).
b.   On peut ne donner qu'une traduction littérale: Tu as raison: you have
right.   La même chose peut se produire aux niveaux de la phonologie et des
structures, comme l'a montré M. Hattori.   C'est pour cette raison sans doute
que les bilingues ont tendance à unifier leur deux systèmes, afin d'être plus à
l'aise dans la langue seconde; très souvent, il en résulte un état de langue é-
tranger à l'un et l'autre des systèmes.

Une longue discussion se déroule sur les techniques issues de ces principes
généraux.   M. Nuytens réitère ses critiques à l'endroit des mesures utilisées,
qui lui paraissent faibles.   Contredit, il se reporte à ce qu'il a déjà dit à la
deuxième séance de travail et de nouveau il se réfère à Coombs.   Un autre

participant fait observer que la notion de mesure est par certains côtés irritante. Déterminer n'est pas mesurer, car celui qui détermine le bilinguisme se sert de normes établies en fonction d'une population donnée, tandis que celui qui le mesure rapporte tout à des absolus. L'une des raisons de l'incompréhension qui subsiste entre linguistes et autres savants réside en ce que les linguistes travaillent d'ordinaire sur des données quantifiées, tandis que les sociologues et les psychologues travaillent sur des données tenant compte de la répartition.

Dans le domaine de la phonétique, un commentateur observe que, d'après lui, la représentation de la production de /ǫ/ de Tatar que suggère M. Hattori est trop simpliste. Pour mettre en lumière l'évolution des voyelles on doit faire appel à une analyse des traits distinctifs. Par exemple, en saramacca et sranan, toutes deux des langues parlées en Surinam, la première retient l'accent tonal des langues de l'Afrique occidentale, tandis que la deuxième recourt à un système d'accentuation apparenté à celui de l'anglais. Il y a une évolution complexe à partir de l'intonation tonale pour aboutir à celle de l'anglais.

Un des participants soutient que le principal problème de méthodologie consiste à savoir par lequel des moyens dont on dispose peut être étudié chacun des aspects socio-linguistiques. Il est difficile de déterminer ceux des éléments composants qui peuvent jouer un rôle dans le self-report, car les composantes dont il s'agit ne sont pas toutes appréhendées par la conscience sociale. Les relations entre self-report et réalité sont bien peu sûres et les relations entre self-report et comportement linguistique n'ont pas la même signification suivant le degré de développement intellectuel du locuteur. On propose diverses manières de contourner cette difficulté. L'une consiste dans le recours à la technique Fries d'analyse des conversations téléphoniques. Cette méthode fournirait toutes les données voulues. Malheureusement la rigueur des travaux de Fries n'a jamais pu être vérifiée, la compagnie de téléphone Bell n'ayant jamais autorisé Fries à rendre publiques ses matières premières, c'est-à-dire les conversations enregistrées. Une autre méthode proposée s'inspire d'une expérience faite en Malaisie. On a demandé à deux cents étudiants un rapport sur le comportement linguistique de leurs familles. Les trois générations devaient, éventuellement, présenter des rapports les unes les autres, accompagnés d'un échantillonnage d'enregistrements de leur comportement linguistique. Une autre idée, née des observations formulées sur la qualité de la langue, serait d'installer des micros dans les usines, à l'insu des travailleurs, et d'enregistrer, par moments, les conversations. L'analyse de celles-ci permettrait de se faire une idée juste des caractéristiques quantitatives et qualitatives du langage employé, et peut-être de mesurer ces caractéristiques.

M. Cooper s'est servi d'une autre méthode encore. Dans une analyse recourant à plusieurs variées, il a eu recours à des conversations supposant des relations de rôle. Il a tenté d'abord de rédiger lui-même ces conversations. A la fin, il s'est fait aider de quatre adolescents auxquels il a proposé des situations hypothétiques et a demandé ce qu'ils pensaient de la possibilité de pareilles situations et de la manière dont celles-ci tourneraient. Par exemple,

un garçon appelle au téléphone la soeur d'un de ses amis et l'invite au cinéma.
Si c'est la mère de la jeune fille qui répond, elle s'enquiert de façon précise
de chaque détail, après quoi la jeune fille est appelée à l'appareil.   Celle-ci
n'accepte pas immédiatement, mais offre de rappeler le jeune homme après
s'être entretenue avec sa mère.   Les quatre adolescents ont proposé un dialogue et l'ont joué comme une sorte de saynète.   Leurs paroles enregistrées ont
été reproduites à l'intention d'autres personnes qui les ont commentées.   Il
s'agit là d'une technique pouvant permettre de découvrir le mécanisme psychologique du passage de l'espagnol à l'anglais et de l'anglais à l'espagnol.

Un participant tient à féliciter M. Cooper de sa communication, attendant
beaucoup des méthodes de ce genre; la question de savoir à quel point les résultats des recherches sont conformes à la situation primitive ressortit avant
tout à la statistique, et aussi longtemps que les trois disciplines qui interviennent dans la détermination et la mesure du bilinguisme ne seront pas d'accord
quant aux variables dont il faut tenir compte, aucun progrès appréciable ne
sera possible.   A l'heure actuelle, ces disciplines ne sont pas d'accord, et
l'on se sert d'une foule de mesures différentes.   Il faut arriver à réduire tous
les facteurs à quelque chose qu'un ordinateur puisse mesurer.   Les solutions
proposées à la présente réunion marquent un début prometteur dans ce sens.

Les participants estiment qu'il faut établir une typologie sociale des situations de bilinguisme.   Il existe une différence fondamentale entre le comportement des bilingues naturels dont on peut dire qu'ils ont deux langues maternelles, et ceux qui sont bilingues parce qu'ils ont fait l'acquisition d'une
deuxième langue à force d'étude.   Les critères d'établissement de règles ne
sont pas les mêmes dans l'un et l'autre cas: il faut étudier les quantums à mesurer qui indiqueront les diverses utilisations des langues et les divers degrés
de connaissance de ces langues, ce qui permettra d'évaluer le cas des bilingues de la seconde catégorie.   A propos de ces derniers, il y a eu en Inde une
situation assez particulière, surtout avant 1947.   Les Indiens qui avaient reçu
leur formation en anglais avaient tendance, dans toutes les situations, à trans-
poser tout simplement dans l'autre langue leur façon de s'exprimer.   Une pareille transposition ne nous aide en rien à distinguer le rôle propre de chaque
langue.   Cette tendance est l'une des raisons qui ont poussé les éducateurs indiens à recommander l'usage des langues des Etats, dans l'enseignements, plutôt que celui de la langue que l'on avait voulu rendre officielle.

Un des participants voit une différence entre le bilinguisme de l'immigrant, et celui de l'indigène.   Dans le cas de l'immigrant, sa langue minoritaire ne peut s'imposer, et c'est la minorité, non pas la majorité, qui devient
bilingue.   Dans le second cas, chaque élément linguistique parle sa propre
langue, à égalité avec les autres.   Il ne reste plus qu'à choisir une langue de
communication entre groupes.   Si l'on apprend bien cette langue auxiliaire,
il n'y aura pas d'interférence nuisible entre les deux.   C'est ce qui se produit en URSS.   Divers participants soulignent le fait que le bilinguisme, quelle
que soit son importance du point de vue linguistique, provient d'abord d'un
état de choses existant sur le plan social.

Un observateur s'efforce de souligner l'intérêt interdisciplinaire du bi-linguisme, faisant observer que du point de vue de la population bilingue, il constitue souvent une condition nécessaire de survivance. Trois situations dif-férentes sont à étudier:

1.   Le bilinguisme individuel de l'homme cultivé;

2.   Le bilinguisme collectif nécessité par la présence sur un même territoire de deux populations tendant à l'égalité de statut;

3.   Le bilinguisme collectif d'une population minoritaire qui cherche à sur-vivre comme nationalité.

D'après l'orateur, les colloques futurs seront mieux orientés si leurs étu-des se font en fonction de l'une ou l'autre de ces trois situations, et de préfé-rence en fonction de la troisième, car la plupart des populations bilingues sont minoritaires.

CHAIRMAN'S SUMMARY/BILAN DE LA SEANCE

Veroboj Vildomec

In principle Dr. Cooper intends to measure the roles played by both languages in the everyday behaviour of a bilingual mainly by measuring the subject's proficiency in each of these languages and his ability and readiness to use them in different domains, roles and situations. To do this Dr. Cooper uses especially word-tests. These tests, like most tests of this kind, contain, we suspect, mainly nouns. A further technique suggested by Dr. Cooper are tests of comprehension of recorded conversation.

Other speakers stress, however, the necessity of studying also pronunciation, grammar, phraseology, and syntax. Let us mention, in addition to that, the importance of spelling, punctuation and (if a subject has mastered languages using different alphabets) of the alphabet, these features usually betraying, among other things, at first glance the role which the school plays or played in a subject's use of languages. After all, why should we not study, in addition to tape-recordings, also written performance of a bilingual, for instance all letters written by him over a certain period of time? Another relatively easy approach is certainly the study of what a subject reads in each language. Comprehension tests of reading may supplement those of recorded conversation.

Professor Hattori gives interesting examples of interference phenomena. If in a subject's performance language A influences language B more than language B influences language A, we can usually assume that—other things such as the prestige of the languages in contact being equal—language A plays a more important role in his everyday life than language B. If the languages are specialized for various domains, roles and situations, it will be interesting to study the varying incidence of interference phenomena.

M. Haudricourt stresses the need of considering how language A and language B are spoken in a milieu before embarking on any further study. In milieus in which the speakers of two languages are blended as a rule neither language is used in its literary form. Professor Pipping's remark asking us to determine how much interaction is with bilingual and how much with monoglot partners is certainly linked with this as, in such milieus, monoglot speakers of language A will usually (even if not always) use fewer features due to the influence of language B than bilingual speakers do when they use language A.

Speech is a phenomenon existing as a means of communication in society. Still, we should not neglect entirely the use of languages for silent thought, for monologues, in dreams, etc. when trying to determine what role each of them plays in the life of a bilingual, however inexact the results of such study may be. Even the reactions of a bilingual patient affected by aphasia may be sometimes linked with the role played by each language in his everyday life.

Professor Katre asks the research worker to state the purpose of his study. Seen from the practical angle, the investigation of "artificial" or "cultural" bilingualism will prove especially important. It will enable us to decide which languages should be taught to whom and which parts of a language should be taught. It will be most probably more useful for a class of waiter apprentices to learn how to speak than how to write a foreign language, but those who plan educational policies in this sphere are usually faced with far more difficult problems than this one. If almost all students have no use whatever for the foreign language which they learned at school for many years, we shall have to consider replacing these languages by subjects for which the students may have more use later in life.

Let us mention that most tests suggested do not seem to reveal the role of a language used exclusively until the age of, say, 20 or 25 and rarely after this age. Even if it does not play any important part in the behaviour of the subject at the age of, say, 30 or 35, the tests may still indicate that it is his dominant language. Self-reports in the form of answers to questionnaires, interviews and other means of gathering information concerning the subject's linguistic history will be especially important in such cases.

Let us sum up the methods suggested: testing oral proficiency in each language and the ability and inclination to use each language in different domains, roles and situations; comprehension tests both of conversation and reading; self-reports in the form of answers to questionnaires and interviews; information gathered from persons knowing the subject; analysis of tape-recordings and of written performance devoting special attention to interference phenomena; study of what a bilingual reads; study of silent thought, monologues, dreams; investigation of the use of languages in aphasic conditions. The investigator will have, of course, to decide which of these methods will be used to gather basic data and which will be used merely to supplement this basic information. If large numbers of subjects have to be studied very simple techniques such as Dr. Cooper's univariate techniques using mainly word-tests will have to be used.

BIBLIOGRAPHY/BIBLIOGRAPHIE

Barker, G. C.
1947   "Social Functions of Language in a Mexican-American Community".
         Acta Americana 5, 185-202
Blom, J.-P., Gumperz, J. J.
1968   "Some Social Determinants of Verbal Behavior", (In) Directions in
         Socio-Linguistics; the ethnography of communication, John J.
         Gumperz and Dell Hymes (eds.), New York, Holt, Rinehart and
         Winston
Carroll, J. B.
1966   "Quelques mesures subjectives en psycholinguistique; fréquence des
         mots, significativité et qualité de traduction", Bulletin de psy-
         chologie 19, 580-590
Coombs, C.
1964   The Theory of Data, New York, Wiley
Eaton, H. S.
1961   An English-French-German-Spanish Word Frequency Dictionary;
         a correlation of the first six thousands Words in four single-
         language frequency lists, New York, Dover Publications
Ervin-Tripp, S. M.
1964   "An Analysis of the Interaction of Language, Topic, and Listener",
         American Anthropologist 66, Part 2, 86-102
Ferguson, C. A.
1959   "Diglossia", Word 15, 325-340
Fishman, J. A.
1964   "Language Maintenance and Language Shift as a Field of Inquiry;
         a definition of the field and suggestions for its further develop-
         ment, Linguistics 9, 32-70

1965   "Who Speaks What Language to Whom and When"? La linguistique
         2, 67-88

1968   "Sociolinguistic Perspective on the Study of Bilingualism",
         Linguistics 39, 20-48
Frey, W. J.
1945   "Amish 'Triple Talk'", American Speech 20, 85-98
Gumperz, J. J.
1964   "Linguistic and Social Interaction in Two Communities", American
         Anthropologist 66, 6, Part 2, 137-153

1967   "On the Linguistic Markers of Bilingual Communication", The
         Journal of Social Issues 23, 2, 48-57

Haugen, E. I.
    1956   Bilingualism in the Americas; a bibliography and research guide,
                    American Dialect Society, University of Alabama Press

----
    1966   "Dialect, Language, Nation", American Anthropologist 68,
                    922-935
Herman, S. N.
    1961   "Explorations in the Social Psychology of Language Choice",
                    Journal of Human Relations 14, 149-164
Hoffman, M. N. H.
    1934   The Measurement of Bilingual Background, New York City, Tea-
                    chers College, Columbia University
Howes, D.
    1954   "On the Interpretation of Word Frequency as a Variable Affecting
                    Speed of Recognition", Journal of Experimental Psychology 48,
                    106-112
Hymes, D.
    1962   "The Ethnography of Speaking", (In) Anthropology and Human
                    Behavior, T. Gladwin and W. C. Sturtevant (eds.), Washington,
                    D. C., 13-53

    1967   "Models of the Interaction of Language and Social Setting", The
                    Journal of Social Issues 23, 2, 8-28
Kloss, H.
    1929   Nebensprachen, Vienna
Mackey, W. F.
    1962   "The Description of Bilingualism", Canadian Journal of Linguis-
                    tics 7, 51-85

    1966   "The Measurement of Bilingual Behavior", Canadian Psychologist
                    7, 75-92
Macnamara, J.
    1967c   "The Bilingual's Linguistic Performance, a psychological overview",
                    The Journal of Social Issues 23, 2, 58-77
Reimen, J. R.
    1965   "Esquisse d'une situation plurilingue, le Luxembourg", La linguis-
                    tique 2, 89-102
Saer, H.
    1931   "An Experimental Inquiry into the Education of Bilingual Peoples",
                    (In) Education in a Changing Commonwealth, Wyatt Rawson
                    (ed.), London, The New Education Fellowship, 116-122
Schmidt-Rohr, G.
    1933   Muttersprache; vom Amt der Sprache bei der Volkwerdung, Jena,
                    E. Diederichs

Thorndike, E. L. & Lorge, I.
  1959   The Teacher's Word Book of 30,000 Words, New York City,
                   Teachers College, Columbia University, 3rd ed.

Weinreich, U.
  1952a   Research Problems in Bilingualism, with Special Reference to
                   Switzerland, Unpublished Dissertation, Columbia University,
                   New York (microfilm)

  1953   Languages in Contact, Findings and Problems, 2 ed.(1963) The
                   Hague, Mouton

West, M. P.
  1926   Bilingualism; with Special Reference to Bengal, Calcutta, Gov-
                   ernment of India, Central Publication Branch

5

HOW CAN WE DESCRIBE AND MEASURE THE BEHAVIOUR
OF BILINGUAL GROUPS?

COMMENT DEFINIR ET MESURER LE COMPORTEMENT DES GROUPES
HUMAINS BILINGUES?

THEME

John Gumperz

In dealing with bilingualism as a group phenomenon, I am concerned with the behavior of individuals in social systems where both languages are in regular use, and where the choice of one language over another conveys clear social connotations. Isolated bilinguals surrounded by speakers of a single language, or even marginal individuals, such as residents of border areas bridging what would ordinarily be regarded as two distinct systems, are excluded from consideration. I will furthermore not deal with questions of degree of bilingualism and of dominance of one language over the other. I do this partly because these issues have already been treated at length in the literature (Weinreich 1953; Haugen 1956; Vildomec 1963; Diebold 1956; 1967) and partly because, as I hope to show in this paper, they are secondary to some of the more general questions about communicative competence I wish to raise here.

Any discussion of bilingualism must take account of the fact that, first of all, verbal interaction is always rule-governed, and secondly, that the rules of verbal interaction go considerably beyond what we normally understand by grammatical rules. (Hymes 1966; Gumperz 1964; Ervin-Tripp 1964) The general linguist who is concerned with grammar only works at a level of abstraction which covers but part of the verbal communication process. A generative grammar of English for example states the basic rules which underly the verbal performance of such socially diverse peoples as Midwestern Americans, speakers of Indian English, Australians, Liberians and many more. It need however not account for what we know to be the many differences in the linguistic performances of these individuals. As Dell Hymes (1966) has pointed out, linguistic competence in the sense in which Chomsky (1965) employs this term must not be confused with the ability to communicate effectively in a particular society.

The linguist's analysis furthermore does not attempt to explain the fact that any encounter between speakers always conveys more than the mere cognitive content of the message. Frequently just a few overheard words or phrases enable a casual hearer to judge, for example, whether his wife is talking to a woman or to a man, friend or stranger on the telephone, and whether she's transacting business, just chatting or having a serious discussion. To some extent information of this type is coded in the so-called paralinguistic features of voice qualifiers, loudness, or sentence speed, etc. (Trager 1958) But it is in large part also a function of choice among lexical alternates and among syntactic or phonological options. Wherever such selection conveys readily understood information it must conform to shared rules, rules which, as recent sociolinguistic research suggests, are like the rules of grammar in that they are internalized and operate largely below the level of consciousness (Labov 1964; Fischer 1964; Gumperz 1964) Bilingualism as a group phenomenon must be analyzed within the context of these rules of verbal interaction.

If bilingual communication then is not a unique phenomenon, but merely a special case of socially determined selection among linguistic variants, what are its distinguishing features? How, for example, do we recognize bilingualism on both linguistic and social grounds? How do we distinguish among different bilingual situations? These and similar questions, which have so far not received adequate attention in the literature, will be discussed here.

Although the answer to the question about the linguistic characteristics of bilingualism may at first glance seem obvious, it is by no means so if we consider the fact that the concept "a language" as it is usually used, is defined by a combination of social and linguistic criteria (Ferguson and Gumperz 1960) Pairs like Serbian and Croatian, Thai and Laotian, Hindi and Urdu, and many other similar pairs throughout the world are merely stylistic variants of each other. A person who controls both members in a set is bilingual in the social sense only. It has been suggested that these problems can be avoided by limiting the term bilingualism to cases where the varieties concerned are mutually unintelligible. Recent studies by Wolff (1964) and Blanc (1960), however, have shown that intelligibility is also a function of social factors.

Even when two speech varieties are obviously grammatically distinct, convergence resulting from language contact over time materially affects their distinctness. The degree and the nature of this effect has long been a matter of dispute. Structural linguists on the whole have tended to doubt some of the late nineteenth and early twentieth century writings on mixed languages. Edward Sapir's view that the grammatical core of a language is relatively immune to diffusion is still widely accepted. Nevertheless, more recent, structurally oriented studies by Weinreich (1952) and Emeneau (1962) reveal a number of clear instances of grammatical borrowings. Such borrowings are particularly frequent in those cases where we have evidence of widespread bilingualism.

Ethnographically oriented work on bilingual behavior further shows that not all varieties of a language are equally affected. Casual styles of either language tend to be less distant than more formal varieties. Diebold, for example, finds that phonological interference is greatest in code switching situations (1963) The colloquial Canadian French expression, "pourquoi tu l'as fait pour," cited by Mackey (1965) is a close translation equivalent of the English, "What have you done that for?" John Macnamara cites a similar example from rural dialects of Irish English, where sentences such as "I have it lost" for "I lost it" can be explained as direct translation equivalents of Gaelic. Both formal Canadian French and educated Irish English avoid such translation equivalents.

The existence of such phonological and syntactic diversity in multilingual communities suggests that what we ordinarily conceive of as two languages do not simply constitute two discrete but internally homogeneous systems. On the contrary, each language is in turn subdivided into varieties showing varying degrees of similarity to the other language. When bilinguals are at ease and not on guard, and when they talk about matters that could equally well be dealt with in either language, translatability between the two languages tends to be increased. As a result multilingual speech communities show considerably more intralanguage diversity than the equivalent monolingual communities. Language distance is not an absolute, it is a function of intensity of contact and social context.

Although the existence of convergence can no longer be in serious doubt, linguistic analysis in bilingual communities continues to employ analytical models derived from the study of monolingual communities. Among the most frequently used measures are interference, the use of elements from one language while speaking or writing another (Mackey 1965) and contrastive analysis, in which the grammars of the two languages are compared directly (Banathy, Trayer and Waddle 1966) In both cases it is assumed that the structure of the languages involved is relatively uniform and is known. Halliday, McIntosh and Strevens (1964) avoid some of these difficulties by direct translation between text in the two languages. But even here the structural categories of the monolingual norms form the main yardstick for measurement. More serious yet than the theoretical orientation is the carryover of traditional elicitation techniques into fieldwork in bilingual situations. If the linguist, as is commonly done, simply seeks out individuals who speak both languages well and asks them to repeat utterances in the two languages, he is likely to elicit formal—i.e., maximally distinct—styles. Colloquial expressions like the French and Irish examples cited above are quite likely to be suppressed as unsuitable. As long as the speakers themselves perceive the situation as a formal encounter, even requests to speak informally are not likely to produce desired results, since the rules of language choice are largely beyond conscious control. In order to elimit a realistic range of styles, new techniques for sampling verbal behavior will have to be devised.

If instead of starting with the a priori assumption that two languages are distinct, we take the opposite view and treat them as part of a single whole, many of the difficulties cited above can be avoided. This means that in his fieldwork the linguist would disregard the speaker's view of the languages as distinct entities, and treat them as part of the same linguistic repertoire (Gumperz 1964) The distinction between grammars and languages current in recent linguistic theory provides some justification for this approach. A grammar is a theoretical construct, a set of rules which underly verbal performance. A language consists of the set of utterances generated by the grammar. Implicit in the notion of grammar is the assumption that some rules are universal, that is, characteristic of human behavior as a whole, and others are language specific. If we then say that grammars may show varying degrees of relatedness, we are only carrying this notion a little bit further. We assume that for the bilingual there exists an underlying general set of rules which apply to all aspects of his behavior.   Nonshared rules can then be regarded as lower order phenomena.

Any such description of highly diverse speech behavior within a single framework will of course contain an unusually large residue of alternates or optional rules.   Labov's recent work in New York suggests a way of integrating such alternations into a linguistic description (1966) His phonetic study of speech in a number of social contexts demonstrates that it is not always possible to segment a speaker's speech performance into a finite number of articulation ranges.   For example, values of the vowel in bad may vary anywhere from [ih] to [æh]   There are no clear grounds for drawing discrete phonetic boundaries.   Labov suggests the concept of a variable for these cases. A variable defines a range of variation rather than a point of articulation. Its values vary along a scale anywhere within this range, depending on the social context.   Although Labov deals primarily with phonetic variables, there is no reason why the same concept cannot apply to variation in morphology and syntax also.   We may thus state that speakers convey social meaning by selecting variants from within the range defined by variables in linguistic structure.

But the value of one variable in a particular utterance is never independent of that of other variables within the same stretch of speech.   It is not enough to say that "X speaker from Y social class selected value 3 of the (Z) variable under certain social conditions."   It is more useful and significant to note that this same speaker who uses value 3 of the (Z) variable also uses value 1 of the (W) variable, value 4 of the (U) variable, etc.

In judging social meaning, speakers take into account whole utterances or sketches of utterances, not individual items.   Suppose a bilingual speaker of Puerto Rican Spanish has three different phonetic variants of the sentence, esta bien, as follows:

[esta bien]

[esta bieŋ]

[hta bieŋ]

The three variants may hypothetically indicate three different degrees of social distance.   They contain two variables, (S) and (N).   If we were to count only the individual instances of a particular varient of either variable taken separately, we would be unable to account for the fact that two sentences with different social meanings, e.g., 1 and 2, had the same phonetic variant,[s], of the (S) variable.   However, if we consider that in sentence 2 the [s] variant co-occurs with the [n] variant of the (N) variable, then we are able to keep them apart.   Variants thus tend to appear in co-occurrent sequences.   It is the variation of each distinctive cluster of values, not a single variant, which cor-relates with distinctive social content or function. Wherever co-occurrence rules are regular and clearly statable we can speak of speech variation as al-ternation between varieties.

Recent work on machine translation suggests a technique for measuring lan-guage distance among varieties within the repertoire as a function of the nature and number of rules needed to translate texts from one variety into the other (Gumperz 1964a; 1967) Application of this technique, which focusses directly on the speaker's code switching performance, provides empirical evidence for the view that what is ordinarily called bilingualism may correspond to linguis-tically quite distinct phenomena. Some extreme cases have been discovered where language contact over many centuries had led to virtual grammatical and phonetic identity among varieties of two genetically distinct languages used in code switching situations. Thus in central India speakers switch from the Indo-Aryan Marathi to the Dravidian Kannada by a simple process of morph for morph substitution. In effect they control one grammar with two lexica. Elsewhere, where language contact is less prolonged and intensive, differences among va-rieties may appear in all components of linguistic structure.

In spite of these differences in degree of linguistic similarity bilingual com-munication of all kinds is alike in two respects: (1) variants tend to be concen-trated at the level of morphonemics—i.e., they affect the phonological real-ization of morphemes, and (2) co-occurrence rules tend to be rigid. As a re-sult the shift between bilingual codes has a quality of abruptness, which sets it off from the more gradual transition between styles in monolingual repertoires (Gumperz 1967)

Although translatability measures have so far been used primarily to deter-mine the language distance between maximally alike varieties, they are equal-ly applicable to the problem of internal diversity. Our discussion of this phe-nomenon so far suggests that whenever a speaker controls several optional con-structions in the two languages, bilingual situations will tend to favor those al-ternates which are most readily translatable. The following example from the speech of Spanish-English bilinguals will show how this may be handled in bi-lingual description:

vamos a [dɛsiɹ]

[digamos]

let us say

Note that in sentence one an English-like periphrastic construction co-occurs with a pronunciation of decir showing English-like [ɹ] and [ɪ]
In sentence two the inflected form digamos, which has no parallel in English,

co-occurs with the Spanish-like tense pronunciation [i].

A bilingual who controls all three varieties has a repertoire characterized by a range of syntactic variables (i.e., digamos vs. vamos a decir) and a range of phonological variables with values [i] [ɩ] and [r] [ɹ] etc.) varying along a scale of decreasing translatability.

Not all members, however, control the entire range of variables. Some may have only varieties one and three, others only two and three. Others again may use Spanish-like pronunciations and syntax in their English. The measurements of translatability among varieties defined by different co-occurrent variant sequences thus becomes an important tool in distinguishing intra-community differences in bilingual performance.

The Social Determinants of Language Choice

Given the purely linguistic description of bilingualism as patterned selection of variants from among the variables within the linguistic repertoire, we must now deal with the question of the social determinants of the selection and their measurement. Although the linguistic literature contains a number of references to the phenomenon of code switching, the question has received relatively little attention so far. Charles Ferguson (1964), in one of the first systematic discussions of the problem, discusses the use of high and low speech varieties in situations of diglossia, mainly in terms of the setting (home, lecture platform, office, etc.) in which they are used. Stewart (1962) attempts to classify the language situations in multilingual countries by means of an index which takes account of the nature of the languages themselves (classical languages, vernaculars, creoles, etc.) The British linguists' concept of "register" also seems to rely on some such notion as Stewart's function (Halliday, McIntosh and Strevens 1964)

A different approach which deals with a new and highly important aspect of the problem is that of Lambert (1967) and of Labov (1966), who measure the speaker's reaction to particular forms or texts in the two languages. Fishman (1965) attempts to account for both attitudinal and situational factors by means of an index called dominance configuration.

All the above writings have done much to deepen our understanding of language usage, but they concentrate on taxonomy of usage rather than on rules of selection. I doubt that questions like Fishman's "Who speaks what language to whom and when?" can be answered in such a way as to account for the many subtle and often momentary shifts in verbal strategy which are so common in everyday talk. In dealing with social factors in verbal behavior furthermore, the aim has been to correlate linguistic data with independently measured social categories. Recent work in ethno-methodology raises some serious objections to the techniques by which such supposedly independent categories are usually determined   (Garfinkle 1967) It points out that the interviews and the test situations in which sociological data are ordinarily collected are also forms of social interaction, and that the investigators' implicit and often unstated

assumptions about these types of interactions seriously affect their interpretation of their data.

To the extent that social factors affect language usage, it must be the
speaker's perception of these factors rather than the social scientist's catego-
rixation of them in terms of class, sex, socio-economic status, etc. which is
important. This calls for a cognitive, rather than a correlational, approach to
the problem. It suggests that we regard social reality as related to the speaker's perception of this reality in somewhat the same way as sounds are related
to phonemes. Just as phonemes are a part of our model of what an individual
must know in order to speak and understand, so also social categories are models of how a speaker symbolizes his relationships to others. There is thus never
a one-to-one relationship between social categories and outside stimuli. The
speaker's categories are rather the result of a process of transformation in which
a variety of stimuli are interpreted in terms of the environment, i.e., the spee
speech event, in which they occur.

Examination of language usage in these terms shows that there are some
instances of bilingual behavior where the variety used is directly predictable
from knowledge of the setting and of the social situation. This is the case, for
example, with certain kinds of ceremonial, such as brahminical rituals, the
Roman Catholic mass, or with the language of government or court records, etc.
In these situations, measurement is relatively simple, either by direct observation or by simulating the event.

Highly determined language use, however, is frequent mainly in traditional, relatively stable situations or in small, closed groups, where to use
Bernstein's term, interaction is status-oriented. One of the effects of the rapid social change in modern urban societies and in the so-called developing
societies is that individuals may share a number of social relationships and are
free to allude to these relationships by language shift. Free conversation collected in such settings thus frequently shows what on the surface looks like almost random variation between languages and varieties. The shift between
values of variables is often so rapid that speakers are unable to report how they
shift and why. It is this type of situation which presents the most serious problems of measurement.

One way of overcoming these problems is through recordings of discussions
in natural friendship groups. Whenever such groups get together, even in the
presence of an outsider, they frequently engage in a discussion of their own
affairs. In the course of a period of time, a skilled investigator meeting with
such a group can induce them to talk about a wide variety of topics and, by
throwing out appropriate comments, can maximize the likelihood that speech
variation will occur. The social significance of what transpires can then be
interpreted either by members of the group or by others close to them. In this
way it is frequently possible to divide up what on the surface seems to be a
single stretch of speech into functionally distinct units. By analyzing the occurrence of variables within such units rather than within the passage as a
whole, it is then possible to extract cases showing a direct relationship between

changes in function and selection of variants (Blom and Gumperz 1967)

Investigations of language behavior in these terms show that speakers within the same community in addition to showing differences in range may also differ greatly in the way in which they react to equivalent social stimuli. With some, a friendly chat at home can be conducted only in informal Spanish; to use English would destroy the informality of the situation. Others, on the other hand, shift freely from English to Spanish in order to validate their expertise about certain topics or to convey degrees of intimacy. For a third group of bilinguals, English is the language of ordinary family interaction. Spanish when used is a sign of deep emotional involvement. Such people avoid speaking Spanish to one another in the presence of outsiders.

By focussing on the linguistic reflections of varying social stimuli and change within a range of variables, rather than on the classification of linguistic variants; we are testing the speaker's ability to manipulate language rather than his syntax or his pronunciation per se. Speakers may differ considerably in actual pronunciation, but if they react in the same way to similar social stimuli, their difference in pronunciation does not affect the interpretation of their performance. This enables us to account for the fact that people whose speech shows a great deal of interference may be very sensitive in conveying social meanings by code switching, and thus be effective communicators.

COMMENTARIES/COMMENTAIRES

William Labov

In these comments, I will be concerned with the relation of Gumperz's paper, and his over-all approach, to general problems of linguistic theory. One need hardly emphasize that the characteristic of Gumperz' empirical work is that it has regularly focussed upon problems of successively greater importance for our view of linguistic structure, in such a way that one result builds on another. We may consider three of his major studies in this light, representing the major research strategy that he has followed. His first reports on the sub-dialects of Khalapur provided the most detailed accounts of the social stratification of language that had been received up to that time. He also turned our attention to the process of alternation between social dialects in India, and wrestled with the problem of over-all sociolinguistic structure. The introduction that he and Ferguson provided for Linguistic Diversity in South Asia has never been surpassed as a statement of sociolinguistic principles. Gumperz then selected Hemnesberget in northern Norway as a point of contrast—a nominally unstratified society—in order to analyze the most general conditions for code-switching, and developed the methods for studying the social control of language behavior. He next located in an Indian village, Kupwar, a limiting case of bilingual contact, where Marathi and Kannada had been in contact among proficient bilinguals for many centuries. In this last case, Gumperz developed the remarkable strategy of using the well-known difficulties of mechanical translation between two standard languages to provide a convincing test of structural equivalence of these two superficially distinct languages. Thus Gumperz has demonstrated an uncanny ability to locate points which Merton would call "strategic research sites". Our current work in urban ghetto areas has been influenced and instructed a great deal by his findings.

In this paper, Gumperz refers to the study of verbal interaction and rules for the description of communicative competence in Hymes' sense. Here I will be concerned more with the narrower range of linguistic theory and the types of linguistic rules which are the usual concern of linguists; within this range we find many deficiencies, moot alternatives and insoluble problems which are illuminated by the considerations that Gumperz brings forth. The literature if full of disputes about marginal phonemes, which have never been settled; about alternative analyses of synchronic or historical problems which oscillage in popularity but are never resolved. There are at least a dozen solutions for the structural problems produced by widespread variation in the speech community and most of these are devices of disposing of variation rather than accounting for it. Many important traditional controversies and problems take on a new aspect in the light of Gumperz' arguments and techniques.

One means of dealing with odd, marginal and unintegrated phonemes is that of "Co-existent systems"(Fries & Pike 1949) While this notion has made little progress in the analysis of monolingual communities, it has been widely used in the study of bilingualism. Gumperz emphasizes the inadequacy of analyses of bilingual situations which rest upon the "co-existent" contrast of two uniform systems and attempt from such a base to predict their interaction. In our own study of monolingual speech communities, we find even more compelling reasons to abandon the traditional notion that structure and homogeneity are indissolubly associated. In a forthcoming paper, on the "Empirical Foundations for a Theory of Language Change", Weinreich, Herzog and I have proposed that a model of linguistic structure adequate to account for the fact of language change must provide for orderly heterogeneity. One must integrate not only the complex rules for code-switching, but also rules for continuous style-shifting and for social and ethnic stratification within each style in order to give a rational account of language change.

Gumperz suggests that we shift our view from the "co-existent systems" concept to that of a single repertoire which includes the entire linguistic competence of the bilingual speaker. It is important to avoid an immediate misunderstanding here. Gumperz does not suggest that the competence of every person who speaks two languages can profitably be described in terms of a single linguistic system. He refers to a bilingual community, in which all the effects of social control, attrition, translation and approximation have been operating upon the systems concerned. In such a context, he argues that we may profitably view the competence of the bilingual as a single system of interrelated rules. Here I think one must emphasize the fact that structure, interrelationship, and systematicity cannot be assumed. It is common for linguists to think of system (like language) as a thing inherently good, to believe that concepts are naturally conjunctive, that interrelationships are omnipresent, complex and immediate in their operation. Hence the emphasis on rules without exception, on the flawlessness of sound change, on the dogma that structural change is instantaneous, and that the loss or addition of a single structural element automatically re-structures the entire system. (1) If intimate structural relations are claimed between linguistic elements, it is reasonable that we ask for an empirical demonstration. The most straightforward type of evidence is

---

(1) Cf, Hockett's account of structural change: "No matter how gradual was the approach of early ME /æ/ and /ɔ/ towards each other, we cannot imagine the actual coalescence of the two other than as a sudden event: on such-and-such a day, for such-and-such a speaker or tiny group of speakers, the two fell together as /a/ and the whole system of stressed nuclei, for the particular idiolect or idiolects, was restructured." A Course in Modern Linguistics (New York: 1958), p.456f.

the establishment of strict co-occurrence rules. Given two sub-systems in alternation:

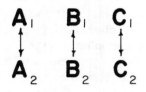

strict co-occurence rules state that we never obtain sentences of the form A_1 B_2 C_1 . . . Whatever subtle conditions determine the shift from one series to another operate equally on all; or in another view, operate upon one item but require the shift of all items because of the tight set of necessary relations that prevail. Thus we might claim that He don't know nothing is possible, and He doesn't have an inkling of the truth, but never He don't have no inkling of the truth.

Such co-occurrence rules do not establish causal relations between A_1 and B_1, since they may indeed be related through a tertium quid, linguistic or extra-linguistic. But they do indicate the existence of a single system. If all the rules governing alternation were of this character, we would have no justification for speaking of a single "repertoire". Indeed, Gumperz' early work stressed such strict co-occurrence in code-switching rules. But as his own research and others produced more exact data, it became apparent that many switching situations did not have this categorical character. We observe co-variation of a less absolute character than strict co-occurrence. We do find A_1 B_2 C_1, though perhaps rarely. In the study of co-variation, the mere frequency of a given form is not the critical fact. Systematic interrelations of A_1, B_1 and C_1 are established by the uniform direction of shift under the same conditions by their response to the same independent variables, and their description by the same quantitative functions. It is clear that many systematic generalizations of change are not instantaneous. Thus in New York City, the raising of the vowel [a] of bad, ask, dance, etc. was not immediately accompanied by the raising of [ɒ] in off, lost, etc. nor was the centralization of Martha's Vineyard [au] the immediate consequence of the centralization of [ai]. These generalizations took time—a generation or so, and in the course of this time, the social structure of the community shifted as well. In each case, other ethnic groups, with different language sub-strata, entered the community and added the indirect influence of their bilingual complication to the network of influence that already prevailed. (Labov 1965)

The demonstration of systematic co-variation by quantative means requires a stricter methodology than the mere assertion that certain forms did or did not occur. We have to know something of the population of utterances from which these forms were drawn, and the social conditions which controlled the linguistic behavior reported. With such precautions, we can construct the linguistic variable, a formal unit which represents predictable and orderly variability within the heterogeneous system. We are dealing with a rich set of such grammatical and phonological variables in our current work on the structural and functional differences which interfere with the acquisition of standard English by non-standard Negro speakers. As Gumperz points out, many of these variables may be governed by the same or similar functions, and may therefore be expressed as functions of one another. To the extent that this can be done, we are justified in speaking of code-switching within a single complex repertoire. It is worth-while pointing out that such variable elements can not be introduced by intuitive or speculative procedure; they are not tolerable within linguistic systems until the quantitative function is established which demonstrates their orderly and predictable character. Secondly, continuous variables do not imply continuous variants. One may have continuous variations based on the oscillation of two discrete variants. Some phonological variables, like palatalization of /l/ in Gumperz' Hemnes dialect, show a continuous range of possible variants which we code into a limited set of choices. Others, including most syntactic variables, give us a clear choice of A_1 or B_1; it is then the frequency of the choice which yields the continuous variable, and we have reason to believe that speakers respond to variable frequencies of this type in a categorial manner.

This mode of reasoning provides us with a more general model of language choice in which bilingualism, bidialectalism, and style-shifting are all seen as examples of the same general phenomenon, and can be studied in the same way. Many investigators of bilingual or bidialectal situations have been baffled by the failure of speakers to show strict co-occurrence rules in their alternation between systems, and they have come to the conclusion that these languages or dialects were not fully structured systems: that they were "hybridized", "pidginized", or "bastardized" forms which were defective in some serious way. This view is the inevitable consequence of the limited theoretical model which sees bilingualism as the all-or-none alternation of two separate systems, each bound by strict co-occurrence rules. If we view these alternating languages or dialects as sub-systems of a single repertoire or over-all system, we are free to study the conditions governing the alternation of any one element as a variable within the system: e.g., the variable (A) with variants A_1 and A_2. The systematic character of the two poles $A_1 B_1 C_1$ and $A_2 B_2 C_2$ can then be established conclusively by the demonstration of co-variation of the variables (A), (B), and (C). The way is then open for deeper studies of the long-range influence of languages in contact upon each other.

In his recent work on bilingualism in Kupwar, Gumperz has contributed to our understanding of the over-all character of linguistic systems, as well as the mechanism of convergence in linguistic evolution. His results challenge the notion, widely held today, that each language forms a single system in which each sub-system is profoundly influenced by the other sub-systems. I have suggested that the assumption of such a holistic grammar, bound by intricate interrelations from phonology to semantics, is not justified by any a priori reasoning.

In our contacts with linguistics, we absorb the notion that language is a tightly interrelated set of oppositions. We read that language is characterized by structures which are "a very complex set of patterns which repeatedly recur..." (2) While it is plain from the beginning that there are several such structures within language, such as the structure of expression and that of content, these separate structures form an over-all structure of their own; they "are intimately related and interacting...", and "the relations between these two complex structures are themselves quite complex."

This concept of an over-all structure, of intricately interrelated rules has been developed in more specific detail in generative grammar. In Chomsky's view, the principle means of selecting one version of a grammar against another is by an evaluation procedure internal to a given theory of language; such an evaluation procedure commonly appears as a simplicity measurement, which is ultimately a convenient means of determining whether the notational conventions involved have captured the most significant generalizations inherent in language structure. It is assumed that the scope of this evaluation measure is large:

> It is the full set of notational conventions that constitute an evaluation procedure... The factual content of an explanatory theory lies in its claim that the most highly valued grammar of the permitted form will be selected, on the basis of given data. Hence, descriptions of particular sub-systems of the grammar must be evaluated in terms of their effect on the entire system of rules. (Chomsky 1965 p. 44)

Thus we find in generative grammars that the phrase structure of the terminal strings, produced by the transformational component, is included in the input to the phonological rules; grammatical categories and boundaries must be taken into account in the most systematic derivation of the phonetic forms of words. As a first hypothesis, it seems likely that an evaluation measure should apply to the entire grammar as a single system, from the deep structure to the lowest level phonetic rules.

Until recently, there has been little evidence that would controvert this view; and on the other hand, little evidence to support it. In the continuation of the quotation given above, Chomsky notes "The extent to which particular parts of the grammar can be selected independently of others is an empirical matter about which very little is known, at present."

We do have some evidence from Creolists that the lexicon can be divorced from the grammatical structure: It is contended that various Creoles have undergone re-lexification one or several times, while the underlying Creole "grammar" has persisted. (Stewart 1962) Although this point of view is not unversally accepted, it is consistent with the data of Gumperz from Kupwar, which shows Marathi and Kannada differentiated in all lexical and morphophonemic rules,

---

(2) This and the following quotations are from Gleason, Introduction to Descriptive Linguistics (2nd. ed. New York: 1961), p.3

but equivalent in all other levels of the grammar. We are forced to contemplate the possibility of an entire section of a grammar following a different path of linguistic evolution from all of the other sections of the grammar, despite the fact that it is presumably bound to the other sections by a complex set of relations. These findings raise the possibility that there are abrupt discontinuities in a grammar. One such discontinuity appears to lie between transformational rules which manipulate general categories and those which insert specific formatives from the dictionary. Most of the sketches of transformational grammars that we have now do not show such a discontinuity: specific grammatical functors like have or be, are inserted by phrase structure rules in the phrase structure, although the tendency is to limit such over-specific phrase structure rules. Linguists have not found any principled reason why the

$$Det \rightarrow the$$

should not appear in the phrase structure instead of being entered from the dictionary; Gumperz empirical work indicates that there may be such a reason.

In these comments, I have tried to indicate some of the theoretical implications of Gumperz' work on the measurement of bilingual behavior. I have not touched on his examples from current research on Spanish-English bilingualism, which is very close to our present research site, since this is too much in progress for us to evaluate now. However firm this paper and other discussions, we expect that our work in the English speaking community will benefit considerably from his results.

P. Pandit

Whether it is stylistic variation among the varieties of one language or whether it is code-switching across mutually unintelligible varieties, variation is rule-governed behaviour and the analyst has to bring out the complex interplay of this patterned behaviour. This involves not only the units of description, but also the techniques of elicitation because all data collection will also be subjected to the same social conditioning.

Professor Gumperz has raised some important problems of the techniques of the description of bilingualism. The models of description of monolingual communication —contrastive, interference or translatibility—are not suitable because they are based on the assumption that the two languages are distinct at all levels, while in fact, convergence of the different varieties in bilingual communication has been frequently noticed; Gumperz rightly observes language distance is not an absolute, it is a function of intensity of contact and social context.

The model suggested is aimed at measuring the speaker as an effective communicator; it measures the speaker's ability to use language varieties.

Bilingualism can be described as a special frame for observation of language change; besides the proposed models of stratified equilibrium, can we not think of a model which measures the dynamics of bilingual situation?

The bilingual's selection of variants (unconscious switch) in off-the-guard, informal ("natural friendship groups") chat or discussion with varying stimuli can be observed and the measurement of "translatibility" of stretches of speech might might prove (despite the contextual diversity) that the "shared rules" in a group like this lead to an able linguistic performance, i.e. communicative effectiveness, with the help of an internally homogeneous single system of apparently two (formally speaking) distant languages.

The description and the measurement would hit upon a situation of fait accompli, after the "homogenisation" has been achieved, is mutually intelligible and is accepted and so internalised that an exposte photostat of achieved (or received?) bilingualism is available (the bilingual tongue is the mother-tongue).

The references to the state of language after "centuries" of language contact does recognise the long span during which the degree of distance, intelligibility, acceptance, internalisation etc. changed, by a linear or perhaps by a vascillating pattern. This process of change, the process of becoming one system out of two languages, is not abrupt, though, at any given moment, the sub-variations (by selecting among variants) are abruptly effected by the speakers according to the context and stimuli for their communication.

Thus, the variation which in a static frame seems to be abrupt is a very gradual (and also patterned) process where the language contact is only one aspect of the social contact over the years. This gradual change is gradual but conscious (to the first generation borrowers-cum-social climbers) at some point of time, as much as the stylistic variation is seen to be gradual and conscious. Both become unconscious or internalised to the groups who belong to the homogenising context, by a normal social conditioning.

To refine our methods of social observation and measurement empirically or to try a historical assessment logically, would be our next job if the dynamics of bilingual situation is our aim.

Félix Kahn

Par rapport au vaste sujet de discussion proposé par le programme du Colloque, Comment définir et mesurer le comportement des groupes humains bilingues?, M. John J. Gumperz a limité l'objet de sa communication à l'examen des problèmes que pose l'étude du "comportement d'individus dans des systèmes sociaux où deux langues s'emploient chacune régulièrement et où la préférence donnée à une langue par rapport à une autre comprend de nettes connotations sociales". Dans Mackey 1966, article que M. Gumperz ne mentionne pas, M. William F. Mackey se borne même au choix du cas d'un seul témoin pour illus-

trer une technique destinée à l'analyse et à la mesure du comportement bilingue de 30 Acadiens.   Les deux chercheurs tentent donc de connaître la nature
du comportement linguistique de collectivités bilingues en partant de l'étude
de cas individuels.

Pour comprendre le phénomène difficile à saisir qu'est le bilinguisme, M.
Gumperz nous invite à nous défaire de l'idée d'un dépôt de deux systèmes linguistiques distincts qui se serait effectué dans le cerveau du bilingue, afin de
n'y voir que des parties d'un seul et même répertoire linguistique, un ensemble
général de règles qui s'appliquent à tous les aspects de son comportement, tout
en laissant subsister un choix exceptionnel de variantes.   - Je me permettrai
d'illustrer cette vue par un exemple emprunté à mon pays: Un collégien suisse-
alémanique parlera son dialecte alémanique dans sa famille et avec ses cama-
rades suisses-alémaniques, mais une variété d'allemand helvétique en répondant
à son professeur pendant une leçon au collège, à moins qu'il ne s'agisse d'une
leçon consacrée à l'apprentissage d'une langue étrangère, auquel cas il s'ef-
forcera de parler la langue étrangère en question.   Pourtant, dès que la cloche
sonne et que la leçon est terminée, une norme sociale et ethnique non écrite
exige qu'élèves et maître suisses-alémaniques s'entretiennent en alémanique
et non plus en allemand.   Cette dernière langue ou une autre ne seraient tolé-
rées que dans une conversation avec une personne qui ne sait pas ou guère parler le dialecte.   En Suisse alémanique, l'emploi du dialecte et de l'allemand
a donc un caractère de complémentarité.   Dans telle situation, un Suisse alémanique utilise son dialecte; dans telle autre, la langue officielle de sa région
linguistique.   Aussi ces deux parlers peuvent-ils être considérés comme faisant
partie d'un seul et même répertoire, de même que plusieurs rôles figurent dans
le répertoire d'un artiste dramatique.

M. Gumperz admet cependant que, sous l'étiquette de bilinguisme, il
peut se cacher des phénomènes bien différents, dont la nature dépend de la durée du contact de deux idiomes, de la faculté et de la volonté des usagers de
les distinguer de façon plus ou moins stricte ou non, et de la situation dans laquelle ils sont amenés à employer tel moyen d'expression linguistique de préférence à un autre.

Le conférencier nous propose une méthode d'enquête sur le comportement
bilingue, en nous suggérant d'enregistrer des entretiens de groupes d'amis et
d'en faire interpréter la signification sociale par des membres du groupe ou par
des personnes qui leur sont proches.   Ainsi il serait possible de diviser en "unités fonctionnellement distinctes" ce qui a l'apparence d'une seule chaîne parlée.   Mais en quoi consistent ces unités?   M. Gumperz ne le précise pas ni ne
l'illustre par des exemples détaillés.   Il se contente de nous annoncer une publication de Blom et de lui-même à paraître en 1968 et il ne nous dit pas pourquoi il préfère analyser la présence de variables à l'intérieur de ces unités plutôt que dans l'ensemble du passage.

Enfin, le conférencier finit par déclarer qu'il s'intéresse moins au classement des variantes linguistiques employées par le ou les bilingues - tâche qui
incomberait pourtant au linguiste -, qu'à la façon dont les bilingues réagissent

à des facteurs sociaux semblables en préférant tel code linguistique à un autre, même si leur parler contient de nombreuses interférences entre deux idiomes. Soit. Mais M. Gumperz n' a traité avec précision et dans le détail ni le sujet qu'il a choisi lui-même pour sa communication, The Measurement of Bilingualism in Social Groups, ni le thème proposé How can we describe and measure the behaviour of bilingual groups? – D'autre part, ce qui me paraîtrait le plus nécessaire pour l'étude approfondie du comportement bilingue, c'est d'inviter les psychologues et les sociologues à scruter le pourquoi de tel et tel comportement, c'est-à-dire à tenter d'élucider les raisons psychologiques, sociales, ethniques et nationales profondes pour lesquelles tel parleur ou groupe de parleurs s'accommode d'un bilinguisme plus ou moins bâtard ou s'y complaît même, alors que d'autre (qui ne constituent qu'une minorité, mais qui peuvent être fort utiles à la société en tant que magistrats et fonctionnaires d'Etats à plusieurs langues nationales, comme représentants diplomatiques et autres à l'étranger, comme interprètes, professeurs de langues, etc.) s'efforcent de séparer proprement deux ou plusieurs systèmes linguistiques et culturels, à la manière d'un acteur qui se met tantôt dans la peau d'un personnage, tantôt dans celle d'un autre, en évitant soigneusement de mélanger les rôles. Le bilinguisme ou le multilinguisme hybrides ne dénoteraient-ils pas une grande inertie, beaucoup d'indifférence, voire de négligence, une incapacité plus ou moins marquée ou même un refus plus ou moins délibéré de s'assimiler sérieusement plusieurs idiomes et cultures et de profiter des immenses possibilités d'enrichissement psychologique, intellectuel et social qu'offre la rencontre de plusieurs univers?

DISCUSSION

English Version

The discussion revolved around the difficulties of analysing bilingual behaviour, which, in the words of one participant, were due to the synchronic fallacy. The dichotomy between synchronic and diachronic is a fiction that can be ignored if:

1. the change is so minute that it can be ignored;
2. the refinement of analysis does not get beyond distinctive features.

Since languages must evolve there must be a sort of variation as described by Labov and Gumperz, otherwise language is dead. In the case they describe evolution is more rapid than usual. In bilingual communities, interference contributes to degree of vacillation and to speed of evolution, so that a change that would take many generations in a unilingual community will take only one in a bilingual community. If this happens in generations a linguist sees, the linguist sees interference or a high degree of free variation. Both are illusions, conditioned by postulated synchronic codes. The code concept becomes more complex as degree of individual variation is a function of the rate of change. Evolution is a two-dimensional continuum, both dimensions of which are alternating in different directions. So nobody knows what is evolution of interference.

This comment was amplified by another participant who remarked that Saussure saw two characteristics in the synchronic/diachronic dichtomy:

1. the synchronic state was viewed as static;
2. there were no systematic relationships in language development.

The second proposition has been under attack for some time. The first point stood longer. Martesius of the Prague school attacked it, showing the importance of potentiality. The neo-grammarian linguists (Chomsky & Company) placed obstacles in the way of the attack. Either real language change is slow and must be observed over hundreds of years or so instantaneous that it can not be mapped. These are not good arguments. In New York City [bæd] went to [bɪəd]   in about 60 years. Social factors are important.

In a bilingual situation is change necessarily in the direction of the other language? The speakers of a lingua franca like Sango tend to choose words not in their own language. Impact draws one away from the first language. This happens in New York too.

Variation in speech, especially in a bilingual situation, is functional. This can be falsified, according to Dr. Gumperz, in an experimental situation as the linguist, being a man of some consequence, is to be pleased, come what may. It is almost a necessary condition of bilingualism itself to have two sets of morpho-phonemic rules; hut not all bilingual situations need have two sets of cognitive, phonetic, semantic, or structural rules. That there are two sets or norms is a matter for empirical investigation. But part of a set of norms could be the ability to decide which linguistic norms apply to a given social situation.

Given this competence we can visualise verbal behaviour as a set of strategies for encoding meaning into linguistic forms. Personal characteristics are not as important as social personalities and an investigator must allow for the possibility of reactions according to two different sets of norms. Dr. Gumperz quoted at this point a conversation between a Puerto Rican father and his daughter who was to go to a New England College. The household was built on the strong authority structure normal in Spanish, but in learning English, the Father had had to rely on his daughter's primary school material. They were discussing the daughter's wish to live in at the college. The father began in English, "I know they have good supervision there," and continued in Spanish, "but I want you to stay here because I want to keep the family together". Dr. Gumperz's theory was that he used English for the first part to show he really know what he was talking about and Spanish for the second to underline the importance of family.

Natural conversations should be studied in terms of relationships between role-relationships, goals and topics. Complicated models tend to be awkward to deal with. We need to find out what meanings various types of language behaviour have in certain environments so that we can compile a "dictionary" of forms of behaviour. To do this we would take samples of natural conversation and ask native speakers to interpret them for us. The social dimension makes it easier for us to sort out and account for "free" variation. We must look to bilingualism to validate concepts of "group".

Variation should be studied in group situations. One participant described the various types of linguistic situation by the following diagrams. In a monolingual situation we have:

□ = the output in surface structure of the same language.

$x_1 = y_1$; $x_2 = y_2$

In these situations there is a large development of abstract rules behind these. Neogrammarian linguistics tended to consider language development as fairly regular, and that a person always spoke the same way—this is certainly not true. We could represent a situation as the following.

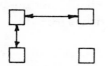

An example of this sort of variation is the position of final [ɹ] in certain dialects of English. Depending on circumstances it may or may not be pronounced, e.g. a person will at times say [faðə]   at others say [faðəɹ].   Sociolinguistics describes the factors entering into the choice between these two. But we must have a linguistic model that accounts for this. We can not write such variants off as expressive variation. There is a fact of variation that cuts across all linguistic lines or across whole language systems, even in individuals. The solution is to measure the phenomenon quantitatively, supply a function for each variable and show how often it occurs. e.g. g=f (age) (style) (ethnicity) (class). Any number of social or linguistic factors can be introduced. We can predict at least the outlines of systematic forms of linguistic behaviour.

In many language situations there is co-variation, expressed by a direct or indirect relationship between g & h. In New York, for instance, the height of the vowels /ɛ/ and /ɔ/ is related. One of the variables must be older than the other and therefore the one which conditions the other. This comes close to Gumperz model. For instance, in Boston English if you raise [ɒ] to [ɔ] you back [a] , so if you say ⌊lɔs]   you say [faðə].   This is not a class or an ethnicity variable; it is strictly related to other linguistic variables. We can begin to speak of co-existent systems. (System implies correlation between at least two linguistic items).

A model of bilingual behaviour would be the following:

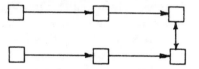

There would be one overall code-switching system, no one-to-one correspondence between elements of different languages. This is why mechanical translation is impossible. We do not have a linguistic model to deal with Dr. Hattori's examples from Tatar unless we speak of interference. This seems to be a violation of the systematic character of language.

Variation is to be accepted as a fact of communication rather than as a residue or deviation. We can not operate with models of description which were intended to describe only constants. Studies in bilingualism tend to start from idea that all that happens is interference between two systems. There is a distinction to be made between standard techniques and Gumperz's ideas. The first are micro-models; Gumperz has produced micro-models in which variants are structured within the social system. The macromodel fits all variations in language behaviour including bilingualism; this is a significant contribution. Techniques of linguistic description have been subjected to social conditioning. Code-switching has been observed through natural friendship groups.

In a given context variation is functional. It helps to preserve one's status. Outside one's own group it helps to clarify identity. Models of speech variation offer an excellent channel of vertical mobility and recognition. Labov's notion of linguistic variable as a formal unit could probably be a step in the direction of using this model for linguistic change.

Dr. Gumperz gave an example of how co-occurence can turn into co-variation. Spanish-speaking teenagers who grow up in New York tend to acquire some English articulation habits which then influence the rest of their speech. In a word like[mira] both vowels are tense compared with the English equivalents. There is also a typical stress pattern that does not occur in English, e.g. ['mɪɹəɹ]   In one type of bilingualism both norm systems are kept separate. What often happens is that the English [ɹ] replaces Spanish [r] . Then the vowels assimilate and we get [mɪɹʌ]   What is happening is collapse of distinctions, not a matter of substitution. There are key points in which substitutions have consequences for the linguistic entourage.

Dr. Gumperz was questioned on his statement that code-switching has a "quality of abruptness". By this he meant that very often, as the switching is effected through grammatical markers with high frequencies, once one notices the frequencies one has the feeling of switching between registers. In one language the linguistic signal is carried more by phonetic variations or by a gradual shift between variants. This is not possible between languages, or at least, not when the two languages are felt as separate norms.

This brought up the question of whether, in a bilingual individual, languages are, in fact, two separate norms. Dr. Gumperz's work would show that in certain pairs of language there is a one-to-one correspondence between items. Which means that all abstractions must be the same. He sees the two languages as one repertoire open to individuals. It is important to see that languages are made up of parts that do not all vary in the same way. In both bilingual and monolingual situations we will get behaviour which ranges widely with us fixed norms on either side. This carries us further into the possibility of explaining linguistic evolution. The idea of a fixed norm does not allow for language change. If we conceive of continuous variation as possible and that co-occurence gives way to co-variation, you can show that people possess two sets of norms and can show the possibility of change. In many situations there could be a fixed norm at one end and general variation at the other. The most systematic form of language behaviour is what a child learns between the ages of 5 & 6. There his language is controlled by his peers. If he uses two languages constantly then he probably has two sets of norms. If only one is learnt then, he will probably have only one set of systematic norms.

According to one participant, it was right to observe two neighbouring languages and their interactions because this was interesting in itself. But he hoped that researchers would ask themselves what was the efficacy of the communication system developed by bilinguals. This was in the domain of linguists and psycho-linguists, rather than in that of the sociologist. The definition of language accepted by many present was that language was patterned behaviour. It was necessary to underline that this behaviour was influenced by the group and by the forces one finds in society. This had been almost denied by the concept of strategies in speech. There are all sorts of limits placed on a bilingual. For example, a French-speaking Montrealer, a few years ago, slipped into

English with English-speakers because their French was hesitant; now, one had the impression of wounding friends if one changed language. This factor was not taken into account in Dr. Gumperz's model. Besides, there are rules reflecting the distribution of power in the society. The question of choice is affected by constraints in the society. There are societies which are sensitive to the proprieties of their language, others which are not. If there are no official constraints, others will develop.

In reply to a critic who taxed him with avoiding consecrated concepts like, caste, class and group, Dr. Gumperz pointed out that he avoided these terms because of the prejudices that go with them. The filter the sociologist uses for separating out aggregates is not the same as Gumperz's, who might see two aggregates where the sociologist sees one. This is something that Basil Bernstein observed. He started by talking about social class and finished by describing different patterns in social relationships which seem to be related to class but which are open to empirical investigation. Dr. Pandit, for instance, had attacked the notion of "caste dialect"; in none of the previous studies has it been proved that there is a necessary connection between caste and the dialect under study. They are rather related to other factors of education and social network. This should be a matter for empirical investigation. Political scientists and anthropologists mean different things by caste. Characteristics of caste politics in urban India are radically different from caste politics in rural India.

The procedure he intends to use on the Puerto Rican population of the New York area is to live in an apartment block in Jersey City in which everybody knows everybody else. He will be sitting in on families with his tape recorder running, watch them going about their daily lives and interacting with the local Spanish-speaking and English-speaking population. He wishes to focus attention on the kinds of repetitive routines and exchanges between individuals. He will take tapes of routines, play them to native speakers and see how the speakers divide them into sub-parts. This is a necessary part of the analysis. Linguistic analysis normally proceeds on basis of sentences. Dr. Gumperz aims at a functional analysis. What does a person intend to do? Persons might express one thought in 3 sentences or 2 thoughts in one. Native speakers can give a good working analysis. The method is the same as that of a linguist doing field work. A linguist takes stretches of speech and segments them to morphs; Gumperz segments them into functional units. Once these units have been isolated we can set up a series of variables for Spanish and English which can be marked over the stretches. There will be certain kinds of co-occurence. The other technique will be organising formal discussions among peer groups and seeing how roles vary between linguistic variations and role-shift.

One participant wondered whether some value judgments should not be made to prepare the ground for language policy. Dr. Gumperz had found that bilingual speakers of Kannada and Marathi speak both languages by morph-by-morph substitution. Bilingual behaviour takes two forms:-

1. one language can be dominant, e.g. Kannada adopts certain features of Marathi or vice-versa;

2. speakers do away with the niceties of both tongues and settle on a
common denominator, a simplified form of speech which amounts to
pidginisation.

Neither is desirable from point of view of language policy.

Much language mixture is conditioned by educational policy. There are
3 possibilities:-

1. if the speakers are illiterate, pidginisation takes place;
2. if only one language is used in school, that language is liable to become dominant;
3. if two languages are used in school, the breakdown in grammatical
categories is not bound to occur.

In the case of the Puerto Ricans of New York, it seems that the second
situation exists. There is a problem not only of fact-finding, but also of establishing desirability or non-desirability. There are possibilities or re-orient-
ing the educational system in the light of this.

This point reminded Dr. Gumperz of a conversation with Katre on his ar-
rival in India. Dr. Gumperz found him and others engaged in a serious attempt
to find a linguistic basis for stating similarities between various Indian languages. It has seemed to many people that the linguistic diversity has produced
some irretrievable divisions. But there are also great underlying unities. Linguistic splits can not be postulated along genetic lines. Experience shows that
Indo-Aryans can learn Dravidian languages more easily than American English.
This is not obvious if you go by the relationships between languages. We may
need to preserve cultural distinctions. These can be preserved in many ways.
Pidginisation is bad only insofar as it is socially disapproved of.

For another participant, Dr. Gumperz presented very little in the way of
methods to deal with the case of Spanish in New York, specifically with the
anecdote on language-switching in a father-daughter conversation. There are
two problems:-

1. How will Dr. Gumperz systematically interpret such phenomena? He
gave one anecdotal instance. How are we to go beyond this step to
provide systematic evidence? We would have to classify events and
infer a certain correlation between a given message and language.
2. How do we go about producing in natural settings a sufficient number
of instances to do something systematic?

These are basic issues.

Linguists tend to neglect the niceties of sampling. The odds are that unless selection is careful one will distort the sample of population one is dealing
with. Dr. Gumperz had also cast doubt on the notion of group, caste or class.
But even in his definition of community the notion of group tended to enter.

The ideas expressed in the first paragraph could be dealt with by cohort
analysis. There is a possibility that some changes over time is repetitive.
Small children evolve linguistic characteristics that are repeated in the next
generation with no long term change in the language. On the other hand, the
possibility of real changes occuring independently of the life-span of the

participants is there. Normally such changes are related to age.

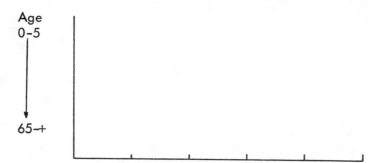

Time 1   Time 2

Over time people will change even if language remains the same; on the other
hand we must recognize possibility of language charge. If we take points 5
years apart, i.e., children of 9 years and then same children at 14 we would
not be able to determine whether changes that occurred were functions of linguistic change or aging. However if we compare 4-year-olds at time 1 with
those at time 2, we can be confident we will find changes of a permanent nature and likewise with other ages.

One participant asked. Why is survey methodology inadequate?

The Gumperz material is not visible to survey methodology. There is no
way of relating answers to survey Questions. Sociologists like Garfinkel and
Saxe recognise the difficulties. Labov's team is applying the ideas behind
Gumperz's work in Norway. It is working with groups in addition to making
surveys. Labov asked for help in enumerating groups, but was told it was too
difficult. His team took a low-income project and worked with young adolescents who helped him enumerate everybody. From this start they observed behaviour. The same thing was done in tenement areas using participant-observer
methods. Groups exist at many levels and the research people managed to locate all the named groups. Gumperz's methods go below the surface caught
by the survey. Age grading by cohort analysis is difficult as interests change
over the years with consequent difficulties in matching up research results.

The discussion was summed up by saying that Gumperz sets out to explore
communicative competence. Because of this, his model has been largely limited to establishing correlations.   It is a model of stratified equilibrium which
gives power to assign a particular variation to a particular social group. Is it
possible to use this model to study language change? Variation marks off boundaries and communication in a speech community. Linguists have operated with
the assumption that there was no other barrier but that of geography. But from
the work of Gumperz and Labov we see that certain social barriers of status
have ingenious ways of communication without assimilation. Language is not
a habit, but a conscious act of distinctive behaviour.

DISCUSSION

Version française

La discussion porte principalement sur la difficulté d'analyser le comportement bilingue, laquelle d'après l'un des participants, tient à l'idée abusive qu'on se fait du synchronisme. La dichotomie en synchronique et en diachronique est une fiction que l'on peut négliger:
1. si la modification est assez faible pour être négligeable;
2. si la finesse de l'analyse ne doit pas aller au-delà des traits distinctifs.

Puisque toute langue évolue, il se produit nécessairement une certaine variation, qu'ont décrite Labov et Gumperz, sans quoi la langue dont il s'agit serait une langue morte. Dans le cas décrit, l'évolution est plus rapide que d'ordinaire. Dans les collectivités bilingues, l'interférence influe sur le degré de vacillation et sur la rapidité de l'évolution, de sorte qu'une transformation qui se serait produite seulement après plusieurs générations dans une collectivité unilingue peut se produire en une seule génération dans une communauté bilingue. Lorsque le fait est perceptible du vivant d'un linguiste, celui-ci l'explique par l'interférence ou par un degré élevé de variation libre. Or il s'agit dans les deux cas d'une illusion, conditionnée par des codes synchroniques postulés. Ces codes sont de plus en plus complexes, car l'importance de la variation individuelle est fonction du rythme de modification. L'évolution est un continu à deux dimensions, dont l'une et l'autre alternent en sens inverse. C'est dire que personne ne sait d'une manière précise si un fait donné est évolution ou interférence.

Un autre participant amplifie ce commentaire en faisant observer que Saussure voyait deux caractéristiques dans la dichotomie synchronique - diachronique:
1. il voyait l'état synchronique comme statique;
2. il ne voyait pas, dans le développement des langues, de systèmes de rapports.

Cette seconde affirmation est contestée depuis quelque temps. La première a été plus longtemps acceptée. Martesius, de l'école de Prague, l'a attaquée en insistant sur l'importance de la potentialité. Les linguistes néogrammairiens (Chomsky et ses confrères) ont cherché à enrayer cette attaque. Ou bien la transformation réelle de la langue se produit lentement et réclame des observations étalées sur des centaines d'années, ou bien elle est tellement instantanée qu'on ne peut en fixer le moment. Ce ne sont pas là des arguments valables. A New-York [bæd] est devenu [bɪəd] en une soixantaine d'années. Les influences sociologiques sont importantes.

Dans une situation de bilinguisme, les transformations qui s'opèrent vont-elles nécessairement dans le sens de l'autre langue? Les personnes qui parlent un sabir du genre du "sango" ont tendance à choisir des mots qui n'appartiennent pas à leur propre langue. La force à laquelle ils obéissent les éloigne de leur langue première. C'est aussi ce qui arrive à New-York.

Les variations du parler, particulièrement dans les situations de bilinguisme, sont fonctionnelles. Dans les situations expérimentales, d'après M. Gumperz, cette règle est parfois faussée, car le linguiste, étant un homme d'un certain prestige, on cherchera à lui plaire. Il est à peu près nécessaire que tout bilinguisme comporte deux ensembles de règles morpho-phonémiques; cependant, ce n'est pas dans toutes les situations de bilinguisme qu'il y a deux ensembles de règles cognitives, phonétiques, sémantiques ou structurelles. L'existence de deux ensembles de normes doit être constatée par voie d'investigation empirique. Il se peut toutefois que l'aptitude à choisir celles des normes linguistiques qui conviennent à telle ou telle situation sociale fasse partie elle-même d'un ensemble de normes.

A partir de cette aptitude on peut voir le comportement verbal comme constituant un ensemble de "stratégies" pour l'expression des significations par des formes linguistiques. Les caractéristiques personnelles n'ont pas la même importance que les personnalités sociales, et l'investigateur doit tenir compte de la possibilité de réactions déterminées par deux ensembles différents de normes. M. Gumperz, à ce propos, cite une conversation entre un Porto-ricain et sa fille qui allait s'inscrire à un collège de Nouvelle-Angleterre. Dans la famille, l'autorité du père était très forte, comme il est habituel dans la tradition hispanique; cependant, pour apprendre l'anglais, le père avait dû se servir des livres utilisés par sa fille à l'école élémentaire. Il était question que la jeune fille, suivant son propre désir, soit pensionnaire au collège. Le père lui dit, en anglais: "Je sais bien que la surveillance est bonne, là-bas." Il continue ensuite en espagnol: "Mais j'aime mieux que tu loges à la maison, parce que je tiens à ce que la famille reste unie". M. Gumperz en déduit que le père s'est servi de l'anglais au début pour bien montrer qu'il savait de quoi il parlait, et de l'espagnol ensuite pour bien faire sentir l'importance qu'il attachait à la famille.

Les conversations naturelles doivent être étudiées du point de vue des rapports entre relations de rôle, objets recherchés et thèmes. Les modèles de conversations, dès qu'ils se compliquent, deviennent peu maniables. Il est nécessaire de connaître la signification que peuvent avoir les divers comportements linguistiques dans certaines conditions de milieu, afin de pouvoir établir une sorte de "dictionnaire" des modes de comportement. Il faudrait à cette fin prélever des échantillons de conversations naturelles et les faire interpréter par des locuteurs indigènes. La dimension sociale facilite le tri des variations "libre" et leur interprétation. Le bilinguisme est la clé des concepts valables de "groupe".

Il faut étudier les variations qui se produisent dans les situations de groupe. Un des participants définit graphiquement de la façon suivante les divers genres de situations linguistiques. Situation de monolinguisme:

□ ◄—————► □

□ = utilisation effective des structures de surface d'une même langue.

$x_1 = y_1$; $x_2 = y_2$

Ces situations comportent un fort développement de règles abstraites qui ne se voient pas en surface. La linguistique des néo-grammairiens a tendance à voir le développement de la langue comme relativement régulier; selon elle, une personne parle toujours de la même façon. Cela n'est certainement pas exact. Une situation peut se représenter de la façon suivante:

$$X_3 = Y_3 \ (g) \quad X_4 = Y_4 \ (h)$$

On trouve un exemple de ce genre de variation dans la position du [ɹ] terminal dans certains dialectes de l'anglais. Suivant les circonstances, il est ou n'est pas prononcé; on prononce parfois [faðə] et parfois [faðəɹ] La sociolinguistique décèle les éléments qui déterminent le choix entre ces deux prononciations. Il faut pourtant établir un modèle linguistique propre à expliquer ce comportement. Ce n'est pas assez de seulement appeler varia- tions d'expression les variantes de ce genre. Il y a telle chose qu'une varia- tion qui recoupe toutes les démarcations linguistiques et tous les systèmes de langue, même chez l'individu. La solution consiste à mesurer quantitativement le phénomène, à attribuer une fonction à chacune des variables et à montrer la fréquence de la variation. Par exemple, g=f (âge) (style) (ethnicité) (classe sociale). On peut faire entrer en jeu un nombre indéfini de facteurs sociaux ou linguistiques. Il est possible de prédire au moins les lignes générales des formes systématiques de comportement linguistique.

Dans de nombreuses situations de langue, on constate une covariation, qu'exprime un rapport direct ou indirect entre g et h. A New-York, par exem- ple, l'ouverture des voyelles /ɛ/ et /ɔ/ obéit à un rapport. Il faut que l'une des variables soit plus ancienne que l'autre et qu'elle soit par consé- quent celle qui conditionne l'autre. Cela se rapproche du modèle Gumperz. Par exemple, dans le parler anglais de Boston, lorsque [ɒ] devient [ɔ], le [a] est modifié; lorsque l'on dit [lɔs] , il faut dire [faðə]. Il ne s'agit pas là d'une variante de classe sociale ou d'ethnicité; la modification est rigoureusement liée à d'autres variables linguistiques. On peut commencer à parler de systèmes coexistants. (En disant système, on suppose une corréla- tion entre au moins deux faits de langue.)

Voici un modèle de comportement bilingue:

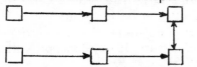

Il y aurait alors un seul système général d'aiguillage, et non pas une corres- pondance point par point entre éléments de langues différentes. C'est pour

cette raison que toute traduction mécanique est impossible. Nous n'avons pas
de modèle linguistique à noyre disposition pour étudier les exemples que M.
Hattori a tirés du tartare, à moins de les considérer comme des faits d'interférence. Il semble y avoir là une violation du caractère systématique du langage.

La variation doit être acceptée comme un fait de communication plutôt
que comme un bas produit ou une déviation. On ne peut rien faire avec des
modèles de description qui ont été conçus à l'origine pour ne décrire que des
constantes. Les études portant sur le bilinguisme partent en général de l'idée
que tout ce qui se produit provient d'une interférence entre deux systèmes.
Il y a lieu d'établir une distinction entre les techniques habituelles et les idées
de Gumperz. Les premières constituent des micromodèles; Gumperz a établi
des micromodèles dans lesquels les variantes sont structurées à l'intérieur même
du système social. Le micromodèle répond à toutes les variations du comportement linguistique, y compris le bilinguisme; c'est là une contribution précieuse.
Les techniques de description linguistique ont été soumises au conditionnement
social. L'aiguillage, ou passage d'un code à un autre, a été observé par recours à des groupes fondés sur une camaraderie naturelle.

Dans un contexte donné, la variation est fonctionnelle. Elle aide l'individu à préserver sa condition sociale. En dehors du groupe dont il fait partie,
elle l'aide à préciser son identité. Les modèles de variation du langage fournissent d'avantageuses possibilités de mobilité verticale et d'acceptation sociale. L'idée que se fait Labov de la variable linguistique comme d'une unité
formelle constitue probablement un pas de plus vers l'utilisation de ce modèle
en vue d'une évolution linguistique.

M. Gumperz a donné un exemple de la manière dont la comanifestation
peut devenir une covariation. Les adolescents de langue espagnole qui gran-
dissent à New-York sont portés à acquérir certains modes d'articulation in-
fluencés par l'anglais, qui retentissent ensuite sur l'ensemble de leur parler.
Dans un mot comme [mira], les deux voyelles sont plus nettes que les voyelles
anglaises correspondantes. L'accentuation du mot est différente aussi de ce
qu'elle serait en anglais, soit [ˈmɪɹəɹ]. Un des genres de bilinguisme
maintient la séparation des deux systemes de normes. Souvent, toutefois, le
/ɹ/ anglais se substitue au [r] espagnol. Dès lors, les voyelles s'anglici-
sent aussi et la prononciation du mot devient [ˈmɪɹʌ].   Il n'y a pas eu
substitution véritable, mais disparition des distinctions. Lorsqu'elles se produisent dans certaines zones de la langue, les substitutions de ce genre retentissent sur l'ensemble du parler.

Quelqu'un demande à M. Gumperz ce qu'il entend par la "qualité abrup-
te" de l'aiguillage d'un code à un autre. Cela signifie, explique-t-il, que
l'aiguillage se fait grâce à des repères grammaticaux de grande fréquence et
qu'une fois conscient de ces fréquences on a l'impression de passer carrément
d'un registre à un autre. Dans chacune des deux langues, le signal linguistique est donné surtout par des variations phonétiques ou par un changement gra-
duel de variante. Cela n'est pas possible d'une langue à l'autre, du moins
lorsque les deux langues nous apparaissent comme constituant des normes distinctes.

La question se pose alors de savoir si, chez le bilingue, les deux langues constituent effectivement deux normes distinctes. Les travaux de M. Gumperz semblent indiquer qu'il y aurait dans certaines langues, examinées deux à deux, une correspondance exacte entre les éléments individuels. Cela signifierait que toutes les abstractions sont identiques dans l'une et l'autre langue. Les deux langues constitueraient un répertoire unique dans lequel chacun pourrait puiser. Il importe de voir que les langues sont constituées d'éléments qui ne varient pas tous de la même façon. Dans les situations de bilinguisme comme dans celles de monolinguisme, on constate des comportements, de part et d'autre, qui varient beaucoup et fort capricieusement. Cela ajoute à la possibilité d'expliquer l'évolution linguistique. L'idée de normes fixes, par opposition à des normes capricieuses, ne permet pas d'expliquer les modifications de la langue. Si l'on conçoit comme possible une variation continue et que l'on voit la covariation se substituer à la comanifestation, on peut démontrer que les bilingues possèdent deux ensembles de normes, et dès lors on démontre la possibilité de la transformation des langues dont il s'agit. Dans bien des situations, on pourrait constater l'existence d'une norme fixe au point de départ et d'une variation générale au terme de l'évolution. La forme la plus systématique du comportement linguistique se présente dans le parler que l'enfant apprend entre les âges de 5 et 6 ans. A cet âge, son parler est contrôlé par les autres enfants. S'il a recours constamment à deux langues, on constatera probablement qu'il observe deux ensembles de normes. S'il n'apprend à cet âge qu'une seule langue, il n'aura probablement qu'un seul ensemble de normes systématiques.

D'après l'un des participants, il est bon d'observer deux langues voisines et l'influence de chacune sur l'autre ne serait-ce que pour l'intérêt de la chose. Il souhaite cependant que les chercheurs se demandent quelle peut-être l'efficacité du système de communication mis au point par les bilingues. Ce sont là les domaines du linguiste et du psycholinguiste plutôt que celui du sociologue. La définition du langage qu'acceptent de nombreux participants en fait un comportement à physionomie typique. On doit souligner que ce comportement est influencé par le groupe et par les forces qui agissent dans la vie sociale, ce dont ne tient à peu près aucun compte la théorie des "stratégies" du locuteur. Le bilingue éprouve de nombreuses contraintes. Par exemple, tel Montréalais de langue française, il y a quelques années, se mettait à parler anglais avec ses interlocuteurs anglais lorsque leur français n'était pas suffisamment assuré; toutefois, lorsque l'on change ainsi de langue, on a l'impression de "lâcher" ses amis. Le modèle de M. Gumperz ne tient pas compte de cet élément. Il existe d'autre part des règles qui naissent de la répartition de la puissance dans la société. Le choix du locuteur est modifié par les contraintes sociales. Certains milieux tiennent plus que d'autres à la qualité de la langue. Lorsqu'il n'y a pas de contraintes officielles, il en apparaît de spontanées.

Répondant à un participant qui lui reprochait de laisser de côté des notions aussi classiques que la caste, la classe sociale et le groupe, M. Gumperz précise qu'il évite ces termes en raison des préjugés qui en sont inséparables. Le filtre dont se sert le sociologue pour disjoindre les éléments intimement mê-lés n'est pas le même que celui de Gumperz, qui verra parfois deux éléments là où le sociologue n'en voit qu'un. Il s'agit d'une observation déjà faite par Basil Bernstein, qui au départ parlait des classes sociales et, au point d'arrivée, décrivait des modes différents de relations sociales paraissant être déterminés par les classes sociales mais qu'une investigation empirique ne confirmait pas toujours. M. Pandit, par exemple, s'en est pris à la notion de "dialecte de caste"; il n'a été prouvé par aucune des études faites jusqu'ici qu'un lien né-cessaire existe entre la caste et le dialecte étudié. Le dialecte se rattache plutôt à d'autres éléments, comme l'instruction et le milieu social. Il fau-drait une investigation empirique de cette question. La caste n'est pas une même réalité pour le politicologue et l'anthropologue. Dans la vie politique de l'Inde, le rôle de la caste est radicalement différent dans les villes et à la campagne.

Pour étudier la population porto-ricaine de la région de New-York, il se propose de s'installer dans un immeuble de Jersey City où chacun connaît ses voisins. Il pénétrera dans les groupes familiaux, enregistrera sur magnétophone les conversations, observera la vie quotidienne de chacun et les divers rapports avec hispanophones et anglophones du quartier. Il souhaite pouvoir concen-trer son attention sur les échanges et les séquences qui se répètent entre mêmes individus. Il enregistrera les séquences, les fera entendre à des Porto-ricains et les leur fera subdiviser. Ce sera là une opération nécessaire de l'analyse. L'analyse linguistique, normalement, travaille d'abord sur des phrases. M. Gumperz entend procéder pour sa part par analyse fonctionnelle. Que cherche à faire la personne dont il s'agit? Certains ont besoin de trois phrases pour exprimer une seule idée, alors que d'autres en expriment deux en une phrase. Les locuteurs indigènes sont capables d'une bonne analyse de travail. La mé-thode à suivre est la même que pour les travaux sur place du linguiste. On prend des fragments de conversation et on les subdivise par mots et formes; Gumperz lui, les subdivise par unités fonctionnelles. Une fois isolées ces u-nités, il devient possible de dresser une liste de variables espagnoles et anglai-ses que l'on inscrit au-dessus des fragments de conversation. On voit appa-raître alors des comanifestations. L'autre technique consiste à organiser des discussions en bonne et due forme entre personnes du même milieu afin de voir la manière dont les rôles varient entre variations linguistiques et déplacements des rôles.

Un des participants demande s'il ne faudrait pas établir certains jugements de valeur pour toute politique linguistique. M. Gumperz a constaté que des locuteurs bilingues de kannada et de mahrate passent d'une langue à l'autre en transposant les phrases mot par mot, forme par forme. Le bilinguisme obéit à deux modes:

1. l'une des langues domine; par exemple, le kannada adopte certaines caractéristiques du mahrate, ou vice versa;

2. le locuteur renonce aux caractéristiques propres de l'une et l'autre

langue et adopte un commun dénominateur, une forme simplifiée de langage, c'est-à-dire ni plus ni moins qu'un sabir.

Du point de vue d'une politique linguistique, ces deux modes d'agir sont déplorables.

Le mélange des langues est souvent conditionné par la politique d'éducation. Il y a trois possibilités:

1. le locuteur est analphabète et l'on voit naître un sabir;
2. une seule langue est utilisée à l'école, et elle tend à l'emporter sur l'autre;
3. deux langues sont utilisées à l'école, et les différences grammaticales subsistent dans l'une et l'autre.

Dans le cas des Porto-ricains de New-York, c'est apparemment la deuxième situation qui règne. Il ne s'agit pas seulement de constater ce qui se fait, mais aussi de savoir si cela est souhaitable ou non. Une réorientation du système d'éducation peut alors intervenir.

Cette question rappelle à M. Gumperz un entretien qu'il a eu avec M. Katre à son arrivée en Inde. M. Katre, avec des confrères, recherchait méthodiquement une base linguistique de définition des ressemblances qui existent entre les langues de l'Inde. On croit souvent que la diversité linguistique a produit des divisions irréparables. Cependant, il subsiste de grandes zones sous-jacentes d'unité. Les divisions sur le plan linguistique ne correspondent pas obligatoirement à des divisions sur le plan des races. L'expérience a démontré que les Indo-Aryens apprennent plus facilement les langues dravidiennes qu'ils n'apprennent l'anglais des Etats-Unis. Cela, pourtant, n'est pas indiqué par les rapports de parenté entre les langues dont il s'agit. Il est parfois souhaitable de préserver les différences culturelles. On peut les préserver de diverses manières. La création des sabirs n'est à regretter que là où la société ne les admet pas.

D'après un autre participant, M. Gumperz n'a pas donné grande indication des méthodes à suivre pour étudier le cas de la langue espagnole à New-York, en particulier avec son anecdote sur le passage d'une langue à l'autre dans la conversation entre le père et sa fille. Deux questions se posent:

1. De quelle façon M. Gumperz interprétera-t-il systématiquement les phénomènes de ce genre? Il n'a donné qu'un exemple isolé, qu'une anecdote. De quelle façon pourra-t-on aller plus loin et trouver systématiquement des preuves? Il faudrait classer les faits, découvrir un certain rapport entre tel message et la langue qui convient pour le transmettre.
2. De quelle façon reproduira-t-on dans des conditions naturelles un nombre suffisant de cas typiques, de telle sorte que l'étude faite soit systématique?

Ce sont là des questions fondamentales.

Les linguistes ont tendance à négliger certaines rigueurs des méthodes d'échantillonnage. Quand la sélection n'obéit pas à une méthode rigoureuse, on a toutes chances de fausser l'échantillonnage de population sur lequel on veut travailler. M. Gumperz a aussi laissé planer un doute sur la notion de groupe, de caste ou de classe sociale. Pourtant, même dans sa définition de la collectivité, la notion de groupe tend à jouer un rôle.

Les idées exprimées dans le premier paragraphe relèvent de l'analyse "par cohortes". Il n'est pas impossible que certaines modifications se répètent à longue échéance. Les enfants en bas âge acquièrent des caractéristiques linguistiques qui se répètent à la génération suivante sans que la langue ne soit modifiée à long terme. D'autre part, il est possible que des modifications réelles se produisent sur une durée plus longue que celle de la vie des participants. Normalement, les transformations de ce genre sont liées à l'âge.

AGE

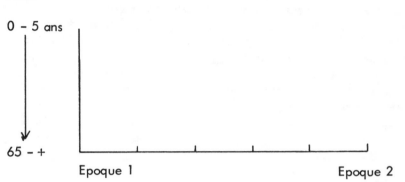

0 – 5 ans

65 – +

Epoque 1   Epoque 2

Sur un long espace de temps, les personnes changent, mais la langue reste la même; il n'est pourtant pas impossible que la langue se modifie. A ne considérer que des intervalles de cinq ans, par exemple chez des enfants à l'âge de 9 ans puis de 14, il ne serait pas possible de savoir si les modifications constatées relèvent d'une modification de la langue ou simplement de la croissance des enfants. Toutefois, si l'on compare des enfants de 4 ans de l'époque 1 et des enfants de 4 ans de l'époque 2, il est certain que l'on constatera des modifications durables. Ce sera la même chose pour les autres âges.

Un des participants demande à M. Gumperz pourquoi la méthodologie des relevés lui paraît insuffisante?

Les matières sur lesquelles travaille M. Gumperz ne sont pas appréciables par la méthodologie des relevés. Celle-ci ne permet pas d'établir le rapport entre les questions posées et les réponses reçues. Des sociologues comme Garfinkel et Saxe reconnaissent cette difficulté. L'équipe de Labov met en pratique les idées qui ont inspiré, en Norvège, les travaux de Gumperz. Cette équipe ne se contente pas d'exécuter des relevés; elle travaille aussi sur des groupes. Labov a fait appel à des concours extérieurs pour l'énumération des groupes, mais on lui a répondu que ce serait trop difficile. Son équipe a choisi un quartier de petits propriétaires où de jeunes adolescents l'ont aidé à faire l'énumération des personnes. L'équipe a ensuite observé le comportement de ces personnes. Elle a fait la même chose d'autre part dans des quartiers de

locataires, avec des méthodes faisant intervenir participants et observateurs.
Les groupes existent à de nombreux niveaux; l'équipe de recherche s'est effor-
cée de distinguer chacun des groupes nommés. Les méthodes de Gumperz permettent de pénétrer par-dessous la surface à laquelle s'arrête le relevé. La
sélection des âges au moyen de l'analyse "par cohortes" est assez difficile,
car les intérêts ne sont plus les mêmes auprès quelques années, ce qui nuit à
la comparaison des résultats.

Pour clore la discussion, on résume en disant que M. Gumperz cherche à
explorer la compétence en matière de communication. Aussi son modèle s'en
tient-il surtout à l'établissement des rapports réciproques. C'est un modèle
d'équilibre stratifié qui permet d'attribuer telle variation à tel groupe social.
Est-il possible de faire servir ce modèle à l'étude des modifications du langage?
Les variations du langage tracent les limites de la communication à l'intérieur
d'une collectivité linguistique. Les linguistes ont toujours travaillé à partir
de l'idée que la seule limite était géographique.   Il ressort cependant des travaux de Gumperz et Labov que certaines limites se situant sur le plan de la
condition sociale donnent lieu à des modes ingénieux de communication d'en-
traînant pas l'assimilation. Le parler n'est pas une habitude, mais un acte
conscient de comportement distinctif.

CHAIRMAN'S SUMMARY/BILAN DE LA SEANCE

Joshua A. Fishman

1. Thesis

Current advanced thinking concerning societal bilingualism—such as that which marked our discussions on this topic during the Moncton Seminar—clearly represents a break with traditional models. Those models viewed societal bilingualism as an <u>inter-</u>group phenomenon resulting from the contact between essentially separate monolingual groups. Given this thesis the basic sociological task was to contrast bilingual "middlemen" with their respective monolingual compatriots to determine when and why the "other tongue" (L_2) was employed and to predict the rate of return to a monolingual outcome which was considered to be the only natural and stable organization of social interaction. Psychological and linguistic research were also held captive by this thesis. Psychologists concentrated on measures of how well L_2 was mastered (i.e. how quickly, how correctly, how complicatedly), since bilingualism was viewed as basically "unnatural" and, therefore, some "price" had to be paid, some toll had to be exacted in comparison with monolingual normality. Linguists too joined in the hunt and found evidence of "interference" at every level: phonetic, lexical, grammatical and semantic. The natural state of languages was that of pristine purity and separation. Bilinguals forced languages into fortunate intercourse and it was rare, indeed, to find that no "damage" had been done to either or both.

It seems clear to me that the thesis which consciously or unconsciously guided so much past research on bilingualism in general, and on societal bilingualism in particular, was, in large part, a result of erroneous generalization from limited Western experience. Bilingualism was confused with some of its atypical concomitants: large scale immigration and other social or personal dislocations related to intergroup contacts. The acculturating immigrant or his offspring, the Westernizing "native", the struggling "foreign language" student, the downtrodden but dedicated cultural nationalist, these were the bilingual subjects on which bilingual research and bilingual theory were based. The notion of widespread, stable intra-group bilingualism (such as exists even today in over half of the world) was unrepresented in the work on societal bilingualism and, as a result, that work was sterile.

2. Antithesis

Our discussions concerning societal bilingualism at Moncton showed how far the pendulum has swung from the initial (conscious or unconscious) theses of bygone years. Instead of being viewed as the temporary or transitional consequence of separate, monolingual societies "in (unfortunate) contact", societal bilingualism is now viewed as a (possibly) stable and widespread phenomenon in its own right. Instead of searching for the differences between the bilingual "middleman" (be they students, elites, traders, assimilators, etc.) and their more normal monolingual compatriots modern sociolinguistic research on bilingualism seeks to determine which members of a bi- (or multi-) lingual society employ which variety (from among a whole repertoire available in the bilingual community) in which functional context. Membership in a bilingual society is viewed as no different from membership in any other in that it results in norm-regulated communicative interaction such that certain usage is considered appropriate (and is, therefore, effective) in certain contexts. Indeed, it is because of this basic similarity between societies marked by widespread and stable bilingualism, on the one hand, and monolingual societies on the other that it is felt that the study of societal (intra-group) bilingualism should be of interest to all students of societal interaction. Since the markers of differentiable varieties (the relative frequencies with which given linguistic variables are realized in particular ways) are somewhat more easily recognizable in bilingual than in monolingual societies the differentiable contexts of social interaction (interactions between specifiable role-relationships, locales, topics and purposes) may also become more recognizable. Thus, those scholars concerned with social process analysis per se, or with the functional demarcation of structural groupings (age groups, occupational groups, educational groups, ethnic groups, religious groups, etc.) may well be attracted to the study of societal bilingualism as an arena which offers easier access to theoretical and methodological clarifications of all-pervading significance.

A very similar counterpart position describes the antithesis linguistic view of bilingualism. Instead of "witch-hunting" for bilingual interferences modern sociolinguistics recognizes the linguistic repertoires of bilingual societies as an instance of the repertoires that characterize all functionally diversified speech communities. Indeed, it is because of this basic similarity that the differentiation of the linguistic repertoires of bilingual speech communities should be of interest to all students of modern descriptive linguistics. Sociolinguistic differentiation may be more recognizable in bilingual than in monolingual repertoires and, as a result, the study of bilingual repertoires may contribute to the solution of basic theoretical and methodological problems facing modern linguistics as a whole.

My, how the worm has turned! However, as with all intellectual revolutions (and modern sociolinguistics is such for both of the parent disciplines involved) the antithesis view of societal bilingualism is marked by certain excesses. These are accidents of intellectual history which derive—as did the thesis model—from the societal and disciplinary problems which happened to co-occur with the rise of modern sociolinguistics itself.

3. Critique

In correcting or counteracting the biases and limitations of the classical ("thesis") approaches to societal bilingualism the modern sociolinguistic "antithesis", so ably presented at Moncton by the speaker, various discussants and several participants, reveals a number of unjustifiable (and unnecessary) biases of its own:

a. At one level the objection to the reality of groups ("groups do not behave; individuals behave. Groups are frequently no more than constructs of the social scientist") merits no particular attention. Social psychology and sociology were forced to demonstrate the reality of groups quite early in their development and this demonstration continues to be performed successfully whenever the consequences of grouping are revealed. The "antithesis" discovery that some groups are structural or analytic devices of the scientist's own making whereas others are functionally real "out there" ("real communities are aggregates whose members exchange messages frequently and who share norms for the interpretation of messages") is truly touching but sadly anticlimactic for anyone who is aware of the intellectual history of sociology, social psychology or political science. The differences between structuralism and functionalism cannot be fruitfully examined on the grounds of "reality", but, rather on the grounds of their contrastive contributions to particular problems to be investigated and answered.

Thus, the only reason why the "antithesis" objection to the reality of groups needs to be taken seriously at all is that it may, in its blindness, make it impossible for sociolinguistics to do that which it is best fitted to do: describe and measure societal bilingualism. To define groups out of existence, to fail to describe functional groups merely because of theoretical bias with respect to structural groups, to fail to seek out the web between process and structure and thereby constantly improve the formulation of structural grouping is to resign from a responsibility rather than to face it responsibly.

b. The reluctance to struggle with structural grouping, and, indeed, the reluctance to consider functional groups to represent the same level of reality as individual functioning is related to another atomistic excess of "antithesis" sociolinguistics in relation to bilingualism (as well as in relation to its other concerns). "Antithesis" sociolinguistics is faced by the Heisenberg-like dilemma of seeking to describe synchronic systems so accurately that all else is lost sight of: above all a parsimonious approach to the notion of repertoire.

Initially the construct of "language" was successfully revealed to be an "abstraction" covering a repertoire of varieties, each with contextually appropriate social meanings. Subsequently the construct "variety" has been revealed to be an "abstraction" covering an (an arbitrary) range and frequency of realizations of particular phonetic and syntactic "variables". As a result, it is no longer deemed sufficiently "refined" or "accurate" to designate the languages or varieties employed in a bilingual setting since any such designation represents a grouping or lumping in contrast to the ultimate descriptive finesse currently attainable.

A similar reluctance characterizes the approach of "antithesis" sociolinguistics to the question of when particular varieties are employed in bilingual societies. The opposition to structural categories leads to a basic reliance on purported inter-personal meanings. Changed frequencies and ranges of variable-realizations are related to phenomenologically experienced changes in "situations" or to phenomenologically experienced changes in "metaphors" (humor, contrast, emphasis, etc.). Just as there is reluctance to engage in grouping risks in designating populations and in designating codes so is there a hypersensitivity to designate the kinds of contexts (situational environments that have societal relevance) in which designated kinds of societal members utilize designated varieties.

The "antithesis" sociolinguistic approach to societal bilingualism is micro-process-oriented with such a vengeance that it not only cannot parsimoniously cope with nomothetic formulations and macro-structure problems but it also defines these formulations and problems as unreal and non-existent. As a result, it often fails to objectify its findings in the sense of reporting frequencies of occurrence or non-occurrence of whatever it is that is being studied ("dependent variable") in precisely defined kinds of individuals, situations or codes in such a fashion as to advance the replicability goals of social science.

c. A final excess of "revolutionary" sociolinguistic antithesis thinking as it applies to the measurement and description of societal bilingualism is its lack of interest (if not active opposition) with respect to attitudinal factors. This opposition has a long prior history in linguistics proper where what an informant actually says rather than what he thinks he says (or what he thinks about what he says, or what he thinks he should say) is the only matter of interest. The opposition to recognizing cognitive-affective self-regulation of usage also has prior social anthropological origins in that the dominant style or research in that field is one of participant and non-directive observation in small communities of very ordinary, unmobilized, "unspoiled" membership. Most directly, however, the reluctance to recognize self-regulation (and self-monitoring or self-report), or to study those social networks in whose bilingualism such factors are most marked, is derived from the prominence of these very factors and these very populations in the earlier work on inter-group bilingualism against which much of sociolinguistics has revolted.

As with the other excesses with which the sociolinguistic revolution has confronted the study of societal bilingualism the reluctance to engage in attitudinal, ideological and self-report inquiry strikes at a worthwhile point. Much earlier work on societal bilingualism (indeed, much of the earlier work in which I myself have engaged) is probably overly removed from the primary data of actual speech because of its well high exclusive preoccupation with self-report. However, if such work failed to examine the relationship between language

attitudes, ideologies and actual language behavior and, furthermore, if such
work dealt almost exclusively with sub-populations selected because of their
particular suitability with respect to the one-sided methodology employed,
these very same charges are now equally (though oppositely) true of the antithesis approach to the study of societal bilingualism.

As a result of its insistence on deriving the speech norms of a bilingual society and its reluctance to study those (teachers, writers, politicians, students
and other sophisticates) who can verbalize these norms and possibly guide their
own language behavior (and that of others) consciously, the antithesis approach
to societal bilingualism cuts itself off from studying important segments of many
bilingual societies. It is false to suppose that only inter-group bilinguals or
"cultural bilinguals" show little switching (due to their more frequent "middleman" role vis-a-vis monolinguals). It is false to suppose that language ideologies and movements arise only as a result of the encounters between conflicting
monolingual populations. Indeed, without studying the ideologically more mo-
bilized segments of bilingual societies where such obtain (and they are not necessarily seeking to disturb the existing functional allocation or variation of
codes), and without contrasting their bilingual attitudes with their bilingual
behaviors in a whole host of contexts, no valid societal description can be
attained.

It is as harmful for the study of societal bilingualism to ignore attitudes/
ideologies as to overemphasize them. As with the other two factors mentioned
above (opposition to societal-grouping and opposition to code-grouping) the
antithesis approach to the role of attitudes and self-report in societal bilingualism has gone too far and has wound up throwing out the baby with the bath
water.

4. Synthesis

Both microsociology and macrosociology represent long and fruitful lines
of inquiry and it would be a pity if the study of societal bilingualism were not
to develop so as to benefit from both, or, at the very least, so as to benefit
from whichever of the two happened to be more appropriate to the problems
clamoring for attention. The "antithesis" approach that was so fully examined
during our deliberations at Moncton is related in its origins and predilections
to the current rejuvenation of microsociology under the general label of ethnomethodology. Ethnomethodology seeks to discover the rules by which members
of a social order carry out their practical, everyday activities. The members
of a social order have knowledge of these rules but, for most of them, it is
knowledge-in-use rather than knowledge that is ideologically organized and
available for accurate and coherent self-report. One of the tasks of ethnomethodology is to discover (and then to formally describe) the rules that organize "talk" in society. As a result of its basic concern with the everyday rounds
of societal behavior in general and its interest in "talk" or conversations in
particular (and the relationship between "talk" and other common social

behaviors) ethnomethodology obviously contributes not only a welcome but a necessary approach to the study of societal bilingualism.

The past decade has also witnessed a revival of interest in macrosociology with its emphases on the structure of total societies as well as their relationships and contrasts or similarities to each other. In macrosociology the processes of social interaction continue to remain of paramount interest but they can no longer be analyzed or comprehended without recourse to social structure. Since its task is (frequently) the characterization of entire nations (rather than only of particular face-to-face inter-action networks) macrosociology faces a very complex task and one admittedly surrounded by methodological problems. In struggling with its problems macrosociology frequently makes use of comparative data and draws upon a greater variety of data than is necessary for ethnomethodological work. At its best—i.e. when it is most penetrating and stimulating—macrosociological research draws upon historical records (including law codes), qualitative impressions, demographic data, attitude and opinion data, behavioral surveys purposely located in terms of a stratified sampling plan, etc. Rather than being at loggerheads with microsociology (including, but not limited to ethnomethodology) macrosociology requires and pursues sure roots at lower-order levels of analysis, otherwise its structural and stratificational categories will be erroneously derived and its findings unenlightening or misleading. Because sociology also needs to be able to comprehend and compare societies and nations as "wholes", because some attributes of societies (and of modern societies in particular) manifest themselves at no other level as clearly as at the national level (e.g. national mobilizatıon and integration) it would be a pity, indeed, if the study of societal bilingualism (or of other sociolinguistic concerns) were so constrained as not to be able to proceed along macrosociological lines.

The study of societal bilingualism is currently an exciting, vigorous area of inquiry for investigators in various countries working in various intellectual traditions. This being the case, I am sure that the next decade will witness many investigations of the kinds that were underrepresented in our deliberations at Moncton. We need studies of societal bilingualism that do not get so lost in the minutia of description in terms of any current equilibrium model that they are unable to demonstrate changes in the pattern as a result of social change. (I underscore demonstrate to emphasize that I do not mean "anecdotal commentary", initially provocative though that may be.) We definitely need studies that contrast intellectual and ideologized groups with more ordinary members of national societies at various stages of modernization. There must certainly be studies of societal bilingualism under stress. There must also be studies that seek a rapprochement with the older tradition of research on intergroup bilingualism since societal bilingualism is not always (and, perhaps, not even usually) entirely of one kind or the other. Degree of mastery is frequently of importance in bilingual societies, particularly when language maintenance or language shift are highlighted in the process of political, economic and cultural conflict.

The study of societal bilingualism is now both too vital and too mature to be long delayed and misled by sectarian biases. It will doubtlessly select what is best from all theoretical and methodological traditions and, in this process, contribute to their enrichment as well.

BIBLIOGRAPHY/BIBLIOGRAPHIE

Banathy, B., Trayer, E. & Waddle, C. D.
   1966 "The Use of Contrastive Data in Foreign Language Course Develop-
           ment". (In) Trends in Language Teaching. A. Vadman (ed.),
           New York, McGraw-Hill, 35-56
Blanc, H.
   1964 Communal Dialects in Baghdad, Cambridge, Harvard University Press
Blom, J. P. & Gumperz, J. J.
   1968 "Some Social Determinants of Verbal Behavior," (In) Directions in
           Sociolinguistics; the Ethnography of Communication, Gumperz
           & Hymes (eds.), New York, Holt, Rinehart & Winston
Chomsky, N.
   1965 Aspects of the Theory of Syntax, Cambridge, Massachusetts Institute
           of Technology Press (Research Laboratory of Electronics, Special
           Technical Report, No. 11)
Diebold, A. R.
   1964 "Incipient Bilingualism,"(In) Language in Culture and Society; a
           reader in linguistics and anthropology, Dell Hymes (ed.), New
           York, Harper & Row, 495-508

   1963 "Code-Switching in Greek-English Bilingual Speech," (In) Report
           of the Thirteenth Annual Roundtable Meeting on Linguistics and
           Language Studies, E. D. Woodworth & R. J. de Pueto (eds.),
           Washington, Georgetown University Press

   1965 "A Survey of Psycholinguistic Research," 1954-65, (In) Psycholin-
           guistics; a survey of theory and research problems, C. E. Osgood
           & T. A. Sebeck (eds.), Bloomington, Indiana, 205-291
Emeneau, M.
   1962 "Bilingualism and Structural Borrowing," Proceedings of the American
           Philosophical Society 106, 430-442
Engler, R.
   1966 Edition critique du cours de Saussure, Weisbaden, Harrassowitz
Ervin-Tripp, S.
   1964 "An Analysis of the Interaction of Language, Topic, and Listener,"
           American Anthropologist 66, 6, Part 2, 86-102
Ferguson, C. A., Gumperz, J. J.
   1960 "Introduction," (In) Linguistic Diversity in South Asia; studies in re-
           gional, social and functional variation, Ferguson & Gumperz
           (eds.), Bloomington, Indiana, (Series: Indiana University Research
           Centre in Anthropoligy, Folklore, and Linguistics, Publication
           No. 13)

   1964 "Diglossia," (In) Language in Culture and Society; a reader in

linguistics and anthropology, Del Hymes (ed.), New York, H
Harper & Row, 429-439

Fischer, J. L.

1964 "Social Influences on the Choice of a Linguistic Variant," (In) Language in Culture and Society; a reader in linguistics and anthropology, Dell Hymes (ed.), New York, Harper & Row, 483-488

Fishman, J. A.

1965 "Who Speaks What Language to Whom and When?", La linguistique
2, 67-88

Fries, C. C., Pike, K. L.

1949 "Co-existent Phonemic Systems," Language 25, 29-50

Gleason, H. A.

1961 An Introduction to Descriptive Linguistics, 2nd ed. New York, Holt,
Rinehart & Winston

Gumperz, J. J.

1964a "Hindi-Punjabi Code-Switching in Delhi," (In) Proceedings of the
9th International Congress of Linguists, H. G. Lunt (ed.), The
Hague, Mouton, 1115-1124

1964b "Linguistic and Social Interaction in Two Communities," American
Anthropologist 66, 6, Part 2, 137-153

1966 "On the Ethnology of Linguistic Change," (In) Sociolinguistics;
proceedings of the UCLA sociolinguistics Conference, 1964, W.
Bright (ed.), The Hague, Mouton, 27-49

1967 "On the Linguistic Markers of Bilingual Communication," The
Journal of Social Issues 23, 2, 48-57

Halliday, M. A. K., McIntosh, A., Stevens, P.

1964 The Linguistic Sciences and Language Teaching, London, Longmans

Haugen, E.

1954 "Problems of Bilingual Description," Georgetown University Monographs on Languages and Linguistics 7: 9-19

1956 Bilingualism in the Americas; a bibliography and research guide,
American Dialect Society, University of Alabama Press

Hockett, C. F.

1958 A Course in Modern Linguistics, New York, Macmillan

Labov, W.

1966 The Social Tratification of English in New York City, Washington,
Centre for Applied Linguistics

1966 "Hypercorrection by the Lower Middle Class as a Factor in Linguistic
Change," (In) Sociolinguistics; proceedings of the UCLA sociolinguistics conference, 1964, W. Bright (ed.), The Hague, Mouton, 84-113

1965c On the Mechanism of Linguistic Change, Georgetown University
        Monographs on Languages and Linguistics, No. 18, 91-114

Lambert, W. E.
  1967 "A Social Psychology of Bilingualism," The Journal of Social Issues
        23, 2, 91-109

Mackey, W. F.
  1965 "Bilingual Interference; its analysis and measurement," The Journal
        of Communication 15, 239-249

  1966 "The Measurement of Bilingual Behavior," Canadian Psychologist 7,
        75-92

Steward, W.
  1962 "Creole Languages in the Caribbean," (In) Study of the Role of Sec-
        ond Languages in Asia, Africa, and Latin America, F. Rice (ed.)
        Washington, Centre for Applied Linguistics of the Modern Lan-
        guage Association of America, 34-53

Stewart, W. A.
  1962 "An Outline of Linguistic. Typology for Describing Multilingualism,"
        (In) Study of the Role of Second Languages in Asia, Africa, and
        Latin America, F. Rice (ed.), Washington, Centre for Applied
        Linguistics of the Modern Language Association of America, 15-25

Trayer, G. L.
  1958 "Paralanguage; a first approximation," Studies in Linguistics 13, 1-12

  1964 "Paralanguage; a first approximation," (In) Language in Culture and
        Society; a reader in linguistics and anthropology, Dell Hymes
        (ed.), New York, Harper & Row, 274-288

Vildomec, V.
  1963 Multilingualism, Leyden, A. W. Sythoff

Weinreich, U.
  1953 Languages in Contact; findings and problems, New York, Linguistic
        Circle of New York (Series: Linguistic Circle of New York,
        Publications, No. 2)

1952b "Sabesdiker Losn in Yiddish; a problem of linguistic affinity," Word
        8, 360-377

Wolff, H.
  1964 "Intelligibility and Inter-Ethnic Attitudes," (In) Language in Culture
        and Society; a reader in linguistics and anthropology, Dell Hymes
        (ed.), New York, Harper & Row, 440-445

6

HOW CAN WE DESCRIBE AND MEASURE THE INCIDENCE AND DISTRIBUTION OF BILINGUALISM?

COMMENT DEFINIR ET MESURER L'INCIDENCE ET LA REPARTITION DU BILINGUISME?

THEME

Stanley Lieberson

The kinds of questions about bilingualism that can be asked in a census or any large scale survey are restricted by certain limitations inherent to such studies. The questionnaire must be constructed so that it can be readily understood not only by the respondents but by interviewers who will normally have no technical competence in linguistics. The goal of censuses is usually to eliminate or minimize the judgements required of the field workers. Moreover, the questions must be completed in a relatively short period of time. This means that there are many facets of bilingualism which, at least at present, cannot be measured on a general purpose census. To expect a census to tap such dimensions as interference, switching, diglossia, dialects, styles and registers would be like listening to a soprano amplified through the sound system of ball park. There are aspects of bilingualism for which the instrument is inadequate. If a population were surveyed about their diglossia, for example, there is reason to believe that many would be unaware of, or would at least deny, their use of the low variety (Ferguson 1964 p.431).

On the other hand, censuses offer certain important advantages. They can yield data on bilingualism for a far larger population than any linguist could possibly hope to interview during a lifetime of work. Moreover, the coverage is relatively more complete and less distorted than what would normally be obtained in the field. In addition, the possibility is presented of linking the data with earlier censuses of the same area as well as with other bilingual settings. In other words, censuses are not appropriate for linguistic analysis per se, but they are an excellent device for determining the frequency, distribution, trends, and social correlates of bilingualism.

One major problem about bilingualism questions in censuses pertains to the validity of the results obtained. There is the possibility of intentional distortion by the respondent because of either prestige, political, or ethnic reasons. Commenting on the adequacy of the linguistic data in the 1940 census of Brazil, Mortara (1950, pp.39-40) observes that the results would have been far less satisfactory after Brazil's neutrality ceased. Census results from some parts of India have been questioned on these grounds (see, for example, the discussion of Kelley 1966 p.306). But even the well-intentioned respondent will often find it difficult to give a correct answer to the census-taker's question about the languages he can speak. If bilingualism is not clearly defined by the profession, ranging from Bloomfield's "native-like control of two languages" on to Diebold's conception of passive-knowledge (Mackey 1962 p.52), what can be expected of the linguistically naive respondent?

Thus, the problem comes down to the optimal questions about bilingualism that will minimize intentional distortion, reduce the subjectivity of the respondents' answers, and provide the researcher with meaningful information about the linguistic capacity of the population which will be most suitable for analysis with other social characteristics obtained in the census. In other words, after deciding on the most desired information about this elusive quality called "bilingualism," the goal is to develop simple questions that will reproduce as nearly as possible the results that would be obtained if expert linguists had interviewed and classified each respondent according to a specific set of criteria.

There are two other major problems in the demographic study of bilingualism besides the development of measures of linguistic ability suitable for censuses. It is necessary to also determine what other social characteristics of the respondents are relevant and worth measuring. Second, one must also know the appropriate descriptive and analytical techniques to use with the data obtained. For the moment, little need be said about these two issues since they mainly involve errors of omission rather than commission.

Attempted solutions

Several different types of language questions have been asked on censuses which are pertinent to measuring bilingualism. These are: mother tongue; language used in the home or most frequently; and ability to speak one or more languages (United Nations 1964 p.39). Although only the latter question deals directly with bilingualism, the first two are important to consider since they provide crucial linguistic information about the population and may, at times, be used to infer some aspects of bilingualism. Information on only the bilingual capacities of a population, unless accompanied by data on their mother tongues, ethnic origins or some other similar characteristic, fail to indicate which segments of the population have been acquiring additional languages. Some of the Belgian censuses provide a good illustration of these difficulties. Although reporting trilingualism as well as bilingualism and monoglots, no information is given on the native tongue of the respondents. Instead data are reported on language preference, a very ambiguous matter. This makes it difficult to determine mother tongues of the multilingual population.

The questions used to measure bilingualism are usually rather simple and, although usually dealing with the skills of speaking and understanding, they are often ambiguous for all but the most fluent and the most ignorant. In most instances the answers are restricted to certain specific languages, although some nations instruct the enumerator to merely record the language(s) reported by the respondent. The question is often of the utmost in simplicity, for example, the 1961 question on Gaelic in the census of Scotland merely asked the enumerator to check off those who speak Gaelic only or both Gaelic and English. The commentary is rather revealing: "'Speaking Gaelic' is itself an expression that was left to the interpretation of the persons supplying the information on the schedule." (General Register Office 1966 p. ix).

In the 1930 census of the United States an effort was made to learn if the foreign born population could speak English. The entire set of instructions for the enumerator were as follows: "Write 'Yes' for a person 10 years of age and over who can speak English, and 'No' for a person who can not speak English. For persons under 10 years of age leave the column blank." (Bureau of the Census 1933 p. 1400). In evaluating these data, the Bureau acknowledged that "determination of this ability has been left to the judgement of the enumerator, and no specific tests of the knowledge of the English language have been prescribed. The standards may therefore be subject to some variations in different parts of the country, but on the whole the replies are believed to indicate the ability or inability to use the English language in ordinary daily activities." (Bureau of the Census 1935 p. 1437).

The question on bilingualism used in Canada for a number of decades is equally simple: "Can you speak English? French?". The Enumeration Manual, at least for the 1951 census, raises no questions about the meaning of the question other than with respect to infants (Dominion Bureau of Statistics 1951 p. p. 40). A slight variation of this approach is evident in the 1960 census of Americans living overseas where the question dealt with ability to speak any of the local languages. The provisal was made, "If he knows only a few words of the language, check 'NO'." (Bureau of the Census 1964 p. xix). Likewise, in the question used for the District of Puerto Rico, "Persons were classified as able to speak English if they reported that they could make themselves understood in English. However, persons who could speak only a few words, such as 'Hello' and 'Goodbye,' were classified as unable to speak English." (Bureau of the Census 1962 p. xx). Thus, there is sometimes an effort made to slightly qualify the question so as to eliminate an affirmative answer among those with very minimal linguistic competence. Nevertheless the illustrations above are by no means exceptional in the degree to which bilingualism is left unclassified.

In passing it should be noted that both the Puerto Rican and Scotland questions, although dealing primarily with the individual's ability to speak a single specified language, can be used to draw inferences about bilingualism. In Scotland, unless a respondent indicates that he can only speak Gaelic, it may be safely inferred that he speaks English. Likewise, if one assumes that virtually everyone speaks Spanish in Puerto Rico, knowledge of the English speaking ability of various segments of the population enables one to classify the population into those who are bilingual in both tongues. In these instances the procedure would involve errors, for example, there will be some Puerto Ricans who know English but not Spanish and there must surely be recent residents of Scotland who know neither English nor Gaelic. But clearly under some circumstances it is possible to gain a great deal of information about bilingualism by only concentrating on one language. To be sure, it would eliminate certain types of data which could prove of value. This lop-sided type of question would not be appropriate in any nation where linguistic pluralism was more complex. Another economical move sometimes employed is to enumerate bilingualism in only one part of a nation, for example, the report on the Welsh speaking population of England and Wales covers Wales only.

Attempts have been made to further restrict, and thereby specify, the meaning of the bilingualism questions. The Republic of the Philippines in their 1960 census used a conversational criterion: "Any person who can carry a simple conversation in Tagalog, English or Spanish on ordinary topics is considered 'able' (to speak) for the purpose of this census." (Bureau of Census and Statistics 1960 p.xxiii). A similar test of speaking ability was used in Ceylon in the 1953 enumeration except that the criteria were either an ability to conduct a short conversation or "understand and answer questions put in that language." (Department of Census and Statistics 1957 p.125).

The Indian censuses have included a question on bilingualism in addition to the inquiry on mother tongue. Respondents in 1961 were asked if they knew any other language(s) with the goal of recording those which the individual "speaks and understands best and can use with felicity in communicating with others. Such language or languages will exclude dialects of the same mother tongue." (Office of the Registrar General 1965a p.437). Although up to two languages were accepted in addition to mother tongue, the published results gave only the first of the two languages. This was rather unfortunate since there was no particular ordering requested in the listings of the additional languages.

Enumerators in the Israeli census of 1948 were instructed to record all of the languages used by the respondents in daily living beginning with the one used most often (Gil and Sicron 1956 p.lxxi). This provides a measure of bilingualism which is distinct from the ones mentioned earlier in two important ways. First the census dealt with the use rather than knowledge of various tongues, making it possible for a completely fluent speaker of a given tongue to not be recorded as bilingual if he did not use the language. Second, it allows for some ranking among the languages of bilinguals since the respondent has hopefully indicated the one used most.

There are several non-census studies of bilingualism which merit attention because of their enumeration procedures. The Reyburns' study of the Mosquito Coast of Nicaragua and Honduras employed an elaborate set of questions for this linguistically complex area. Two items of particular interest here are those dealing with "Communication Elements" and "Chronological Bilingualism." Communication elements are reading, writing, understanding, and speaking. The individual's ability in each language for each of these were to be determined, leading to series of different combinations which could be constructed, for example, only reading, writing and reading, understanding-reading-speaking, etc. (Reyburn 1956 pp.10-11).

The concept of "Chronological Bilingualism" deals with both the degree of mastery of each language and the age at which it was first acquired. Distinctions were drawn between full and partial mastery of a tongue, as well as between whether a language was first learned before or after the age of 14 (Reyburn 1956 p.12). In addition, the Reyburns propose obtaining these data for four generations by asking each respondent about two preceding and one descending generation.

However, as interesting as these questions may be, nowhere is there any indication of how the interviewer is to determine the actual degree of ability in each tongue for the various communication elements. In the questionnaire used for the Nicaragua survey, for example, the interviewer simply checks off whether the respondent is fluent, satisfactory, minimal, or has forgotten (Reyburn 1956 p.50). Thus Reyburn fails to give us any idea about handling the validity issue or how the naive respondent is to answer or even what the interviewer is supposed to look for in making a judgement.

The Center for Applied Linguistics in Dakar employed a worthwhile set of questions to survey the linguistic abilities of school children in Senegal. For each child, the ethnic origin of the father and mother was obtained along with the language spoken at home and any additional tongues used by the child (Wioland 1965 p.20). This procedure, although less elaborate than Reyburn's, also permits determination of linguistic shifts between generations if the mother tongues of the parents can be assumed on the basis of their ethnic origin. However, again I could not find any indication of the validity of the data obtained. Incidentally, this more limited procedure for determining inter-generational shifts is probably more practical in most cases than questions dealing with two generations back.

Diebold, in his study of San Mateo, Mexico, developed a 100-word lexicostatictics list in Huave which he presented to the native Huave speaking villagers. Having previously classified the respondents into monolinguals, subordinate bilinguals, and coordinate bilinguals with respect to their Spanish speaking ability, he then asked them to indicate the Spanish correspondence to each Huave word on the list. The mean number and range of correct responses for his three categories of speaking ability of Spanish differed in the direction which might be expected. The fact that the monolingual group, that is, those classified as able to speak only Huave, were able to give correct answers to about a third of the words on the list suggested to Diebold the importance of recognizing incipient bilingualism. In addition, the possibility was raised of using this procedure in other linguistic surveys. But, for the moment, it should be noted that the initial classification of speakers into the three categories of Spanish speaking ability was made on what were admittedly "highly impressionistic" grounds (Diebold 1961 p.104).

Critique of Attempts to Date

Questions on mother tongue deal with a linguistic characteristic which most respondents should have little difficulty in answering. To be sure there are certain improvements that could be made, for example, censuses seem to never recognize the possibility that a respondent could have more than one mother tongue. Moreover, although the United Nations has recommended that mother tongue be defined as "the language usually spoken in the individual's home in his early childhood, although not necessarily spoken by him at present" (Department of Economic and Social Affairs 1959 p.21), it would be worth knowing exactly why this is preferable to asking for the first language which the respondent learned as a child. In particular, the first question would be rather inappropriate for bilingual parents who elect to raise their off-spring in their acquired language despite the fact that they prefer to use their native tongue among themselves. This, it seems to me, would be an important consideration in countries with a sizable immigrant population.

Census enumerations of the single language most frequently used have varied widely, including such characteristics as language usually spoken, language best spoken, language spoken fluently, language spoken with the family, language spoken in addition to mother tongue or official language, etc. (Department of Economic & Social Affairs 1959 p.23). Most of these questions, which I assume are aimed at determining the primary language used by the population, are clearly ambiguous and demand difficult judgements by the respondents. It seems to me that the optimal solution would be to ask a question on language used most frequently at home. Not only is this less ambiguous than many alternatives, but it provides information on an extremely important factor in determining the bilingual character of the nation. Moreover, the linguistic situation in many other socially important settings such as work and school can be inferred if the results of the bilingualism question are cross-tabulated with suitable social characteristics of the population. Nevertheless, there is a serious consideration about the language used at home which has not received sufficient attention. Namely, a not insignificant segment of the population of many western and urbanized nations probably live alone and hence could not answer such a question without publicly admitting that they talk to themselves! In such instances, I would favor asking an alternative question such as the language favored in thinking or among friends or socially.

But the main difficulties pertain to the questions asked in connection with bilingualism. In a number of instances we have observed that the question is put so simply as to make it very unclear to the respondent or the interviewer exactly what is meant. Although linguistic ability is an admittedly difficult question to ask at best, since second language skills range so greatly, such ambiguous questions more or less court erratic responses, considerations of prestige, and nationalistic fervor. Census reports on this problem, as some of the earlier quotations suggested, have often been rather casual about the ambiguity of their questions while at the same time confident about the validity of the results obtained.

There has been very little effort made to determine the distortions due to extraneous factors influencing the respondents. One notable exception is India, which published careful reports on the accuracy of the linguistic returns for each State, recognizing the political and ethnic agitation which occurred in some parts of the nation. Likewise, Gil and Sicron point out that the frequency

in which Hebrew was indicated in the 1948 census of Israel may have been intentionally exaggerated because of the national pride during the early days of
the new nation (Gil & Sicron 1956). This undoubtedly is a consideration in
other countries as well.

Nevertheless, little effort has been made to examine the data on bilingualism in San Mateo disclosed that 19 per cent were either subordinate or coordinate bilinguals, but all that is told about the results from the 1950 census
is that less than 20 per cent were bilingual in the village and surrounding area
(Diebold 1961 p.104). Thus, there is reason to think that the census was not
too far off from the results obtained by a trained linguist, assuming that the
former was not trying to include cases of incipient bilingualism.

A desirable procedure in censuses is to conduct a post-enumeration survey
of a small sample of the population to probe further into their responses and
then make some estimates of the accuracy of the census results with respect to
the various questions asked. Although the United States Census Bureau has
published a series of technical papers dealing with the 1960 census, I have not
been able to find any evaluations of the mother tongue question asked. Fishman (1966 p.422) reports a "correction factor" of 1.4 for mother tongue data
in 1960, claiming these data are therefore more reliable than those for age by
sex, color or race, residence in 1955, and year moved into present house.
Unfortunately, he is apparently referring to the adjustments used to deal with
sampling variability, a rather different matter from the issue at hand (see Bureau of the Census 1966 pp.xii–xiii). Another failure has been in the absence
of techniques for the evaluation of the internal and external consistency of the
language data in censuses. In the case of age returns, the Indian census was
able to use Myer's Index of Digital Preference and Whipple's Index of Con-
centration to evaluate the accuracy of the data. By contrast, very little has
been done to develop measures of the reliability and validity of language returns, although the present author has outlined some techniques (see Lieberson
1966 pp.272–278).

Recent statistical developments have made it possible to infer the response
variance in census questions. The Dominion Bureau of Statistics experimented
in the 1961 census with re-enumeration and interpenetrating samples to derive
some estimates of the consistency of the results obtained. I. P. Fellegi reports
results for the mother tongue, bilingualism, and ethnic origin questions which
are relatively poor compared to other items in the census. "These questions,"
he observes, "are quite emotionally charged in Canada, and as it turns out,
the interviewers did not seem to be detached." (Fellegi 1964 p.1037). It
would be particularly worthwhile to know what the results might be if a less
ambiguous question on bilingualism were used. Nevertheless, the results are
probably not that bad by normal standards of social research. These pioneering efforts in Canada should be tried out in other countries as well. However,
it should be noted that these techniques cannot be used to estimate systematic
but consistent errors on the part of respondents and interviewers.

There are certain errors of omission in the gathering and reporting of bilingualism data which could be readily corrected. Some countries will not collect linguistic data for some segments of the population. Thus, for example, the Union of South Africa censuses did not ask about the African languages spoken by Europeans. Likewise, Weinreich (1957, p.231) has criticized the Indian census for not accepting English as a second language—a shortcoming which was corrected in the 1961 census. I have already alluded to the frequent failure of countries to report cross-tabulations when two or more different language questions were asked on the census. But another important difficulty that could be readily corrected is the failure to cross-tabulate the language data with a wide range of social characteristics aside from just sex and age.

Based on his conception of incipient bilingualism, Diebold has criticized census data for "concealing in the category 'monolingual' some very real measure of bilingualism." (Diebold 1961 p.111). In this regard, I do not think that the censuses can be properly criticized since it does not seem to me that incipient bilingualism is an appropriate dimension for censuses to tap. If the goal is to determine the social correlates of bilingualism, then to a certain degree a limited knowledge of some words in a second language is of little significance. Virtually everyone in the United States or Canada, for example, would have to be classified to some minute degree as incipient bilingual speakers of German, French, and Spanish since probably most know a few words in these languages. Rather, it seems to me that the basic issue is whether a language is known well enough to use conversationally or in reading, etc. To be sure an incipient bilingual is closer to this state of affairs than one who is completely monolingual, but only as a special measure of potential, rather than actual bilingualism, can I find much reason for demographic and other institutional studies of bilingualism to obtain such data.

What Remains to be Done

The most glaring weakness of census procedures is the failure to consider the validity of the data obtained on language questions. One particular difficulty is due to the fact that linguists themselves would probably not be in agreement on the definition of the term "bilingual." It would be foolhardy to develop here a single most adequate definition. Rather, what has to be done is select a relevant target and then figure out how best to measure it. I would suggest that serious consideration be given to measuring bilingualism on censuses in terms of an ability to carry on a social conversation in the language(s). This would measure both the ability to understand and speak a given tongue. In my opinion these are the kinds of linguistic skills which would be most suitable for enumeration in censuses, given the limitations described earlier. Along with information gathered on the language used most frequently at home and the mother tongue of the respondent, a wide range of problem could be studied which deal with bilingualism in its demographic and institutional context. Information on the mother tongue of the respondents' parents, would be of enormous help in inferring inter-generational shifts.

These three (or four) items, when analyzed along with the social characteristics of the population, would provide the investigator with many possible
inferences as to language use. Many of the linguistic domains that might be
studied through a lengthy questionnaire such as that proposed by several investigators recently (Fishman 1966; Lieberson 1966) could also be inferred by cross-
tabulating linguistic information with the relevant social characteristics. For
example, occupational pressures could be inferred by cross-tabulating linguistic ability with the occupations reported by respondents. The impact of education could be inferred by means of the linguistic associations with age and years
of school completed. Indeed it is one thing to ask individuals what languages
are used in the schools and it is quite different to ask whether they can engage
in a social conversation in the language. Many of the influences of various
domains could be determined by cross-tabulation between linguistic ability and
both age and sex. For example, it was possible to compare the degree of bilingualism by these two characteristics in Montreal and infer the influence of
social contacts between small children, second language learning in schools,
occupational pressures, and the experiences in middle and older ages of life
(Lieberson 1965). The Scottish census of 1961 drew all kinds of inferences
about the use and position of Gaelic by means of only a handful of cross-tabulations with relevant social characteristics.

My point is not that censuses and other surveys of this type are cure-alls
for determining the social context of bilingualism, for obviously there are too
many subtleties to both bilingualism as a linguistic phenomenon and to social
contexts or domains to make this possible. Rather, it is that sociolinguists have
generally failed to utilize the linguistic data available to them in censuses except for the most elementary descriptive purposes. Several important exceptions
come to mind, to be sure, for example, Weinreich (1957), Fishman (1966),
Kelley (1966), Arès (1964), Deutsch (1953), and Coates (1961), but overall the
data remain neglected.

It also follows that the study of bilingualism in its demographic and institutional contexts have failed to employ all of the descriptive and inferential
techniques that are available. I have already indicated the failure to develop
sufficient rigor in testing the validity of the data as well as their internal and
external consistency. What I have in mind here are the wide range of statistical techniques developed in demography and human ecology for dealing with
census data. There are all sorts of controls that are possible, to say nothing of
descriptive methods for describing spatial distributions of social phenomena
(see, for example, Duncan 1957; Duncan, Cuzzort, & Duncan 1961). Many
of these are readily applicable to the study of bilingualism. It is even possible
to draw inferences about linguistic phenomena even when the data are not presented in a fully satisfactory fashion as has been demonstrated with the Canadian
censuses (Lieberson 1966 pp.264-66). Finally, I must confess to considerable
enthusiasm about the measures proposed by Greenberg for quantitatively describing the linguistic properties and diversity of social aggregates (see Greenberg 1956; Lieberson 1964). These measures do not describe the actual inter-

action within a population in a social psychological sense. But they do provide a quantitative measure of diversity, the communication potential in a multi-lingual setting, and the role of bilingualism in raising intelligibility.

But whatever the dimension of bilingualism measured on a census, Diebold's development of the concept of incipient bilingualism makes it all the more apparent that greater specification of bilingualism must be employed, both in terms of skills and medium. Further, any definition implies a number of different ways in which it could be measured or indexed in a survey. Thus, it is absolutely crucial that the issue of validity be examined both before and after a census. In particular, pilot tests should be made on a wide range of possible questions to determine which one gets closest to what linguists would have concluded had they been interviewing the entire population. These experiments should make it possible for investigators to determine what question elicits the best set of answers in the sense that they most closely correspondent with the results obtained by linguists who interviewed the respondents afterwards. Likewise, there is no question that more attention must be paid to post-enumeration surveys in order to determine how closely the results correspond to the goals of the census questions. After all it is one thing to observe popular agitation for certain linguistic response or to speculate that biases may have crept into the census, but it is quite another to find out in quantitative terms just how widespread and significant these distortions actually were.

COMMENTARIES/COMMENTAIRES

Heinz Kloss

Prefatory Notes: Core Problems and Marginal Problems

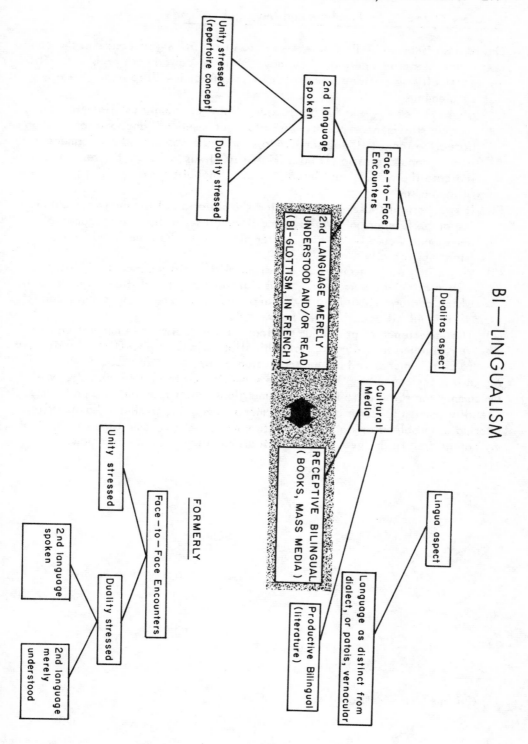

BI—LINGUALISM

Unity stressed (repertoire concept)

Duality stressed

2nd language spoken

Face—to—Face Encounters

Dualitas aspect

2nd LANGUAGE MERELY UNDERSTOOD AND/OR READ (BI-GLOTTISM, IN FRENCH)

Cultural Media

RECEPTIVE BILINGUAL (BOOKS, MASS MEDIA)

Lingua aspect

Language as distinct from dialect, or patois, vernacular

Productive Bilingual (literature)

FORMERLY

Unity stressed

Face—to—Face Encounters

Duality stressed

2nd language spoken

2nd language merely understood

Prefatory Notes: Core Problems and Marginal Problems

The topics discussed by Prof. Lieberson are of central significance in the context of the Moncton meeting, they may rightly be called core problems. There
are practically no critical remarks I have to offer. I wish to underline a few
of his statements.

(1) Where the census asks for the language most commonly used we frequently
     receive statements recording the informant's second language rather than
     his native tongue (Lieberson p.446). In these cases, if the informants live
     in a monopaidoglossic (1) area (Haiti; rural Alsace) such figures actually
     indicate the extent, and intensity, of bilingualism—frequently replacive
     bilingualism.

(2) It is important that we bear in mind the situation of the many persons liv-
     ing alone (Lieberson p.453); to me it would seem that the language of in-
     ner speech would be an even better alternative than that used among
     friends or socially.

(3) While it is useful to have at our disposal Diebold's concept of "incipient
     bilingualism" Lieberson (p.456) is right in stating that this is a dimension
     which censuses should not try to explore. The same holds for my concept
     of residual bilingualism (see below 1.4).

(4) The importance of post-enumeration or rather between-enumerations sur-
     veys (Lieberson p.459, cp. also his illustrations on pp.450–451) will have
     to be re-emphasized at the conclusion of my paper (see sub. 3.1).

My own notes concerning bilingualism submitted on the following pages will
by comparison turn out to touch upon marginal rather than on core problems.
I readily admit that some of the phenomena I am going to sketch have little
bearing on problems of statistical measurement. At the same time I claim that
my categories are derived from life-situations; they are not constructs.

---

(1) On this term see Kloss 1966a p.138

1 Language and Dialect

1.1 The Problem as Seen From a Linguistic, Sociological, and Juridical Viewpoint

The term bi-lingualism consists of two components denoting what might be called the "dualitas aspect" and the "lingua aspect" (see diagram on p. 297).
So far this seminar's papers and discussions have dealt chiefly with the problem
indicated by "bi-" i.e. the duality of the languages used. But we cannot do
without a close, if short, look into the other problem—that of "lingua". Are
we always certain that the speechform listed in a statistical handbook constitutes an autonomous system deserving to be called a language? And may not
conceivably occur instances where it would be preferable to have not a language listed but a dialect? (2) At any rate it is important that in investigating the languages spoken by the inhabitants of a certain area, we make sure
whether the "mother-tongues" we are confront ed with are languages or just
dialects.

By and large we may say that as a rule census enumerators need not be
interested in dialects but in languages. Unfortunately there is no absolute
agreement as to what constitutes a language and what a dialect or a "patois".
Some authors use this dichotomy from an exclusively sociological angle,
speaking e.g. of "Indian dialects" when referring to the languages of the A-
merican Indians. This attitude has been widespread among Anglo-Saxon scholars and perhaps even more so among those writing in French. Among the latter
some have gone even further by adopting not a sociological but a juridical
viewpoint, withholding the appellation "language" from any tongue which is
not an official language in any country. One of the great linguists and socio-
linguists of our time, André Martinet, tells us that in French to be called a
mere patois it matters little whether the 'parler' in question is of Romance
origin and thus closely akin to the dominant tongue, or the member of a completely different family of languages like Breton (3) . And without voicing the
slightest criticism he states that in common French usage a person is called bilingual if he is considered able to handle two different national languages with
equal ease while a peasant from the Basse Bretagne who speaks both Breton and
standard French is not held worthy to be called a 'bilingue' (Martinet 1963
p. 134). This statement entails one factual error as well as two of method. In
the first place Breton today is no longer an uncouth vernacular but has undergone the same transformation as Welsh and Irish, having been made over into
a modern cultural tongue. In the second place Breton would have to be called
a language even without this transformation because of its intrinsic language
distance from all other living tongues. In the third place the fact that a

----

(2) For a first glimpse at this problem see Bilingualism 1965 p. 126
(3) A. Martinet 1960, here quoted from the translation, Martinet 1963 p. 139-
    140

language is not recognized as the national official language of some country in the world gives no indication of the degree of its development. Czech, Slovak, and Polish were full-fledged standard languages at a time when they were not national official languages. Applying juridical criteria would mean that an imperialistic government could oust the tongue of any conquered people from the ranks of true "languages" by simply decreeing that henceforth it would no longer be national and official.

It should be noted that the juridical viewpoint has received support from a group of experts convened by UNESCO who in an otherwise highly meritorious monograph have defined as vernacular language "a language which is the mother tongue of a group which is socially or politically dominated by another group speaking a different language. We do not consider the language of a minority in one country as a vernacular if it is an official language in another country." (Use 1953 p.46) It would seem that this definition is untenable from both a linguistic and a sociolinguistic viewpoint. Equally untenable would be the policy of confining recognition to those languages which are fully modernised (regardless of whether they are national official tongues) while refusing this designation to let me say the vernaculars of the Indians and Eskimos of Canada.

1.2 Language Becomes (Near-) Dialect: a Problem of Diglossic Bilingualism

In the foregoing it was suggested that in drawing a demarcation line between languages and dialects we should completely eliminate juridical aspects and that we should give equal weight to linguistic and to sociological data. Even so there remains a set of rather intricate problems. Among those vernaculars which linguists group with the 'independent' languages there are some which are rather closely akin to the dominant language. For this reason those who speak such languages natively feel and even claim they are mere branches, mere dialects of the latter. Thus the following vernaculars are held to be dialects by politicians, statisticians and by the speakers themselves, but languages by linguists:

Low Saxon (Sassisch) in Germany
Occitan (more commonly but erroneously called Provençal) in France
Sardinian in Italy
Kashubian in Poland
Créole in Haiti.

At least two of these languages pride themselves on a brilliant literary past, namely: Low Saxon and—much more so—Occitan. Among the members of the Occitan élite some endeavour even today to revive the language as a tool for modern thought and modern writings.

Languages of this type may perhaps be called abstand languages (c. Kloss 1952 pp.15-24; Kloss 1964) (languages by distance) because of their intrinsic distance from all other languages, including the superposed one. They may become near-dialectized, they never become fully dialectized; the language corpus distance remains as long as the language exists in an unadulterated form.

The pairing of a vigorous standard language with a near-dialectized abstand language is one of the three possible instances of diglossic bilingualism, the two others being the pairing of a standard with an outright dialect (e.g. German with Alemanic in Switzerland) and the pairing of two variants of a polycentric standard language (e.g. Demotiki and Katharevousa in Greece) (4)

Other languages there are which are "mere" dialects linguistically but "languages" sociologically i.e. because they have been reshaped into standard languages; they may perhaps be said to be "mere" ausbau languages or "languages by elaboration" (cf. 1.3).

Of course most occidental "languages" enjoy their status because of both their distance and their degree of elaboration.

All of these near-dialectized languages cause trouble for the statistician because whatever he may do about them will be misleading. If he sets them apart statistically he may satisfy the linguists but he shall misrepresent the sociological situation. If he omits them the picture he gains will again remain incomplete and—in a way—warped (see also 1.5).

Some confusion may be caused by the fact that occasionally some members of these speech communities are not yet or no longer willing to consider their native tongue a branch of the victorious language. While almost no speakers of Low Saxon would today declare not German "but" Sassisch to be their mother tongue there are some few members of the Occitan elite who might decide against identifying themselves with French linguistically.

There is no way of foretelling where this problem may come up tomorrow or soon after tomorrow. In 1960 the Low Saxon scholar A. Strempel demanded that future German census questionnaires should include questions regarding command of Low Saxon, his argument being that unlike Swabian, Bavarian etc. Low Saxon is not a dialect but a language in its own right (5).

Five years ago only the linguists knew that the vernacular spoken by the Sardinians is a Romance language in its own right. The other month I received a pamphlet "Rapport sur la communauté sarde" edited by an organization called "Sardegna Libera" where we read (Rapport 1967 p. 10-11) "Un mouvement pour

---

(4) My interpretation of the term diglossic differs from that of Fishman 1967 p. 29-30 but tries to remain close to the one originally advanced by Ferguson 1959

(5) Strempel 1960 p. 271. This request probably did not aim at setting aside a separate Low Saxon speech community. Strempel rather thought in terms of members of the German speech community (Sprachgemeinschaft) who in addition to the received standard speak also the Low Saxon sister tongue. In North Germany there is no movement on foot comparable to those spearheaders of the Occitan language who founded the Institut D'Estudis Occitans in Toulouse and the PEN Club de lenga d'oc.

l'accueil de l'enseignement de la langue sarde dans les écoles primaires avec la langue officielle ... est en train de se développer à tous les niveaux ... Sardegna Libera demande donc que le problème de l'enseignement de la langue sarde dans les écoles primaires, parallèlement à ce qui se fait dans la vallée d'Aoste pour la langue française, soit résolu selon l'esprit des principes de l'UNESCO." I do not mean to predict that this movement which at present has roughly 600 members will some day carry away the inhabitants of the island but I claim that it is not out of the question.

Nor is the problem restricted to Europe. The Ryukyuan language is considered by some linguists to be not a dialect but a dialectized sister-language of Japanese (6). In the Indian territory of Goa a plebiscite held on January 16, 1967 turned down the proposed fusion of Goa with the state of Maharashtra. Among the causes that brought about this outcome is said to have been fear on the part of the Goanese that many speakers of Marathi might not respect the dignity and 'independence' of Konkani, the mother tongue of the Goanese which some Marathi claim to be a mere dialect of Marathi. In the state of Madras or, as it is now called, Tamizagham speakers of Sourashtra petitioned the government to have primary schools conducted in their own language but were brushed off on the grounds that Sourashtra is but a dialect; as a matter of fact it was listed among the languages of India at the 1950 census but among the dialects of Gujarati in 1960.

The problem of dialectization assumes gigantic proportions in the cases of these Indo-Aryan languages for which the terms Rajastani and Bihari have been accepted and even more in the case of some of the languages of Southern China as Wu, Cantonese or Hakka. In India and China together the number of persons involved in near-dialectization issues may be not much below 200 millions (7).

We have instances where abstand languages have held their own in some parts of the speech area but became "near-dialectized" in others. It is well known that the rulers of Spain have tried to foist Spanish upon their Catalan-speaking subjects as their only cultural medium. While they failed in Catalonia proper Spanish seems to be accepted as the standard language naturally corresponding to their local dialect among many Catalan-speakers in Valencia and on the Baleares. Similarly while in Eastern Galicia (belonging to Austria until 1918, thereafter to Poland until World War II) Ukrainians had a clear consciousness of their separate linguistic identity those in adjacent "Carpatho-

---

(6) See e.g. Anthropological Linguistics v.7, no.1, Jan. 1965, pp.119-121; ibid. v.7, no. 3, March 1965, pp. 1-3. (=Languages of the World, Boreo-Oriental Fasc. 1; Sino-Tibetan Fasc. 2)

(7) Some figures (in millions) indicative of the size of the problem: Speakers of Wu 50, Cantonese 46, Hakka 17 (all acc. to Janet Roberts), Bihari 41 (S. K. Chatterji) or 17 (1961 census), Rajasthani 15 (1961 census). Cf. also the comparison between Occitan and Rajasthani by Kloss 1966b pp.324-325

Russia" (belonging to Hungary until 1918, thereafter to Czechoslovakia until World War II) were split on the issue, some favoring Russian, others standard Ukrainian, and a third party the local dialect of Ukrainian. Statements by emigrants from these linguistically ambivalent sections may have been bewildering to some of the more conscientious census enumerators.

1.3 Dialect Becomes Language—a Case of Implicit Passive Bilingualism

Besides genuine "languages by distance" which have become near-dialectized we have genuine dialects which have become fully developed standard languages—language by elaboration (ausbau languages). The problems they present in our context are of minor importance.

Linguistically, Slovak, Macedonian, and Gallego are nothing but dialects of Szech, Bulgarian, and Portuguese, respectively. But all of them have been made over into tools of all kinds of non-narrative prose—Macedonian only since World War II—so that sociologically they have attained the status of outright "languages". Obviously the census enumerator will have to list separately speakers of Czech and Slovak, Bulgarian and Macedonian, Portuguese and Gallego.

As a rule this raises no particularly difficult problems. They may come up however where a portion of this speech community does not adhere to this ausbau language. In that part of the Macedonian speech area which belongs to Bulgaria (Pirin section) not Macedonian but Bulgarian is the language used and accepted in the schools and in administration.   Similarly the Slovak dialect speakers living in East Moravia have accepted and retained Czech as their sole literary vehicle. Emigrants from these regions will probably give Bulgarian or Czech as their mother-tongue but one has to be watchful.

Perhaps the main significance, if any, this problem has for the investigation of bilingualism lies in the fact that for most speakers of ausbau languages we may assume that they can understand—though probably not use—the standard language to which their mother tongue linguistically stands in a dialect-like relationship. That is to say: for all Slovaks, Macedonians, Gallegos, we may implicitly assume that more or less they are possively bilingual with regard to Czech, Bulgarian, Portuguese.

1.4 Dialect Survives Language: a Problem of Replacive Bilingualism (8)

All over the world we have a large number of cases where the bilingual situation is but the forerunner of a final phase where what originally was a second language will have become the mother tongue of a population which in this way returns to its former state of monolingualism—with a different language though.

(8) Bilingualism 1965 p.128 speaks of "recessive bilingualism" which seems to be broadly co-terminous with "replacive b."

In this connection one major and one minor problem deserve to be discussed (9). In any given geographical area frequently two forms of a language exist side by side or rather on top and underneath: a spoken dialect and a written standard language that in daily conversation is used either by no one or only by members of a small upper stratum of society. (Here I mean by dialect not a dialectized language but a "true" dialect). Let me call the language A1, the dialect A2. Supposing now A is gradually being replaced by B—the language of the dominant ethnic majority group. In many cases what disappears first is A1—the standard language—, while A2, the dialect, may as yet live on for decades, being a "roofless dialect" (10) i.e. a dialect no longer overlaid, and thus protected, by the received standard naturally corresponding to it.

Here again the statistician who is trying to come to grips with the situation is facing a dilemma. If he groups these dialect speakers with those of the standard which naturally corresponds to it the extension and influence of the latter loom larger than is warranted by actual circumstances. On the other hand listing the dialect separately means treading on unsafe ground and exposes the statistician to the objection that he artificially "creates" new linguistic units.

What is meant becomes clear when we think of

the Masovian (or Masurian) dialect as spoken prior to World War II, in
    East Prussia (Germany),
the Alsatian dialect as spoken today in France,
the Pennsylvania German (Pennsylvanish) dialect as spoken in Eastern
    Pennsylvania,
the Acadian dialect of Southwestern Louisiana.

To have stated, in 1939, that the Masovians were part of the Polish speech community would have been both correct and yet misleading. Today to proclaim that the Alsatians and the Pennsylvania Germans form part of a worldwide German speech community would be equally correct and equally distorting.

There are two ways out. One would be to have not the standard, but either the dialect or both entered into the lists. France in her censuses conducted in Alsace since 1926 has asked separate questions concerning command of standard and dialectial German. The other would be to ask two questions, one regarding the mother tongue, the other concerning the ethnic affiliation. Just as the pre-1939 Masovians would have called themselves Germans, today nearly all young Alsatians would call themselves French. This distinction is customary in many Old World censuses. Thus e.g. the Soviet census of 1959 asked for

_____

(9)   On the minor problem see below 1.6
(10) Kloss 1952 p.21 ("dachlose Mundart")

a) Mother tongue
b) "nationality" (= ethnic affiliation)
with the result that (in rough numbers) there were

	by ethnic affiliation abs. (mill.)	by language abs.	%
Ukrainians in the Ukr. SSR	32.2	30.1	94
Ukrainians in other parts of the USSR	5.1	2.6	51
Germans (entire USSR)	1.6	1.2	
Germans (entire USSR)	1.6	1.2	75
Poles (" ")	1.4	0.65	46

Romania makes a similar distinction between language and ethnic nationality.

1.5 (Near-) Dialectized Language Survives Dialectizing Language: a Prob-
      lem of Both Diglossic and Replacive Bilingualism

Just as dialects sometimes locally survive the standard languages naturally corresponding to them so may near-dialectized languages outlive their superposed sister tongues and for the same reason. In Canada knowledge of the
German language is receding among the Mennonite groups in the Prairie Provinces but in some instances they seem to hold on to Plautdietsch as they call
their particular branch of the Low Saxon language. (11)
Counting the speakers of low Saxon separately—or at least listing both the
use of German and the use of Plautdietsch—might make more sense in some parts
of Canada than in Germany. It might make even more sense in northern Mexico
where we have roughly 20,000 Mennonites (12) who because of their plain-
minded aversion against secular education are said to have become almost illiterate in High German so that grouping them with the genuine German-
speakers would yield an even more inaccurate picture. Similarly listing a
knowledge of Occitan might be more appropriate in Spain (Aran valley) or

----

(11) The Plautdietsch spoken by these Mennonites—cp. Thiessen 1963—is a va-
      riety of Low Saxon which is particularly deviant from the better known
      Low Saxon dialects: "Plautdietsch" and standard German are by no means
      mutually comprehensible. There is a measure of literary activities going
      on in this dialect including an attempt at translating part of the Bible into
      it. Specimens of the dialect contained in Kloss 1961. Specimens from
      the Bible-translation in J. H. Goerzen: Germanic Heritage. Edmonton:
      the author, 2nd ed. 1965 pp.327-34
(12) Pferdekamp 1958 (esp. the appended contribution by Klaus G. Wust)

Italy (certain Alpine valleys in Piemont) than in France.

1.6   Vestiges of Extinguished Tongues: the Case of Residual Bilingualism

A minor problem that might be discussed in connection with replacive bilingualism is that of the last vestiges of a language (or dialect) in a geographical area where it has been replaced by another language in fairly recent
times. Diebold has spoken of "incipient bilingualism"; similarly we might now
speak of residual bilingualism. Two features might be significant: the ability
still to understand simple sentences spoken in the lost language and the ability
to produce primitive but meaningful utterances slightly above the "Good Mor-
ning" and "How are you"-level. Residual bilingualism probably is very frequent among the European or Soviet citizens whose ethnic affiliation (see 1.4)
differs from that indicated by their mother-tongue; their "ethnicity" may be at
least co-conditioned by residual bilingualism e.g. by a passive knowledge of
the language of their ancestors.

Of course, not all facts that occur are worth being collected, let alone
published, and it is open to debate whether attempts to isolate instances of
residual bilingualism would be worth the effort. They might become useful
e.g. in connection with FLES projects. In Louisiana conceivably the introduction of French into elementary schools might give promise of better success
in those "Créole" parishes where vestiges of the formerly dominant French language are still to be found (13).

2   Bilingualism Outside the Sphere of Face-to-Face Encounters

2.1   Bilingualism In the Use of Mass Media: the Case of Receptive Bilin-
gualism

Most questions raised and discussed in the context of this seminar bear on
bilingualism as practiced in the sphere of face-to-face encounters. While their
preeminence is not to be doubted we must not overlook the significance cultural tools such as books or mass media often have for bilingual groups. They
may simply utilize them passively; here we may speak of receptive bilingualism. Or they may actively, creatively produce books and/or scripts in two
languages, thus performing feats of what may be called productive bilingualism.

In a good many cases the consumption of periodicals, books, discs, broadcasts, telecasts, and movies in the "other-tongue" will supply a good parameter
for the extent and degree to which a speech community has become bi- or even
plurilingual. Figures are often easily obtainable for the inhabitants of islands—
Malta, or Iceland, or Puerto Rico for example—or for those of small countries

---

(13) In Louisiana, French has lost more ground in "Créole" than in "Acadian"
parishes.

like Luxembourg who share the same mother-tongue, i.e. who are "monopaido-glossic".   From Luxembourg e.g. we have the following figures (14):
Statistical data bearing on   "Receptive Plurilingualism in Luxembourg

A.   Circulation of Dailies 1966
    1. German language dailies published in Luxembourg   98.000
    2. Special editions of French language dailies
       published abroad   17.500

B.   Listeners to Radio Luxembourg 1966
    (based on a 1.494 persons sampling)

	Broadcasts in		
	Letseburgish	German	French
daily	1.156	414	126
several times a week	211	500	146
at most once a week	79	150	229
never	19	132	238
no answer	29	488	755
	1.494	1.494	1.494

C.   Films shown in city of Luxembourg 1966
    English   180   German   125
    French   130   Other   78

D.   Sale of discs with popular songs 1966
    (in the two leading specialist stores)

	Store no. 1	Store no. 2
German	25%	13%
French	40%	40%
English	20%	30%
Letseburgish	15%	17%

It will be seen that only in the realm of dailies we are dealing with a bi-lingual situation (French/German). Radio broadcasts and films are trilingual (French/German plus Letseburgish for the radio and English for the films) while in the realm of popular songs we even encounter an outright quadrilingualism. (Needless to underline that because of the musical aspect involved data on discs are less conclusive than those on periodicals etc.; I would not admit how-ever that they are irrelevant). I might just as well have taken my figures from Lebanon (15)—but for the 6% Armenian minority—also a "monopaidoglossic" country—or from Paraguay (Rubin 1963 e.g. pp.122, 118-119) or from Malta.

---

(14) Figures taken from an unpublished essay "Esquisse du trilinguisme au Grand-
    Duché" by A. Verdoodt (with the author's kind permission)
(15) Abou 1962, esp. his chapter II 'Morphologie sociale du bilinguisme liba-
    nais', pp.88-156, which is richly studded with statistical data.

To isolate figures for larger geographical areas inhabited by members of two or more juxtaposed speech communities is much more difficult than to obtain figures for monopaidoglossic populations. In India we have the following significant figures for some of the major speech communities:

		Number of inhabitants (%) 1	Circulation of all newspapers (%) 2	Dailies (%) 3	Number of films (%) 4	Number of non-English books published in 1963/64 (%) 5
				Share in		
1.	Assamese	1.5	0.3	0.01	0.9	1.1
2.	Gujarati	4.6	6.7	7.8	0.3	7.8
3.	Oriya	3.6	5.7	0.1	0.7	5.2
4.	Punjabi	1.9	1.0	0.6	0.5	2.3

This would seem to indicate that we are dealing with receptive bilingualism
    with regard to films only in Gujarat,
    films and dailies in Orissa and Punjab,
    films and all kinds of newspapers in Assam.

The statistics give no clear indication whether the films, newspapers etc. consumed by these bilingual speech communities are composed in another Indian language or in English. It is however highly probable that both English and Hindi are used as second languages with the exception of Assam, where Bengali may be better known than Hindi. The problem whether there exists for Gujarati, Oriya, and Assamese a longrange danger of becoming dialectized deserves careful examination.

There is a definite correlation between receptive bilingualism and what some authors writing in French have dubbed "bi-glottisme"—that halfway house between incipient and active bilingualism where a person can speak only his mother-tongue but can understand the second language when he reads and/or hears it (16). (It should be noted that not infrequently people understand only the written but not the spoken word or vice versa.) "Biglottisme" denotes a stage below that of active bilingualism but is well compatible with receptive bilingualism i.e. the habit to exploit the second language without being able to employ it (cf. the diagram on p.297). Productive bilingualism on the other hand is conceptually linked up, if only loosely, with an ability to speak both languages.

(16) Abou 1962 p.217, referring to Haje 1951 p.207 who in turn quotes Rees 1939 p.241 as speaking of "duoglossie impressive et monoglossie expressive" or the ability to "lire en deux langues mais de n'en parler réellement qu'une seule".

2.2 Literature Written in Several Languages: the Case of "Productive" Bilingualism

The meaning of the term "productive" will, in the present context, be strictly confined to literary and kindred activities making use of the written word, to the exclusion of the activities of painters, musicians, architects, technicians etc.

There is no doubt that among bilinguals we find no fewer people who are productive in this—restricted, arbitrary and admittedly superficial—sense than among monolinguals. But the concept of productive (or literary) bilingualism has little to do with that of productive bilinguals. It refers to the literary activities of those bilingual groups whose authors are equally able to write their books and edit their periodicals in two languages, the mother tongue as well as the second language.

We have numerous bilingual groups whose literary output is largely written in the group's original language; bilingual Frenchmen in the state of Quebec e.g. probably seldom write in English. There are just as many bilingual groups whose literary activities are more or less confined to the second language—the Pennsylvania Germans and the Louisiana Frenchmen, the Cap Breton Gaels and the New Mexico Spaniards all write in English almost exclusively. These two types have in common that they are monolingual with regard to literary output.

Besides we have other ethnic groups or speech communities whose writers use two languages with equal, or near-equal facility. A case in point is again Luxembourg where the mother tongue fo all inhabitants is a Franconian i.e. German dialect and where books have been published in the following languages (17).

	1947	1960
German	51	58
French	83	57
Letseburgish	18	11
Other	5	–

The significant feature hidden behind these dry figures is that in Luxembourg plurilingualism is not restricted to the domain of scholarly research but extends to the domains of poetry and fiction as well, with Letseburgish firmly entrenched in these fields but excluded from learned prose.

Actually we have to distinguish between two basic types of productive bilingualism, the one comprising all secondary school graduates and the other more or less restricted to university graduates. The first type we met with in Luxembourg, and we would find a similar situation in Malta and among many minority groups all over the world whose elementary schools are conducted in the mother tongue but whose secondary schools make use of both the minority tongue and the dominant language, or perhaps even of the dominant language

---

(17) Acc. to A. Verdoodt (see footnote 14)

alone. Wales would be a good case in point. Of this first type of productive
bilingualism it is characteristic that it frequently embraces not merely scholars,
but poets, novelists, essayists as well. With regard to non-narrative prose it
is useful to have separate data for the various disciplines. It has been said that,
in 1955, 36% of all books published in the Soviet Union were written in non-
Russian languages—but only 9% of those dealing with science; the principal domains of books in minority tongues were (a) original poetry, (b) original fiction, and (c) translated political writings.

An even more widespread type of productive bilingualism is that obtaining
among scholars in small or medium-sized speech communities resorting to languages of wider communication. Among them we find a number of—frequently
interlinked and overlapping—motivations, such as

(a) the necessity to use a language which reaches a broader market than the
     author's own speech community, which simply cannot absorb books on
     specialized scholarly topics—the case of a Faroese author writing in Danish;
(b) the desire to use a language which reaches a wider international reading
     public than the author's home tongue which may be a fully developed tool
     for scholarly research and yet little known as a second language—the case
     of a Swedish scholar writing in English;
(c) the necessity to use a language which is more fully elaborated and disposes
     of a more comprehensive technical terminology than the author's mother
     tongue—the case of an Indonesian physicist writing in English.
From Sweden we have the following figures for the production of original
books (no translations incl.)

Language	1960	Original Works Published in 1965	1958–65
Swedish	3310	4241	28650
English	620	804	5706
	(15%)	(15%)	(16%)
French	22	17	185
German	99	94	682
Other	52	58	425
	4103	5214	35648

These figures go to prove that roughly 1/5 of all books by Swedish authors
are written in languages other than Swedish; the percentage is even higher if
we consider only books written in non-narrative prose (Sw. "facklitteratur")(18)

The occurrence of productive ("bi-literary") bilingualism raises an interesting problem. Among the scholars of the world's leading speech communities,

(18) In 1965 of 804 books written in English only 4 belonged to the realm of
     fiction and poetry.

only a select few are in a position to write in two tongues, and these are usually considered as unusually gifted linguistically. Among these few scholars,
professional linguists would probably turn out to be heavily over-represented.
But in the smaller nations and speech communities productive bilingualism seems
to be expected from almost any normal scholar. Could it be that the smaller
nations are more gifted than the larger ones with regard to linguistic expression? Or are we dealing with another instance where motivation transforms itself into achievement? An American educator once stated that "80% of aptitude is motivation" and much of this motivation is of necessity lacking among
native speakers of English or French.

2.3 Bilingualism in Governmental Agencies: a Case of Impersonal Bilingualism

There are countries with two juxtaposed major speech communities whose
two languages are both considered national or official, so that it is customary
to call them bilingual countries. Yet it may be that in the daily life of the
citizens the second language is almost never heard. This is a situation prevail-
ing in many parts of Switzerland and eagerly desired by many Belgians with
many Flemings trying to expel French, and many Walloons trying to lock Dutch
out of their respective speech areas. The Belgian, M. R. Bourgeois, speaks
about "bilingualisme des services et bilinguisme des individus" which must not
be confused (Berquet 1963 p.46). In officially trilingual Switzerland "trilingualism is largely an affair of official forms, postal cards, posters, etc. for
most Swiss citizens—and even here trilingualism is sometimes avoided through
the use of Latin." (Kloss 1966a pp. 141-142)
      In a former article of mine I have dubbed this type of bilingualism "imper-
sonal bil." (Kloss 1966a p. 141). It is indispensable to mention this category
in any attempt to sketch a tentative typology of bilingualism. But I hasten to
add that impersonal bilingualism is almost irrelevant in connection with most
statistical surveys. Still special studies in bilingual countries isolating the
degree of bilingualism among the leading bureaucrats in the upper brackets of
government might be revealing and rewarding.
      "Impersonal bil." probably is more suitable a term than "national bilin-
gualism", the term used by the rapporteur of the Aberystwyth Conference (Bilingualism 1965 pp. 108-110). For while bilingualism at the level of national
government is certainly by far the most important instance of the phenomena
in question, I would hesitate to use the term "national" even for all instances
of use of two languages by the machinery of government. For besides national
government, we have regional (state, provincial) and local districts (county,
municipal) government and bilingualism may be absent at the national but established practice at the municipal level. Therefore it seems advisable to
speak of governmental rather than of national bilingualism.
      Besides, impersonal bilingualism may as well occur within the framework
of non-governmental organizations.
      The fact that of the members of a churchbody, or of a federation of credit

unions, 40% may speak the language A, and 60% the language B, may necessitate the headquarters of the denomination, or federation, to become fully bilingual while all local branches (congregations or credit unions) remain monolingual. "Impersonal bilingualism" has as its natural counterpart "personal bilingualism" a coverterm for both individual or group bilingualism.

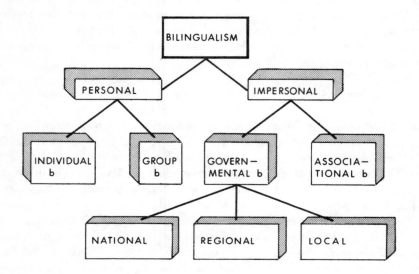

2.4 Languages Used In U. S. Church Services: an Example of Associational Bilingualism

For a government's central statistical office the usual way to collect linguistic as well as other demographic data is to question the individual citizens.

We must, however, not lose sight of the alternative of having the statistical office interrogate not the citizens but some of their chief organizations, for example, their various religious bodies. There are two advantages going with a survey of this type. In the first place the questionnaire to be submitted to the denominational headquarters may contain a great many questions bearing on the life of the denominations at large, their congregations, colleges, magazines etc. In our present context the question concerning the language(s) of church services would be of paramount importance.

Besides, this way of collecting data would be much less expensive than the usual one since we do not need thousands of local enumerators but merely a handful of experts to draw up, and to make use of, the comprehensive questionnaires to be sent to the various church bodies.

The U. S. Census has conducted a number of surveys among the country's religious bodies and has repeatedly (1906-1916) included a question concerning the use of languages in church services. The question was dropped in the 1926 census. Also I am under the impression that language data contained in those surveys have not been much used by American scholars (19).

While only indirectly linked up with the problem of individual bilingualism the question whether or not the example set by those early US censuses should be imitated deserves to be pondered on. The data thus assembled would shed considerable light on many aspects of bilingualism, especially if compared with mother tongue data taken from the preceding population census. We might find that some groups whom we know to have actually switched to English as the language of daily intercourse have retained the ancestral language—and thereby a measure of bilingualism—to a surprising degree when worshipping— and vice versa (20).

While and since information on languages used in church services cannot be used for external verification of extant data concerning the degree of individual mono- or bilingualism among the parishioners, it would open up a new and independent dimension of bilingualism—that of the professional use of two languages by the ministers in question (21), though in the case of large congregations there exists the possibility of one of the ministers using language A and the other language B to the exclusion of the other tongue. We may come

---

(19) For a foreigner's attempt to compile from this source basic data concerning a specific speech community see H. Kloss: 'Deutsch als Gottesdienstsprache in den Vereinigten Staaten'. In Der Auslanddeutsche, 14 (1931) pp. 630-634, 689-692, 715-721

"Censuses of religious bodies were conducted by the US Bureau of the Census for 1906, 1916, 1926, and 1936; reports concerning the language used in church services were included only in 1906 and 1916. In March, 1957, the Bureau conducted a sample survey on religion as reported by the civilian population (cf. Doc. Series P-20, No. 79, dated Feb. 2, 1958). By and large the date on languages in church services seem to have remained completely untapped so as to fall into oblivion even within the walls of the Bureau o.t.C.—witness a letter dated Oct. 25, 1961 which denies such inquiries ever to have been made."

(20) In 1937 I visited, on behalf of the Carl Schutz Memorial Foundation (Philadelphia), a number of German speech islands in the U. S. and found areas—e.g. among the Mennonites in Kansas—where German was still the only language of church services (the childred already had only a passive knowledge of it), and others—particularly in Pennsylvania—where German had been dropped decades ago as a language of worship but where still many youngsters spoke the local German dialect.

(21) This will be particularly obvious where religious services make use of a language like Latin, Hebrew or Church Slavonic.

across congregations where two languages, A and B, are customary in services without knowing for sure whether the constituency

    (a) embraces two generationally complete speech groups, both embracing all age brackets, but one preferring English, the other German,

    (b) embraces two linguistically differentiated age groups, with English dominant among the younger and German among the older generation,

    (c) consists of fully bilingual persons who alternately attend services conducted in English and German, or, in other words, whether this is a case of

a) the living side by side, within the same congregation, of two linguistic groups (22), or of

b) an intergenerational shift from language A to language B, or

c) of stabilized all-round bilingualism on the part of all parishioners.

And there is the additional likelihood of one of four major possible combinations (a + b; a + c; b + c; a + b + c) beclouding the picture.

    In short, inferences to be drawn with regard to group bilingualism are tenuous and we have to admit that a census of this kind may instead of greatly reinforcing our knowledge concerning of personal bilingualism constitute an end in itself by clarifying hitherto unidentified issues of associational bilingualism.

    Surveys of this type can easily be extended to secular organizations. What with the dearth of nationwide federations among these clubs, societies etc. this extension may be feasible only where the survey is confined to a single locality or district.

3 Concluding Remarks

3.1 The Need for Private and Semi-Private Surveys

    Most of the problems discussed in the present paper are of too subtle a nature to fit into the framework of a decennial census. They require special surveys such as those recommended, or quoted, in Professor Lieberson's paper. Therefore I plead even more strongly than Professor Lieberson for private and semiprivate surveys and studies to be conducted by universities, research institutes, or individual scholars. Some of these investigations might be undertaken on the basis of a contract with a public agency. To the illustrations given by Professor Lieberson I wish to add just two more. In connection with his doctoral thesis Clyde Stine conducted a survey, in the thirties, concerning use of the Pennsylvania German dialect by monolingual or bilingual school-

---

(22) The two linguistic groups may represent

    aa) either two ethnic stocks, e.g. one of Irish and one of German descent, resp.,

    bb) two subgroups belonging to the same ethnic stock, e.g. one German immigrant group of recent and another of 19th century origin, the latter having lost the ancestral tongue shile the other still retains it.

children in certain counties of Eastern Pennsylvania. The questionnaire was distributed by the county school authorities among the teachers and contained detailed questions concerning the use of dialect among the children as well as their parents which no census enumerator could hope to get answered (23).

A pace-setter in the field of statistics has been for decades the German, Paul Selk, who has done much to explore the use of

standard German
Low Saxon
standard Danish
the local Danish dialect in Slesvig-Holstein South of the Danish border.
(see e.g. P. Selk 1937/1940-1942; 1950; 1960)

3.2 Additional Hints

Future research on the statistico-demographic aspects of bilingualism may do well to tap pertinent research traditions of the various continents. From 1923 until Hitler forced him out of office in 1938, Professor Wilhelm Winkler headed an "Institut fur Statistik der Minderheitsvolker an der Universitat Wien" which has brought out a number of relevant publications, notably a "Statistisches Handbuch der Europaischen Nationalitäten" (1931) (24). Earlier we find an important doctoral thesis by R. Kleeberg "Die Nationalitatenstatistik" (1915) (25). The preoccupation of Central European statisticians may be said to have been with the problem of ethnic nationality ("Nationalitat" see above 1.6) rather than with bilingualism, but there is considerable overlap.

I wish to state once more (26) my conviction that it would be a good thing to have experts agree on two different terms for

a) individual bilingualism as occurring in "monopaidoglossic" countries like Haiti and Luxembourg where all educated persons speak French in addition to the local vernacular,

b) bilingualism as obtaining in a country where we have two major speech communities (Belgium, Canada, Ceylon, Cyprus)—a bilingualism that is fully compatible with wholesale individual monolingualism.

Some thought might be given to the question whether it would be advisable to recommend (by means of a resolution or otherwise) to some supranational bo body, preferably UNESCO, that governments be requested to include in their censuses questions regarding bilingualism. That however would be wise policy

---

(23) Stine 1938, some of his figures repr. in Der Auslanddeutsche, Stuttgart, 21, 1938 p.488

(24) See also Winkler 1923 (here e.g. pp.41-42 on plurilingualism (Mehrsprachigkeit)

(25) For full title see bibliography; his thesis reviewed by Wurzburger 1917 is rich in bibliographical data

(26) As I did first in Kloss 1966a p.137

only if we are in a position to offer a model set of reasonable questions so that censuses stand a chance to yield results that can be compared with those from other countries.

K. D. Macrae

I should like to begin by complimenting Professor Lieberson for having written a paper that promises to open some interesting discussion. He has touched on a range of topics that open a good many doors to further inquiry, and the vistas that he offers us within a few pages are both exciting and varied. Personally, I am acquainted with a far narrower range of phenomena relating to bilingualism, and I think it will be most useful if I concentrate my comment on the areas of my acquaintance. I hope that others will take up some of the other questions raised by Professor Lieberson's paper.

The Canadian background. Let me begin by calling attention to the fact that in the past Canadians have not made intensive use of the linguistic questions in their census, at least for purposes of academic research. Considering the importance of language issues to the survival of Canada as a political entity, this may seem at first glance somewhat surprising, but to keep the matter in perspective, it might be asked whether other officially bilingual or plurilingual countries have done very much more. If my information is correct, the census of Switzerland has never attempted to measure the incidence of bilingualism there at all—perhaps in recognition of the difficulties of quantitative measurement of this phenomenon. My first suggestion, then, which seems to be confirmed by a glance through Professor Lieberson's bibliography and others, is that the countries which are officially bilingual or plurilingual do not seem to have been significantly ahead of some officially unilingual countries in research on bilingualism or even on socio-linguistics generally. Canada seems to fall within this broad pattern. Until very recently the field of socio-linguistics—as I understand the term—was almost totally undeveloped in Canada. Yet the political difficulties of the last few years, and the research to which they have given rise, may indicate that we have come at least to the threshold of a clearer understanding of linguistic behavior in Canada.

The Canadian asks three questions relating to language. They concern the respondent's ethnic origin, his mother tongue, and his knowledge of the two official languages. This last question provides the only direct measurement of bilingualism in the census, and it measures only English-French bilinguals. The question on ethnic origin has, of course, limited relevance to languages spoken currently today, though it may be related, with certain adjustments, to the presumed original languages of immigrants. This question, it might be noted, is the oldest one in the census, dating from the first federal census of 1871 and being found in some provincial censuses before Confederation. The questions on mother tongue and official languages are relatively recent, having been as asked only since 1931.

Canada is a country of immigrants, and many of these have brought with them languages other than English and French. This fact may help to explain why in the past Canadian interest has been not so much in the sociology of language generally, but rather in language transfer and language maintenance, particularly mother tongue transfer and mother tongue maintenance. There was a time not too long ago (to be exact, 1941) when official census publications explicitly identified mother tongue transfers to English or French with progress, and mother tongue maintenance, by implication, with backwardness. Both transfer and maintenance have been linked—perhaps somewhat too naively—with cultural affiliation in other aspects. In this context, it is not too difficult to see a possible reason why the study of bilingualism as much has been relatively neglected in Canada. If the acculturation of immigrants is seen as involving a shift of mother tongue to one of the official languages, bilingualism (other than English-French bilingualism) will be regarded as a transitory phenomenon, a price to be paid by the generation or two that is involved in the language transfer. The possible benefit that these bilinguals may bring to the country at large has never, so far as I am aware, been seriously considered.

Before mentioning current research, I should like to note that Professor Lieberson's remarks about failure to correlate linguistic with other census variables are certainly applicable to Canada. However, I am not sure that individual researchers—had there been any working in the area—could have achieved much without further publication of data by the federal Bureau of Statistics. The Census of Canada does cross-tabulate ethnic origin and official languages spoken, but it does not do so for mother tongue and official languages. In the published census materials some other social and economic variables have been broken down by ethnic origin, but rather fewer by mother tongue, even in the 1961 census. On the whole the mother tongue and official language variables have been relatively neglected in the past, and it is difficult to decide whether this accounts for the paucity of research, or whether the relationship is the other way round.

The present: the work of the Royal Commission on Bilingualism. In speaking of the Royal Commission on Bilingualism, I should state that I have been involved in development of the Commission's research programme but not in policy discussions arising from the research findings. My conclusions, therefore, are personal opinions only. As a further caveat, I do not wish to suggest that the only work on socio-linguistics presently going on is that being done by the Royal Commission on Bilingualism and Biculturalism. Far from it. But there does seem to be discernible a sort of pause in certain areas of academic research to see what the research studies of the Commission will bring forth.

In one sense, the Royal Commission reflects the traditional Canadian concerns of cultural identity and cultural maintenance. The Commission's first concern, as its Preliminary Report makes clear, is with the development of an "equal partnership" between English-speaking and French-speaking Canadians within a bilingual polity characterized by bilingual institutions, rather than with bilingual individuals as such. Of course, the successful working of bilingual institutions presupposes a certain proportion of bilingual individuals; hence the first question necessarily implies some interest in the second, and the terms of reference do invite recommendations on second-language learning.

Canada, however, is not today a country of bilingual citizens, at least in the official languages. Only about 12 per cent of the population reported a knowledge of both official languages in 1961; three quarters of these were of French mother tongue. To set this in perspective, this is comparable with the 11 per cent of Finnish citizens who reported a knowledge of Finnish and Swedish at the 1950 Census of Finland, but somewhat below the 18 per cent of Belgians who spoke Flemish and French (or all three national languages) at the Belgian census of 1947. All three countries are strikingly below the figure for South Africa, where 73 per cent of the European population (of 7 years or over) was classified as bilingual in English and Afrikaans in 1951. Clearly whatever solutions are to be recommended for Canada must presuppose, for the short run at least, a comparatively low level of official bilingualism among the general population.

The apparent implications of this for the subject of this seminar are reasonably clear. Bilingualism among individuals or groups have not been the primary focus of most of the research studies, through many will undoubtedly afford interesting insights into the social and economic roles of bilinguals in Canadian society, their educational experience, their geographical distribution, etc.

But what are the contributions to socio-linguistic research that may be expected in the work of the Commission? More specifically, what will be its contributions to the study of bilingual persons or groups? Basically, I should like to mention two kinds of data arising from the Commission's work that may provide a take-off point for a good deal more understanding of linguistic behavior.

In the first place, the Commission was able, with the cooperation of the Bureau of Statistics, to obtain print-outs of material based on several sample tapes run from census records, material which for various populations cross-tabulated census data on ethnic origin, official language, and sometimes mother tongue, with a variety of other social characteristics, including age, sex, birthplace, education, occupation, industry sector, income levels, and few others. Many Commission research studies have been based on these print-outs, but the print-outs themselves, which are physically rather bulky, represent an enormous further source of research material of which only the surface has been scratched during the research programme. We have here in raw form the sort of cross-tabulation of linguistic and non-linguistic variables that Professor Lieberson has touched on in his paper. (p.294)

In the second place, the Commission's research programme collected other kinds of linguistic data. In particular, it undertook several surveys of selected populations, including two country-wide samples (one of adults, one of young people), the federal public service, the armed forces, and certain provincial and municipal public services. On all of these surveys linguistic questions were asked, and usually in a more specialized way than in the census. For example, among the questions will be found some that ask for self-assessed degrees of fluency, some that are functionally specialized (reading, writing, speaking, understanding) some that probe the respondent's volition (desire or perceived advantage of knowing a second language), some that ask for language used at home, or at work, or in specific types of inter-personal contact. Most of the surveys gathered a number of other variables at the same time, and numerous cross-tabulations are possible.

This is not to suggest that the vast array of research results will settle immediately a very wide range of questions. Most of the questionnaires were devised with rather practical aims in view, and sometimes the linguistic data appear to raise more questions than they solve (1). Nevertheless, the data so gained are likely to suggest fresh insights and hypotheses that may well lead to a more comprehensive understanding of many language phenomena in Canada than we have hitherto possessed.

Possibilities for the future. What can be done to increase our understanding of linguistic behavior in Canada? I should like to suggest—and I emphasize that I am speaking in a personal capacity only—two lines of development.

First, while it may be assumed that many of the research studies of the Royal Commission on Bilingualism will be published, the richest resource for linguistic or socio-linguistic research undoubtedly lies in the raw data upon which the studies were based. The latter, as indicated earlier, frequently had practical and specific objectives, and did not utilize the language data to the fullest extent possible. It would therefore be immensely valuable, in my opinion, if the data themselves were placed at the disposal of the entire academic community. In making this suggestion I have in mind specifically

(1) the tabulations or print-outs of census material (the tapes themselves were not available even to the Commission staff, because of the Census require-

---

(1) For example, the more results, the more variations in response patterns. One survey of a group of public servants found that those surveyed of English mother tongue reported a knowledge of French in the following proportions:

Reading	6.4 per cent
Writing	2.9 per cent
Understanding	4.2 per cent
Speaking	2.6 per cent

At the 1961 census the corresponding figure for this group in reply to the question "Can you speak French?" was 4.7 per cent, which suggests as one hypothesis that some English-speakers may interpret the census question not as ability to speak French, but rather to understand or read it.

ment of anonymity of individuals) and

(2) the cards or tapes containing results of Commission surveys. To have even these two categories of material available for academic research might well yield fruitful results for several years to come.

In the second place, in the light of all that we have learned in the last few years, some serious thought should be given to the possibility of improving or supplementing the linguistic questions on the Canadian census. I would tentatively list the priorities more or less as follows:

1. We need most of all an indicator of current language usage, since mother tongue, while useful for some purposes, is of little relevance on this point. For this purpose the South African concept of "home language" seems preferable to the Finnish concept of "main language". The latter seems rather ambigous and open to a wide range of interpretations, while "home language" is more closely linked to individual preverence, or at least family preference.

2. In addition—or perhaps as an alternative to the first point—we need some means of separating those fluently bilingual from those whose second language is obviously imperfect, stilted, limited, or halting. Having lived in Ottawa for the past 12 years, I have been fascinated by the number of children who grow up from earliest childhood with full fluency (for general purposes at least) in French and English. They constitute a category of bilingual that is far removed from the limited knowledge of a second language that most Canadians achieve. I am unable to suggest how this question should be approached, though I suspect that the kind of fluency I am thinking of virtually requires a bilingual childhood environment. Though it may sound heretical, I have sometimes wondered if the concept of a double mother tongue, or of two languages learned at pre-school level, should be considered as a starting point.

3. One question that may be related to the preceding one is the notion that the census might ask for the mother tongue (or mother tongues) of the respondent's father and mother. In addition to clarifying inter-generational language transfers, this information would help to explain the context in which bilingualism occurs.

4. Canada has a very inadequate inventory of linguistic skills in languages other than English and French. We can make some inferences about "semi-official" bilingualism by correlating those knowing English or French (or both) as official languages against those of mother tongues other than English or French. But this is a minimum level only; it cannot measure those of English or French mother tongue who learned another language at school, or from parents, or in any other way. At the moment, apart from English-French bilinguals, we have very incomplete data on the number of Canadians who know two languages.

5. Finally, it may be typical of Canada's disregard of her aboriginal cultures that the Census does not separately identify the Eskimo or the various Indian languages, even though the latter belong to several distinct families. Probably one useful tool for research in several disciplines would be a more exact listing of these languages as sub-categories of the present umbrella heading

of "Indian and Eskimo".

I realize, of course, that the above points raise technical problems. A census must ask simple questions, and it is incapable of great precision in some of the areas that I have mentioned. But perhaps through further discussion some agreement will emerge as to the best line of approach both for Canada and for other countries.

Everett C. Hughes

As you all know from having read Mr. Lieberson's paper, he has limited his discussion to the general purpose census; a census in which large numbers of people are asked simple questions by questioners who are not expected to have much skill or much knowledge of the subject-matter of the questions. Such censuses are taken throughout much of the world. Mr. Lieberson seems to me, who know not much about censuses, to have covered the problem of gathering information about bilingualism in such censuses very well indeed. He has also, in various papers published earlier, dealt with exploitation—the mining—of the data concerning bilingualism in Montreal, Canada, contained in the Canadian censuses of several decades back. Such censuses are necessary. They serve many purposes. I do not find fault with Mr. Lieberson for having dealt with them in a detailed way; quite the contrary. Nor do I suggest that he should have gone beyond his assignment.

But we must eventually get beyond this means of describing and measuring bilingualism, for the reason that the aim of the study of language is to understand systems of social communication. In modern urban and industrial societies the systems of communication are very complex indeed. Mr. Greenberg's index of the probability that two randomly chosen persons could talk to each other would be more useful somewhere where there is some randomness in the probability that any one person will meet any other. Randomness of contact is not a feature of our highly organized society. Nor am I at all sure of the importance of proximity of place of residence as a factor in the likelihood that two people will frequently talk to each other. Even if it is an important factor, one still wants to know a good deal more about the people with whom a given person is likely to talk in course of his day,¬with its work, travel, listening to and reading of mass media, and shopping for goods and services; in short, a day more replete with transactions, probably, than with conversations.

You will have foreseen that I am about to suggest the study of bilingualism in relation to on-going social organization. A step in that direction lies in the relating of bilingualism, and other features of linguistic behavior, to the other characteristics of people,—their education and occupations notably. But it is only a step, for a person in any occupation is likely to have a variety of contacts; in a multilingual society, each kind of contact brings its own problems of language.

Steps in the direction of seeing bilingualism in on-going social life are taken in the work of many students. Let me mention but one. Mr. Mackey says

It is not only the person that determines the language that the bilingual uses at any one time; it is also the place in which he uses it, the role or register he assumes in using it, the style and context of what is said. (Mackey 1966 p.77)

Mr. Fishman has followed out this point further, in speaking of a society as presenting "a finite set of culturally specific categories, social occasions and constituent encounters."

When the Canadian Royal Commission on Bilingualism and Biculturalism first approached me to give them my bit of advice, I suggested that a team be deployed to observe, on a given day, the use of French and English in a large sample of the institutions and meeting places, formal and informal, in the city of Montreal. It was perhaps an outlandish proposal, but I think it could be done and that much could be learned from it. It would require fantastic organization and preparation. But a kind of sampling of situations could be done on a more limited scale, and not necessarily on a single day or in a short time; from it we could learn the functions of the two languages and of bilingualism in a modern city where both the current languages are of the western European type and when the population is practically all literate and all engaged is essentially one and the same economy and society.

Suppose we take Montreal as a model. As Mr. Lieberson shows, it is a huge city in which more than three-quarters of the population are of French mother-tongue and ethnic identity. A large proportion of the remainder are of English mother-tongue. They go about their daily affairs to some extent in institutions which they share, but also to some extent in separate systems of institutions. There are, in effect, separate systems of educational and religious institutions, inside of which communication can go on in one language or the other. From kindergarten to the doctorate of law, medicine or philosophy one may be taught in one language or the other, so far as the daily contact of pupil, and of teacher with teacher are concerned. Indeed, students in my seminar at l'Université de Montréal two years ago said they could travel to and from the university for weeks on end and never have occasion to speak or listen to English. But one might answer the telephone and hear an English voice, and be more angry than if some French person had got his number by mistake.

The radio, the television, the newspapers, the theatre are systems of unilingual communication. But all of them have some point of contact with the world of the other language. Newsgathering and translating are one such frontier where some people must be bilingual. In the world of education there is also a bilingual frontier where fiscal matters are discussed and arranged. Science and letters depend upon world-wide communication. In a time when about three-quarters of the findings in science are first published in English, and when all scientists must know what others are doing, and immediately, there is a language frontier of the greatest importance. The scientists of the world read English these days, and so do a large proportion of those physicians who are engaged in medical innovation and research. Thus one feature of a great city of two or more languages is that there is a point of meeting of the languages in any large institutional system; in certain of them there can be a great and elaborate system of internal communication in a single language, with certain points of contact with systems of communications involving the other language.

Medicine and the personal services of religion can be delivered from professional to client of his own language in a large proportion of cases; there is evidence that in most multi-language societies people prefer a person of their own language for their more intimate services. With the increasing complexity of the institutions which deliver these services, (clinics, hospitals, etc.) a greater variety of professional people are required. The newer techniques which they use are generally internationally developed and transmitted, so that here again there is a language frontier. Someone must be bilingual. In Quebec, the schools of physio-therapy, of specialized nursing, of librarianship, and others have either sent out their own people for training in other countries or have engaged bilinguals from other countries to come as temporary or permanent teachers. Again, there is a language frontier at a certain level in the system.

But there are of course systems of common institutions. There is but one set of factories producing economic goods and but one set of public utilities.

Given the fact that more than three-quarters of the adult male labor force of Quebec is French, and the other fact that the manufacturing industry is largely part of the general North American system, it is to be expected that the main body of labor in any industry will be French while the management tends to be English-speaking. In most industries the communication system at the top is English, while the day to day talk of the workers, even of the office is more likely to be in French. At some point as one goes down the line of command, the language frontier is crossed. At that point there is bilingualism. It may be that great care is taken at the top to see that written instructions are put into French; that too requires bilingualism. One has to find, in any organization, the point, of formal and of effective bilingualism.

One may speak here of two kinds of bilingualism. One is 'line' bilingualism, the translation of commands and instructions downward in the organization past a language frontier. The other may be called 'liaison' bilingualism. In the 'line' bilingualism, a foreman or supervisor of some rank passes the word received in one language on to his subordinates in another language. Sometimes,—we do not know how often—he may use translation to create a monopoly of communication between those below him and those above him in the organization. In fact, we have very little systematic observation and description of this kind of use of bilingualism, although it occurs in many organization in many parts of the world. Liaison bilingualism is found, for example, in the

work of the private secretary or personal assistant to people of managerial rank.
In Montreal, for instance, there is a convent school which trains young women
of good social standing for precisely this kind of work. She does more than
translate her employer's letters; she subtly saves him from errors in dealing with
people of the other language and culture. Wherever communications go from
one language to another more than literate accuracy is required; the proper nu-
ance of phrase and mood must be found.

I think it characteristic of the large organizations which produce goods
and services on a mass scale in two-language societies that these two kinds of
bilingualism—the line, and the liaison—will be found. The one passes the word
down; the other passes it across.

There is still another kind of system; these organizations which distribute
goods or services to a mass public. They will generally have a large body of
employees who do not meet the public, but they also will have a large number
of daily contacts with the small customer or client. Insofar as the people of
the two languages seek similar goods and services in the same places and from
the same organizations an army of bilinguals is required. The point of language
contact is here at the bottom outward edge of the organization, where rank and
file employees meet the common public. Here of course the geographic distribution and movements of people come into play. Anyone who has ridden in a
taxicab in various parts of the world can testify to the eagerness of the cab
driver to speak the language of his foreign client. He uses the client as a
teacher so that he, the driver, can enlarge his clientele. In other situations
the reciprocal attitudes of sales person and customer may be quite different.
There is sometimes a struggle between them as to which language shall prevail.
We must remember that while the customer is always right in any trade, some
customers are righter, and more desired, than others. Furthermore the relative
power of one party or the other to determine the language of a transaction varies greatly.

On public transport—busses, trams, trains,—communication may be reduced
to signals. On the telephone, dialing and the recording of standardized messages on tape in two or more languages reduce the amount of transaction requiring personnel capable of immediate choice of language. The vending machine
and serve-yourself devices have the same effect. They put bilingualism back
inside the organization where technicians must work out simple codes for communicating with their publics. The aim of modern merchandising of goods and
services frequently purchased and in small quantities appears to reduce personal
encounter,—talk,—with the customer. They ask of him a minimum literacy and
familiarity with simple machines.

General censuses of language spoken or read by populations of cities, regions and countries will certainly continue to be essential. We can hope, with
Mr. Lieberson, that they will be greatly improved. Certainly there is need of
a great deal more study of bilingualism in small groups and in various social
roles. But I also think that at this point in the world's history, we require systematic and detailed study of the functions of various languages in urban and

industrial societies and of the frontiers where languages meet in complicated social systems, the points where there is bilingualism of one kind and degree or another. What we need for such study is not so much a definition of bilingualism, but a catalogue of the kinds which occur in terms not merely of relative fluency of hearing, speaking, reading, writing and translation, but also in terms of social function (1).

E. G. Malherbe

My comments on Dr. Lieberson's paper are based on my experience as Director of Census and Statistics for the Union of South Africa more than two decades ago. The nature and number of the questions which go on to a census form are usually decided by a Statistical Council which is supposed to judge the degree of tolerance which the public will have in answering the questions which have to be replied to by the whole of the population. These questions have therefore to be as simple and straightforward as possible. I don't think anybody has succeeded in drawing up a national questionnaire which is completely foolproof. For example, perfectly straightforward questions dealing with Marital Condition have elicited answers such as "Happy" and "Unhappy", "Could be better"! One item labelled Sex which required the response "Male" or "Female" elicited the response "Sometimes"!

Methods of census taking differ from country to country; in some countries trained enumerators are used to visit homes and record the responses themselves. In South Africa, for example, the blank forms are left in homes for about a week or so and later merely collected by the enumerators. In each case it is essential to emphasise that strict secrecy will be observed in regard to the responses and that only the machines will deal with the tabulation of the results, otherwise fear of consequences of particular responses or alternatively a desire to please may cause a bias to the answers.

In most bilingual countries the Census asks two types of question, (a) on home language or mother tongue and (b) on the official languages spoken.

The decision as to which is the better term to use, "Home Language" or "Mother Tongue" is a difficult one. I personally would prefer using "Home

---

(1) I have left out of account bilingualism in administering the law and the services of the state. It seems likely that the western idea of a single system of police and law for all people who live in a given territory will replace the 'communal' system found in many parts of the world. The points of language contact become very crucial when that happens. I leave the problem for those who know more about it.

Language" as it is the sociological unit which has a significance. "Mother Tongue" can be taken too literally with consequent wrong impressions being conveyed.

In South Africa the formula is as follows: "State the language most commonly used by each person in the home". Results of the 1960 Census were as follows:

Afrikaans	58%
English	37%
Both	1.6%
Neither	3.2%

The 1.6% has sometimes been interpreted as an index of the bilinguality of the population. It is, however, nothing of the sort, but rather an index of the error in interpretation of the question, where the word "language" is explicitly put in the singular. Moreover, this 1.6% can hardly reflect reality in view of the fact that (a) 66% of the population speak both languages, and (b) I found in a survey which I made in 1938 covering the homes of 18,000 school children spread all over South Africa, that the number of homes where both English and Afrikaans was spoken was 43%.

There is always a margin of error in all responses given on a general census form and the margin of error depends very largely on how unambiguously the question is framed. For example, the margin of error in South Africa was reduced from 2% to 1.6% when the version of the question was varied from "What language is most commonly spoken in the home?" to "State the language most commonly spoken by each person in the home".

Here a note of warning must be sounded. It is unwise to vary the wording of census questions very much from year to year, because any variation makes comparison from one census to another very difficult, if not impossible. Some refinement of the question should be introduced in order to eliminate ambiguity on the lines suggested by Dr. MacRae by adding a question: "What other languages are commonly spoken in the home?".

Census figures dealing with language can have important economic and political significance in a bilingual country. For example, the placing of advertisements for commodities in newspapers with a certain language circulation. In South Africa, the political implications have always been most important. The Census figures reflect as well as determine Government policy as regards education and the medium to be used in schools. For example, the percentage of people speaking both English and Afrikaans dropped from 73% in 1951 to 66% in 1960 as a result of separating Afrikaans English-speaking children at school and students at Universities in separate institutions. Formerly, Universities and school were much more mixed.

The scope of a census is considerably limited where one deals with illiterate and underdeveloped peoples, thus, for example in South Africa, we have to use a separate census form for the Bantu population. The Coloured and Asiatic populations make their Census returns on the same forms as the Whites. In the case of the Bantu, the question on the language is whether the subject speaks English, Afrikaans or one of the Bantu languages.   (The results of these Censuses are given in the Appendix).

I feel that the suggestions made by Drs. Lieberson and MacRae in regard to using statistical and computer techniques in correlating various sociological data with those obtained in respect of language are very useful indeed.

Census data can be supplemented as well as validated by the use of Sample Surveys which can be designed to go into far greater detail than a general Population Census can do. The Census office should therefore establish close liaison with Universities, particularly in conducting Sample Surveys where it is essential to have a wide range of expert advice readily available.

APPENDIX

Censuses in a Bilingual Country (i.e. where there are two or more <u>official</u> <u>languages</u>) usually include two types of question pertaining to:

(a) <u>Home Language</u> (or mother-tongue)
For example, in the South African Census the question is framed as follows: "State the language most commonly spoken by each person at home"
This yielded in respect of the white population (about 3 million) the following results in the 1960 Census:

Afrikaans   only 58.1%
English   only 37.1%
Both English & Afrikaans 1.6%
other languages, e.g. German, Netherlands, Italian, Portuguese, etc. 3.2%

(b) Official Languages spoken: Here the question was framed as follows and the percentages for 1960 in respect of the white population of 7 years and over given in brackets:

"If able to speak –

1. Both English & Afrikaans, state <u>BOTH</u> (66%)
2. English only, state <u>ENGLISH</u> (15%)
3. Afrikaans only, state <u>AFRIKAANS</u> (18%)
4. Neither English nor Afrikaans, state <u>NEITHER</u> (1%)

Growth of Bilingualism as reflected in the percentages of <u>whites</u> who could speak both English and Afrikaans (official languages):

1918 – 43%
1921 – 52%
1926 – 61%
1936 – 66%
1946 – 69%
1951 – 73%
1960 – 66%

In the <u>non-white population</u>:
$2\frac{1}{2}$ million can speak English
3-3/4 million can speak Afrikaans
1 million can speak both English & Afrikaans
8 million can speak neither (these speak only a Bantu language).

DISCUSSION

English Version

The general question of methodology was discussed at some length. One participant attacked the whole question of censuses. Their main fault was that they were complete enumerations. That means that the questions have to be simple and limited in number. As well, a large number of enumerators have to be trained. Sampling is now so well developed that samples give more accurate results than complete censuses. He would predict that most countries will move away from the complete census to sampling methods. This will make question shedules more comprehensive and one will have the chance to have better questions on bilingualism.

The meeting was warned by Dr. Lieberson that any survey has inherent limitations: distortions inherent in the method and the very cavalier fashion in which questions on bilingualism are asked. This affects validity and reliability. Pilot projects could be run before censuses so that the final questions would elimit the right data. Another speaker commented on the lack of sensitivity to language evinced by many censuses, pointing out that this made the results less useful to the scholarly community. We need more information on what kinds of people answer what kinds of question. We need confrontation of self-report and analyses of usage. Both for functional-contextual reality of usage and repertoire that would enable us to realise what kinds of populations can accurately answer what kinds of question. This is most important to know what segments of the population can validly answer what kinds of question on language use.

Several speakers pointed out that, inadequate as census data is, it can be milked further. In addition to the present cross-tabulations we could extrapolate from the present information to finding out about the influence of education, work pressures, neighbourhood contact, adult social support for bilinguals and infer the social dominance of French over English. We must also compare the figures for ethnicity and mother tongue. In a city population we get the following configuration. (See Figure 1). Except for cities where there are a large number of people who speak French the influence of French on those of another mother tongue is declining. This should be examined as we look at the changing positions of languages in society. If people want to claim that they have changed their mother tongue, we can check this tendency if we have tables of ages according to mother tongue and cross-tabulate with later censuses. We can also project from these figures, compare with the results actually got, and isolate factors in change.

Figure 1

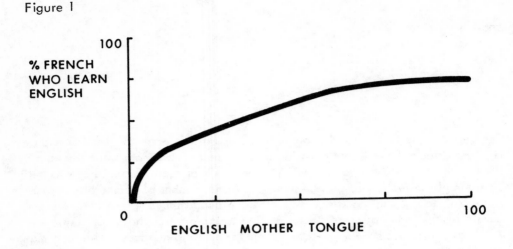

A census must be cross-tabulated with mortality and birth rates and then related to data from other sources. The Government Printer and Education Department are important to get details of class size, of entries to Training Colleges and examination statistics.

One way of cross-tabulation is through mobility in a multi-lingual society. One would assume that a Punjabi living in Bengal would be able to speak Bengali, even if it was not entered on his form. He warned about the pitfalls in the last Indian census. The questions were:

1. What language is spoken at home?
2. What language do you know?

In multiple replies only the first language was kept in assessing the statistics. The educated middle class entered English first. These figures have to be taken with a grain of salt and must be cross-tabulated with birthplace.

The question of the need for validation was raised. When asked how one would go about validating census and survey questions, Dr. Lieberson suggested that one should run a pilot project on a sample of the population and use a group of independent linguists to examine each member of the sample and compare results.

The term, "mother-tongue" vs "home language" produced some discussion. Though it was pointed out that several countries had opted for one or the other, one speaker reminded the meeting that in some parts of the world many people have two or three mother tongues they use in different circumstances, and also two or three home languages. One can not generalise on this question. In some cases, it might be better to avoid both terms. In support of this view one French-speaking participant married to an English-speaker, said that his home language was not his mother tongue. What was probably wanted was the language used in the home.

The question was asked: What was the difference between a language and a dialect? Was there any reason why census takers should not write down any name given for a language or a dialect? This would demand a team of skilled linguists to analyses the questions. How would one deal with mythical languages like *slavish?

The finest possible classification could have the danger of encouraging languages frowned on by the government. In the United States one of the most serious problems is illiteracy. Teachers are faced with classes whose basic dialect is different from theirs. <u>Dialect</u> is a term of stigma for the language spoken by Negroes.

Negroes and whites in United States have diametrically opposed attitudes for evaluating Northern and Southern dialects. Surveys should be run with the following questions: What do you speak now? What did you speak when growing up? Differences found are important for education. Linguistically a person's formative years are between five and thirteen. If a person started learning a school language at the age of 11, he has had only two or three formative years for the language.

We should think of a taxonomy:

a. Is your language a kind of another language?
b. Do you speak a particular kind of your language?
c. Are there any people you meet and do not understand?
d. Have you ever tried to learn a language?
e. How did you do? Is there any reason for the result?
f. What was the reaction to your attempts?

About the last question, reactions tend to differ: French people tend to react adversely to a foreign accent while with Hungarians a smattering will produce a flattering enthusiasm.

The comment was made that, though it would be useful to have a spread of terms in the census, that this presupposed a competent staff at the office. This was possible in multilingual areas but in unilingual countries it could pose problems of recruitment. Dr. Fishman's proposals would overtax the census office and the citizenry at large. He reminded the meeting that in one of the private work sessions Dr. Vildomec suggested that an agency should be commissioned to do the work on a sampling basis and be financed from outside.

Dr. Lieberson defended the Greenberg index in the face of Dr. Hughes' comment, saying that it is a valuable tool for describing bilingualism and linguistic skill in a population. It is not meant to be entirely accurate as people's interaction is never 100% random, but it assumes randomness as a working hypothesis, in order to measure the potential of communication within a bilingual society. By it we do observe some actual events in the society and we have some idea of language change.

Another participant described the work of Grootaers in Japan. He took a given village as centre and asked how far one had to move away to get into

another language area. Lenehan had sampled the attitudes to integration in
Ridgewood, New Jersey. He asked what the respondent thought about integration, and then, what he thought his neighbour thought. Most people assumed
that their neighbours were opposed, when in fact they were not. Both these
techniques could be used in assessing incidence of bilingualism and attitudes
to it. Where surveys and censuses were made by leaving the form in the household, the design allows for much gathering of information. If alternative answering channels are given, the channel chosen will reveal much about the
subjects.

The profile we get from the census data could be widened by other indicators. One could even begin from another standpoint: pattern of newspaper circulation, Radio and T.V. listenership, advertising, commercial sections of
phone directories, volume of books published, applications for broadcasting li-
cences, language of forms used. In the case of broadcasting the language of
the form is an indicator of group size and of the determinant of the amount of
revenue allocated to broadcasting services. By starting from the census and
other data one can construct a very elaborate profile on the pattern of bilingualism in society.

There was a suggestion that we should get away from the distinction between people who spoke A, those who spoke B and those who spoke both. What
we need to ask is who speaks what language with whom, where, and what a-
bout. We need to get to situational uses. Staying with the crude data forces
us to overlook special contexts. Language must be viewed with sensitivity.
We must look to the kinds of English, or the kinds of French used in certain
areas. In compiling a survey a sociologist needs a linguist to help him on this
question. For if 40% of the population use a certain language in different a-
reas, it may not be the same kind of language.

One commentator stressed the interdisciplinary nature of discussions of this
nature and called for new methods to analyse the function of bilinguals in modern technological society. To do this we need first to distinguish between industries that produce culturally neutral goods (insofar as this is possible) and
those that produce culturally biassed goods.

Relationships in the first type of industry conform to the following diagram
(Figure 2) (as far as French Canada is concerned). The line staff in this situa-
tion are charged with cultural and linguistic translation from top to bottom.
The key man here is very often the foreman: "Be here at 9 a.m." becomes
"Don't be late too often. You know how the English revere punctuality."
The foreman very often has a monopoly of communication in this direction, and
will go to any length to keep it. The staff on the other hand, are charged with
cultural and linguistic translation goes higher in staff than in line.

In a commercial situation the pattern is somewhat different. (See Figure
3). In the first situation customers are distant from the operation, in the second, they are part of it, hence the bilingual contact point is at the bottom.
In Montreal one can go for weeks on end with no English contact, except when
one has to buy scientific books.

Figure 2

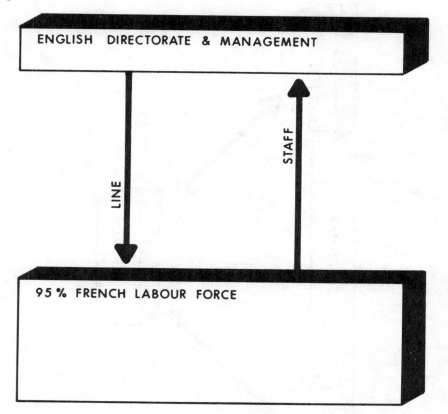

The culturally peculiar services are religion, education, theatre, social services and news. These vary according to their degree of peculiarity. In these it is possible to go from top to bottom and stay in one's own ethnic group. In education, most careers are conducted in one language or the other with some points of contact. As late as 1927 social services in Montreal were divided according to language and religion, now they are breaking down. Several companies, Bell Telephone, Imperial Tobacco, among them, now have operational analyses showing where bilingualism is needed. We must understand a bilingual society as it is.

One of the most interesting occupations is that of bilingual secretary. There There is a convent which specialises in training these girls. They act as liaison officers between unilingual bosses and their French subordinates. They are intercultural agents. We should be able to sample situations and develop infor-

Figure 3

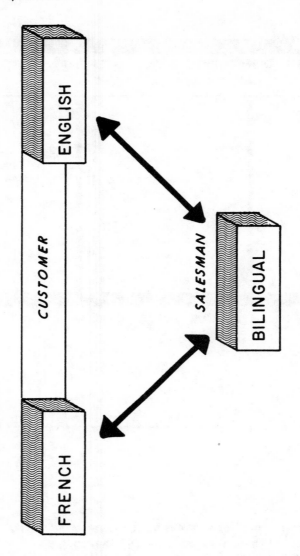

mation along these lines. For instance their are many culturally peculiar industries disappearing in Montreal, like the modistes for mourning clothes.
    Bilingual groups usually have a strong identity. They usually have one
language for communication with outsiders, and another for communication a-
bout outsiders within the group.
    Another commentator remarked that the conference speakers seemed to be
operating on different wavelengths, according to their country. There was a
fundamental difference of approach between unilingual and plurilingual countries. In unilingual countries the matter of incidence and distribution of bilingualism was taken as a natural occurence and the problem could be dealt
with some detachment. In other countries it was a part of political life and

dispassionate study was not really possible. In plurilingual countries language patterns are seen as valid areas for public policy, like education. Unilingual countries are hardly likely to agree. The speaker was interested in the wider applications of bilingualism in the wider social unit. This implied rising above group considerations to the impact of bilingualism on politics. This could need cruder techniques of study.

It was pointed out by Dr. Kloss that Dr. Lieberson was dealing with enumeration universals. His own comment was intended to cover material not treated by Lieberson. The dimensions of bilingual contact were important, even if, as far as the seminar was concerned, face-to-face encounters were more important. In most countries it is not impossible to assemble specific data on this dimension. He would suggest the term biglottism to describe the state of affairs where the first language is spoken and the second merely understood. There is a definite rapport between biglottism and receptive bilingualism.

In Alsace the knowledge of standard German has definitely declined since World War II. At one stage it was almost zero among the young, but now it is staging a comeback through the mass-media. It is not used in speaking, though passive knowledge of standard German is widespread. There are two types of productive bilingualism:

a. in secondary schools, pertaining not only to non-narrative prose but to fiction as well;
b. in scholars, as given in the diagram.

We must look both to the duality and the linguistic aspect of bilingualism. In the matter of distinguishing between a language, a dialect and a patois, we must not let juridical factors impinge on this matter. We can divide languages into four groups in duscussing this division:

a. A language can become dialectalised: (Provençal)
b. A dialect can become a standard language;
c. A dialect can survive a standard language;
d. A dialectalised language can survive a dialectising language.
    (e.g. Mennonite German in Canada and the United States has survived
    the standard language in this environment)

The census-taker has many difficulties. For instance in a plebiscite taken in Goa over fusion with the neighbouring state of Maharashtra, many voters were against it as they spoke Konkani, and they were afraid that in the new state, Konkani would be militated against. There are Marathis who hold that Konkani is a dialect of Marathi. During the 1950s the government of Madras was petitioned by Saushastra speakers for schools in the mother tongue. It was rejected on the grounds that Saushastra was a dialect, not a language. In the 1960 census it had been listed separated, but was later listed among the dialects of Gujarati. In Germany there is the problem of Low German or Saxon. There are demands that the quest ion on speaking Low German be included in the Census, on the argument that Saxon is a language in its own right. A group of Sardinians is demanding that Sardinian be taught in schools—the problem is world-wide.

DISCUSSION

Version française

La question de méthodologie est discutée assez longuement. L'un des participants s'en prend à l'idée même des relevés. Leur défaut principal consiste en ce qu'ils sont des énumérations complètes. Les questions doivent donc être très simples et peu nombreuses. D'autre part, il faut former des recenseurs en nombre considérable. Les méthodes d'échantillonnage sont tellement au point maintenant qu'elles donnent des résultats plus exacts que les recensements complets. A son avis, la plupart des pays abandonneront les recensements complets pour recourir aux échantillonages. Cela permettra de diversifier davantage les questions et en particulier de poser des questions plus utiles sur le bilinguisme.

M. Lieberson fait observer que tout relevé comporte ses limites: il ne peut qu'apparaître des distorsions, du fait de la méthode même que l'on emploie et de la désinvolture avec laquelle on pose les questions relatives au bilinguisme. Les réponses en sont moins valables et moins sûres. Il serait bon avant les recensements, de procéder à des opérations pilotes afin de s'assurer que les questions seront propres à faire obtenir les données désirées. Un autre participant déplore la faible valeur de beaucoup de recensements en ce qui concerne les faits de langages, ce qui rend les résultats de recensements moins utiles pour le monde de la science. Nous avons besoin de plus de précisions quant aux catégories de personnes qui répondent à chacune des catégories de questions. Nous avons besoin d'une comparaison critique du self-report et des analyses de l'utilisation des langues, aussi bien pour vérifier la réalité de leur utilisation et du répertoire employé, du point de vue fonctionnel comme du point de vue du contexte, afin de savoir quels éléments de la population sont en mesure de répondre avec justesse à chacune des catégories de questions. Il importe beaucoup, en effet, de savoir quels secteurs de la population peuvent répondre utilement à chacune des catégories de questions au sujet de l'utilisation de chaque langue.

Plusieurs participants font observer que les données fournies par les recensements sont peut-être insuffisantes, mais qu'on n'en a pas tiré tous les renseignements qu'elles recèlent. Au-delà de ce que fournissent les tableaux comparés, on peut chercher par l'extrapolation des données acquises ce que sont l'influence de l'enseignement, les pressions exercées par le milieu de travail, celles qu'exercent le voisinage, l'estime que portent les adultes aux personnes bilingues, et par là juger de la prédominance sociale du français sur l'anglais. Il faut aussi comparer les chiffres du recensement relatifs à l'origine ethnique et à la langue maternelle. Une population urbaine présent la configuration qui suit:

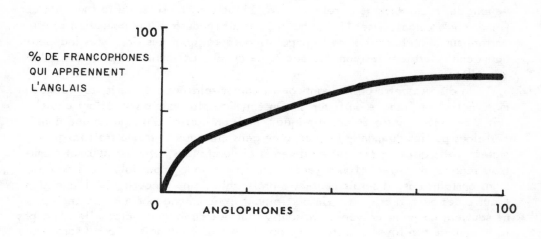

Sauf dans les villes où les francophones sont nombreux, l'influence de la langue française sur les personnes dont la langue maternelle est autre marque un déclin.   Il y a là un fait qui demande à être examiné, pour autant qu'il constitue une modification des positions linguistiques dans la société.   Là où des gens ne déclarent pas la même langue maternelle que précédemment, cette tendance sera révélée par la comparaison des tableaux des recensements successifs indiquant l'âge et la langue maternelle.   On peut aussi établir a posteriori des prévisions fondées sur les tendances que revèlent les recensements précédents, comparer ces prévisions avec les données des recensements postérieurs, et par là découvrir les facteurs des modifications constatées.

Il faut comparer les tableaux du recensement avec les taux de mortalité et de natalité, de même qu'avec les données provenant d'autres sources.   Les publications de l'Etat, en particulier celles des ministères de l'Education fournissent d'utiles données: chiffres des classes d'âge, inscriptions aux écoles professionnelles, statistiques docimologiques.

Un des indices qui permettent l'examen critique des tableaux des recensements est la mobilité des personnes au sein d'une société multilingue.   Qu'une personne originaire du Pendjab et habitant le Bengale sachant parler le bengali paraît tout à fait probable, même si le recensement n'en fait pas mention.   Le participant qui donne cet exemple met ses confrères en garde contre certaines lacunes du dernier recensement indien.   On posait les questions suivantes:

1.   Quelle langue se parle chez vous?
2.   Quelle langue savez-vous?

Certaines réponses nommaient plusieurs langues, mais seule la première figurait dans les statistiques. Les gens instruits de classe moyenne indiquaient d'abord l'anglais. On ne doit donc pas attacher de valeur absolue aux chiffres du recensement, mais les comparer avec ceux des lieux de naissance.

Quelqu'un pose la question de la confirmation nécessaire des données provenant des recensements et relevés. M. Lieberson, au sujet de la façon de confirmer ces données, émet l'idée qu'il faudrait recourir à une opération pilote portant sur un échantillon de la population, après quoi des linguistes indépendants contrôleraient les données auprès de chaque personne comprise dans l'échantillon.

On discute entre participants de la valeur relative des rubriques "langue maternelle" et "langue du foyer". On énumère plusieurs pays qui ont choisi soit l'une soit l'autre de ces rubriques, mais un participant signale que dans certaines parties du monde beaucoup de gens ont deux et même trois langues maternelles, qui leur servent en diverses circonstances, et aussi deux et même trois langues du foyer. Toute généralisation est donc impossible à cet égard. Dans certains cas, il serait peut-être préférable de ne recourir ni à l'une ni à l'autre des deux rubriques. Un participant francophone marié à une anglophone soutient ce point de vue en faisant valoir que sa langue maternelle n'est pas la langue de son foyer. En fait, ce que l'on désire connaître, c'est sans doute la langue employée à la maison.

Quelqu'un pose la question de la différence qui existe entre langue et dialecte. Y a-t-il une raison pour laquelle les recenseurs ne devraient pas inscrire telle ou telle langue, tel ou tel dialecte? Il faudrait pour cela qu'une équipe de linguistes analyse les questions. Et que ferait-on dans le cas des langues plus ou moins mythiques, comme le slave?

Une classification trop précise risquerait d'apporter des encouragements à certaines langues contre le voeu des gouvernements. Aux Etats-Unis, l'analphabétisme pose un problème difficile. Certains instituteurs se trouvent devant des classes entières d'élèves dont le langage de base n'est pas le leur. Le mot dialecte est employé péjorativement lorsqu'il s'agit de la façon de parler des Noirs.

Aux Etats-Unis, Noirs et Blancs observent des attitudes diamétralement opposées pour l'évaluation des dialectes du Nord et du Sud. Il faudrait faudrait faire des relevés en posant les questions suivantes: Quelle langue parlez-vous actuellement? Que parliez-vous à l'âge de la croissance? Les différences que l'on relèvera seront importantes à connaître du point de vue de l'enseignement. Pour l'apprentissage d'une langue, l'âge de formation se situe entre cinq et treize ans. Celui qui n'a commencé qu'à onze ans à apprendre la langue de l'enseignement n'a eu que deux ou trois de ses meilleures années de formation pour apprendre cette langue.

Il faudrait établir une taxonomie du genre de la suivante:
a. Votre parler est-il une variété d'une autre langue?
b. Parlez-vous une variété particulière de votre langue?
c. Rencontrez-vous des gens que vous ne pouvez comprendre?
d. Avez-vous déjà essayé d'apprendre une langue?

e. Quels résultats avez-vous obtenu? Savez-vous à quoi tiennent ces résul-
    tats?

f. De quelle façon réagissait-on à votre effort?

A propos de cette dernière question, les manières de réagir ne sont pas toutes
les mêmes: les personnes de langue française ont tendance à réagir de façon
défavorable devant un accent étranger; les Hongrois, au contraire, réagissent
avec un enthousiasme flatteur devant la personne qui prononce quelques mots
dans leur langue.

Les participants sont d'avis qu'il pourrait être utile de faire figurer dans
le questionnaire du recensement une liste de termes, mais qu'il faudrait alors
prévoir un personnel compétent au bureau de recensement. On arriverait à
trouver un tel personnel dans les régions multilingues, mais beaucoup plus difficilement dans les pays unilingues. Les propositions de M. Fishman imposeraient un fardeau excessif à l'administration du recensement et aux citoyens
eux-mêmes. M. Fishman rappelle que M. Vildomec, au cours d'une séance
de travail en petit comité, a émis l'idée que la tâche pourrait être confiée à
un service spécial, procédant par voie d'échantillonnage et financé de l'extérieur.

M. Lieberson a pris la défense de l'indice Greenberg contre les critiques
de M. Hughes, y voyant un précieux instrument de description du bilinguisme
et du développement linguistique d'une population. On ne doit pas s'attendre
à ce qu'il soit rigoureusement exact, car l'influence des gens les uns sur les
autres ne s'exerce jamais absolument au hasard; le principe de hasard est retenu seulement comme hypothèse de travail en vue de mesurer le potentiel de
communication au sein d'une société bilingue. Cela permet d'observer certains faits réels dans cette société, et donne une idée des transformations qui
interviennent sur le plan linguistique.

Un autre participant fait état des travaux poursuivis au Japon par Grootaers. A partir d'un village déterminé, Grootaers s'est demandé à quelle distance il fallait se rendre pour passer dans une autre région linguistique. M.
Lenehan a fait un échantillonnage des attitudes des gens vis-à-vis de l'intégration des races à Ridgewood (New Jersey). A celui qu'il interrogeait, il de-
mandait d'abord ce qu'il pensait de l'intégration, puis ce qu'il croyait que
son voisin en pensait. La plupart des gens étaient persuadés que leurs voisins
s'y opposaient, alors qu'en fait il n'en était rien. Les deux techniques pourraient servir à évaluer l'incidence du bilinguisme et les attitudes entretenues
à son égard. Dans le cas des recensements et relevés comportant un formulaire
que l'on laisse entre les mains des personnes interrogées, il est possible de con-
cevoir le formulaire d'une manière qui permette d'obtenir d'abondants renseignements. Lorsque diverses manières possibles de répondre sont indiquées, le
choix qui est fait peut être très révélateur.

Le profil tracé par les données du recensement pourrait être élargi grâce
à l'emploi d'indicateurs complémentaires. On pourrait même partir d'un autre
point de vue: configuration de la diffusion du journal dans la population, é-
coute de la radio et de la télévision, publicité, annonces commerciales dans

les annuaires du téléphone, tirage des livres édités, demandes de permis de télédiffusion, langue utilisée sur les formulaires. Dans le cas de la télédiffusion,
la langue utilisée sur les formulaires constitue un indicateur de l'importance
numérique du groupe considéré et elle indique la proportion des revenus qui est
attribuée aux services de télédiffusion. On peut, à partir des données du recensement et d'autres données dont on dispose, tracer un profil très détaillé
d'une situation de bilinguisme au sein d'une société.

Un participant soutient qu'il faudrait renoncer à la distinction entre ceux
qui parlent une langue A, ceux qui parlent une langue B et ceux qui parlent
les deux. Ce qu'il faut savoir, c'est lequel parle A ou B avec telle personne,
en tel lieu et à propos de telle chose. Il faut en arriver à examiner les situations d'usage de chaque langue. Les données trop sommaires nous masquent
divers contextes spéciaux. Il faut considérer la langue avec une certaine sensibilité de perception. Il faut tenir compte du genre de langue anglaise, du
genre de langue française qui se parlent dans certaines régions. Le sociologue
qui étudie les données d'un relevé a besoin d'un linguiste auprès de lui. Telle
langue est peut-être parlée par 40% de la population dans un certain nombre
de régions, mais est-ce tout à fait la même langue?

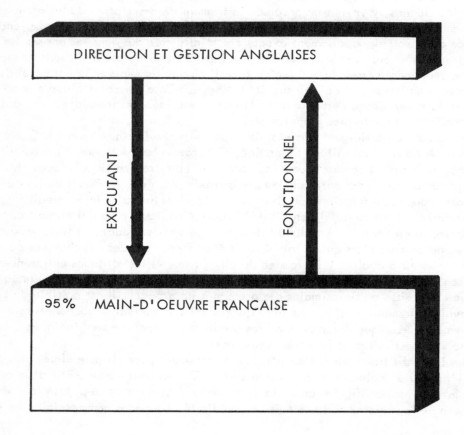

Un des commentateurs souligne l'aspect interdisciplinaire des discussions de ce genre et souhaite que de nouvelles méthodes soient utilisées pour l'analyse du rôle joué par les bilingues dans la société technique de notre temps. Il faut pour cela établir une distinction entre les industries qui produisent des biens culturellement neutres (à supposer que cela soit possible) et celles qui produisent des biens à caractère culturel.   Dans les industries du premier genre, les relations observent le schéma sur la page en regard.

Le personnel d'exécution, dans cette situation, doit assurer une traduction culturelle et linguistique du sommet à la base. Le contremaître joue souvent un rôle-clé. L'ordre donné d'en haut d'arriver à 9 heures le matin devient par exemple: "N'arrivez pas trop souvent en retard; vous savez comme les Anglais ont la religion de la ponctualité". Le contre-maître a souvent le monopole des communications du sommet vers la base, et il fait en sorte de le conserver. Le personnel auxiliaire, pour sa part, remplit des tâches de traduction culturelle et linguistique entre la base et le sommet. D'ordinaire, les fonctions de traduction s'exercent jusqu'à un niveau plus élevé dans la hiérarchie du personnel auxiliaire que dans celle du personnel d'exécution.

Dans les entreprises commerciales, la situation se présente d'une manière quelque peu différente:

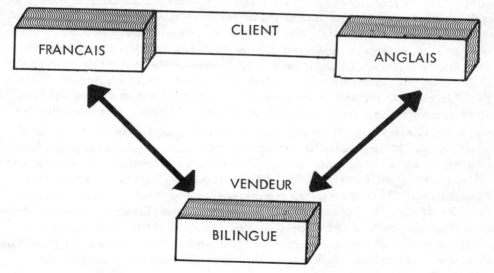

Dans la première situation, les clients étaient éloignés du fonctionnement de l'entreprise; dans la seconde, ils y pressent part. Aussi le point de contact où doit s'exercer le bilinguisme se trouve-t-il à la base. A Montréal, on peut passer des semaines sans venir en contact avec l'anglais, à moins d'avoir à se procurer, par exemple, des ouvrages scientifiques.

Les services particulièrement culturels sont le culte, l'enseignement, le

théâtre, les services sociaux et l'information. Tous ne sont pas culturels au
même degré. On peut y circuler du sommet à la base sans quitter l'élément
ethnique dont on fait partie. Dans l'enseignement, la plupart des carrières se
font dans une seule des deux langues, quelques points de contact intervenant
avec l'autre langue. En 1927 encore, les services sociaux de Montréal étaient
compartimentés suivant la langue et la religion; on tend maintenant à les re-
grouper. Plusieurs grandes sociétés, comme la Compagnie de téléphone Bell
et l'Imperial Tobacco, disposent d'analyses de leurs opérations qui leur indi-
quent les cas où le bilinguisme est nécessaire. Une société bilingue doit être
comprise telle qu'elle existe.

S'il est une profession intéressante, c'est celle de secrétaire bilingue.
Une institution de jeunes filles se spécialise dans la formation de sujets pour
cette profession. La secrétaire bilingue joue un rôle de liaison entre le patron
unilingue et ses subordonnés de langue française. Elle est un agent intercul-
turel. Il faudrait que nous puissions opérer un échantillonnage de situations
et accroître nos connaissances à cet égard. Par exemple, plusieurs industries
à caractère culturel particulier sont en voie de disparition à Montréal, notamment les modistes de vêtements de deuil.

Les populations bilingues ont d'ordinaire une personnalité fortement marquée. Une de leurs langues, bien souvent, leur sert à communiquer avec l'extérieur, tandis que l'autre leur sert à parler entre eux des gens de l'extérieur.

Un autre participant fait observer que les auteurs des communications présentées à la conférence paraissent utiliser des longueurs d'ondes différentes
d'un pays à l'autre. Le point de vue est fondamentalement différent lorsqu'il
s'agit d'un pays unilingue et d'un pays plurilingue. Dans les pays unilingues,
l'incidence et la répartition du bilinguisme sont considérées comme des faits
naturels dont on peut parler avec un certain détachement. Dans certains des
autres pays, elles constituent des aspects essentiels de la vie politique, et il
n'est pas possible en réalité de les étudier sans passion. Dans les pays pluri-
lingues, la carte des langues est considérée comme présentant des données valables pour l'établissement de la politique publique, notamment en matière
d'éducation. On ne peut guère compter sur les pays unilingues pour adopter
ce point de vue. L'orateur se dit intéressé par l'élargissement des applications
du bilinguisme dans le cadre social, ce qui oblige à s'élever au-dessus des
points de vue du groupe pour examiner l'influence du bilinguisme sur l'activité
politique. Cet examen demanderait peut-être des techniques moins fines.

M. Kloss signale que M. Lieberson a traité des caractéristiques universelles des énumérations. Il se propose, dans son commentaire, de traiter de questions que M. Lieberson n'a pas abordées. L'ampleur relative des contacts bilingues a son importance, même si, du point de vue du colloque, les rencontres
de personne à personne ont plus d'importance. Dans la plupart des pays, il
n'est pas impossible de réunir des données spécifiques sur l'ampleur relative
des contacts bilingues. Il aimerait voir adopter le terme diglossie lorsqu'il
s'agit d'un état de choses dans lequel on parle la première langue et l'on ne

fait que comprendre la seconde. Il existe un rapport certain entre diglossie et bilinguisme de réception.

En Alsace, la connaissance de l'allemand officiel a nettement diminué depuis la seconde guerre mondiale. Il y a même eu un temps où les jeunes ne savaient presque plus l'allemand, mais celui-ci revient maintenant par les moyens de grande information. On ne le parle pas, mais la plupart des gens le connaissent de façon passive. Il existe deux genres de bilinguisme productif:

a. à l'école secondaire, non seulement pour la prose didactique, mais aussi pour celle des récits;

b. chez les universitaires, comme le fait voir le tableau (p.297).

On doit considérer aussi bien la dualité que l'aspect linguistique, en ce qui concerne le bilinguisme. Lorsqu'il s'agit de distinguer entre langue, dialecte et patois, il importe de ne pas se laisser influencer par des considérations juridiques. Les langues peuvent à cet égard, se répartir en quatre groupes:

a. Langues en voie de devenir dialectes (comme le provençal)

b. Dialectes en voie de devenir langues

c. Dialectes qui survivent à une langue

d. Langues devenues dialectes et qui survivent à la langue qui les a fait devenir dialectes (par exemple, l'allemand des Mennonites, au Canada et aux Etats-Unis, qui survit à la langue du milieu général)

Celui qui fait un recensement doit surmonter bien des difficultés. Dans le plébiscite qui a eu lieu à Goa au sujet de la fusion avec l'Etat voisin du Maharashtra, nombreux furent ceux qui s'opposèrent à la fusion parce qu'ils parlaient le konkini et redoutaient une action du nouvel Etat contre ce parler. Certains Mahrates soutiennent que le konkini n'est qu'un dialecte du mahrate. Dans les années 1950, des populations de langue soushastra présentèrent des pétitions au gouvernement de Madras en vue d'obtenir l'enseignement à l'école dans leur langue maternelle. Cette demande fut repoussée, le gouvernement de Madras considérant le soushastra comme un dialecte et non une langue. Au recensement de 1960, le soushastra fut compté comme une langue parmi les autres, mais par la suite il fut inscrit parmi les dialectes du gujarati. En Allemagne se pose le problème du saxon ou bas-allemand. Certains voudraient que le recensement fasse mention de l'utilisation du bas-allemand, car on soutient que le saxon est une langue à l'égal des autres langues modernes. En Sardaigne, certains voudraient que le sarde soit enseigné à l'école. C'est un problème qui se pose un peu partout dans le monde.

BIBLIOGRAPHY/BIBLIOGRAPHIE

Abou, S.
1962   Le bilinguisme arabe-français en Liban, Paris
Arès, R.
1964   "Comportement linguistique des minorités françaises au Canada –
        II". Relations 281, 41-144
Berquet, Ch. (ed.)
1963   Le bilinguisme en Suisse, en Belgique. Brussels
Bilingualism and Education, Report on an International Seminar. Aberysthwyth,
1965   Wales, 1960, organized by U. K. National Commission for
        UNESCO. E. G. Lewis (ed.), London, H. M. Stationery Office
Bureau of the Census
1933   U. S. Census of Population, 1930, Volume 2, General Report,
        Statistics by Subjects, Washington, Government Printing Office

----
1962   U. S. Census of Population, 1960 Detailed Characteristics, Puerto
        Rico. Washington, Government Printing Office

1964   U. S. Census of Population, 1960, Selected Area Reports, Ameri-
        cans Overseas. Washington, Government Printing Office

----
1966   U. S. Census of Population, 1960, Subject Reports, Mother Tongue
        of the Foreign Born. Washington, Government Printing Office
Bureau of the Census and Statistics
1960   Census of the Philippines, Population and Housing, Summary, Ma-
        nila, Department of Commerce and Industry
Clyde, S.
1938   Problems of Education among the Pennsylvania Germans. Cornell,
        Ph. D. Thesis
Coates, W. A.
1961   "The Languages of Ceylon in 1946 and 1953." University of Ceylon
        Review 19, 81-91
Ceylon, Department of Census and Statistics
1957   Census of Ceylon 1953. Vol. I. Colombo, Department of Census
        and Statistics
Department of Economic and Social Affairs
1959   Handbook of Population Census Methods, Vol. 3, Demographic and
        Social Characteristics of the Population. New York, United
        Nations
Deutsch, K. W.
1953   Nationalism and Social Communication; an inquiry into the foun-
        dations of nationality. Cambridge, Published jointly by the Tech-
        nology Press of the Massachusetts Institute of Technology, and
        Wiley, New York

Diebold, R. A.
   1961   "Incipient Bilingualism." Language 37, 97-112
Dominion Bureau of Statistics
   1951   Enumeration Manual, 9th Census of Canada, 1951. Ottawa,
           Edmond Cloutier
Duncan, O. D.
   1957   "The Measurement of Population Distribution." Population Studies
           11, 27-45
-------, Cuzzort, R. P., Duncan, B.
   1961   Statistical Geography; problems in analysing areal data. Glencoe,
           Illinois, Free Press
Fellegi, I. P.
   1964   "Response Variance and its Estimation." Journal of the American
           Statistical Association 59, 1016-1041
Ferguson, C. A.
   1959   "Diglossia." Word 15, 325-40

   1964   "Diglossia." (In) Language in Culture and Society; a reader in lin-
           guistics and anthropology. D. Hymes (ed.), New York, Harper
           & Row, 429-439
Fishman, J. A. et al
   1966   Language Loyalty in the United States; the Maintenance and Per-
           petuation of Non-English Mother Tongues by American Ethnic and
           Religious Groups. The Hague, Mouton

   1967   "Bilingualism with and without Diglossia; Diglossia with and without
           Bilingualism." Journal of Social Forces 23, 29-38
General Register Office
   1966   Census 1961 Scotland, Volume 7, Gaelic. Edinburgh, Her Ma-
           jesty's Stationery Office
Gil, B. & Sicron, M.
   1956   Registration of Population (8XI 1948), Part B, Special Series No.
           53. Jerusalem, Israel Central Bureau of Statistics
Greenberg, J. H.
   1956   "The Measurement of Linguistic Diversity." Language 32, 109-115
el-Haje, K.
   1951   "Le bilinguisme, est-il possible?" Conférences du Cénacle V,
           (Beirut) 191-213
Hoffmann, G. & Jürgensen, G. (eds.)
   1960   Hart, Warr nich mööd. Festschrift für Christian Boeck, Hamburg
Kelley, G.
   1966   "The Status of Hindi as a Lingua Franca." (In) Sociolinguistics;
           proceedings of the U. C. L. A. sociolinguistics Conference,
           1964. W. Bright (ed.), The Hague, Mouton, 299-308

Kleeberg, R.
1915   Die Nationalitatenstatistik, ihre Ziele, Methoden und Ergebnisse
        Doctoral Thesis, Weida (Thüringen)

Kloss, H.
1931   "Deutsch als Gottesdienstsprachs in den Vereinigten Staaten," Der
        Auslanddeutsche 14, 630-634, 689-692, 715-721

1952   Die Entwicklung neuer germanischer Kultursprachen von 1800 bis
        1950. München, Pohl

------- (ed.)
1961   Ahornblätter. (Maple Leaves). Deutsche Dichtung aus Kanada
        Würzburg

1964   A Few Words Concerning Abstand Languages and Ausbau Languages.
        Paper Submitted at the Bloomington (Ind.) Seminar on Sociolin-
        guistics, July 6 and 7 (mim.)

1966a   "Types of Multilingual Communities; a discussion of ten variables."
        Sociological Inquiry 36, 135-145

1966b   "Problèmes linguistiques des Indes et de leurs minorités", Revue de
        Psychologie des Peuples 21, 310-349

Lieberson, S.
1964   "An Extension of Greenberg's Linguistic Diversity Measures. Lan-
        guage 40, 526-531

1965   "Bilingualism in Montreal; a demographic analysis." American
        Journal of Sociology 71, 10-25

1966   "Language Questions in Censuses." Sociological Inquiry 36, 262-
        279

Mackey, W. F.
1962   "The Description of Bilingualism," Canadian Journal of Linguistics
        7, 51-85

1966   "The Measurement of Bilingual Behavior," Canadian Psychologist
        7, 75-92

Martinet, A.
1960   Eléments de linguistique générale. Paris, Colin. (Collection Ar-
        mand Colin, No 349, Section de littérature

Mortara, G.
1950   "Immigration to Brazil; some observations on the linguistic assimila-
        tion of immigrants and their descendants in Brazil." Population
        Studies 3, supplement, 39-44

Office of the Registrar General
1965   Census of India, 1961, Volume 1, Part II-C(ii). Language Table
        (No city or publisher indicated)
Pferdekampf, W.
1958   Auf Humbolts Sparen-Deutsche im Sporen jungen Mexico, Munich

1967   Rapport sur la communauté sarde, Sassari
Rees, W. H.
1939   Le bilinguisme dans les pays celtiques, Rennes
Reyburn, W. D.
1956   Problems and Procedures in Ethnolinguistic Surveys, New York,
        American Bible Society
Rubin, J.
1963   National Bilingualism in Paraguay. Unpub. Yale Dissertation
Selk, P.
1937   Die Sprachlichen verhältnisse im deutsch-dänischen Sprachgebiet
        südlich der Grenze; eine statistisch-geographisehe Untersuchung
        von Paul Selk. Flensburg, Verlag Heimat und Erbe

1942   "Mehrsprachigkeit in Schleswig ", Volksforschung 5, 226-235

1950   "Der Sprachwechsel in Schleswig--eine Kultur begegnung. Aus
        Schleswig-Holsteins Geschichte w. Gegenwart...Festschriften
        für Volquart Paals, Neumünster, 281-297

1960   "Hundert Jahre Sprachwechsel im Kirchspiel Wallsbull." vide
        Hoffman and Jürgensen 260-259
Stine, C. S.
1938   Problems of Education among the Pennsylvanian Germans, Unpub.
        Ph.D. Thesis, Cornell
Strempel, A.
1960   Von einer wiewohl unbillig abgewürdigten Sprache. vide Hoffman
        and Jürgensen, 270-281
Thiessen, J.
1963   Studien zum Wortschatz der Kanadischen Mennoniten, Marburg

1953   The Use of Vernacular Languages in Education. UNESCO, Paris.
        (Monogr. on Fundamental Education, No. 8)
United Nations
1964   Demographic Yearbook, 1963, New York, Statistical Office, De-
        partment of Economic and Social Affairs
Verdoodt, A.
        Esquisse du trilinguisme au Grand-Duché. Unpublished Essay

Weinreich, U.
  1957   "Functional Aspects of Indian Bilingualism." Word 13, 203-233
Winkler, W.
  1923   Die ledeutung der statistik für den Schutz der nationalen Minder-
          heiten. Leipzig und Wien, F. Deuticke
Wioland, F.
  1965   Enquête sur les langues parlées au Sénégal par les élèves de l'en-
          seignement primaire. Dakar, Centre de linguistique appliquée
          de Dakar
Würzburger, E.
  1917   "Die Sprachenstatistik" Deutsches Statistiches Zentralblatt 9,
          No. 5, 138-144, No. 9-10, 244-254

ADDITIONAL COMMENTS/COMMENTAIRES DE PORTEE GENERALE

The following two statements were made by Drs. Nuytens & Siertsema at a free session held near the end of the seminar. As they are comments on the entire field covered by the seminar rather than on the six topics discussed, they find their place here.

Editor

Les deux exposés qui suivent furent présentés par M. Nuytens et Mlle Siertsema lors de la séance libre. Puisqu'ils concernent l'ensemble des matières discutées au colloque, ils trouvent leur place ici.

Editeur

Emile-Th. Nuytens

My statements are only meant as a positive contribution to the study of bilingualism. I have worked too long in the field of bilingualism to make personal
attacks.

In my opinion, we have to distinguish between linguistics studying language merely as a system; and linguistics studying the act, the use of language,
focussing on language behaviour. The first aspect we find in the work of
Bloomfield, Hockett, Harris, etc. and also in the methods of the generative
and transformational grammarians, Chomsky, Fodor, Greenberg, Lees, etc.
I believe we would be wise when we are studying Chomsky, first of all to know
something of the background of his ideas; that means studying the work of phi-
losophers as Goodman, Quine, Wittgenstein, and paying attention to the great
differences between e.g. Goodman and Carnap. When you notice the same
influence on many psychologists, it becomes clear that cooperation between
Chomsky and Miller is possible. Anybody who wishes to know something about
the place of glossematics must read the work of Professor Siertsema.

Structural linguistics can contribute to solving the problem of bilingualism
in that it focusses on the common core of two systems. The phenomenon of bilingualism is independent of nation, country, region or group. The only method we can use in this field is a synchronic one. Synchronic description will
yield data which don't fit into the systems, and these data we have to analyse
with the diachronic method. The compound word, wastafel (washstand) must
be analysed as was (wash) + tafel (table), but the object is no longer a table.
This change of meaning must be described and explained by a diachronic method in that we have to explain the change of meaning of wastafel in connection with other elements, while remaining within the system. In the American
Structural approach it is impossible to use a term like interference; in this field
we can only use terms like diaphone, diamorpheme, etc.

I see possibilities of cooperation between the school of Bloomfield and the
school of Chomsky through mathematics, mathematical psychology and information theory that such cooperation is desirable as is already clear from forms
as code, encoding, decoding. I believe that in future this cooperation might
be especially fruitful in the study of bilingualism. In the field of structuralism
there may also be cooperation between linguists and social psychologists and
between linguists and sociologists. I think it will be cooperation on a theoretical basis, on matters like open and closed systems, infrastructure, supra-
structure, etc.

But first of all we have to distinguish between the American form of structuralism and the European one, as we have to distinguish between the school
of Bloomfield and the work of Pike. European structuralism, e.g. Saussure,
Frei, Reichling, Uhlenbeck, Siertsema, Schultink, etc. is interested not merely in a system, as such, and does not observe the data of the system and the

rules of grammar, but focusses on language as an action, the use of language, the situation. I do not think it was by accident that at the last congress (1966) of social psychology it was concluded that cooperation with linguistics may be possible only on the basis of linguistic theories of Uhlenbeck.

This school of linguistics (Uhlenbeck, Pike) may cooperate with social psychology, pharmaco-psychology and neurology. About the very difficult problem of meaning, i.e. meaning of a word, we will probably get our information especially from pharmaco-psychology and neurology. Through the work of neurologists we already know how words are stored up in our brains and we have a new notion of the problem of the Gestalt. In addition we can not work in this area without any notion of information theory. I should like to refer to the fascinating work of Mol (1955). It will probably be useful for scholars who try to measure hearing or listening.

I should like to mention the work of Osgood and Suci in connection with bilingualism. Mathematically there are some problems. The distances between meanings can be measured, but I can also measure the difference between the angles of the vectors. The results are not the same. In mathematical psychology we now

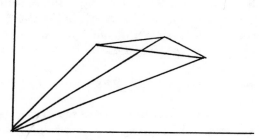

prefer to use city block models and not the Euclidian model. In measuring the meanings of prepositions and adverbs I use only city block models. I would refer to the work of Slama-Cazacu (1961) which gives us a lot of information about Russian investigations in the field of psycholinguistics.

What I read in the papers of this congress and what I heard here was first of all on the level of applied linguistics and applied psychology. What I missed here was a sound basis, founded on linguistics and psychology as sciences. That is the reason I said we have gone wrong.

A teacher of French at a secondary school has to explain the rules of grammar, to observe the use of these rules. But his task is not in the field of science. Applied psychology has to use tests; but using tests is the same as using a school grammar. A psychologist who has to use tests is not in the field of science. This work is not scientific because he has to make a diagnosis in a non-experimental situation. Measuring is inherent in the experimental sciences, but I can't see that testing is the same as measuring. I think that, first of all, we have to distinguish between the pure scientific approach and the more pragmatic and practical one well known in applied psychology. We also have to distinguish between the psychologist working in the field of science and the psychologist working in the field of education. I don't believe that applied psychology can give us a better insight into the problem of bilingualism.

Let me compare the use of tests and testing with a school grammar and the use of a school grammar. By teaching a language we don't get more knowledge of the scientific grammar of the language. There will always be a distance, a gap between the true scientific grammar and the school grammar. In a scientific grammar, the word fast in he walks fast may be called an adverb, but it is also possible to call it an adjective, because from a morphological point of view it is an adjective. But in teaching English as a language, it would not be wise to say: "Call it an adjective or an adverb, it does not matter." In teaching we work with ten word classes; in a scientific approach it is not clear why there should be ten classes or three or thirty classes.

I should like to say something of my results in the field of studying bilingualism. For forty years I worked at a study about the bilingual person in the East of the Netherlands: bilingualism of standard Dutch and dialect. I found out that contact between dialect and the standard language can cause a very strong levelling of both. The bilingual person might speak Dutch almost without mistakes or confusion, but it remained a levelled Dutch. Here we see a very striking resemblance between my results and those of Osgood who analysed the style of suicide letters. We both found as the most important factors of style:

(a) word repetitions, which means very high frequency of a small number of words;

(b) very high redundancy in sentence structure, a feature quite easily measured. The high redundancy had a very close correlation with the simple syntactical patterns we found.

We both concluded that the speakers preferred to use the present of a verb, had a poorish morphology and use of language which did not, however, affect communication, and that they preferred to use short sentences and tried to avoid subordinate clauses. We both gave the same explanation: social stress.

Now I would like to say something about what I call, in connection with Magnetic Hill, acoustical illusion. Magnetic Hill is a very good example of optical illusion (1). It is well known nowadays that optical illusions are caused by too much information from the background, so that the information from the details of the figure will be distorted. It is also well known that the style of perception has a very high correlation with the personality and character of the subjects. In studying bilingualism I found that many persons who spoke dialect in their youth could not hear that they used wrong syntactical or pho-

---

(1) Magnetic Hill is a small hill near Moncton where, due to an optical illusion caused by the configuration of the slope, vehicles seem to be able to roll up part of the slope without power.

nological patterns. Even in the studies of a rather good linguist born in the east of Holland, I found altijd niet instead of niet altijd and om in the meaning without, a meaning only possible with the preposition zonder. Still more amazing is the adverb weg: Where were you born? Where do you come from? are in Dutch, Waar kim ji vandaan? but in the Dutch of a bilingual person Waar kim ji weg? although in the dialect he says Woǒr kom ic vandan? I should like to call this phenomenon acoustical or lingual illusion. The person who thinks that he speaks rather good Dutch can not perceive that his Dutch is not normal. It is my opinion that this phenomenon may be interesting to linguists, information theorists and psychologists. If we can not measure it, what then?

I should like to ask everybody to make it possible for scholars of the whole world to cooperate. It has become very difficult for European scholars to go the way we see in the papers presented here.

B. Siertsema

In the course of this congress, non-linguists have made quite a number of remarks on linguistics. On what linguists think, and want to do and on their way of working, which to my mind do not seem to do quite justice to this branch of study. I cannot resist this opportunity to defend myself and my colleagues and try to remove any false impression you may have got. Before doing so, I want to say emphatically that I do hope that my criticism on statements will not be interpreted as a personal attack on the maker of the statements as it was the other day, for whenever that is done there is an end of all scholarly discussion. What has struck me most throughout the congress is the idea non-linguists seem to have, that linguists are only interested in phonology and grammar. This idea transpired again and again. It is expressed among others on page 254 of the paper where Chomsky is mentioned as more or less representative of modern linguistics.

Now it is true that generative transformational grammar concentrates on the field of grammar, but generative transformational grammar is only one grammatical theory amidst many and grammar covers only a minute part of the vast field of general linguistic studies. In fairness to Chomsky it should be pointed out that his is a developing theory, that he keeps changing it and especially that in his last publication Topics in the Theory of Grammar, he gives evidence of realizing very well that there are areas he has hardly begun to tackle. Still Chomsky is not the be-all and end-all of general linguistics. The anthropologist Dell Hymes, quoted on page 242 of the papers has pointed out that "linguistic competence" in the sense in which Chomsky employs this term must not be confused with the ability to communicate effectively in a particular society".

For other examples I refer you to several papers written in English by linguists Reichling and Uhlenbeck in Lingua; International Journal of General Linguistics in which the importance of context and situation for the interpretation of any utterance are continually stressed, to Kingdon 1956; 1958 and to Pike 1945; 1967. I draw your attention to the excellent books and papers by Nida, especially Nida 1947; 1949; 1950; 1964; which continually warn their readers against this very limitation to grammar and words only. Further, I would like to draw your attention to the great many publications from members of the so-called SIL, the Summer Institute of Linguistics of whom, by the way, I am surprised to see not one at the conference. Most of them work in the field for Bible translation. There are teams working on, I am not sure whether 228 or 128, but we keep on the safe side, on 128 languages which is a great number at this very moment. Many of them are bilingual, in the language of their tribe and many of the tribes they are working are partly bilingual. These people, the members of the Summer Institute of Linguistics have a vast store of experience and published many excellent studies because the Summer Institute of Linguistics in the United States give excellent training in which attention is specially focussed on the inter-cultural contact situations on the things to be aware of when working with informants on the importance of distinguishing the different styles of spoken language and all the other things for which papers say we need new sampling techniques. You will find publications of the linguists mentioned in IJAL, International Journal of American Linguistics, in the International Journal of African Linguistics, in the International Journal of West-African Languages, in Word and Language and Phonetica, and, for instance, the excellent paper by Sarah Gudschinsky twelve years ago, on the "A.B.C. of lexical statistics." She is one of the members of the Summer Institute of Linguistics.

As to the more detailed statements made on linguistics by non-linguists, I will confine myself to a sampling. First of all, I know of no linguist who, and I quote "thinks of a system like language as a thing inherently good" (Session 5, first Commentary). The idea that sound-change is flawless, taken from the same commentary, came up last century but was refuted early in this century and as regards to the idea that the loss or addition of a single structural element automatically restructures the entire system, taken from the same commentary, this depends on the point of view. But in the way de Saussure put it, for logical systems as he called them, it is true. His notion of value should be taken into account as is no doubt the case in Hockett's statement quoted in the same commentary. I could go on like this for quite a while, but I won't. Having mentioned de Saussure I would like to close with a word in defense of him. It is true that he advocated the complete independence of synchronic from diachronic studies, at least in some places of his book. But he did go against the background of linguistics of his time when only historical linguistics was something. He wanted to stress the equal importance of synchronic linguistics as a science in its own right.

It is true he over emphasized this independence in some places, but de

Saussure's statement should not be taken in isolation, less so than any other statements, and it is equally true that in other places, especially the pages 195 to 200 of his <u>Cours de linguistique générale</u> de Saussure stressed the mutual inter-dependence of the two approaches. That is what he illustrates with his two axes, <u>l'axe de la simultanéité et l'axe de succésivité</u> where he says "everything in one axe is also situated on the other" and that is what he illustrated with his transverse cut through the stalk of a plant.

But enough of linguistic details: you can read about the interpretation of these pages in Rulon Wells' excellent article (Wells 1946), and in some german publications before 1940. What I want to say in this statement to non-linguists dealing with language is simply: please read our publications, read and read and you will stop accusing us all of mistakes that only one or two of us have made or sometimes only seem to have made to superficial readers and that the rest of us object to as much as you do.

BIBLIOGRAPHY/BIBLIOGRAPHIE

Chomsky, N.
   1967   Topics in the Theory of Grammar, The Hague, Mouton

Gudschinsky, S. C.
   1956   "The ABCs of Lexicostatistics (Glottochronology)," Word 12, 175-210

Kingdon, R.
   1956   The Groundwork of English Stress, London, Longmans

   1958   The Groundwork of English Intonation, London, Longmans

Mol, H.
   1963   Fundamentals of Phonetics 1; The Organ of Hearing, The Hague, Mouton

Nida, E. A.
   1947   Bible Translating, an Analysis of Principles and Procedures, New York, American Bible Society
-----
   1949   Morphology, Ann Arbor, Michigan U. P.

   1950   Learning a Second Language, 2 ed., New York, National Council of the Churches of Christ
-----
   1964   Toward a Science in Translating with Special Reference to Principles and Procedures Involved in Bible Translation, Leiden, Brill

Pike, K. L.
   1945   Intonation of American English, Ann Arbor, Michigan U. P.

   1967   Language in Relation to an Integrated Theory of Human Behavior, The Hague, Mouton

Saussure, F. de
   1915   Cours de linguistique générale, Bally, C. & Sechehaye, A. (eds.) Paris, Payot

Wells, R. S.
   1946   "De Saussure's System of Linguistics," Word 2, 1-31

RESOLUTIONS/RESOLUTIONS

1

QUE dans le but de prolonger le travail amorcé au cours du présent colloque et d'en exploiter les résultats, soient organisés conjointement par les organismes nationaux intéressés et le Centre international de recherches sur le bilinguisme des colloques qui étudieraient les aspects spécifiques du bilinguisme et auxquels participeraient à la fois des spécialistes et les observateurs selon la formule appliquée cette fois.

1

THAT, in order to continue the work begun at this seminar and to make the best use of its results, interested national organisations in conjunction with the International Centre for Research on Bilingualism organise seminars to study specific aspects of bilingualism. To these seminars should be invited specialists and observers according to the formula applied this time.

2

Les participants au Colloque souhaitent que soient établis et soutenus (par des organismes nationaux ou internationaux) des centre de recherches interdisciplinaires sur le bilinguisme et le multilinguisme. Ils souhaitent vivement que soient développées les recherches et les sciences appliquées, dans ces domaines, par

a) l'encouragement et l'appui apportés à la préparation d'un personnel supplémentaire pour les centres du genre de celui qui existe déjà à l'Université Laval, à Québec, et pour ceux qui seraient créés ultérieurement;

b) la mise en place ou l'accroissement des moyens propres à faciliter les échanges d'information et de personnel entre les centres de ce genre.

2

The conference welcomes the establishment and support (by national and international agencies) of centres in which interdisciplinary research on bilingualism and multilingualism is to be done. It considers very desirable the furtherance of such appropriate research and applied science by

a) encouraging and supporting the preparation of additional personnel for such centres as that already established at l'Université Laval (Québec) and for others yet to be founded;

b) establishing or increasing means of exchanging information and personnel among such centres.

3

QUE le Centre international de recherches sur le bilinguisme reçoive des Etats membres de l'UNESCO la documentation sur le bilinguisme et le multilinguisme publiée dans leurs pays respectifs.

3

THAT the International Centre for Research on Bilingualism receive from the members of UNESCO the documentation on bilingualism and multilingualism published in their respective countries.

4

Le Colloque souligne la nécessité urgente d'instituer des systèmes de documentation utilisant les méthodes de l'informatique en vue de permettre une dissémination internationale et interdisciplinaire des résultats des recherches concernant le bilinguisme et le multilinguisme.

4

THAT the Conference stress the urgent need for developing documentation systems based on automatic storage and retrieval techniques that will provide international and interdisciplinary dissemination of research findings in the area of bilingualism and multilingualism.

5

QUE soient étudiés scientifiquement les parlers résultant du croisement de deux langues dans certaines situations bilingues par rapport à tous les facteurs politiques, sociaux, économiques et culturels et l'incidence de ces parlers sur le développement intellectuel et la sensibilité des sujets parlants.

5

THAT scholars make scientific studies of means of expression resulting from contact between two languages in certain bilingual situations to relate all the political, social, economic and cultural factors to each other and to assess the influence of these languages on the intellectual and emotional development of the speakers.

6

Vu l'ampleur du phénomène du bilinguisme dans le monde, l'UNESCO devrait chercher à obtenir des divers pays de plus abondantes données diagnostiques provenant des recensements, ainsi que des enquêtes méthodiques sur ce phénomène.

6

In view of the prevalence of bilingualism in the world, UNESCO should seek to obtain from countries more diagnostic data, based on censuses and for surveys of the phenomenon.

7

Les participants au Colloque insistent auprès de l'UNESCO sur l'utilité que présenteraient des données de recensement sur la langue du foyer, la langue maternelle, le bilinguisme et le multilinguisme. Ils souhaitent en particulier que soient examinées attentivement les propositions et la discussion de la séance intitulée "Comment décrire et mesurer l'incidence et la répartition du bilinguisme?" du Colloque international sur la description et la mesure du bilinguisme. Les recensements démographiques devraient être complétés par des enquêtes sur les langues, effectuées à l'aide de techniques d'échantillonnage scientifique et suivant les méthodes de la linguistique et les autres disciplines intéressées, de façon que soient élargies et confirmées les données que fournissent les recensements des divers pays.

7

RESOLVED that the members of the seminar wish to express to UNESCO the desirability of census data about home language, mother-tongue, bilingualism and multilingualism.   In particular we recommend careful consideration of the proposals and discussion presented at the session entitled "How can we describe and measure the incidence and distribution of bilingualism?" of the International Seminar on the Description and Measurement of Bilingualism.   Population censuses should be supplemented by language surveys conducted in accordance with scientific sampling techniques and with the methods of linguistics and other relevant disciplines, in order to extend and validate the date obtained by the census in a particular country.

8

QUE de tels colloques sur le bilinguisme et le multilinguisme soient tenus régulièrement.   Ce sera à la Commission canadienne pour l'UNESCO d'entrer en pourparlers avec d'autres commissions nationales pour ces fins.

8

THAT such seminars on bilingualism and multilingualism be held regularly.   It will be the responsibility of the Canadian National Commission for UNESCO to initiate discussions with other National Commission for this purpose.

CONCLUSION

W. F. Mackey

Maintenant que nous sommes arrivés au terme de ce colloque, il m'incombe d'y apporter la conclusion et, si possible, la synthèse.

Mais avant de dresser le bilan scientifique de nos discussions, j'aimerais mentionner le bilan humain. Je dirai donc quelques mots sur ce qui reste après que les discussions, les interventions et les résolutions seront terminées, après la publication des actes et la lecture du rapport final. Ce qui resterait c'est toutes ces choses qui nous ont apporté le contact humain, les rencontres personnelles et les discussions intimes de personnes qui nourissent les mêmes intérêts, les mêmes liens établis entre les spécialistes d'une même préoccupation scientifique.

L'établissement de tels liens et de tels contacts sont en soi une justification suffisante d'un colloque. A ce point de vue je crois que notre colloque a eu un grand succès. On a noué durant ces quelques jours des rapports humains qui vont certainement durer pendant des années, et qui vont peut-être apporter à l'étude de nos problèmes les fruits de la collaboration internationale et interdisciplinaire.

De retour dans nos foyers, nos bureaux ou nos laboratoires, nous allons pouvoir lire avec un renouveau d'intérêt et de compréhension les travaux de ceux qui ont bien voulu venir nous adresser la parole.

Au point de vue scientifique, il faut d'abord se demander dans quelle mesure le colloque a-t-il atteint le but qu'il s'est proposé.

On aura souhaité comme résultat d'un colloque international de ce genre, une élaboration de mesures universelles du bilinguisme. Pourquoi n'a-t-on pas réussi à établir de telles mesures? Si on examine de près la question, on se rend compte du fait que l'on n'a pas réussi d'abord à établir un accord préalable concernant l'identification de nos unités de base. Puisque toute mesure suppose une conception préalable de la matière à mesurer, cette conception, une fois arrêtée, empêche l'adoption et l'utilisation de toutes mesures basées sur des conceptions différentes. C'est que chaque conception engendre des typologies de la matière, basées sur la discipline que pratique le chercheur. N'empêche que les typologies utilisées par des chercheurs à l'intérieur de la même discipline peuvent différer énormément les unes des autres.

Nous avons parmi nous des spécialistes de l'étude du bilinguisme venant de disciplines diverses, et à l'intérieur de chaque discipline des chercheurs, éloignés dans le temps et dans l'espace, qui travaillent plus ou moins isolément et qui ont réussi à élaborer pour les fins de leurs recherches leur propre typologie.

C'est aussi que nous avons éprouvé quelques difficultés à nous entendre sur la description du bilinguisme préalable à sa mesure. Mais puisqu'il s'agit seulement d'un premier colloque sur la mensuration du bilinguisme, c'est peut-être trop demander.

Même si nous n'avons pas réussi à élaborer un système universel pour la mensuration du bilinguisme, nous y avons tout de même apporté une contribution positive.

D'abord, le fait même que nous avons pu identifier les préjugés, les faiblesses et le manque de rigueur dans les mesures actuellement en usage, permettra aux chercheurs de réévaluer et d'améliorer leurs mesures ou d'en inventer d'autres. Un tel examen périodique est fort salutaire pour une discipline, parce qu'elle décourage l'utilisation continue de mesures fautives, préjugées ou peu rentables.

Ayant critiqué nos mesures actuelles, on était peut-être dans l'obligation d'en fournir des meilleures. Mais malheureusement nous n'en avons pas d'autres à proposer. Et ceci constitue une des faiblesses ou une les lacunes de ce colloque.

On aura espéré que, faute d'un système de mesures universelles, on aura au moins pu contribuer à l'évolution et au perfectionnement des mesures actuelles qui constituent nos outils de découverte. Si nous voulons progresser dans l'étude du bilinguisme, il faut forger des outils de plus en plus puissants et à la fois de plus en plus délicats. Si nous n'avons pu élaborer de nouvelles mesures, nous n'avons pas hésiter à proposer d'autres variables à mesurer, et à poser des problèmes - voire, des dilemmes - pour ceux qui entreprendront des recherches scientifiques sur le bilinguisme.

Sous le chapitre de l'acquisition linguistique, on a souligné l'invalidation des tests qui utilisent des représentations d'objets dans le cas des enfants bilingues qui n'ont pas encore atteint l'âge de la généralisation mentale. On a demandé aux chercheurs de tenir en ligne de compte dans leur mesure la proportion de l'utilisation des deux langues dans le milieu de celui qui subit le test, de ne pas oublier de mesurer les attitudes envers la langue, les changements de la personnalité qui accompagnent l'individu quand il s'exprime dans la langue seconde.

On nous demande de décrire et de mesurer les types et les degrés du bilinguisme nécessaire pour toute une gamme de fonctions individuelles et d'élaborer des tests qui nous permettront de prédire le progrès linguistique d'un unilingue qui se trouvera placé dans un milieu où on n'utilise que l'autre langue.

On nous demande de mesurer le comportement physique, les gestes et les mouvements expressifs des bilingues, leur intelligibilité, leur répertoire et variétés de bilinguisme, et en même temps le prestige social des différents types de bilinguisme. On propose également l'étude quantitative des rôles que peut jouer dans chaque langue l'individu bilingue. Les membres du colloque, qui ont tous longuement réfléchi à ces questions de la mesure du bilinguisme, n'ont pas hésité à poser des problèmes.

Dans le domaine de l'acquisition des langues, on se demande comment il est possible de mesurer la connaissance d'une langue en mesurant la performance linguistique du sujet. Et dans la mesure des performances on se demande s'il est légitime de mesurer séparément des automatismes, tels que l'utilisation des systèmes grammaticaux et lexicaux, qui fonctionnent toujours simultanément dans le sujet parlant. On a également critiqué la valeur des tests d'un seul automatisme qui présuppose des habitudes non pas encore formées, par exemple, les tests d'expression qui supposent un certain degré de compréhension de la langue.

On a également critiqué les tests qui supposent une connaissance analytique de la langue, comme si l'on voulait mesurer le rendement d'un ouvrier en lui demandant de décrire les fonctions de ses outils.

En ce qui concerne la capacité linguistique des bilingues, certains l'ont mesurée en utilisant comme base le rendement linguistique des deux groupes unilingues. Et ici se pose la question du choix d'un groupe unilingue pour servir de norme. D'autres préfèrent une mesure de l'équilibre des deux langues à l'intérieur de chaque individu, de sorte que, ce qui importe, ce n'est pas les connaissances de chacune des langues, mais plutôt les différences entre ses connaissances, nous permettant ainsi d'établir, pour chaque individu, le degré d'équilibre de son bilinguisme.

Ce qui complique l'interprétation de toutes ces mesures du bilinguisme, c'est le rapport intime entre la langue et la pensée. Si la langue sert comme instrument essentiel de la représentation mentale, la performance intellectuelle réalisée dans une langue ne peut pas avoir la même valeur que dans l'autre.

Mais ce qui a touché le plus profondément nos inquiétudes pour l'avenir des études sur le bilinguisme, est le fait que ce colloque a réussi à ébranler la confiance de certains collègues dans la validité de quelques notions fondamentales de nos disciplines. En linguistique, par exemple, quelle que soit la théorie de base, la plupart des linguistes ont toujours accepté la distribution entre langue et parole et la dichotomie analogue qui séparent la synchronie de la diachronie. Maintenant, paraît-il, ces distinctions s'appliquent difficilement à l'étude du bilinguisme.

Chers collègues, pour sauver le principe du bilinguisme que ce congrès à adopté, j'estime que le temps est venu de continuer ces propos dans l'autre langue.

Out of respect for the principle of official bilingualism adopted by the seminar, I shall now continue my remarks in English.

As I was saying, this seminar, which was designed as a study of the description and measurement of bilingualism has ended up as a discussion on theory and method, since what we have been discussing are the basic conceptual problems of the study of bilingualism.

One of these, is the concept of interference. Since the verbal behaviour of bilinguals has been measured in terms of interference, it was important to delimit this basic notion. We have still to determine the point at which interference becomes borrowing. It has been suggested that if interference is either constant or consistent it ceases to be interference. Although we do not all agree on what constitutes interference, one of its characteristics, on which most of us do agree, is that it is some sort of deviation from the norm. But there is still uncertainty about what exactly constitutes a norm. Is it what people do or what people expect? Is it what a person usually says in relation to what others usually say? How can it be determined? Must it be arrived at quantitatively in order to be of any use?

It has been suggested that the more defined the norm is the more definite the interference (for example, two patois vs standardized national languages). To give an accurate picture of bilingualism we may have to measure linguistic and situational norms together.

But we cannot measure interference until we can assign items to different codes. And we cannot do this until we know what constitutes the code of each language. But since the languages are in contact, the codes themselves are not stable and evolve rapidly within the same community, while varying in time and space within and between individuals. The analysis and measurement of such situations is far beyond the capacity of the conventional synchronic techniques of description and requires new theories and methods. It has been suggested that the elaboration of a sort of quantum linguistics, designed to deal with interrelated and evolving codes and norms is what is most needed.

But before we can quantify bilingualism, we need to know more about roles and role-expectation data of monolinguals. In recent years, researchers have attempted to define the notion of role in the study of situations and to define its relationship to the concepts of domain, topic and interaction, in the construction of models for the study of bilingual behaviour. A number of different models have been suggested, including in addition to these variables, those of social situation (time and setting), self-evaluation, sensitivity, proficiency, attitude, the presence of other persons and their personel relationship to the bilingual individual. What we need, therefore, is a multi-dimensional typology of multi-lingualism.

In attempting to describe the roles which a bilingual's languages play in his behaviour, a number of quite contradictory methods have been used, including those of the theoretical and experimental sciences. Some of us construct models, test them, modify and re-test, until an acceptable approximation has been achieved. Others are satisfied to pursue an empirical, down-to-earth, self-correcting approach, consisting mostly in the identification and measurement of variables. The value of survey methodology, however, has been questioned as a useful tool in the social study of bilingualism. So has the interview technique, which some field-workers have now replaced with taped samples of free or guided verbal behaviour, mostly in the form of conversation, reflecting social behaviour and analysed into socially functional units of speech. Still others are proposing the use of the techniques of modern mathematical psychology, information theory, and modern mathematical models.

In the study of bilingual behaviour, we may need a concept of language proficiency quite different from the conventional notions of linguists and language teachers. We may have to describe proficiency in terms of communicative competences, each for a specific function, while measuring the communicative efficiency of an evolving code.

We must check the data supplied both by reports made by one generation on the behaviour of another, and that supplied by self-reports of bilinguals; these may vary considerably when the bilingual community is under some form of pressure.

In the study of the behaviour of bilingual groups, the very usefulness of the notion of language has been brought into question. We are asked to go beyond language in order to investigate the behaviour of bilinguals. And if we focus our attention on their different speech events, we are permitted to forget about their language differences. This may be true, provided firstly that we can establish standard units of speech events, and secondly, that we can create a grammar including two languages, two sets of rules by which syntatic material may be encoded into phonetic manifestations with sets of norms applying to particular social situations. This is the concept of bilingualism as rule-governed behaviour in contradiction to bilingualism as a set of strategies for encoding meaning into linguistic form.

Whether bilingualism is indeed governed by rules or motivated by strategies, we must develop quantitative techniques for the description of language choice, and for the study of the inhibition of bilinguals in different types of situations.

We must also investigate those social rules of bilingualism governed by the distribution of power in society of which language itself is a faithful reflection. Finally, we have been asked to measure how effective the language may be controlled from above in a bilingual society.

Techniques for measuring the incidence and distribution of bilingualism have also been suggested. Among these are cohort analysis, refined sampling techniques, and the exploitation of multiple cross-tabulations based on conventional census data, permitting a comparison of bilinguals with unilinguals according to such variables as occupation, education, birth place and income.

Other useful sources of data include readership and listenership surveys of the mass media, data from telephone directories and publication figures. We could also measure the distribution of what and how much has been translated and how quickly. We cannot, however, solely rely on census questions, which are severely limited by the degree of tolerance that the public is judged to possess. The trouble with census data is that they tend to be only enumeration. Some controlled samples can to-day be simpler, more reliable, and more efficient, while at the same time yielding more information. It has been suggested that professional polling institutions be hired to do such surveys of bilingual communities, in conjunction with specialists in the field. This would permit us to find out with whom bilinguals speak each language, and in what variety. It would also help us spot the strategic points for bilingual contact in a multi-lingual society, in order to plot on various communication models the amounts of line bilingualism and liaison bilingualism in a number of different areas. Investigations along these lines are likely to be most fruitful and could have far-reaching practical consequences for those who will base language policy on refined and quantitative studies of communication in a bilingual society.

All these far-off and attractive horizons, however, can only be reached through a great effort of inter-disciplinary co-operation between the theorists and experimentalists of several fields of knowledge and such professions as those of statistics and the communication sciences, using both quantitative and distributional techniques and a common and rigorous terminology—all agreed to accept the same rules of this game of measurement. When this day arrives, a seminar on the measurement of bilingualism will be quite different from the present one. But let us hope that it will have been made possible by our work here, for it is in theory and method which is prerequisite to all scientific description and measurement that we have, I believe, made our greatest contribution. And because of this, it would be most appropriate if we could include this fact in the title of the proceedings of this useful and most stimulating seminar.

PROBLEMES DE BILINGUISME AU CANADA

par
Jean-Paul VINAY, m.s.r.c.,
University of Victoria, B. C.

NOTE LIMINAIRE

"Dans le cas de pays bilingues   il s'agit toujours du même problème:
abolir la distance. Ici, le fonds commun est pour ainsi dire inexistant: les
codes sont de plus en plus différents. Mais il subsiste toujours une certaine
correspondance, une certaine relation entre les deux codes. Il reste possible
d'atteindre à une compréhension au moins partielle, et c'est ici qu'interviennent des médiateurs linguistiques, des interprètes, - les bilingues. Nous tou-
chons à un point très important, un point décisif. Le bilinguisme est pour moi
le problème fondamental de la linguistique."

Roman Jakobson,
in "Results of the Conference of Anthropologists and Linguists,"
IJAL, Supplement, Memoir No. 8, 19-2
(April, 1953)

Traduction N. Ruwet,
Editions de Minuit, Arguments No. 14, 1963

Le présent article a été suscité par le comité d'organisation des journées d'études sur le bilinguisme et doit, dans l'esprit des membres de ce comité, souligner certains aspects du bilinguisme au Canada, de nature à éclairer les travaux des participants tout en restant dans le cadre du colloque.

Dans le document préparatoire au colloque se trouvent les grandes lignes du programme qui intéresse, rappelons-le, "la description et la mesure du bilinguisme". On y retrouve les points principaux de la pensée précise et nourrie d'exemples du président du colloque, mon collègue William F. Mackey, de l'Université Laval. Je ne pouvais mieux faire que de conserver les cadres principaux de ses divers exposés pour présenter ici un tour d'horizon rapide sur le bilinguisme canadien. Comme le souligne le Secrétariat (Annonce préliminaire, page 1), la plupart des travaux spécialisés consacrés au bilinguisme ont été l'oeuvre d'isolés ou de quasi-isolés. Ceci est parfaitement exact, et peut s'expliquer à la fois par le peu d'intérêt que les linguistes ont porté jusqu'ici aux problèmes du bilinguisme, - à quelques brillantes exceptions près - et sans doute aussi par le fait que ces problèmes se situent à la frontière de plusieurs disciplines: psychologie, sociologie, communication, linguistique et même politique. On sait que les travaux interdisciplinaires ne datent que de quelques années, que la psycholinguistique et la sociolinguistique se cherchent encore, et que les cloisons à l'intérieur des Facultés restent la plupart du temps très étanches.

Le colloque vient donc parfaitement à point, et il faut féliciter les organisateurs du choix du thème. Il le faut d'autant plus que les études sérieuses sur le bilinguisme franco-anglais au Canada sont extrêmement rares (pratiquement inexistantes du côté anglais), ce qui ajoute une difficulté supplémentaire à la rareté des travaux sur le bilinguisme en général.

En préparant ces quelques brèves remarques, mon propos était de souligner, à l'intention des experts rassemblés par l'UNESCO, l'intérêt qu'il y aurait à appliquer le concept de mesure du bilinguisme à des domaines très divers, pour lesquels je n'ai relevé, jusqu'ici, que des notations qualitatives. Les exemples cités n'ont d'autre excuse que de vouloir rappeler à ces mêmes experts l'existence d'un problème très réel au sein même de l'Amérique du Nord, dont la solution, quelle qu'elle soit, intéresse la santé mentale et le développement intellectuel de plus de cinq millions d'individus. Eu égard à l'indifférence de la majorité anglophone vis-à-vis de ce problème, il sera presque exclusivement question du bilinguisme franco-anglais, - mais ces mêmes remarques pourraient s'appliquer, mutatis mutandis, à d'autres types de bilinguisme, et toute conclusion prend de ce fait une portée beaucoup plus vaste.

Enfin, plutôt que de citer des textes, d'ailleurs rares ou d'accès difficile, j'ai cru préférable de puiser dans une expérience de 20 années passées en milieu bilingue, avec tous les avantages et les inconvénients que cela comporte. Il faut noter à ce sujet que le bilinguisme au Canada se colore en outre de certaines nuances qui tiennent à la personnalité des deux langues en présence. Il y aurait là un domaine où les techniques de mesure pourraient peut-être s'exercer utilement: je suis porté à croire que si le bilinguisme est en tout temps générateur de frictions sociales et de souffrances personnelles chez l'individu, il revêt un aspect encore plus aigu selon les langues considérées. Cette dernière hypothèse est peut-être illusoire, bien qu'il m'ait toujours semblé discerner des nuances importantes dans le climat du bilinguisme amérindien (par exemple, montagnais-français au Québec, cowichan-anglais en Colombie britannique) et européen (par exemple, breton-français (1), basque-français, gallois-anglais). Il est possible qu'en dernière analyse, il s'agisse seulement du comportement politique de la majorité et de l'image que se fait de celle-ci la minorité en question. De toute façon, si ce n'est pas du domaine de la psycholinguistique, c'est sans doute un problème qui intéresse la sociolinguistique, ou, comme on dit plus simplement en français et depuis plus longtemps, un problème de psychologie des peuples (2).

1. Définitions et données du problème

Le Maréchal Foch avait une manie, dit-on, qui caractérise bien l'esprit cartésien: il voulait toujours partir d'une définition. A son exemple, nous pourrions commencer cet exposé en posant la question "Le bilinguisme, qu'est-ce que c'est?" C'est d'ailleurs, d'après le programme, ce que le professeur Mackey se propose de faire au début du Colloque. Il n'est donc pas inutile de rappeler ici quelques définitions antérieures, et même d'en proposer de nouvelles.

N'ayant pu assister au Colloque d'Aberystwyth, je dois me fier aux dires

---

(1) Presque tous les grands linguistes français depuis un demi-siècle ont prédit la mort imminente du breton ou insistent sur les avantages évidents qu'il y aurait à en hâter la disparition (Cf. Martray 1947). Ces mêmes linguistes soulignent avec complaisance l'intérêt que présente la présence d'une zone bilingue bascophone en France. On peut voir là plusieurs causes en jeu: religieuses, politiques, démographiques, culturelles. Leur étude, et leur dosage, serait important. Il n'est pas inutile de noter ici que les mêmes prédictions pessimistes ont été formulées à l'égard du canadien-français par d'éminents linguistes français tels que Meillet, et qu'aucun des grands instruments de travail chers aux philologues (Dictionnaires, thesaurus, grammaires comparées, atlas linguistiques) ne tient compte des formes canadiennes. Toutefois une réaction se dessine actuellement en France, qui se penche plus volontiers sur le sort de ses minorités linguistiques en Suisse (Valais), en Belgique, et au Canada. Mais il s'agit surtout d'articles de vulgarisation, au sens étymologique du mot, qui n'auront de valeur que pour l'histoire du bilinguisme, si tant est que cette discipline devienne un jour diachronique.
(2) Consulter les études qui paraissent régulièrement dans l'intéressante publication havraise La Revue de Psychologie des Peuples et qui passent trop souvent inaperçues des linguistes.

des observateurs (3), qui parlent de "bilinguisme organisé ou non-organisé, mélangé ou à l'état pur, généralisé ou accidentel, régressif ou équilibré, etc." Je crois en effet qu'un examen attentif des faits permet d'établir ces distinctions entre différents types de bilinguisme; mais toutes ces définitions ont le tort de présenter exclusivement le phénomène sur le plan géographique ou social. Si cette démarche est parfaitement légitime, comme nous le verrons plus loin, on doit néanmoins chercher le point de départ d'une définition là où réside la coexistence de plusieurs langues, à savoir le cerveau d'un individu.

Bien entendu, il faut avoir des interlocuteurs pour pouvoir échanger des propos, et on peut se demander jusqu'à quel point Willyam Bodener, dernier représentant du cornique en Angleterre, faisait du bilinguisme alors qu'il ne pouvait plus se parler qu'à lui-même. Cependant, dans la mesure où il connaissait le cornique et l'anglais, c'était en fait un bilingue et il devait en offrir toutes les caractéristiques. En particulier, il posait à lui seul le problème essentiel: Dans quelle proportion était-il bilingue?, avec le corollaire inévitable: Dans quelle mesure les deux systèmes linguistiques avaient-ils gardé chez lui leur individualité?

Plutôt que de s'inspirer des dichotomies d'Aberystwyth, il semble préférable de partir des cadres tracés par Mackey 1956, 1966 et de rechercher des définitions qui mettent en relief, dès le départ, les notions essentielles de degré, d'alternance et d'interférence, ces dernières permettant au linguiste de se faire une idée de l'importance des pressions socio-culturelles qui s'exercent sur un sujet ou une population donnés.

1.1 Définitions du bilinguisme

1 Connaissance des deux langues

"Etat d'individus qui ont en commun de ne pas être unilingues". (Haugen 1956 "A bilingual person can be said to have two coding systems for his intentive

_____

(3) Taillon 1961. Le Colloque d'Aberystwyth a également défini le bilinguisme selon le type de langues en présence:

dialecte / langue nationale

langue du foyer / langue nationale

langue vernaculaire / langue étrangère (avec variantes selon que ces langues possèdent ou non une littérature écrite)

langue non officielle / langue officielle

deux langues officielles (avec degrés dans leur application pratique)

système fédéral de langues, dont l'une tend à fonctionner comme langue commune.

behavior, and two sets of decoding responses leading into interpretative behavior." Caroll 1953, 99
"Any contact with possible models in a second language and the ability to use
these in the environment of the native language." Diebold 1961
"Toute personne capable de comprendre et de se faire comprendre dans une autre langue que la sienne". JPV. (Cette définition prend langue dans un sens
très général; pour moi, toute personne vivant dans une région autre que celle
où elle a été élevée est obligée d'acquérir des caractéristiques linguistiques
nouvelles qui peuvent parfaitement coexister avec les structures anciennes.
C'est alors un bilingue, même si l'écart entre les deux "langues" est relativement faible (Cf. le cas du Français venant se fixer au Québec). "

2 Connaissance poussée des deux langues

"The ability to produce complete meaningful utterances in the other language." Haugen 1953
"Qualité d'un sujet ou d'une population qui se sert couramment de deux langues, sans aptitude marquée pour l'une plutôt que l'autre". Marouzeau 1951
"The native-like control of two languages." Bloomfield 1933
"By bilingualism I mean the use of two or more languages by anyone at any
time. This does not limit bilingualism, as certain linguists maintain, to the
simultaneous mastery of two languages." Mackey 1953
"This insistence on a criterion of indistinguishability from native usage has
been /..../ one of the greatest theoretical obstacles to the advancement of
research in bilingualism." Mackey 1956, 4
"Il n'existe pas de bilingues parfaits". Vinay 1952

3 Bilinguisme et contacts linguistiques

"It is important not to confuse bilingualism—the use of two or more languages
by the individual—with the more general concept of language contact, resulting in changes /..../ which become the permanent property of monolinguals
and enter into the historical development of the language." Mackey 1962, 51.

4 Bilinguisme et société: position officielle

"On s'entend pour le moment sur la définition du bilinguisme comme la coexistence et l'utilisation de deux langues par un individu ou un groupe social".
Taillon 1961
"Bilingualism, in Canada, involves the status and the use of the two official
languages: English and French; no other language can be considered official
at the national level." Royal Society of Canada, Working Paper (Feb.1964)
"... Des Canadiens entendent parvenir à une égale possession des deux langues et de deux cultures. Mais on peut tout de suite affirmer, en thèse générale, que le bilinguisme d'un pays n'implique pas le bilinguisme de tous les

individus. Ceci peut conduire à accepter comme normale l'existence, des deux côtés, de larges secteurs unilingues". (4) C.R.B.B. 1964

Il serait possible d'ajouter d'autres définitions et d'en donner des commentaires abondants. Mais, pour nous limiter au concept de mesure du bilinguisme, je me contenterai de présenter quelques remarques sur le degré de perfection dans le maniement des deux langues, en pensant avant tout aux groupes francophones du Canada.

1.1.1 Degré de perfection dans le maniement des deux langues

Cette perfection peut se mesurer à différents niveaux, et ces niveaux peuvent varier d'une langue à l'autre. Nous avons dit qu'il n'existe pas de bilingues parfaits ou du moins que ce sont des oiseaux rares: une expérience de vingt ans d'enseignement dans un milieu bilingue nous permet de dire que pour chaque bilingue étudié, il y avait toujours un plan sur lequel on pouvait relever une faiblesse quelconque (phonème étranger, intonation, calques, solécismes, etc.) même si, sur le plan culturel, les bilingues de Montréal sont relativement homogènes. (5)

Il n'est pas indifférent non plus de constater que, parmi les bilingues montréalais que j'ai pu observer, ceux qui étaient parvenus à une maîtrise vraiment exceptionnelle de l'anglais parlaient tous un français qui laissait fortement à désirer, - ceci indépendamment des caractéristiques purement canadiennes que présentent également les monolingues canadiens-français. Inversement, d'excellents écrivains, conférenciers, professeurs, artistes de télévi-

---

(4) Dans son premier Document de travail, la Commission précisait notamment que l'idée-force du mandat était "l'égalité entre les deux peuples qui ont fondé la confédération canadienne" (an equal partnership between the two founding races). Deux jugements sont implicites dans les termes du mandat (1) la création même de la Commission implique qu'aux yeux d'un grand nombre de Canadiens, cette égalité n'existe pas; (2) mais qu'elle est réalisable, au moins jusqu'à un certain point. L'idée d'égalité n'est pas limitée à tel secteur géographique particulier, non plus qu'à la seule politique fédérale. La CRBB devra examiner surtout les difficultés et les handicaps suscités par la coexistence de deux langues et de deux cultures au Canada; mais aussi, de souligner les aspects positifs, les avantages d'une telle situation.
(5) Inutile de dire que le caractère hautement désirable du bilinguisme en matière de commerce, d'administration, etc., pousse les individus à se dire "parfaits bilingues". On rencontre cette expression presque à chaque page des annonces des journaux. Cependant, il est rare que les Anglo-Canadiens se disent "perfectly bilingual." Le terme lui-même était peu répandu au Canada avant ces dernières années, comme le prouvent les dictionnaires publiés au Canada.

sion, etc., qui avaient de toute évidence porté une grande attention à la perfection de leur langue maternelle (le français), savaient généralement bien
l'anglais, – mieux que ne le savent les Européens francophones occupant des
positions équivalentes, – mais le parlaient avec toutes les petites fautes caractéristiques du francophone: accentuation hésitante, intonation étrangère, tour-
nures stylistiques inusitées, etc.

Le problème de la définition d'une "bonne" ou d'une "très bonne" connaissance d'une langue seconde, qui s'accompagne au Canada du problème de
la connaissance plus ou moins parfaite de la langue maternelle – n'est pas seulement académique. Comme c'est le cas dans tous les pays de bilinguisme officiel, certains postes sont offerts en priorité à des bilingues et de grands efforts s'accomplissent en ce moment pour former des candidats à ces postes bilingues. Malheureusement, pour le moment, sans vouloir donner des statistiques
sans doute difficiles à recueillir, on peut affirmer que les seuls bilingues à Ottawa sont des francophones, à quelques brillantes exceptions près. On a pu
ainsi définir le bilinguisme au Canada "comme l'obligation imposée aux Canadiens français de parler anglais". (Vinay 1964, 50) On raconte à ce sujet
l'histoire d'un haut fonctionnaire recevant une délégation québécoise et qui
commence ainsi son discours: "Puisque nous sommes tous bilingues ici, nous
pouvons parler anglais". Cette remarque rejoint celle de W. F. Mackey sur
le monolinguisme des majorités.

La mesure du bilinguisme est donc, au Canada, une nécessité pratique (6),
car le gouvernement et certaines grandes administrations font déjà des distinctions importantes entre "monolingues" et "bilingues", accordant un boni ou autres avantages aux personnes capables d'exercer leurs fonctions dans les deux
langues. On pourrait d'ailleurs discuter du bien fondé de cette égalité dans
le travail linguistique, et se demander s'il ne vaudrait pas mieux généraliser
le principe adopté par les Nations Unies selon lequel les traducteurs travaillent
toujours vers leur langue maternelle. On pourrait aussi prôner un système semblable à celui adopté par l'administration belge, selon lequel chaque fonctionnaire important possède un fonctionnaire homologue dans l'autre langue, ce
qui entraîne la dualité des voies d'acheminement et la dualité du dossier. A
Ottawa, jusqu'à présent, la tradition veut qu'il y ait dossier unique, ce qui
oblige les fonctionnaires francophones à s'écrire mutuellement en anglais. (7)

_____

(6) Voir la déclaration de M. Pickersgill, ministre des Transports à Ottawa,
à l'effet que les téléphonistes du Parlement fédéral doivent parler anglais "mais
qu'il est important également qu'elles puissent répondre aux appels en français". Les téléphonistes unilingues de la Compagnie Bell auraient été dès lors
mutées à d'autres postes. "On n'a pas cherché à n'employer que les personnes
couramment bilingues, mais des personnes qui peuvent répondre aux principales
questions ordinairement posées au téléphone" (Le Devoir, 26-11-66)
(7) Cette tradition a peut-être changé récemment dans certains services. Elle
demeure pourtant vivace, par la force de l'habitude et par suite de l'indifférence de la majorité envers les problèmes (suite de la note à la page suivante)

La mesure du degré de perfectionnement dans les deux langues est donc d'actualité au Canada, et présente les difficultés que l'on sait. Comme le recommande W. F. Mackey, il faut effectuer des mesures à tous les niveaux (phonologique, graphémique, syntaxique, lexical, stylistique) et à propos des quatre types de connaissances (skills): compréhension orale, compréhension écrite, maniement de la langue parlée, maniement de la langue écrite (Listening, Reading, Speaking & Writing) (Lado 1960). Faute de bien distinguer ces quatre types, on risque d'exiger trop des personnes appelées, par leur métier, à un bilinguisme qu'on aurait tout intérêt à limiter à tel domaine précis: compréhension des chiffres pour un garçon d'ascenseur, compréhension de groupes de chiffres et de lettres et quelques phrases stéréotypées pour les standardistes; connaissance des chiffres, du nom des rues et de quelques phrases stéréotypées pour les chauffeurs de taxi, etc. (8). On aperçoit tout ce que la linguistique appliquée aurait à gagner à la définition de ces micro-systèmes, qui pourraient d'ailleurs constituer une première étape pour ceux qui voudraient pousser plus loin leurs études.

1.2   Le biculturalisme

Puisque nous venons de rappeler certaines définitions du bilinguisme qui, sans prétendre épuiser le problème, le cernent néanmoins avec suffisamment

---

(suite de la note de la page précédente)
(7) de la minorité. Il ne s'agit pas ici de critique unilatérale. On observe au Québec, depuis quelque temps, la même tendance au sein de la majorité francophone. Les libéraux anglophones, par exemple, se plaignent de ce que leur récent Congrès n'ait pas fait suffisamment de place à l'anglais; des Canadiens de l'Ouest se plaignent, parce que la signalisation routière sur certains tronçons de la route transcanadienne est monolingue, et uniquement en français. Les traducteurs fédéraux à Ottawa travaillent presque uniquement vers le français, et leurs collègues anglophones, fortement minoritaires, se plaignent de ce que la langue de travail de leur Association professionnelle soit uniquement le français, etc.
(8) A ma connaissance, la seule expérience qui ait été tentée systématiquement dans ce domaine, le fut à McGill par les soins du professeur A. Rigault (présentation du micro-glossaire de l'ascenseur avec différents accents français et canadiens). Le problème a été également étudié par le Dr G. Rondeau, alors directeur du Bureau de recherches en linguistique appliquée, à Ottawa. Il mériterait une étude complète, car il a des conséquences pratiques insoupçonnées. Le choix des termes figurant sur les panneaux de signalisation, les avis officiels, les plaques de rues, etc. ne doit pas être laissé au hasard - comme c'est le cas pour presque toute la publicité commerciale où abondent les fautes de français les plus grossières, même si les originaux anglais sont correctement rédigés.

d'approximation, il n'est pas inutile d'en rapprocher deux définitions concurrentes du biculturalisme. Ce problème, qui occupe la majeure partie du chapitre 5 du manuel de Haugen (1956), rentrerait sans doute maintenant dans le domaine de la sociolinguistique. Il convient également de relire le mandat de la Commission royale d'enquête sur le bilinguisme et le biculturalisme pour comprendre la totalité du climat qui a présidé aux travaux de cette commission. Ce document devra désormais figurer en bonne place dans tout programme de recherche sur la question. Peu de pays, me semble-t-il, ont aussi courageusement posé le problème de la coexistence possible ou impossible de deux cultures, et il faut en féliciter le gouvernement canadien, même s'il est encore trop tôt pour juger de la portée de ce geste politique sans précédent.

Les définitions qui vont suivre m'ont été fournies par un linguiste versé dans le domaine de la linguistique différentielle, Jean Darbelnet, professeur à l'Université Laval, et par un humaniste de talent, Maurice Lebel, également professeur à Laval. Elles intéresseront notamment les participants de la discussion sur les incidences culturelles et sociales du bilinguisme, mais il ne m'apparaît pas possible, pour le moment du moins, d'appliquer à cette matière très fluide des critères quantitatifs.

Voici la première définition du biculturalisme, celle de M. Darbelnet, qui a le grand mérite de la clarté, de la brièveté, et qui a également le non moindre mérite d'être articulée sur la langue, véhicule primordial de la pensée et de la culture:

"Biculturalisme est un terme parallèle à bilinguisme et destiné à le compléter. Il devient nécessaire quand on se rend compte qu'un pays qui a deux langues a généralement deux cultures. Il a fallu un certain temps pour qu'on comprenne qu'une langue suppose une culture dont elle est l'expression, et qu'on change de culture quand on change de langue. En d'autres termes, le bilinguisme est l'aspect immédiatement apparent d'une dualité dont le biculturalisme est la réalité sous-jacente." (1-10-1963)

Et voici la seconde, plus complexe:

"Biculturalism is a new and .... nebulous term. The individual is seldom bicultural; but a country, a province, a city or a community may be bicultural, the coexistence of two cultures in them may be seen. There may be an interplay between the two cultures, but these are seldom fused or integrated. It is practically impossible, or naive, to try to discuss biculturalism as a separate subject from bilingualism. ... Biculturalism is more complex than bilingualism. It implies a whole set of values, traditions and institutions not contained in bilingualism. It means fundamentally the respect, the appreciation, the acceptance and the knowledge, as far as possible, of the two cultures and ways of life, English and French, in Canada..." The Royal Society of Canada, Feb. 14, 1964

Nous pouvons essayer maintenant de mieux comprendre le mandat de la Commission. Fidèle à son titre, elle a publié ce document dans les deux langues, ainsi que ses documents de travail, qui méritent de figurer au Rapport final:

MANDAT de la Commission royale d'enquête sur le bilinguisme et le biculturalisme (extrait de l'arrêté-en-Conseil 1963-1106, approuvé par Son Excellence le Gouverneur général le 19 juillet 1963)

"....pour faire enquête et rapport sur l'état présent du bilinguisme et du biculturalisme au Canada et recommander les mesures à prendre pour que la Confédération canadienne se développe d'après le principe de l'égalité entre les deux peuples qui l'ont fondée, compte tenu de l'apport des autres groupes ethniques à l'enrichissement culturel du Canada, ainsi que les mesures à prendre pour sauvegarder cet apport; en particulier,

1. faire rapport sur l'état et la pratique du bilinguisme dans tous les services et institutions de l'administration fédérale – y compris les sociétés de la Couronne – ainsi que dans leurs contacts avec le public, et présenter des recommandations de nature à assurer le caractère bilingue et fondamentalement biculturel de l'administration fédérale;

2. faire rapport sur le rôle dévolu aux institutions, tant publiques que privées, y compris les grands organes de communication, en vue de favoriser le bilinguisme, de meilleures relations culturelles ainsi qu'une compréhension plus répandue du caractère fondamentalement biculturel de notre pays et de l'apport subséquent des autres cultures; présenter des recommandations en vue d'intensifier ce rôle; et

3. discuter avec les gouvernements provinciaux, compte tenu de ce que la compétence constitutionnelle en matière d'éducation est conférée aux provinces, les occasions qui sont données aux Canadiens d'apprendre le français et l'anglais et présenter des recommandations sur les moyens à prendre pour permettre aux Canadiens de devenir bilingues."

2. L'histoire

La coexistence au sein d'une même communauté de deux langues (ou plus) est toujours un fait historique. Le bilinguisme canadien ne fait pas exception. Mais le maintien d'une telle situation devient difficile, sinon impossible, sans l'appui du gouvernement ou sans un texte de loi. On pourra objecter que bien des langues ont coexisté dans le passé sans qu'il y ait eu appareil juridique; cette remarque est cependant moins vraie depuis l'instruction obligatoire, le service militaire obligatoire et l'avènement des grands moyens de diffusion de la parole et de la pensée: journaux, cinéma, radio, télévision. Alors qu'en France même les dialectes se maintenaient assez bien dans les familles jusqu'au début du XXe siècle, l'alphabétisation et la télévision ont eu raison des résistances – même si certains particularismes mineurs tendent à se perpétuer (9).

(9) Le cas des parlers régionaux du Royaume-Uni est caractéristique; on constate un nivellement de la morphologie et du vocabulaire, mais une résistance sur le plan phonologique, grâce à la contre-offensive des postes régionaux de la BBC.

Mais justement un texte de loi, l'article d'une constitution, peuvent faire obstacle à cette évolution ou du moins la ralentir. A cet égard, il est instructif de constater la différence entre l'histoire des groupes francophones de l'Ouest du Canada, qui n'ont pas d'existence légale, en quelque sorte, et celle du bloc québécois. La question du bilinguisme au Canada repose donc en partie sur un texte de loi.

L'article 133 de l'Acte de l'Amérique du Nord britannique garantit l'usage de l'anglais et du français dans le Québec, ainsi qu'au Parlement canadien et dans les cours fédérales. C'est là un principe général, qui prête encore à des interprétations divergentes; pour ne pas allonger le débat, je me contenterai de citer l'opinion d'un juriste distingué (et bilingue), le professeur Frank R. Scott, qui résumait la position officielle du français au Canada en 1953 en ces termes:

"A la première session de la première législature, qui se réunit à Québec en 1792, la langue française fut placée sur un pied d'égalité légale avec la langue anglaise.   ....   Plus d'un homme d'état anglais ou canadien, particulièrement Lord Durham, espérait qu'éventuellement les Français (10) accepteraient la langue, les lois et peut-être la religion anglaises. Cependant, une seule fois on a tenté d'établir l'anglais comme seule langue officielle; l'incident se situe immédiatement après les soulèvements de 1837-38 et fut de courte durée. Le principe du bilinguisme fut rétabli en 1848 et inscrit dans la constitution de 1867, tant pour le Québec que pour le Parlement et les cours fédérales. Toutefois, ce principe était soumis à des limites géographiques que l'expansion des établissements français hors du Québec ne tarda pas à rendre évidentes; dès lors, elles furent une source de conflit qui ne s'est pas encore tarie. Le Québec est la seule province où les deux langues aient un statut officiel pour les questions provinciales; le Manitoba est revenu à l'usage (exclusif) de l'anglais en 1890..." (Scott 1952, 181)

Puisqu'il est question de mesure du bilinguisme, on peut commencer ici à pied d'oeuvre: comment se mesure le bilinguisme officiel d'un Etat? Sans doute par la proportion de langue A et de langue B utilisée par les fonctionnaires et les hommes politiques, ou encore par le niveau de connaissances linguistiques que possèdent les dirigeants, ou enfin par les signes extérieurs d'utilisation des deux langues. La lecture du billet familier d'un dollar (canadien) permet de

---

(10) Il est bon de noter que l'usage canadien peut prêter à confusion, en raison de l'extension particulière donnée aux termes français/Français; anglais/Anglais; French/English (cf. pour le détail le Dictionnaire canadien, Toronto 1962). D'une façon générale, ces termes désignent les populations d'origine française et anglaise du Canada, ainsi que les langues qu'elles parlent. Lorsqu'on veut préciser, on ajoute un qualificatif (parfois péjoratif): français de France, "Parisian French" sic, Canadian (par opposition à Canadien et encore plus à Canayen, etc.)

s'assurer que tout y est bien bilingue, puisque l'émission de la monnaie est une prérogative du gouvernement central; sur ce point, d'ailleurs, le Canada pourrait en remontrer à d'autres pays bilingues, la Suisse par exemple (11). Ce bilinguisme bancaire, qui n'est pas inscrit dans la constitution, ne s'est d'ailleurs pas réalisé sans luttes, non plus que celui des timbres-poste: le passage du monolingue POSTAGE à la formule actuelle POSTES/POSTAGE a dû se faire, si j'en juge d'après ma collection, sous le règne d'Edouard VII. On a pu se gausser, à tort croyons-nous, de ce "postage-stamp patriotism", qui est de nature à orienter plus fermement les membres de la minorité. Mais cette mesure du bilinguisme est encore bien faible (cf. Gouin 1960; Poisson 1960; Vie française 1961, et presque quotidiennement dans Le Devoir); faibles également les arguments des Canadiens qui voudraient pouvoir traverser leur pays a mari usque ad mare, en trouvant des services officiels capables de les comprendre. Le récent livre de Mme Solange Chaput-Rolland, publié à la demande expresse de la Commission du centenaire (!), constate en effet la faillite de cet idéal de citoyen à part entière: "Dans toutes les provinces, écrit-elle, les Canadiens français existent, luttent et survivent. Mais le Canada français n'existe nulle part, sauf au Québec." (Cité par Le Devoir du 31-12-66)

Cette constatation est essentielle à notre propos, puisque la coexistence des langues suppose une certaine égalité des pressions sociales, culturelles ou économiques, qu'il appartient sans doute au linguiste de déceler, d'apprécier, de mesurer. La thèse des "deux nations", qui seule donnerait ce poids égal aux deux langues (12), officiellement du moins, n'a fait à peu près aucun progrès chez les Canadiens anglophones. Il est possible (si l'on songe à la Belgique) qu'il ne puisse en être autrement.

Le frère Léopold Taillon, observateur au séminar d'Aberystwyth de 1960, avait regretté l'absence totale de renseignements sur les groupes linguistiques du Canada. Ses collègues canadiens ont exprimé, avec lui, leur surprise devant ce manque d'intérêt de spécialistes en matière de bilinguisme; c'est sans doute pourquoi il a offert les ressources d'une jeune université sise en pays bilingue pour la tenue d'un nouveau Colloque sur le même sujet. Cependant, il est impossible, dans les quelques pages qui nous sont allouées, de brosser un tableau suffisamment précis. Force nous est de renvoyer le lecteur à certains mémoires qui évoquent parfaitement le cadre historique, géographique et sociologique dans lequel se posent les problèmes du bilinguisme au Canada. Je pense notamment au mémoire de la Société royale, à celui de l'Université de

_____

(11) La seule mention qui ne soit pas bilingue est au moins bi-culturelle. Il s'agit du nom de la compagnie qui imprime ces intéressants documents, la British American Bank Note Ltd.

(12) Voir l'article de P. M. Lapointe dans l'édition française de Maclean (décembre 1966) et la longue citation du ministre québécois Jean-Noël Tremblay que donne Le Devoir du 15-11-66. "L'usage de la langue est une question de droit à partir du moment où cet usage est devenu un fait accompli."

Montréal et, dans une moindre mesure, à celui de l'Université McGill; il faut également citer les rapports relativement spécialisés du Conseil des Arts du Canada et de l'Association des professeurs de l'Université de Montréal. On peut espérer que ces textes figureront en entier dans le Rapport final de la Commission royale d'enquête sur le bilinguisme et le biculturalisme. Ils resteront ainsi des documents essentiels, non seulement pour le Canada, mais pour toute étude sur le bilinguisme dans le monde.

3. Géographie et démographie

Le véritable bilinguisme, dit Wm. F. Mackey (1962, 51) est celui de l'individu. Soit; mais pour qu'il y ait bilinguisme synchronique, il faut une certaine disposition dans l'espace des locuteurs, et cette disposition n'est pas indifférente. Ce n'est pas le lieu de s'étendre sur ces considérations de géographie linguistique; rappelons seulement qu'on a pu souligner la force de conservation des groupements francophones canadiens qui sont, ou qui furent longtemps, séparés du reste du monde anglophone par des obstacles naturels: "bosse" du Maine pour la région du Bas du Fleuve, parcs nationaux pour Chéticamp en Nouvelle-Ecosse, forêt subarctique autour du Lac St-Jean et de l'Abitibi, etc. Inversement, les groupes de l'Ontario occidental, dans l'entre-deux-mers qui relie Montréal à Ottawa, adossés à la province de Québec offrent un exemple frappant d'homogénéité linguistique malgré l'absence d'obstacles naturels. Cette région est d'ailleurs traversée par la route trans-canadienne, voie de communication rapide qui protège encore les populations rurales contre les contacts prolongés avec des anglophones. Les groupes francophones de l'Ouest sont au contraire fortement dispersés et en position de faiblesse linguistique.

Or, pour qu'il y ait bilinguisme, il faut qu'il y ait des monolingues. "A self-sufficient bilingual community has no reason to remain bilingual, since a closed community in which everyone is fluent in two languages could get along just as well with one language". (Mackey 1962, 51)

Il serait donc utile de publier des cartes, basées sur les renseignements démographiques les plus récents montrant la répartition des groupes francophones "d'un océan à l'autre" (Trudel & Grenier 1955; Vinay 1955) et précisant les échanges linguistiques et économiques qu'ils peuvent avoir avec les groupes allogènes environnants. Dans l'étude des pressions linguistiques, ces chiffres sont essentiels:

"The numerical strength of monolinguals in each language communities involved determines the extent of the bilingualism.... The greater the imbalance between monolingual groups, the greater the percentage of bilinguals in the minority. In Wales, 82% of the Welsh are bilingual by the age of twelve, but only 4% of the English." (13)

(13) Herbert Pilch (Miscelania Homenaje a André Martinet) cite des chiffres encore plus frappants. D'après lui, la proportion de monolingues gallois ne dépasserait pas 1.7% (cf. Vinay 1957, 88-89)

3.1 Quelques chiffres

Le paragraphe suivant, extrait du Document de travail préparé par la CRBB, résume bien la situation démographique des groupes linguistiques au Canada. Puisqu'il s'agit ici de langues et de cultures, la CRBB a cru devoir utiliser les statistiques relatives à la langue maternelle et non à l'origine ethnique – laquelle ne saurait renseigner, de toute évidence, sur le type de langue parlée par les individus recensés. On trouve dans le Recensement du Canada, (1961) qu'en fonction de leur langue maternelle, les Canadiens se divisent de la façon suivante:

Population totale (en 1961)   18,238,247
Langues maternelles

	Langue maternelle	Pourcentage de bilingues
1. Anglais..........	10,660,534 (58%)	318,463 (3.98%)
2. Français.........	5,123,151 (28%	1,665,979 (30.06%)
3. Autres	2,454,562 (14%)	246,730 (5.24%)

Cette dernière rubrique se subdivisait alors comme suit: Allemand (3%), ukrainien (2%), italien (2%), hollandais (1%), langues amérindiennes y compris l'esquimau (1%), polonais (1%), divers (4%).

On aura noté la proportion extrêmement faible des anglophones bilingues (4% de la population totale), ce qui confirme la thèse de Mackey. Cependant, il faudrait sans doute nuancer ces chiffres et c'est là encore un point où des mesures exactes du bilinguisme pourront éclairer la situation d'un jour nouveau. En fait, tout anglophone (comme d'ailleurs tout francophone) de moins de 40 ans a forcément eu des contacts – scolaires, livresques certes – avec une langue seconde, le français dans la grande majorité des cas. C'est donc la définition du bilinguisme qui est en jeu ici, celle du moins qui prévaut dans les milieux officiels chargés du recensement. (Voir le Catalogue 92-651, volume I, 3e partie: "Population: Langue officielle par groupe ethnique" et le Catalogue 92-549, volume I, 2e partie: "Population: Langue officielle et langue maternelle".) Toute précision, dans ces notions, apportée par le Colloque de Moncton, pourra avoir d'importantes répercussions sur le prochain recensement, dans la mesure où Ottawa songera à faire appel aux linguistes.

3.2 Autres bilinguismes

Et que faut-il penser des 5.24% de bilingues qui sont étiquetés "Autres"? Qui dit en effet "bilinguisme" ne dit pas forcément "bilinguisme franco-anglais". Au Canada, on pense spontanément à ce dernier à cause de l'histoire, à cause de l'émergence récente d'une littérature canadienne-française et d'un mouvement séparatiste, qui n'est d'ailleurs pas nouveau. Mais il y a d'autres bilinguismes, en général orientés dans le même sens, l'anglais exerçant presque partout sa force d'attraction. Ces bilinguismes posent plusieurs problèmes particuliers, dont certains ont été notés dans le Rapport préliminaire de la CRBB. On peut leur attribuer les origines suivantes:

(a) Groupes allogènes fixés au Canada au siècle dernier, en quantités non négligeables, anciennes colonies ayant conservé une certaine identité culturelle et linguistique, surtout dans la mesure où il y a eu renforcement par immigration récente: Islandais, Allemands, Ukrainiens, Italiens. Il n'existe pratiquement plus de groupements linguistiques gaéliques ou gallois, mais les communautés écossaises et irlandaises, bien qu'anglophones, continuent à exercer une influence sur la langue anglaise au Canada et sur une certaine conception de la vie, un Anglo-Canadian way of life qui est une partie précieuse de l'héritage britannique.

(b) Néo-Canadiens encore non assimilés et parlant une langue seconde très hésitante; à Montréal, à Toronto, à Vancouver et dans les Prairies, ces groupes ethniques sont très actifs. Ils ont leurs journaux, leurs cinémas et leurs restaurants, souvent leurs programmes de radio: Hongrois, Allemands, Grecs, Italiens, Hollandais, Dano-Norvégiens; Finlandais et Baltes; Japonais, Chinois. L'absence d'écoles et les fortes pressions socio-économiques qui s'exercent en faveur de l'anglais tendent à précipiter leur assimilation, généralement vers le groupe anglophone.

Ces deux types de Canadiens (même si certains montrent encore un réel attachement à leur culture) tendent à considérer le Canada comme un nouvel exemple de melting pot; ils ne comprennent pas les étapes successives de la formation de l'unité canadienne, s'irritent de la présence des provinces et s'opposent à la division entre Canadians et Canadiens: "Why don't they all consider themselves Canadians first and treat their ancestry as something that belongs to the past?" (The Canadian, 17-12-66).

La motivation très forte dont nous venons de parler pousse la grande majorité des jeunes Néo-Canadiens vers une assimilation totale au milieu ambiant. Il serait intéressant d'encore connaître le détail, dans la mesure où des tests d'assimilation linguistique et psychologique pourront être préparés. C'est en somme l'histoire de l'américanisation des nouveaux arrivants qui se répète, avec 100 ans de décalage, dans l'oekoumène canadien.

(c) Il ne faut pas oublier que les provinces de l'Ouest ont été colonisées dans une large mesure par des Américains du Middle West. Culturellement plus proches des anglophones, ces colonies made in USA tendent plutôt à assimiler leurs concitoyens qu'à s'aligner sur des traditions qui leur sont étrangères, parfois hostiles. Il y a là un facteur important pour expliquer les pressions linguistiques qu'exerce l'américain sur la langue de l'Ouest canadien.

(d) Les Amérindiens - il aurait sans doute fallu commencer par eux! - posent des problèmes différents, mais qu'il ne faudrait pas négliger pour autant. La langue des groupes vivant en vase clos ou dans des vastes territoires (Keewatin, Nouveau-Québec) est généralement très vivace, et il y a bilinguisme grâce à l'apprentissage d'une langue seconde, anglais ou français. Mais ailleurs, on note toute la gamme des étapes d'acculturation chez les Indiens en contact avec les Blancs; cela peut aller jusqu'à la perte totale de la langue d'origine. On assiste alors à des cultures monolingues sur un substrat (faible) amérindien, résultats d'un génocide culturel témoignant souvent d'une excellente intention de la part des gouvernements.

Les linguistes n'ont pas à porter de jugement de valeur, et dans la mesure où il n'y a plus bilinguisme chez les Hurons ou les Salish, il n'y a plus de problèmes pour les experts de Moncton. Au moins fallait-il leur rappeler que les langues, comme les civilisations, sont mortelles.

4. Conséquences linguistiques

Dans une première partie, nous avons tenté de faire toucher du doigt quelques réalités quotidiennes qui ont été au Canada le climat du bilinguisme. Il nous appartient maintenant de présenter brièvement quelques réflexions sur les conséquences de cet état de choses, notamment les conséquences linguistiques, psychologiques et culturelles que le Colloque sera sans doute amené à envisager.

Les conséquences linguistiques peuvent se résumer en un seul mot: "interférences". Tout le problème est là; l'homme n'est pas fait pour être bilingue, et il lui est très difficile de maintenir distincts deux codes linguistiques cohabitant dans son cerveau. Cette difficulté ne tient d'ailleurs pas à des caractéristiques du code; j'ai eu l'occasion de noter fréquemment des difficultés semblables à propos de codes bien différents: conduite à gauche et conduite à droite; alphabet latin et alphabet gréco-cyrillique; notation musicale sur portée de 5 lignes et notation tonic sol-fa, etc.

Ces conflits entre deux (ou plusieurs) systèmes ont été notés depuis longtemps par les linguistes, qui n'y ont cependant pas porté toute l'attention que ce problème mérite. Une relecture d'ouvrages très au fait des conséquences sociales du bilinguisme, par exemple celui d'Otto Jespersen, Mankind, Individual & Nation, ceux de Weisgerber, Bally, Lewis, etc., entreprise dans le cadre du présent article, m'a permis de constater que plusieurs principes essentiels du phénomène d'interférence avaient été dégagés déjà dans les premières années du XXe siècle (14).

Qu'est-ce donc que l'interférence? Je rapprocherai deux textes, émanant d'un linguiste et d'un psychologue, qui semblent de nature à éclairer le problème:

"Interference is the use of elements from one language while speaking or writing another. It is a characteristic of the message, not of the code. It varies quantitatively and qualitatively from bilingual to bilingual and from time to time in the same individual, ranging from an almost imperceptible stylistic variation to the most obvious sort of speech-mixture

---

(14) Des faits très significatifs sont également rapportés dans la biographie de Jespersen (1938), qui mériterait de ce fait une plus grande diffusion en français ou en anglais.

/...../ Interference therefore is a divergence from the local standard as a result of the inclusion in the message of features from another code." (Mackey 1965b)

Il ressort de cette définition que Mackey envisage l'interférence comme un processus actif, un devenir qui se situe à la frontière de deux codes linguistiques. Il est important de se souvenir, dans cette perspective, de la distinction posée par l'auteur (cf. page 7.3) entre les contacts linguistiques et l'interférence. Dans le premier cas, il y aurait création de formes nouvelles dans un des codes (ou dans les deux? - point extrêmement important); dans le deuxième cas, les interférences se traduiraient par des formes aberrantes non encore intégrées à l'un ou l'autre des codes. C'est une distinction d'aspect, destinée à faciliter le dépistage des faits d'interférence, qui autrement ne seraient sensibles qu'aux seuls diachroniciens.

Et voici la deuxième citation:

"Le bilinguisme implique d'une part une situation indiscutablement sociale, où deux systèmes linguistiques se côtoient dans un même groupe humain; la situation de bilinguisme relèverait d'une analyse sociologique. D'autre part les individus de ce groupe ajustent leurs usages à l'état linguistique existant: le fonctionnement de l'individu dans une telle situation relèverait d'une analyse multidimensionnelle qui irait de l'étude des lois de l'interférence phonologique de deux systèmes linguistiques à l'étude des processus de tri nécessaire dans l'alternance des deux systèmes." (Tabouret-Keller 1963, 206)

Cette deuxième citation nous rappelle fort à propos que le bilinguisme joue constamment sur deux plans, coexistence physique, coexistence intellectuelle, tout en mettant l'accent principal sur l'aspect neuro-physiologique. A cet égard, il faut noter que, de l'avis de Haugen, il paraît certain que les langues maniées par un bilingue sont entreposées dans les mêmes parties du cerveau (in Saporta 1961, 403). Le problème de leur séparation n'est donc pas simplement une question de structures linguistiques - (il est possible que la coexistence soit d'ailleurs plus facile selon le type de langues en présence) - , mais aussi et surtout de cheminements nerveux. Le mélange des codes se fait à la sortie, au niveau du message, et l'engramme qui en résulte tend à son tour à modifier les codes eux-mêmes: c'est bien dans ce sens qu'il faut comprendre la remarque de Jakobson, citée en exergue "Le bilinguisme est /.../ le problème fondamental de la linguistique".

Ces constatations soulignent encore l'urgence qu'il y a d'aboutir à une mesure du bilinguisme. Il est en effet remarquable que tout contact, fût-il passager, de notre cerveau avec un système linguistique allogène peut causer une interférence. Tous les professeurs confirmeront que l'exercice mal compris de la traduction, appliquée aux premiers stades de l'apprentissage, amène toujours barbarismes, solécismes et calques qui ne se présenteraient pas naturellement dans un exercice monolingue de rédaction. Si cette observation devait se confirmer, cela signifierait qu'on ne doit utiliser qu'avec une extrême prudence des tests de mesure du bilinguisme basés sur le relevé d'erreurs de structure dans la langue maternelle (version).

Bien au contraire, il semble que la coexistence parfaite de deux systèmes
linguistiques chez un même individu (fait d'ailleurs exceptionnel) exige un effort constant, volontaire pour garder ceux-ci distincts; cet effort croît avec
l'âge (15), l'état de santé, le moment de la journée, etc. Autrement dit, un
grand nombre de fautes chez un individu n'est pas forcément l'indice d'une
grande familiarité avec la langue seconde, mais trahit plutôt l'extrême fragi-
lité du bilinguisme chez la majorité des individus. Il faut sans doute nuancer
cette remarques en se demandant si elle vaut pour les deux grands types de bilinguisme décrits par Ervin & Osgood (1954): les types mixtes (compounds) et
parallèles (coordinate):

"The compound system would be developed through experience in fused
contexts, as with vocabulary training in school, or where the same family
members use two languages interchangeably to refer to the same situational events /.../ The coordinate system would be developed through experience in different linguistic communities where languages are rarely
interchanged." (cf. Saporta 1961, 108)

Au Canada français, dans les parties géographiquement bilingues, il s'a-
git sans doute plutôt du "compound system". La culture des deux ethnies est
différente, mais tend à se rapprocher constamment (16), alors qu'un individu
monolingue faisant à l'âge adulte des études poussées en Angleterre ou aux
Etats-Unis tend à acquérir un "coordinate system". On pourrait schématiser
des faits par les dessins de la page suivante, basés sur la structure du signe linguistique selon de Saussure. (Tableau I)

La position B, où les interférences se situent dans la partie supérieure du
signe saussurien, explique bon nombre de faits canadiens tant psychologiques
(culturels) que linguistiques, et notamment l'assertion fréquemment relevée
dans la documentation consultée voulant que les Canadiens français soient des
individus "différents des autres", "des Français d'Amérique". (17)

Terminons ce paragraphe sur cette constatation. Pour les Canadiens d'expression française, le bilinguisme est un phénomène-Janus, tourné à la fois
vers le français européen et l'anglo-américain, fait que l'on pourrait schématiser comme illustré à la page suivante. (Tableau 2)

---

(15) Voir les notations intéressantes chez Epstein 1915 et naturellement les
auteurs plus récents qui ont étudié les phénomènes d'acquisition et d'oubli des
langues: Buhler, Decroly, Piaget, Oleron, etc., pour ne citer que des noms
qui n'apparaissent pas souvent dans les bibliographies américaines.
(16) On a noté le fait que les Canadiens des deux groupes, qui ne se fréquen-
tent pas volontiers dans leur propre pays, se recherchent instinctivement à l'é-
tranger et sympathisent tout de suite.
(17) Cf. Darbelnet 1964. Cette position est à la base des arguments que l'on
avance parfois en faveur d'une nouvelle langue canadienne, dont on exagère
sans doute les caractéristiques différentielles, mais qui permettraient théoriquement aux sujets parlants de retrouver un signe saussurien binaire et non plus
ternaire (type B).

Tableau I

Tableau 2

Il s'agirait alors d'un trilinguisme, et pareille constatation devra être prise en considération lors de l'établissement de tests de mesure. J'ai eu l'occasion d'examiner à Strasbourg, à la demande du Conseil culturel de l'Europe, des tests de ce genre dont un en provenance de Montréal. La principale critique qu'on pouvait lui adresser était un manque de définition quant aux interférences possibles (F sur A? F sur CF? A sur CF?, etc.). Il est indubitable que le couple langue-culture est différent en France et au Canada, et que l'histoire de ces interférences est également différente. Nous le redirons au paragraphe 6; il fallait le souligner ici, puisque le programme prévoit un rapport spécial sur "les effets exercés par une langue sur l'autre dans le langage des bilingues" (Document préparatoire, S4).

5. Conséquences psycholinguistiques

Il n'est pas question de brosser ici un tableau détaillé des problèmes qui attendent les experts du Colloque de Moncton: éminents spécialistes en la matière, on peut attendre d'eux des vues nouvelles sur le domaine relativement inexploré de la psycho-linguistique. D'ailleurs, le point de vue d'ensemble adopté ne permet pas d'apporter toujours une distinction nette entre les conséquences psychologiques purement fonctionnelles du bilinguisme, et ses conséquences sociales, étant donné précisément que la langue est à la fois le phénomène intellectuel et le fait social par excellence. On ne saurait donc mieux faire que de renvoyer aux travaux qui se multiplient un peu partout à l'heure actuelle, aux Etats-Unis, en France et au Canada (18). Rappelons, en tout cas, l'urgence d'une collaboration sur ce point entre linguistes et psychologues:

"Linguistic techniques alone /...°/ cannot solve the problem of bilingualism. Since the locus of bilingualism is in the individual mind the psychological aspects of bilingualism are of prime importance." (Mackey 1958, 97)

Je voudrais me contenter de quelques brèves indications sur les rapports du bilinguisme et de l'intelligence. Il arrive trop fréquemment que l'on enseigne des matières importantes et difficiles à des élèves réputés bilingues sans que l'on se soit assuré au préalable de l'état véritable de leurs connaissances

---

(18) Cf. les travaux de Saporta, Rosenberg, Jenkins, Carroll, Leopold aux Etats-Unis; ceux de Lambert, Peal, Spilka, Bibeau, Spreen au Canada; ceux d'Oléron, Bresson, Fraisse, Tabouret-Keller en France. Ce dernier auteur annonce la parution prochaine aux P. U. F. d'un volume sur le bilinguisme dans la collection Le Linguiste, publiée sous la direction D'André Martinet. Certains travaux récents publiés en France mériteraient d'être mieux connus, en particulier le texte des colloques de l'Association psychologie scientifique de la langue française. Le dernier paru porte sur des Problèmes de psycho-linguistique (Paris, PUF., 1963)

en matière de langue seconde. Dans ces conditions, comme le font remarquer Mackey et Noonan, on a tendance à porter un jugement défavorable sur le développement intellectuel des sujets bilingues, alors qu'on s'appuie en fait sur des tests de connaissances qui portent à faux: "The fundamental point of whether the bilingual learner has really understood the lesson is ignored." (19)

Il est donc nécessaire de mettre au point, le plus tôt possible, des tests spécialement conçus pour les deux populations scolaires canadiennes, (20) qui permettront de juger de la connaissance scolaire des langues dans lesquelles l'instruction sera donnée. Ces tests devront tenir compte (a) des données culturelles propres au Canada, (b) des données culturelles propres à chacun des groupes linguistiques, enfin (c) des données psycholinguistiques actuellement en cours d'élaboration qui doivent permettrent de préciser sous quelle forme ces tests ont le plus de chance d'être appliqués avec succès.

Pour respecter les conditions ci-dessus, il faudra examiner six cas théoriquement possibles qui se traduiront sans doute par six types de tests fort différents:

	Connaissance du français		Connaissance de l'anglais
1	population CF monolingue	4	population CA monolingue
2	population CA en cours d'apprentissage	5	population CF en cours d'apprentissage
3	population CA bilingue	6	population CF bilingue

Il semble que ces tests soient difficiles à préparer pour les cas 3 et 6 étant donné qu'il s'agit de populations adultes ayant terminé leur scolarité et de niveaux très différents. Les élèves en cours d'apprentissage présentent au contraire des conditions idéales, et c'est là que les tests pourraient s'appliquer utilement, à condition de noter que les populations CF en cours d'apprentissage ont subi de fortes pressions linguistiques vers l'anglais depuis leur jeunesse, lesquelles se traduisent soit par une avance réelle par rapport aux élèves

---

(19) Pour la détermination du bilinguisme chez un individu, voir notamment Peal & Lambert 1961. La bibliographie présentée par Saporta à propos des articles de Wienreich, Haugen et Lambert est très riche; elle mériterait d'être développée pour englober les travaux en cours en France et en Allemagne.
(20) Nous omettons pour simplifier les groupes allogènes, qui mériteraient pourtant des tests appropriés (en particulier Indiens et Esquimaux).

monolingues de même âge, soit par des conflits et des blocages divers (21).

D'après mon expérience, les Canadiens français dits "bilingues" auxquels j'enseignais la traduction ou la rédaction publicitaire se répartissaient en deux groupes. Un premier utilisait surtout le français dans la vie quotidienne et montrait fréquemment des faiblesses, toujours les mêmes (et les mêmes qu'en France) en morpho-syntaxe et en stylistique; leur vocabulaire anglais était rudimentaire. La langue maternelle de ce groupe (F) était généralement bonne, tout en présentant les anglicismes et autres calques qui figurent généralement dans le français du Canada sans être pour cela le fait d'une interférence linguistique chez les locuteurs. Le deuxième groupe, qui employait l'anglais pour leurs affaires, montrait au contraire de grandes faiblesses en langue maternelle (F) et une connaissance limitée et stéréotypée de la langue seconde (A). Grâce à cette forme stéréotypée de connaissances, ces personnes étaient capables de manier correctement des textes faciles relevant de leur spécialité, un peu à la façon d'un ordinateur qui synthétise à partir d'un corpus fini. Il est intéressant de noter à cet égard que dans les pays bilingues qu'il me fut donné d'étudier, j'ai toujours constaté que les textes rédigés dans la langue dominante (p. ex. le français à Bruxelles, l'anglais à Montréal) sont corrects à tous les points de vue (vocabulaire, grammaire, stylistique), même si leurs auteurs ne parlent pas ces langues à titre de langue maternelle, alors que les textes français rédigés par des Canadiens français ou par les rares Canadiens anglais capables de manier le français sont généralement incorrects dans leur conception et leur rédaction (22). On aura noté que cette interférence à sens unique est implicite chez les auteurs qui décrivent le bilinguisme; par exemple, le récent article de Mackey 1965b ne mentionne nulle part la possibilité d'interférences linguistiques ou culturelles dans le sens minorité-majorité; mais, songeant peut-être à ses lecteurs monoglottes américains, il ne cite que des exemples d'interférences vers le français.

---

(21) Les cours d'anglais de certains collèges classiques ou écoles secondaires ont été de tout temps l'objet de chahut organisé. Cela pourrait s'expliquer aussi par la qualité médiocre des méthodes employées et la formation insuffisante du corps professoral. Ajoutons que cette même désaffection des élèves se constate également en pays anglophone, pour le français cette fois; l'absence de toute pression détruit alors les motivations possibles des élèves. Les manuels, là encore, ne poussent guère à la connaissance des groupes francophones du pays qui jouissent, si l'on peut dire, de préjugés souvent défavorables.

(22) On pourrait multiplier les exemples, et cela vaudrait la peine de le faire. Qu'il suffise de rappeler qu'on ne voit jamais de boîtes et emballages portant des inscriptions anglaise erronées, même si le fabricant est Canadien français (alors que le cas est fréquent, par exemple, avec des marchandises japonaises présentées en anglais). Un des rares exemples de la situation inverse (erreur
(suite de la note à la page suivante)

6. Conséquences socio-culturelles

Le titre de la Commission royale d'enquête n'est pas un vain mot. Sans trop savoir si le terme était justifié ou non (voir page 372), les législateurs ont senti qu'une langue allait de pair avec une culture, en était à la fois l'expression et la limite. La reconnaissance de facto du couple langue/culture est la pièce essentielle de toute éducation bilingue. L'oubli de ce couple est la source de tous les problèmes posés par la diversité des langues. Et la majorité, comme toutes les majorités, a tendance à passer outre à la diversité des cultures. Comme le rapporte le frère Taillon, "les représentants de pays à langue nationale de grande diffusion à Aberystwyth s'étonnent quelque peu des querelles menées autour du bilinguisme: "Ils s'en balancent bien, du bilinguisme!.." Le rapport final du Seminar a dû faire mention du fait qu'on n'a pas pu s'entendre en terre galloise, c'est-à-dire bilingue, sur un principe applicable à tous les milieux fonctionnellement bilingues, quant aux moyens susceptibles de garantir aux minorités une priorité au moins relative de leur langue maternelle.

On sait pourtant depuis longtemps - et la question a rebondi lors de la querelle autour de l'hypothèse whorfienne, que la langue est le miroir d'une culture; "quand on change de culture, on change de langue", disait J. Darbelnet dans sa définition du biculturalisme. La chose est fréquente au Nouveau Monde. Certains parents peuvent désirer voir leurs enfants changer de langue pour

(22) (suite de la note de la page précédente)
dans la langue seconde par suite de la dominance de la langue maternelle) m'a été fourni par un poteau situé à Cap Saint-Jacques, sur l'Ile de Montréal, près d'un tournant brusque, sur lequel un fermier bienveillant rappelle aux touristes anglophones la présence possible de piétons: ATTENTION AT FOOTWALKER. Il s'agit évidemment du calque de ATTENTION AU PIETON, lui-même bon exemple de l'absence de pluriel (ATTENTION AUX PIETONS) caractéristique des écriteaux rédigés par des Canadiens français peu cultivés (cf. FRAISE A VENDRE).

Il faut toutefois ajouter que depuis un certain temps, des erreurs de traduction, véritables interférences dues au bilinguisme, se glissent dans des textes anglais. Sur la route no 9, on a longtemps vu des panneaux anglais SLOW MEN AT WORK accompagnés de panneaux français incorrectement rédigés LENTEMENT HOMMES AU TRAVAIL (1960); depuis que le français devient la langue de rédaction des ministères québécois, on observe des panneaux français correctement rédigés RALENTIR - TRAVAUX (1965), et des traductions incorrectes en anglais SLOW WORKS (Vinay 1965, 125). De même, certains panneaux officiels dans la ville de Montréal présentent maintenant des incorrections dans le texte anglais, ce qui n'était sans doute jamais arrivé auparavant. Ce sont de petits faits de ce genre qui peuvent orienter le chercheur sur le moyen de mesurer le bilinguisme d'une population.

des raisons politiques, sociales, ou de prestige.   On cite souvent le cas de
jeunes Flamands (avant la guerre) élevés dans des écoles francophones qui deviennent, à leur majorité, francophones eux-mêmes.   Ce fut certainement le
cas des enfants de la deuxième génération d'émigrants aux Etats-Unis, tout au
moins dans les groupes linguistiques non homogènes; ces enfants désiraient se
fondre dans le tout linguistique anglo-saxon (23).

Cette "allégeance linguistique" dont parle A. Martinet est bien en fait
une allégeance culturelle, et l'un des ministres de l'immigration d'Ottawa le
comprenait parfaitement lorsqu'il disait préférer un Néo-Canadien né au Canada à dix immigrants nés en Europe.   Passé un certain seuil d'âge et d'expérience, il est difficile à l'individu de se refaire un deuxième loyalisme: et
pourtant, sans ce loyalisme, pas de véritable bilinguisme, étape vers une assimilation totale des jeunes générations.

Il faudra donc envisager un classement des faits et des individus qui tienne
compte du rapport langue/culture.   Les paramètre de ces classements seraient
non plus le degré de connaissance plus ou moins poussée des deux langues en
présence, mais leur liaison avec telle culture plutôt que telle autre et surtout
leur insertion dans telle culture particulière.   On ne peut s'arrêter longtemps
à ces considérations, qui mériteraient pourtant d'être développées.   Voici
quelques-unes de ces catégories possibles; des types intermédiaires pourraient
naturellement être envisagés.   La partie de gauche symbolise la langue maternelle en précisant le climat culturel dans lequel elle s'est développée; la partie de droite indique comment s'effectue l'apprentissage d'une seconde langue,
et le climat culturel qui l'accompagne.   (Tableau 3)

Chacune des combinaisons illustrées à la page suivante doit poser des problèmes différents, car les pressions culturelles ne s'exercent pas de la même
façon et sont d'ailleurs différentes; cela conditionne le type de bilinguisme
auquel on aboutira.   Comme le remarque Mackey, "In the study of bilingualism, no solution is adequate which does not take into account the socio-cultural setting, for bilingualism alone does not arise except in response to social
necessities" (Mackey 1958, 97).   Les facultés dites des "Sciences sociales" ont
bien reconnu la prépondérance de l'élément culturel dans l'image globale que
donne un peuple à ceux qui l'observent; un coup d'oeil aux Annuaires en cours
permettra de relever les titres de recherches dans ce domaine, dont on peut espérer qu'elles seront articulées sur des études linguistiques (Psychologie sociale
de la communication; organisation sociale et culture; traits culturels d'une communauté; langue et culture, etc., voir Annuaire de l'Université de Montréal,
1966-67:   607 sqq.) (24).

(23) Ce ne fut pas le cas des groupes franco-américains, dispersés dans les E-
tats de la Nouvelle-Angleterre, qui bénéficiaient de la présence de la masse
francophone du Québec (journaux, radio, puis télévision, congrégations ensei-
gnantes, vacances en pays francophone, etc.)
(24) Il existe naturellement des formes de culture paralinguistiques ou métalin-
guistiques.   Mais ces dernières s'accompagnent en général de formules linguistiques qui ramènent le sujet parlant à ce couple langue/culture dont on peut
difficilement faire abstraction.

Tableau 3

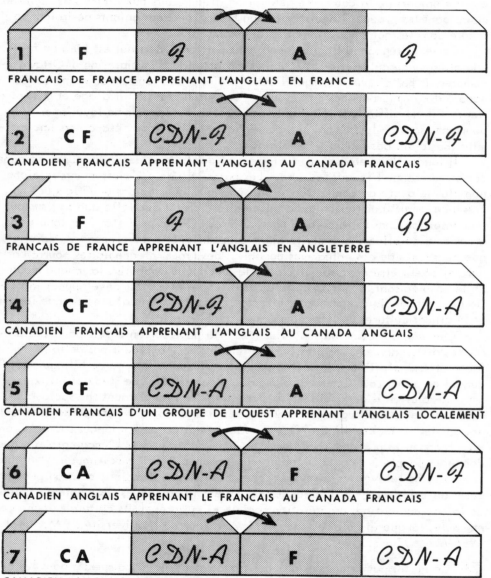

1   F   𝓕   A   𝓕
FRANCAIS DE FRANCE APPRENANT L'ANGLAIS EN FRANCE

2   C F   CDN-𝓕   A   CDN-𝓕
CANADIEN FRANCAIS APPRENANT L'ANGLAIS AU CANADA FRANCAIS

3   F   𝓕   A   GB
FRANCAIS DE FRANCE APPRENANT L'ANGLAIS EN ANGLETERRE

4   C F   CDN-𝓕   A   CDN-A
CANADIEN FRANCAIS APPRENANT L'ANGLAIS AU CANADA ANGLAIS

5   C F   CDN-A   A   CDN-A
CANADIEN FRANCAIS D'UN GROUPE DE L'OUEST APPRENANT L'ANGLAIS LOCALEMENT

6   C A   CDN-A   F   CDN-𝓕
CANADIEN ANGLAIS APPRENANT LE FRANCAIS AU CANADA FRANCAIS

7   C A   CDN-A   F   CDN-A
CANADIEN ANGLAIS APPRENANT LE FRANCAIS AU CANADA ANGLAIS

Or, qui dit culture dit école, dans la mesure du moins où cette dernière dispense l'éducation en même temps que l'instruction. Avec un sens très sûr des valeurs, les Canadiens français lient la survivance de leur langue à l'existence d'écoles où tout l'enseignement se donne en français (sauf les cours d'anglais, bien entendu). Cette attitude se justifie d'autant mieux dans le cas d' d'une langue possédant une abondante culture écrite, mais on pourrait citer des régions bilingues où il n'existe pas d'écoles séparées, où d'ailleurs la langue de la minorité ne s'écrit pas, et où le bilinguisme survit ou même se développe.

Avec cette réserve, il convient d'accorder une grande attention aux conséquences scolaires du bilinguisme et d'étudier attentivement les résultats d'une éducation entièrement monolingue, ou monolingue puis bilingue, ou bilingue depuis le Jardin d'Enfants. Les résultats les plus encourageants ont été relevés semble-t-il, chez les anglophones minoritaires du Québec; ceux-ci, bien protégés par les pressions sociales, économiques et culturelles qui s'exercent au Canada en faveur de l'anglais, n'ont rien à craindre du français et peuvent l'apprendre sans arrière-pensée, sans craindre une gallicisation des cadres lexicaux ou syntaxiques de leur langue maternelle. Les résultats obtenus à la Weston School de Montréal, par exemple, montrent que dans une atmosphère détendue, le bilinguisme s'acquiert de très bonne heure, comme le recommande Penfield, et très efficacement. Dans cette école, on enseigne certaines matières en français, d'autres en anglais et l'intérêt que portent les enfants à la géographie ou au calcul est une motivation plus importante que celui qu'ils portent (ou qu'on voudrait qu'ils portent) à la langue véhiculaire de ces matières. Evidemment, on obtient ainsi des cloisonnements; toute sa vie durant, un enfant aura tendance à calculer dans une langue, à parler de géographie dans une autre, – mais il le fera chaque fois avec un haut degré de perfection. C'est dans un tel milieu qu'il conviendrait de mener des enquêtes sur le degré de perfection dans le maniement simultané de deux langues, afin d'assurer au départ un climat de sérénité qui fait totalement défaut ailleurs.

Sur le plan des principes, il est piquant de constater que depuis la "révolution tranquille" au Québec, les anglophones minoritaires de cette province s'inquiètent de la position de l'anglais (pourtant solidement installé à tous les niveaux de la vie sociale) et invoquent pour leur défense les "Droits de l'Homme" auxquels on ne songe guère à Ottawa. Dans une lettre au Devoir du 19-11-66, un "rapatrié" des provinces de l'Ouest rappelle à M. John Humphrey de l'Université McGill que, s'il y a violation des droits de l'homme à vouloir imposer le français à tous les Québécois, cette pratique a débuté dans l'Ouest, où les gouvernements "ont pratiqué à ciel ouvert, d'une façon préméditée et ordonnée, la violation des droits de l'homme envers les Canadiens français depuis 1896." Et ce correspondant de rappeler que même au Manitoba, dont la constitution prévoyait l'usage du français, on a institué une loi "providing that the English language shall be the Province". Il en est de même au Saskatchewan, où l'article 203 de la loi scolaire précise que "no language other than English shall be taught during school hours". Dans aucune des quatre provinces de l'Ouest, dit l'auteur, on ne trouve d'écoles françaises subventionnées par l'Etat.

A la suite de contacts plus fréquents, de prises de conscience souvent courageuses et d'une certaine crainte de la minorité bruyante des séparatistes, les Canadiens anglais commencent à évoluer de leur côté. Le Premier ministre de l'Ontario, M. John Robarts, déclarait récemment (Le Devoir, 24-11-66) son désir de réduire les tensions au Canada, et soulignait "la popularité des études de français en Ontario chez les citoyens anglophones"; il promettait en outre aux Franco-Ontariens une meilleure part du système scolaire de la province "tout en affirmant qu'un système scolaire exclusivement français n'est ni désirable ni possible en Ontario, l'anglais y possédant une place prépondérante." On ne saurait dire les choses plus aimablement. Le Manitoba de son côté annonce par la voix de la Winnipeg Free Press (19-11-66) que les libéraux de cett cette province "recommandent l'usage du français comme langue d'enseignement dans les écoles publiques là où la demande le justifie". (Cité par Le Devoir du 26-11-66). Les conclusions du Colloque pourraient être diffusées dans les provinces afin d'alerter l'opinion sur la nécessité de fournir à la minorité des moyens de culture qui seuls, à longue échéance, assureront sa survie.

Dans le cas contraire, le bilinguisme est mortel, car il tue la culture. Il n'y a gain pour les individus que dans la mesure où ceux-ci peuvent conserver leur culture propre tout en s'enrichissant au contact d'une culture seconde. C'est dans cette dernière hypothèse que l'étude des langues est un humanisme. Peut-être fallait-il que le latin et le grec fussent des langues mortes pour que l'on puisse boire sans danger à leur coupe. Il est amusant de rappeler ici que l'un des deux Commissaires de la Commission royale d'enquête sur le bilinguisme et le biculturalisme, André Laurendeau, en était venu au début de sa carrière à conclure au caractère éminemment nocif du bilinguisme tel qu'il est trop souvent pratiqué au Canada (Laurendeau 1940). (25)

7. Conséquences politiques

Enfin, les ultimes conséquences du bilinguisme se situent sur le plan poli-

---

(25) Vouloir dresser une liste des faits d'interférence culturelle, entre CF et CA nous entraînerait trop loin. Ce serait pourtant chose utile, car les faits de culture donnent la clef de bien des difficultés et interférences linguistiques. Les observateurs les plus clairvoyants l'ont reconnu depuis longtemps, cf. notamment Lortie, M. 1952. Dans le même numéro des Contributions à l'étude des sciences de l'Homme le RP N. Mailloux, psychologue, mesure ainsi la force de résistance d'un groupe social: "Ce qui témoigne... le plus clairement de la vitalité des individus et des groupes /..../, c'est aussi la capacité d'opposer une résistance ferme et efficace à tout ce qui menace d'obnubiler ou d'édulcorer ces valeurs inaliénables" (p. 8)

tique. C'est là que les luttes se font le plus âpre, parce que psychologie, sociologie, linguistique et doctrines juridiques descendent dans l'arène où s'af-
frontent quotidiennement les points de vue minoritaires et majoritaire. Cette
situation se reflète dans bon nombre de pages du Rapport préliminaire de la
C.R.B.B. L'impression générale que donne ce rapport n'est pas sereine – et
il serait étonnant qu'il en soit autrement, si l'on songe que la langue et la
culture qu'elle véhicule est sans doute la barrière la plus remarquable à se
dresser entre les peuples. L'enquête elle-même semble bien révéler que la
grande majorité des anglophones ne comprend pas ce qu'on attend d'elle en
matière de bilinguisme. On pourrait composer une véritable anthologie de
l'incompréhension de ce problème en publiant les Letters to the Editor les plus
représentatives. Dans un second volume, d'ailleurs, on trouverait dans les
journaux d'expression française une abondante moisson de Lettres au Devoir,
etc., qui révèlent, chez les francophones, une incompréhension tout aussi totale, sinon plus grande encore, des problèmes de la majorité vis-à-vis de la
minorité. (26)
     Toutes les considérations mentionnées dans le présent article sont en effet
plus sensibles (et paraissent plus valables) aux yeux de la minorité. Comme le
faisait remarquer M. M. Lewis

"the ultimate aim of every state, in its political structure and functioning,
is to secure the union of all its members, in thought, feeling, and action,
towards the maintenance of the society as a characteristic polity. A primary condition of the growth of vast polities, – whether democratic or to-
talitarian – is the existence of a single common language, which shall be
made the means of common education." (Lewis 1948, 147, 168)

     Du côté fédéral, on ne trouve guère de raisons d'encourager un dévelop-
pement économique, fiscal et administratif qui pourrait renforcer les cadres du
Canada français et, par voie de conséquence, sa culture et sa langue. Comme
le soulignait récemment le Globe and Mail de Toronto,

"... some of those around the Minister of Finance (Mr. C.D. Sharp) are
basically assimilationists. They have no animosity to the French language
and culture in Canada. Indeed, they view them as virtues. But they
simply do not believe that a French culture can survive as an island in an
English-speaking North America. As the "quiet revolution" opens up

---

(26) Il ne faut donc pas sous-estimer la valeur, l'importance et l'influence
de ces documents quotidiens, apparemment éphémères, mais qui sont à leur façon un moyen de mesurer l'opinion. Bien sûr, il ne faudrait pas y rechercher
une doctrine solide du bilinguisme; ce serait trop demander, puisque même les
linguistes ne s'y intéressent pas outre mesure, malgré les objurgations de Roman
Jakobson. Mais il y a là une masse de documents qui méritent d'être analysés
(On pourrait en faire un recueil thématique) parce qu'ils ponctuent l'évolution
de la conscience linguistique des différents groupes en présence – et même,
parfois, de l'ensemble du pays.

Quebec and economic standards rise, they believe it is inevitable that
French Canadians will be assimilated and they see no point in federal policies that could only slow down the process and make it more difficult."
(31-10-66)

Ce à quoi les gens du Québec rétorquent que la seule façon de riposter
est de prendre toutes les dispositions administratives pour faire du français la
langue d'usage (the working language?) de la nation canadienne-française.
M. Jean-Noël Tremblay, ministre des Affaires culturelles du Québec, ajoutait: "Je sais qu'il s'en trouvera pour objecter que ce serait faire litière des
droits de la minorité anglophone et décourager, par des provocations, les in-
vestisseurs étrangers.   .....   C'est là un faux problème, une équivoque
dangereuse entretenue par les partisans d'un bilinguisme et d'un biculturalisme
qui sont appelés à devenir les prétextes officiels, politiques, intellectuels et
mondains de l'unilinguisme que nous a imposé la Confédération." (Cité par
Le Devoir du 15-11-66).

On voit par ces deux extraits qu'il y a bien peu de chances pour que les
deux camps se rejoignent, sinon en éclairant attentivement, et sans esprit de
partisanerie, les différents niveaux du problème, afin de mieux comprendre
quelles sont les forces en jeu, quels sont les véritables problèmes à la fois linguistiques, sociologiques et culturels qui séparent la minorité souffrante de la
majorité indifférente.

8. Conclusion

Nous voici arrivés au terme de ce tour d'horizon à la fois trop bref et trop
long. Le problème est immense, les conséquences innombrables et - sauf pour
les membres de la majorité, d'une portée personnelle angoissante. Le bilinguisme au Canada divise le pays, bouleverse des familles, retarde la promotion
sociale et le développement intellectuel d'un tiers du pays. Et pourtant, comme l'écrit W. F. Mackey, "bilingualism, one of the most important problem
of linguistics, is also one of the most neglected." (Mackey 1956) La tenue
en territoire acadien, où la défense des intérêts culturels de la minorité revêt
depuis 300 ans un caractère particulièrement tragique, doit obliger les participants du Colloque à méditer sur les faits cités dans les pages qui précèdent.
Leurs travaux ne se situent pas dans l'abstrait, mais au niveau de la personne
humaine. La mesure du bilinguisme est au Canada, comme dans beaucoup de
régions du globe, la mesure de l'individu. Cela vaut qu'on s'y arrête; et je
ne puis que m'associer à la récente déclaration de mon collègue Mackey (dont
les écrits, on l'aura vu, dominent vraiment la question) qui préface admira-
blement le Colloque de 1967:

"... Relationships between the bilingual individual and the linguistic,
social and psychological factors which influence his bilingualism need to
be studied by specialists in the relevant disciplines capable of analyzing
this much-neglected phenomen (sic) of human behaviour." (Mackey 1966,
91)

BIBLIOGRAPHY/BIBLIOGRAPHIE

Association des professeurs de l'université de Montréal
  1965   Mémoire soumis à la Commission d'enquête sur le bilinguisme et la
              dualité de culture, Montréal (polygraphié)
Avis, W. S.
  1965   A Bibliography of Writings on Canadian English (1857-1965). To-
              ronto, Gage
Barbeau, R.
  1963   Bilinguisme-Biculturalisme, Montréal, Institut canadien et éduca-
              tion des adultes (polycopié)

  1965   Le Québec bientôt unilingue, Montréal, éd. de l'Homme
Bibeau, G.
  1966   Nos enfants parleront-ils français?, Montréal, les éd. Actualité
Bloomfield, L.
  1933   Language, New York, H. Holt & Co.
Bruchési, J.
  1957   Introduction, Chronique sociale de France 5
Butcher, W. F.
  1963   "Les Canadiens anglais désirent la sauvegarde du français au Cana-
              da". (In) Conférences Bardy. Québec, Société Saint-Jean-
              Baptiste, 33-35
Canada
  1962   Canadian Government Style Manual for Writers and Editors, Ottawa,
              The Queen's Printer
Commission royale d'enquête sur le bilinguisme et le biculturalisme
  1965   Rapport préliminaire, Ottawa, Imprimeur de la Reine

  1964   "Mandat", (In) Rapport préliminaire, 143-144
Carroll, J. B.
  1953   The Study of Language; a Survey of Linguistics and related discip-
              lines in America, Cambridge Mass., Harvard U. P.
Conseil de la vie française
  1961   "Mémoire sur le bilinguisme des traités signés par le Canada", Vie
              française 15, 136-141

  1961   "Mémoire sur la situation du français au ministère des Transports
              dans le Québec, Vie française 15, 268-270
Conseil des Arts du Canada
  1965   Mémoire soumis à la Commission royale d'enquête sur le bilinguisme
              et le biculturalisme, Ottawa, mars
Cox, D. M.
  1961   "Canadian Bilingualism," Culture 22, 185-190

Darbelnet, J.
   1963   "The French-Canadian Linguistic Tradition and Canada," Culture
           24, 217-224

   1964   "Réflexions sur le bilinguisme", Culture 25, 255-266

   1966   "The French Language in Canada", Culture 27, 9-27
Diebold, A. R. Jr.
   1961   "Incipient Bilingualism," Language 37, 97-112
Domenach, J.-M.
   1965   "Le Canada français; controverse sur un nationalisme", Esprit fév.
           290-331
Dulong, G.
   1966   Bibliographie linguistique du Canada français, Québec, Presses de
           l'Université Laval; Paris. C. Klincksieck
Epstein, I.
   1915   La pensée et la polyglossie; essai psychologique et didactique, Pa-
           ris, Payot & Cie
Ervin, S. M. & Osgood, C. E.
   1954   "Second Language Learning and Bilingualism," Journal of Abnormal
           and Social Psychology Suppl., 139-146
Esprit
   1952   "Numéro spécial sur le Canada français", 8-9, 169-408
Le français dans le monde
   1964   "Numéro spécial sur le Canada français, 23, 1-56
Gouin, P.
   1960   "Le bilinguisme des édifices du gouvernement à Ottawa", Vie fran-
           çaise 15, 25-45

   1961   "Le français dans le service civil", Vie française 15, 273-275
Hamel, R.
   1965   "Bibliographie des lettres canadiennes-françaises", Etudes françai-
           ses 1, 2, XXXI
Haugen, E.
   1950   "The Analysis of Linguistic Borrowing", Language 26, 210-231

   1953   The Norwegian Language in America; a study in bilingual behavior,
           Philadelphia, University of Pennsylvania Press

   1956   Bilingualism in the Americas; a bibliography and research guide,
           Gainesville, Fla., American Dialect Society. (Publication of
           the American Dialect Society, No. 26)
Jakobson, R.
   1953   "Results of the Conference of Anthropologists and Linguists," Inter-
           national Journal of American Linguistics, Memoir 8

Jesperson, O.
1938   En sprogmands lerwed, Kobenhaw, Gyldendal
Lado, R.
1960   "Testing Proficiency in Writing a Foreign Language", Canadian
           Journal of Linguistics, 21-28
Lambert, W. E.
1955   "Measurement of the Linguistic Dominance of Bilinguals," Journal
           of Abnormal and Social Psychology 50, 197-200

1959   "Linguistic Manifestations of Bilingualism," American Journal of
           Psychology 72, 77-82
Laurendeau, A.
1940   "La mort par le bilinguisme", Action nationale 16, 314-317
Lefebvre, G. R.
1962   "L'étude de la culture: la linguistique," Recherches sociographi-
           ques 3, 233-249
Léger, J.-M.
1962   "L'état de la langue, miroir de la nation", Journal des traducteurs
           7, 39-51
Lewis, M. M.
1947   Language in Society, London, New York, T. Nelson
Lortie, L.
1965   Projet de mémoire de l'Université de Montréal, soumis à la Com-
           mission royale d'enquête sur le bilinguisme et le biculturalisme,
           Montréal (polycopié)
Lortie, M.
1952   "Les relations bi-culturelles au Canada", (In) Contributions à l'é-
           tude des sciences de l'homme, Montréal
Mackey, W. F.
1953   "Bilingualism and Linguistic Structure," Culture 14, 143-149

1956   "Towards a Redefinition of Bilingualism," Canadian Journal of Lin-
           guistics 2, 4-11

1962   "The Description of Bilingualism," Canadian Journal of Linguistics
           7, 51-85

1965b   "Bilingual Interference; its analysis and Measurement," The Journal
           of Communication 15, 239-249

1966   "The Measurement of Bilingual Behavior," The Canadian Psychol-
           ogist 7, 75-92

1967   Bilingualism as a World Problem/Le bilinguisme, phénomène mon-
           dial, E. R. Adair Memorial Lectures, Montréal, Harvest House

Marouzeau, J.
    1951   Lexique de la terminologie linguistique français, allemand, anglais,
            italien, 3 éd. augm. et mise à jour, Paris, 8, Geuther
Martray, J.
    1947   Le problème breton et la réforme de la France, La Baule, Edit. de
            Bretagne
Peal, E. & Lambert, W.
    1962   "The Relation of Bilingualism to Intelligence," Washington, Amer-
            ican Psychological Association. (Psychological Monographs:
            General and Applied V. 76, whole No. 546
Pellerin, J.
    1962   "Le Canada français," Esprit 11, 669-690
Philip, D.
    1957   Chronique sociale de France 5, 475-479
Pilch, H.
    1957   "Le bilinguisme au pays de Galles", (In) Miscelanea Homenaje a
            André Martinet, Universidad de lo Laguna, Canarias, I, 223-241
Pilon, J.-G.
    1966   "Québec ou Canada?", Le Devoir 31, 12, II
Poisson, J.
    1960   "Mémoire sur le bilinguisme des édifices fédéraux à Ottawa," Vie
            française 14, 159-167
Rolland, S. (Chaput)
    1966   Mon pays, Québec ou le Canada?, Montréal, Cercle du Livre de
            France
Saporta, S. & Bastian, R.
    1961   Psycholinguistics; a Book of Readings, New York, Hold, Rinehart
            & Winston
Scott, F. R.
    1952   "Canada et le Canada français", Esprit 20^2 , 178-189
Spilka, I. V.
    1965   Le bilinguisme et la fonction publique; plan de recherche, Univer-
            sité de Montréal (polycopié)
Tabouret-Keller, A.
    1963   "L'acquisition du langage parlé chez un petit enfant en milieu bi-
            lingue", (In) Problèmes de psycho-linguistique; symposium Neu-
            chatel, 1962, Paris, Presses universitaires de France, 205-219
Taillon, L.
    1959   Diversité des langues et bilinguisme, 2e éd. Montréal, les Editions
            de l'Atelier

    1961   Le Seminar international sur le bilinguisme en éducation, Aberystwyth
            1960; rapport d'un observateur canadien, Moncton (texte dacty-
            lographié)

Tougas, G.
   1957   "The Language Problem in a Dual Culture", Bulletin of the Human-
            ities Association of Canada 21, 8-9
Trudel, M. & Grenier, F.
   1955   "Répartition des groupes français au Canada depuis deux siècles",
            (In) Etudes sur le parler français au Canada, Québec, Presses de
            l'Université Laval, 49-60
Unesco
   1966   Annonce préliminaire au Colloque de Moncton, Ottawa (polycopié)
Vildomec, V.
   1963   Multilingualism, Leyden, A. W. Sythoff
Vinay, J.-P.
   1949   "Problèmes et méthodes de la linguistique", L'action universitaire
            16, 4-25
----- (ed.)
   1952   Traductions, Montréal, Institut de traduction

   1955a   "Aperçu des études de phonétique canadienne", (In) Etudes sur le
            parler français au Canada, Québec, Presses de l'Université Laval
-----
   1955b   "Le français au Canada. Répartition des groupes francophones",
            La classe de français 5, 312-317

   1964   "Contacts linguistiques au Canada et en France", Le français dans
            le monde 23, 47-52

   1965   "Editorial", Journal des traducteurs 10, 115-127
Weinreich, U.
   1953   Languages in Contact; findings and problems, New York, Linguis-
            tic Circle of New York (Publications of the Linguistic Circle of
            New York, No. 1)

           "Research Frontiers in Bilingualism Studies," (In) Proceedings of the
           VIIIth International Congress of Linguists, 786-797

ANNEX II

LIST OF PARTICIPANTS

LISTE DES CONGRESSISTES

ORGANIZING COMMITTEE/COMITE D'ORGANISATION

William F. Mackey
  (Chairman)

Executive Director,
International Centre for Research
 on Bilingualism,
Université Laval,
Québec 10, P. Q., Canada.

Jean Darbelnet

Professeur,
Faculté des lettres,
Université Laval,
Québec 10, P. Q., Canada.

President,
Canadian Linguistic Association.

Joshua A. Fishman

Professor of Social Sciences,
Ferkauf Graduate School of Humanities
 and Social Sciences,
Yeshiva University,
55 Fifth Avenue,
New York, N. Y., 10003, U.S.A.

William W. Gage

Acting Director of Languages Program,
Centre for Applied Linguistics,
1755 Massachusetts Avenue, N. W.,
Washington, D.C. 20036, U.S.A.

Einar Haugen

Germanic Languages and Literature,
406 Boylston Hall,
Harvard University,
Cambridge, Mass., 02138 U.S.A.

Wallace E. Lambert

Chairman,
Department of Psychology,
McGill University,
Montreal, Canada.

Werner F. Leopold

Professor,
Department of German,
Bascom Hall,
University of Wisconsin,
Madison 6, Wis. 53715 U.S.A.

Veroboj Vildomec

Hilchenbach,
West Germany,
Attached to International Centre for
 Research on Bilingualism,
Université Laval,
Québec 10, Canada.

Brother Léopold Taillon

Directeur,
Ecole des langues vivantes,
Université de Moncton,
Moncton, Canada.

OFFICIAL GUESTS/INVITES

BOILEAU, Armand

Suppléant,
Université de Liège,
Philologie germanique,
Membre de la Commission royale de
   toponymie et de dialectologie de Belgique.

BRAZEAU, Jacques

Directeur,
Département de sociologie,
Université de Montréal.

COOPER, Robert L.

Research Associate,
Ferkauf Graduate School of Humanities
  and Social Sciences,
Yeshiva University.

CORMIER, R.P. Clément, c.s.c.

Recteur de l'Université de Moncton,
Moncton, N.-B., Canada.

ERVIN-TRIPP, Susan

Department of Speech,
University of California,
Berkeley, California 94720.

GUMPERZ, John J.

Linguistics and Anthropology,
University of California,
Berkeley, California 94720.

HASSELMO, Nils

Linguistics, Scandinavian,
University of Minnesota,
Minneapolis, Minnesota 55455.

HATTORI, Shirô

Department of Linguistics,
Faculty of Letters,
University of Tokyo,
Bunkyo-ku, Tokyo, Japan.

HAUDRICOURT, André Georges

Directeur de recherches,
Centre national de la recherche
  scientifique,
Paris, France.

HUGHES, Everett C.

Professor of Sociology,
Brandeis University,
Waltham, Massachusetts 02154.

JAKOBOVITS, Leon A.

Co-director,
Institute of Communications Research,
Center for Comparative Psycholinguistics,
University of Illinois,
Urbana, Illinois 61801.

JONES, Robert Maynard

Senior Lecturer,
Department of Welsh Language and
   Literature,
University of Wales,
Aberystwyth, Wales.

KAHN, Félix

Privat-docent et Assistant de linguistique,
Faculté des lettres,
Université de Genève,
Genève, Suisse.

KATRE, S. M.

Director,
Postgraduate and Research Institute,
Deccan College,
Poona 6, India.

KLOSS, Heinz

Director of Research Institute,
Forschungsstelle für Nationalit'äten und
   Sprachenfragen,
21 Rotenberg,
D-355 Marburg, Germany.

LABOV, William

Department of Linguistics,
Columbia University in the City of
   New York,
New York, N.Y. 10027.

LE BLANC, Napoléon

Doyen de la faculté des sciences sociales,
Université Laval,
Québec 10, Canada.

LEGRAND, Albert

Programme Specialist,
Teaching of Modern Languages,
Department of School and Higher Education,
Unesco, Place de Fontenoy,
Paris 7e, France.

LE PAGE, Robert B.

Department of Language,
University of York,
The King's Manor,
York, England.

LIEBERSON, Stanley

Professor,
Department of Sociology,
University of Wisconsin,
Social Science Building,
Madison, Wisconsin 537706.

MACKEY, I. S.

Directrice,
Département des langues étrangères,
Université Laval,
Cité universitaire,
Québec 10, Canada.

MACNAMARA, John

St. Patrick's College,
Dublin, Eire.

MALHERBE, E. G.

University of Natal,
Durban, South Africa.

MACRAE, Kenneth D.

Professor of Political Science,
Carleton University,
Ottawa, Ontario, Canada.

NUYTENS, E. Th. G.

Psychological Institute,
University of Nijmegen,
Nijmegen (Netherlands).

OKSAAR, Els

General and comparative linguistics,
University of Hamburg, Germany.

PANDIT, Prabodh B.

Head,
Department of Linguistics,
University of Delhi, India.

PIPPING, Knut

Professor of Sociology and Statistics,
Abo Akademi (Swedish University of Abo),
Finland.

REFEROVSKAIA, Elizaveta

Académie des sciences de l'URSS,
c/o Dr. Vasily Vakhrushev,
Commission of the USSR for Unesco,
9, Kalinine Avenue,
Moscow, USSR.

RIVERS, Wilga

Senior Lecturer,
Department of Modern Languages,
Monash University,
Clayton Victoria,
Australia.

SIERTSEMA, Berthe

Professor of Linguistics,
Free University,
Amsterdam, Holland.

TABOURET-KELLER, Andrée

Chargée de recherche au Centre national
   de la recherche scientifique,
Institut de Psychologie,
Faculté des lettres et sciences humaines,
Université de Strasbourg,
25, rue du Soleil,
Strasbourg, France.

VINAY, Jean-Paul

Department of Linguistics,
University of Victoria,
Victoria, B. C.

OBSERVERS/OBSERVATEURS

ADIVE, John R.

Center for International Programs,
College of Education,
Ohio University,
Athens, Ohio 45701.

ARSENAULT, Adrien

C. P. 12,
R. R. 5, Moncton, N.-B., Canada.

BELANGER, Rita

3620, rue Sherbrooke est, app. 15,
Montréal 4, Québec, Canada.

BOUDREAU, Jacques J.

Commission de la fonction publique du
    Canada,
Moncton, N.-B., Canada.

BOUDREAU-NELSON, Léone

Professeur de phonétique,
Université de Moncton,
Moncton, N.-B., Canada.

CARON, André

Bell Telephone du Canada,
Montréal, Québec, Canada.

CHALIFOUX, Jean-Pierre

Bibliothécaire,
Centre d'études canadiennes-françaises,
Université McGill,
Montréal, Québec, Canada.

CORMIER, Gérard

Psychologie,
Université de Moncton,
Moncton, N.-B., Canada.

COSTELLO, Raymond F.

Chef de la division de l'anglais comme
    langue seconde,
Ministère de l'Education,
Québec, Québec, Canada.

CYR, Hervé W.

Division des plans d'études,
Ministère de l'Education de l'Ontario,
Toronto, Ontario, Canada.

DESILETS, Guy

Conseiller linguistique,
Ministère de l'Education,
Québec, Québec, Canada.

DORIAN, Nancy

Associate Professor,
Department of German,
Bryn Mawr College,
Bryn Mawr, Pennsylvania, U.S.A.

DUGAS, Donald

Professeur de langues et de linguistique,
University of Michigan,
Michigan, U.S.A.

ELIE, Robert

Directeur associé,
Secrétariat spécial du bilinguisme,
Edifice de l'Est,
Colline parlementaire,
Ottawa, Ontario, Canada.

FATA, Julia

Program Researcher,
Bilingual Education Resources Center,
University of Michigan,
Ann Arbor, Michigan, U.S.A.

FEENSTRA, Henry J.

Educational Research Assistant,
London Ontario Board of Education,
University of Western Ontario,
London, Ontario, Canada.

FRANCIS, Bahgat

Professeur,
Séminaire de Saint-Jean,
Saint-Jean, Québec, Canada.

GAGNE, Raymond Clovis

Linguiste,
Ministère des Affaires indiennes et du
   Nord canadien,
Ottawa, Ontario, Canada.

GUTIERREZ, Medardo

Associate Professor,
Foreign Language Department,
State University College,
Oneonta, New York 13820.

HARRIS, Richard M.

Assistant Professor of Linguistics,
Director of Hindi Instruction,
University of Rochester,
Rochester, New York 14627.

HAUMONT, Roland

Ministère de l'Education,
Hôtel du Parlement,
Québec, Québec, Canada.

JACOBSON, J. V.

Department of Indian Affairs and Northern
 Development,
Ottawa, Ontario, Canada.

LACROIX, Léopold F.

Surintendant adjoint,
Ministère de l'Education de l'Ontario,
Division de la formation des maîtres,
Toronto, Ontario, Canada.

LaPLANTE, Corinne

Professeur-étudiante en histoire,
Université de Moncton,
Moncton, N.-B., Canada.

LAVERGNE, Roger

Directeur général des programmes
 d'enseignement,
Ministère de la Défense nationale,
Ottawa, Ontario, Canada.

LEBLANC, Lorraine

Professeur de français,
Université de Moncton et Moncton High,
Moncton, N.-B., Canada.

LUSIGNAN, Gérard

Librairie Beauchemin Ltée,
Montréal, Québec, Canada.

LYNAM, Josephine

Advisor on Bilingualism,
Department of Manpower & Immigration,
Bourque Building,
Ottawa, Ontario, Canada.

MACLEOD, Finlay

Professor,
Psychology Department,
University of Aberdeen,
Aberdeen, Scotland.

MEPHAM, Michael

Assistant,
International Centre for Research on
 Bilingualism,
Laval University,
Quebec 10, Quebec, Canada.

MEYERSTEIN, Goldie P.

Lecturer in Slavic Languages,
University of California,
Los Angeles, Cal., U.S.A.

NOEL de TILLY, Louis

Commandant d'aviation,
Conseiller – Entraînement et bilinguisme,
Pièce 2445 "A",
Ministère de la Défense nationale,
Ottawa, Ontario, Canada.

O CIOSAIN, Séamus

Principal Officer,
Department of Finance,
Dublin 2, Ireland.

O'HUALLACHAIN, Colman L.

Directeur,
Institut national de langue,
Irlande (Institiuid Teanga Eireann),
Baile-Mhic-Ghormain,
Co. na Mi, Irlande.

OYELARAN, Olasope

(Doctoral Candidate),
Stanford University,
Box 4063,
Stanford, California, U.S.A.

PREFONTAINE, Gisèle

Le Sablier,
250, de la Saudrays,
Boucherville, Québec, Canada.

QUIRION, J. M.

Doyen,
Faculté des arts,
Université d'Ottawa,
Ottawa, Ontario, Canada.

RANGONGO, Mabela Percy

Language Officer,
Public Service Commission of Canada,
71 Bank Street,
Ottawa, Ontario, Canada.

REID, Marcel

Conseiller en bilinguisme,
Ministère de la Santé et du Bien-être,
   (Ottawa),
240, boulevard Taché,
App. 505,
Hull, Québec, Canada.

RUDNYCKYJ, J. B.

Linguist,
University of Manitoba,
Winnipeg, Manitoba, Canada.

SAINT-ONGE, Armand

Ministère de l'Education,
Frédéricton, N.-B., Canada.

SAVARD, Jean-Guy

Assistant,
Centre international de recherches sur le
  bilinguisme,
Université Laval,
Québec 10, Québec, Canada.

SMITH, George W.

International Centre for Research on
  Bilingualism,
Laval University,
Quebec 10, Quebec, Canada.

SURDUCKI, Milan

Assistant Professor,
Department of Slavic Languages and
  Literature,
University of Toronto,
Toronto 5, Ontario, Canada.

THERIAULT, George F.

Professor,
Sociology,
Dartmouth, N.S., Canada.

TUCKER, Richard

Psychologist,
(Assistant Professor, Philippine Normal
  College, Manila),
Department of Psychology,
McGill University,
Montreal, Quebec, Canada.

UPSHUR, John A.

Research Associate in English Language
  Measurement,
University of Michigan,
3020 North University Building,
Ann Arbor, Michigan, U.S.A.

VINCENT, Michel

Commission de la Fonction publique du
  Canada,
Ottawa, Ontario, Canada.

WONG, Irene

Post-Graduate Student,
University of Alberta,
Edmonton, Alberta, Canada.

STAFF/PERSONNEL

Canadian National Commission for Unesco

BARTLETT, David W.   Secretary-General,
                                       Canadian National Commission for Unesco.

CULL, Shirley   Associate Secretary-General,
                                       Canadian National Commission for Unesco.

KELLY, Louis G.   Acting-Chairman,
                                       Department of Modern Languages and
                                         Linguistics,
                                       University of Ottawa.

PARE, Micheline   Canadian National Commission for Unesco.

Université de Moncton

BERUBE, Rhéal   Directeur,
                                       Extension de l'enseignement,
                                       Université de Moncton.

Interpreters

BECCAT, Jean-Paul   Montreal.

MORRISON, Jeannette   New York.

RAINERI, J.   Montreal.

ANNEX III

INDEX LIBRORIUM

(Numbers refer to Section Bibliographies, FS stands for Free Session;
  A1, Annex 1)

Abou, Sélim
    Le bilinguisme arabe-français en Liban   6
Akhmanova, O. S. et al.
    Exact Methods in Linguistic Research   3
Albright, R. W. & J. B.
    "The Phonology of a Two-Year-Old Child"   1
Anderson, Theodore
    The Teaching of Foreign Languages in the
    Elementary School   1
Arès, Richard
    "Comportement linguistique des minorités
    françaises au Canada"   6
Arlitt, Ada Hart
    Psychology of Infancy and Early Childhood   1
Arsenian, Seth
    Bilingualism and Mental Development; a study of
    the intelligence and the social background of
    bilingual children in New York City   1 2
Asher, James V.
    "The Strategy of the Total Physical Response; an
    application to learning Russian"   1
Association des professeurs de l'Université de Montréal
    Mémoire soumis à la Commission royale d'enquête
    sur le bilinguisme et le biculturalisme   A1
Avis, W. S.
    A Bibliography of Writings on Canadian English
    (1857-1965)   1
Banathy, B., Trayer, E. & Waddle, C. D.
    "The Use of Contrastive Data in Foreign Language
    Course Development"   5
Barbeau, R.
    Bilinguisme-Biculturalisme   A1

    Le Québec bientôt unilingue?   A1
Barbeau, V.
    Le français du Canada   A1
Barker, G. C.
    "Social Functions of Language in a Mexican-
    American Community"   4
Bateman,
    "Papers on Language Development"   1

Bellugi, V., & Brown, R. (eds.)
　　The Acquisition of Language   1
Berko, J.
　　"The Child's Learning of English Morphology"   1
----- & Brown, R.
　　"Psycholinguistic Research Methods"   1
Bendix, E. H.
　　"Componential Analysis of General Vocabulary; the
　　semantic structure of a set of verbs in English, Hindi
　　and Japanese"   3
Berquet, Ch. (ed.)
　　Le bilinguisme en Suisse, en Belgique   6
Bertrang, A.
　　Grammatik der Areler Mundart   3
Betz, W.
　　"Zur Erfarschung des 'inneren Lehnguts'"   3

　　Deutsch unde Lateinisch; die Lehnbildungen der
　　althochdeutschen Benediktinerregel   3
Bibeau, G.
　　Nos enfants parleront-ils français?   A1
Bilingualism in Education   1   6
Blanc, H.
　　Communal Dialects in Baghdad   5
Blancquaert, E.
　　Practische Vitspraakleer van de Nederlandstaal   3
Blom, J. P. & Gumperz, J. J.
　　"Some social determinants of Verbal Behavior"   1   4   5
Bloomfield, L.
　　Language   3   A1
Boileau, A.
　　"Les procès sémantiques de l'emprunt populaire
　　observés à travers quelques verbes wallons d'origine
　　germanique"   3

　　Notes sur les parlers du nord-est de la province de
　　Liège   3

　　Enquête dialectale sur la toponymie germanique du
　　nord-est de la province de Liège   3

　　"Het noordoosten van de provincie Luik, kriusfunt
　　van drie kulturen"   3

　　"Le problème du bilinguisme et la théorie des substrats"   3

Bolinger, D.
      "Transformulation; structural translation"   3
Borsu, A.
      La bonne forme; sens des mots, prononciation, ortho-
      graphe, expressions vicieuses   3
Bottequin, A.
      Le français contemporain, incorrections, difficultés,
      illogismes, bizarreries, ou le bon usage du français
      d'aujourd'hui   3
Braine, M. D. S.
      "The Ontogeny of English Phrase Structure; the first
      phase"   1

      "The Acquisition of Language in Infant and Child"   1
Braunshausen, N.
      Le bilinguisme et les méthodes d'enseignement des
      langues étrangères   3
Breunig, M.
      Foreign Languages in the Elementary Schools of the
      United States, New York   1
Brière, E.
      "An experimentally Defined Hierarchy of Difficulties
      of learning Phonological Categories"   1
Brown, R. & Bellugi, U.
      "Three processes in the Child's Acquisition of Syntax"   1
----- & Berko, J.
      "Psycholinguistic Research Methods"   1
----- & Fraser, C.
      "The Acquisition of Syntax"   1
Bruch, R.
      "Aspects linguistiques du Luxembourg"   3
Bruchési, J.
      "Introduction". Chronique sociale de France   5
Buhler, K.
      The Mental Development of the Child; a summary of
      modern psychological theory   1
Bureau of the Census, U.S. Census of Population, 1930,
      Volume 2, General Report, Statistics by Subjects   6
-------   U.S. Census of Population, 1960,
      Detailed Characteristics, Puerto Rico   6
-------   U.S. Census of Population, 1960,
      Selected Area Reports, Americans Overseas   6
-------   U.S. Census of Population, 1960,
      Subject Reports, Mother Tongue of the Foreign Born   6
Bureau of the Census and Statistics, Census of the Philippines,
      Population and Housing, Summary   6

Burling, R.
    "Language Development of a Garo and English Speaking   1
    Child"
Butcher, W. F.
    "Les Canadiens anglais désirent la sauvegarde du
    français au Canada"   A1
Buxbaum, E.
    "The Role of a Second Language in the Formation
    of Ego and Superego"   1
Canada, Canadian Government Style Manual for Writers and
    Editors   A1
------- Commission royale d'enquête sur le bilinguisme et le
    biculturalisme, Rapport préliminaire   A1
------- Mandat de la Commission royale d'enquête sur le
    bilinguisme et le biculturalisme   A1
Cape Provincial Department of Public Education, Report on
    the Experiment Involving the Use of the Second Language
    as a Medium of Instruction   1
Carroll, J. B.
    "A Factor Analysis of Verbal Abilities"   2

    "Language Acquisition, Bilingualism and Language
    Change"   1

    "Language Development"   1

    "Quelques mesures subjectives en psycholinguistique;
    fréquence des mots, significativité et qualité de
    traduction"   4

    The Study of Language; a survey of linguistics and
    related disciplines in America   A1
Cassirer, E.
    An Essay on Man; an introduction to a philosophy
    of human culture   1
Cazden, C.
    Environmental Assistance to the Child's Acquisition
    of Grammar   1
Ceylon, Department of Census and Statistics. Census of
    Ceylon 1953, Vol. I   6
Chomsky, N.
    Aspects of the Theory of Syntax   5

    Syntactic Structures   3

"Some Methodological Remarks on Generative Grammar"   3

"Degrees of Grammaticalness"   3

Topics in the Theory of Grammar   FS

Chukovskii, K.

Ot Dvukh Do Piati   1

Clarke, F.

Quebec and South Africa; a study in cultural adjustment   1

Closset, F.

"Le problème du bilinguisme et l'enseignement des
langues vivantes"   3

Didactique des langues vivantes   3

Clyde, S.

Problems of Education among the Pennsylvania Germans   6

Coates, W.

"The Languages of Ceylon in 1946 and 1953"   6

Cohen, M.

"Sur l'étude du langage enfantin"   1

Coleman, E. B.

"Responses to a Scale of Grammaticalness"   3

Conférence internationale sur le bilinguisme et l'éducation   1

Conseil des Arts du Canada, Mémoire soumis à la Commission
royale d'enquête sur le bilinguisme et le biculturalisme   A1

Conseil de la vie française, "Mémoire sur le bilinguisme des
traités signés par le Canada"   A1

-------, "Mémoire sur la situation du français au ministère des
Transports dans le Québec"   A1

Coombs, C.

The Theory of Data   2   FS

Cox, D. M.

"Canadian Bilingualism"   A1

Darbelnet, J.

"The French Canadian Linguistic Tradition and Canada"   1

"The French Language in Canada"   A1

"Réflexions sur le bilinguisme"   A1

Darcy, N. T.

"A Review of the Literature on the Effects of Bilingualism
upon the Measurement of Intelligence"   2

Dauzat, A.

Les patois; évolution-classification-étude   3

Dawes, T. R.
    Bilingual Teaching in Belgian Schools   1
Daherveng, S. V.
    Corrigeons-nous; aide-mémoire et additions   3
Department of Economic and Social Affairs, Handbook of
    Population Census Methods, Vol. 3, Demographic and
    Social Characteristics of the Population   6
Deroy, L.
    "L'emprunt linguistique"   3
Descoeudres, A.
    Le développement de l'enfant de deux à sept ans;
    recherches de psychologie expérimentale   1
Des Marez, G.
    Le problème de la colonisation franque et du régime
    agraire en Belgique, avec cartes, plans et figures   3
Deutsch, K.
    Nationalism and Social Communication; an inquiry
    into the foundations of nationality   6
D'Harve, G.
    Parlons mieux! Nouvelles recherches et trouvailles
    lexicologiques   3
Diebold, R. A.
    "Code-Switching in Greek-English Bilingual Speech"   3 4

    "Incipient Bilingualism"   3 4 6

    "A Survey of Psycgolinguistic Research", 1954-64   1 3 4
Dimitrijevic, N. R.
    "A Bilingual Child"   1
Dingwall, W.
    "Transformational Generative Grammar and Contrastive
    Analysis"   3
Domenach, J.
    "Le Canada français; controverse sur un nationalisme"   A1
Dominion Bureau of Statistics, Enumeration Manual, 9th Census
    of Canada, 1951   6
Draye, H.
    De studie van de Vlaams - Waalse taalgrenslijn
    in Belgie   3

    De gelijkmaking in plaatsnamen   3
Dulong, G.
    Bibliographie linguistique du Canada français   A1
Duncan, O. D.
    "The Measurement of Population Distribution"   6

-------, Cuzzort, R. P. & Duncan, B.
Statistical Geography; problems in analyzing areal data   6

Earle, M. J.
"Bilingual Semantic Merging and an aspect of acculturation"   1

Eaton, H.
An English-French-German Spanish Word Frequency
Dictionary   4

El'konin, D. B.
Detskaia Psikhologiia   1

"Nekotorye itogi izucheniia psikhicheskoyo razvitiia
detei doshkol nogo vozrasta"   1

Elwert, W. T.
Das zweisprachige Individuum; ein Selbstzeugnis   3

Emeneau, M.
"Bilingualism and Structural Borrowing"   5

Engler, R.
Edition critique du cours de Saussure   5

Epstein, I.
La pensée et la polyglossie; essai psychologique et
didactique   3   A1

Ervin-Tripp, S. M. (see also Ervin)
"An Analysis of the Interaction of Language, Topic,
and Listener"   4   5

"An Issei Learns English"   1

"Language Development"   1

Ervin, S. M.
"Imitation and Structural Change in Children's Language"   1

"Semantic Shift in Bilingualism"   2

The Verbal Behavior of Bilinguals. The Effect of
Language of Report on the Thematic Apperception
Test Content of Adult French Bilinguals   1

"When should Second Language Learning Begin?"   1

------- & Miller, W. R.
"Language Development"   1

------- & Osgood, C. E.
"Second Language Learning and Bilingualism"   3   A1

Esprit
Numéro spécial sur le Canada français   A1

Fellegi, I. P.
     "Response Variance and its Estimation"   6
Ferguson, C. A.
     "Diglossia"   6
------- & Gumperz, J.
     "Introduction". International Journal of American
     Linguistics 26   3   2   4

     "Introduction." (In) Linguistic Diversity in South Asia,
     studies in regional, social and functional variation   5
Fischer, H.
     "A New Approach to the Measurement of Meaning"   3
Fischer, J. L.
     "Social Influences on the Choice of a Linguistic Variant"   5
Fishman, J. A.
     "Bilingualism with and without Diglossia"   2   6

     "Language Maintenance and Language Shift as a Field
     of Inquiry; a definition of the field and suggestions
     for its further development"   3   4   5

     "Sociolinguistic Perspective on the Study of Bilingualism"   4

     "Who Speaks What Language to Whom and When?"   4   5
Fishman et al.
     Language Loyalty in the United States   6
Fodor, J.
     "How to Learn to Talk"   1
Le français dans le monde
     Numéro spécial sur le Canada français   A1
Fraser, C., Bellugi, U. & Brown, R.
     "The Control of Grammar in Imitation, Comprehension
     and Production"   1
Frey, W. J.
     "Amish 'Triple Talk'"   4
Fries, C. C. & Pike, K. L.
     "Co-existent Phonemic Systems"   5
Galand, V.
     Les 600 expressions vicieuses belges recueillies et
     corrigées   3
Gali, A. M.
     "Comment mesurer l'influence du bilinguisme"   3
Gallup, J. R.
     "An Approach to the Theory of Declension"   1

General Register Office, Census 1961 Scotland, Volume 7
    Gaelic   6
Geschiere, L.
    Eléments néerlandais du wallon liégeois   3
Gil, B. & Sicron, M.
    Registration of Population (8XI 1948), Part B
    Special Series No. 53   6
Gleason, H. A.
    An Introduction to Descriptive Linguistics   5
Glees, P.
    Experimental Neurology   1
Goldstein, K.
    Language and Language Disturbances   1
Gouin, P.
    "Le bilinguisme des édifices du gouvernement à Ottawa"   A1

    "Le français dans le service civil"   A1
Green, E.
    "On Grading Phonic Interference"   3
Greenberg, J. H.
    "The Measurement of Linguistic Diversity"   6
Grégoire, A.
    L'apprentissage du langage   1
Grootaers, L.
    "Tweetaligheid"   3
Gudschinsky, S. C.
    "The ABCs of Lexicostatistics"   FS
Guildford, J. P. et al.
    "The Nature of the General Reasoning Factor"   1
Guillaume, G.
    Langage et science du langage   1
Gumperz, J. J.
    "Hindi-Punjabi Code-Switching in Delhi"   5

    "Linguistic and Social Interaction in Two
    Communities"   1 2 3 4 5

    "On the Ethnology of Linguistic Change"   5

    "On the Linguistic Markers of Bilingual C
    Communication"   1 2 4 5
Gurrey, P.
    Letter to English Language Teaching 13   1

Hertzler, J. V.
    A Sociology of Language   3

Hill, A. A.
    "Grammaticality"   3

Hill, T.
    "Institutional Linguistics"   3

Hockett, C. F.
    A Course in Modern Linguistics   5

Hoffman, M. N. H.
    The Measurement of Bilingual Background   1 2 4

Hoffman, G. & Jürgensen, G. (eds.)
    Hart, Warr nich mööd. Festschrift für Christian Boeck   6

Hoistätter, P. R.
    "Uber sprachliche Bestimmungsleistungen?"   3

Howes, D.
    "On the Interpretation of Word Frequency as a
    Variable Affecting Speed of Recognition"   4

Hughes, J.
    "The Social Psychology of Bilingualism"   1

Huse, H. R.
    Reading and Speaking Foreign Languages   1

Hymes, Dell
    "The Ethnography of Speaking"   3 4

    "Introduction: Toward Ethnographies of Communication"   3

    "Models of the Interaction of Language and Social
    Setting"   2 4

Irwin, O. C. & Chen, H. P.
    "Development of Speech during Infancy; survey of
    phoneme types"   1

Jakobovits, L. A. & Lambert, W. E.
    "Semantic Satiation among Bilinguals"   3

Jakobson, R.
    Kindersprache; aphasie und allgemeine Lautgesetze   1

    "Results of the Conference of Anthropologists and
    Linguists"   A1

    "Les lois phoniques du langage enfantin"   1
------- & Halle, M.
    "Phonemic Patterning"   1

Jenkins, J. V. & Palermo, D. S.
    "Mediation Processes and the Acquisition of
    Linguistic Structure"   1 3

Jespersen, O.

En sprogmands lerwed   A1

Language; its nature development and origin   1

"Mankind, Nation and Individual"   A1

Johnson, G. B.

"Bilingualism as Measured by a Reaction Time Technique
and the Relationship Between a Language and a Non-
Language Intelligence Quotient"   2

Johnson, N. F.

"Linguistic Models and Functional Units of Language
Behavior"   3

Jones, R. M.

Astudiaeth o ddatblyiad icithyddol plentyn hyd at
dair blwydd oed mewn cartref cymraeg   1

"Situational Vocabulary"   1

Kainz, F.

Psychologie der Sprache   1

Kelley, G.

"The Status of Hindi as a Lingua Franca"   6

Kingdon, R.

The Groundwork of English Stress   FS

The Groundwork of English Intonation   FS

Kleeberg, R.

Die Nationalitätenstatistik   6

Kloss, Heinz

Nebensprachen   4

"Deutsch als Gottesdienstsprache in den Vereinigten
Staaten"   6

Die Entwicklung neuer germanischer Kultursprachen
von 1800 bis 1950   6

A Few Words Concerning Abstand Languages and
Ausbau Languages   6

"Problèmes linguistiques des Indes et de leurs
minorités"   6

"Types of Multilingual Communities; a discussion
of ten variables"   6

          Ahornblätter   (Maple Leaves)   6
Kotze, W. J.
          "Bantu Languages in Education"   1
Krauthammer, M.
          A Comparison of Performance on Linguistic and
          Non-Linguistic Tasks in English-French Bilinguals   2
Kurth, G.
          La frontière linguistique en Belgique et dans le nord
          de la France   3
Labov, W.
          "Hypercorrection in the Lower Middle Classes as a
          Factor in Linguistic Change"   5

          On the Mechanism of Linguistic Change   5

          Progress Report for Office of Education   1

          Phonological Indices to Social Stratification   3

          The Social Stratification of English in New York City   5

          Stages in the Acquisition of Standard English   1
Lado, R.
          Language Testing   2   3

          "Testing Proficiency in Writing a Foreign Language"
Lambert, W. E.
          "Measurement of the Linguistic Dominance of Bilinguals" 2   3   A1

          "Psychological Approaches in the Study of Language,
          Part II"   2

          Psychological Studies of the Interdependencies of the
          Bilingual's Two Languages   2   3

          "A Social Psychology of Bilingualism"   5
-------, Gardner, R. C., Tunstall, K. & Barik, H. C.
          "Attitudinal and Cognitive Aspects of the Study of
          Bilingualism"   1
-------, Havelka, J., & Crosby, C.
          "The Influence of Language-Acquisition Contexts on
          Bilingualism"   3   A1
-------, Havelka, J., & Gardner, R.
          "Linguistic Manifestations of Bilingualism"   2

Landreth, C.
    "The Psychology of Early Childhood"   1
Langer, S. K.
    Philosophy in a New Key   1
Lanham, L. W.
    "Teaching English to Africans"   1
Larew, L. A.
    "The Optimum Age for Beginning a Foreign Language"   1
Learned, M. D.
    The Pennsylvania German Dialect   3
Lee, W. R.
    "Letter"   1
Lefebvre, G. R.
    "L'étude de la culture"   A1
Léger, J.-M.
    "L'état de la langue, miroir de la nation"   A1
Legros, E.
    La frontière des dialectes romans en Belgique   3
Leisi, E.
    Der Wortinhalt, seine Struktur im Deutschen und
    Englischen   3
Lenneberg, Eric H.
    Biological Foundations of Language   1

    "The Capacity for Language Acquisition"   1

    "A Probabilistic Approach to Language Learning"   1

    New Directions in the Study of Language   1
Leopold, W. F.
    Bibliography of Child Language   1

    "Kindersprach"   1

    "Patterning in Children's Language Learning"   1

    "Roman Jakobson and the Study of Child Language"   1

    Speech Development of a Bilingual Child   1
Lewis, E. G.
    "Conditions Affecting the Reception of an Official
    (Second/Foreign) Language"   3
Lewis, M.
    How Children Learn to Speak   1

    Infant Speech   1

    Language in Society   A1
Lieberson, S.
    "Bilingualism in Montreal"   6

    "An Extension of Greenberg's Linguistic Diversity
    Measures"   6

    "Language Questions in Censuses"   6
Lisker, L., Cooper, F. S. & Liberman, A. M.
    "The Uses of Experiment in Language Description"   1
Lortie, Léon
    Projet de Mémoire de l'Université de Montréal, soumis
    à la Commission royale d'enquête sur le bilinguisme et
    le biculturalisme   A1
Lortie, M.
    "Les relations bi-culturelles au Canada"   A1
Lowie, R.
    "A Case of Bilingualism"   1
Luelsdorff, P. A.
    "Applicational Generative Grammar"   3
Luriia, A. R.
    The Role of Speech in the Regulation of Normal
    and Abnormal Behaviour   1
Mackey, W. F.
    "Bilingual Interference"   3   5   A1

    "Bilingualism and Linguistic Structure"   3   A1

    Bilingualism as a World Problem   A1

    "The Description of Bilingualism"   4   6   A1

    "The Measurement of Bilingual Behavior"   3   4   5   6   A1

    "Towards a Redefinition of Bilingualism"   A1

    Language Teaching Analysis   1   3
Maclay, H. & Sleator, M. D.
    "Responses to Language"   3
Macnamara, J. T.
    Bilingualism and Primary Education   2

      "The Bilingual's Linguistic Performance"   4

      "The Effects of Instruction in a Weaker Language"   2

      "The Linguistic Independence of Bilinguals"   2
------- & Kellaghan, T.
      "Reading in a Second Language"   2
McCarthey, D. A.
      "Language Development in Children"   1
McConkey, W. G.
      "An Experiment in Bilingual Education"   1
McNeil, D.
      "Developmental Psycholinguistics"   1
McRae, K. D.
      Switzerland; example of cultural coexistence   1
Malherbe, E. G.
      The Bilingual School; a study of bilingualism
      in South Africa   1 3

      Demographic and Socio-Political Forces Determining
      the Position of English in South Africa   1
Marouzeau, J.
      Lexique de la terminologie linguistique   A1
Marshall, M. V. & Phillips, R. H.
      "Effect of Bilingualism on College Grades"   1
Martinet, A.
      Eléments de linguistique générale   6
Martray, J.
      Le problème breton et la réforme de la France   A1
Meillet, A.
      Linguistique historique et linguistique générale   3
Menyuk, P.
      "Syntactic Structures in the Language of Children" 1

      "A Preliminary Evaluation of Grammatical Capacity
      in Children"   1

      "Comparison of Grammar of Children with Functionally
      Deviant and Normal Speech"   1
Miller, W. & Ervin, S.
      "The Development of Grammar in Child Language" 1
Milner, P. M.
      "Book Review of Penfield and Roberts"   1

Moignet, G.
          L'adverbe dans la location verbale   1
Mol, H.
          Fundamentals of Phonetics, 1; the Organ of Hearing   2   FS
Moore, O. K.
          "Comments and Conclusions"   1
Mortara, G.
          "Immigration to Brazil"   6
Nichol, L.
          "Réalités psycho-sociales et degrés du bilinguisme"   3
Nida, E. A.
          Bible Translating   FS

          Morphology   FS

          Learning a Second Language   FS

          Toward a Science in Translating   FS
Nostrand et al.
          Research in Language Teaching   1
Office of the Registrar General, Census of India, 1961,
          Volume 1, Part II-C(ii). Language Table   6
Oksaar, E.
          "Kaksikielisyyden ongelmaste"   3

          "Om tvasprakighetens Problematik"   3
Ollman, M. J.
          "MLA Selective List of Materials"   1
Osgood, C. E., Suci, G. & Tannenbaum, P. H.
          The Measurement of Meaning   1   2
Pap, L.
          Portuguese-American Speech   3
Parker, W. R.
          The National Interest and Foreign Languages;
          a discussion guide   1
Paton, A.
          "New Schools for South Africans"   1
Paul, H.
          Prinzipien der Sprachgeschichte   3
Pavlovitch, M.
          Le langage enfantin, acquisition du serbe et du
          français, par un enfant serbe   1
Peal, E. & Lambert, W.
          "The Relation of Bilingualism to Intelligence"   A1

Pée, W.
Anderhalve eeuw taalgrensverschuiwing en
taaltoestand in Frens-Vlaanderen   3
Pellerin, J.
"Le Canada français"   A1
Penfield, W.
"A Consideration of Neurophysiological Mechanisms
of Speech and Some Educational Consequences"   1
------- & Roberts, L.
Speech and Brain Mechanisms   1
Perren, G. E.
"Bilingualism or Replacement? English in East Africa"   1
Petri, F.
Germanisches volkserbe in Wallonien und
Nordfrankreich   3
Pferdekampf, W.
Auf Humbolts Sparen-Deutsche im Sporen jungen Mexico   6
Philip, D.
"Chronique sociale de France"   A1
Pike, K. L.
Intonation of American English   FS

Language in Relation to an Integrated Theory of
Human Behavior   FS
Pilch, H.
"Le bilinguisme au pays de Galle"   A1
Pilon, J.
"Québec ou Canada?"   A1
Pintner, R. & Arsenian, S.
"The Relation of Bilingualism to Verbal Intelligence
and School Adjustment"   1
Plath, W.
"Mathematical Linguistics"   3
Poisson, J.
"Mémoire sur le bilinguisme des édifices fédéraux
à Ottawa"   A1
Preston, M. S.
Inter-Lingual Interference in a Bilingual Version
of the Stroop Color-Word Test   2
Preyer, W.
The Mind of the Child   1
Public Service Commission Report 1950, Union of South Africa   1
Rao, T. S.
"Development and Use of the Directions Test for
Measuring Degree of Bilingualism"   2

Smith, F. L. & Miller, G. A. (eds.)
    The Genesis of Language; a psycholinguistic approach   1
Smith, M. E.
    "Some light on the Problem of Bilingualism as Found
    from a Study of the Progress in Mastery of English among
    Pre-School Children of Non-American Ancestry in
    Hawaii"   3
Sommerfelt, A.
    "Phonetics and Sociology"   3
Spilka, I. V.
    "Le bilinguisme dans la fonction publique"   A1
Spoerl, D. T.
    "Bilinguality and Emotional Adjustment"   1
Springer, O.
    "The Study of the Pennsylvania German Dialect"   3
Stegman von Pritzwald, K.
    "Sprachwissenschaftliche Minderheitenforschung"   6
Stengers, J.
    "La formation de la frontière linguistique en Belgique,
    ou de la légitimité de l'hypothèse historique"   3
Stern, H. H. (ed.)
    Foreign Languages in Primary Education; the teaching
    of foreign or second languages to younger children   1
Stern, W.
    Psychology of Early Childhood up to the Sixth Year
    of Age   1
Steward, W.
    "Creole Languages in the Caribbean"   5
Stewart, W. A.
    "An Outline of Linguistic Typology for Describing
    Multilingualism"   3   5
Stine, C. S.
    Problems of Education among the Pennsylvanian Germans   6
Stone, L. J. & Church, J.
    Childhood and Adolescence; a psychology of the
    growing person   1
Strain, J. E.
    "Difficulties in Measuring Pronunciation Improvement"   3
Strempel, A.
    Von einer wiewohl unbillig abgewürdigten Sprache   3
Strunk Sachs, J.
    Recognition Memory for Syntactic and Semantic Aspects
    of Connected Discourse   1
Sully, J.
    Studies of Childhood   1

Swanepoel, J. F.
   The Teaching of the Second Language in the Primary
   School   1
Tabouret-Keller, A.
   "L'acquisition du langage parlé chez un petit enfant
   en milieu bilingue"   A1
Taillon, L.
   Diversité des langues et bilinguisme   3   A1

   Le Seminar international sur le bilinguisme en éducation,
   Aberystwyth 1960; rapport d'un observateur canadien   A1
Taute, B.
   "Die befaling van die mondelinge beheer van
   skoolkinders oor die tweede taal"   1   3
Templin, M.
   Language Skills in Children   1
Thiessen, J.
   Studien zum Wortschatz der Kanadischen Mennoniten   6
Thorndike, E. L. & Lorge, I.
   The Teacher's Word Book of 30,000 Words   4
Thurstone, L. L. & Thurstone, T. G.
   "Factorial Studies of Intelligence"   2
Tireman, L. S.
   "Bilingual Children"   1

   Teaching Spanish-Speaking Children   1
Tomb, J. W.
   "On the Intuitive Capacity of Children to Understand
   Spoken Language"   1
Tougas, G.
   "The Language Problem in a Dual Culture"   A1
Toussaint, M.
   La frontière linguistique en Lorraine; les fluctuations
   et la délimitation actuelle des langues française et
   germanique dans la Moselle   3
Trayer, G. L.
   "Paralanguage; a first approximation"   5
Treisman, A. M.
   "The Effects of Redundancy and Familiarity on
   Translating and Repeating Back a Foreign and a
   Native Language"   2
Trettien, A. W.
   "Psychology of the Language Interest of Children"   1

Trudel, M. & Grenier, F.
    "Répartition des groupes français au Canada depuis
    deux siècles"   A1
Thorne et al.
    "A Model for the Perception of Syntactic Structure"   1
Turner, J. D.
    Language Laboratories and the Teaching of English
    in South Africa   1
Ullman, S.
    Language and Style; collected papers   3
Unesco, Annonce préliminaire au Colloque de Moncton   A1
------ The Use of Vernacular Languages in Education   6
United Nations, Demographic Yearbook, 1963   6
Van Doorne, A.
    "De Franse woorden in het dialect van Wingene"   3
Van Loey, A.
    "Tweetaligheid"   3
Van Zyl, H. J.
    "Interesting Experiment by Unesco on Mother Tongue
    Instruction"   1
Velten, H. V.
    "The Growth of Phonemic and Lexical Patterns in
    Infant Language"   1
Verdoodt, A.
    "Esquisse du trilinguisme au Grand-Duché"   6
Verheyen, J. E.
    "Le bilinguisme en Belgique"   3
Verlinden, C.
    Les origines de la frontière linguistique en
    Belgique et la colonisation franque   3
Vernon, P. E.
    The Structure of Human Abilities   2
Vildomec, V.
    Multilingualism   3   5   A1
Vinay, J.-P.
    "Aperçu des études de phonétique canadienne"   A1

    "Contacts linguistiques au Canada et en France"   A1

    "Editorial Journal des traducteurs 10"   A1

    "Le français au Canada. Répartition des groupes
    francophones"   A1

    "Problèmes et méthodes de la linguistique"   A1

      "Sabesdiker Losn in Yiddish; a problem of linguistic
      affinity"   5

Weir, G. M.
      The Separate School Question in Canada   1

Weir, R. H.
      Language in the Crib   1

Weiss, A. von
      Hauptprobleme der Zweisprachigkeit; eine
      Untersuchung auf Grund Deutsch/estnischen
      Materials   6

Wells, R. S.
      "De Saussure's System of Linguistics"   FS

Weksel, W.
      The Acquisition of Language. By V. Bellugi and
      R. Brown (Review)   1

West, M. P.
      Bilingualism; with special reference to Bengal   1   4

Whitney, W. D.
      "On Mixture in Language"   3

Wind, B.
      "Les contributions néerlandaises au vocabulaire
      du français belge"   3

Windisch, E.
      "Zur Theorie der Mischsprachen und Lehnworter"   3

Winkler, W.
      Die Ledeutung der Statistik für den Schutz der
      nationalen Minderheiten   6

Winthrop, H.
      "A Proposed Model and Procedure for Studying
      Message Distortion in Translation"   3

Wioland, F.
      Enquête sur les langues parlées au Sénégal par les
      élèves de l'enseignement primaire   6

Wittwer, J.
      Les fonctions grammaticales chez l'enfant; sujet,
      objet, attribut   1

Wolff, H.
      "Intelligibility and Inter-Ethnic Attitudes"   5

Würzburger, E.
      "Die Sprachenstatistik"   6

Wyatt, J. L.
      "Contrastive Analysis Via the Chomskyan Verb-
      Phrase Formula"   3